Provence

J.-Ch. Géard/DIAF

O, for a draught of vintage! That hath been
Cooled a long age in the deep-delved earth,
Tasting of Flora and the country green,
Dance, and Provençal song, and sunburnt mirth!
O, for a beaker full of the warm South,
Full of the true, the blushful Hippocrene,
With beaded bubbles winking at the brim,
And purple-stained mouth.

John Keats
Ode to a Nightingale

Travel Publications

38 Clarendon Road – WATFORD Herts WD1 1 SX - U.K.
Tel. (01923) 415 000
www.michelin-travel.com
TheGreenGuide-uk@uk.michelin.com

Manufacture française des pneumatiques Michelin
Société en commandite par actions au capital de 2 000 000 000 de francs
Place des Carmes-Déchaux – 63000 Clermont-Ferrand (France)
R.C.S. Clermont-Fd B 855 200 507

Michelin et Cie, Propriétaires-éditeurs, 2000
Dépôt légal juin 2000 – ISBN 2-06-000029-7 – ISSN 0763-1383

Printed in the EU 06-2000 – 4/1

Compogravure : Nord Compo, Villeneuve d'Ascq
Imprimeur : KAPP /LAHURE-JOMBART, Évreux
Brocheur : DIGUET-DENY, Breteuil-sur-Iton

Maquette de couverture extérieure : Agence Carré Noir à Paris 12ᵉ

THE GREEN GUIDE:
The Spirit of Discovery

The exhilaration of new horizons, the fun of seeing the world , the excitement of discovery: this is what we seek to share with you. To help you make the most of your travel experience, we offer first-hand knowledge and turn a discerning eye on places to visit.

This wealth of information gives you the expertise to plan your own enriching adventure. With THE GREEN GUIDE showing you the way, you can explore new destinations with confidence or rediscover old ones.

Leisure time spent with THE GREEN GUIDE is also a time for refreshing your spirit and enjoying yourself.

So turn the page and open a window on the world. Join THE GREEN GUIDE in the spirit of discovery.

Contents

Using this guide
Key
Map of principal sights
Map of touring programmes
Map of places to stay

Introduction   9

Description of the country   10
Historical table and notes   20
Language and literature   25
Legends and tales   27
Christmas cribs   28
Festivals and costumes   30
Food and wine in Provence   32
A passion for play   35
Furniture and faience   36
Art and architecture   38

Sights   56

Aigues-Mortes 58 - Aix-en-Provence 61 -
Allauch 73 - Les Alpilles 73 - Ansouis 76 -
Apt 76 - Ardèche gorges 79 - Arles 84 -
Aubagne 94 - Auriolles 95 - Avignon 96 -
Bagnols-sur-Cèze 111 - Barben château
113 - Barbentane 114 - Les Baux-de-
Provence 115 - Beaucaire 119 - Berre
lagoon 121 - Bollène 125 - Bonnieux
126 - Brantes 126 - Cadenet 127 -
Calanques 127 - Calès 131 - La Camar-
gue 132 - Carpentras 139 - Cassis 141 -

19C Arlésienne
(A. Hesse, Museon Arlatan, Arles)

Green and black olives
of Provence

Cavaillon 142 - Château-bas 143 - Châteauneuf-du-Pape 144 - Château-renard 145 - La Ciotat 145 - Cocalière cave 146 - Comtat Venaissin 147 - Les Concluses 147 - Corniche des Crêtes 148 - La Crau plain 148 - Dentelles de Montmirail 149 - La Durance (lower valley) 151 - Estaque cliffs 155 - Étoile mountains 157 - Fontaine-de-Vaucluse 157 - Fos 159 - Les Garrigues 160 - Gordes 161 - Le Grau-du-Roi 162 - Grignan 163 - L'Isle-sur-la-Sorgue 165 - Labeaume 166 - Lourmarin 167 - Le Luberon 167 - La Madeleine cave 172 - Maillane 173 - Marcoule 173 - Marseille 174 - Martigues 194 - Marzal chasm 196 - Ménerbes 197 - La Montagnette 197 - Abbaye de Montmajour 198 - Moulin de Daudet 199 - Nages oppidum 200 - Nesque gorges 201 - Nîmes 202 - Nyons 210 - Orange 212 - Orgnac chasm 216 - Orgon 218 - Bois de Païolive 218 - Pernes-les-Fontaines 219 - Peyrolles-en-Provence 220 - Pont du Gard 221 - Pont-Saint-Esprit 222 - Rochefort-du-Gard 224 - La Roque-sur-Cèze 224 - Roussillon 225 - Saint-Blaise 225 - Saint-Gilles 226 - Saint-Julien-le-Montagnier 229 - Saint-Marcel cave 230 - Saint-Maximin-la-Sainte-Baume 230 - Saint-Michel de Frigolet 232 - Saint-Rémy-de-Provence 233 - Sainte-

Baume mountains 237 - Sainte-Victoire mount 240 -Les Saintes-Maries-de-la-Mer 242 - Salon-de-Provence 244 - Sault 246 - Abbaye de Senanque 247 - Abbaye de Silvacane 250 - Suze-la-Rousse 251 -Tarascon 251 - Le Thor 254 - La Tour-d'Aigues 255 - Uzès 256 - Vaison-la-Romaine 259 - Valbonne chartreuse 264 - Vallon-Pont-d'Arc 264 - Valréas 265 -Venasque 266 - Mont Ventoux 267 - Villeneuve-lès-Avignon 269 - Vitrolles 273 -

Practical information

Planning your trip	276
Getting there	277
Getting around	278
Accommodation	279
Basic information	280
Conversion tables	282
Notes and coins	283
Telephoning	284
Shopping	285
Sports and recreation	287
Thematic trips	292
Books and films	296
Calendar of events	297
Useful French words and phrases	301
Admission times and charges	303
Index	323

Traditional music is played on a galoubet

Varnished earthenware dish from Aubagne, 1676

A. Favix/Ville de Marseille

Maps and plans

COMPANION PUBLICATIONS

Motorists who plan ahead will always have the appropriate maps at hand. Michelin products are complementary: for each of the sites listed in The Green Guide, map references are indicated which help you find your location on our range of maps. The image below shows the maps to use for each geographic area covered in this guide. To travel the roads in this region, you may use any of the following:

• the **regional maps** at a scale of 1:200 000 no 245 and 246, which cover the main roads and secondary roads, and include useful indications for finding tourist attractions. These are good maps to choose for travelling in a wide area. In a quick glance, you can locate and identify the main sights to see. In addition to identifying the nature of the roadways, the maps show castles, churches and other religious edifices, scenic view points, megalithic monuments, swimming beaches on lakes and rivers, swimming pools, golf courses, race tracks, air fields, and more.

• the **detailed maps** are based on the regional map data, but with a reduced format (about half a region), which makes them easier to consult and fold. These maps are recommended for tourists who plan to stay within a limited area, without travelling far. For Provence, use maps 80, 81, 83 and 84.

• **departmental maps** (at a scale of 1:150 000, an enlargement of the 1:200 000 maps). These maps are very easy to read, and make it easy to travel on all of the roads in the following departments: Bouches-du-Rhône (4013), Vaucluse (4084). They come with a complete index of place-names and include a plan of the towns which serve as administrative seats *(préfectures)*.

And remember to travel with the latest edition of the **map of France no 989**, which gives an overall view of the region of Provence, and the main access roads which connect it to the rest of France. The entire country is mapped at a 1:1 000 000 scale and clearly shows the main road network. Michelin is pleased to offer a route-planning service on the Internet: **www. michelin-travel. com.** Choose the shortest route, a route without tolls, or the Michelin recommended route to your destination; you can also access information about hotels and restaurants from The Red Guide, and tourists sites from The Green Guide.

There are a number of useful maps and plans in the guide, listed on the following page.

Bon voyage!

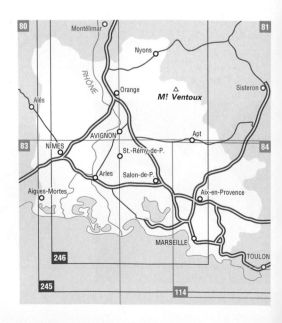

THEMATIC MAPS

Relief map	11
Occitanian dialects	25
Greco-Roman Marseille	175
Carmargues coastline	133
Orgnac chasm	216

TOWN PLANS

Aigues-Mortes	60
Aix-en-Provence	65, 68, 71
Apt and excursions	77, 78
Arles	90
Avignon	104-105
Bagnols-sur-Cèze	111
Beaucaire	120
Bollène	125
Bonnieux	126
Carpentras	140
Cassis	142
Cavaillon	143
La Ciotat	145
Port-Calargue	163
L'Isle-sur-la-Sorgue	165
Marseille	180-181, 182-183, 192
Martigues	195
Nîmes	207, 208
Nyons	211
Orange	213
Pernes-les-Fontaines	220
Pont-St-Esprit	223
Roussillon	225
St-Gilles	227
St-Rémy-de-Provence	236
Stes-Maries-de-la-Mer	243
Salon-de-Provence	244
Tarascon	253
Uzès	257
Vaison-le-Romaine	263
Valréas	265
Villeneuve-les-Avignon	271

MONUMENTS AND SITES

Arles cathedral façade	88
Arles, Roman baths	91
Avignon, Palais des Papes	100, 102
Les Baux	117
Fos docklands	159
Montmajour Abbey	199
St-Gilles façade of the abbey church	228
St-Maximin Basilica	231
St-Rémy, excavations	234
Sénaque Abbey	249
Silvacane Abbey	251
Tarascon castle	252
Vaison-la-Romaine, Roman ruins	260, 262
Chartreuse du Val de Bénédiction	270

LOCAL MAPS FOR TOURING

Les Alpilles	74-75
Gorges de l'Ardèche	80
Étang de Berre	123
Les Calanques	128
La Camargue	136
Tour from Vaison-la-Romaine	150
La-Tour-d'Aigues to Avignon	152-153
Luberon	170-171
Corniche du Chassezac	218
Ste-Baume mountains	238-239
Ste-Victoire mountains	241
Mont Ventoux	268

Using this guide

• The summary maps on the following pages are designed to assist you in planning your trip: the **Map of principal sights** identifies major sights and attractions, the **Touring programmes** propose regional driving itineraries and the **Places to stay map** points out pleasant holiday spots.

• We recommend that you read the **Introduction** before setting out on your trip. The background information it contains on history, the arts and traditional culture will prove most instructive and make your visit more meaningful.

• The main towns and attractions are presented in alphabetical order in the **Sights** section. In order to ensure quick, easy identification, original place names have been used throughout the guide. The clock symbol ⊙, placed after monuments or other sights, refers to the **Admission times and charges** section at the end of the guide, in which the names appear in the same order as in the Sights section.

• The **Practical information** section offers useful addresses for planning your trip, seeking accommodation, indulging in outdoor activities and more; opening hours and admission prices for monuments, museums and other tourist attractions; festival and carnival dates; suggestions for thematic tours on scenic railways and through nature reserves etc.

• The **Index** lists attractions, famous people and events, and other subjects covered in the guide.

Let us hear from you. We are interested in your reaction to our guide, in any ideas you have to offer or good addresses you would like to share. Send your comments to Michelin Travel Publications, 38 Clarendon Road, Watford, Herts WD 1 1SX, U.K. or by e-mail to thegreenguide-uk@uk.michelin.com.

Cloisters, Sénanque Abbey

Key

	Sight	Seaside Resort	Winter Sports Resort	Spa
Worth a journey	★★★	⚐⚐⚐	❅❅❅	⚕⚕⚕
Worth a detour	★★	⚐⚐	❅❅	⚕⚕
Interesting	★	⚐	❅	⚕

Tourism

⊙ Admission Times and Charges listed at the end of the guide

◉⇒ Sightseeing route with departure point indicated

🛐⛪🛐⛪ Ecclesiastical building

✡ 🕌 Synagogue – Mosque

🏛 Building (with main entrance)

■ Statue, small building

✝ Wayside cross

◎ Fountain

●—■—■ Fortified walls – Tower – Gate

►► Visit if time permits

AZ B Map co-ordinates locating sights

🛈 Tourist information

⚰ ⁂ Historic house, castle – Ruins

◡ ☼ Dam – Factory or power station

☆ ∩ Fort – Cave

⊤ Prehistoric site

▼ Ⱳ Viewing table – View

▲ Miscellaneous sight

Recreation

🏇 Racecourse

⛸ Skating rink

≋ ▨ Outdoor, indoor swimming pool

⛵ Marina, moorings

⌂ Mountain refuge hut

▫—▪—▫ Overhead cable-car

🚂 Tourist or steam railway

🏃 Waymarked footpath

♦ Outdoor leisure park/centre

🎭 Theme/Amusement park

Ⴤ Wildlife/Safari park, zoo

❀ Gardens, park, arboretum

🕊 Aviary, bird sanctuary

Additional symbols

═ ═ Motorway (unclassified)

❶ ❶ Junction: complete, limited

⊏⊐ ══ Pedestrian street

ⵉ═══ⵉ Unsuitable for traffic, street subject to restrictions

⸬⸬⸬ ---- Steps – Footpath

🚆 🚌 Railway – Coach station

▫+++++▫ Funicular – Rack-railway

─●─ 🚇 Tram – Metro, Underground

Bert (R.)... Main shopping street

✉ ◉ Post office – Telephone centre

✉ Covered market

⋅✕⋅ Barracks

⟁ Swing bridge

◡ ✕ Quarry – Mine

Ⓑ Ⓕ Ferry (river and lake crossings)

⛴ Ferry services: Passengers and cars

⛵ Foot passengers only

③ Access route number common to MICHELIN maps and town plans

Abbreviations and special symbols

A Agricultural office (Chambre d'agriculture)

C Chamber of commerce (Chambre de commerce)

H Town hall (Hôtel de ville)

J Law courts (Palais de justice)

M Museum (Musée)

P Local authority offices (Préfecture, sous-préfecture)

POL. Police station (Police)

🛡 Police station (Gendarmerie)

T Theatre (Théâtre)

U University (Université)

ⓐ Hotel

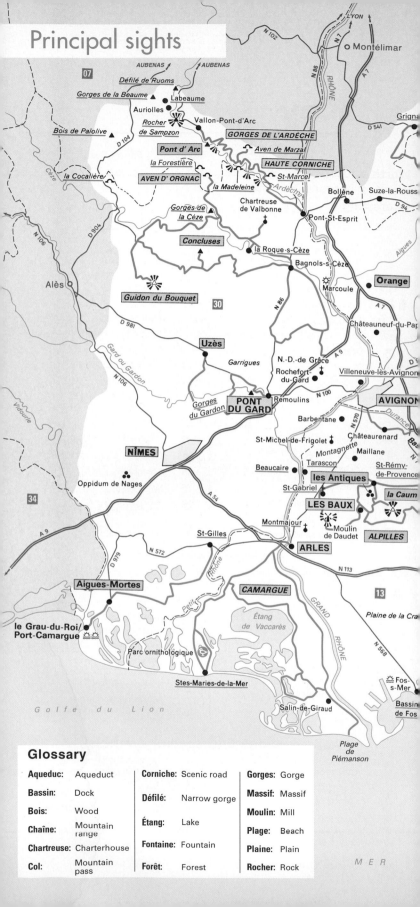

Principal sights

Glossary

Aqueduc:	Aqueduct	**Corniche:**	Scenic road	**Gorges:**	Gorge
Bassin:	Dock	**Défilé:**	Narrow gorge	**Massif:**	Massif
Bois:	Wood			**Moulin:**	Mill
Chaîne:	Mountain range	**Étang:**	Lake	**Plage:**	Beach
Chartreuse:	Charterhouse	**Fontaine:**	Fountain	**Plaine:**	Plain
Col:	Mountain pass	**Forêt:**	Forest	**Rocher:**	Rock

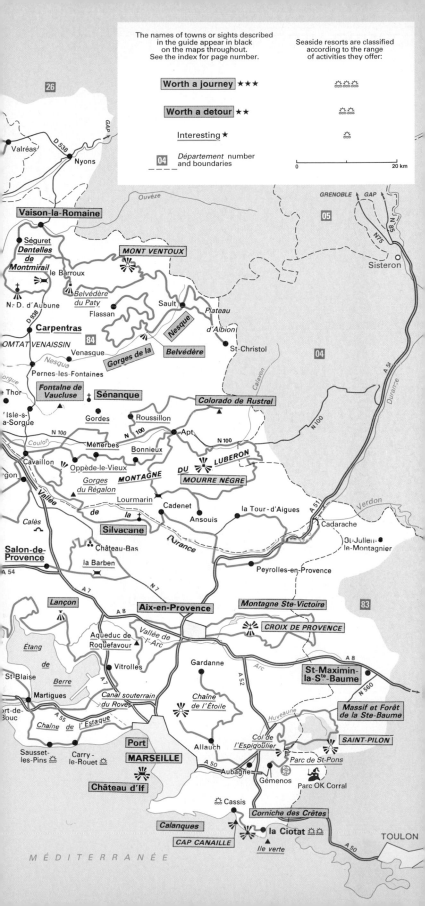

The names of towns or sights described
in the guide appear in black
on the maps throughout.
See the index for page number.

Seaside resorts are classified
according to the range
of activities they offer:

Worth a journey ★★★

Worth a detour ★★

Interesting ★

04 *Département* number
and boundaries

0   20 km

26

Valréas

D 538

GAP

Nyons

Ouvèze

GRENOBLE   GAP

05

N 85

N 75

Sisteron

Vaison-la-Romaine

Séguret

Dentelles
de
Montmirail

le Barroux

N.-D. d'Aubune

D 538

MONT VENTOUX

Belvédère
du Paty

Sault

Flassan

Plateau
d'Albion

Carpentras

OMTAT VENAISSIN

84

Nesque

Venasque

Gorges de la

Belvédère

St-Christol

04

Durance

A 51

Pernes-les-Fontaines

Nesque

orgue

Thor

Fontaine de
Vaucluse

Sénanque

Colorado de Rustrel

'Isle-s-
a-Sorgue

N 100

N 100

Gordes

Roussillon

Coulon

Apt

N 100

Ménerbes

Bonnieux

N 100

Cavaillon

Oppède-le-Vieux

MONTAGNE

DU   LUBERON

gon

Gorges
du Régalon

MOURRE NÈGRE

Vallée

de   la

Lourmarin

Cadenet

la Tour-d'Aigues

Calès

Ansouis

Verdon

A 51

Silvacane

urance

Cadarache

Château-Bas

St-Julien-
le-Montagnier

Salon-de-
Provence

la Barben

Peyrolles-en-Provence

A 54

A 7

N 7

Lançon

A 8

Aix-en-Provence

Montagne Ste-Victoire

83

Étang

de

Berre

Aqueduc de
Roquefavour

Vallée de
l'Arc

CROIX DE PROVENCE

St-Blaise

Vitrolles

Gardanne

Arc

A 8

St-Maximin-
la-Ste-Baume

Martigues

A 7

A 52

N 560

ort-de-
Bouc

Canal souterrain
du Rove

Chaîne
de l'Étoile

Huveaune

Massif et Forêt
de la Ste-Baume

A 55

Chaîne   de   l'Estaque

SAINT-PILON

Sausset-
les-Pins

Carry-
le-Rouet

Port

Allauch

Col de
l'Espigoulier

Parc de St-Pons

MARSEILLE

A 50

Aubagne

Gémenos

Parc OK Corral

Château d'If

Cassis

Corniche des Crêtes

Calanques

la Ciotat

CAP CANAILLE

Ile verte

TOULON

A 50

M É D I T E R R A N É E

Touring programmes

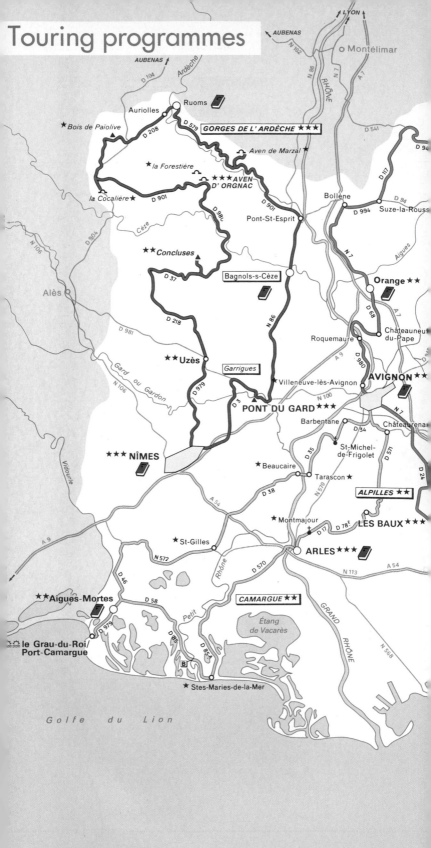

LYON

AUBENAS

Montélimar

AUBENAS

Ardèche

D 104

Ruoms

Auriolles

★ *Bois de Païolive*

GORGES DE L' ARDÈCHE ★★★

D 208

D 579

D 541

D 94

la Forestière ★

Aven de Marzal ★

★★★ AVEN D' ORGNAC

D 901

Bollène

D 117

D 94

Suze-la-Rousse

la Cocalière ★

D 901

D 980

Pont-St-Esprit

D 994

Cèze

N 106

D 904

★★ *Concluses*

Bagnols-s-Cèze

D 37

N 7

Aigues

Alès

D 218

Orange ★★

D 68

A 7

Châteauneuf-du-Pape

D 981

N 86

Roquemaure

D 980

★★ Uzès

Garrigues

A 9

Villeneuve-lès-Avignon

AVIGNON ★★

N 106

Gard ou Gardon

D 979

D 5

PONT DU GARD ★★★

N 100

N 7

★★★ NÎMES

Barbentane

D 34

Châteaurenard

★ St-Michel-de-Frigolet

D 35

D 571

D 24

★ Beaucaire

D 38

Tarascon ★

Vidourle

A 54

N 570

ALPILLES ★★

★ Montmajour

✝ D 17 D 78ᴱ

LES BAUX ★★★

A 9

★ St-Gilles

N 572

Rhône

ARLES ★★★

N 113

A 54

D 46

D 570

GRAND

★★ Aigues-Mortes

D 58

CAMARGUE ★★

D 979

Petit

Étang de Vacarès

le Grau-du-Roi/ Port-Camargue

D 85

RHÔNE

N 568

B

D 85ᴬ

★ Stes-Maries-de-la-Mer

Golfe   du   Lion

0   20 km

MER

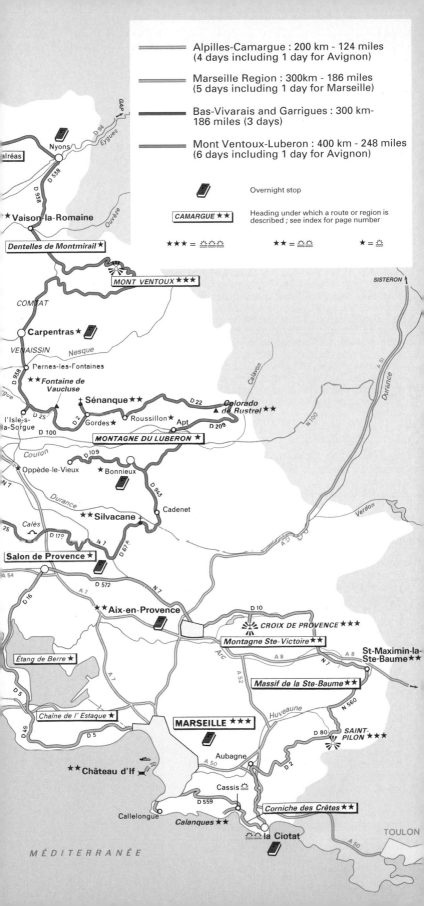

Alpilles-Camargue : 200 km - 124 miles
(4 days including 1 day for Avignon)

Marseille Region : 300km - 186 miles
(5 days including 1 day for Marseille)

Bas-Vivarais and Garrigues : 300 km-
186 miles (3 days)

Mont Ventoux-Luberon : 400 km - 248 miles
(6 days including 1 day for Avignon)

Overnight stop

CAMARGUE ★★   Heading under which a route or region is
               described ; see index for page number

★★★ = 🛁🛁🛁   ★★ = 🛁🛁   ★ = 🛁

SISTERON

GAP

Nyons

alréas

Eygues

D 94

D 538

★ Vaison-la-Romaine

Ouvèze

Dentelles de Montmirail ★

MONT VENTOUX ★★★

COMTAT

Carpentras ★

VENAISSIN

Nesque

Pernes-les-Fontaines

Calavon

Durance

A 51

★★ Fontaine de
Vaucluse

+ Sénanque ★★

D 22

Colorado
de Rustrel ★★

l'Isle-s-
a-Sorgue

D 938

D 25

D 2

Gordes ★   Roussillon ★   Apt

D 100

D 209

N 100

MONTAGNE DU LUBERON ★

Coulon

D 109

★ Oppède-le-Vieux   ★ Bonnieux

N 7

Durance

D 943

Cadenet

Verdon

Calès

★★ Silvacane +

25

D 17ᴰ

N 7

D 67⁴

Salon de Provence ★

A 54

A 7

D 572

N 7

A 7

D 16

★★ Aix-en-Provence

D 10

Étang de Berre ★

A 7

CROIX DE PROVENCE ★★★

Montagne Ste-Victoire ★★

A 8

A 8

St-Maximin-la-
Ste-Baume ★★

Arc

A 52

N 7

Chaîne de l'Estaque ★

D 5

Massif de la Ste-Baume ★★

N 560

D 49

D 5

MARSEILLE ★★★

Huveaune

D 80

SAINT-
PILON ★★★

★★ Château d'If

Aubagne

A 50

D 2

Cassis 🛁

D 559

Corniche des Crêtes ★★

Callelongue

Calanques ★★

🛁🛁 la Ciotat

TOULON

A 50

MÉDITERRANÉE

Places to stay

The mention "Facilities" under individual headings or after place names in the body of the guide refers to the information given on this page.

The map below indicates towns selected for the accommodation, pleasant surroundings and leisure facilities which they offer to the holiday-maker. It also indicates seaside resorts, towns in which a particularly high-quality summer festival takes place, towns of a reasonable size with a good range of accommodation choices and tourist attractions suitable for an overnight stop and cities which are ideally suited for a weekend break, by dint of the historical and artistic heritage and range of cultural activities they offer.

To help you plan your route and choose your hotel, restaurant or camp site, consult the following Michelin publications.

CHOOSING WHERE TO STAY

Accommodation – **The Red Guide France** to hotels and restaurants and the **Michelin Guide Camping Caravaning France** are annual publications, which present a selection of hotels, restaurants and camp sites. The final choice is based on regular on-the-spot enquiries and visits. Both the hotels and camp sites are classified according to the standard of comfort of their amenities. Establishments which are notable for their fortunate set-

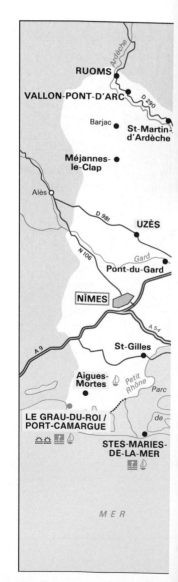

ting, their decor, their quiet and secluded location and their warm welcome are distinguished by special symbols. There are plenty of other kinds of accommodation available (furnished flats for rent, self-catering country cottages, etc.). To find out further details, contact the Tourist Information Offices and *Syndicats d'Initiative*. The most significant of these are listed in The Red Guide France and in the Admission times and charges section at the end of this guide.

THE SEASONS

Climate – Poets and writers have acclaimed Provence's temperate climate, low rainfall and exceptional light.

Nevertheless, weather conditions are changeable from year to year (freezing winters – the most recent one being winter 1985-86 – do occur), while the rhythm of the seasons fluctuates somewhat, especially in the spring; even in winter the temperature can rise or fall dramatically in one day.

Provence's land relief and the sea play an important role. Maritime Provence enjoys a more agreeable climate (less rain and hotter) than Provence's hinterland, where altitude modifies the temperature considerably.

But the dominant factor remains the long periods of sunshine (more than 2 500hr per year) in the region.

Summer – This is "the" season. During those three or four months which give Provence both its appeal and charm, the heat and lack of rain attract the sun-loving tourists. It rains no more than 70mm/2.5in and the temperature rarely drops below 30°C/86°F. This dry heat is neither depressing nor overpowering; its constancy is explained by the presence of a hot air mass from the Sahara, protected from the west's humid depressions by the Massif Central.

Autumn – The reflux of high pressure of tropical origin opens the way to Atlantic depressions. From mid-September to late-November rain appears; sometimes violent rainstorms provoke flash floods. The rainfall can amount to more than 100mm/3.75in in 1hr (for a total of 600mm/23.5in annually).

Winter – The cold season, which is often sunny, is relatively mild and dry. The temperature can drop 10°C/50°F in a few hours because of the *mistral*. The Mediterranean's liquid mass reduces the cold front and prevents snow falls except on the peaks.

Spring – High pressure from Siberia abates from February, allowing the Atlantic rains to fall. These rains are less violent than those in the autumn and fine bright and clear days are frequent. The *mistral*, especially in March, can provoke a surprising chill for those who are not used to the whims of a Provençal spring.

Winds – The wind is an essential part of the Provençal climate. The most famous is the **mistral** (*mistrau* means master in Provençal, thus master-wind); this strong, dry, cold north-northwesterly wind sweeps down when the pressure is high over the mountains from the Massif Central to the Mediterranean, funnelling through the narrow Rhône valley, clearing the sky of clouds and purifying the soil; the farmers call it *mange fange* (mud eater) as it dries up the mud pools. When the *mistral* rages a storm-like atmosphere reigns: the Rhône makes waves, the lagoons and ponds foam and just moving about becomes difficult. The master-wind disappears as suddenly as it arrives; in a couple of hours nature goes back to normal. Alphonse Daudet counted some 30 different winds from the mill at Fontvieille. Besides the *mistral*, two other winds are common: the *marin*, a southeast wind bringing rain and fog, and the *labech*, a southwest wind bringing rainstorms. All the other winds are local.

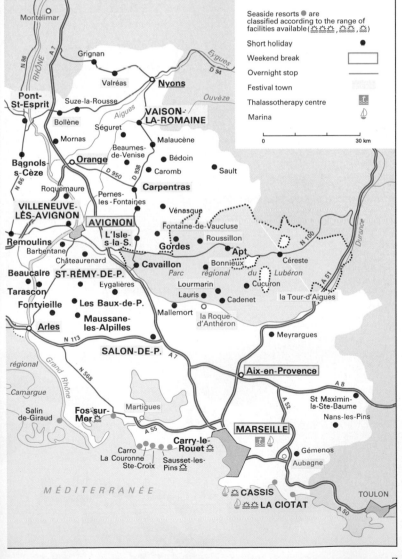

Introduction

Description of the country

LOCAL GEOGRAPHY

Formation of the land – During the Primary Era (c 600-220 million years ago) what is now Provence was covered by a sea which surrounded the continent of Tyrrhenia, contemporary with the Massif Central. It was formed by crystalline rocks, and vestiges of this land mass included the Maures, Corsica, Sardinia and the Balearic Islands. During the Secondary Era (220-60 million years ago), Tyrrhenia was gradually levelled by erosion; the Cretaceous Sea covered practically the whole region. Variations in sea level were caused by the materials from the Primary strata carried down by rivers and deposited at the bottom of the sea, forming sedimentary deposits composed either of limestone (e.g. from Orgon) or marl and transformed into regular and parallel layers of rock (strata) in a strip of land lying east to west; this was the Durancen Isthmus surrounded by the sea.

Primary Era: Tyrrhenia

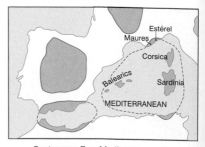

Quaternary Era: Mediterranean Sea

The Tertiary Era (60-2 million years ago) was marked by important tectonic upheavals creating the young folded mountains of the Alps and Pyrenees by uplifting the sedimentary cover. The strata were uplifted and folded in an east-west direction creating the Provençal secondary mountains; to the north of Marseille (Ste-Baume, Ste-Victoire, Mont Ventoux, Baronnies, Alpilles, Luberon), Toulon and Draguignan. The sea level rose to the present-day Rhône valley and while the Alpilles chain was thrust upwards, the Crau plain sank.

During the Quaternary Era (beginning about 2 million years ago) land mass development continued: Tyrrhenia was submerged beneath the present-day Mediterranean Sea leaving such outliers as the Maures, Esterel and Canaille mountains. The relief adopted the form it has now, the Rhône corridor emerged, widened and became an important routeway.

The course of the River Durance was modified by the subsiding of the Crau plain and deviated to join the Rhône. Erosion during glaciation and interglacial periods put the final touches to the landscapes *(calanques)*.

Plains – The plains were formed by reclaiming territory from the sea with the constant deposits of alluvial sediments, i.e. the Rhône delta. They first spread over the Rhône's east bank, **Comtat Venaissin**, then they spread over both banks. On the west side of the river the plains extended to the Lower Languedoc dominated by the *garrigues* near Nîmes; to the east they became the fertile **Petite Crau** and **Grande Crau**. Romans, medieval monks and small property holders throughout the centuries have improved the land with drainage and irrigation schemes. Two regions, especially, have profited from such schemes: Comtat Venaissin and Petite Crau. Market gardens now cover the land creating a fine pattern of tiny plots separated by windbreaks of tall cypress and lower screens of reeds.

The **Grande Crau**, separated from Camargue by the Grand Rhône, is an immense desert of pebbles and boulders between which grow tufts of grass known locally as *coussous*. It was used traditionally for the winter pasturing of large flocks of sheep. The expansion of Fos' industrial zone and the clearing of the land of stones as well as the irrigation schemes have transformed the area; it has lost its pastoral image and with it much of its charm.

Olive groves, almond trees, vineyards and undulating grassland make up the new wealth of these areas.

The **Camargue** is a delta of recent alluvium or silt formed by the Rhône. This delta regained from the sea is salt-impregnated, and is one of France's most picturesque regions. The *sansouires*, vast salt-marshes, bring to the area an immense wild appearance.

Plateaux, hills and massifs – The Provençal plains are flanked or penetrated by folded mountain chains lying east to west which rise quite abruptly, blocking the horizon. The relief often appears confused presenting an undisciplined alternation of limestone heights and partitioned-off fertile basins: Apt country, Aigues country (south of

Luberon), Aix country (irrigated by the Provence canal) where very varied crops (grain, vineyards, fruit, market gardening) are cultivated. East of the Rhône, from north to south, different landscapes follow one after the other.

The western fringe of the **Baronnies** form a complicated structure of hills and slopes of real beauty where olive groves and the hybrid *lavandin* reign. The rocky summits of the **Dentelles de Montmirail** display a finely carved-out relief (*dentelle* means lace) which is unique in Provence: oak and pine forests with vineyards carpeting the slopes. Backed up against the Baronnies is **Mont Ventoux**, an imposing limestone massif, which dominates the Comtadin plain at a height of 1 909m/6 263ft.

The **Vaucluse plateau** – also known as the Vaucluse hills – a vast arid area devoted to sheep raising and the cultivation of lavender *(photograph p 17)*, is a land of karstic relief. This limestone countryside is potted with chasms *(see p 18)* and carved out by gorges. A mysterious underground hydrographic network penetrates through the limestone and opens out at the Fontaine de Vaucluse.

The **Montagne du Luberon** stretches over some 60km/37mi; cut in half north to south by the Lourmarin coomb, it culminates in the Grand Luberon at Mourre Nègre (alt 1 125m/3 691ft). This region has some enchantingly beautiful rugged mountain sites to which villages cling precariously; there is a striking contrast between its forest-clad, wild north face and its more cultivated south face. In the middle of the Rhône plain stand two picturesque ranges: La **Montagnette** and Les **Alpilles**.

East of Aix, **Montagne Ste-Victoire**, a limestone mass pock-marked with caves and chasms, dominates the Aix basin, whereas to the southeast the Trévaresse and Vitrolles ranges bar it from the Étang de Berre. The lagoon is closed to the south by **Chaîne de l'Estaque** separated from the St-Mitre hills by the Caronte depression.

The **Chaîne de l'Étoile**, Chaîne St-Cyr and Massif Marseilleveyre surround Marseille whereas on the horizon looms the long rocky barrier of the **Massif de la Ste-Baume** which reaches an altitude of 1 447m/3 763ft at the Ste-Baume signal station.

West of the River Rhône, the Cévennes foothills lie north to south receding in the river's direction and the vine-carpeted plain via the *garrigues* of Nîmes. A series of desolate limestone plateaux cut by canyons and gouged out by sometimes huge chasms succeed in tiers; it is an arid, rocky terrain only fit for sheep grazing. In the past, harvesting the plant-life (aromatic plants, olives, almonds...) and making goats'

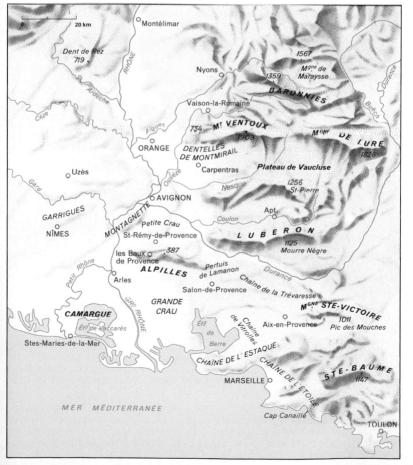

cheese *(migou)* constituted ways of raising income. The countryside is criss-crossed by a multitude of dry-stone enclosures in the middle of which stood a modest hut *(mazet)* or *capitelle* (similar to the dry-stone huts known as *bories*). There are, however, a couple of isolated fertile areas: Uzès basin, Vistre plain and Vaunage (southwest of Nîmes) which are devoted to crop growing (orchards, vineyards etc).

Waterways – On its Provençal flow, the Rhône receives from the west the Ardèche and Gard rivers, which come down from the Cévennes, and from the east the Aigues, Ouvèze and Durance rivers, which come down from the Alps. They all have the same torrential appearance: a trickle of water in a stony bed too wide during periods of drought which transforms itself into an avalanche of foaming water during rain storms. The Cévennes receive rainfalls of unusual violence – a single downpour exceeds the annual rainfall of Paris. The rivers expand dramatically, the Ardèche has been seen to rise 21m/69ft in one day and its flow from 2.5m³ per second to 7.500m³/88.3 cubic ft to 264855 cubic ft; often enough the water rises 10m/33ft and more. Frequently the flow of the Ardèche cuts through the Rhône like a rocket striking the dikes of the left bank, across the way; these flash-floods 5m/16.5ft high are known as the blows of the Ardèche *(les coups de l'Ardèche)*.

For the tributaries of the east bank which come down from the Alps, it is the melting snows which considerably multiply the volume of water. For the Durance, for example, it expands proportionately from 1 to 180. Fortunately these spates occur in the spring, when the Ardèche and Gard rivers are low. On the other hand, the Durance is almost dry in winter and autumn while the rains from the Cévennes expand the tributaries of the west bank.

Coastline – From the Languedoc coast to the Marseille *calanques* the coastline often changes form. As far as the Golfe de Fos, the shoreline is marked by vast **lagoons** separated from the sea by narrow sand bars: the mass of alluvial deposits dropped by the Rhône and shaped by the coastal currents has formed offshore bars closing off the lagoons. The encroachment of sand has pushed inland old ports like Aigues-Mortes.

With the Chaîne de l'Estaque reappears the limestone relief which cuts the coastline. From Marseille to La Ciotat the littoral is cut into a great number of coves of which the deepest and most uneven are called **calanques** – they are in fact the submerged extremities of the valleys, when the sea level rose after the Quaternary Era's glacial period. Steep cliffs, brown and reddish rocks plunge vertically into the deep, blue sea from which emerge a number of islands not far out. With small well-sheltered ports and lovely wild creeks, the *calanques* are the kingdom of deep-sea divers and climbers alike.

The sea – This is the bluest of European seas. This deep tint – cobalt, the painters call it – arises from the great limpidity of the water.

The temperature of the water surface varies from 20°-25°C/68°-77°F in summer falling to only 12°-13°C/53°-55°F in winter (at a depth of 200 to 4000m/656 to 13123ft, the temperature is a constant 13°C/55°F). This is an important factor in the climate; this great liquid mass cools in summer, warms in winter. As a result of very rapid evaporation the water is noticeably more salty than that of the Atlantic.

The tide is very slight: averaging 0.25m/9.5in, and yet variation in height caused by strong winds can be as much as 1m/3ft. This relative stability has singled out the Mediterranean as base level for all the French coast's altitudes.

A calm sea, with small short choppy waves, the Mediterranean can suddenly become violent: in the lapse of a couple of hours a *mistral*, which can rise and provoke dangerous storms often surprises careless yachtsmen.

LOCAL ECONOMY

The Provençal economy is, perhaps, the regional economy of France which has encountered the most impressive mutations in the past 50 years: agricultural revolution, increased industrialisation especially along the coast, adaptation to large-scale tourism and runaway urbanisation.

The different facets of agriculture

Rural life in the past depended on three crops – wheat, vineyards, olives – which, with sheep raising and a variety of other products gathered locally (herbs, almonds), ensured the existence of a mass of small farmers very attached to their native soil. This traditional polyculture has almost disappeared, replaced by modern speculative agriculture, making the most out of Provence's natural resources, thus enabling it to become the garden of France.

Early produce – The alluvial soil of the Rhône plain, the high mean temperature and irrigation schemes have favoured the development of early market gardening and fruit growing, producing several crops a year in the Comtat Venaissin and Petite Crau. The whole region is now divided up into little parcels of land protected from the *mistral* by screens of cypress and reeds.

Strawberries, tomatoes and melons from Carpentras, asparagus, new potatoes and melons from Cavaillon, cabbage from Rognonas, asparagus from Lauris, cherries from Remoulins, peaches, pears and apricots from the Rhône valley are all sold in the markets of Paris, northern and eastern France as well as foreign countries.

Early produce, picked in the morning, is either sold to a private packer or sent to a cooperative where it is sorted, graded, packed and conditioned (cooperatives have been established at St-Rémy, Châteaurenard, Barbentane, Cabannes and St-Andiol, west of Cavaillon etc).

From the main railway heads – Châteaurenard, Cavaillon, Carpentras, Barbentane, Avignon – fast trains transport the early produce up the Rhône valley to Paris and other large cities.

Cereals and vineyards – The area between Arles and Tarascon, hitherto the main centre for growing wheat in Provence, is now producing maize, rape and rice as well, and the windmills so dear to Alphonse Daudet have been replaced by modern milling machinery in the towns.

Vineyards occupy some 110 000ha/424sq mi and in the plains produce large quantities of table wine *(vin ordinaire)*; whereas on the hillside, where the vineyards are cultivated with more care, a more delicate wine is produced carrying the general name Côtes du Rhône. The Côtes du Rhône's most celebrated vintage is Châteauneuf-du-Pape *(see p 144)*. It has an estimated 15 000ha/37 050 acres of vineyards which produce high quality wine.

Lavender and lavandin – The delicate scent of lavender is characteristic of Provence. This plant is well suited to the climate and calcareous soils of Provence and Haute-Provence *(see Michelin Green Guide Alpes du Sud, in French only)*. *Lavandin*, a more productive but less fragrant hybrid, is cultivated on the lower slopes (400-700m/1 312-2 297ft) and in the valleys. Today, about 8 400ha/20 748 acres of lavender are cultivated as well as 2 350ha/5 805 acres of *lavandin*. The harvest takes place from July to September according to the region; most of the picking is now done by machinery but the inaccessible or closely-planted older fields are still picked by hand. After drying for two to three days, the picked lavender is sent to a distillery equipped with the classic still. One hundred kilos of lavender blossom are needed to produce one litre of essence (as against only 10 litres in the case of *lavandin* flowers). Lavender essence is reserved for the perfume and cosmetic industries whereas the hybrid *lavandin* perfumes laundry soap and cleaning products. The lavender flower can also be dried and placed in scent bags.

Superb lavender fields can be spotted on the Vaucluse plateau and in the Drôme and Gard *départements*, north of Nîmes.

Almonds and olives – Almond trees which grow all round the shores of the Mediterranean were first imported into France from Asia in 1548; the development of later-blossoming varieties has led to increased cultivation. The most famous of the local almond confectionery are *calissons* from Aix and Salon, lozenge-shaped sweetmeats coated in white sugar icing.

The silver-green of the olive groves is a common sight in the country round Salon, Nyons and the mountains' southern slopes.

Sometimes, in the olive plantations, old trees have been cut low to the ground and four suckers can be seen growing in a crown-like shape; these are kept as they create handsome new trees. The black olives of Nyons, preserved in brine, are a delicacy.

Truffles – The truffle is an edible, subterranean fungus which develops from the mycelium, a network of filaments invisible to the naked eye. They live symbiotically in close association with the root of the downy oak, known in Provence as the white oak. The truffle is harvested in the winter when it is ripe and odorous.

These small stunted oaks are planted in rows in fields called *truffières*.

They are found mainly in south Tricastin, Comtat Venaissin, the Claparèdes plateau and in the Luberon. A superficial breaking-up of the soil and a specified pruning favours the truffle crop which is harvested from November to April and marketed mostly in Apt, Carpentras, Richerenches, Uzès and Valréas, where several tons of this "black diamond" pass through annually.

Lime trees and herbs – Although found in most parts of France, the lime tree is cultivated mainly in Provence between Buis-les-Baronnies and Carpentras. At the end of the 19C, the lime tree grew alongside most French roads, whereas today it is planted in orchards and pruned. The flower is picked in June, depending on the blooming, dried in a shaded, airy dry room, then sold in bags or by the ounce for tea. Aromatic plants also called *herbes de Provence* (Herbs of Provence) have doubled in popularity in recent years. Certain varieties are cultivated traditionally: basil and marjoram are cultivated around St-Rémy-de-Provence, tarragon on the Vaucluse plateau, whereas other varieties such as thyme, rosemary and savory are still gathered from the hillsides where they grow wild, and supply a large proportion of the herbs gathered.

Stock raising – Provence is centred on sheep raising, an essential resource of all Mediterranean rural economics. Wool, no longer profitable, was discarded and the sheep are now reared for meat. The Merino variety from Arles is predominant in the Bouches-du-Rhône *département*; however, the area allocated to it diminishes daily. It grazes on the meagre *coussous* from Plaine de la Crau from 15 October to 15 June and then transhumes to the Alps; the transhumance, once a picturesque procession, is now done in trucks. In the *garrigues* there again the flocks of sheep graze on the meagre vegetation that they find when roaming these vast territories; they spend the summer in Larzac or in the Lozère mountains.

Camargue is the land of large plantations and concentrates on the rearing of black bulls and white horses living in liberty and grouped in herds called *manades (see p 134)*.

Fishing

Fishing is a traditional activity which takes place in the ports of Languedoc (Le Grau-du-Roi) and Provence (Port-St-Louis, Martigues, Carry-le-Rouet, Marseille, Cassis), and yet it occupies a minimal position and frequently suffers from water pollution. Nevertheless, several thousand tons of sardines, anchovies, mackerel and eel are caught annually. The coming and going of these sailor-fishermen unloading their catch and drying their nets still remains one of the ports' most attractive scenes.

At Marseille, the recent port of Saumaty, located at the foot of the Estaque, can shelter as many as 180 trawlers (1 400m/4 593ft of quays) and offers all the necessary equipment for the preservation of fish.

Small fishing boats still supply the fishmongers of Marseille's Vieux Port whose cries echo in an atmosphere so vividly rendered in several of Marcel Pagnol's novels.

Industrialisation

Provence has benefited from a geographical location propitious to commercial exchange and witnessed a spectacular industrial development in the 1930s.

Around Étang de Berre a vast industrial complex was built – oil refineries, chemical, aeronautic and iron and steel (today threatened) works – with the Bassins de Fos complex, inaugurated in 1968, as its centre. From Marseille to Aix industrial zones have multiplied and offer a vast range of activities from soapmaking plants to the most modern electronics factories including the Gardanne thermal power station.

The hydroelectric installations of the lower valleys of the Rhône and Durance have also contributed to the profound economic upheavals. Hydroelectric production combined with nuclear (Marcoule) production has allowed France to strengthen its energy potential. Moreover, the domestication of the two undisciplined rivers has resulted in the possibility of irrigating an immense agricultural area, until then hindered by drought.

All these transformations have made Provence one of France's great industrial areas juggling between two types of industry:

– traditional: minerals (ochre, bauxite, lignite), shipbuilding, foodstuffs, soapmaking (Marseille area), building materials, construction and saltworks;

– modern: petroleum and its derivatives, aeronautics, electronics, nuclear (Cadarache Centre for Nuclear Studies), chemicals.

Light industries have also developed: packaging in Valréas and Tarascon, confectionery in Aix, Apt and Nyons, fruit preserving, garment and shoe making in Nîmes.

Ochre quarries of Roussillon

Ochre – The Apt-Roussillon area is one of the main mining and treatment regions in France for ochre (an earthy red or yellow and often impure iron ore essentially used as a pigment for paints or as a wash applied for its protective value). The mineral beds can at times be 15m/49ft thick. Ochre in its natural state is a mixture of argillaceous sand and iron oxide. To obtain a commercially-pure ochre product, the mineral is first washed and the impurities which tend to be heavier settle to the bottom; whereas the lighter weight "flower", which is made of iron oxide and clay, is passed through the filter and into settling tanks where after drying it assumes the look of ochre, which is then cut into blocks. After drying, the ochre is crushed, sifted and at times baked in ovens to darken the pigmentation and obtain a reddish orange colour. This process is called ochre calcining; it then becomes an unctuous, impalpable powder used commercially. The quality of the ochre from Vaucluse has made France one of its most important producers – annual production is about 3 000 metric tons.

Olive oil – Typically Provençal oil has always been olive oil. Olives are treated when they are ripe and are picked while still green if used for food preservation. The quality of the oil depends on the quality of the fruit and treatment (number of pressings). Once picked, the olives are crushed whole with the pit either by a millstone, hammer mill or roller. The paste obtained is then distributed on a trolley's nylon discs. The trolley, now loaded, is placed on the sliding piston of a hydraulic press, pressure is exerted and the resulting mixture of oil and water is collected in tanks and then pumped into centrifugal machines where the oil and water will be separated. The oil which comes out of the machine is a virgin oil obtained by a first cold water pressing. The residual pulp *(grignon)* can be pressed again.

In the past the olive paste was spread by hand onto coconut mats *(scourtins)* which were stacked under the press. For a long time the presses were worked by hand and the horse turned the millstone. The residual pulp was remashed with lukewarm water: a mixture of refined and virgin oil was obtained, classed as second quality and called second pressing. Today, as in the past, the residual pulp treated with chemical solvents in Italy produces oil used for cutting or soap-making. Before this last pressing the stone can be separated from the pulp: the stone is ground down into powder and is used by the baker and pastry cook; the pulp is used for compost.

Salt marshes – Two large salt marshes are worked in Camargue: one south of Aigues-Mortes spreads over 10 000ha/24 700 acres; the other south of Salin-de-Giraud spreads over 11 000ha/27 170 acres. Already improved by the monks in the 13C, the salt marshes *(see p 133)* increased production in the mid-19C, progressed and then decreased. The present-day global annual production is evaluated at 850 000 metric tons.

VEGETATION

In addition to its beautiful countryside, underlined by an always (or almost) luminous sky, Provence possesses a highly original natural habitat.

Trees and plants – All vegetation is closely dependent on climatic conditions. In Provence, as elsewhere, flowering occurs during the spring, although there is a second blossoming in the autumn which goes on well into winter; the dormant period is during the summer when the heat of the climate only permits plants which are especially adapted to resist drought to grow: long taproots, glazed leaves which reduce transpiration, bulbs which act as reservoirs of moisture and a protective perfumed vapour. The olive tree and holm oak mark out the Mediterranean area as such, which is dotted with *garrigues*. In Haute-Provence the *garrigues* disappear, to be replaced by the forest cover (downy oak, Scots pine, beech) and the moors (broom, lavender, boxwood).

In Vivarais chestnut trees add an unusual touch to the landscape.

Olive trees – The Greeks brought olive trees to Provence 2 500 years ago because they grow equally well in limestone or sandy soils. The olive has been called the immortal tree as, grafted or wild, it will continually renew itself. Those grown from cuttings die relatively young at 300 years of age. Along the coast the trees reach gigantic dimensions attaining 20m/65.5ft in height, their domes of silver foliage 20m/65.5ft in circumference and trunks 4m/13ft round the base. The olive tree, of which there are more than 60 varieties, will grow at up to altitudes of 600m/1 968ft and marks the limit of the Mediterranean climate. It grows mainly on valley floors and hillsides, often mingling with almond and fig trees. The olive tree begins to bear fruit at between 6 and 12 years and is in full yield at 20-25 years; it is harvested every two years. Under the light, evergreen foliage of the olive tree early vegetables are cultivated.

Olive tree

Oak trees – There are several varieties of oaks.

The **holm oak** *(quercus ilex)* has a short thick-set trunk with a wide-spreading thick dome. It grows on arid calcareous soil at less than 1 000m/3 281ft. It is an evergreen oak, the leaves of which remain a fine dark green. In stunted form it is a characteristic element of the *garrigues* in association with all sorts of shrubs and aromatic plants.

The **kermes** or scrub oak is a bushy evergreen shrub rarely exceeding 1m/3ft in height. It has a trunk of grey bark with a thick dome of shiny, tough, ragged, prickly leaves. Its name, kermes, comes from the scale-insect which lives on its branches and from which a bright red dye is obtained. The tree grows on stone-free dry soil but prefers a fertile, cool soil.

The **downy oak** or **white oak** *(quercus pubescens)* is a deciduous tree (the undersides of the leaves are covered with dense short white hairs) which requires more water than the evergreens above. It can be found in the valleys and on the more humid mountain slopes. It is at times associated with the maple, service tree and rowan. In its undergrowth a variety of shrubs and flowers, notably the orchid, grow. It is also on the root of this tree that the truffle lives.

Umbrella pine

Pine trees – The three types of pine to be found in the Mediterranean can be easily distinguished by their outline.

The **maritime pine** *(pinus pinaster)* grows on limestone soil; its foliage is dark blue-green and the bark a purply red.

The **umbrella** or **stone pine** *(pinus pinea)* is one of the Mediterranean's most characteristic sights; it owes its name to its easily-recognisable shape. It is often found growing alone.

The **Aleppo pine** *(pinus halepensis)* is a Mediterranean species which grows well in the chalky soil along the coast. Its foliage is light and graceful with a trunk covered with a grey bark and twisting as it grows.

Other Provençal trees – In towns and villages the streets and squares are shaded by the smooth-barked **plane trees** or the dark green canopy of the branching **lotus tree** *(micocoulier)* which yields a fruit mentioned by Homer in the *Odyssey* as inducing a state of dreamy forgetfulness and loss of desire to return home – hence lotus-eaters. It has also been identified by some as the jujube tree.

The outline of the dark **cypress,** a coniferous evergreen, marks the Mediterranean landscape with its tapered form pointed towards the sky. Planted in serried ranks, the pyramid-shaped cypress forms a windbreak.

The variety with scattered branches is used for reforestation programmes. The rosaceous species, the common **almond tree** prevalent in Provence, delights the eye with its lovely early-spring pink blossoms.

The noble elm tree has practically disappeared.

Forest cover – There are not many forests in Provence and those that exist grow especially in the mountain ranges below 1 600m/5 249ft.

Fine forests of holm or downy oak grow in Grand Luberon, on Montagne Ste-Victoire and the Vaucluse plateau.

Petit Luberon is covered with a fine cedar forest; on the north face of the Massif de la Ste-Baume grow forests of beech trees. Spread along the limestone peaks is a moor of broom.

The designation of the word forest beyond these areas indicates copses carpeting vast areas north of the Durance.

Almond tree

Cypress

Oleander

A. Carrara/JACANA

Yellow everlasting

M. Viard/JACANA

Globe thistle

Y. Szymczac/JACANA

Thyme

M. Viard/JACANA

Garrigues – In Provence this word is used to describe vast expanses of rocky, limestone moors. Small *garrigues* can be found in most parts of Provence; however, the *garrigue* as such is found especially north of Nîmes where it was carved deeply by the Gardon river. It is generally made up of a stretch of low limestone hills with minute parcels of land between the outcrops of white calcareous rock; sometimes the rain has washed the soil down into the valleys leaving vast rocky table-lands.

Vegetation is sparse consisting mostly of holm oaks, stunted downy oaks, thistles, gorse and cistus as well as lavender, thyme and rosemary interspersed with short dry grass which provides pasture for flocks of sheep.

In addition to the wild aromatic plants which grow in the *garrigues*, such herbs as basil, marjoram, savory, sage, melissa, mint, laurel and absinth, which are cultivated commercially and sold for herbal and medicinal use, also appear *(see "Lime trees and herbs" above)*.

Environmental battle – The influx of tourists, industrial and urban development are the cause of constant attacks against the Mediterranean and Provence's natural habitat.

Forest fires – The Provençal forest is particularly exposed to fires (those of 1979, 1985 and 1986 were catastrophic), the majority of which are due to negligence or arson. The fire has two natural allies: drought and wind.

During the summer the dried-up plants of the underbrush, pine needles, resins exuded by leaves and twigs are highly combustible and sometimes catch fire spontaneously. Once a fire has started, it spreads to the pines, and if the wind is strong, disaster may follow. Enormous walls of flame, sometimes more than 10km/6mi long and 30m/98ft high, spread at speeds of 5-6kph/2-3mph. When the fire has passed, nothing remains standing except the blackened skeletons of the trees while a thick layer of white ash covers the ground.

Often the fire wins, stopping only at the coast, unless the wind drops or alters direction. These fires gradually disrupt the ecological balance; for example, the oak forests are receding and the soil remains barren for a long time. The many different means of fighting forest fires will not solve the problem; fire prevention (systematic watch, periodically clearing the underbrush, creation of fire-breaks etc), public awareness, especially that of tourists, should help combat this enemy of nature.

Dial 18 to reach the Fire Department (pompiers).

Pollution – The fast-developing urbanisation and industrialisation programmes which occurred in Provence have dealt a heavy blow to the beauty of several natural sites. The Fos-sur-Mer industrial complex spreads out over the Plaine de la Crau; the area around Étang de Berre, especially its eastern side, has become the bustling suburb (airport, refineries etc) of Marseille. Already in 1957 owing to the high level of polluted water, fishing was strictly forbidden in the lagoon. The discharge of used water from the surrounding towns, the St-Martin-de-Crau rubbish tip and the Marseille main sewer flowing into the Calanque Cortiou etc are all very harmful.

The flow of traffic (constantly on the increase) in the region has resulted in the construction of more and more road networks which are cutting up the countryside and leaving a smaller and smaller area to nature.

CAVES AND CHASMS

In contrast to the deeply-dissected green valleys with their many settlements, the Bas Vivarais limestone plateaux roll away to the far horizon, stony, grey and deserted. The dryness of the soil is due to the calcareous nature of the rock which absorbs rain like a sponge.

At the end of the last century, the methodical and scientific exploration of the underground world, with which the name of **Édouard-Alfred Martel** is associated, led to the discovery of a certain number of caves and their organisation as a tourist attraction. In 1935 **Robert de Joly** explored Aven d'Orgnac and discovered its wealth of cave formations; later on the discovery of a gaping hole in the chasm led to the discovery in 1965 of a vast network of upper galleries. Our knowledge of the underground system is at present very incomplete and a great many chasms remain unknown to speleologists.

Water infiltration – Rainwater, charged with carbonic acid, dissolves the carbonate of lime to be found in the limestone. Depressions, which are usually circular in shape and small in size and are known as **cloups** or **sotchs**, are then formed. The dissolution of the limestone rocks, containing especially salt or gypsum, produces rich soil particularly suitable for growing crops; when the *cloups* increase in size they form large, closed depressions known as **dolines**. Where rainwater infiltrates deeply through the fissures in the plateau, the hollowing out and dissolution of the calcareous layer produces wells or natural chasms which are called **avens** or **igues**. Little by little the chasms lengthen and branch off, communicating with each other and widening out into caves.

Underground rivers – The infiltrating waters finally produce underground galleries and collect to form a more or less swift flowing river. The river widens its course and often changes level, to fall in cascades. Where the rivers run slowly they form lakes, above natural dams, known as **gours**, which are raised layer by layer by deposits of carbonate of lime. The dissolution of the limestone also continues above the water-level in these subterranean galleries: blocks of stone fall from the roof and domes form, the upper parts pointing towards the surface of the earth. Such is the case with the Upper Chamber at Orgnac which lies only a few feet beneath the surface of the plateau. When the roof of the dome wears thin it may cave in, disclosing the cavity from above and opening the chasm.

Cave formation – As it circulates below ground, the water deposits the lime with which it has become charged, thus building up concretions of fantastic shapes which seem to defy the laws of gravity and equilibrium.

In some caverns, the seeping waters produce calcite (carbonate of lime) deposits which form pendants, pyramids and draperies. The best known formations are stalactites, stalagmites and eccentrics.

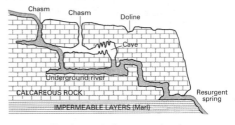

Development of a resurgent spring

Stalactites are formed from the cave roof. Every droplet of water seeping through to the ceiling deposits on it some of the calcite with which it is charged, before dripping off. Gradually the concretion builds up layer by layer as the drops are attracted and run down its length, depositing particles before falling.

Stalagmites are formed in the same way but rise from the floor towards the roof. Drops of water, dripping from the roof always in the same place, deposit the calcite particles they are carrying which build up to form a candle-like shape. This rises towards a stalactite with which it ultimately joins to form a pillar linking the cave floor with the ceiling. Concretions form very slowly indeed; the rate of growth in a temperate climate is about 1cm/0.4in every 100 years.

The **eccentrics** are very fine protuberances which seldom exceed 20cm/8in in length. They emerge at any angle either as slender spikes or in the shape of small, translucent fans. They are formed by crystallisation and seem to disregard the laws of gravity. Aven d'Orgnac, Aven de Marzal and Grotte de la Madeleine contain remarkable examples.

Historical table and notes

Events in italics indicate milestones in history

From prehistory to the Roman conquest

BC

c 6000	Neolithic impressed pottery: the first potters begin turning to agriculture and settle on the sites of Châteauneuf-les-Martigues and Courthézon.
c 3500	Chassey culture: the appearance of true stock-raising farmers living in villages.
1800-800	Bronze Age. Ligurian occupation.
8-4C	Progressive installation of the Celts.
c 600	Founding of Massalia (Marseille) by the Phocaeans *(see MARSEILLE)*.
4C	Massalia is at its apex; travels of the Massaliote, Pythéas, into the northern seas.
218	Hannibal passes through Provence and crosses the Alps.
125-122	Conquest of southern Gaul by the Romans. Destruction of Entremont and founding of Aix.
102	Marius defeats the Teutons at Aquae Sextiae (Aix).
58-51	Conquest of long-haired Gaul by Julius Caesar.
55	Caesar lands in Britain.
27	Augustus establishes the Narbonensis.

AD

2C	Nîmes at its apex.
284	Narbonensis is divided into two provinces: Narbonensis on the west bank of the River Rhône, and Viennoise on the east bank.
4C	Arles at its apex; establishment of the dioceses.
416	Jean Cassien, from the Far East, founds the Abbaye de St-Victor in Marseille.

Establishment of the County of Provence

471	Arles taken over by the Visigoths.
476	Fall of the Roman Empire.
536	Provence ceded to the Franks.
843	By the *Treaty of Verdun* Provence, Burgundy and Lorraine are restored to Lothair (one of Charlemagne's grandsons).
855	Provence is made a kingdom by Lothair for his third son, Charles.
879	Boson, Charles the Bald's brother-in-law, is king of Burgundy and Provence.
2nd half of 9C and 10C	Saracens, Vikings and Magyars terrorise the land.
1032	Provence is annexed by the Holy Roman Empire; the counts of Provence, however, retain their independence; the towns expand and assert their autonomy.
1066	William the Conqueror lands in England.
1125	Provence divided up between the counts of Barcelona and Toulouse.
c 1135	First mention of a consulate in Arles.
1215	*Magna Carta.*
1229	By the *Treaty of Paris* Lower-Languedoc returns to France; founding of the royal seneschalship in Beaucaire.
1246	Charles of Anjou, brother of St Louis, marries Beatrice of Provence, the count of Barcelona's daughter, and becomes count of Provence.
1248	St Louis embarks from Aigues-Mortes on the Seventh Crusade.
1274	Cession of the Comtat Venaissin to the papacy.
1316-1403	The popes and schismatic popes at Avignon. Great Schism of the West (1378-1417).
1337-1453	Hundred Years War.
1348	Clement VI buys Avignon from Queen Joan I. Great Plague epidemic.
1409	University of Aix founded.
1434-80	Reign of Good King René, Louis XI's uncle.
1450	Jacques Cœur sets up his trading-posts in Marseille.
1481	Charles of Maine, nephew of René of Anjou, bequeaths Provence to Louis XI.

The Estates of Provence

1486	The Estates of Provence meet at Aix to ratify the union of Provence to the crown.
1492	Christopher Columbus discovers America.
1501	Inauguration of the Parliament of Aix as Supreme Court of Justice with limited political authority.
1509-47	Henry VIII's reign.
1524-36	Provence is invaded by the Imperialists (soldiers of the Holy Roman Empire).
1539	Edict of Villers-Cotterêts decrees French as the language for all administrative laws in Provence.
1545	Suppression of Vaudois heretics from Luberon.
1555	Nostradamus publishes his astrological predictions, Centuries.
1558-1603	Elizabeth I's reign.
1558	The engineer Adam de Craponne builds a canal.
1567	Michelade tragedy occurs in Nîmes.
1588	Defeat of the Spanish Armada.
1622	Louis XIII visits Arles, Aix and Marseille.
1660	Solemn entry of Louis XIV into Marseille.
1685	Revocation of the Edict of Nantes. Huguenots flee France.
1713	Under the Treaty of Utrecht the Principality of Orange is transferred from the House of Orange-Nassau to France.
1714-27	George I's reign.
1720	The great plague which originated in Marseille decimates Provence.
1763	Peace of Paris ends French and Indian War (1754-63); it marks the end of France's colonial empire in North America.
1771	Suppression of Aix's Parliament.

From the Revolution to the present

1790	The constitutional Assembly divides southeast France into three *départements*: Basses-Alpes (capital: Digne), Bouches-du-Rhône (capital: Aix-en-Provence), Var (capital: Toulon).
1791	Avignon and Comtat Venaissin are annexed to France.
1792	500 Marseille volunteers parade in Paris to the song of the Rhine Army, called *La Marseillaise*.
1805	Battle of Trafalgar.
1815	Battle of Waterloo; Napoleon's fall.
1837-1901	Victoria's reign.
1854	Founding of the Provençal literary school: Félibrige.
1859	Frédéric Mistral publishes the Provençal poem *Mirèio*.
1861-65	American Civil War.
1886	Statue of Liberty erected.
1899	Second Boer War.
1933	Founding of the Compagnie Nationale du Rhône for the harnessing of the river.
1942	German forces invade Provence.
1944	15 August: Allied troops land on the Côte d'Azur.
	22-28 August: General de Montsabert and his troops aided by the Resistance movement liberate Marseille from German occupation.
1962	First hydroelectric power stations of the Durance begin operating.
1965	Construction of Bassins de Fos complex begins.
1970	A 6-A 7 motorways link Paris and Marseille.
	Creation of the Parc Naturel Régional de Camargue.
1977	Marseille's underground begins service.
	Creation of the Parc Naturel Régional du Luberon.
1981	The TGV, France's high-speed train, links Paris to Marseille.
1991	Discovery in the Calanque de Sormiou, south of Marseille, of cave paintings and engravings dating from the Upper Paleolithic era, now known as the Grotte Cosquer *(see p 131)*.
1993	Olympique de Marseille become the first French football club to win the European Cup.
1994	A painted cave, known as the Grotte Chauvet, is discovered in the Ardèche gorges *(see p 83)*.

A RICH PAST

Southern Gaul before the Roman conquest

Origins: a melting pot – During the Bronze Age (1800-800BC) the region was inhabited by Ligurians, probably descendants of the native Neolithic population. In the 7C the Celts began infiltrating while the first Greeks were settling. Massalia (Marseille) was founded in 600 (or 620) by the Phocaeans in agreement with a Celtic tribe. And yet the arrival of Celts in hordes did not come about until the 5C-4C. This resulted in a mixture of populations which provided ancient Provence with roots in the Celtic-Ligurian civilization. These diverse populations settled progressively on *oppida*, fortified hill sites. Nages, near Nîmes, St-Blaise overlooking the Golfe de Fos, Entremont near Aix were important settlements, in reality fortified townships.

Greek presence – It is seen as an essential part of the history of Provence's civilization. The Rhodians most likely gave their name to the great Provençal river (Rhodanos); however, the Phocaeans from Asia Minor (Ionia) were the first to establish a permanent colony: **Massalia**. Massalia rapidly became a powerful commercial city which founded in turn a number of trading posts: Glanum, Avignon, Cavaillon, and had commercial exchanges with the people of the north (wine and pottery for pewter from Armorica and agricultural products and livestock from Brittany). And yet Greek culture spread slowly; not before the 2C, a period when relations between the natives and the Phocaeans from Massalia were deteriorating. The Salian Confederation (which had grouped together the Provençal population) rose against Massaliote imperialism.

Rome and Massalia – During the Second Punic War (218-201), Massalia supported Rome whereas the Salian Franks helped Hannibal cross the region in 218. In 154 Massalia, worried about the threat of attack by the Gauls, obtained the protection of Rome. In 130 the powerful Arverni empire posed a problem of security to southern Gaul, the key trading centre between Italy and Spain. In 125 Rome came to Massalia's aid and the Roman legions conquered with ease the Vocontii and Salian Franks whose capital, Entremont, fell. In 122, date of the founding of Aquae Sextiae (Aix-en-Provence), the Arverni and Allobroges suffered a bloody defeat. The consul Domitius Ahenobarbus delimited the boundaries of a new province, **Transalpine**, which became **Narbonensis** (from the name of the first Roman colony of Narbonna) in 118. Massalia remained independent and it was recognised as a territory. The Roman domination, which at one time was threatened by the Cimbrian and Teuton invasions in 105 (disaster at Orange) and halted by Marius near Aix in 102 spread irreversibly over the region, not without abuse and pillaging.

Roman colonisation

Pax Romana – Gaul Transalpine rapidly became integrated in the Roman world and actively supported the Proconsul Caesar during the Gallic Wars (58-51BC). Marseille, as a result of having supported Pompey against Caesar, was besieged in 49BC, fell and lost its independence. The important towns were Narbonne, Nîmes, Arles and Fréjus. Romanisation accelerated under Augustus, the Narbonensis *(see above)* was reorganised in 27BC. Antoninus Pius' *(see NÎMES)* reign (2C) marked the apogee of Gallo-Roman civilization. Agriculture remained Provence's principal activity and trade enriched the towns, of which Arles profited the most from Marseille's disgrace. Urban affluence was reflected in the way of life which was entirely focused on comfort, luxury and leisure. Excavations have given us a glimpse of that life.

Arles, the favoured city – After the troubled times of the 3C, the 4C and 5C brought considerable religious and political transformations. Christianity, which did not seem to appear before the end of the 2C, triumphed over the other religions after the conversion of Constantine, who went on to make Arles his favourite town in the west. Marseille remained a commercial centre, Aix became an administrative capital while Nîmes declined and Glanum was abandoned. Rural areas suffered from the general impoverishment of the Gallo-Roman world; large landowners placed heavy demands, and insecurity led to the resettlement of fortified hill sites such as St-Blaise.

Head of Apollo from the Maison des Messii, Vaison-la-Romaine

From the fall of the Roman Empire to the Popes at Avignon

Invasion after invasion – Until 471, the date Arles was taken by the Visigoths, Provence had been relatively free from invasions. After the Burgundian and Visigoth domination, which lasted from 476 to 508, followed the Ostrogoth restoration, a period of some 30 years whereupon the Ostrogoths considered themselves the mandatories of the Far Eastern emperor and revived Roman institutions: Arles thus recovered its praetorian prefects. Religious life continued to progress; several synods were held in Provence towns (Vaison-la-Romaine).

The bishop of Arles, Saint Caesarius, had a vast following in Gaul. In 536, Provence was ceded to the Franks and followed the same uncertain destiny as other provinces, tossed from hand to hand according to the Merovingian dynastic divisions. Decline was rapid.

The first half of the 8C was confusion and tragedy: Arabs and Franks transformed the region into a battleground. **Charles Martel** went through it with an incredible brutality from 736 to 740.

The Saracens were a constant threat. In 855 Provence was made a kingdom, its limits corresponding more or less with the Rhône basin. It was weakened by the Saracens and Vikings terrorising the land. It, thus, soon fell into the hands of the kingdom of Burgundy, whose possessions spread from the Jura to the Mediterranean and were under the protection of the Holy Roman Emperors, who inherited it in 1032. This was a major date in the history of Provence as it made Provence a part of the Holy Roman Empire, with the area west of the Rhône under the yoke of the counts of Toulouse.

Occitanian Provence – The 10C and 11C marked a break in the evolution of Provence's civilization, until then dependent on its Greco-Roman past. A new society developed out of the feudal anarchy. Rural life, henceforth, was concentrated in the perched villages Luberon, Ste-Baume and the Vaucluse mountains – which depended upon the seigneuries. The towns attempted to recapture their expansion and began administrating themselves. The Oïl language spread... Close links were established between Provence and Languedoc.

The failure of Occitania facilitated Capetian intervention. The Albigensian heresy resulted in the delayed union of the Catalan and Toulousain peoples who until then had been fighting over Provence, against the invaders from the north; but the defeat at Muret in 1213 dashed all hope of a united Occitania.

Louis VIII's expedition (siege of Avignon in 1226) and the Treaty of Paris in 1229 brought about the founding of the royal seneschalship in Beaucaire: the west bank of the Rhône was part of France. In the east the Catalan Count, Raimond Bérenger V maintained his authority and endowed Provence with an administrative organisation. The towns became powerful locally: as early as the 12C they elected their own consuls, whose power increased to the detriment of the traditional lords (bishops, counts and viscounts); in the 13C they were seeking to gain independence.

House of Anjou's Provence – The marriage of **Charles of Anjou**, St Louis' brother, to Beatrice of Provence, Raimond Bérenger V's heir, in 1246 linked Provence to the House of Anjou. Charles had large political ambitions: he interfered in Italy and conquered the kingdom of Naples in 1266 before turning towards the Far East.

In Provence, Charles of Anjou's government was very much appreciated: security was re-established, honest administration managed public affairs and prosperity returned. Concerning the territories, Comtat Venaissin was ceded to the papacy in 1274, by the king of France, and evolved separately.

Charles I's successors, Charles II and Robert I, continued their father's and grandfather's political ideas and political order, and peace reigned during the first half of the 14C. Aix was raised to administrative capital with a seneschal and a court where the officers who presided were in charge of the finances of the county.

The key city was henceforth Avignon, where the Bishop Jacques Duèse, elected Pope in 1316 under the name John XXII, established himself. Clement V was already resident in Comtat Venaissin and benefited from the protection of the king of France; thus John XXII's decision was confirmed by his successor Benedict XII, who began the construction of a new papal palace. The popes' stay in Avignon, which lasted almost a century, brought expansion and extraordinary brilliance to the city.

From annexation to the French crown to the present day

The end of Provence's independence – After the second half of the 14C, Provence entered a difficult period. Famine and the plague (which struck in 1348), the pillaging road bandits and the political instability brought about by the slackness of Queen Joan (granddaughter to King Robert; she was assassinated in 1382) badly damaged Provence's stability. The population was decimated, the country in ruins. After a violent dispute over succession, Louis II of Anjou (nephew to the king of France, Charles V) aided by his mother, Marie of Blois, and the pope re-established the situation (1387).

Pacification was temporarily slowed by the activities of a turbulent lord, Viscount Raymond de Turenne who terrorised the country (1389-99), pillaging and kidnapping. His lairs were the fortresses of Les Baux and Roquemartine. Peace was not achieved until the early 15C.

Louis II of Anjou's (d 1417) youngest son, **King René**, inherited the county at the death of his brother in 1434. He was primarily concerned with the reconquest of the kingdom of Naples but every attempt of his failed, whereupon he turned all his attention to Provence (1447) and came to love it. His reign left happy memories; it coincided with a political and economic restoration which was felt through all of France. He was a poet and had a cultivated mind fed by his love of art; he attracted a number of artists to Aix, who came to take up where the popes' Avignon had left off.

His nephew Charles of Maine briefly succeeded him and in 1481 ceded Provence to Louis XI. The history of Provence was henceforth interlaced with that of the kingdom of France, in spite of the Rhône boatmen who, for a long time, continued to distinguish between the Holy Roman Empire and the kingdom of France.

Vaudois and Huguenots – As early as 1530, the Reformation spread in the south of France, owing for the most part to merchants and pedlars; through the Rhône and Durance valleys and Vivarais, Protestantism was stimulated by the brilliance of the Vaudois church located in the Luberon village communities.

The Vaudois heresy went back to the 12C: a certain Vaudès or **Valdès**, a rich merchant from Lyon, had founded a sect in 1170 preaching poverty, Evangelism and refusal of the sacraments and ecclesiastical hierarchy. Excommunicated in 1184, the Vaudois had since been pursued as heretics. In 1530 they were targeted by the Inquisition, and in 1540 the Aix Parliament decided to strike hard by issuing a warrant for the arrest of 19 Vaudois from Mérindol. François I temporised and prescribed a deferment. Instead of calming things down, the religious controversy was brought to a head. The Abbaye de Sénanque was pillaged by the heretics in 1544; as a riposte, the Parliament's president obtained royal authorisation to enforce the Mérindol warrant and organised a punitive expedition. From 15 to 20 April 1545 blood ran through the Luberon village streets: 3000 people were massacred, 600 were sent to the galleys and many villages were razed.

Nevertheless, Protestantism continued to spread, especially west of the Rhône in Vivarais, Cévennes, Nîmes and Uzès; east of the Rhône it was Orange (a Nassau Family principality since 1559) which became a Reformation stronghold. In 1560 the inevitable happened. Numerous churches and abbeys (St-Gilles, Valbonne charterhouse) were pillaged by the Huguenots; violence gave rise to more violence and with it the capture of Orange (1563) by the Catholic partisans, which was answered by the fall of Mornas.

During these tumultuous times Provence and Languedoc-Cévennes split, taking different paths. Provence opted for Catholicism, and the Catholic League recruited fervent partisans in such cities as Aix and Marseille (both of which would have liked to become an independent republic). On the Rhône's opposite shore the situation was different. The people, influenced by the merchants and textile craftsmen who kept the Reformation alive, generally tended to believe in the Protestant movement with Nîmes as its capital.

The violent Wars of Religion in southern France brought about a conflict between two peoples of opposing mentalities who were to clash again during the Camisard Insurrection (1702-04) and who were never able to forget this crucial period of their history.

The 17C to 20C – Provence licked its wounds and revived, particularly in the 18C, which was the golden age for agriculture and commerce. However, the 19C was a less successful period: industrialisation progressed but rural life suffered from the failure of the silkworm farms and phylloxera which spread through the vineyards.

In the face of these changes, Mistral sought to defend the Provençal identity and its traditions. When he died in 1914, Provence was nevertheless wholeheartedly engaged in modernisation, and is now highly successful in heavy industry, speculative agriculture and tourism.

Language and literature

Provence is an ancient civilized land, Greco-Latin then Occitanian, which has never stopped influencing poets and writers alike, who expressed themselves in Provençal (a group of South Occitan dialects).

OCCITANIAN DIALECTS

Language of the troubadours – From Vulgar Latin spoken at the end of the Roman Empire evolved the Romance languages: Italian, Romanian, Catalan, Spanish, Portuguese and in France the Oïl language *(langue d'oïl)* in the north and the Oc language *(langue d'oc)* in the south. Oïl and Oc were the words used for yes in the north and south, respectively. This distinction, which was formed as early as the Merovingian period, was advanced enough in the 10C and 11C for the two languages to enter into literature separately. Occitan, which appeared in Latin texts for the first time in the 11C, owed its place and influence to the success of 12C courtly literature. In fact the art of the **troubadours**, which developed in the feudal courts of Périgord, Limousin and Gascony, was not confined purely to Provence but encompassed all of Occitania, from Bordeaux to Nice.

These troubadours *(trobar = to find)*, inventors of musical airs, both melodies and words in the Oc language, created a linguistic community independent of political divisions: Jaufré Rudel from Blaye, Bernard de Ventadour, Peire Vidal from Toulouse and from Provence Raimbaut of Orange, the countess of Die, Raimbaut of Vaqueiras and Folquet of Marseille.

Under the Provençal or Limousin name, Occitanian was appreciated by noble foreigners and most of the European courts. The essential inspirational force of the troubadours was love, not passionate love but courtly love where the patience and discretion of the poet-lover finally won over the lady who accepted the homage of her vassal. Using sound, word pattern and stanza-structure these poems told of the troubadours' anxieties and hopes.

The courtly poem declined in the 13C, its themes having been exhausted. It was replaced by satirical poems known as *sirventès* and prose which told of the lives of the troubadours (the famous *vidas*). This period is marked by the European influence of French, by the setting up of the Inquisition and by the expansion of the Capetian monarchy.

Occitan, nevertheless, retained its importance; it is said that Dante (1265-1321) almost used it to write his *Divina Commedia* and it was the language spoken at the pontifical court of Avignon. With Latin, Occitan was, in the Middle Ages, the only written administrative language. And yet beginning in the 14C regional differences began appearing in written texts and French was gradually adopted in its place.

Occitanian literature became popular in Italy where it was revived thanks to Dante and returned in force into the Rhône valley in the form of a sonnet with **Petrarch** (1304-74). Exiled in Avignon, Petrarch fell passionately in love with the lovely Laura de Noves in 1327. His love was personified at her death (1348): his *Canzonière* were a group of sonnets where he expressed his unrequited love for Laura. The poet, who had retired to Fontaine-de-Vaucluse, also wrote in his letters descriptions of Provençal life; he spoke of shepherds, the Sorgue fishermen and his climb to Mont Ventoux.

The Occitan language's fatal blow was in 1539 with the adoption of the Edict of Villers-Cotterêts which decreed that for all administrative purposes the French language – the dialect spoken in the Île de France, and thus Paris – should be used. In spite of that, Occitan survived until the 19C in the theatre, poetry, short stories and legends, chronicles, didactic and erudite works (dictionaries and anthologies). The popular writers of the period were: Bellaud de la Bellaudière and Nicolas Saboly.

Bellaud de la Bellaudière – Born in Grasse in 1534, Bellaud de la Bellaudière lived a very active life as a soldier; he was opposed

Folquet of Marseille (13C manuscript)

B. N. Paris

to the Huguenots. When he was in prison, he wrote 160 sonnets, his *Œuvres et Rimes*. His poetry, inspired by Marot, Rabelais and Petrarch, was essentially personal owing to its familiar realism. It brought to the Occitan language a renewal. He was joined by Claude Bruey, Raynier from Briançon and François de Bègue.

Nicolas Saboly – In the 17C, while the moralist Vauvenargues was born in Aix and Madame de Sévigné resided at Grignan, Nicolas Saboly was composing Provençal **Noëls**, charming, simple works of popular poetry. These happy yet pious canticles depicted beside the angels the touching characters of an entire small world running in the night towards the newly-born baby Jesus.

As a popular language, however, Occitan declined, breaking up into different provincial dialects.

In the 17C services were still said in Occitan in rural villages as well as in the cities. When Racine resided in Uzès in 1661, he had a great deal of difficulty making himself understood. Until the Revolution, Occitan was the language spoken daily; only a small elite spoke French, and even then they were bilingual.

The Félibrige – In the late 18C, Occitan, weakened by the centralised state, was reborn through literature. In 1795, Abbot Favre made history with his *Siège de Caderousse* (Caderousse's Seat), a satirical poem written in dialect, amusing because of its Rabelais-like truculence. In the 1840s there was an explosion: **Joseph Roumanille** (1818-91), a teacher in Avignon and the author of a work *Li Margarideto* (1847), awakened in the young **Frédéric Mistral** a passion for Provence, its culture, history and Oc language. As early as 1851, Mistral began writing *Miréio* and in 1852 the first congress of future *Félibres* was held in Arles. The decisive date was 21 May 1854 at the castle of Fort-Ségugne; seven young poets, writing in Provençal (Roumanille, Mistral, Aubanel, Mathieu, Tavan, Giéra and Brunet), founded the Félibrige (*félibre* was a word taken from an old song meaning doctor), an association whose goal was to restore the Provençal language and to codify its spelling; it published a periodical *Armana Provençau* which was to spread its ideas, making them widely known.

In 1859 Mistral, published *Mirèio*, an epic poem of twelve cantos which brought him immense success – Lamartine praised his work and Charles Gounod made it into an opera in 1864. His literary works included: *Calendau* (1867), *Lis Isclo d'Or* (1875), *Nerto* (1884), *La Reino Jano* (1890), *The Song of the Rhône* (1896), *Lis Oulivado* (1912). In 1904 he was awarded the Nobel Prize for Literature. Mistral was also a fine philologist who patiently collected the scattered elements of the Oc language and recorded its spelling in a monumental dictionary *Lou Trésor du Félibrige*, published in 1878-86, which still serves as a reference book. The Félibrige grouped Occitanian poets and novelists as different as: Alphonse Daudet, Paul Arène, Félix Gras, Baptiste Bonnet, Joseph d'Arbaud, Charles Rieu, Dom Xavier de Fourvière, Jean-Henri Fabre, Folco de Baroncelli-Javon and Charles Maurras (political theorist). At the same period, renowned writers of French included Jean Alcard (a member of the Academy, he wrote *Maurin of the Moors*); and on a totally different level, Émile Zola (went to secondary school in Aix), who in his Rougon-Macquart series described the evolution of a family from the south; and Edmond Rostand (born in Marseille) who wrote the unforgettable *Aiglon*.

In the present – Although Provence is always present in their works, the contemporary writers have gone beyond the regional level and attained the ranks of top French writers: Jean Giono from Manosque *(see Michelin Green Guide Alpes du Sud, in French)*, Marcel Pagnol *(Jean de Florette, Manon des Sources)* from Aubagne, René Barjavel from Nyons, René Char (one of France's greatest poets) from Isle-sur-la-Sorgue and Marie Mauron, to name but a few. Among the English and American writers who settled in Provence are: Lawrence Durrell, Graham Greene, F. Scott Fitzgerald, and H.G. Wells.

Paradoxically, Provençal as a spoken language regressed, whereas as a language of culture (successor to the *troubadours* and *Félibres*) it progressed. Admittedly the local dialects remain but they are most often ignored by the young and are more prevalent in rural than urban areas; while the centralising and unifying role of the state, instead of weakening it, has enhanced the language: the Oc language is, henceforth,

Marcel Pagnol

recognised in the official teaching programmes. A harmonious language, Occitan, and therefore Provençal, has a wealthy vocabulary, which allows for an infinite variety of nuance.

Continuing with the work of the Félibrige society, the goal of the Institut des Études Occitanes (Institute of Occitanian Studies), while still promoting the use of authentic everyday speech, is to seek the unity of a common language, similar to what Occitania's influence was in the Middle Ages when it extended beyond political limits from the Atlantic to the Mediterranean.

Legends and tales

The legends and tales of Provence are a colourful account of history and geography; these stories depict men, customs, institutions, lifestyles, beliefs, monuments and sites. Perhaps Greco-Roman heritage must be recognised in Provençal tradition, in which the wonderful accompanies daily life in its humblest activities, as in the ancient Roman and Greek myths where the gods were omnipresent and miracles occurred at their behest.

Ancient myths – For the ancient Greeks the western Mediterranean was awe-inspiring and at the same time frightening and wonderful, where each evening the sun set with Apollo's chariot. **Heracles**, son of Zeus, had been to this land and had married Galathea from Gaul. Endowed with incredible strength he had opened the passages through the Alps; to protect his son's passage through Provence, Zeus had showered his enemies with stones and boulders which became a desert, the Crau. The attraction of this western Mediterranean land inspired the Phocaeans later to found a colony here. The legend of **Protis** and **Gyptis** illustrates this episode *(see MARSEILLE)*. The Marseille navigator, **Pytheas**, is said to have sailed in the 4C BC, between the columns of Heracles (Straits of Gibraltar), across the waters to Cornwall and on to Iceland.

Legends of the Saints – Christianity, too, brought its collection of stories. A thousand-year-old tradition ascribes the conversion of Provence in the 1C to the miraculous landing of a boat from Judaea bearing Lazarus, Mary Magdalene and Martha and their saintly companions, disciples of Christ. With St Victor and Cassien they formed a sort of mystic Provençal state and are credited with many wondrous acts including the overcoming by Martha of the Tarasque monster *(see TARASCON)*.

Local saints were not in short supply either. **Eleazarius de Sabran** was so precocious that every Friday he refused milk from his milk nurse for mortification. **St Mitre**, the beheaded martyr, as the legend goes, picked up his head, kissed it and bore it to the cathedral where he placed it on the altar. Then there is **St Caesarius**, who captured in his glove a puff of sea air and carried it back to Nyons country, locked in an amphitheatre of impenetrable mountains. From then on a light wind blew over the region; the local people took heart and began to cultivate the land. The prosperity of Nyons country dates from this period and its privileged climate has allowed it to cultivate olives.

Troubadour tradition – The legends of Provence were inspired by epic poetry *(chansons de geste)* and courtly prose.

Pierre of Provence, a valiant knight and talented troubadour, lived at his father's court in the Château de Cavaillon. Simply on seeing her portrait, the knight fell in love with Princess Maguelone, daughter of the king of Naples, and set out to fetch her. Received at the Neapolitan court, he was victorious in a series of tournaments where he wore Maguelone's colours. But one day Pierre was kidnapped by Barbary pirates and taken to Tunis where he was imprisoned for seven years. Having served his term he was finally able to set sail for Provence, but his boat sank not far from Aigues-Mortes. Mortally wounded, he was brought to the Aigues-Mortes hospital, headed by Princess Maguelone herself, who had sought through charitable works a way to forget her unhappy love. The lovers met and recognised each other; Pierre was cured...

Not all endings were so happy. One day **Guillem de Cabestaing**, a son of a noble and well-known troubadour, came to sing at the court of the lord of Castel-Roussillon, an ugly, vulgar old man who had a lovely young wife named Sérémonde. Love kindled quickly between these two young people. The lord, having discovered this, killed the handsome Guillem in an ambush, ripped out his heart and served it to his wife as dinner; Sérémonde responded with: "My lord, you have served me such delicious fare that nothing could ever equal it and so I swear before Christ, in order to keep the taste fresh for all time, I will never eat again". She then threw herself from the top of a cliff in Roussillon; her blood as it spread coloured the soil; that is the origin of ochre!

Sorcery – Rare were the villages that did not have at least one *masc* or *masco*. These people had the power to bewitch men and animals. If a baby stopped suckling, if horses stopped for no apparent reason, if hunting dogs lost their scent, they had been *emmasqués*. Méthamis in Vaucluse is still, even today, a sanctuary of Provençal sorcery. To fight against evil spells a *démascaire* was called in. This person was often a shepherd, because the shepherd was a holder of supernatural powers but was said to be a sworn enemy of sorcerers, someone who held the secrets of nature. The *demascaire* was good and broke the evil spell; he was also a bonesetter and cured sickness with plants. Other ways of warding off the evil spell were possible, such as wearing a piece of clothing inside out or back to front, throwing salt into the hearth or reciting different invocations while crossing oneself at the same time. To protect houses from the evil eye the custom was to cement into the wall a vitrified pebble; on the sheep-pen door was nailed a magic thistle. Some places are totally magical and mysterious, such as Garagaï at Vauvenargues, a bottomless chasm where strange things happen. Between Arles and Montmajour is the fairies' hole, peopled with supernatural beings.

Child heroes – A great number of Provençal legends recount the memorable exploits of children and adolescents gifted with a force and extraordinary ingenuity; they generally appeal to Almighty God, the intervention of the saints or magic. This is the case of little **Bénézet** from Avignon, who built the bridge at Avignon. **Jean de l'Ours**, so-called because he had been brought up with a bear, was another. At the age of 12, he conceived the idea of journeying round France. He forged himeslf a stout iron staff and thus armed killed the horrible dragons which kept a young princess in an enchanted castle. He married the princess and lived happily ever after... **Guihen l'Orphelin** (the orphan), thanks to his mysterious white hen, which he would stroke while murmuring a special incantation, could become invisible. He was able to free a king and his daughter imprisoned by a wicked baron. To thank him the king promised his daughter to Guihen and they lived happily ever after.

Christmas cribs

Christmas cribs (*crèche* means crib) have a long tradition in Provence although it was not until the late 18C that they became at all common and developed a typically local character – a few 18C groups, often highly original and beautifully modelled, may still be seen at a collector's or a few rare churches but most are now in museums (Musée du Vieil Aix, Musée du Vieux Marseille, Museon Arlaten in Arles, and the Musée National des Arts et Traditions Populaires in Paris).

Church cribs – Christmas was not an important festival in the early church nor did cribs form part of the medieval celebrations except for rare low reliefs of the Adoration of the Shepherds or the Kings as in the St-Maximin crypt.
In 1545 the Council of Trent sought to advance the Counter-Reformation through the encouragement of popular piety. The practice of setting up a crib in church arrived in Provence from Italy in the 17C. There is a particularly beautiful crib from this period in the church of St-Maximin; the carved figures, about 50cm/20in high, are of gilded wood. In the 18C, bejewelled wax figures were introduced with glass eyes and wigs. Only the head, arms and legs were carved and attached to a richly-dressed articulated frame. The 19C saw the employment of printed or painted cardboard cut-outs with gaily coloured clothing, or figures made from spun glass, cork or other materials.
By the 19C all the Provençal churches had adopted the Christmas crib of dressed figures; this kind of Christmas crib can still be seen nowadays.

Live cribs – At midnight mass in many churches today – Séguret, Allauch, Isle-sur-la-Sorgue and Marseille – there is an actual Nativity play. In Gémenos, children in costume place the Infant Jesus in a straw-filled manger. In Les Baux, a little cart, decorated with greenery and bearing a new-born lamb, is drawn into church by a ram and accompanied by shepherds. The procession is headed by angels and fife and tabor players while the congregation sing old Provençal carols. The lamb is offered to the church and the cart stands on one side in the aisle throughout the year.

Talking cribs – The 18C passion for marionettes was adapted to produce talking cribs in which mechanical figures enacted the Nativity to a commentary and carols; people came from far and wide to see and hear the talking cribs of Marseille and Aix. Characters were added to the already numerous cast and, as imagination ran wild, historical accuracy and relevance vanished: reindeer, giraffes and hippopotamuses joined the other animals in the stable, even the pope arrived in a carriage ahead of his time to bless the Holy Family.
In the 19C, Napoleon, accompanied by his soldiers and a man-of-war firing salvoes, brought the scene up to date! Another new idea came to those presenting a crib close to Marseille station: the Three Kings travelled to the scene in a steam train! Some of these talking cribs functioned until the late 19C.

Santon cribs – The *santon* cribs are the most typical of Provence. They first appeared in 1789 at the time of the Revolution when the churches were closed and cribs, therefore, inaccessible. **Jean-Louis Lagnel**, a church statue-maker from Marseille, had the idea of making small figures which families could buy at little cost. Labelled *santouns* (little

Santons of Provence

Gaspard

The Shepherd and his sheep

The Miller and his donkey

The Gypsies

Bartoumieu

Grasset and Grasseto

The drummer

The Village Idiot

Santons based on old models by Ateliers Marcel Carbonel, Marseille

29

saints) in Provençal and *santoni* in Italian, abbreviated from *santibelli* (beautiful saints), these figurines had an immediate and wide appeal. They were modelled in clay, fired and naïvely painted in bright colours. Limited at first to Biblical personages, they were soon joined by men and women from all walks of life, dressed, of course, in the local costume; the Holy Family, the Shepherds and their sheep, the Three Kings occupied the stage, together with the knife grinder, the fife and tabor player, the smith, the blind man and his guide, the fishwife, wetnurse, milkmaid, the huntsman, fisherman and even the mayor! So great was the figurines' success, as virtually every family began to build up a collection, that a Santons Fair was inaugurated in Marseille, which is still held on the Canebière from the last Sunday in November to Epiphany. Aubagne was

Provençal Christmas Crib

also famous for its *santons*. *Santon* makers established workshops in towns throughout Provence whereas in the country men and women made figures in the long winter evenings. The craft reached its peak in the 1820-30s, which is why so many of the characters, now mass-produced, appear in the dress of that period.

The *santons* of Provence are now known the world over and many a family seeks its own Christmas crib peopled with *santons*.

Festivals and costumes

Festivals – The people of Provence have always had a taste for celebration. In the past it was the men who were in charge of the festivities. The fairs, either secular or religious (remnants of solemn Christian celebrations mixed with pagan tendencies), were numerous; there are the classic feast days which happen throughout the year and the larger festivals, more or less traditional, attracting thousands of people in a typically colourful Provençal atmosphere.

From April to September, Nîmes and Arles rival each other in the organisation of their famous *férias* attracting *aficionados* whether it be the *corrida*, bullfights with picadors and the kill, or simply making the bull run through the streets (the bulls wear a *cocarde*, a rosette between their horns: it must be removed by the *razeteurs*, handrake holders). In Camargue the roundup *(ferrade)* is always an exciting time: the young calves are thrown to the ground and branded with the mark of their owner; there are also horse races between *gardians*.

The Venetian Water Festival is held at Martigues and includes a nocturnal procession of decorated boats.

And of course there are theatre, opera and dance festivals which take place in Provence; be it Avignon, Aix-en-Provence, Orange, Vaison-la-Romaine, Carpentras, Salon-de-Provence or Arles, each of these cities is the venue for an annual artistic festival of top quality. *See the Calendar of events at the end of the guide.*

Farandoles – Most of the festivals are a wonderful opportunity to listen to the fife and *tambourin so delightfully characteristic of the Provence region*. The **farandole** is a Mediterranean dance which dates back to the Middle Ages if not to Antiquity, and was danced throughout Arles country. Young men and women, either holding each other's hands or a handkerchief, dance to a six-beat rhythm. The typically Provençal instruments played by the *tambourinaires* are the **galoubet**, a small 3-holed flute which produces a piercing sound, and the **tambourin**, a type of drum 75cm/29.5in high and 35cm/13.5in wide, beaten by a *massette* held in the right hand while the other hand

30

holds the *galoubet*; on the drum itself, the head of which is made from calf-skin, is stretched the *chanterelle*, a thin strand of hemp or a violin string which produces a rasping sound poetically called the song of the cicada.

Christmas in Provence – Celebrations surrounding the end of the year begin on 4 December, the feast day of Ste Barbe and end at Candlemas on 2 February. The locals start by sowing their "Christmas wheat" (*lou blad de Calendo*) on 4 December: when it starts to sprout, it is placed above the fireplace. Three weeks later, it will be used as decoration beside the crib or as a centrepiece for the long banquet table. Preparations for the crib take place on the Sunday before Christmas but it is only at midnight on 25 December that the Infant Jesus is laid down inside the crib. That same night, the whole family ritually performs *Cacho-Fio*, a ceremony during which a Christmas log (*bûche de Noël*) is blessed with a fortified wine and taken round the house three times, before being burnt. The family may then be seated to begin their Christmas feast. The table, covered with three overlapping tablecloths, is laid with three chandeliers and three saucers containing the Christmas wheat, as well as 13 loaves of bread. The meal ends with the 13 desserts (*mendiants*: walnuts and hazel nuts, figs, almonds and raisins; fresh fruit; black and white nougat; *pompe à huile*, a flat, brittle loaf made with olive oil). Midnight Mass starts with *lou Pastrage*: the shepherd, the miller and the ancestors enter the church, where the priest lays down the Infant Jesus in the crib. Then the bells are rung, inviting the procession of shepherds to enter the church: they draw a small cart with a lamb, an offering made to the Infant Jesus. Mass continues with a series of Christmas songs and carols. Boxing Day heralds the start of the Pastorales, which retrace the steps of Joseph who was seeking refuge for the night. On 31 December, Provençal people always celebrate the New Year (*an nou*) together as a family. On the first Sunday in January, they pay tribute to the Magi and throughout the month of January, in honour of the Three Wise Men, they eat Twelfth Night cake (*galette des rois*), a crown-shaped bun decorated with crystallized fruit and containing a lucky charm (*fève*). These Christmas festivities end on 2 February with Candlemas (*Chandeleur*), the feast marking the Purification of the Virgin Mary and the presentation of Christ in the Temple 40 days after the birth of Jesus. Celebrations involve a procession of green church candles. In Marseille, one also eats *navettes*, small boat-shaped biscuits that evoke the arrival of the Saintes Maries in Provence.

Provençal fabric and costumes – Thanks to the commercial relationship between Marseille and the Mediterranean ports of the Levant, Provence discovered oriental fabrics and, since the end of the 17C, has made these its own by adopting printed floral calicos and stitching and quilting techniques. The characteristic patterns of colourful motifs which are now known as "Provençal prints" are the result of a long evolution of methods and fashions.

Traditional costume in Arles is but one of the several different costumes worn all over Provence. It is one reminder of the diversity of the clothing worn by the various social milieux of days gone by: the fishwife of the Vieux Port of Marseille, with the flaps of her coif blowing about in the wind; the flowergirl; the country farmer's wife; the washerwoman; or the peasant woman with her striped underskirts, her huge apron of deep purple canvas and the *capuch* or *capelino* enveloping her head.

Taking as an example, then, the traditional costume of women from Arles (there is an excellent collection in the Museon Arlaten in Arles), the women wear long colourful skirts and a black under-blouse *(eso)* with long tight sleeves; on top a pleated shirt is covered with a shawl either made of white lace or matching the skirt. There are different varieties of headdress; they are all, however, worn on top of a high bun: *à la cravate* involves a white percale handkerchief being knotted like rabbits' ears; *à ruban*: the bun is fitted with a wide velvet ribbon hemmed with lace on the front and running down the back, at the crown of the head, there is a flat ribboned surface (held with cardboard); *en ailes de papillon*, a lovely old lace ribbon knotted around the head in the form of butterfly *(papillon)* wings *(ailes)*. The fan accompanies the Arles traditional costume.

The men's costume is less colourful. They wear a white shirt knotted at the collar by a thin tie or ribbon, sometimes covered by a dark-coloured vest upon which hangs a watch chain; canvas trousers are held at the waist by a wide red or black woollen belt. They wear black felt hats with a wide slightly-raised rim. The peasants' dress consists of a lovely brightly-coloured shawl and small white hat on top of which is a wide flat straw hat for the women, whereas a black velvet vest and straw hat are worn by the men.

Traditional Arles costume

Food and wine in Provence

A succulent cuisine

Provençal cooking is characterised by garlic and food fried in oil. Garlic was praised by poets: the "truffle of Provence", the "divine condiment", this "friend of man", while oil – preferably olive oil – replaced butter in all the Provençal dishes. An old Provençal saying states "A fish lives in water and dies in hot oil".

Bouillabaisse – This most famous of Provençal dishes traditionally comprises "the three fishes": the spiny, red hog-fish, gurnet, and conger eel *(rascasse, grondin, congre)*. To these are added as many others as are available – sea bass *(loup)*, turbot, sole, red mullet *(rouget)*, monkfish *(lotte)* – a selection of crustaceans: crabs, spider crabs *(araignées de mer)*, mussels *(moules)* etc and in very special cases, spiny lobsters *(langoustes)* or crawfish.
These are all cooked together very rapidly in a *bouillon*, emulsified with a small quantity of olive oil and seasoned with salt and pepper, onion, tomato, saffron, garlic, thyme, bay *(laurier)*, sage, fennel, orange peel, maybe a glass of white wine or cognac – the magic of the results depends on the seasoning.
A *rouille* or paste of Spanish peppers, served at the same time, sharpens the sauce and gives it colour.
In a restaurant one is usually presented with a soup plate and toast with which to line it. Some people then spread some of the toast with the *rouille* paste, others mix it directly into the by now thickened bouillon-soup which arrives in a tureen. To your plateful of toast, *rouille* and soup, you then add titbits from the dish of assorted cooked fish and crustaceans. *Bouillabaisse* is a main dish. The fish must be fresh and the dish freshly prepared (it is not a stew – the actual cooking time is only 10 minutes).

Aïoli – *Aïoli* (pronounced exactly as it is written), the other great Provençal speciality, is a mayonnaise made with freshly pounded, mild, Provençal garlic to which are added the usual egg yolks, olive oil and condiments.
It is served with *hors-d'œuvre*, asparagus and other vegetables, and also as a sauce with *bourride*, the fish soup made from angler fish *(baudroie)*, sea bass *(loup)*, whiting *(merlan)* etc, and preferred by many to *bouillabaisse*.

Fish and crustaceans – Local fish dishes include red mullet *(rouget)* cooked whole, sea bass *(loup)* grilled with fennel or vine shoots and *brandade de morue*, a heavy, cream of pounded cod, olive oil and milk, seasoned with crushed garlic and slivers of truffle.
Fish specialities associated with individual towns include, for Marseille, in addition to *bouillabaisse*, clams *(clovisses)*, ascidia or iodine-tasting sea-squirts *(violets)*, mussels *(moules)* and edible sea urchins *(oursins)* – all to be found most easily in the small restaurants around the Vieux Port; in St-Rémy, the *catigau*, a dish of grilled or smoked Rhône eel in sauce; in the Camargue, *tellines* or sand crustaceans served with a pungent sauce.

A dish of *bouillabaisse*

Vegetables and fruit – Raw onion and tomatoes, common favourites among vegetables, are followed closely by cardoons (vegetable related to the artichoke, served in white sauce), fennel, peppers, courgettes and aubergines. The art of Provençal cuisine resides in the wide variety of its cooking methods: gratin dishes baked in the oven (*tians*), soups, salads, stews, fritters, stuffed vegetables etc. The most popular fruit is the small green fig or Marseille fig, a juicy, sweet fruit. Peaches, apricots, strawberries, cherries and grapes are all top quality, not to mention the deliciously fragrant melons from Cavaillon and also watermelons. *(Details on how to recognise and prepare the different types of olives can be found in the chapter on Practical information.)*

Olives – Local olives are the small, meaty green and black varieties which are left whole, pitted or stuffed; there is the green olive, picked early then marinated, which comes from Nîmes, and the black olive of Nyons preserved in brine. Nyons and Carpentras are the main production centres.

Specialities – Among the numerous Provençal specialities are the *pieds-paquets* (a kind of tripe) of Marseille; Arles' sausages or saucissons; Gardian beef stew from Camargue; Avignon's preserved melons; Aix's *calissons* or almond paste sweets with sugar icing; Carpentras' *berlingots* or humbugs; Nîmes' *brandade de morue (see above)*, small almond cakes or *caladons* and crisp Villaret biscuits; Tarascon's *tartarinades* or special chocolates; the crystallised fruits of Apt; the nougat of Sault, the black olives of Nyons and Modane bread (bread split and stuffed with crystallised fruit...).

The Herbs of Provence

The famous *herbes de Provence*, an integral part of the Provençal countryside, form, along with garlic and olive oil, the basis of the region's cuisine. Coupled with the magic touch of the cook, these fresh ingredients will add their own personality to the frugal, yet fully flavoured and characteristic cooking of Provence. Among these note: **savory**, often used to flavour goats' or sheep's cheeses; a mix of **thyme** and **bay**, which combined with tomatoes, aubergines, courgettes, red and green peppers and onions, is used to make the popular ratatouille, as well as being an ideal addition to grilled and roast meats; **basil**, which, crushed with garlic, olive oil and occasionally bacon and parmesan cheese, is an important ingredient in the preparation of the famous *pistou*; **sage**, its clear, velvety leaves boiled with garlic to make the traditional *aigo-boulido* broth to which nothing more than olive oil and slices of bread are added; **rosemary**, a perfect seasoning for vegetable gratins and baked fish, is also used in herbal teas to ease digestion; **wild thyme**, particularly suited to wild rabbit dishes, but which also brings out the best in vegetable soups and tomato-based recipes; **juniper**, an irreplaceable seasoning for pâtés and game; **marjoram**, ideal for stews; **tarragon**, used to spice up white sauces; **fennel**, with its aniseed taste, a superb accompaniment to fish dishes.

Thanks to each chef's personal culinary skills, these ingredients all lend character to Provençal cuisine, whose simplicity does not detract from its strongly aromatic nature, earning it a fine reputation among all dedicated gourmets.

Three traditional recipes

Tapenade – This olive, anchovy and caper-flavoured paste is eaten either as an hors-d'œuvre or as an accompaniment to an aperitif and is generally spread on slices of bread. Place equal quantities of stoned black olives, anchovy fillets and capers in a mortar. Crush, then add a dessert spoon of mustard. Mix, at the same time slowly adding a dash of olive oil.

Artichauts à la barigoule – Serves 4. The term *barigoule* is Provençal for mushroom; the name of the dish comes from the manner in which the artichokes are cut, giving them the appearance of mushrooms. Select a dozen small fresh artichokes and remove the largest leaves. Cut off the top two-thirds of the remainder and cook in an open casserole dish over a low heat with some sliced onions and carrots; add some olive oil. After 20-25min, add two glasses of dry white wine, two glasses of stock, two cloves of garlic and a few bacon cubes. Add salt and pepper, then cover once more and simmer for 50 min. Serve the artichokes coated with the sauce.

Daube provençale – Allow two days for the preparation of this dish. Marinate half a pound of beef cut up into pieces in red wine together with an onion cut in four, a clove of garlic, a bunch of mixed herbs (*bouquet garni*), salt and pepper. The next day, fry some bacon (*lard*) in hot olive oil, using either a casserole dish (preferably made of clay with a shallow lid). Add a chopped onion and two sliced carrots as well as two crushed tomatoes. After browning these, mix in with the meat and continue to fry. Pour in a glass of red wine and bring to the boil. Add two more glasses of water and the garlic, the *bouquet garni* and the peel of an orange. Season with salt and pepper. After boiling point is reached, turn the heat down and leave to simmer for five hours.

Provençal Wines

It was the Greeks who first cultivated vines in Provence on the hills around Massalia (present-day Marseille); the lower Rhône valley also received an early initiation in the art of viticulture.

During the Middle Ages, it was the honest, full-bodied red wines of Provence that enjoyed the greatest renown. It was only when King René encouraged the production of rosé in the 15C that their domination was halted. Following the spread of phylloxera, it was not until 1918 that the vineyards of Provence regained prominence. Over the past 20 years, huge leaps in quality have been made, largely due to strict selection processes and to an often highly complex blending of grapes. Provençal wines are characterised by the blending of several grape varieties in the same wine. This technique was devised in order to anticipate extreme climatic changes (such as drought, which can be aggravated by the mistral winds) since these, under certain circumstances, can have an unpredictable effect on the ripening of the grape. In the course of time, Mediterranean French stock has been mixed with Spanish and Italian transplants, with the following drawback: the wines occasionally lack consistency and there are doubts about their ability to age.

The delightful, fruity rosé wines of Provence, with their sparkling colour and recollections of sunshine and summer holidays, have become immensely popular in recent years. Having fully benefited from the introduction of the new vinification process, the wines are now developing greater balance, possess a delightful bouquet and are exceedingly fresh on the palate, especially when enjoyed young.

The mainly dry whites, with a similarly delicate bouquet, are a perfect accompaniment for fish and seafood dishes.

The contrasting Provençal vineyards have led to a wide variety of rapidly improving reds, ranging from generous and full-bodied to supple, delicate wines.

Southern Côtes du Rhône wines – They feature many prestigious appellations such as Lirac, Tavel, Châteauneuf-du-Pape, Gigondas, Vacqueyras, Rasteau, Muscat de Beaumes-de-Venise, Côtes du Ventoux and Côtes du Luberon, as well as the regional appellation Côtes du Rhône-Villages.

The right bank of the Rhône offers some fine wines such as **Tavel**, one of the most popular French wines sold abroad - a smooth, crystalline rosé, described as "sunlight trapped in a bottle" by the Poet Ronsard, north of Tavel, the coteaux de **Lirac** yield delicate, full-bodied reds and rosés. **Listel** is a rosé wine (*vin gris du sable*) from the Aigues-Mortes region.

To the west, the well-balanced **Costières de Nîmes** reds are both elegant and powerful although they are not strictly speaking part of the Côtes-du-Rhône appellation.

On the left bank, the warm, structured **Châteauneuf-du-Pape** appellation is one of the most famous names in the Côtes-du-Rhône area. The reds, characterised by a dark robe as well as spicy, woody and peppery aromas, are definitely wines for laying down. The whites, more scarce, have a bouquet reminiscent of flowers.

Vacqueyras produces well-constructed reds and elegant whites. The Séguret vineyard yields heady, scented wines, that of **Cairanne** tannic wines that will improve with age.

Gigondas is a red wine which needs to age in oak casks for a few years; in this respect it can be likened to Châteauneuf-du-Pape.

The **Côtes du Lubéron** reds are light and should be drunk young whereas the whites tend to be fresh and fine. Red wines from the **Côtes du Ventoux** are both structured and tannic, made with grapes that have ripened on the exposed slopes of Mont Ventoux; the lighter varieties should be drunk very young, barely a few months after the harvest (vins de primeur).

Dessert wines are represented by **Rasteau**, with its red or amber robe, and by **Muscat de Beaumes-de-Venise**, renowned for its golden robe and strong bouquet with notes of flower and fruit. They are made by adding alcohol to the must (the grape juice) during the fermentation process, which ensures that the wine is rich in sugar. The Rasteau and Beaumes-de-Venise vineyards are also used to produce red and rosé Côtes du Rhône.

Provence appellations – In the hills of southern Provence, the wines of **Cassis** have an excellent reputation, particularly the flower-scented dry whites; the velvety reds are equally exceptional.

The outskirts of Aix-en-Provence are home to the small **Palette** appellation (200 hectolitres a year), a smooth, tannic red, often referred to as the "Claret of Provence"; only two landlords share this vineyard, which features the famous Château Simone. The **Coteaux d'Aix-en-Provence** produce warm, robust reds and dry, lively whites.

The **Baux-de-Provence** appellation is used for red, white and rosé wines that may be drunk young.

As for the **Côtes de Provence** appelation, on the boundary of this guide around the Massif de la Sainte-Baume, it is best represented by its many different rosés, offering a wide choice of flavours and textures.

Finally, you can also sample many pleasant country wines (*vins de pays*), including those made in La Petite Crau and the Principality of Orange.

A passion for play

The game of boules

This is the favourite popular game. It is played with balls weighted with iron. Contests are played between teams of three *(triplettes)* or four *(quadrettes)*, amid attentive and enthusiastic spectators. The *pointeurs* have to throw their balls as near as possible to a smaller ball *(cochonnet)*, which has been set at the end of the bowling ground; the *tireurs* have then to dislodge the balls of the opposing team by striking them with their own, and the most skillful succeed in doing this and in taking the exact place of their adversary *(faire le carreau)*. Over short distances play is *à la pétanque*, which means with the feet together placed in a circle. Over longer distances, above 10m/30ft, the game is called *la longue*; the *tireurs* take a running start and throw their balls after having made three hopping steps from the throwing-point.

Among all these shirt-sleeved players the two Provençal types form a piquant contrast. The one, a native of the mountains, somewhat reserved and distant, shows his pleasure or his disappointment by a smile or a frown; the other, a descendant of the traditional Marius, enacts quite a little drama, which has been happily described: "Here, then, is the last ball; it rolls out before the player and you can watch its progress in his face; he broods over it, protects it with his gaze; gives it advice, strives to make it obedient to his voice, hurries or slows its course, encourages it with a gesture or urges it on with a heave of his shoulder, slackens it with his hand; perched on tiptoe, his arm flung out, his face animated by a wealth of varying emotions, he wriggles his body in bizarre undulations; one could almost say that his soul had passed into the ball." Play is frequently held up by noisy, heated arguments about the distances separating the various balls from the *cochonnet*; play resumes once measurements have been taken, often with small branches or twigs broken off a nearby tree.

P. d'Argence/PIX

Card games

The unforgettable scene in the Bar de la Marine, where a group of locals take part in a game of *manille*, indulging in the colourful dialogue that typified Pagnol's work, is a telling example of the importance of card games in Provençal society. Moreover, it must be known that it was in Provence that the first mention of playing cards was made in France. The discovery of the minutes drawn up by a Marseille notary public, dated 30 August 1381, prohibiting a merchant of the city from playing *nahipi* or *naïbi*, a sort of Happy Families for Venetian children, attest to the fact. In the last quarter of the 14C this card game became a favourite table recreation which, nowadays, is considered as being the ancestor of modern-day *tarot*. Following their likely origins in the Imperial Chinese court, playing cards reached the Occident during the course of the 13C, either in the luggage of Venetian passengers, bankers or merchants, or via the hordes of Tartars from central Asia. Venetian artists, hitherto devoted to reli-

---

Pastis in Provence

Inextricably linked to the game of *boules*, *pastis* is usually drunk around apéritif time, on the outdoor terraces of cafés. Pastis made its first appearance in Marseille in 1922, after aniseed beverages were rehabilitated (they had been banned since 1915 because they were likened to absinth). Proper *pastis* is produced by leaving various aromatic plants (anise, star anise, liquorice etc) to macerate in alcohol. By the late 1930s, a host of brands had already made a name for themselves in France: Capon, Pernod, Cap Anis, Pasty-Anis, Bisanis, Stop-Anis... but especially Ricard. During the Second World War, *pastis* was sold in small packets on the black market: mixing the concentrated powder with half a litre of 90° proof alcohol and the same quantity of water would produce a litre of *pastis*. Demand for "liquid" pastis soared once again in the 1960s with such brands as Casanis and Poncié ou Janot, which is still made in Aubagne today. However, the unquestionable leader remains Ricard, whose rhyming slogan associating the drink with apéritif time will never be forgotten by all those who have a fondness for the delicious pale yellow nectar: "*Midi et quart, sept heures et quart, l'heure du Ricard*".

Marseille tarot card

gious and secular canvases, eagerly succumbed to this growing trend of painting on card and parchment, leading to Venice becoming the main distribution centre in Europe. Marseille, with its openings on both the Mediterranean and the Orient, fell early to the charms of this new pastime, as did the Comtat Venaissin, with its close ties with Italy. The 15C gave rise to the game *cinq cents*, also known as the *Marseillais*. By the 17C, the popularity of card games in the city was considerable, paving the way for the appearance of the first "professional" card makers around 1631. Their numbers fluctuated according to the laws and taxes of the period, however with the development of new xylographic and typographic processes, replacing wooden printing moulds with copper ones, production continued to increase dramatically, reaching a rate of 180 000 packs a year by the end of the 17C. The 18C was, for Marseille, the epoch of **tarot**, which originated in Italy. Apart from the set manufactured by Jean Noblet in Paris during the 17C, the oldest tarot cards, which were said to have been made in Marseille, did in fact appear in Avignon in 1713, a city where card makers were exempt from tax. This privilege was removed in 1754, at which time Marseille established itself as the leading manufacturer. Marseille Tarot, the French version of Venetian Tarot, from which it copied 78 signs, provided the game with its definitive form, principally under the aegis of the master tarot maker **Nicolas Conver**, who produced a particularly attractive set of cards in 1760. The *Tarot de Marseille*, which was adopted by clairvoyants and soothsayers alike, was also to act as a support for another regional game in the 18C; the **portrait de Marseille**. By this time, production in the city was relatively evenly divided between eight card manufacturers.

However, the following century, the Camoin company, with its exports world-wide, was to distance itself from its competitors by producing over a million sets a year, based on traditional expertise acquired over more than two centuries. The company finally closed its doors in 1974, though its sparkling creations can still be admired in the large collection housed in the Musée du Vieux-Marseille *(see p 179)*.

Furniture and faience

Provençal furniture – It was during the 15C that Provençal furniture, until that time considered to be of unsophisticated design, began to follow the lead set by Italy, with the introduction of delicate sculptures, finished off with Spanish-influenced style of heavily-chiselled wrought iron and copper key-holes. The 18C and beginning of the 19C heralded the *grande époque* of Provençal furniture, with the main production centres scattered between the lower valley of the Rhône and the mid-section of the Durance; the period from the Second Empire onwards was characterised among other things by excessive sculptured decoration.

In lower Provence, the Louis XV style reigned absolute from the middle of the 18C onwards. Artisans preferred working with walnut, resorting if necessary to the use of box, olive or cherry or pear wood. The pieces of furniture, with their irregular curves, pronounced bends and curled legs and bases are generally of quite slender proportion, with an abundance of storage units and include: the **paneiro** or openwork bread bin *(see photograph)*; **manjadou** or meat safe decorated with ornamental spindles; **estagnié** or pewter cupboard; **verriau**, for glasses; **saliero** or salt container etc. The following original items also stand out: the elegant **buffet à glissants** or sliding sideboard; **radassié**, a large straw-seated sofa adorned with esparto leaves or sprigs of rye, such as those of the so-called *à la capucine* armchairs, distinguishable by their trapezoid seat, set back arm rests and concave-strutted back. Ornamentation is based on abundant and deep mouldings and sculpted motifs with overriding importance given to vegetation in different forms: acanthus leaves, flower baskets, branches of olive or oak; the addition of small, curved candle-rings to the angles and to the crest tops. The decorative style of Arles, a production centre of particular character, from where the *paneiro* or bread container, the first mobile cabinets and *à la capucine* chairs derived, is the best known.

In upper Provence, the sobriety of both the lines and the decor triumph over furniture of a more rustic style, remaining steadfast throughout the period of influence of the Renaissance and Louis XIII styles. Craftsmen in this part of the region preferred working with mulberry, pine or limewood; furniture not seen in lower Provence such as the *vaisselier* or dresser, and the *banc à dossier* or backed bench are a testimony to the influence of the neighbouring Dauphiné; simple wall cavities also tend to replace the use of small storage units in evidence in lower Provence.

The supremacy of clay – The abundance of excellent quality clay in Provence has given rise to a number of large ceramic centres in the region: the mottle decoration of **Apt** and **Avignon** faience; **Allemagne-en-Provence** and **Moustiers** *(see Michelin Green Guide Alpes du Sud, in French)*, **La Tour-d'Aigues** *(see p 255)*, and above all, **Marseille**, which received confirmation of its pioneer status with the archeological discovery of the market town of Les Olliers *(see p 179)*. Under Louis XIV, the wars which emptied the kingdom's coffers resulted in the banning of the use of gold and silver dishes, thus providing a fillip for the faience industry. In 1679, the Fabre pottery works at **St-Jean-du-Désert** between Aubagne and Marseille transformed its production to that of faience under the impetus of **Joseph Clérissy**, from an Aubagne

Bread bin (Museon Arlaten, Arles)

family which had moved to Moustiers. As in Nevers and Rouen, its blue "Chinese-style" cameos drew inspiration from the first pieces of porcelain imported into France from China. Although St-Jean-du-Désert saw its importance decline after the Great Plague, other earthenware works started to spring up, many of which employed the sharp fire technique, such as: **Fauchier**, who created both the *fleurs jetées* technique, whereby flowers would be painted in a seemingly haphazard fashion, and yellow enamel background decoration; **Leroy**, a true artist whose star-shaped flower motifs did their utmost to usurp those compositions filled with characters and fantastic animals.

The second half of the 18C represented the zenith of Marseille earthenware, mainly as a result of the activities and talent of Pierrette Candellot, a colourful personality originally from Lyon, and the wife of the Marseille pottery manufacturer Claude Perrin. Following his death in 1748, his widow, known as **La Veuve Perrin**, guided the family business towards the mild firing technique, consequently obtaining pieces of exceptional quality, exploited this by developing the ornamental Marseille style even further, lent her letters patent of nobility to fish-inspired decoration, introduced sea landscapes, developed an unusual sea-green coloured background, and evolved the shape of forms by drawing from the new ideas in gold and silver-making.

After Veuve Perrin, the last great Marseille earthenware producers were **Joseph-Gaspard Robert** and **Antoine Bonnefoy** both of whom were able to give to faience an ornamental refinement which until that time had been the prerogative of porcelain; the former with his famous floral black butterfly decoration and borders, and Bonnefoy with his refined medallions either with their *"bouillabaisse"* motifs or representing pastoral scenes reminiscent of Boucher. Ultimately, a combination of the competition from porcelain makers, the Revolution and the blockade by the English naval fleet sounded the death knell for Marseille's faience industry. The red, white and blue bordered plates by Gaspard Robert were to signal the end of an era for the city's illustrious earthenware.

Faience ware from St-Jean-du-Désert
(Musée Cantini, Marseille)

Art

ARCHITECTURAL TERMS

Ancient architecture

ORANGE – Roman Theatre (early 1C BC)

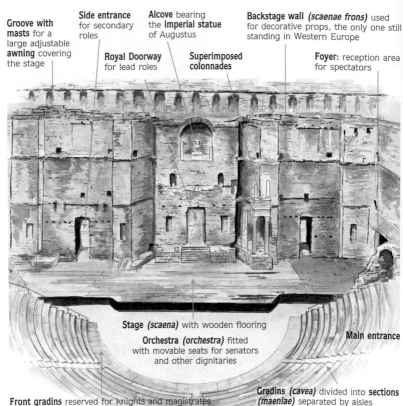

Groove with masts for a large adjustable **awning** covering the stage

Side entrance for secondary roles

Royal Doorway for lead roles

Alcove bearing the **imperial statue** of Augustus

Superimposed colonnades

Backstage wall (*scaenae frons*) used for decorative props, the only one still standing in Western Europe

Foyer: reception area for spectators

Stage (*scaena*) with wooden flooring

Orchestra (*orchestra*) fitted with movable seats for senators and other dignitaries

Main entrance

Front gradins reserved for knights and magistrates

Gradins (*cavea*) divided into **sections (*maeniae*)** separated by aisles

NÎMES – Maison Carrée (late 1C BC)

The Maison Carrée in Nîmes is a temple consecrated to the Imperial cult: it consists of a vestibule lined by a colonnade and a room housing a statue of the divinity, the *cella*.

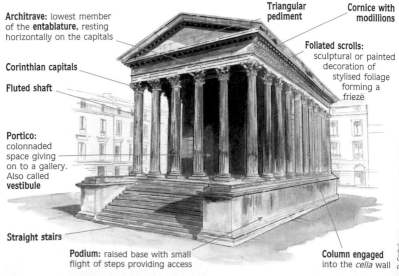

Architrave: lowest member of the **entablature,** resting horizontally on the capitals

Corinthian capitals

Fluted shaft

Portico: colonnaded space giving on to a gallery. Also called **vestibule**

Straight stairs

Triangular pediment

Cornice with modillions

Foliated scrolls: sculptural or painted decoration of stylised foliage forming a frieze

Podium: raised base with small flight of steps providing access

Column engaged into the *cella* wall

Religious architecture

VAISON-LA-ROMAINE – Plan of the Ancienne Cathédrale Notre-Dame-de-Nazareth (11C)

This cathedral is a typical example of Provençal church architecture, consisting of a nave without a transept ending in a semicircular apse.

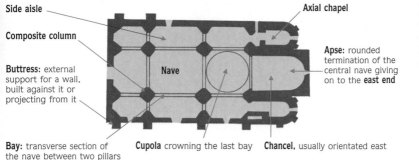

Side aisle

Composite column

Buttress: external support for a wall, built against it or projecting from it

Bay: transverse section of the nave between two pillars

Nave

Axial chapel

Apse: rounded termination of the central nave giving on to the **east end**

Cupola crowning the last bay

Chancel, usually orientated east

Vertical section of a Romanesque Provençal church

The two following drawings reflect the type of Romanesque church most frequently encountered in Provence.

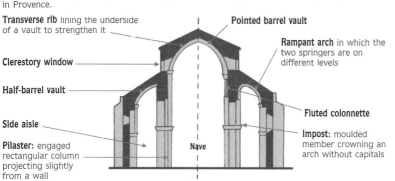

Transverse rib lining the underside of a vault to strengthen it

Clerestory window

Half-barrel vault

Side aisle

Pilaster: engaged rectangular column projecting slightly from a wall

Nave

Pointed barrel vault

Rampant arch in which the two springers are on different levels

Fluted colonnette

Impost: moulded member crowning an arch without capitals

Abbaye de SILVACANE   Vaulting in the Chapterhouse (13C)

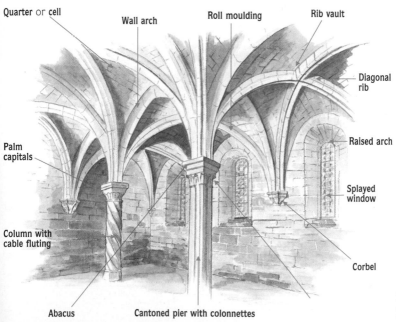

Quarter or cell

Wall arch

Roll moulding

Rib vault

Diagonal rib

Palm capitals

Raised arch

Column with cable fluting

Splayed window

Corbel

Abacus

Cantoned pier with colonnettes

R. Corbel

Abbaye de MONTMAJOUR – Chapelle Ste-Croix (12C)

The quadrilobed plan of the Chapelle Ste-Croix, based on a Greek cross and representative of 12C Provençal architecture, can be seen in several other buildings of the area.

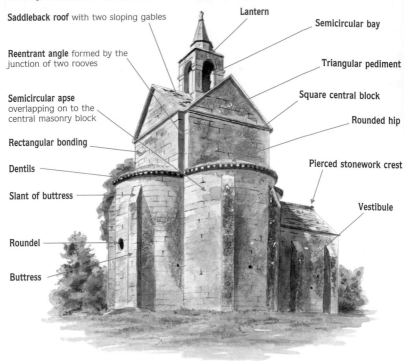

Saddleback roof with two sloping gables

Reentrant angle formed by the junction of two rooves

Semicircular apse overlapping on to the central masonry block

Rectangular bonding

Dentils

Slant of buttress

Roundel

Buttress

Lantern

Semicircular bay

Triangular pediment

Square central block

Rounded hip

Pierced stonework crest

Vestibule

CARPENTRAS – South Door of the Ancienne Cathédrale St-Siffrein (late 15C)

The South Door, known as the Jewish Door, is Flamboyant or late Gothic: this is evidenced by the window tracery and its sinuous, tapering lines evoking tongues of flame.

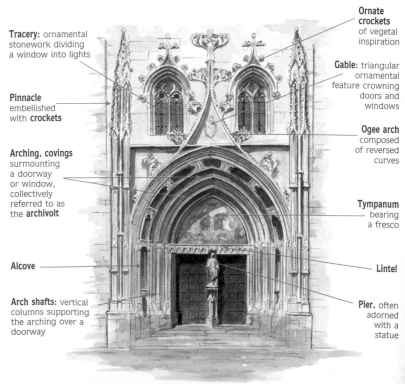

Tracery: ornamental stonework dividing a window into lights

Pinnacle embellished with **crockets**

Arching, covings surmounting a doorway or window, collectively referred to as the **archivolt**

Alcove

Arch shafts: vertical columns supporting the arching over a doorway

Ornate crockets of vegetal inspiration

Gable: triangular ornamental feature crowning doors and windows

Ogee arch composed of reversed curves

Tympanum bearing a fresco

Lintel

Pier, often adorned with a statue

Abbaye de ST-MICHEL-DE-FRIGOLET – Retable in the Chapelle Notre-Dame-du-Bon-Remède (17C)

This 11C chapel is richly decorated with Baroque panelling dating from the 17C. At the far end stands an imposing altarpiece.

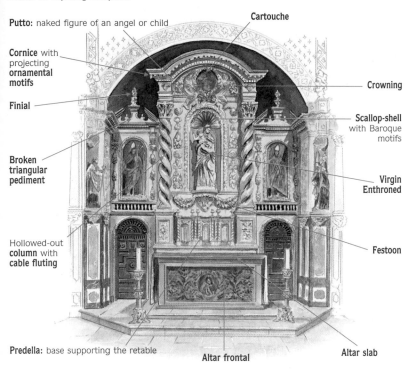

Putto: naked figure of an angel or child

Cornice with projecting **ornamental motifs**

Finial

Broken triangular pediment

Hollowed-out **column** with **cable fluting**

Predella: base supporting the retable

Cartouche

Crowning

Scallop-shell with Baroque motifs

Virgin Enthroned

Festoon

Altar slab

Altar frontal

UZÈS – Organ in the Cathédrale St-Théodorit (18C)

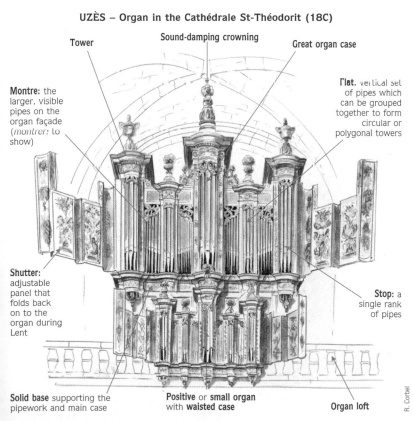

Tower

Sound-damping crowning

Great organ case

Montre: the larger, visible pipes on the organ façade (*montrer:* to show)

Flat: vertical set of pipes which can be grouped together to form circular or polygonal towers

Shutter: adjustable panel that folds back on to the organ during Lent

Stop: a single rank of pipes

Solid base supporting the pipework and main case

Positive or **small organ** with **waisted case**

Organ loft

R. Corbel

41

Military architecture

TARASCON – Fortified castle (14-15C)

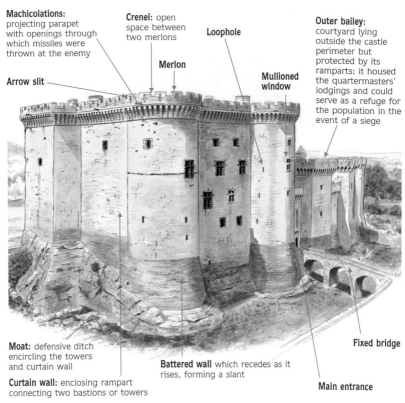

Machicolations: projecting parapet with openings through which missiles were thrown at the enemy

Crenel: open space between two merlons

Loophole

Merlon

Arrow slit

Mullioned window

Outer bailey: courtyard lying outside the castle perimeter but protected by its ramparts; it housed the quartermasters' lodgings and could serve as a refuge for the population in the event of a siege

Moat: defensive ditch encircling the towers and curtain wall

Curtain wall: enclosing rampart connecting two bastions or towers

Battered wall which recedes as it rises, forming a slant

Fixed bridge

Main entrance

PORT-DE-BOUC – Fort (17C)

This fort was built by Vauban in 1664. Its defensive system allows for a great many salients and bastions in order to avoid both dead angles and areas lacking artillery.

Rampart walk

Square keep converted into a lighthouse

Steep, narrow flight of steps backing on to the fort

Barracks

Look-out turret

Reentrant angle in an outer rampart formed by the junction of two wings

Raised terreplein reserved for heavy artillery pieces

Battered wall

Curtain wall

Parade ground

Salient

R. Corbel

Civil architecture

AIX-EN-PROVENCE – Pavillon de Vendôme (17-18C)

The main façade features the "great order" advocated by Palladio as early back as the Renaissance, characterised by the display of three superimposed orders: Doric, Ionic and Corinthian.

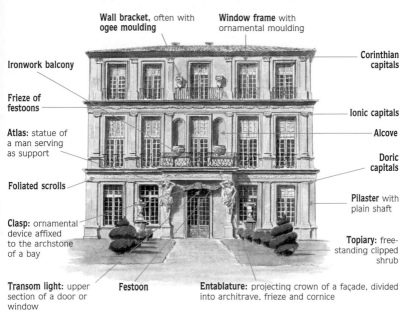

Wall bracket, often with **ogee moulding**

Window frame with ornamental moulding

Corinthian capitals

Ironwork balcony

Frieze of festoons

Ionic capitals

Atlas: statue of a man serving as support

Alcove

Doric capitals

Foliated scrolls

Pilaster with plain shaft

Clasp: ornamental device affixed to the archstone of a bay

Topiary: free-standing clipped shrub

Transom light: upper section of a door or window

Festoon

Entablature: projecting crown of a façade, divided into architrave, frieze and cornice

MARSEILLE – Water tower of the Palais Longchamp (19C)

Seeking inspiration from Bernini's work in Rome, the architect Espérandieu built a monumental fountain whose decoration draws heavily upon the aquatic theme.

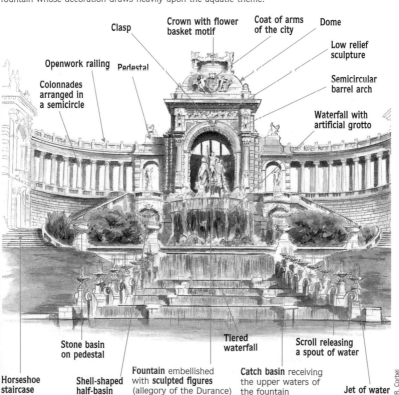

Clasp

Crown with flower basket motif

Coat of arms of the city

Dome

Low relief sculpture

Openwork railing

Pedestal

Colonnades arranged in a semicircle

Semicircular barrel arch

Waterfall with artificial grotto

Horseshoe staircase

Shell-shaped half-basin

Stone basin on pedestal

Fountain embellished with **sculpted figures** (allegory of the Durance)

Tiered waterfall

Catch basin receiving the upper waters of the fountain

Scroll releasing a spout of water

Jet of water

R. Corbel

43

ART AND ARCHITECTURAL TERMS USED IN THE GUIDE

Acroterion: ornaments placed at the apex and ends of a pediment of a temple.

Aisle: lateral division in a church flanking a nave or chancel.

Ambulatory: aisle running around the east end of a church.

Apse: rounded termination of the central nave giving on to the east end.

Archivolt: arch moulding over an arcade or upper section of a doorway.

Barrel vault: vault in the form of a half-cylinder.

Basket-handled arch: depressed arch in late medieval and Renaissance architecture.

Bay: transverse section of the nave between two pillars.

Blind arcading: sequences of arches, sometimes intersecting, applied to a blank wall for decorative effect.

Brattice: a temporary wooden gallery or parapet for use during a siege.

Caryatid: carved female figure used for support.

Chevet: French term for the east end of a church.

Cippus: small pillar used to mark a burial place or serve as a sepulchral monument.

Claustra: stone railings with vertical bars.

Coffered ceiling: vault or ceiling decorated with sunken panels.

Crocket: carved ornament in the form of a curled leaf or cusp used in Gothic architecture.

Crypt: underground chamber or chapel.

Diaphragm arch: transversal arch used to relieve side walls.

Entablature: projecting crown of a façade, divided into architrave, frieze and cornice.

Exedra: niche, usually semicircular, with a bench around the wall.

Flamboyant: latest phase (15C) of French Gothic architecture; the name was taken from the tapering (flame-like) lines of the window tracery.

Fluting: vertical shallow grooving decorating a column or pilaster.

Foliated scrolls: sculptural or painted ornamentation depicting foliage, often in a frieze.

Fresco: mural paintings executed on wet plaster.

Gable: triangular part of an end wall carrying a sloping roof; the term is also applied to steeply-pitched ornamental pediments in Gothic architecture.

Génoise: decorative frieze under the eaves, composed of a double or triple row of tiles embedded end-on in the wall.

Historiated: decorated with figures of people or animals.

Hypocaust: an underground furnace to heat the water for the baths or rooms of a house.

Jambs: pillars flanking a doorway and supporting the arch above.

Keystone: middle and topmost stone in an arch or vault.

Lintel: horizontal beam or stone slab surmounting a door or window frame.

Mascaron: medallion carved in the shape of a human head.

Modillion: small console supporting a cornice.

Mullion: vertical post dividing a window.

Narthex: interior vestibule of a church.

Peristyle: range of columns surrounding or fronting a building.

Pietà: Italian term designating the Virgin Mary with the dead Christ on her knees.

Piscina: basin for washing the sacred vessels.

Pilaster: engaged rectangular column.

Pinnacle: slender upright structure crowning a buttress, gable or tower.

Portico: a colonnaded space in front of a façade or in an interior courtyard.

Predella: base of an altarpiece, divided into small panels.

Pulpitum: front section of the stage in an antique theatre.

Retable: ornamental structure set up above and behind an altar, often used as a setting for a religious picture or carving.

Rood screen: open screen, often richly painted or carved, separating areas reserved for clergy (chancel) and laity (nave).

Rosette: circular window with ornamental tracery radiating from the centre to form a symmetrical rose-like pattern.

Stucco: mixture of powdered marble, plaster and strong glue; used for decoration.

Transom light: upper section of a door or window.

Triptych: three panels hinged together, chiefly used as an altarpiece.

Voussoir: wedge-shaped stone forming part of an arch or vault.

ANCIENT ART

Before the Roman conquest: Celtic-Ligurian civilisation

Ligurians and Celts settled in fortified hill sites *(oppida)* such as Nages, Entremont and Roquepertuse *(see p 185)* and created towns organised on a regular plan. Within the fortified walls stood a group of uniform dwellings, a type of hut in unfired stone and brick. Celtic-Ligurian sculpture honoured, above anything else, the cult of the dead warrior, the town's hero, which was represented in the form of warriors' statues seated cross-legged with people either free-standing or in relief. An important ritual consisted of setting in the stone lintels the severed heads of the conquered peoples, or at least the carved version. The sculpture exhibited at Roquepertuse demonstrates perfectly the Celtic form of expression.

Analysis of pottery shards confirms that the site was densely occupied from the final Neolithic Era (3000 BC) to around 200 BC, date of the last destruction of the site. The most prosperous period was between the end of 4 BC to the end of 3 BC, characterised by the widespread use of delicate Mediterranean dishes (cups and pitchers of either painted or unpainted clay, Italic black glaze from 3C). From being confined to a single sanctuary, as was long believed, Roquepertuse, which is still the subject of detailed research, is in fact a vast complex stretching from the oppidum in the north to the sloping village in the south.

Hellenistic influence was crucial for the region; it directly influenced the native peoples, accelerating the development of their economy and society. Greek construction techniques are evident in the building of St-Blaise *(see p 225)* and Glanum *(see p 234)*. Numerous pottery fragments and Greek black figure vases were excavated at Arles, and the stelae found in Rue Négrel in Marseille are the oldest examples (second half of the 6C BC) of Greek sculpture in France.

Roman towns

Throughout Provence towns were built on the Roman urban plan. They all boasted remarkable public and private buildings, some of which are still well preserved, giving them a charm all of their own.

Towns – The great Provençal towns, without totally dropping all Hellenistic influence, took Rome as their model.

Urban plan – Most of the towns were built either on native Hellenistic or Gallic sites. And yet, very often, the desire to settle in a particular spot was that of a colony of veteran legionnaires, as was the case in Nîmes and Orange, who were soon after joined by the civilian population. The foundation was laid according to precise rules: having determined the future town centre two major streets were traced – the *cardo maximus* (north-south orientation) and the *decumanus maximus* (east-west orientation) which created a regular grid pattern in which the grids were squared with sides some hundred square yards wide. In fact this geometric exactitude could only appear on sites where the local topography was suitable, such as in Orange or Arles as opposed to Nîmes and Vaison-la-Romaine.

Where previous edifices had existed, they were razed as at Glanum, to make room for the new buildings. These towns were not surrounded with walls except at Nîmes, Arles and Orange, which were granted the honour of surrounding themselves with ramparts (permission obtained from Rome). Defensive walls did not appear until the end of the 3C; they were then built with towers and gates corresponding to the main streets.

Streets – The main streets were lined with pavements, at times 50cm/19.5in high and bordered by porticoes which protected the people from sun and rain. The roadway, paved with large flagstones laid diagonally, was crossed at intervals by stepping-stones laid at the same level as the pavements but between which horses and chariot-wheels could pass and pedestrians could cross over above the dust and mud. Gutters also ran alongside the road and were slightly rounded.

Forum – The forum, a large paved open space surrounded by an arcade, was the centre of public and commercial life in a Roman town. Government offices were located round the forum; these included a temple devoted to the imperial cult, a civil basilica (a type of town hall where judicial and commercial affairs were conducted); the curia or headquarters of local government, and at times a prison.

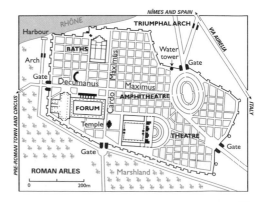

ROMAN ARLES

At Arles the forum had the particularity of being lined with a vast underground gallery, *cryptoporticus*, the origin of which remains a mystery.

The art of building – The art of building was very advanced with the Romans. The rapidity with which their buildings went up was not so much due to the number of people working on a site as to the special training of the workers, their organised working methods and the use of lifting devices such as levers, hoisting winches and tackles, to move heavy material into place.

Building materials – For building material the Romans used the local limestone, which was not hard to dress; the stone was easily extracted and shaped into blocks. They originally adopted the method of using large blocks of stone without mortar, that is to say the stones were held together by their weight, and with dowels or cramps. But they then revolutionised wall construction by introducing the use of concrete, a manufactured material not unique to any one country; it could, therefore, be used in the construction of buildings throughout the Empire giving a uniformity and similarity to their buildings.

It could be used to fill in the cracks or joints, or give to a public building a uniform surface such as at the Maison Carrée and Amphitheatre in Nîmes, or to wedge the stones together allowing the expansion of the vault.

Orders – The Roman architectural orders derived from the Greek orders but with some variation. Roman Doric, still called the Tuscan Order, the simplest and most solid, was found on the monuments' lower storeys; too severe, it was rarely used by the Romans. The Ionic Order was very elegant but not ornate enough for the Roman architects. However, the Corinthian Order was used frequently for the richness of its ornamentation. The Composite Order was a combination of the Ionic and Corinthian Orders.

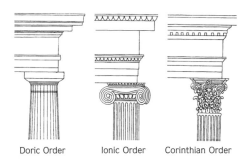

Doric Order   Ionic Order   Corinthian Order

Roofs – The public buildings sometimes had rectangular-shaped roofs held by colonnades inside the rooms. But more often the Romans used rounded vaulting in corridors and galleries where the walls were parallel, groined vaulting in square rooms and the dome in circular rooms.

Public Buildings – The inhabitants of Roman towns enjoyed bloody combats as much as more peaceful theatrical representations *(see NÎMES)*.

The gladiator fights were forbidden in 404 under the influence of Christianisation; the games were abandoned at the same time.

Amphitheatres – The amphitheatre, also known as **arena**, had on the outside two tiers of arcades surmounted by a low storey called the attic. On the attic were fixed posts to carry a huge adjustable awning, the *velarium*, to shelter the spectators from the sun and rain. The arcades were divided by rectangular pillars decorated with engaged half-columns on the first storey. Inside, enclosing the arena, a wall protected the spectators in the front rows from the wild animals released in the ring. The *cavea* – terraces for the spectators – was divided into *maenia* – tiers of seats generally in groups of four, individually separated by a passage. The seats were strictly allocated, those nearest the arena being for the men with a superior social station: the first *maenia* were reserved for consuls, senators, magistrates and members of local guilds (such as the boatmen of Arles) who arrived in litters. In another section sat priests, knights and Roman citizens whereas freedmen and slaves sat in the attic. The arcades and three circular gallery-promenades, the hundreds of staircases and passages enabled spectators to reach or leave their stepped seats directly – at Nîmes it took less than five minutes for the audience of 20 000 to leave.

Theatres – The Roman theatre, in the form of a half-circle lengthened by a deep stage, was divided into three sections: the *cavea* (auditorium) built in the hollow of a hillside, as in Orange and crowned by a colonnade; the *orchestra*, the semicircular section in front of the stage with movable seats reserved for dignitaries; the stage flanked by side rooms, rectangular in shape, which were higher in level than the orchestra. At the back of the stage was a wall (which was as high as the *cavea*) with three doors through which the actors entered.

The stage wall was the finest part of the building; its decoration included several tiers of columns, niches containing statues (the central niche contained the emperor's statue), marble facing and mosaics. Behind this the actors' dressing-rooms and store rooms were situated. Beyond these again was a portico open to the garden, through which the actors entered the theatre. In it the spectators would stroll during the intermissions or take shelter from rain. As in the arenas, a huge adjustable awning which was known as the *velum* could be opened to shelter the spectators from the sun and rain.

Scenery and machinery were ingenious. Some scenes were fixed; some were superimposed and uncovered by sliding others sideways.

The curtain was only 3m/10ft high. It dropped into a slit at the beginning of the play and rose at the end. The basement contained the machinery and communicated with the stage through trapdoors on which the actors could rise from or sink into the ground. Other machines, mounted in the flies, lowered gods or heroes from the heavens or raised them into the clouds.

The effects men knew how to create were smoke, lightning, thunder, ghosts and the accompaniment of apotheoses.

All sorts of means were used to obtain perfect acoustics. The mouths of the actors' masks were little megaphones; the large sloping roof over the stage threw the sound downwards, the upward curve of the seats received it smoothly, the colonnades broke up the echo and carefully graduated sounding-boards under the seats acted as loud-speakers. One detail shows how far these refinements were carried: the doors on the stage were hollow and made like violins inside. When an actor wished to amplify his voice he would stand against one of these sound-boxes. *(See illustration under Art and Architectural Terms)*.

Circuses – These were huge rectangular arenas, one end of which was oval-shaped, where chariot and horse races were held. All that remains of the circus at Arles is the obelisk which stands in front of St-Trophime.

Temples – The temple stood on a podium surrounded by columns and consisted of two rooms: the *pronaos* (a vestibule) and the *cella* (a place for the statue of the divinity).The prime example of a temple is the Maison Carrée at Nîmes *(see illustration under Art and Architectural Terms)*. In the countryside there were small local temples, *fana* (singular *fanum*).

Triumphal arches – The arches in Orange, Glanum, Carpentras and Cavaillon resemble the triumphal arches of Rome, raised in honour of victorious generals, but were built to commemorate the founding of the cities in which they stand and the exploits of the veterans who settled there. They had either one or three openings; the columns decorating the four sides and flanking the central arch were all engaged; later on they became detached. The upper storey was decorated with statues, horse drawn chariots and their feats of arms, usually in gilt bronze.

Baths – The Roman baths, which were public and free, were also centres of physical culture, casinos, clubs, recreation centres, libraries, lecture halls and meeting-places, which explains the amount of time people spent in them. Decoration in these great buildings *(see plan of La Trouille baths under ARLES)* was lavish: columns and capitals picked out in bright colours, mosaic ornaments, coloured marble facings, richly coffered ceilings, mural paintings and statues.

Central heating – The bath's functioning demonstrated the Romans' understanding of the canalisation of water and its subsequent heating. Water was brought from the mountains via aqueducts and placed into cisterns and then distributed by a lead-pipe and cement system of canals; evacuation was conducted through a network of drain pipes.

Orange – Arc de Triomphe

To heat air and water a number of underground furnaces (hypocausts) like bakers' ovens, in which roaring fires were kept going, were used. The hot gases circulated among the brick pillars supporting the stone floors of rooms and baths, and rose through flues in the walls to escape from chimneys. In this way the rooms were heated from below and from the sides as in modern buildings. The warmest room, facing south or west, had large glazed windows and was used as a solarium. Water at three different temperatures, cold, lukewarm and hot, circulated automatically by thermo-siphon.

Bather's route – The bather followed a medically-designed route. From the changing room where he would have left his clothes and anointed his body with oil, he entered the *palestra* (a gymnasium of sorts) where he would warm up performing physical exercises; then came the *tepidarium* (a lukewarm room) where he thoroughly cleaned himself by scraping his skin with small curved metal spatulas *(strigiles)*, which prepared him for the *caldarium* (hot room) where he took a steam bath; he then proceeded into the hot swimming-pool. Having been massaged, he once again returned to the *tepidarium* before continuing on to the *frigidarium* (cold bath) to tone up the skin.

Thoroughly revived he dressed and proceeded to take advantage of the baths' other activities (such as lectures, sports, gossip...). The private baths located in the wealthy urban dwellings and *villae* were not as spacious but did possess a comparable level of luxury.

The Roman townhouse – Excavations at Vaison-la-Romaine, Glanum or the Fountain quarter in Nîmes have uncovered Roman houses of various types: the small bourgeois house, a dwelling (several storeys high) for rent, shops open to the street and finally large, luxurious patrician mansions.

The latter had a modest external appearance owing to their bare walls and few windows. But the interiors, adorned with mosaics, statues, paintings and marbles and sometimes including hot baths and a fish pond, reflected the wealth of their owners.

R. Corbel

A vestibule and a corridor led to the *atrium*.

The **atrium** (**1**) which opened on to the street through a vestibule containing the porter's lodge was a large rectangular court, open in the middle, to the sky *(compluvium)*; a basin called the *impluvium*, under the open section, caught rainwater. Rooms opened off the *atrium*: reception room (**2**), private oratory, *tablinum* or study and library of the head of the family.

The **peristyle** (**3**) was a court surrounded by a portico (a gallery with a roof supported by columns) in the centre of the part of the house reserved for the family. It was reached from the *atrium* along a corridor called the *fauces*. Here the peristyle was generally made into a garden with basins lined with mosaics, fountains and statues. The living quarters opened all around it: bedrooms, *triclinium* (dining room-**4**), and *oecus* (main drawing room).

The annexes included the kitchen with a sink and drain, baths, flush lavatory; other buildings housed slaves' quarters, attics, cellars, stables etc.

Rural housing – This kind of dwelling is just beginning to be examined. The towns must have been numerous and the settlement of these sites by Romans was done on pre-existing sites. The cadastral plan of Orange seems to show that the Romans tried to organise their territory into square-shaped lots called centuries.

The most common type of house was the *villa*, 40 of which have been discovered in Provence.

Aqueducts – Grandiose like the Pont du Gard or more modest like Barbegal, aqueducts played an important role in daily life as they carried the water from their source to the town.

Roman roads – As soon as they settled in Provence, the Romans decided to design and build a reliable network of terrestrial means of communication that would ensure supremacy over the lands they had conquered, while at the same time encouraging the exchange of both goods and ideas. The layout of these roads usually coincided with that undertaken by the Gauls or with the paths *(drailles)* traditionally used by herds of cattle. They were cobbled only at the entrance to cities (country ways were surfaced with small, flat stones arranged tightly together) and dotted with stone or wooden bridges (Pont Julien at Bonnieux, Pont Flavien at St-Chamas), military milestones (1 Roman mile = 1 481m/0.92mi) and relay posts. Three great Roman roads cut across Provence: the Aurelian Way *(Via Aurelia)*, the Domitian Way *(Via Domitia)* and the road to Agrippa. The first connected Rome to the River Rhône, running along the coast through the towns of Antibes *(Antipolis)*, Fréjus *(Forum Jilii)*, Aix-en-Provence *(Aquae Sextiae)* and Salon-de-Provence *(Salo)* before joining up with the Domitian Way in Tarascon *(Tarusco)*. The *Via Domitia*, which headed towards Spain, helped link northern Italy to southern Gaul. It served the cities of Briançon *(Brigantium)*, Gap *(Vapicum)*, Sisteron *(Segustero)*, Apt *(Aptia Julia)*, Cavaillon *(Cabello)*, Tarascon *(Tarusco)*, Nîmes *(Nemausus)*, Béziers *(Julia Baeterrae)*, Narbonne *(Noarb)* and Perpignan *(Ruscino)*. Finally, the road to Agrippa started at Arles *(Arelate)* and extended towards Lyon, following the left bank of the Rhône and crossing Avignon *(Avenio)* and Orange *(Arausio)*.

ROMANESQUE ART

The brilliant Gallo-Roman civilization took a long time to disappear after the fall of the Western Empire. The ancient public buildings remained standing and the architects of the Middle Ages took inspiration from them to build churches and monasteries. A dark age followed (5C-10C) when few buildings were erected, of which only isolated specimens now remain, such as the small baptistries at Aix and Venasque. Early Romanesque art, which developed from Catalonia to northern Italy in the 10C and 11C, did not leave significant examples, either.

The 12C was for Provence one of its most outstanding historic periods during which it underwent a brilliant architectural renaissance. Churches, remarkable for the bonding of their evenly-cut stones with fine mortar work, appeared everywhere. Their style was closely-linked to a School which had evolved in the area between the River Rhône, the Drôme, the Alps and the Mediterranean. This School was more original than innovative and knew how to capture different influences: from Roman Antiquity came the use of vaults and especially decoration; from Languedoc came the carved portals; from Lombardy came the Lombard arcade or the lions adorning the base of doors; from Auvergne came the dome on squinches over the nave and in front of the apse.

Given below are the essential characteristics of this style, the best examples of which were the great sanctuaries in the Rhône valley: Cathédrale de la Major in Marseille, St-Trophime in Arles, St-Gilles, Cathédrale Notre-Dame-des-Doms in Avignon, Cathédrale Notre-Dame in Orange and the church in Le Thor.

Churches and chapels

Plan – Provençal Romanesque churches have descended directly from the Roman basilica and Carolingian church. Their general appearance was of a solid mass. Transepts were rare and shallow. Often there was a single nave with side chapels hollowed out of the thickness of the walls. The east end took the form of an apse with two flanking apsidal chapels, where there were side aisles. Only the great pilgrimage churches of St-Gilles and St-Trophime, Arles, have ambulatories. Minor buildings (Chapelle Ste-Croix in Montmajour – *see illustration p 40* – St-Sépulcre in Peyrolles) present a quadrilobed plan.

E. Baret

Abbey of St-Gilles: Romanesque doorway

Exterior

Bell towers – The bell tower is, an imposing, most often square, sometimes octagonal structure, that dominated the dome above the transept crossing.

It was sometimes placed above the bay preceding the apse or on the façade. It was decorated with blind arcading known as Lombard arcades or fluted pilasters in the Antique style, or sometimes both.

Side walls – The walls were usually bare except for the cornice and the plain side doors. Massive buttresses, between which were set the windows of the nave, relieved the austere monotony of the exterior.

West fronts and doors – The west front was generally plain, opened by a door surmounted by an oculus as the main door was often located on the south side sheltered from the *mistral*.

The doors were probably the architectural element most influenced by ancient Greek and Roman art; sometimes they were decorated with a fronton directly influenced by the ancient temples, such as the porch at Notre-Dame-des-Doms and the Chapelle St-Gabriel near Tarascon.

During the 12C, façades became more ornate preceded at times by a porch: a large carved tympanum over a horizontal lintel began to feature. The doorways of St-Gilles and St-Trophime, superb carved examples, rivalled in quality, size and beauty the Gothic cathedral masterpieces of northern France.

Interior

Upon entering the Provençal Romanesque church the visitor is struck by the simplicity and austerity of the inside structure enhanced only by some carved mouldings and cornices, barely visible in the dimly lit interior.

Chancel – This is the part of the church reserved for the clergy. It was usually oven vaulted and linked to the transept crossing with rounded barrel vaulting.

Nave and vault – The lofty – moderate though it was – structure of the building's interior was remarkable for the purity of its lines.

The nave was roofed with pointed barrel vaulting in which the downward thrust was more direct than that of the rounded arches which tended to splay the wall outwards. The barrel vaulting had already been used in the Roman era, having replaced the easily flammable wooden roofing, used from the 5C to the 11C, which had caused the destruction of many buildings. It was buttressed by pointed arches, also called transverse arches, which came down on thick engaged pilasters in the side walls or down onto slender pillars lining the nave.

The nave was sometimes lined with aisles with quarter-circle or pointed barrel vaulting, which acted as buttresses.

Owing to the height of the side aisles there were no tribunes but a decorative band of blind arcading, made of rounded arches, with three arches to each bay, the central arch pierced by a lancet window, which let in very little light. Where the churches had but a single nave the side walls were quite thick in order to compensate for the missing side walls and balance the whole structure.

Transept and dome – The construction of the transept was a difficult problem for the architects in the Romanesque period. The groined vaulting made by the crossing of the nave and aisle vaulting had to be of great height in order to support the heavy weight of the central bell tower; the problem was solved by placing a dome on squinches over the crossing in the style of the Auvergne School.

Decoration – Interior decoration was as austere as exterior decoration: decorated capitals usually ornamented with stylised leaves, friezes with interlacing and foliated scrolls, fluting and rope moulding.

The capital with leaves of the Romanesque style was an adaptation of the ancient Corinthian capital: it was formed by a group of leaves arranged according to the style of the Romanesque period (interlacing and stylised decoration). The most picturesque of these capitals were historiated, inspired by religious stories taken from the Old and New Testaments. The cloisters offer the best examples: St-Trophime with its magnificent corner pillars adorned with statues of saints is remarkable. Fine capitals can also be found in the cloisters of Montmajour and St-Paul-de-Mausole (fantastic animals) and the apse of the church at Stes-Maries-de-la-Mer. There are also fragments of carved decoration worth seeing: in Avignon's cathedral there is the bishop's throne; in Apt's cathedral there is the altar.

Abbeys – Provence boasts several fine abbeys. The Benedictine Abbaye de Montmajour near Arles, founded in the 10C, forms a superb architectural ensemble illustrating the evolution of Romanesque forms from the 11C to 13C. It includes two churches (an upper church and crypt or lower church), two chapels, cloisters and its annexes in the characteristic Provençal style: simplicity in the monumental size, the volumes of which were inspired by the Antique style, carved decoration similar to St-Trophime, and perfection in the stone bonding. Cistercian art was represented by three sister abbeys: Sénanque (see *p 247*), Silvacane (see *p 250*) and Le Thoronet *(see Michelin Green Guide French Riviera)*.

Sober elegance, austerity and lack of ornamentation were the required rules of the Cistercians, a reformed monastic order founded by St Bernard of Clairvaux. St Bernard had denounced the fanciful nature of Romanesque sculpture which could distract the monks at prayer. The Cistercians imposed an identical plan everywhere, and they themselves directed the construction.

GOTHIC ART

Architecture – The Gothic style is marked by the systematic use of quadripartite vaulting and pointed arches. This innovative style, which originated in northern France, revolutionised construction by concentrating the weight of the structure on four pillars directed by stringers and transverse arches. Due to the absence of flying buttresses (characteristic of Northern Gothic) the thrust of the vaults was assured by the massive buttresses between which chapels were built.

Inside, the nave was relatively dark, almost as wide as it was high and ended in a narrower polygonal apse. Its width made it easier for the church, intended primarily for Dominican preaching. The wall surfaces required painted decoration.

Église St-Didier in Avignon is considered the best example of Southern Gothic in the region, whereas in a building like the basilica in St-Maximin-la-Ste-Baume southern and northern influences appear; the church of the Couvent des Célestines in Avignon is entirely Northern Gothic in style.

Religious edifices were not the only examples of Gothic art in Provence; civic and military buildings also held an important place. The Palais des Papes in Avignon was one of tildings in the 14C, combining the demands of luxury and comfort with those of defence and security.

Evolution – Romanesque art survived longer in Provence than it did in the rest of France. In spite of the relatively early appearance of Gothic, limited to two buildings (crypt of St-Gilles, porch of St-Victor in Marseille) and quadripartite vaulting as early as pre-1150, Gothic art was late in taking hold in Provence.

In the early 13C the new vaulting was used to cover buildings only in the Romanesque style. The only buildings entirely in the 13C Gothic style are to be found in Aix: central nave of Cathédrale St-Sauveur and Église St-Jean-de-Malte, the former priory of the Knights of Malta. The Gothic style finally caught on under the influence of two historic factors: Capetian presence in the south, as a result of the Albigensian Crusade and the marriage of Charles of Anjou with Beatrice of Provence, and the settling of the mendicant orders in the towns.

In the mid 14C, there began a new step in Gothic evolution: a school of architecture called the Papal Gothic style began developing in Avignon. The popes attracted to their court artists from different regions of France, Germany, Flanders and Italy.

During the 15C the cardinals embellished Villeneuve-lès-Avignon with palaces *(livrées)*, churches and cloisters; aisles and chapels were added to certain churches. St-Trophime was altered, the Romanesque apse was replaced by an ambulatory and radiating chapels.

The main Gothic churches include: Palais des Papes (Clementine, Grand or Clement VI Chapel), St-Didier, St-Pierre, St-Agricol, Couvent des Célestines, all in Avignon; St-Laurent in Salon-de-Provence; Cathédrale St-Siffrein in Carpentras; the basilica of St-Maximin-la-Ste-Baume; the church in Roquemaure and especially the charterhouse and church in Villeneuve-lès-Avignon.

Decoration – The austere elegance of Provençal Gothic churches is underlined by the lack of decoration.

Painting – The Avignon region was for over two centuries (14C-15C) the great centre of Provençal painting. Already in the 13C the frescoes of the Ferrande tower recalled the miniatures painted during St Louis' reign. In the 14C the popes decorating the palace sought out the great Italian masters: Simone Martini from Siena and Matteo Giovanetti from Viterbo *(see Michelin Green Guide Italy)*. The charterhouse in Villeneuve-lès-Avignon also contains fine works by Giovanetti. Once the popes had left Avignon, Italian influence diminished, but artistic life underwent a renaissance in the mid 15C; Good King René was a patron of the arts and attracted mastercraftsmen – artists and architects – to his court. Fresco painting lost ground to the Avignon School of panel painting. Artists from the north, Flanders and Burgundy painted splendid masterpieces such as the Triptych of the Annunciation (1443-45) in Aix's Ste-Marie-Madeleine Church and the Coronation of the Virgin (1453-54) by Enguerrand Quarton, which is exhibited in the Musée Pierre de Luxembourg in Villeneuve-lès-Avignon.

Annunciation by Taddea di Bartolo

51

Nicolas Froment, King René's court painter from Languedoc, painted the famous *Triptych of the Burning Bush* (in Aix's Cathédrale St-Sauveur). Avignon's Petit Palais contains a remarkable collection of lovely 14C and 15C paintings (Avignon and Italian Schools).

Sculpture – In the 14C, sculpture consisted of recumbent figures (John XXII in Avignon's Notre-Dame-des-Doms, Innocent VI in Villeneuve-lès-Avignon's charterhouse and Cardinal Lagrange in the Petit Palais in Avignon), corbels, keystones and slender capitals; archaic in style, they tended to derive from the Romanesque tradition. The reason for this penury was that mural painting was occupying an increasingly important role in the interior decoration of churches.

FROM THE RENAISSANCE TO THE PRESENT DAY

Renaissance – Although the Rhône valley was the principal route by which personalities of the Italian Renaissance entered France, Provence remained virtually untouched by the movement. Such buildings as were erected in the 16C were in the Gothic style, except for a few chapels and châteaux.

Classical Period – The 17C and 18C, by contrast, produced a large number of buildings. They were dignified and austere in design without distinctive regional characteristics. The so-called Jesuit style developed in the Comtat Venaison churches, bringing with it Italian monumental features such as ornate retables or altarpieces, panelling and baldachins, often obscuring the church's architectural lines. Avignon became the major centre once more, with local artists such as the Mignards and Parrocels producing religious pictures and **Jacques Bernus** of Mazan carving for churches throughout the region.

In the Gard, there was a great drive to rebuild churches damaged during the Wars of Religion (Église St-Gilles). An entirely novel element was the building of town houses by the old and new moneyed nobility, the magistracy and others: a few remain in Avignon and Nîmes but the finest line the streets of Aix. These well-proportioned, dignified stone houses are distinguished by doorways coroneted with ironwork balconies often supported by robust caryatids or muscular atlantes. The artists of these works were sculptor-decorators **Jean-Claude Rambot** (1421-94) and **Bernard Toro** (1672-1731), both contemporaries of Pierre Puget. **Pierre Puget** (1620-94), an artist and architect from Marseille, became one of the great Baroque sculptors of 17C France.

The 18C saw the continuation of the towns' and cities' embellishment programme which had begun the previous century: in Nîmes the engineer J.-P. Mareschal designed the splendid Jardin de la Fontaine.

Among the painters of that period two stand out: **Carle Van Loo**, who was susceptible to Provençal charm, and **Joseph Vernet**, the painter of seascapes and ports.

19C – The art of architects and civil engineers was mostly practised in the Marseille region where **Espérandieu** erected the new Cathédrale La Major and Basilique de Notre-Dame-de-la-Garde, in the fashionable late-19C Romano-Byzantine style, and Palais Longchamp. Roquefavour Aqueduct is a superb civil engineering project which brings to mind the ancient Roman Pont du Gard. The Rove Underground Canal also represents an incredible feat.

Pierre Puget (1620-1694)

This highly-skilled, multifaceted artist began his career as a young sculptor in Italy, where he trained under Pierre de Cortone. In 1645, Fouquet commissioned him to execute the doorway for the town hall in Toulon – it was to be one of his first great masterpieces. Between 1660 and 1668, the most brilliant period in his career, he was living in Genoa. He was called back to Paris by Colbert, who entrusted him with the decoration of ships' prows belonging to the fleet in Toulon. Wary of the plots and intrigues of Versailles, he chose to live away from the French Court and devoted himself to the ornamentation of several Provençal cities such as Aix and Marseille. His work is said to be forceful rather than elegant, and his statues, often of monumental proportions, artfully convey power, movement and pathos. His style is strongly reminiscent of Italian Baroque (Bernini, Cortone) and he succeeded in gracing Provence with a personal and highly original touch at a time when the country was largely dominated by Classicism.

His paintings (*Achilles' Education*) and sculptures (*The Faun, The Plague in Milan*) *(see right)*, are displayed at the Musée des Beaux-Arts in Marseille, as well as at the Louvre Museum in Paris (the famous *Milon de Crotone* sculpture). His architectural feats include the ovoid dome of the Vieille Charité chapel in Marseille.

Y. Gallois/Musée des Beaux-Arts, Marseille

Around this time painting benefited from an explosion of talented artists all fascinated by the luminous beauty of the Provençal countryside. The first to study the landscapes of Provence were J.-A. Constantin (1756-1844) and **François-Marius Granet** (1775-1849). The Landscape School inspired by **Émile Loubon** (1809-1863) also explored the notion of light with painters such as **Paul Guigou** (1834-1871), a forerunner of Impressionism, and the Marseille artist Adolphe Monticelli (1824-1886). This School ceased to exist around 1870 and was replaced by the painters known as "Naturalists": Achille Emperaire (1829-1898) and Joseph Ravaisou (1865-1925) in Aix; Clément Brun (1868-1920) and Paul Sain (1853-1908) in Avignon; Joseph Garibaldi (1863-1941), J.-B. Olive (1848-1936) and Alphonse Moutte (1840-1913 - strong realistic scenes of local fishermen) in Marseille, the first artists to paint L'Estaque. Finally **Félix Ziem**, a resident of Martigues, one of the first to paint in the hills beyond the fishing village of L'Estaque, chose to use colour in its own right and not to create light effects; his concerns were echoed by the great painters of the late 19C and the early 20C.

Van Gogh – Vincent Van Gogh (1853-90), son of a Dutch Calvinist pastor, admirer of Millet and Rubens and influenced by the art of Japanese prints, was attracted to Impressionism, despite his turbulent, strong personality.

In February 1888, he decided to settle in Arles *(see p 85)*, seeking a "different light". The two years he spent discovering Provence (Arles, Stes-Maries-de-la-Mer, Les Baux, St-Rémy) correspond to an intense period of creativity: he sought to express with colours and dramatic forms the "terrible human passions" which tormented him and caused him to suffer. He painted intensely, with genius, the light and forms of Provence: landscapes *(View of Arles with Irises, The Alyscamps, Starry Night, Crau Plain, Boats along the Beach...)* and portraits *(Portrait of an Old Provençal Peasant, L'Arlésienne, Madame Ginoux...)*. His quarrel with **Paul Gauguin**, who had joined him in October 1888, plunged him into despair and madness; he was cared for at St-Paul-de-Mausole *(see p 235)* near St-Rémy-de-Provence and continued painting *(Wheatfields, Cypresses, Olive Trees, Self-Portrait...)*. He returned to Paris in May 1890 and committed suicide two months later. Precursor of the Fauves and Expressionism, Van Gogh left an enormous legacy of work where his Provençal period is perhaps the most intense and fascinating.

Cézanne – Cézanne (1839-1904), unlike Van Gogh, was from Provence. Son of an Aix-en-Provence banker, he left his studies to take up painting *(see AIX-EN-PROVENCE)*. Introduced to the Parisian Impressionists by his friend, the writer, Émile Zola, he began as a Romantic studying Delacroix, whose theory of colours he adopted. Having assimilated the Impressionist techniques, he rapidly went beyond them as early as 1879 and began his constructive period; he experimented with large dabs of luminous colour and simple geometric forms: "Everything in nature is modelled after the sphere, the cone and the cylinder", he wrote. He painted still lifes and portraits where colour and form determined the painting's organisation.

After 1890, he hardly ever left his native Provence and devoted all his energy to capturing the Montagne Ste-Victoire on canvas, painting it some 60 times without ever being entirely satisfied with his work; his research continued until his death and opened the way to Cubism.

20C – Clearly, for Cézanne, it was impossible for a painting to convey the full brilliance and subtleties of light; only colour could presume to fulfil that role. These views gave rise to a movement that influenced many late 19C and early 20C painters. Provence was now attracting many artists who settled in L'Estaque, following in the footsteps of Cézanne. First **Paul Signac** (1863-1935), who applied his Pointillist technique to Provençal colour (instead of the fine brushwork used in the north of France, here he opted for square, oblong touches, more suitable for catching the vivid sunlight). The Fauves found inspiration in this radiant Provençal setting. Their works played with colours and lines ignoring perspective and chiaroscuro. Matisse, Dufy and Derain all spent time in Provence, together with native artists from the region like **Charles Camoin** (1879-1965), **Auguste Chabaud** (1882-1955), **Alfred Lombard** (1884-1973) and **L.-M. Verdilhan** (1875-1928). Around 1906-08, L'Estaque (Cézanne had painted views of it) became the privileged meeting-place of those artists who were later dubbed the Cubists. **Georges Braque** and **Pablo Picasso** worked together closely in Sorgues; the product of this joint venture was revolutionary pictorial compositions touching on abstraction.

After the Second World War, a new generation was experimenting with novel theories, such as Expressionism and Surrealism. **André Masson**, father of spontaneous drawing (a technique which enabled him to break from figurative conventions), settled in the Aix region until his death in 1987 and drew a series entitled *Provençal Landscapes*. Other prestigious names were also linked to Provence: **Max Ernst, Nicolas de Staël, Yves Brayer** and **Vasarely**, who at Gordes has opened a foundation destined to make known his research into optics and kinetics.

At present, the École d'Art de Lumigny in Marseille attracts and develops France's new talents.

*Travel with **Michelin Maps**, at a scale of 1:200 000.*
They are constantly revised.

Traditional rural architecture

The Provençal house in the country, whether a *mas*, a *bastide* or an *oustau*, features the following characteristics:

– a shallow sloping roof of Roman style; curved terracotta tiles, with a decorative frieze under the eaves, composed of a double or triple row of tiles embedded end-on in the wall and known as a **génoise**;

– stone walls, more or less smoothly rendered (pink or lavender), with no windows on the north side and those on the other three sides just large enough to let in light but keep out the summer heat;

– a north-south orientation, with sometimes a slight turn to the east to avoid the direct blast of the *mistral*, and a serried row of cypresses to serve as a windbreak to the north, whereas plane and lotus trees provide shade to the south;

– floors covered with red or brown terracotta tiles *(mallons)*;

– vaulting in dried stone or masonry which completely replaced floor boards.

The **Provençal mas** *(photograph below)* was a large low farmhouse rectangular in plan with a sprawling low roof covering the living quarters and annexes. The walls were made of stone taken from the fields or from the Plaine de la Crau, ashlar-stone surrounding the openings. It was divided into two parts by a corridor, one for the master and the other for the farmer *(bayle)*; this was repeated on the ground floor and on the upper storey.

Provençal *mas*

The kitchen was level with the courtyard, and was the centre of the house in spite of its small size; with little variation all Provençal *mas* kitchens were the same, with the obvious sink, hearth and wall oven, whereas the furnishings varied (tables, chairs, cupboards, shelves etc and receptacles for the making and preserving of bread; *panetière* – a type of wooden cage at times beautifully worked). On the upper floor were the tiled-floor bedrooms and attic. The outbuildings and rooms were used for various purposes according to the importance of the *mas* and the agricultural vocation of the region. The ground floor could have a vaulted cellar orientated to the north, stables, shed, storeroom, sheep's pen (at times separated from the *mas*), bread oven and cistern; above were the attics containing the cocoonery (silkworms), barn (above the sheep's pen) and dovecote.

The **mas of the Bas Vivarais** was slightly different from the Provençal *mas*; it had an attractive pattern of stonework and had an added storey. The ground floor covered by solid vaulting contained the stables for the smaller animals and storeroom for wine-making tools; in the cold-room harvested products as well as hams and sausages were kept.

A stone staircase which opened on to a **couradou**, a terrace, generally covered, led to the stone or terracotta-tiled kitchen; the cocoonery (silkworms) was often off the *couradou* and was until c 1850 an essential part of the Vivarais *mas* architectural

---

Provençal Bell Cages

Built to resist the mistral which would blow through the wrought iron instead of blowing and knocking down the stones, the Provençal bell cage crowned buildings: religious, civic or military. Either simple (bell shaped or spherical) or elaborate in shape (bulbous, cylindrical or pyramidal), these wrought-iron cages grace the Provençal sky with their delicate silhouettes.

conception. From the kitchen, off which were the sleeping quarters, a small wooden staircase led to the attic. In the wealthier *mas* it became a spiral staircase in a turret and was visible from the exterior; it led to the sleeping quarters.

Annexes were often added to the living quarters: bread oven, barn and in the chestnut region a chestnut dryer, **clède** (or *clédo*).

The **oustau**, was the typical Provençal farmhouse smaller in size compared to the *mas* but with the same layout. In the upper Comtat it was called a *grange* and was progressively enlarged to house the family, which formed a clan, and the workers; it constituted an intermediary type of building between the *mas* of the plain and the village house, small but compensating for the lack of surface area by adding on upper storeys.

The **bastide** was built of fine ashlar-stone and displayed regular façades with symmetrical openings. Most often its layout was square in plan with a hipped roof.

Unlike the *mas*, the *bastide* was not necessarily a farmhouse; thus its conception was more luxurious using decorative elements such as wrought iron balconies, exterior staircase, sculpture etc.

The **gardian's cabin** *(photograph opposite)*, the typical Camargue dwelling *(cabane)*, was a small building (10m x 5m/33ft x 16.5ft) with a rounded apse at one end. The cob walls were low; only the front façade, with its entrance door, was built in rubble to hold a long ridge beam supported

Cabin of a *gardian*

by another piece of wood sloped at a 45° angle and crossed by a piece of wood to form a cross. Thatched with marsh reeds, *sagnos*, the cabin consisted of two rooms divided by a wall of reeds; the dining room and bedroom.

Sights

AIGUES-MORTES★★

Population 4999

Michelin map 83 fold 8 or 245 fold 27 – Local map see La CAMARGUE – Facilities

Aigues-Mortes (from *Aquae Mortuae* meaning dead water), with its large towers and defensive curtain wall, stands in a melancholy landscape of pools, sea marshes and salt pans. This solitary fortified city is a glorious sight, especially during the long sunsets of the summer evenings.

HISTORICAL NOTES

St Louis' creation – In the early 13C the king of France, Louis IX (St Louis), possessed no Mediterranean seaport as such. As he was preparing to set out on a crusade to Palestine, Louis IX did not want to embark from a "foreign" seaport like Marseille for example (foreign, because Marseille was ruled by the counts of Provence and thus separate from central government); he was seeking a site on the coast where he could set up a port of embarkation and city which would serve to establish and reassert Capetian influence in the region.

In 1240 he obtained, from the monks of the Abbaye de Psalmody, a tract of virgin land frequented only by fishermen, on which he rapidly built the powerful Tour de Constance *(see below)*. In order to encourage people to settle on this rather desolate site, the king granted a charter in 1246 which offered many advantages such as tax exemption and other commercial privileges. Like the southern *bastides (see Michelin Green Guide Dordogne)*, the new town was built on a regular grid plan within a rectangle (550m x 300m/1804ft x 984ft) cut across by five straight streets which in turn were cut by five cross streets. Clusters of settlements developed in the vicinity of three religious establishments (Notre-Dame-des-Sablons, the Franciscan monastery and the Psalmody monks' residence), which offered protection from the local winds.

Setting off for the crusades – In 1248 a huge armada chartered from Venice and Genoa gathered at Aigues-Mortes, which at that time was linked to the sea by the channel of Grau Louis. An estimated 1500 ships, carrying 35000 men plus horses and equipment – the Seventh Crusade – set sail for Cyprus on 28 August. On the flag ship, St Louis' suite included a spacious room with large portholes, the queen's chamber, as well as a room for her attendants and a chapel. The ships' passengers were obliged to have a long chest which served as a trunk bed, and in the event of a death, as a coffin, which was thrown into the ocean. They were also told to bring a small barrel of pure water as well as miscellaneous provisions. The crusaders arrived in Cyprus 23 days later and met with some success before being defeated at al Mansurah; the king was captured in 1250. In 1270 a sick St Louis embarked with a fleet from Marseille which sailed to Tunis. It was there that he died of the plague, a disease he contracted while attending to his sick crusaders.

The salted Burgundians – In 1418, during the Hundred Years War, the Burgundians captured Aigues-Mortes by surprise. The Armagnacs laid siege to the town and were desperate to seize it. A handful of their partisans within the city walls succeeded, at the dead of night, in killing the garrison guarding one of the gates; the city gates were opened to the besieging army. The Burgundians were decimated; so numerous were the dead that the corpses awaiting burial were thrown into a tower, named ever since the Tour des Bourguignons. To prevent putrefaction, the dead bodies were covered with salt until the Armagnacs could bury them.

Decline – Aigues-Mortes stayed prosperous until the mid 14C. It had a population of 15000 and Jacques Cœur (Charles VII's master of the mint) even set up a counting house. However, the sea withdrew and the channels silted up in spite of dredging. Even the construction of a canal to the coast was unable to prevent the decline.

The town participated in the Wars of Religion and became a Protestant stronghold. In the 18C the founding of Sète dealt the port a final blow.

The town's activities now include wine growing, which extends over 75% of the municipality, and the extraction of salt.

★★FORTIFICATIONS *1hr 30min*

★★**General view** – To admire the site of Aigues-Mortes from the best angle before beginning the tour of the town itself, drive along the road towards Le Grau-du-Roi (D 979) until about 1500m/1mi before this town (turn around just before a small bridge). On the return journey there are superb views of the Aigues ramparts on the south side of the town.

Some modern buildings have unfortunately been set up in front of the age-old walls, which have remained unchanged since medieval times, creating a somewhat unusual contrast.

Porte de la Gardette – This, the town's northern gate, was used by travellers coming along the only road from the north through marshy country. Some 3km/2mi beyond, spanning the road, stands the barbican of the Tour Carbonnière *(see p 138)*, the first defensive structure encountered.

Go through Porte de la Gardette, turn right, cross Place Anatole-France and go to the ticket office at the foot of the tower.

Aerial view of Aigues-Mortes

★★**Tour de Constance** ⊘ – This tower is a massive circular keep 22m/72ft in diameter and 40m/13ft high (including the turret), with walls 6m/20ft thick.

Located northwest of the town, from which it was originally isolated, the tower was built between 1240 and 1249. The entrance fort and bridge, which connected the tower to the ramparts, date from the 16C. An elaborate defensive system protected the entrance; there remain the portcullis and the embrasures through which missiles were hurled onto assailants.

The lower room with fine pointed arches has kept its bread oven. The upper floors are approached by a spiral staircase: St Louis' oratory, a minute chapel built into the wall and the upper room, which served as quarters for well-known prisoners; a display case presents various documents covering a period of 500 years and concerning these famous detainees, many of whom were political opponents of the regime, Templars, rebel barons and Huguenots. Two Protestants held in the tower were **Abraham Mazel**, a leading Calvinist who escaped down knotted bedclothes with 16 co-religionists in 1705, and **Marie Durand**, whose indomitable courage finally secured her release together with 10 of her companions from the cell in which she had been incarcerated for 38 years (1730-68) – note her graffito: *Register* (the verb to resist in Vivarais dialect).

Climb to the summit of the watchtower (53 steps) crowned by a wrought iron cage. In the 13C-16C this protected a lantern, which served as a beacon. An immense **panorama**★★ extends over the town and its grid-patterned streets, the surrounding plain punctuated right to left by the Cévennes, the Grande-Motte "pyramids", Montagne de Sète, the Midi saltmarshes and the Camargue.

★★**Remparts** ⊘ – The ramparts were built after 1272 with stone quarried from Beaucaire and Les Baux. Four-sided, and of remarkable unity, the fortifications are a typical example of 13C military architecture. The walls, topped by a watchpath, are flanked by towers of different size and importance. The more massive towers defending the main gates contained two vaulted rooms with terraces.

Inside, a wide street ran between the curtain wall and the town's houses, allowing the garrison swift access to any point. Outside, the moat, now filled, was another element of defence. The curtain wall, pierced by two rows of arrow slits, included hoarding, traces of which are visible at the base of the crenellations.

The ramparts were punctuated by only two gates to the north whereas, to the south, five gates or posterns offered access to the town from its loading docks. The towers in order of approach are: Tour des Bourguignons *(see above)*; Porte de l'Organeau, an *organeau* being the great iron ring to which the ships were moored; Porte des Moulins (Mill Gate) where grain was ground for the garrison; Porte des Galions (Galleons Postern), in front of which moored the galleys; Porte de la Marine (Maritime Gate), a ceremonial entrance; Tour de la Poudrière (the powder magazine); Tour de Villeneuve; Tour de la Mèche (Wick Tower), where a light was kept constantly burning to ignite firearms; finally, Tour du Sel (Salt Tower).

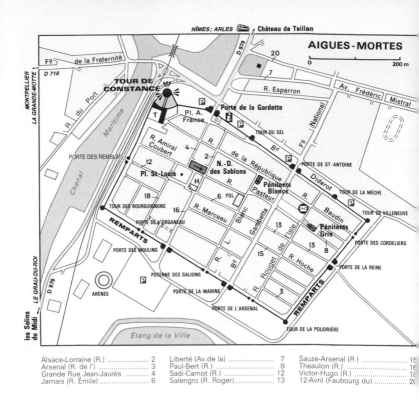

Alsace-Lorraine (R.)	2	Liberté (Av. de la)	7	Sauze-Arsenal (R.)	18
Arsenal (R. de l')	3	Paul-Bert (R.)	8	Theaulon (R.)	16
Grande Rue Jean-Jaurès	4	Sadi-Carnot (R.)	12	Victor-Hugo (R.)	18
Jamais (R. Émile)	6	Salengro (R. Roger)	13	12-Avril (Faubourg du)	20

ADDITIONAL SIGHTS

Place St-Louis – On this lovely shaded square, the heart of the town, stands the statue of St Louis (1849) by Pradier.

Notre-Dame-des-Sablons – This Gothic church was often remodelled. Inside, its timber-framed nave adds to the simplicity of the decor: 14C Christ, altar table from the former Abbaye de Psalmody and Chapelle St-Louis.

Chapelle des Pénitents Blancs ⊘ – A service is held in this Baroque chapel once a year on Palm Sunday. It houses a number of mementoes (liturgical vestments, penitents' attributes) belonging to this brotherhood established at Aigues-Mortes in 1622.

Chapelle des Pénitents Gris ⊘ – This 17C chapel contains an imposing altarpiece (1687) carved by Sabatier.

EXCURSIONS

Salins du Midi ⊘ **and Caves de Listel** ⊘ – *3km/2mi south of Aigues-Mortes on D 979 (access signposted by a small road on the left).*

Salins du Midi ⊘ – This tour enables visitors to follow the various stages of salt production (both past and present procedures).

Caves de Listel ⊘ – Enjoy this visit to the cellars of the Domaine de Jarras, which produces the local rosé wine (*vin gris du sable*). Among the Russian oak casks note a special 16C press (*pressoir à perroquet*), in operation until 1883; the name refers to the small cross-bars resembling parrots' perches which the press-hands had to climb in order to operate the wheel.

Château de Teillan ⊘ – *13km/8mi northeast on D 979, left on D 34 then right on D 265 in Marseillargues. Just after the bridge take an unsurfaced road on the right.*

Built on the site of a Gallo-Roman stronghold, this former priory of the Abbaye de Psalmody was sold in the 17C and subsequently enlarged.

A watchtower (15C) surmounts the main part of the building. The terrace view embraces the Cévennes, Languedoc plain, Aigues-Mortes and the Camargue.

On the ground floor, there is a large vaulted hall with 17C and 18C furnishings. The outbuildings, rebuilt in the 18C, house a vast dovecote, containing 1 500 nests: it has preserved its interior arrangement and especially its revolving ladder. In the park, landscaped with a fine variety of plants and trees, can be found a number of Roman altars and milliary columns; note as well the remarkable chain pump in small vaulted outbuildings.

AIX-EN-PROVENCE★★

Population 123 842
Michelin map 84 fold 3 or 114 folds 15and 16 or 245 fold 31 or 246 fold J
Local map see Montagne STE-VICTOIRE

This old capital of Provence has kept a great deal of the character imparted to it in the 17C and 18C. The sober elegance of its mansions, the graceful charm of its squares, the majesty of its avenues and the loveliness of its fountains are impressive. In 1995 this historical centre was officially listed as a cultural site belonging to UNESCO's World Heritage.

Around old Aix a new town has developed, which is both a spa and an industrial complex – it is the largest centre in France and Europe for processed almonds. Part of the production is used to make the cakes and confectionery of Aix, including the local speciality, a lozenge-shaped almond sweetmeat, *calisson*.

Aix-en-Provence is birthplace to the moralist Vauvenargues (1715-1747), the painters Jean-Baptiste Van Loo (1684-1745) and Paul Cézanne (1839-1906) and the musicians André Campra (1660-1744) and Darius Milhaud (1892-1974).

HISTORICAL NOTES

The origins of Aix – In 3C BC, western lower Provence was inhabited by the Celtic-Ligurian Confederation of the Salian Franks, whose capital, the *oppidum d'Entremont (see Additional Sights below)*, crowned a plateau to the north of Aix, near the Puyricard road. The excavations undertaken in this area have uncovered traces of a fairly advanced urban civilisation, as is testified by the layout of the buildings and the sophisticated statuary exhibited at the Musée Granet *(see Quartier Mazarin below)*.

These brutish peoples hindered the expansion of the merchants of Marseille, who appealed to the Roman army to break their neighbours' resistance. In 124 BC, the Consul Sextius seized and destroyed the town of Entremont; the inhabitants were condemned to slavery (900 of them were spared) and their king fled. To consolidate the conquered region, the following year, Sextius set up an entrenched camp called *Aquae Sextiae* (the waters of Sextius) near the thermal springs (which were already known); this camp site was the origin of Aix.

Marius the First (2C BC) – Twenty years later the Teutons, on their march to Italy, arrived at the gates of Aix, where they encountered Marius at the head of a Roman army. The Barbarians, from the Baltic Coast, travelled with their families and animals, living in carts covered with hide canopies; they were said to be tough fighters.

It was in the environs of Aix, in the Arc valley, perhaps at the foot of the height which has since been known as Montagne Ste-Victoire, that, according to tradition, the stroke which stopped the invaders and which developed into a great Roman victory (102 BC) was delivered. According to Plutarch, Marius, entrenched, at first refused battle and let the Teutons parade before his troops for six days. Then, dividing his army into three corps, he opposed the enemy, opening a converging attack with devastating results: 100 000 Teutons killed, 100 000 prisoners taken. The last survivors of the Barbarians used their grouped chariots as a barricade; the women were massed there: they had such a fierce nature that they themselves killed the fleeing warriors. Then they strangled their own children and committed suicide to avoid being captured. In memory of the Roman general, first conqueror of the Teutonic hordes, many Provençal families adopted the custom of calling one of their children Marius.

Good King René (1409-80) – At the end of the 12C, the counts of Provence held a refined and literate court at Aix. The development of the town continued during the 13C, and yet in the 14C its surface area diminished. In 1409 Louis II of Anjou founded the university but Aix's golden age occurred later, in the second half of the 15C under the reign of Good King René.

A city of 4 000 to 5 000 people, a bishopric and county seat, Aix exerted a strong influence over the neighbouring countryside, occupied by wealthy townspeople and enhanced by Italian craftsmen. Within the walls lived the burghers, aristocrats and farmers; this category included the shepherds responsible for ensuring a return on livestock investments made by a handful of powerful merchants.

Second son to Louis II and Yolanda of Aragon, René became duke of Anjou, count of Provence, titular king of Sicily and Naples at the death of his older brother, Louis III, in 1434. René spoke Latin, Greek, Italian, Hebrew and Catalan; he played and composed music, painted illuminations with meticulous detail, wrote verses, understood mathematics, astrology and geology. In short, René possessed one of the most universal minds of his time. He was an enlightened patron of the arts surrounded by artists, in particular Flemish painters. Dating from his rule are the famous triptychs of the *Annunciation* (said to be by the Master of King René) and the *Burning Bush* painted by Nicolas Froment (of Languedoc origin, he studied in Flanders and Burgundy). By the end of the 15C some 40 artists of quality lived and worked in Aix under contract to René and his nobles. They produced prestigious works of art and contributed to the decoration of mystery plays and popular festivals (such as Corpus Christi, which underwent a brilliant revival).

A man of arts and letters, René did not neglect his obligations as a ruler; he legislated, stimulated commerce and encouraged agriculture. He introduced the Muscat grape into Provence and on occasion cultivated his own vineyards. He was concerned with the health standards of his people and instituted a public service of doctors and surgeons, promulgated a sanitation law and ordained the cleaning up of the different quarters of the city. He was, however, criticised for his heavy taxation as well as his weak currency; the coins he minted, called *parpaillottes*, were of rather base alloy.

At the age of 12, René married Isabelle of Lorraine, who brought him as dowry the duchy of Lorraine. Their younger daughter, Margaret of Anjou (1429-82), married the English king, Henry VI (1421-71) in 1445. Two years after the death of Isabelle (at 44) to whom he had remained tenderly attached during the 33 years of their union, he married Jeanne of Laval, aged 21. This second marriage, which seemed a challenge to fortune, was as happy as the first. Queen Jeanne, who should not be confused with the 14C Queen Joan I of Sicily, was as popular as her elderly husband among the people of Provence.

King René

Having lost both his son and two grandsons, King René sadly observed Louis XI annex Anjou to the kingdom of France.

Thereafter, instead of dividing his time between Angers *(see Michelin Green Guide Châteaux of the Loire)* and Provence, René never set foot outside the land of sunshine and died at Aix in 1480, aged 72. His nephew Charles of Maine, who had been chosen as his heir, died one year later.

A capital – After the union of Provence to France in 1486, a governor appointed by the king lived in Aix. In 1501, the city thus became the seat of a newly-created parliament (a royal court of justice); it was also where the Estates General chose to meet to vote on taxes.

In contrast to René's golden age in the preceding century, the 16C appeared quite gloomy, marked by incessant wars (repeated hostilities instigated by Charles V's army from 1524 to 1543), and both religious and political disputes (Mérindol Affair, p 24, commitment to the Holy League etc).

And yet in the 17C, the city made great strides which radically changed its appearance. Totalling approximately 27 000 people, its population mingled several social classes, one of which became prominent – the men of law. The parliament, a strong advocate of local liberties in face of the centralist trend of the monarchy, was a breeding ground of well-to-do judges and lawyers (the majority of these appointments were procured by financial inducements). These men of law led stimulating and active lives and consequently proceeded to build magnificent townhouses *(hôtels)* worthy of their name and rank.

At the same time the urban landscape was transformed: new areas of the city sprang up and developed rapidly (notably the Quartier Mazarin, south of the city), the old ramparts were razed and replaced by an avenue for carriages, which later became Cours Mirabeau. During his stay in 1660, Louis XIV was able to admire these renovations in person.

In the 18C, the city continued its transformation, with its wide avenues, squares, fountains and new buildings (the old county palace was demolished and a new law court was built in its place). The conception of the *hôtel* had changed: more attention was paid to simplicity and comfort; decoration became more subdued while retaining a strong element of fantasy.

Parliament was living its last hours; the conflict of opinions and clan rivalry created a constant scene of dissent which nurtured gossip and epigrams. In 1763 it decreed that the Jesuits be banned from the land. This was its last great legal act: parliament was dissolved in 1771 (re-established in 1775), to no one's regret, as stated in the couplet:

> *Parliament, mistral and Durance*
> *Are the scourges of Provence.*

The marriage of Mirabeau (18C) – Aix played an important role in the life of Mirabeau. He married here in 1772 and was divorced here in 1783. It was here, too, that he was elected to the Estates General in 1789.

The fiery Mirabeau was only 23 when he married Mlle de Marignane. The bride was a rich heiress, and among her suitors featured the best of Provence nobility. Mirabeau, although a count, was ill-favoured: with a monstrous great head and a face disfigured by smallpox, he was penniless and moreover had a scandalous reputation. But he was aware of the mysterious attraction he held for women. He entered the competition and swept off with the prize. Cynically, he made a show of his good fortune and left his coach at the door of the Hôtel de Marignane *(see Quartier Mazarin below)* before spending the night there. After this scandal, a marriage had to take place. But Mirabeau's father-in-law showed resentment by cutting off the young couple's allowance. Mirabeau displayed no embarrassment at this blow and promptly ran up 200 000 *livres* of debts with Aix merchants. Their complaints were such that a warrant was issued sending him under house arrest to Château d'If and subsequently Fort Joux, where he published his *Essay on Despotism.*

No sooner was he freed than he seduced the lovely young Mme Monnier and fled to Holland with her. Mirabeau returned to Aix in 1783 to answer a summons for separation instituted by his wife. The eminent orator presented his own defence. His prodigious eloquence secured him victory at a first hearing but he lost on appeal, although it is said that his pleading aroused such enthusiasm and the violence of his language was such that the opposing counsel fainted!

1789 dawned and with it the elections to the Estates General. The count of Mirabeau, who had encountered only contempt and rebuff among his peers, decided to represent not nobility but the Third Estate. His election was a triumph and his historic role as an orator began; however it was also the beginning of Aix's downfall.

In Cézanne's Footsteps – Born in Aix in 1839, **Paul Cézanne** studied at the Collège Bourbon, where he became friends with Émile Zola. He chose "humanities", then enrolled at the Faculty of Law in accordance with the wishes of his father, while at the same time painting and writing poetry in the countryside around Jas de Bouffan. This residence in the midst of parkland, acquired by his father in 1859, was a propitious setting for the development of his artistic work. His reputation owed little to his frequent visits to Paris.

It was at Aix that fame crept up on him, thanks to the good name he had made for himself among painters such as Monet, Manet, Sisley and above all Pissarro. During his youthful period spent in their company, his palette brightened, and he then further enriched it as his contact with the natural setting around Aix deepened. Like these other artists, Cézanne wanted to capture the vibrancy of light, the shimmering quality of reflections and shadows, the depth of the sky and the softening effect of light on different hues.

However, it was not long before Cézanne shook off Impressionist techniques. Using large, luminous patches of colour and juxtaposing colours in new associations, he created shapes with exaggerated outlines and relief, but simple in form. Fauvism, Cubism and modern schools of paintings were to draw their inspiration from his work. Nostalgia for his native region frequently drew him back to Aix. He would go to the banks of the Arc and the Pistachio Tree Courtyard at Château Noir, the country house with its lone cypress overlooking the Bibemus plateau. The countryside around Aix became the dominant subject of his painting *(Montagne Ste-Victoire)*. Fleeing Paris in 1870, he settled at Estaque in his mother's house *(Sea at Estaque).*

A **Cézanne Tour** ⊘ has been set up by the Tourist Information Centre, which includes a visit to the parts of the town habitually frequented by the artist and the particular areas of the surrounding countryside from which he drew inspiration.

Decline and renaissance – In the 19C, as Marseille developed, Aix declined: the provincial capital became a *sous-préfecture*, the parliament a court of appeal, the university a faculty of law and letters. In 1914, Aix's population numbered no more than 30 000 people.

The modern city is undergoing a noticeable expansion, and its population figures are increasing. Industrial activity, spas and the tourist trade, as well as a flourishing cultural life (university, festival) have all assured the renewal and future growth of its influence. Several industrial zones have been set up since 1970, including that at Milles southwest of the city, in which a number of businesses in the tertiary, information technology and electronics sectors have established a base. There are plans for further technological centres, for example Duranne and Europole de l'Arbois (in collaboration with the municipalities of Vitrolles and Marseille). Furthermore, an extensive urban development project is underway on an old industrial site in the extension of the Cours Sextius and the Cours Mirabeau; this includes, among other things, the construction of a conference centre, a large entertainment hall, a new casino, hotels and a major transport road interchange. The Cité du Livre *(see Additional Sights below)*, which is part of this project, has already been completed.

Aix-en-Provence Festival – Aix has been transformed into one of the main musical centres in Europe, every summer since 1948 with the **International Festival of Opera and Music** *(see Calendar of events at the end of the guide)*. Based on great operas (in particular those by Mozart), the festival is also devoted in part to Baroque operas and 20C music. The courtyard of the old archiepiscopal palace is converted into a theatre for the event; concerts and recitals are given in the cathedral and the Hôtel de Maynier d'Oppède. Among the many talented artists who have contributed to the excellent reputation of the festival are conductors Hans Rosbaud and Carlo Maria Giulini and singers Renato Capecchi, Teresa Stich-Randall, Teresa Berganza, Gabriel Bacquier and Jean Piland. Working with the musicians, world-famous directors (Jorge Lavelli, Pier Luigi Pizzi) and set designers (Cassandre, Balthus, Derain, Masson) have also signed some unforgettable performances.

STAYING IN AIX

Cafés and Bars – Cours Mirabeau: several pavement cafés in the shade of the plane trees, including the famous Café des Deux Garçons with decor dating from the Consular period (1792). **Place de l'Hôtel-de-Ville:** La Cour de Rohan tea rooms, with an attractive interior extended by a patio. **Place Richelme/Rue Fauchier:** Le Brigand bar, the Scat-Club jazz club, 11 Rue de la Verrerie. **Cours Sextius:** Bistrot Aixois or Café des Deux Mondes bars, Le Petit Verdot wine bar, 7 Rue d'Entrecasteaux. Le Cintra with a selection of 140 different beers. **Boulevard Carnot:** Jungle Café holds evening rock concerts.

Markets and Shops – Every morning there is a market of fresh fruit and vegetables on Place Richelme. The main market (fresh fruit and vegetables, clothes, bric-à-brac) is held on Tuesday, Thursday and Saturday mornings on Place des Prêcheurs. On the same days there is a flower market on Place de l'Hôtel-de-Ville and a flea market on Place de Verdun.
The narrow pedestrian streets of the old town are dotted with many shops catering for all tastes: antiques, luxury goods (Rue Espariat and Rue Papassaudi) and confectionery (Calissons du Roi René, 7 Rue Papassaudi). The famous *santon* maker Paul Fouque, a native of Aix, has set up his workshop at no 65 Cours Gambetta. The old city also features a great many art galleries.

Entertainment – Classical plays and farce at the Théâtre du Jeu de Paume, Rue de l'Opéra; avant-garde performances at the Théâtre 108, 37 Boulevard Aristide-Briand and at the Théâtre Jacques Prévert, 24 Boulevard de la République; café-theatre at the Théâtre de la Fonderie, 14 Cours St-Louis and at La Fontaine-d'Argent, 5 Rue de la Fontaine d'Argent; avant-garde cinema at Studio Keaton, 45 Rue Manuel; International Festival of Opera and Music in the courtyard of the bishop's palace and St-Sauveur cathedral and cloisters.

★★OLD AIX *allow half a day*

The ring of boulevards and squares which encircles the old town marks the line of the ancient ramparts. North of Cours Mirabeau, the town's focal point, lies old Aix tucked between the cathedral and Place d'Albertas. The many pedestrian streets crisscrossing this area make it the perfect setting for an exploratory stroll. *Start from Place du Général-de-Gaulle, more commonly known as the "Rotonde".* In the centre of this square stands a monumental fountain erected in 1860.

Detail of the fountain on Place du Général-de-Gaulle (Rotonde)

LE VIEIL AIX

Agard (Passage)	**EY** 2	
Bagniers (R. des)	**DY** 4	
Clemenceau (R.)	**DY** 18	
Cordeliers (R. des)	**DY** 20	
Espariat (R.)	**DY** 26	
Fabrot (R.)	**DY** 28	
Méjanes (R.)	**DY** 51	
Mirabeau (Cours)	**DY**	
Paul-Bert (R.)	**DX** 66	
Thiers (R.)	**EY** 80	

Aude (R.)	**DY** 3	
Bedarrides (R.)	**DY** 5	
Bellegarde (Pl.)	**EX** 6	
Bon-Pasteur (R. du)	**DX** 9	
Cabassol (R. Joseph)	**DY** 14	
Curie (R. Pierre-et-Marie)	**DX** 22	
De-la-Roque (R. J.)	**DX** 25	
Foch (R. du Maréchal)	**DY** 30	
Gaulle (Pl. du Gén.-de-)	**DY** 36	
Martyrs-de-la-R.		
(Pl. des)	**DX** 47	
Matheron (R.)	**DY** 49	
Montigny (R. de)	**DY** 55	
Nazareth (R.)	**DY** 58	
Opéra (R. de l')	**EY** 62	
Pasteur (Av.)	**DX** 64	
Portalis (R.)	**EY** 69	
Prêcheurs (Pl. des)	**EY** 70	
Richelme (Pl.)	**DY** 72	
St-Honoré (Pl.)	**DY** 73	
Saporta (R. Gaston-de-)	**DX** 75	
Vauvenargues (R.)	**DY** 82	
Verdun (Pl. de)	**EY** 85	
Victor-Hugo (Av.)	**DY** 86	
4-Septembre (R. du)	**DY** 87	

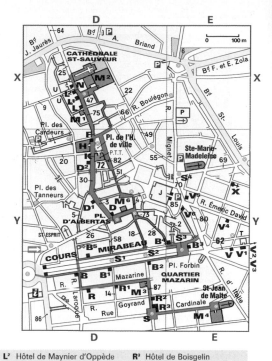

B	Hôtel d'Isoard de Vauvenargues	
B¹	Hôtel de Forbin	
B²	Hôtel Maurel de Pontevès	
B³	Hôtel du Poët	
B⁴	Ancienne chapellerie	
B⁵	Hôtel d'Arbaud-Jouques	
D	Hôtel d'Albertas	
D¹	Hôtel Peyronetti	
D²	Hôtel d'Arbaud	
F	Tour de l'Horloge	
H	Hôtel de Ville	
K	Ancienne halle aux Grains	
L	Hôtel de Châteaurenard	
L¹	Hôtel Boyer de Fonscolombe	
L²	Hôtel de Maynier d'Oppède	
M¹	Musée du Vieil Aix	
M²	Musée des Tapisseries	
M³	Musée bibliographique et archéologique Paul-Arbaud	
M⁴	Musée Granet (Beaux-Arts et Archéologie)	
M⁶	Hôtel Boyer d'Eguilles (Muséum d'Histoire naturelle)	
N	Cloître St-Sauveur	
R	Hôtel de Marignane	
R¹	Hôtel de Caumont	
R²	Hôtel de Villeneuve d'Ansouis	
R²	Hôtel de Boisgelin	
S	Fontaine des Quatre Dauphins	
S¹	Fontaine des 9 canons	
S²	Fontaine d'eau thermale	
S³	Fontaine du roi René	
S⁴	Fontaine des Prêcheurs	
V	Hôtel de Lestang-Parade	
V¹	Hôtel de Bonnecorse	
V²	Hôtel de Grimaldi	
V³	Maison natale de Cézanne	
V⁴	Hôtel de Panisse-Passis	
V⁵	Hôtel d'Agut	
V⁶	Hôtel de Roquesante	
X	Ancienne chapelle des Jésuites	

★★Cours Mirabeau (DY)

This wide avenue, shaded by fine plane trees, is the hub of Aix; a verdant tunnel of foliage protects against the hot Provençal sun.

Built in the 17C on the site of the medieval ramparts, the avenue originally had no shops or boutiques; yet now Aix's life revolves around this very area. Lining the north side of the street are cafés (namely the Café des Deux Garçons, once an important meeting-place for artists and writers) and shops; a number of bookshops show the intellectual and scholarly vocation of Aix. On the other side stand the aristocratic façades of the old *hôtels* with their finely-carved doorways and wrought iron balconies supported by caryatids or atlantes from the Puget School.

Walk up the avenue on the south side.

Hôtel d'Isoard de Vauvenargues (DY B) – *No 10.* This mansion was built around 1710 with a wrought iron balcony and fluted lintel. The Marchioness of Entrecasteaux, Angélique de Castellane, was murdered here by her husband, the president of Parliament.

Hôtel de Forbin (DY B¹) – *No 20.* Ornamenting the 1656 façade is a balcony with lovely wrought iron work. Received in this hôtel were the dukes of Berry and Burgundy, grandsons of Louis XIV, Pauline Borghese, the ill-favoured Fouché, the future duchess of Berry and the duke of Angoulême.

Fontaine des Neuf Canons (DY S¹) – Midway, at the junction with Rue Joseph-Cabassol, stands a fountain (1691).

Fontaine d'eau thermale (DY S²) – Further up Cours Mirabeau, at its junction with Rue Clémenceau, is a natural hot water fountain covered with moss, dating from 1734. Its waters, which gush out at 34°C/93°F, were appreciated by the Romans some 2 000 years ago on account of their healing properties.

Hôtel Maurel de Pontevès (DY B²) – *No 38.* Pierre Maurel, Diane de Pontevès' husband, is a telling example of social success: an ordinary shopkeeper, he received confirmation of his hereditary peerage at the end of his life.

In 1660 the *hôtel* was the residence of Anne-Marie Montpensier, known as La Grande Mademoiselle; it now houses an annexe of the Aix-en-Provence Court of Appeal.

Aix-en-Provence – Place d'Albertas

Fontaine du Roi René (**EY S³**) – This fountain marks the end of the avenue. Carved by David d'Angers (19C), the fountain portrays King René holding a bunch of muscat grapes, which he had introduced into Provence.

Hôtel du Poët (**EY B³**) – This dates from 1730 and closes off the view down Cours Mirabeau to the east. The three-tiered façade is decorated with mascarons, and some pretty ironwork adorns the first floor balcony.

Go round the statue of King René, leaving it to the right, and cross the avenue.

Number 55 (**EY B⁴**) is where the hat shop opened by Cézanne's father in 1825 used to be; the shop's original sign is still on display.

Rue Fabrot (first street on the left), a pedestrian and shopping street, leads to Place St-Honoré (on the corner of a house, a 19C statue of St Vincent).

Bear left on Rue Espariat.

Hôtel Boyer d'Éguilles (**DY M⁶**) – *No 6.* This townhouse was built in 1675, most probably by Pierre Puget. Entrance is through a large porte cochère which opens into the main courtyard. The Musée d'Histoire Naturelle is housed here.

Musée d'Histoire Naturelle ⊘ – This Natural History Museum houses interesting collections of mineralogy and paleontology. The paleontology section includes general exhibits as well as exhibits from Provence, notably a collection of dinosaur eggs from the fluvial and lacustrine basin of Aix-en-Provence, as well as a cabinet of "curios". In addition, the *hôtel* is embellished with fine 17C doors, paintings and interior panelling from the bedroom of Lucrèce de Forbin Solliès, the "Belle du Canet", as well as busts by Gassendi, Peiresc, Tournefort and Adanson.

★**Place d'Albertas** (**DY**) – This square was opened in 1745 and was embellished by a fountain in 1912. It is arranged very much in the style of Parisian squares and has lovely mansions all around it. Every summer concerts are held here.

Hôtel d'Albertas (**DY D**) – *No 10.* Built in 1707, this *hôtel* includes carvings by the sculptor Toro.

Bear right into Rue Aude.

Hôtel Peyronetti (**DY D¹**) – *No 13.* Italian Renaissance in style, it dates from 1620.

Follow Rue du Maréchal-Foch.

Hôtel d'Arbaud (**DY D²**) – *No 7.* Fine atlantes frame the doorway.

Place Richelme (**DY 72**) – The south façade of the old grain market runs alongside this square, which is broken into sections by two corner statues. Every morning there is a fresh fruit and vegetable market here.

★**Place de l'Hôtel-de-Ville** (**DY**) – The northwest corner of this attractive square is overlooked by the **clock tower** (**F**), which used to be the town's belfry (16C). A bell in a wrought iron cage also dates from the 16C; each season is represented by a different character.

Hôtel de Ville (**DY H**) – Built between 1655 and 1670, the town hall was designed by the Parisian architect Pierre Pavillon. Both the lovely wrought iron balcony and entrance gate are from the 17C. Around the splendid paved **courtyard**★, the buildings are divided by pilasters of the classical order *(see Introduction: Ancient Art)*; there is a niche with scrolls on the inside façade.

Ancienne Halle aux Grains (DY K) – This former grain market was built to the south of the square in the mid 18C. The central part of the building projects forward and is embellished with a pediment carved by Chastel, depicting the Rhône and the Durance. This sculptor spent his life in Aix, a fact evidenced by the many works of art left behind by him. The grain market now houses a post office and administrative centre.

Go along Rue Gaston-de-Saporta.

Musée du Vieil Aix ⊘ **(DX M¹)** – *No 17.* Located in the Hôtel d'Estienne de St-Jean (17C), attributed to Laurent Vallon, the museum presents local memorabilia. On display is a collection of marionettes evoking the talking cribs and the local Corpus Christi procession, porcelain from Moustiers, *santons...*
The lovely wrought iron banister and ceiling attributed to Daret's workshop in the boudoir are admirable.

Hôtel de Châteaurenard ⊘ **(DX L)** – *No 19.* It houses the Social Services Office. Just after the mansion was completed, Louis XIV was received here during his visit in 1660. The splendid stairwell decorated with views in *trompe-l'œil* by Daret draws the attention.

Hôtel Boyer de Fonscolombe (DX L¹) – *No 21.* This townhouse dates from the 17C and was modified in the 18C. It has a long façade. The small inner courtyard is decorated with a Louis XV fountain.

Hôtel de Maynier d'Oppède (DX L²) – *No 23.* The *hôtel* was built in 1490 and remodelled in the 18C. Its wrought iron balcony is supported by a basket-handle arch and pilasters crowned with acanthus leaves.

Rue Gaston-de-Saporta ends on Place des Martyrs-de-la-Résistance; at the end stands the Musée des Tapisseries, to the left the Cloître St-Sauveur.

★**Musée des Tapisseries** ⊘ **(DX M²)** – *Take the stairs on the left underneath the monumental porch.* Housed in the former bishop's palace, built in the 17C and enlarged in the 18C, the Tapestry Museum presents collections found here in the 19C. The vast courtyard is the scene of the annual International Festival. Note the 19 magnificent tapestries made in Beauvais in the 17C and 18C, six of which were based on designs by Monnoyer in the style of Bérain; nine famous panels illustrating the life of Don Quixote, after cartoons by Natoire, preserved at the Château de Compiègne; four panels of Russian Games produced after Leprince in 1769.

★**Cloître St-Sauveur** ⊘ **(DX N)** – These Romanesque cloisters are a delight; they are roofed with tiles instead of being vaulted like the cloisters at Arles and the Abbaye de Montmajour. Because the arcades are not buttressed, the cloisters seem delicate; the small paired columns and the capitals adorned with leaves or historiated add a great deal of elegance to the construction. For the most part the carvings on the capitals are badly damaged; however, on a fine corner pillar stands a remarkably carved St Peter.

A door northwest of the cloisters gives access to the adjoining cathedral.

★**Cathédrale St-Sauveur** ⊘ **(DX)** – St-Sauveur is a curious building where all styles from the 5C to the 17C may be seen side by side. The Romanesque nave *(access via the cloisters)* dates from the 12C. The furthest chapel to the west, transformed into a lapidary museum, contains a 5C white marble sarcophagus, said to be the tomb of St Mitre. The two bays which follow open onto the **baptistery**★ of the Merovingian period; it was built on the site of the old Roman forum in front of a basilica, in which six of the eight Roman columns surrounding it have been used to hold up the Renaissance dome. On the east side are traces of the cardo, the old Roman street, orientated north-south. In the vast Gothic central nave hang two 15C triptychs. Of the first triptych, depicting the Passion, only the central panel is from the 15C. The second series, the **Triptych of the Burning Bush**★★ *(currently undergoing restoration)*, is a masterpiece wrongly attributed to King René. In fact it was the work of his

Triptych of the Burning Bush by Nicolas Froment (detail) in the Cathédrale St-Sauveur

67

court painter Nicolas Froment. King René and Queen Jeanne are shown kneeling on either side of the Virgin. The Virgin holding the Infant Jesus is in the Burning Bush, from which the triptych takes its name. It was in a burning bush that God appeared to Moses; in the Middle Ages the Bush, which burned but was not consumed, symbolised the virginity of Mary. In the 13C chancel are 16C stalls and fine tapestries (1511) made for Canterbury Cathedral, illustrating the life of Christ and the Virgin Mary. Behind the altar, in the Chapel of St-Mitre, hangs a painting on wood (Martyrdom of St Mitre) attributed to the School of Nicolas Froment. The north aisle was refurbished in the 17C.

The great doorway is closed by **panels**★ *(masked by false doors)* in walnut; this masterpiece (1504) of sculpture in wood by Jean Guiramand of Toulon represents the four prophets of Israel and 12 pagan sibyls.

The cathedral's west front includes to the right a small door in the Romanesque Provençal style, in the middle a Flamboyant Gothic part (early 16C) and to the left a Gothic bell tower (14C-15C). Only two of the statues are old: the lovely *Virgin and Child* on the pier and *St Michael Slaying the Dragon* above the main window.

Return to Cours Mirabeau via Place de l'Hôtel-de-Ville and Rues Vauvenargues, Méjanes, des Bagniers and Clemenceau.

Hôtel d'Arbaud-Jouques (DY B⁵) – *No 19 Cours Mirabeau.* Built in 1700, this *hôtel* displays a finely decorated façade with a carved frieze underlining the first floor, a medallion on the impost underneath the balcony and carved oak doors.

Turn left into Rue Laroque and then left again into Rue Mazarine.

AIX-
EN-PROVENCE

Agard (Passage)	CY 2	Mirabeau (Cours)	BY	Minimes (Crs des)	AY 52
Bagniers (R. des)	BY 4	Paul-Bert (R.)	BX 66	Montigny (R. de)	BY 55
Clemenceau (R.)	BY 18	Thiers (R.)	CY 80	Napoléon
Cordeliers (R. des)	BY 20	Bon-Pasteur (R.)	BX 9	Bonaparte (Av.)	AY 57
Espariat (R.)	BY 26	Boulégon (R.)	BX 12	Nazareth (R.)	BY 58
Fabrot (R.)	BY 28	Brossolette (Av.)	AV 13	Opéra (R. de l')	CY 62
Méjanes (R.)	BY 51	Cardeurs (Pl. des)	BY 16	Pasteur (Av.)	BX 64
		De-la-Roque (R. J.)	BX 25	Prêcheurs (Pl. des)	CY 70
		Hôtel-de-Ville (Pl.)	BY 37	Richelme (Pl.)	BY 72
		Italie (R. d')	CY 42	Saporta (R. G.-de)	BX 75
		Lattre-de-T (Av.)	AY 46	Verdun (Pl. de)	CY 85
		Matheron (R.)	BY 49	4-Septembre (R.)	BZ 87

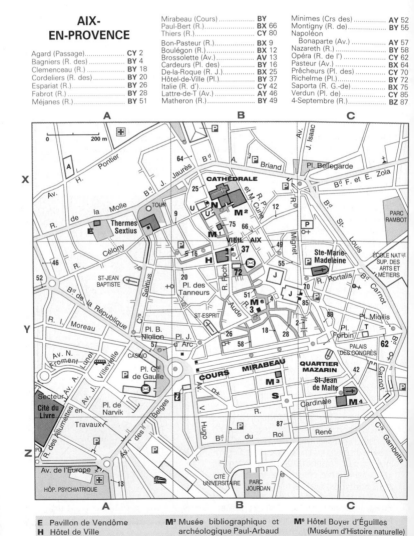

E Pavillon de Vendôme
H Hôtel de Ville
M¹ Musée du Vieil Aix
M² Musée des Tapisseries
M³ Musée bibliographique et archéologique Paul-Arbaud
M⁴ Musée Granet (Beaux-Arts et Archéologie)
M⁶ Hôtel Boyer d'Éguilles (Muséum d'Histoire naturelle)
N Cloître St-Sauveur
S Fontaine des Quatre-Dauphins

★QUARTIER MAZARIN (DEY) *1hr 30min*

This district of orderly design was built (1646-51) by the Archbishop Michel Mazarin, brother of the famous cardinal of the same name, south of the old town.

Hôtel de Marignane (DY R) – *No 12 Rue Mazarine.* Late 17C. This *hôtel* was the scene of Mirabeau's scandalous behaviour towards Mlle de Marignane *(see above).*

Hôtel de Caumont (DY R¹) – *No 3 Rue Joseph-Cabassol.* An elegant mansion built in 1720, it presents a lovely façade adorned with balconies and pediments. It houses the Darius Milhaud Music and Dance Conservatory.

Musée Bibliographique et Archéologique Paul-Arbaud ⊘ **(DY M³)** – *No 2a Rue du 4-Septembre.* This bibliographical and archeological museum is located in the home of a collector; it was built at the end of the 18C on the site of a Feuillant Convent. Exhibited are books concerning Provence, a lovely collection of porcelain from the region (Moustiers, Marseille, Allemagne-en-Provence), and some fine paintings and sculptures.

Hôtel de Villeneuve d'Ansouis (DY R²) – *No 9 Rue du 4-Septembre.* Early 18C. Birthplace of Folco de Baroncelli, marquis of Javon, the *hôtel* is decorated with balconies and carved mascarons.

Hôtel de Boisgelin (DY R³) – *No 11 Rue du 4-Septembre.* A vast building built in 1650, designed by Pierre Pouillon and decorated by J.-C. Rambot.

★**Fontaine des Quatre Dauphins (DY S)** – This delightful fountain (1667), depicting four dolphins, is by J.-C. Rambot.

Église St-Jean-de-Malte (EY) – The church, dating from the late 13C, was the chapel of the former priory of the Knights of Malta, and was Aix's first Gothic building. The 67m/220ft bell tower stands to the left of the austere façade. The **nave★** presents the elegant simplicity of the High Gothic with its wide arches, clerestory windows, without triforium, and its lovely quadripartite vaulting. In the past, the church housed the tombs of the counts of Provence; they were destroyed in 1794 and partially rebuilt (1828) in the north arm of the transept.

★**Musée Granet** ⊘ **(EY M⁴)** – *During restoration work, the main wing of the museum will remain open to the public.* The Fine Arts and Archeology Museum is located in the former priory of the Knights of Malta; it contains a fine collection of paintings acquired through various legacies including those of the Aix painter, **François-Marius Granet** (1775-1849).

Exhibited beside the Flemish, Italian and Avignon (panels of a triptych by Matteo Giovanetti) Primitives are the paintings characteristic of the great European Schools and covering the 16C-19C.

The French School is represented by a series of paintings by Géricault, Philippe de Champagne, Le Nain, Rigaud, Largillière, Van Loo, Greuze, David, Ingres... A number of works by the Provençal School are also on display, note in particular Granet, Constantin, Loubon, Parrocel, Emperaire.

The Italian (Guercino), Flemish (Rubens, Master of Flémalle) and Dutch (Rembrandt's studio) Schools are also worth admiring. Note the lovely allegory of Peace by the Fontainebleau School. *During restoration work these paintings are not on display, except for* Jupiter *and* Tétis *by Ingres and* Christ Appearing Before St Teresa *by Guercino.*

A gallery devoted entirely to Cézanne presents eight of his paintings: *Still Life* (1865), *Naked Woman Before a Mirror* (1872), *The Bathers* (1895), *Portrait of Madame Cézanne* (1885)...

Another room will contain works by contemporary artists such as Estève, Tal Coat, Masson (*Montagne Ste-Victoire Emerging from the Fog* – 1949, *Young Chimera* – 1956) Lasne, Aubrun, Léger, Sorgue, Forat, Vasselin...

The archeological galleries display objects found at the Entremont and Aquae Sextiae (Archbishopric, Grassi gardens and Pasteur parking) sites. The statues unearthed at Entremont typify a unique native Celtic-Ligurian art, although influenced by Greek and Etruscan forms. The statues usually represent effigies of people squatting, busts of warriors (a tunic-clad torso showing a breastplate and buckle), male and female heads and low and high reliefs. It has been suggested that the squatting warrior held on his knees several severed heads (note the hand placed on some of them).

ADDITIONAL SIGHTS

Rue de l'Opéra (EY 62) – In this street houses of interest include *no 18* **(V)** Hôtel de Lestang-Parade built around 1650 by Pavillon and Rambot and remodelled in 1830; *no 24* **(V¹)** Hôtel de Bonnecorse (or Arlatan-Lauris) dates from the 18C; *no 26* **(V²)** Hôtel de Grimaldi was constructed in 1680 after drawings by Puget; *no 28* **(V³)** was Cézanne's birthplace.

Doorway of
Hôtel de Panisse-Passis (18C)
Aix-en-Provence

Hôtel de Panisse-Passis (**EY V⁴**)– *No 16 Rue Émeric-David*. Built in 1739, the façade is enhanced by fine wrought iron and corbelled balconies with fantastically carved heads.

Ancienne Chapelle des Jésuites (**EY X**) – Dating from the 17C, the former Jesuit chapel has an imposing façade pierced with five niches.

Église Ste-Marie-Madeleine (**EY**) – The church's west front is modern although the church itself is 17C. At the end of the south aisle, in the fourth chapel, an 18C marble **Virgin★** by Chastel can be seen. In the chapels hang 17C and 18C paintings. A massive picture attributed to Rubens adorns the north transept.

The central panel of the 15C **Triptych of the Annunciation★** in the north aisle, near the altar to Our Gracious Lady, is all that remains of the triptych *(the other two panels are elsewhere)*. Ordered around 1443-45 by Pierre Corpici, this work is attributed to the Master of King René (a relative of the famous Van Eycks), an artist who used chiaroscuro effects subtly and inventively.

Fontaine des Prêcheurs (**EY S⁴**) – An 18C work by Chastel.

Hôtel d'Agut (**EY V⁵**) – *No 2 Place des Prêcheurs*. This townhouse was erected in 1676 by Pierre d'Agut, a parliament counsellor. Its doorway is decorated with atlantes.

Hôtel de Roquesante (**EY V⁶**) – *No 2 Rue Thiers*. Dating from the first half of the 17C, the *hôtel*'s façade displays friezes and pediments, which underline the different floors, and a monumental doorway.

Thermes Sextius (**AX**) – *Currently under renovation*. The 18C spa complex stands close to the site of the Roman baths. The 34°C/93°F waters are recommended for people with circulatory problems.

A tower from the 14C city walls has been preserved in the park.

Pavillon de Vendôme ⊘ (**AX E**) – *Entrance at no 13 Rue de la Molle or no 32 Rue Célony*. The mansion was built in 1667 from plans by A. Matisse and P. Pavillon, as Cardinal de Vendôme's country home.

The façade, unfortunately heightened in the 18C, offers a dignified decor with the three classical orders represented: Ionic, Doric and Corinthian. The central balcony, supported by atlantes, has kept its original wrought-iron work (*see illustration on p 43 under Art: Architectural Terms*). Displayed inside are Provençal furnishings and objets d'art. The staircase is adorned with 17C wrought iron work.

A slide show recounts the history of this house and its residents.

Cité du Livre ⊘ (**AZ**) – *Nos 8-10 Rue des Allumettes*. Built on the site of an old match-manufacturing plant, the **Cité du Livre** complex hosts a number of cultural departments: the **Bibliothèque Méjanes**, a library which houses beneath its glass and metal architecture an original collection of books bequeathed by the marquis of Méjanes, consul of Aix in the 18C; the **Fondation St-John-Perse** ⊘, a collection of manuscripts, publications and photographs retracing the life of this diplomat and poet, who was awarded the Nobel Prize in 1960 (exhibitions concerning his work and contemporary writing), the **Vidéothèque Internationale d'Art Lyrique et de Musique** ⊘ (International Video Library of Opera and Music) and the **Centre de Documentation Historique sur l'Algérie** (Historical Information Centre on Algeria). The complex, which, in addition, contains two exhibition galleries and a multi-purpose lecture theatre, is also home to training organizations in the literary field, and associations such as the Institut de l'Image.

★ Fondation Vasarely ⊘ (**AV M⁵**) – *2.5km/1.5mi west*. The foundation is to be found on a hill to the west of Aix, in an area known as the Jas de Bouffan, where Paul Cézanne used to live. This was the place selected by Victor Vasarely for the foundation that was to bear his name. This visual artist, who was born in Pécs in Hungary in 1908, made no secret of his great admiration for the Aix painter.

The vast building, consisting of 16 hexagonal structures, has sober façades, decorated with circles on alternately black and white squares. This rather surprisingly tones in well with the surrounding Aix countryside. The ground floor is devoted to 44 architectural groups by the master, linking mural panels made from a variety of materials (anodized aluminium, wood, glass, enamel, cardboard, ceramics) and enormous tapestries in geometric designs. Vasarely's research, as early as 1930 (also the year he left Hungary for Paris), led him to geometric abstractions via lines

Berger (Av. G.)	**BV**	7
Brossolette (Av.)	**AV**	13
Club Hippique (Av.)	**AV**	18
Dalmas (Av. J.)	**AV**	23
Ferrini (Av. F.)	**AV**	30
Fourane (Av. de la)	**AV**	32
Galice (Rte de)	**AV**	33
Isaac (Av. J.)	**BV**	41
Malacrida (Av. H.)	**BV**	48
Mauriat (Av. H.)	**BV**	50
Minimes (Crs des)	**AV**	52
Moulin (Av. J.)	**BV**	56
Pigonnet (Av du)	**AV**	62
Poilus (Bd des)	**BV**	67
Prados (Av. E.)	**AV**	68
Solari (Av. Ph.)	**AV**	76

M⁸ Fondation Vasarely
Z Atelier Paul-Cézanne

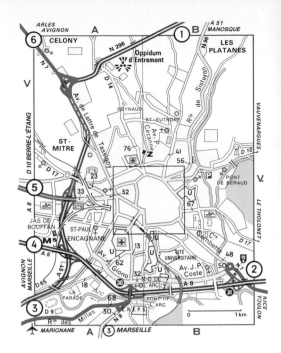

and graphics. In 1955, the artist evolved into a more kinetic field where by various optical means he was able to produce visual illusion with the use of movement (the viewer moves about the work and the subject depicted moves and changes). The first floor features a succession of visual displays (22 screens containing 798 mobile documents; by pressing a button the works inside the case move), through which the works of this master of Optical Art unfold, spanning half a century of research. Exhibitions featuring the work of modern and contemporary artists are organised every year, together with conferences and concerts.

Atelier Paul-Cézanne (Cézanne's Studio) ⊘ **(BV Z)** – *No 9 Avenue Paul-Cézanne*. When his mother died in 1897, Cézanne had a traditional Provençal-style house built about 500m (just over 500yd) from the cathedral, outside the ramparts. It was surrounded by a garden with colourful leafy plants growing up to the level of the first floor, where the artist worked.
The studio, called the "Lauves", in which he painted *The Bathers*, among other works, has been left as it was at his death in 1900 and houses a few items of his memorabilia.

Oppidum d'Entremont (**ABV**) – *2.5km/1.5mi then 10min return on foot. Leave Aix going north by D 14 uphill; after 2.5km/1.5ml, walk up the path on the right to the plateau.*

Fouilles (Excavations) ⊘ – Entremont *(see Origins of Aix above)* in the 2C BC already looked like the fortified town it was (surface area 3.5ha/9 acres). It was naturally defended by steep slopes on one side and to the north by ramparts with strong curtain walls reinforced by large round towers set at regular intervals. Inside these walls a series of fortifications served to define a first town known as the "upper town" showing a remarkably even texture. The former, an elevated area, was built to a regular grid pattern with a street network and sewage and drainage systems. The small dwellings with walls of dried stone and unbaked brick, were built against the ramparts or grouped together to a pre-established plan. Between two towers, part of the old ramparts, stood a portico building; probably a sanctuary where enemy skulls were displayed. The lower town seems to have been the district of artisans and tradesmen (vestiges of ovens and oil presses have been found).
The excavations have uncovered a great many of objects and works of art, proving that the *oppidum* possessed quite a high level of civilization and explaining how the town fell (stone balls, buried hoards) under the Romans. Entremont statuary is of capital interest for the history of art and may be seen at the Musée Granet *(see above)*, whose visit is a fitting complement to the tour of the site.
The low relief carvings and statues on display represent scenes of people making offerings, warriors on horseback or seated cross-legged, full-length figures or women with long veils.

Viewing Table *(Table d'orientation)* – From the plateau there is a wide view of the Aix basin, Montagne Ste-Victoire, Ste-Baume massif and the Étoile chain.

EXCURSIONS

Éguilles – *10km/6mi west – about 45min. Leave Aix-en-Provence by ⑥ on the map, N 7, towards Salon-de-Provence. After 2.5km/1.5mi turn left on to D 543 for the village of Éguilles.*

The village, which has a wonderful view of the Arc valley, is situated on the old Aurelian Way, the present D 17. The town hall, an old castle bought by the Boyer d'Éguilles family in the 17C, has a beautiful façade interspersed with mullioned windows on four levels. From the esplanade, there is a magnificent **view** of the Étoile chain and Les Milles. Stroll through the village to explore the old wash houses.

Jardins d'Albertas ⊘ – *11km/7mi – about 1hr. Leave Aix-en-Provence by ③ on the map, N 8. After 8km/5mi take D 8 towards Marseille. Turn left for the Jardins d'Albertas car park.*

These gardens were laid out in 1751 by the Marquis Jean-Baptiste d'Albertas. The section east of D 8, open to visitors, blends together different styles: Italian (terraces, antique statues, artifical cave where visitors can enjoy the cool, Triton fountain); French (flower beds, canals, perspective); Provençal (rows of plane trees). From the viewpoint, to the right, there is a pretty view of the site.

VALLÉE DE L'ARC

Round tour of 43km/26.5mi – about 2hr

Leave Aix-en-Provence southwest of the conurbation plan on D 9.

The road offers lovely views of the Étoile chain, in particular the characteristic peak of Pilon du Roi and, further to the right, Grande Étoile.

Château de la Pioline ⊘ – Set in the Milles industrial zone, this manorhouse dates partly from the 16C; it also received Charles V in 1536. Enlarged and embellished in the 17C and 18C, it served as the Aix parliamentarians' summer residence. A main building flanked by two wings opens on to a great courtyard decorated with a pool. Inside, a vestibule precedes a succession of richly-decorated and furnished rooms, especially the Louis XVI Room with its gilt work and columns. Across the drawing room, a vast hall of mirrors evokes its opulent past. In the back is a lovely park with a terrace.

Réservoir du Réaltor – This pleasant stretch of water (58ha/143 acres) is surrounded by luxuriant foliage. This is the settling tank for the water which has come from the Grand Torrent (brought from the River Arc) and the Durance (brought via the Canal de Marseille).
After the reservoir, bear right on D 65ᴰ on its western shore skirting radio station buildings and crossing the Canal de Marseille.
After La Mérindolle turn left.

★**Aqueduc de Roquefavour** – This fine aqueduct was constructed to transport the Canal de Marseille across the Arc valley at a point 12km/7.5mi west of Aix-en-Provence. Built from 1842 to 1847 under the direction of Montricher, the aqueduct is a spectacular example of a 19C civil engineering project. Made up of three stages – three tiers of arches – supporting the water channel, it is 375m/1230ft long and 83m/272ft high (Pont du Gard: 275m/902ft high and 49m/161ft high). Its lower level has 12 arches, the middle level 15 arches, and the top level with its 53 smaller arches carries the canal which transports the waters of the Durance to Marseille.

Follow D 65 towards Salon-de-Provence and 300m/328yd further on bear right on the D 64 uphill.

A lovely view opens out to the right of the aqueduct before entering a wooded area of pine and oak trees.

Top level of Roquefavour Aqueduct (Sommet) – *After 2.1km/1mi bear right on a path towards Petit Rigouès and right again to the keeper's house located on the aqueduct's topmost level.*

Drive past the ruins of Marius' Roman camp *(excavations under way)*. From the plateau's edge there is a lovely view of the Aix basin, Montagne Ste-Victoire and the Étoile chain.
From the car park walk to the aqueduct's top level where the canal runs.
Return to D 64 and turn right.

Ventabren – This tiny village is dominated by Queen Jeanne's castle, now in ruins. Take Rue du Cimetière to the foot of the castle ruins to enjoy the splendid **view**★ of the Berre lagoon, Martigues, the Caronte gap and the Vitrolles chain.
Take D 64ᴬ then right on D 10 to Aix-en-Provence.

ALLAUCH

Population 16 092

Michelin map 84 fold 13 or 114 fold 29 or 245 folds 44 and 45 or 246 fold L

A large suburb of Marseille, Allauch (pronounced Allau) rises in tiers up the foothills of the Étoile chain *(see p 157)*. From Allauch you may follow a series of footpaths leading up to the Garlaban hills, steeped in the memory of the great Provençal writer **Marcel Pagnol** *(see AUBAGNE)*.

Esplanade des Moulins – Appropriately named (*moulin* means mill), this esplanade, with its five windmills (one of which has been restored), offers a good **view★** of Marseille.

Musée du Vieil Allauch ⊘ – *Near the church*. This museum contains objects and documents pertaining to local history.

Chapelle Notre-Dame-du-Château – *30min return on foot*. This chapel is a relic of an 11C and 12C castle of which only some ramparts remain. The terrace affords a fine view of Marseille.

EXCURSION

Musée des Arts et Traditions Populaires du Terroir Marseillais – *7km/4mi northwest on D 44ᶠ. See MARSEILLE: Excursions.*

Les ALPILLES★★

Michelin map 83 fold 10 or 84 fold 1 or 245 fold 29

The limestone chain of the Alpilles, a geological extension of the Luberon range, rises in the heart of Provence between Avignon and Arles. From afar these jagged crests, rising 300-400m/984-1 312ft, appear to be really lofty mountains.
The arid, white peaks of these summits standing out against the blue sky remind us of some Greek landscapes. At the mouth of the dry valleys, which cross the mountain chain, olive and almond trees spread their foliage over the lower slopes. Occasionally a dark line of cypress trees breaks the landscape. In the mountains the gently sloping lower areas are planted with kermes oaks and pines, but often the rock is bare and peppered with a few scraggy bushes covered by maquis or poor pasture suitable only for sheep.

★★LES BAUX ALPILLES

① Round Tour starting from St-Rémy-de-Provence

40km/25mi – allow 4hr

★**St-Rémy-de-Provence** – *See ST-RÉMY-DE-PROVENCE.*

Leave St-Rémy-de-Provence going southwest on Chemin de la Combette; turn right into Vieux Chemin d'Arles.

J.F. Devaud/TOP

Alpilles landscape

Tour du Cardinal – This tower is, in fact, a 16C country house with an attractive Renaissance balcony and ornamental windows and friezes.

Turn left onto D 27.

The road winds between cypress-enclosed fields before rising through a rock landscape in the heart of the Alpilles. Towards the end of the climb, the view extends to the left and behind over the Comtat Venaissin bounded by Mont Ventoux.

Just before reaching the top of the hill turn left on a surfaced corniche road; after 1km/0.5mi, park the car.

★★★**Les Baux Viewing Table** (Table d'orientation) – *See Les BAUX-DE-PROVENCE.*

Return to D 27; bear left on it.

The road winds through Val d'Enfer *(See Les BAUX-DE-PROVENCE).*

★★★**Les Baux-de-Provence** – *See Les BAUX-DE-PROVENCE.*

Continue along D 27 through Paradou to D 78ᴱ.

The road winds through olive groves.

Aqueducs de Barbegal – *15min return on foot.* Note the impressive ruins *(on the left in particular)* of a pair of Gallo-Roman aqueducts.

The aqueduct which branches off to the west supplied Arles with water from Eygalières some 50km/31mi away. The other one cut through the rock and served a 4C hydraulic flour mill on the slope's south side, the ruins of which provide a rare example of Gallo-Roman mechanical engineering: a triangular-shaped cistern fed two channels which then activated eight successive mills with their water wheels and millstones. The mill occupied $1\,200m^2/12\,900$sq ft and could grind 300kg/661lb of flour an hour!

Continue along D 78ᴱ then D 82; turn right on D 33.

Moulin de Daudet (Daudet's Mill) – *See MOULIN DE DAUDET.*

A lovely avenue of pines leads to Fontvieille.

Fontvieille – Facilities. For centuries, the main industry in this small town where Alphonse Daudet is remembered for his *Lettres de mon Moulin* has been the quarrying of Arles limestone. In the 18C parish church, the old ceremony of the shepherds' bringing the offering of the lamb is celebrated on Christmas Eve.

Continue along D 33.

The road runs through a countryside of olive groves, pinewoods and fields of early vegetables cut by long rows of poplars.

★**Chapelle St-Gabriel** ⊘ – Located originally on the site of this chapel was a Gallo-Roman town, Ernaginum. Surrounded by marshland, it was a port for rafts (called *utriculaires*) as well as being the junction of commercial and military roads. The small, late-12C chapel has a west doorway framed within a rounded arch by antique-style columns and a pediment. The pediment and tympanum are richly, if

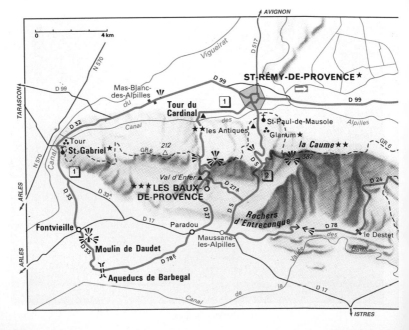

somewhat naïvely, carved with the Annunciation, the Visitation, Adam and Eve, and Daniel in the lions' den. The symbols of the four Evangelists frame the richly-decorated oculus.

The interior, by contrast, is plain; it comprises a single aisle and three bays covered by broken-barrel vaulting and an oven-vaulted apse, resulting in a great unity of style. In the nave, to the right, note the cippus dating from Augustus' time.

Further on are the ruins of a 13C square tower, which belonged to the fortifications of a village long gone.

Take D 32 and D 99 to return to St-Rémy-de-Provence.

After Mas-Blanc-des-Alpilles there is a fine view of Mont Ventoux on the left.

★★EYGALIÈRES ALPILLES

② Round Tour from St-Rémy-de-Provence
73km/45mi – allow about 5hr

★**St-Rémy-de-Provence** – *See ST-RÉMY-DE-PROVENCE.*
Leave St-Rémy-de-Provence by ③ on the map, D 5.

The road passes the old monastery of St-Paul-de-Mausole and the Roman Monuments of Glanum, before continuing deep into the mountains where one can observe the regular lines of the rock strata. From a bend, a wide view opens out onto the Montagnette hills and Durance valley.

After 4 km/2.5mi leave the car by the side of D 5 and take the left footpath leading up to the Caume.

★★**Panorama de la Caume** ⊙ – Alt 387m/1 270ft. A television relay mast is located at the top. Walk to the southern edge of the plateau to enjoy a vast panorama of the surrounding countryside, including the Alpilles in the foreground and the Crau and Camargue plains; from the northern edge, the view encompasses the Rhône plain, the Guidon du Bouquet with its characteristic beak-like outline, Mont Ventoux and the Durance valley.

Visitors should bear in mind that the Panorama de la Caume is a preserved area for Bonelli's eagle, the Egyptian vulture and the eagle owl. Therefore it is not permitted to stray from the signposted trails and some paths may be temporarily closed owing to the presence of protected species.

Return to D 5 and turn left.

The road traverses a pinewood and several small gorges.

Rochers d'Entreconque – Lying to the left of the road, these rocks are, in fact, former bauxite quarries, as can be seen from their characteristic dark red colour. The road then runs through olive, apricot, almond and cherry orchard country.

Turn right into D 27ᴬ for Les Baux.

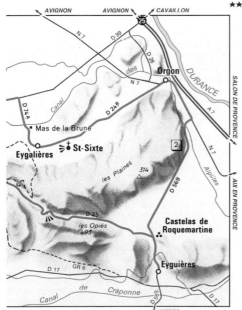

★★★**Baux-de-Provence** – *See Les BAUX-DE-PROVENCE.*

Turn round and by way of D 5 make for Maussane-les-Alpilles (facilities). At the town entrance bear left and immediately left again onto D 78.

The road runs through olive groves at the foot of the Alpilles before rising gently to a low pass from where there is a view of Les Opiès, a hillock crowned by a tower. At Le Destet, turn left onto D 24 which, as it rises, reveals the crest of La Caume. After 5km/ 3mi bear right onto D 25 which circles the Plaines massif.

Castelas de Roquemartine – This castle comprises ruins of various ages perched on the hillside. At the end of the 14C the fortress was, with Les Baux, the hide-out of Raymond de Turenne's band of thieves *(see Les BAUX-DE-PROVENCE).*

Eyguières – *2km/1mi from Castelas de Roquemartine on D 569.* At the edge of the Salon plain, this delightful small Provençal town is enhanced by its many splashing fountains.
Turn left onto D 569, a picturesque stretch of road which runs through olive groves, to N 7 which leads to Orgon.

Orgon – *See ORGON.*
D 24⁸ skirts the north flank of the Plaines massif.

Chapelle St-Sixte – This 12C chapel, crowning a stony hill, stands on the site of a pagan temple erected to the spirit of the local spring *(see below)*. The arch separating the nave from the fine oven-vaulted apse rests on boar's head consoles. A small 16C hermitage stands next to the chapel. There is a lovely view of Eygalières and the Alpilles.

Eygalières – Facilities. The small town of narrow winding streets rises in tiers up the hill to an ancient castle keep. Once a Neolithic settlement, it was later occupied by a Roman legion sent to divert the local spring waters to Arles. Park the car in the square and walk through Porte de l'Auro up to the clock tower: 12C church surmounted by a 19C bell tower. From the top of the village a pleasant view opens out onto La Caume mountains, the Alpilles and Durance valley.
Take D 74ᴬ, which near Mas-de-la-Brune (16C) crosses the Canal des Alpilles.
Bear left on D 99 for St-Rémy-de-Provence.

ANSOUIS

Population 892
Michelin map 84 fold 3 or 114 fold 2 or 245 fold 31
Local map see Montagne du LUBERON

Located between the River Durance and the Grand Luberon foothills, the town was built on the southern slope of a rocky spur crowned by a castle.

★Château ⊘ – At the beginning of the 12C the barons of Ansouis built a medieval castle on the foundations of an old fortress. The castle lost its defensive character, particularly in its southern section, during the 17C and 18C. The castle is of great interest as it has been in the Sabran family for centuries and each generation has left its imprint. Stone steps and a ramp lead to a spacious chestnut walk, dominated by a monumental and harmonious façade in gold-coloured stone. The main door, lavishly decorated with pyramidal bosses and over which hangs the Sabran crest, is worthy of particular note. The coffer-vaulted grand staircase, dating from the Henri IV period, leads to the guardroom embellished with 17C-19C arms and armour. This room is connected, via a narrow corridor, to the well room, adjacent to the former guardroom, now a chapel. Cross the dining room, in which hang 17C Flemish tapestries depicting the story of Aeneas and Dido, the Charles X Room, and the St Eleazarius' and St Dauphine de Sabran's rooms, which contain memorabilia of the two saints. The Provençal kitchen, the prison and the chapel nicely round off the visit. The terrace affords a beautiful view of the Durance gap and Trévaresse range.
The gardens are a delightful surprise: hanging gardens planted with boxwood and dark-leafed trees fill every corner; and the "Garden of Eden", cultivated during the Renaissance on the castle's former cemetery.

Church – This former courtroom of the counts of Forcalquier and the counts of Sabran was constructed in the 13C on the original fortifications of the castle, as can be seen by its south wall pierced by thin arrow slits, contrasting with the round-arched doorway that dominates the nine semicircular steps.

Musée Extraordinaire ⊘ – 15C vaulted cellars house this small museum devoted to underwater life. Works of art by G. Mazoyer (first floor: artist's workshop) are displayed. An underwater cave has been recreated. Provençal furniture is also exhibited.

APT

Population 11 506
Michelin map 81 fold 14 or 114 fold 2 or 245 fold 31
Local maps overleaf and see Montagne du LUBERON – Facilities

Apt, a small bustling town in the Calavon valley, is known for its crystallized fruit and preserves *(it is possible to attend a guided tour of a* **crystallized fruit factory** ⊘ *in the Solignan district via road ③ on the map)*, lavender essence and truffles; it is the main centre for ochre mining *(see Introduction: Local economy)* in France. The town is also considered a good excursion centre for trips to the Luberon range. A colourful, animated market is held on Saturday mornings. The Roman colony of Julia Apt was a prosperous ancient city and a bishopric in the 3C.
Its cathedral is the first sanctuary dedicated to St Anne in France and holds the saint's reliquaries brought back from the Orient in the 3C and, according to legend, miraculously found by Charlemagne during a trip in 776. It is the scene of a traditional pilgrimage which takes place on the last Sunday in July.

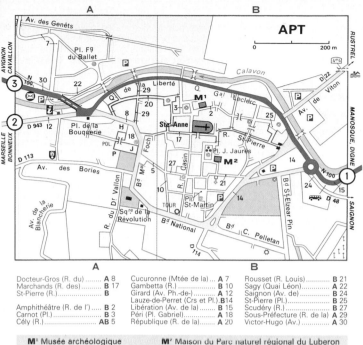

Docteur-Gros (R. du) .... **A** 8	Cucuronne (Mtée de la) ... **A** 7	Rousset (R. Louis) .... **B** 21
Marchands (R. des) .... **B** 17	Gambetta (R.) .... **B** 10	Sagy (Quai Léon) .... **A** 22
St-Pierre (R.) .... **B**	Girard (Av. Ph.-de-) .... **A** 12	Saignon (Av. de) .... **B** 24
	Lauze-de-Perret (Crs et Pl.).**B**14	St-Pierre (Pl.) .... **B** 25
Amphithéâtre (R. de l') .... **B** 2	Libération (Av. de la) .... **B** 15	Scudéry (R.) .... **B** 27
Carnot (Pl.) .... **B** 3	Péri (Pl. Gabriel) .... **A** 18	Sous-Préfecture (R. de la) **A** 29
Cély (R.) .... **AB** 5	République (R. de la) .... **A** 20	Victor-Hugo (Av.) .... **A** 30

M¹ Musée archéologique   **M²** Maison du Parc naturel régional du Luberon

SIGHTS

Ancienne Cathédrale Sainte-Anne ⊘ (**B**) – The present building was constructed in the 11C or 12C and was remodelled many times. The south aisle is Romanesque, the north aisle is 14C Gothic and the nave was rebuilt in the 17C. Covering the transept crossing is a dome on squinches similar to the one at Notre-Dame-des-Doms Cathedral in Avignon. At the end of the apse, a 14C stained glass window, given by Pope Urban V, depicts St Anne holding the Virgin and Child in her arms.

Chapelle Sainte-Anne – The first chapel off the north aisle was built in 1660, when Anne of Austria came on pilgrimage. The furnishings include: above the wooden gilt altarpiece, a large reliquary bust of St Anne; on the left, under the dome, a marble group of St Anne and the Virgin by the Italian Bonzoni; and across the way the family tomb of the dukes of Sabran.

Treasury (Trésor) ⊘ – In the sacristy of St Anne's chapel are displayed 11C and 12C liturgical manuscripts, shrines decorated with 12C and 13C Limoges enamels, 14C Florentine gilded wood caskets and St Anne's shroud, and an 11C caliph's coat brought back from the First Crusade (1096-99). In the second chapel off the north aisle, above the altar which rests on a 4C sarcophagus, hangs a painting from the Byzantine School portraying St John the Baptist against a gold background. In the Corpus Domini Chapel, south of the chancel, stands the cathedral's former high altar, with its fine Antique-style decoration.

Crypt – Composed of two floors: the upper crypt is in the Romanesque style and contains an altar supported by a Romanesque capital and 13C sarcophagi; the lower crypt is Pre-Romanesque. At the back of the two crypts stand two tombstones.

Musée archéologique ⊘ (**B M¹**) – An 18C *hôtel* houses this archeological museum. On the ground floor are displays covering prehistory (flint, stone implements), proto-history (arms and tools, large jar, earthenware) and Gallo-Roman carvings (funerary inscriptions, capitals, various fragments). The first floor includes displays of the Gallo-Roman period (mosaics, pottery, glassware, funerary furnishings, jewellery, coins) and items (tools, votive objects, especially oil lamps dating from 2C BC) excavated from the *oppidum* of Chastellard-de-Lardiers, near Banon in the Alpes-de-Haute-Provence. The second floor covers 17C-19C ceramics (Apt, Moustiers, Allemagne-en-Provence, Castellet, some originally from the former hospice). Works by Léon Sagy (1863-1939), the ceramist from Apt, complete the collection. A number of 17C-19C ex-votos are also exhibited.

Maison du Parc Naturel Régional du Luberon ⊘ (**B M²**) – Visitors to the centre learn about the natural environment and rural life in the Luberon Nature Park through various exhibitions, documents, local products and walking tours. The caves house a **Museum of Paleontology** explaining the evolution of living specimens and geological phenomena. The displays include illuminated panels, an aquarium, animated tableaux of prehistoric landscapes and sculptures of primitive animals. The ground floor exhibition is devoted to the region's geological heritage, the different types of natural environment, habitat and perched villages...which are the main distinguishing features of the Luberon area.

★★OCHRE TOUR *49km-30mi – about 3hr 30min*

Leave Apt by ③, on the map,N 100.

Pont Julien – Spanning the River Coulon (or Calavon) in the 3C BC, this 3-arched bridge was on the ancient Domitian Way linking Italy to Spain. It was mounted on two piers pierced to allow flood-waters to pass swiftly through them.

D 108 and D 149 on the right lead to Roussillon.

★**Roussillon** – *See ROUSSILLON.*

D 227 offers fine views to the right onto the ochre cliffs and Luberon range, and to the left onto the Vaucluse plateau.

Cross D 4, bear right on D 2 and right again on D 101.

In a field to the right of the road some twenty settling tanks used for the processing of ochre, extracted from neighbouring quarries, can be seen.

On entering Gargas bear left on D 83 and left again on D 943.

St-Saturnin-lès-Apt – The village, perched on the first foothills of the Vaucluse plateau, is overlooked by old castle ruins and a Romanesque chapel. Take the alley left of the village church and climb to the chapel for a view of the Apt countryside and Luberon range. The upper Porte Ayguier (15C gate) still preserves some of its defences.

Return south along D 943 and turn left along D 179 towards Rustrel.

On the way, the flowering cherry orchards on the plain are a glorious sight in season.

★★**Colorado de Rustrel** – *Steep and slippery paths.* The gigantic ochre quarry can be explored on several walks; two are outlined below.

– 1hr return: at D 179, 22 and 30 crossroads, turn left onto D 22; after 2.5km/1.5mi bear right, downhill. Leave the car in the small car park running along the bank of the Dôa, or, a little further on, in the car park located before the hamlet of Bouvène. Cross the river, level with the first car park, and follow the yellow signposts.

After the departure ramp and a curve to the right, the path cuts through a pinewood to come out at some natural viewpoints overlooking the old quarry workings, an ochre-coloured landscape of cliff faces, clay-capped earth pillars ("Cheminées de Fées" – fairies' chimneys), often with jagged sawtooth edges. Return along the way you came. D 22 takes you back to Apt.

– 2hr return: from D 22, take the road towards Colorado camp site, leave the car there and follow the yellow indicators.

Leave the old workings of the Rustrel iron foundry to the right. The steep slope down into the little valley of the Lèbre contains vermilion rocks. Climb back up the valley to the foot of the old phosphate quarries, known as "Terres vertes" (green earth). The countryside of pine forest and heathland leads to the rose-coloured cliffs of the Istrane quarry. Return to the car via the footpath from Rustrel to Caseneuve and a small country road.

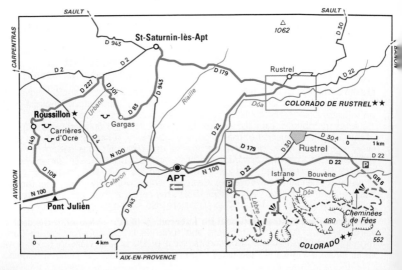

Gorges de l'ARDÈCHE★★★

Michelin map 80 folds 9 and 10 or 245 folds 1, 2, 14 and 15 or 246 fold 23

The Ardèche gorges, overlooked by an audaciously engineered road, rank among the most imposing natural sites in the south of France; the main part of the gorges is now a nature reserve and in 1993 the whole area was listed as a Major Site belonging to France's national heritage.

A temperamental river – The Ardèche rises in the Mazan massif (alt 1 467m/4 813ft). After a 119km/74mi journey, it flows into the River Rhône, 1km/0.5mi upstream from Pont-St-Esprit. The river slope has a steep gradient, particularly so in the upper valley *(see Michelin Green Guide Vallée du Rhône, in French)*, but it is in the lower valley that the most surprising examples of erosion can be observed as the river carved a passage through the limestone strata of the plateau, already hollowed out by underground rivers. The Ardèche's tributaries flowing down from the mountain accentuate its sporadic yet typically Mediterranean flow: autumn spates give way to a shallow rivulet in winter, then swell into spring torrents, before subsiding to a comparative trickle during the summer. During the peak flow there is a formidable convergence of flood-waters at Vallon-Pont-d'Arc. A powerful wall of water advances down the valley at 15-20kph/ 9-12mph! The strength of these erratic flood-waters is such that the river pushes the flow of the Rhône eastwards and deposits a pile of rubble in its river bed. In 1890, the overflow of the Ardèche was so strong that it cut through the Rhône and broke the Lauzon breakwater on the opposite bank. Its drainage is just as erratic.

FROM VALLON-PONT-D'ARC TO PONT-ST-ESPRIT
58km/36mi – allow 1 day

On leaving the Vallon basin, the Ardèche reaches the lower Vivarais limestone plateau which it divides by its deep course into two plateaux: the Gras to the north and the Orgnac *(see Plateau d'Orgnac on p 81)* below to the south, covered with evergreen oak and scrub and riddled with caves.
A **panoramic road**, D 290, overlooks (in *corniche* style) the gorge along the Gras plateau side, giving wonderful views from the many viewpoints *(belvédères)* along its way.

Vallon-Pont-d'Arc – *See VALLON-PONT-D'ARC.*
Leave Vallon for Pont-d'Arc.

The road makes for the Ardèche, past the Château du Vieux Vallon *(restoration in progress)* and across the River Ibie. On the left is the **Grotte des Tunnels**, a cave which once had an underground stream, and then the **Grotte des Huguenots** ⊘, which houses an exhibition on speleology and prehistory.

★★**Pont-d'Arc** – *See p 264. Leave the car in one of the car parks on either side of the viewpoint.* The river flows under the natural arch (34m/112ft high, 59m/194ft wide), which it once skirted (the road just taken in the car). Thousands of years ago, the arch was most likely a narrow passage through which ran a subterranean stream. Infiltration and erosion isolated it and thus when the flood-waters caused the river to alter its course, it adopted the passage already made, which it has since been making wider. *To reach the foot of Pont-d'Arc, there is a path on the Vallon side 150m/164yd from the viewpoint.*
The scenic splendour begins immediately after Pont-d'Arc: the river flows in wide curves punctuated by rapids, all in the framework of a 30km/20mi gorge enclosed by rock walls 300m/984ft high in some places, dramatically coloured in tones of white, dark and light grey and overgrown with scrub oak and vegetation; the river is jade green.
Beyond Chames, on the floor of the Tiourre valley, the road curves to the left creating a grandiose rocky **cirque**★ before climbing to the plateau's edge.

★★**Belvédère du Serre de Tourre** – The viewpoint, poised almost vertically 200m/656ft above the Ardèche, offers a superb **picture** of the river winding round the **Pas du Mousse rock** on which stand the few remaining ruins of the 16C Château d'Ebbo. Also to be seen are the Falaises de Saleyron (Saleyron cliffs). Standing out on the horizon, to the right, is Mont Lozère and, to the left, the wide expanse of the Orgnac plateau.
On the left bank, the tourist road follows the tormented relief of its cliffs and passes through forests of evergreen oaks, first the Bois Bouchas and then the Bois Malbosc.

★★**Belvédères de Gaud** – The **view** upstream takes in the Gaud meander and the turrets of its small 19C castle.

★**Belvédères d'Autridge** – To reach the two viewpoints take the panoramic curve. The Aiguille de Morsanne (Morsanne needle) soars above the gorges like the prow of a ship.
500m/0.3mi beyond the coomb, Combe d'Agrimont, new **vistas**★★ open up of the bend in the river with the Aiguille de Morsanne in the foreground.

★★ Belvédères de Gournier –
The viewpoints are well
situated 200m/656ft
above the river. Below, Le
Gournier farm lies in ruins
in a small field bordering the
Ardèche, which carves its
course through the Rochers
de la Toupine (*toupine*
means cooking pot).

★ Grotte de la Madeleine –
*See Grotte de la MADE-
LEINE.*

*Approach Aven de Marzal
by the road running along
Gras plateau.*

**★ Aven de Marzal (Marzal
chasm)** – *See Aven de
MARZAL.*

*Return to La Madeleine
crossroads and the car
parks of Belvédère de la
Madeleine.*

★★★ La Haute Corniche – This,
the most outstanding sec-
tion of the drive, affords unrivalled views, in close succession, of the gorges.

*Drive to the Aven de Marzal
by the road running across
the Plateau des Gras.*

**★ Belvédère de la Made-
leine** – There is a fine view
of the "Fort" de la
Madeleine which bars the
succession of gorges downstream: these cliffs are the
highest to be found in the
gorges and they dominate
the valley from a height of
300m/984ft.

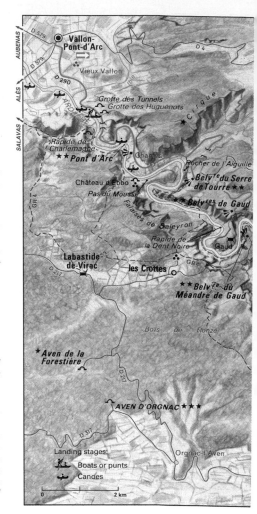

**★★ Belvédère de la Cathé-
drale** – *15min on foot.* This affords a breathtaking view of one of the most curious sight of these gorges, the "Cathedral", a huge rock resembling a building in
ruins whose stone spurs proudly overhang the river.

Balcon des Templiers – The viewpoint offers impressive views of a tight loop in
the river flanked by the magnificent high rocky walls of the cirque. Down below,
crowning a small spur, are the ruins of the Maladrerie des Templiers (Templars'
Leper Hospital).

Belvédère de la Maladrerie – View of the Rocher de la Cathédrale.

Belvédère de la Rouvière – Facing the Garn "Ramparts".

Belvédère de la Coutelle – The viewpoint overlooks the river from a dizzying height
of 180m/590ft. To the right are the last of the Garn ramparts; to the left the
Castelviel rocks and along the river's course, up and downstream, the swift-flowing Fève and Cadière rapids.

★ Grand Belvédère – View of the end of the gorges and the Ardèche's final bend.

★ Grotte de St-Marcel – *See Grotte de ST-MARCEL.*

★ Belvédère du Colombier – View down into the bend enclosed by rocky banks.
The road follows a loop along a dry valley, skirts the Dona Vierna promontory and
makes a wide detour around the small Louby valley to reach the next viewpoint.

★★ Belvédère du Ranc-Pointu – The viewpoint, perched at the end of the Louby valley slope, overlooks the Ardèche's last enclosed bend. Note the different types of
erosion, striation, potholes and caves.
Leaving the gorge, the countryside changes completely: the bare defile is replaced
by a cultivated valley which opens out as it approaches the Rhône. On the far bank
stands the village of **Aiguèze** (*see below*).

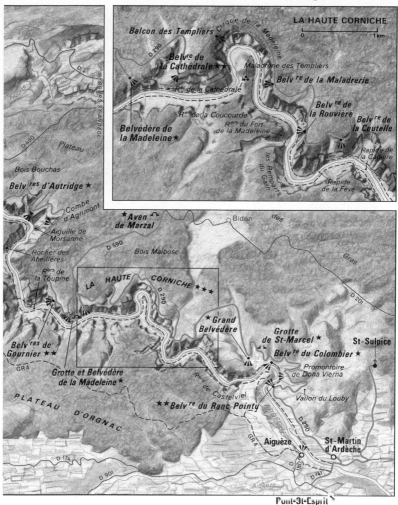

St-Martin-d'Ardèche – The first village on the north bank since Vallon.

Chapelle St-Sulpice – *4km/2.5mi via Trignan from St-Martin-d'Ardèche.*
The dazzling white Romanesque chapel (12C-17C) stands on a slight hillock rising amid a sea of vines. The south wall is built of re-used stones carved with interlacing designs.
Cross the Ardèche by the suspension bridge (pont suspendu St-Martin).
Take D 901 on the left, which joins N 86 slightly before the confluence of the Ardèche and the Rhône.
N 86 goes to Pont-St-Esprit.

Pont-St-Esprit – *See PONT-ST-ESPRIT.*

PLATEAU D'ORGNAC (south bank)

Aiguèze ⊘ – This medieval village with its paved streets is set on top of the last cliffs of the gorges. After passing under an arch cut into the rock, one comes out into an old 14C fortress. From the watchpath there is a pretty **view**★ of the end of the canyon to Mont Ventoux, the ruined towers and the suspension bridge linking Aiguèze to St-Martin-d'Ardèche.

Les Crottes – A village deserted since 3 March 1944, when all the villagers were shot by the Nazis; a stele commemorates this event.

★**Aven de la Forestière** ⊘ – Explored by A. Sonzogni, this chasm was opened to tourists in 1968. It is not far below ground and is easily accessible. The dramatically lit chambers are rich in fine concretions such as the cauliflower-like shapes and macaroni-like strips, which hang from the roof, variegated stalactite curtains, phantasmagoric and eccentric formations and floors bristling with stalagmites.
A small zoo presents a variety of crustaceans, fish, frogs, toads and insects.

Gorges de l'ARDÈCHE

Gorges de l'Ardèche – Cirque de la Madeleine

Labastide-de-Virac – North of this fortified village, located on the boundary line between Languedoc and Vivarais, and an ideal departure point for outings to the Aveyron gorges or the Orgnac plateau, stands the 15C **castle** ⊙ belonging to the Roure family, which guarded the passage through the gorges at Pont-d'Arc. The two round towers were pulled down in 1629 during the Wars of Religion.

Since 1825 the castle has belonged to the family of the sculptor James Pradier (1795-1825; he carved the statues representing Lille and Strasbourg on the Place de la Concorde in Paris), whose forebears were tenant farmers to the Counts of Roure. During the visit note the Florentine-style courtyard, spiral staircase and great hall *(first floor)* with its fine chimney. The watchpath overlooks the Ardèche and Gras plateaux; during clear weather the Lozère mountains and Mézenc mount can be seen to the north. A fully operational silkworm farm enlightens visitors on the traditional breeding of silkworms. The visit ends with an exhibition of local hand-made silks.

★★**Belvédère du Méandre de Gaud** – This commands an excellent **view**★★ of the river at the foot of the Gaud cirque.

★★★**Aven d'Orgnac** – *See Aven d'ORGNAC.*

★★★DESCENDING THE GORGES BY BOAT OR CANOE OR ON FOOT

From Vallon-Pont-d'Arc to St-Martin-d'Ardèche

Descent by boat or canoe ⊙ – *This can be done at any time between March and late November, but is best in May-June. Be sure to find out the level of the water before setting out; prefectural laws have been passed in an attempt to reduce the number of accidents.*

After a long calm stretch, the river bends and one enters the gorges. Almost immediately, the impressive Charlemagne rapid is passed, dominated on the right by the large rock of the same name. The river then passes under the natural porch of the famous Pont d'Arc. To the left extends the Estre cirque onto which opens a cave known as the Grotte Chauvet *(see inset below)*. Shortly after, to the right, are the Grotte d'Ebbo and Pas du Mousse rock, a narrow passage through the cliff to the plateau; the rock on the north bank is the Rocher de l'Aiguille. The first rapids, Rapide de la Dent Noire, are just below the immensely tall Saleyron cliffs and are followed by the wide Gaud meander and cirque with its small château.

Rapids and smooth flowing stretches, overlooked by canyon-high cliffs, alternate as landmarks such as the Aiguille de Morsanne, a needle-like rock on the north bank, and the jagged red and black spikes of the Rocher des Abeillères appear on the south bank.

After approximately 4hr you should have negotiated the Rochers de la Toupine, rocks strewn in the river's course, which in places is 18m/60ft deep, and be able to see Rocher de la Cathédrale in the distance. Before you actually reach Rocher de la Cathédrale you pass one of the natural openings of Grotte de la Madeleine, on the left. Shortly afterwards, the river flows below the enormous Rocher de la Cathédrale and past the Templars peninsula (12C remains), a popular spot with naturists.

The Cirque de la Madeleine is among the most spectacular on the trip, when seen from water level. Straits, rapids and smooth iridescent reaches follow one another as the river continues downwards between sheer cliff walls, bare of all but occasional evergreen oaks. Below the peculiar-looking Coucourde (Provençal for crane) rock and the Castelvieil cliff, the opening of the Grotte St-Marcel can be seen on the left, and, as you round the bend, the Dona Vierna promontory and the Belvédère de Ranc-Pointu. The cliffs melt away, the valley widens out, Aiguèze's tower can be seen on the edge of the rock escarpment to the right.

Descent on foot ⊙ – Only the south bank, leaving from Salavas or Aiguèze, offers the possibility of a "dry" walk. Taking the north bank, leaving from St-Martin or Chames, involves crossing two fords. Passable only when the water level is low.

A New Prehistoric Shrine

At the end of 1994, a collection of cave drawings and paintings of exceptional interest was discovered on the site of the Combe-d'Arc, in the Ardèche gorges. Part of a vast network of underground galleries, the cave, named the **Grotte Chauvet** after its discoverer, has almost 300 black or red paintings and just as many engravings on its walls. These depict a variety of animals, including horses, mammoths, bears, woolly rhinoceroses, cats, and aurochs; rare drawings of a hyena and an owl have also been discovered. Geometric signs and positive or negative hands appear alongside these figures which bear witness to great skill in the portrayal of features and the depiction of movement or relief.

Initial studies of these works of art place them in the Upper Paleolithic Age, about 30 000 years before the present. Because of the number, quality and originality of these drawings, the Vallon-Pont-d'Arc cave has an important contribution to make to the study of cave paintings worldwide, along with the Cosquer cave in the Calanques range and the Lascaux cave in the Dordogne. Furthermore, as the cave has been left untouched since the Paleolithic Age, it provides a wide field of investigation for paleontologists to analyse the bones of ursine mammals found scattered in the cave, and for archeologists to attempt to discover those activites practised by our ancestors through the many remains on the site: hearths, cut flint, footprints etc.

For the time being only specialists are allowed access to the cave. However, in Vallon-Pont-d'Arc, an **exhibition** *(see p 264)* displays the many treasures found in the painted caves of the Ardèche region, including the Grotte Chauvet.

Michelin on the Net: www.michelin-travel.com

Our route planning service covers all of Europe – twenty-one countries and one million kilometres of highways and byways – enabling you to plot many different itineraries from wherever you are.

The itinerary options allow you to choose a preferred route – for example, quickest, shortest, or Michelin recommended.

The network is updated three times weekly, integrating ongoing road works, detours, new motorways, and snowbound mountain passes.

The description of the itinerary includes the distances and travelling times between towns, selected hotels and restaurants.

ARLES★★★

Population 54 309
Michelin map 83 fold 10 or 245 fold 28 or 246 fold 26
Local map see La CAMARGUE

Roman capital and a major religious centre in the Middle Ages, Arles preserves, from its glorious past, two fine Gallo-Roman antiquities, its amphitheatre and theatre, and two gems of Romanesque art, the cloisters and doorway of St-Trophime.

The development of the Camargue as a protected natural environment has made Arles the rice capital, and yet the city depends not only on its vocation as a central market for agricultural produce (market gardening, breeding and raising of Crau sheep and rice growing) but also on its diversified light industry and administrative and cultural functions. It is also the largest *commune* in France, encompassing 77 000ha/30sq mi.

The Arles Festival, which has now gained a solid reputation for quality and Provençal originality, holds folklore events, concerts, opera, dance and theatre. In addition there are the traditional Camargue bullfighting festivals: Easter Feria, Fête des Gardians etc.

The Rencontres Internationales de la Photographie (International Photography Show), founded by Lucien Clergue (a famous photographer born in Arles in 1934), takes place annually. It consists of a series of quality exhibitions and events. This, with the École Nationale de la Photographie (National School of Photography), founded in 1982, has made Arles one of the capitals of photography.

Arles women inspired the praise in poetry or music of Mistral, Daudet, Gounod and Bizet. Although their splendid costumes can be seen only during the festivals, the beauty of these women survives from one generation to the next.

HISTORICAL NOTES

Arles and Marseille – The site of Arles, amid the marshes, at the tip of Camargue, was originally an island-like rocky eminence, which overlooked the Rhône delta. It controlled navigation along the river, the course of which was not yet established. The excavations undertaken in 1975 under the Jardin d'Hiver have revealed the existence of a Celtic-Ligurian town (known as Theline) colonised by the Greeks from Marseille as early as the 6C BC.

The town, which soon took the name of Arelate, met with new prosperity when the Consul Marius, in 104 BC, built a canal which joined the Rhône to the Fos gulf, greatly facilitating navigation. And yet Arles stayed economically dependent on the Massalians who levied a toll on ships using the canal. This situation continued until 49 BC when Caesar defeated Marseille. Arles had provided Caesar with 12 ships for his campaign and Caesar, thus, transferred to the town Marseille's possessions and ordered them to found a Roman colony. Thereafter, Arles supplanted its rival and developed its own economy.

It possessed the southernmost bridge on the Rhône *(see Pont Julien under Gorges de l'ARDÈCHE)* and, on the Domitian Way, the direct road between Italy and Spain. Other roads leaving from the city united the Mediterranean with northern Gaul and other western provinces. These land routes were complemented by a number of waterways. Arles, closer to the sea than it is now, became a sea and river port: the largest ships could dock there easily.

Roman Arles – *Town plan under Introduction: Ancient Art.* A colony of veterans of the Sixth Legion, Arles was granted the privilege of building a fortified wall around the 40ha/99 acres of the official city; on the Rhône side stood a triumphal arch, razed in 1687.

The town was divided into two main streets: the *cardo* (north-south axis; located Rue de l'Hôtel-de-Ville) and the *decumanus* (east-west axis; located in part in Rue de la Calade) and included the forum (on the site of the Cryptoporticus, *see below*), most likely several temples, a basilica, baths (under Place de la République) and a theatre. The streets (4-7m/13-23ft wide), dividing the town into a chequered pattern, were all paved and often lined with footpaths; whereas the *cardo*, with a total width of 12m/39ft (4m/13ft of which was street), was lined with porticoes.

An aqueduct (vestiges near Porte de la Redoute to the east) brought water in abundance from the Alpilles. From a central cistern, water was distributed to three points: local fountains, baths and private houses. A remarkable drainage system (the masterpipe being 3.5m/11ft in diameter) evacuated the used water: the public lavatories were built of white marble and equipped with running water. The town was spreading at the end of the 1C beyond the fortifications: parts of the ramparts were destroyed to build the amphitheatre.

To the south lay the Roquette shipyards and, beyond the circus (the obelisk standing in front of St-Trophime originates from it); further to the east the Jardin d'Hiver district and the Esplanade were residential (two villas were discovered); on the right bank of the Rhône, at Trinquetaille, was the large bustling dockland frequented by sailors, boatmen and merchants. A bridge of boats joined the two banks of the river northeast of the town, level with the Bourg-Neuf district.

The expansion of Arles reached its maximum in the 4C and 5C. Under Emperor Constantine the northwest district was remodelled; an imperial palace and the La Trouille baths were built. The ground plan of the fortifications was hardly modified; the ramparts are still visible to the east where two towers from the Redoute Gate (Porte de la Redoute) still stand *(see p 93)*.

Rome of the Gauls – Trade was such that in the 5C it was written that "Everything produced by the Orient, perfumed Araby, luxuriant Assyria, fertile Africa, beautiful Spain and fecund Gaul is to be found in Arles, and in as great quantity as in the countries of origin".

The town was made up of five guilds of boatmen. Some sailed the Rhône, the Durance and the lagoons around Arles' hill, using rafts carried on inflated goatskins called utriculaires; others sailed the Mediterranean.

It was an active industrial centre as well: textiles and gold and silver work were manufactured, ships were built, sarcophagi and arms were made. Imperial money was minted. Wheat, pork butcher's meat (already famous), olive oil, dark and thick wine from the Rhône hills, were all exported. Stonecarvers, masons and architects were famous for the quality of their work.

Prosperity brought political importance: Emperor Constantine established himself and was succeeded by his sons. In 395 Arles became the political and administrative capital of the Gauls (made up of Spain, Gaul as such, Brittany) and obtained in 417 the primacy transferred from Lyon.

It was a great religious centre where 19 synods were held. The first bishop of Arles, Trophimus, was most likely sent from Rome around 225 and legends rapidly grew around him *(see p 87)*. Christianisation dates from this period (mid 3C), illustrated by the martyrdom of St Genesius around 250. In the 4C and 5C the bishops were constantly acquiring importance under the protection of imperial rule and hoped to control all the other churches of the Gauls.

The decline – Arles suffered from the Barbarian invasions at the end of the 5C, but rediscovered a certain illustriousness under the Ostrogoths from 508-36. More than the insignificant and temporarily re-established praetorian prefects, it was the brilliance of the bishops, notably St Caesarius, which continued to make Arles a great religious centre where important synods were held, as in 524. But Frankish domination led to Arles' decline.

In the 8C, the Franks and Saracens fought over the country and as a result caused a great deal of destruction. In the 9C Arles was but a shadow of its former self, when it became the capital of the Kingdom of Arles, which included Burgundy and part of Provence. It was not until the 12C that the town experienced a political and economic revival and acquired the status of a district governed by elected consuls. Its prestige was considerable as the Germanic Emperor Frederick Barbarossa came to the town in 1178 to be crowned king of Arles in the newly completed, superb Romanesque Cathedral of St-Trophime. In 1239 the burghers of Arles submitted to the count of Provence. From that time onwards, the town followed the fortunes of the province: political status was transferred to Aix, and Marseille took its revenge and surpassed Arles in economic prosperity.

As long as the Rhône remained the main commercial route, Arles continued to be relatively prosperous and even more so when the land was upgraded by the Crau irrigation project and drainage of the marshland. However, the arrival of the railway made river traffic obsolete and dealt a severe blow to trade. Until 20 years ago it was only the agricultural market centre of Camargue, Crau and Alpilles.

Van Gogh in Arles – Vincent Van Gogh (1853-90) came to Arles from Paris on 21 February 1888. He first lived at the Hôtel-Restaurant Carrel, Rue de la Cavalerie and then rented a small house, "Yellow House", on Place Lamartine: both buildings were destroyed during the war.

He adapted quickly and his health improved; he made friends and received Gauguin in October. His style changed as he moved away from Impressionism. He sought to find "another Japan", as Japanese wood prints fascinated him. The Provençal countryside and its luminosity provided the answer. He painted non-stop: nature, working in the fields, portraits, views of Arles and its surroundings, producing in all more than 200 paintings and 100 drawings. His Arles subjects, including: *House of Vin-*

Self-Portrait with Bandaged Ear and Pipe
by Van Gogh (private collection)

cent, The Alyscamps, L'Arlésienne, Crau Plain and *Langlois Bridge* (this, the so-called Van Gogh bridge, was destroyed in 1926 and rebuilt on the Arles canal at the Fos-sur-Mer port – 3km/1.5mi by ③ on the map, D 35, then a small road to the left), were some of the most exciting works of his Arles period.

Plagued increasingly by fits of madness, made worse by his brutal break with Gauguin (24 December 1888, when he cut off part of his left ear, *Self-Portrait*), Van Gogh was hospitalised. His fortunes went from bad to worse: Gauguin abandoned him, his friend Roulin, the postman, was sent to Marseille, and in February 1889 a petition circulated in Arles demanding that he be confined. He finally decided to leave Arles for the asylum at St-Rémy-de-Provence, where he arrived on 3 May 1889 *(see p 235)*.

STAYING IN ARLES

Cafés and Bars: Place du Forum: several pavement cafés, including the Van Gogh once frequented by the famous artist. **Boulevard des Lices and Boulevard Clémenceau:** several possibilities such as the Malarte, the Maison de la Bière, the Grande Brasserie Arlésienne, the Wilson or the Clémenceau; jazz or salsa at weekends at the Tropicana, 7 Rue Molière. **Rue Porte-de-Laure:** Le Tropical snack-bar and ice-cream parlour, for a drink or snack before or after a performance at the Roman theatre. **Place Nina-Berberova and Quai Marx-Dormoy:** the café-restaurant L'Entrevue, located inside the avant-garde cinema run by the publishing house Actes Sud. **Avenue Sadi-Carnot:** Cargo de Nuit, a café-restaurant with live music offering jazz concerts.

Photography: Rencontres Internationales de la Photographie: evenings at the Roman theatre, exhibitions, courses, talks, activities in the field of photography in various locations throughout the town, 10 Rond-Point des Arènes, 13200 Arles ☎ 04 90 96 76 06; **Journées de l'Image Professionnelle:** presentation of the latest technical developments and public display of the work of internationally renowned photographers, 1 Rue Copernic, 13200 Arles ☎ 04 90 96 44 44.

Stage Performances: Théâtre de la Calade, Grenier à Sel, 49 Quai de la Roquette ☎ 04 90 93 05 23.

THE CENTRE'S PUBLIC BUILDINGS *1 day*

★★Amphitheatre (Arènes) ⊘ **(YZ)** – *See p 46 in the Introduction.* This is, strictly speaking, an amphitheatre dating most probably from the end of the 1C. Transformed into a fortress during the early Middle Ages, it constituted a system of defence. Later on, under the filled-in arcades, in the galleries, on the tiers and in the arena itself arose a small town of 200 houses and two chapels. In order to carry out these transformations, the materials were taken from the building itself which was mutilated but saved from complete destruction. The excavation and restoration began in 1825. Three out of the four medieval watchtowers remain.

The amphitheatre measured 136m x 107m/446ft x 351ft and could seat more than 20 000 spectators. Two storeys, each made up of 60 arches, had a total height of 21m/65.5ft. Corinthian half-columns back to back adorned the pillars on the first floor. The third floor, the attic storey, which was preserved at Nîmes, has completely disappeared. The arena (69m x 40m/226ft x 131ft) as such, was separated from the tiers by a protective wall; the arena was floored and underneath it were machinery, animal cages and the backstage area.

Climb to the platform of the tower dominating the entrance to appreciate the grandeur of the building and to enjoy an all-round view of the amphitheatre's architecture and an interesting view of Arles, the Rhône, the Alpilles and the Abbaye de Montmajour. Wander through the upper level of arches of half the amphitheatre in order to understand the building's construction; finally go around the arena at the lower level of arches. This allows you to grasp the strength of this ancient structure and the originality of the trabeated form of construction, where in fact the circular galleries are covered with enormous flat slabs which replaced the traditional Roman vault and prove Greek influence in Arles.

★★Roman Theatre (Théâtre Antique) ⊘ **(Z)** – This theatre, built during Augustus' reign c 27-5 BC, was much more badly damaged than the amphitheatre. As early as the 5C it was used as a quarry for the construction of churches, and in the 9C was transformed into a redoubt before disappearing completely under houses and gardens. Rediscovered in the 17C, it was excavated from 1827 to 1855.

Smaller in size than the one in Autun or Lyon, the theatre measured 102m/335ft in diameter and had a seating capacity of 12 000. Unlike the one in Orange, which was built on a natural height, this theatre was backed up by a 27-arched portico made up of three levels of arcades, of which only one bay (part of the medieval ramparts, the Tour de Roland) remains.

L. But/FOC

Roman Amphitheatre, Arles

All that is preserved of the stage wall are two columns in African breccia and Italian marble standing whole amid the ruins, as a reminder of the theatre's great past. The stage, curtain slit, orchestra and part of the tiers are still visible. The tiers of seats went up to and were level with the Roland Tower; the attic level was added onto the topmost rows.

In 1651 excavations in the pit unearthed the famous Venus of Arles (a cast is in the Musée de l'Arles antique – *see below*) given to Louis XIV. One hundred years later, a naked torso, part of a colossal statue of Augustus, was discovered; it was most likely set in the large niche of the stage wall; in 1834 its head was uncovered (now in the Musée de l'Arles Antique).

★**Église St-Trophime** (Z) – Around St Trophimus, possibly the first bishop of Arles in the early 3C, were born a number of legends: sent by St Peter, cousin and disciple of St Paul; received the St Marys when they landed *(see STES-MARIES-DE-LA-MER)*; and Christ Himself appeared before him at the Alyscamps, etc.

The early cathedral, initially consecrated to St Stephen, was destroyed and then rebuilt during the Carolingian era (part of the façade built of rubble remains). It was again rebuilt at the end of the 11C (transept) and in the first half of the 12C (nave) in order to house the relics of St Trophimus, to whom it was then consecrated.

In c 1190 the building was enhanced by a magnificently-carved doorway, set against the façade and raised, which required raising the nave. The construction was completed just after the bell tower. The former bell tower was replaced by a square tower of bands and arcades and fluted pilasters, the last storey of which was remodelled in the 17C; St-Trophime, thus, presents a masterpiece of the late Provençal Romanesque style.

In the 15C the cathedral underwent extensive transformations: the chancel with its ambulatory and radiating chapels was reconstructed, enlarging the church by a third. In the 17C two classical doors were added on either side of the main doorway, two windows were pierced to illuminate the transept crossing, and galleries were added.

★★**Doorway** – Owing to the beauty of its carved decoration, this doorway *(portail)* can be compared to the façade of the old abbey church at St-Gilles.

It displays an ancient classical arrangement, suggesting the form of a triumphal arch, often used in 12C Provence. Its archaic appearance recalling the Roman tradition has not evolved in comparison with the main French Romanesque works of art, especially those works from the north.

Flanking the doorway near the side doors are images of, on the left, St Michael weighing souls and, on the right, some demons from hell.

Interior – Inside, the main body of the building is surprisingly high and the aisles very narrow. The nave, lit by a rounded clerestory, is roofed with pointed-barrel vaulting; the aisles feature half-barrel vaulting. The Romanesque severity contrasts with the rib and moulding work of the Gothic chancel. Among the works of art of particular interest are:

– in the second bay of the north aisle: 4C Christian sarcophagus with two carved registers; some of the carvings are in high relief.

– in the north arm of the transept an admirable Annunciation by Finsonius; in the transept chapel, called Chapel of Grignan, another sarcophagus which served as an altar and represents the crossing of the Red Sea.

1) Tympanum of the Last Judgement, Christ crowned, in glory, holding the book of the Evangelists in one hand and raising the other in benediction: his physiognomy suggests a great deal of formalism. He is surrounded by the attributes of the four Evangelists – the winged man (St Matthew), the eagle (St John), the ox (St Luke), the lion (St Mark). Crowding the recessed arches are a procession of angels with, at the top, the three angels of the Last Judgement.
2) The elect, clothed, advance towards Christ.
3) An angel receives the elect and drops their souls in the aprons of Abraham, Isaac and Jacob.
4) Joseph's vision and the Annunciation.
5) Twelve Apostles.
6) Christ's birth and the bathing of the newborn child.
7) An angel guards the Gates to Paradise from where a group of sinners (prelates, men, women) are refused admission.
8) The condemned, naked, held closely by one chain, carried by a demon, are led to hell.
9) St Bartholomew.
10) St James the Lesser.
11) St Trophimus (in bishop's robes); two angels are placing the mitre on his head.

12) St John the Evangelist, unbearded.
13) St Peter with his keys.
14) St Paul. This statue with its deeply cut and closely set folds was inspired by the central doorway of St-Gilles.
15) St Andrew.
16) The stoning of St Stephen: two angels bear off his soul (represented by a child) and take it to Paradise.
17) St James the Greater.
18) St Philip.

– in the Chapelle du Saint-Sépulcre (right of the axial chapel) the sarcophagus of Geminus, who died c 400, surmounted by a 16C Entombment.

– in the south arm of the transept a long painted panel (16C) shows a synod assembled around the Virgin.

– in the Chapelle des Rois (south side aisle) Adoration of the Magi by Finsonius.

– on the wall of the north aisle Aubusson tapestries illustrate the Virgin's life.

– in the nave above the triumphal arch the Stoning of St Stephen by Finsonius.

** **Cloître St-Trophime** ⊘ (**Z**) – These cloisters, the most famous in Provence for the elegance and richness of their carved decoration, may have been carved with the collaboration of the craftsmen of St-Gilles. Developed for the cathedral's canons at the same time as the surrounding conventual buildings, their construction spanned several stages: the Romanesque north and east galleries in the last third of the 12C, the Gothic south and west galleries in the 14C.

The best work is to be found in the north gallery (on the left on entering), particularly on the magnificent corner pillars decorated with large statues and low relief.

Statues on the doorway of St-Trophime

The capitals are adorned with scenes from the Resurrection and the origins of Christian Arles, as well as foliage. Note especially, on the northeast pillar, the statue of St Paul, with the deeply-incised folds, very long under the elbows, the work of a craftsman who was familiar with St Gilles' central doorway. Of a later period the east gallery's capitals and pillars recount the major episodes of Christ's life. The south gallery tells of the life of St Trophimus and the west gallery concentrates on typically Provençal subjects such as St Martha and the Tarasque. From the south gallery can be seen the cloisters and, above, the former chapter premises, the church nave. Dominating the whole stands the stout plain bell tower. Above the gallery runs a walk.

The chapterhouse, opening onto the north gallery, vaulted with pointed-barrel vaulting, houses, on the ground floor, Flemish and Aubusson (17C) tapestries and upstairs some Romanesque capitals and various lapidary fragments. Along the east gallery the refectory and dormitory display temporary exhibitions.

A Pilot Restoration Project

Following important and delicate restoration work, the doorway of St-Trophime church, a masterpiece of Provençal Romanesque art on UNESCO's world heritage list, has regained its former splendour.

Threatened by wind, rain and pollution, the sculptures on the doorway have benefited from the work carried out by many specialists, whose joint expertise has managed to save them just in time. Petrographical research establishing the number and quality of the different materials used in the doorway and a precise diagnosis of the condition of these materials were conducted before setting up a highly-sophisticated cleaning and consolidation operation: milling with diamond-pointed heads, micro-sandblasting, the application of ethyl silicate to ensure good levels of porosity, and a waterproofing product to prevent the penetration of rain water.

To clean the cloister capitals (second phase of the programme), the laser method recently used on Amiens Cathedral, which was not fully operational when work started on St-Trophime, will be applied. To ensure that the beneficial effects of this restoration will last, it is now necessary to place guttering over the doorway to protect it from water run-off, to install a net to discourage birds and to control traffic levels around the site.

Hôtel de Ville (Z H) – The town hall was rebuilt from 1673 to 1675 after plans by Hardouin-Mansart and the architect Peytret from Arles. It includes the **clock tower**, a vestige of the original building, which was built from 1543 to 1553 and inspired by the Glanum mausoleum. The vestibule's (which gives onto Plan de la Cour, *see below*) flat **vaulting★** is a masterpiece; at one time it was studied by the craftsmen touring France (before they became master craftsmen). The setting is completed by the town hall's Versailles-like classical façade overlooking Place de la République and the fountain, in the middle of which stands a fine **obelisk** from Arles' Roman circus which was moved here in the 17C.

The Plan de la Cour *(access via the vestibule)* is an unusual small square lined with old buildings including the 12C-15C Hôtel des Podestats. Leaning against one of the walls is the judgement bench from where the magistrates pronounced sentence.

★ **Cryptoporticus** ⊘ (Z V) – *Enter via the former Chapelle des Jésuites* (17C). The Cryptoporticus, the forum's substructure, is a double, horseshoe-shaped, underground gallery, 90m/295ft long and 60m/197ft wide. The two rounded-arched corridors were divided by a line of massive rectangular pillars; ancient air shafts let the light in. The north corridor, cut in the 2C by a temple, the ruins of which can be seen on the Place du Forum, was flush with and opened onto the *decumanus* by two doors; it was doubled in the 4C by a new covered gallery.

The use of the Cryptoporticus is unclear, apart from the fact that the galleries enhanced and ensured the stability of the forum's monuments. The specialists have often imagined that they were huge granaries or more prosaically just walkways. During the excavations several fine sculptures were found, now displayed in the Musée de l'Arles Antique, especially the bearded head of Octavius and a votive shield, a marble copy of the gold shield offered to Augustus by the Senate in 27 BC.

★ **Museon Arlaten** ⊘ (Z M³) – This fascinating Provençal Ethnographic Museum was created by Frédéric Mistral in 1896 and installed, from 1906 to 1909, in the 16C Hôtel de Castellane-Laval, bought by Mistral with the money he was given when awarded the Nobel Prize for Literature in 1904. Worried by the loss of Provençal identity before the national centralisation policy, Mistral wanted to preserve the details of Provençal daily life for future generations. At the entrance to the courtyard is a small tiled forum with exedra which led to a small 2C basilica.

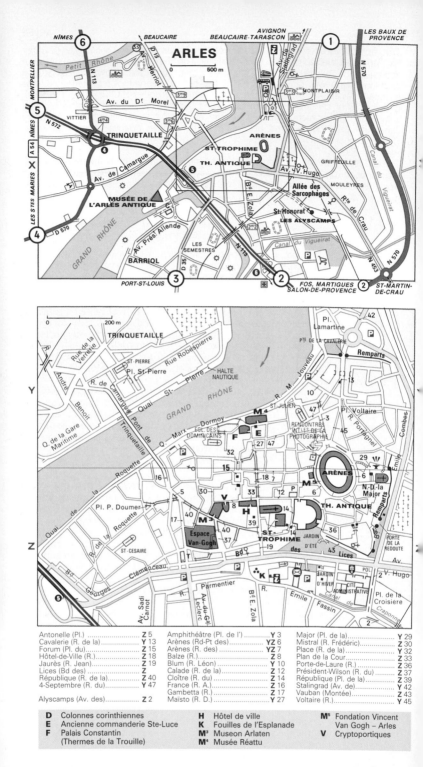

Antonelle (Pl.)	**Z** 5	Amphithéâtre (Pl. de l')	**Y** 3	Major (Pl. de la)	**Y** 29
Cavalerie (R. de la)	**Y** 13	Arènes (Rd-Pt des)	**YZ** 6	Mistral (R. Frédéric)	**Z** 30
Forum (Pl. du)	**Z** 15	Arènes (R. des)	**YZ** 7	Place (R. de la)	**Y** 32
Hôtel-de-Ville (R.)	**Z** 18	Balze (R.)	**Z** 8	Plan de la Cour	**Z** 33
Jaurès (R. Jean)	**Z** 19	Blum (R. Léon)	**Y** 10	Porte-de-Laure (R.)	**Z** 36
Lices (Bd des)	**Z**	Calade (R. de la)	**Z** 12	Président-Wilson (R. du)	**Z** 37
République (R. de la)	**Z** 40	Cloître (R. du)	**Z** 14	République (Pl. de la)	**Z** 39
4-Septembre (R. du)	**Y** 47	France (R. A.)	**Z** 16	Stalingrad (Av. de)	**Y** 42
		Gambetta (R.)	**Z** 17	Vauban (Montée)	**Z** 43
Alyscamps (Av. des)	**Z** 2	Maïsto (R. D.)	**Y** 27	Voltaire (R.)	**Y** 45

D	Colonnes corinthiennes	**H**	Hôtel de ville
E	Ancienne commanderie Ste-Luce	**K**	Fouilles de l'Esplanade
F	Palais Constantin	**M³**	Museon Arlaten
	(Thermes de la Trouille)	**M⁴**	Musée Réattu
M⁵	Fondation Vincent Van Gogh – Arles		
V	Cryptoportiques		

The Museon, with its attendant in traditional Arles costume as Mistral had wished, consists of some thirty rooms devoted in the main to the Arles country and organised according to theme or scene. Furnishings, costumes, ceramics evoking local customs, crafts and music, items of popular devotion, documents on the Félibrige and the history of Arles and its surroundings make this museum the most comprehensive of its kind in Provence.

Not to be missed are the reconstructed interiors (delivery room, Christmas Eve in the dining room of a *mas*) displayed in a delightful atmosphere of days past.

Also noteworthy is the Frédéric Mistral Room containing a moving display of the poet's personal belongings (cradle, hat, cane, clothes). An area has been set aside for traditional farming, shipping activities along the Rhône and the regions of Crau and Camargue *(gardian's* hut).

Place du Forum (Z 15) – The actual Place du Forum is not on the site of the ancient forum; it borders it. Left of the Hôtel Nord-Pinus, two Corinthian columns (**D**) surmounted by a fragment of pediment are all that remains of a 2C temple which straddled the north corridor of the Cryptoporticus. Augustus forum lay more to the south. On this very animated square, lined with cafés, stands a statue of Mistral surrounded by a railing of Camargue *gardians'* pitchforks.

★**Musée Réattu** ⏲ (**Y M⁴**) – The museum is located in the former Grand Priory of the Order of the Hospital of St John of Jerusalem (15C). The façade, overlooking the Rhône, was once part of the medieval walls. Before becoming the property of Arles in 1867, the priory belonged to the painter **Jacques Réattu** (1760-1833). Five of the museum's galleries exhibit his work. There are also works from the Italian (16C and 17C), French (17C), Dutch (18C) and Provençal (18C) Schools.

The other galleries contain a large collection of modern and contemporary art. Displayed are watercolours, engravings and paintings by Gauguin, Dufy, Prassinos, Léger, Marchand, Vlaminck, Vasarely, Singier, Sarthou, Marquet, Rousseau and Degottex; sculpture by César, G. Richier, Zadkine, Bury and Toni Grand.

The **Picasso Donation★** is exhibited in three galleries: 57 drawings executed in 1971 show the variety of techniques (pen, pencil, felt-tip pen, chalk and wash drawing) mastered by Picasso, demonstrating his outstanding pictorial skills.

The Hospitallers have their own gallery.

An imposing collection of photographs is presented in the form of temporary exhibitions.

Note the former **Commanderie Ste-Luce** (**Y E**) that stands opposite the museum.

★**Palais Constantin – Thermes de la Trouille** ⏲ (**Y F**) – *See p 47 for details on baths and how they work.*

The baths of Arles are the largest (98 x 45m/ 322 x 148ft) remaining in Provence. They date from Constantine's era, the 4C.

The plan on the right shows the lay-out and specifies the location of the non-excavated part in relation to present-day Arles. Enter by the *tepidarium*, through to the *caldarium*, which still has its hypocaust. The

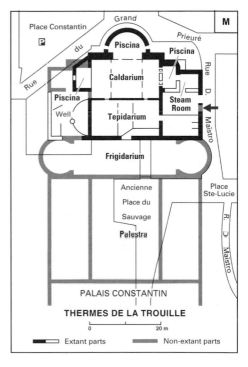

PALAIS CONSTANTIN

THERMES DE LA TROUILLE

0   20 m

■■■□ Extant parts   ▬▬ Non-extant parts

oven-vaulted wall and apse, completing the building towards the Rhône, are made of alternate courses of brick and stone.

★★MUSÉE DE L'ARLES ANTIQUE (X) ⏲ 1hr 30min

Built on the edge of the Roman circus on the peninsula surrounded by the Rhône and the canal linking Arles to the port of Fos, this bold triangular construction, designed by Henri Ciriani, houses behind its blue enamel walls the extensive Arles collection of ancient art.

The visitor is greeted by the sight of the **Arcoule Lion** (1C BC), together with a quotation by Mistral; a large single room then groups together large statues and models illustrating Roman civilisation in Imperial times. Town plans are presented, marked with the important monuments of the Augustan (forum, theatre), Flavian (amphitheatre), Antonine (circus) and Constantine (baths) eras. Around the **colossal statue of Augustus** (marble torso, limestone drape), which decorated the theatre stage wall, are organized statues of dancers, altars dedicated to the god Apollo and a cast of the famous **Venus of Arles**, which is the copy of a masterpiece of Hellenistic statuary; the statue is now displayed in the Louvre. The **bust of Aphrodite** (copy of a Greek work dating from the 4C BC) and the **bust of a young prince** (2C) are striking for the purity of their features. The large **votive shield of Augustus** (26 BC), a marble copy of the golden Roman shield, shows the extent and speed of Romanization in Arles.

The daily life of the people of Arles (household equipment, jewels, medical care) is presented alongside traditional activities (agriculture, breeding, craftwork, trade) either through objects: tools for weaving, bronze, glass and clay dishes, or with sarcophagus reliefs: scenes of hunting and the olive harvest. Two models demonstrate the operation of the large Barbegal flour mill and a series of lead pipes illustrate water conveyance. The economic role of Arles is evoked through the presentation of its road network (military limits) and both its land and sea trade (set of amphorae and marine anchors, lead, tin and copper ingots). One area is given over to religions of the time: a small faun in bronze (1C BC), torso of Sarapis (2C), around which a serpent is coiled.

The splendour of the Imperial age is evident in the sumptuous nature of the **mosaics**, taken from the rich villas of Trinquetaille (late 2C). A footbridge allows visitors to explore the patterns and colours of the mosaics, which are either geometrical or illustrate a theme, such as the Abduction of Europa, Orpheus or the Four Seasons. In the central medallion of the Aiön mosaic, the god of time can be seen holding the wheel of the zodiac in his hand.

Next to the collection of funerary steles, typical of incineration rites, is the dazzling display of **sarcophagi★★**, both pagan and Christian, which constitutes one of the most important collections in the world after that of Rome. These magnificent marble works, carved predominantly in the 4C by craftsmen from Arles and some of which originate from the Alyscamps necropolis, exalted the new triumphant Christian faith. As well as the sarcophagus known as Phaedra and Hippolytus, note that of the Trinity or the spouses. The visit ends with late Antiquity and the presentation of the 6C ivory shield of St Caesarius, which depicts soldiers asleep in front of Christ's tomb.

From the terrace, there is a **view** of the old town of Arles, the bell tower of St-Trophime rising above the roof-tops, and the remains of the immense Roman circus *(excavation under way)* dating from the 2C, whose central obelisk has been moved to the Place de l'Hôtel-de-Ville.

The building is also home to organisations devoted to research activities, such as the Institut de Recherche sur la Provence Antique and to culture (library, photo library, computer databank, auditorium, temporary exhibition hall).

★★LES ALYSCAMPS ⊘ (X) *30min*

From Roman times to the late Middle Ages, the Alyscamps was one of the most famous necropolises of the western world.

In ancient times, when a traveller arrived by the Aurelian Way to the gates of Arles, he made his way to the city's entrance passing along a line of inscribed tombs and mausoleums. And yet the Alyscamps' great expansion occurred during the Christianisation of the necropolis around the tomb of St Genesius.

Genesius was a Roman civil servant, beheaded in 250 for having refused to write down an imperial edict persecuting the Christians. Miracles began to happen on this site and the faithful, more and more numerous, asked to be buried here; added to that was the legend of St Trophimus, which confirmed that he too was buried here.

Les Alyscamps, Arles

As early as the 4C the tombs numbered several thousand and sarcophagi piled up on several levels (three to be exact: 4C-5C, 9C-10C and 12C-13C). The religious buildings multiplied, too, and in the 13C there were 19churches and chapels.

From far and wide, recount the chroniclers, coffins were sent down the Rhône, with a coin for the gravediggers, who stopped them at the Trinquetaille bridge, and from there they were delivered to the Alyscamps. In the 10C the legend stating that the knights of Roncevaux were buried here heightened its popularity. The transfer of St Trophimus' relics to the cathedral in 1152 removed part of the prestige of this immense necropolis.

From the time of the Renaissance the necropolis was desecrated. The city council-lors took to offering their honoured guests one or several of the better carved sar-cophagi as presents; monks in charge of the necropolis took funerary stones to build churches and convents and enclose monastery grounds.

Thanks to the Musée de l'Arles Antique some of the admirable sarcophagi, which enable us to get an idea of the splendour of the Alyscamps in the past, were saved and are exhibited. Finally, the remaining tombs – empty and of no artistic inter-est – were assembled into an avenue but even these have not survived unscathed; the railway cuts through the approach, housing projects line the right side and on the left the canal and workshops are barely hidden by trees.

Allée des Sarcophages (**X**) – The visitor cannot help but be awestruck, when he realises that he is walking where for over 2000 years 80 generations have been buried. This funerary alley is bordered by tall trees interspersed with two rows of sar-cophagi and with St-Honorat church in the background. A 12C porch, all that remains of the Abbaye St-Césaire, opens onto the avenue also lined with chapels. A large num-ber of the sarcophagi are Greek in style: double-pitched roof with four raised cor-ners; the Roman-style ones are identified by the flat top. Some are carved with the three symbols: a plumb line and a mason's level, signifying the equality of man before death, and a trowel, a type of axe, intended to protect the sarcophagi from robbers.

Église St-Honorat (**X**) – Rebuilt in the 12C by the monks of St-Victor of Marseille, keepers of the necropolis, this church is dominated by a powerful 2-storey bell tower (13C), or lantern tower, opened by eight round-arched bays. Besides the bell tower, the chancel, to which several chapels were added at a later date, and a carved doorway remain. Sarcophagi have been placed to show the former location of the nave and aisles, since disappeared. In the apse are three Carolingian sar-cophagi adorned with S-shaped fluting. Across from the entrance is a 4C white mar-ble sarcophagus and in the south chapels are a group of five sarcophagi. Note, also, the powerful round 16C pillars in the transept crossing.

ADDITIONAL SIGHTS

Remparts (**YZ**) – Across from the cemetery are the Porte de la Redoute, also known as the Porte d'Auguste, and the southeast corner of the stronghold, with the ruins of a paleo-Christian church.

Ramparts from the barbarian period can be seen near the public gardens; near the 16C Porte de la Cavalerie the fortifications are medieval.

Collégiale Notre-Dame-de-la-Major (**Z**) – This Romanesque church was built on the site of a Roman temple dedicated to Cybelius. It was enlarged in the 14C (aisles), 16C (chancel) and 17C (façade).

From the adjacent terrace there is a good **view** from west to east of the Cévennes, the Montagnette hills, Mont Ventoux and the Crau plateau.

Boulevard des Lices (**Z**) – The favourite promenade of the local people, this broad avenue lined with cafés and their plane tree-shaded terraces presents the charac-teristic Provençal avenue *(see Cours Mirabeau under AIX-EN-PROVENCE)*.

Fouilles de l'Esplanade (Esplanade Excavations) (**Z K**) – Skirting Boulevard des Lices, a Gallo-Roman district – baths, shops, houses (one features a lovely mosaic, illus-trating Leda and the Swan) – has been uncovered. Also discovered is the southern continuation of the *cardo*, which crossed town following the present-day Rue de l'Hôtel-de-Ville and Rue de la République. Destroyed in the late 3C, this district was only partially rebuilt in the 4C and 5C.

Fondation Vincent Van Gogh-Arles ⊘ (**Z M⁹**) – This foundation, the physical mani-festation of the "artists' community" that Van Gogh had spoken of so enthusiasti-cally during his time in Provence, is to be found at the heart of the old town beneath the ogee mouldings of the Palais de Luppé. The permanent collection includes works of art executed in homage to Van Gogh by some of the greatest names in con-temporary art, be they painters (Francis Bacon, David Hockney, Fernando Botero, Olivier Debré), sculptors (Karel Appel, César), photographers (Lucien Clergue, Robert Doisneau), writers (Viviane Forrester, Michel Tournier), musicians (Henri Dutilleux) or even fashion designers (Christian Lacroix).

Every year, while the permanent collection is on tour in France and abroad, there is an exhibition on the subject of one of these artists who have made a donation to the foundation.

Espace Van-Gogh ⊘ (**Z**) – This centre was originally a hospital where Van Gogh was treated in 1889; the courtyard is lined with arcades. The artist painted the garden which has been recreated on the basis of his painting entitled *Garden of Arles Hospital* and of a letter to his sister containing details of the plants grown. The buildings house various organisations: multimedia reference library, academic centre, school for literary translators, archives etc.

The Carte Triangle d'Or is a 10-day pass which provides cheaper entrance fees to museums and other cultural sites located in Arles, Nîmes and Avignon. It is available from the Tourist Information Centre in any of these three towns.

AUBAGNE

Population 41 100

Michelin map 84 folds 13 and 14 or 114 folds 29 and 30 or 245 fold 45 or 246 fold L

In the Huveaune valley, Aubagne lies in a verdant basin, dominated to the northwest by the Chaîne de l'Étoile. Its location is favourable to industrial expansion and local food production (important agricultural market centre). The once fortified town has preserved some of its old ramparts and a 12C church remodelled in the 17C.
Born in Aubagne (birthplace: 16 Cours Barthélemy), **Marcel Pagnol** (1895-1974) was at the same time a writer of novels, poems, short stories and scenarios; he was also elected to the French Academy.
Other French celebrities born in Aubagne are Urbain Domergue and Abbé Barthélemy, both members of the Académie Française, as well as Dr Fallen, an authority on the Provençal language, and Claude Sicard, who invented the earthenware cicada, known throughout the world.

Légion Étrangère (French Foreign Legion) – Founded by King Louis-Philippe on 10 March 1831, the legion was to be a light infantry regiment that accepted all foreigners on the verge of receiving their naturalisation papers. For more than a century the legion has been in continuous combat. On 30 April, the legion celebrates the heroic stand of one of its regiments in **Camaron**, Mexico, in 1863. In this village, 64 men under the orders of Captain Danjou stood out, without hope, against 2 000 Mexicans for more than 9 hours. On this commemorative day tradition has it that the youngest officer reads before the other *légionnaires* the account of this battle.

Clay quarries – Aubagne's pottery tradition, which developed as a result of its clay quarries, dates back to Antiquity. This tradition became established during the Gallo-Roman period with the manufacture of amphorae and ceramics and turned to tile production in the Middle Ages.
In the 19C, the production of *santons* was started, carried on today in a score of cottage industries dotted throughout the old town. The ceramic coating of ships such as the *Normandie*, the *France* or the *De Grasse* originates from Aubagne's workshops.

Events Commemorating the Clay Industry in Aubagne
Every two years (odd years) in August the town hosts "Argilla", an important religious celebration where a great many potters congregate to present their prestigious ceramics.
Every two years (even years) in May faience makers from all over France meet in Aubagne to attend the Journées Nationales de la Faïence.
All summer and during the month of December a santon fair is held along Cours Maréchal-Foch.

SANTON AND FAIENCE MANUFACTURERS IN AUBAGNE

Historical Centre – It lies within the ancient fortified ramparts of which a few vestiges remain, namely the 14C Gachiou doorway, one of the seven original gates that gave access to the medieval city. The small, narrow streets reveal a number of architectural curiosities – the quaint triangular belfry of the late 17C Chapelle de l'Observance (*Place de l'Observance*), the Tour de l'Horloge and its superb wrought iron bell tower, the fine white Baroque front of the Chapelle des Pénitents Blancs and the more Classical façade (1551) of the Chapelle des Pénitents Noirs (*Chemin de St-Michel*), not to mention the 11C Eglise St-Sauveur, which houses a *Virgin with Child* sculpted by followers of the artist Puget.
Set up in the heart of this district, the **santon and ceramics workshops** ⊘ open their doors to visitors all year round. See illustration of *santon* figurines *(p 29)* and workshop *(p 294)*.

Ateliers Thérèse-Neveu ⊘ – This huge exhibition hall occupies the former workshop of Thérèse Neveu, who was a famous *santon* maker from Aubagne. It is devoted to the art of clay and other related industries. It features a standing retrospective on the history of ceramics in Aubagne and hosts temporary exhibitions on a variety of themes associated with *santons* and pottery.

CELEBRATING THE MEMORY OF MARCEL PAGNOL

Birthplace of Marcel Pagnol – It was in this house, situated at no 16 Cours Barthélemy, that Marcel Pagnol – author, playwright, film director and member of the Académie Française – spent his early childhood days.

Le Petit Monde de Marcel Pagnol ⊙ – This Small World of Marcel Pagnol consists of a panoramic crib with *santons* illustrating the popular characters that feature in Pagnol's films and literary works. In December these figurines are replaced by traditional religious personalities to form an impressive Christmas crib *(a similar crib is set up along the Cours Foch around the same period)*.

Marcel Pagnol Walks ⊙ – Three circuits organised by the Tourist Information Office will take visitors to some of the writer's favourite spots, accessible either by foot or by coach: Raimu's well, Manon grotto, Grosibou grotto, La Treille, Bastide Neuve... One can also choose to visit these places on one's own by following the signposted paths, allowing for either half a day or a whole day depending on one's destination *(explanatory brochure available from the Tourist Information Centre)*.

ADDITIONAL SIGHT

★Musée de la Légion Étrangère ⊙ – *Access via D 2 towards Marseille, turn right on D 44ᴬ.* On the ground floor, the great hall opens onto the **salle d'honneur** which exhibits memorabilia belonging to the legion's great leaders; further on, the crypt contains a touching list of the dead. The **museum**, on the first floor, presents numerous historical documents, photographs, arms and uniforms. In the main courtyard, the Sacred Way (*Voie Sacrée*) from the Viénot district in Sidi-Bel-Abbès (Algerian headquarters) has been recreated; the way ends with a memorial to the legion's dead, brought back from Algeria.

EXCURSIONS

Chapelle St-Jean-de-Garguier – *5.5km/10mi northeast on D 2, turn left on D 43ᶜ and right on D 43ᴰ.* Rebuilt in the 17C, this chapel, consecrated to St John the Baptist, is the object of an annual pilgrimage on 24 June. More than 300 ex-votos (painted on wood, canvas or zinc), mainly dating from the 18C and 19C, although some go back to the 15C, hang on the chapel walls. A small museum giving off the chapel displays documents relating to this small priory's history (17C missals, 18C religious art, two carved low reliefs).

Parc d'Attractions OK Corral ⊙ – *16km/10mi east on N 8.* Below N 8, in the centre of a pine forest clearing with the Ste-Baume massif serving as a backdrop, lies this exceptional amusement park (loop-the-loops roller coaster, Titanic, Tokaido Express, scenic railways, looping star).However there are also more restful activities and games for visitors of all ages. A chairlift and a small train provide a quick, comfortable tour of the park. Snack bars, *crêperies* and picnic areas have been set up.

AURIOLLES

Population 166
Michelin map 80 fold 8 or 245 fold 1 or 246 fold 22

On the plateau separating the lower Chassezac valley from the Beaume gorges, not far from Auriolles, stands the isolated Languedoc *mas*, the Mas de la Vignasse, which contains **Alphonse Daudet** memorabilia.

Mas de la Vignasse ⊙ – *When you draw level with the church in Auriolles, bear right on the uphill road from Ruoms; about 500m/0.3mi further on an effigy of the author announces the entrance to the* mas.

Restored and transformed into a museum (**Lou Museon dou Bas-Vivarès**), this farmhouse belonged to the Reynauds, Alphonse Daudet's cousins on his mother's side, who were sericulturists and merchants. In the cocoonery and courtyard is housed the **Musée des Arts et Traditions** Rurales which displays thousands of objects (17C olive oil press, 18C still, wine press, ploughs 18C-20C, bread and lime ovens, tools used in chestnut cultivation, 16C loom, lace, workshop for wool, hemp and silk spinning, sericultural tools...) evoking daily life in an important *mas* of yesteryear.

The sericulturist's home (1714) contains the **Musée Alphonse-Daudet**, which revives the author's epoch (1840-97). It was here that Daudet wrote his only book of poems *Les Amoureuses* (1858). Manuscripts, documents and newspaper cuttings are exhibited alongside family portraits. Note the photograph of Henri Reynaud, Daudet's cousin, whose hunting stories served as inspiration for the famous Tartarin in *The New Don Quixote or the Wonderful Adventures of Tarascon*.

★Walk to Labeaume – *30min return on foot. On leaving Mas de Vignasse turn right and 800m/0.5mi further on leave the car near a group of houses. At the crossroads take the left path and 500m/0.3mi further on a path through a pine forest and acacia copse. On the way down, the path opens out facing Labeaume.*

AVIGNON★★★

Population 181 136
Michelin map 81 folds 11 and 12 or 245 fold 16 or 246 fold 25
Local map see Basse Vallée de la DURANCE
Plan of conurbation in the Michelin Red Guide France

City of art and culture, on the borders of three *départements* (Bouches-du-Rhône, Gard and Vaucluse), Avignon stretches in all its beauty along the banks of the River Rhône. Peppered with bell towers emerging from a mass of pink roofs, the city is surrounded by ramparts and dominated by the Rocher des Doms, on which stand, majestically, the cathedral and Palais des Papes. It is from the City of the Cardinals, Villeneuve-lès-Avignon, opposite, that Avignon should be admired, especially at sunset.

Owing to its administrative *(Préfecture of the Vaucluse)* and cultural functions, Avignon is essentially concerned with tertiary activities. Already placed at the head of an important agricultural region – Comtat Venaissin – the city is equally developing a number of commercial and industrial activities (chemicals, fertilisers, ceramics, foodstuffs) concentrated east of town (Le Pontet, Montfavet and airport). **Boat trips on the Rhône** ⊘ are organised leaving from Avignon (**DY-FY**).

Avignon – Pont St-Bénézet and Palais des Papes

Festival d'Avignon – The bustling atmosphere which pervades the city is due, for the most part, to the annual **Festival d'Art Dramatique** (Festival of Theatre, Dance and Music) founded in 1947 by Jean Vilar (1912-71: actor and director). Attracting a cosmopolitan crowd flocking here from all over the world, the festival is the source of a cultural explosion which other Provençal towns have tried to recreate. Aside from the great theatrical events, the many and varied spectacles of both the mainstream and the fringe festival, which tend to recall the popular pageants of the Middle Ages, illustrate various art forms (dance, music, cinema etc) They make use of the enchanting historical monuments, which are a hive of activity, and overflow into the street where a festive atmosphere is much in evidence. The city has adapted over the years and acquired appropriate cultural facilities: Conference Centre (in the Palais des Papes), Petit Palais, Livrée Ceccano (Media Library).

HISTORICAL NOTES

Before the popes – The presence of man has been noted on and around the Rocher des Doms since the Neolithic Era (4 000 BC). In the 6C or 5C BC, the Massalians founded a settlement establishing Avignon as a river port; it began to flourish. On becoming a Gallo-Roman settlement with a Gallic, then Roman code of law, the town developed and prospered; unfortunately there remain only a few ruins of the monuments which embellished it (in the area around Place de l'Horloge, which covers the forum).

Following the invasions of the 5C, Avignon fell into oblivion through the early Middle Ages. We do know, however, that Avignon took sides with the Arabs and that it was therefore pillaged by Charles Martel's soldiers in 737. The rebirth occurred in the 11C and more so in the 12C. Avignon took advantage of the feudal rivalries between the Houses of Toulouse and Barcelona to protect and reinforce its independence: like its Italian counterparts, Avignon formed a small city state. Its commitment in favour of the Albigensians brought about royal reprisals: in 1226, Louis VIII seized the town, ordering it to raze its defences. Nevertheless, Avignon rose again quite quickly, and, in spite of losing its independence, regained its former prosperity under the rule of the House of Anjou.

The popes at Avignon – Avignon's destiny changed in the early 14C with the exile of the pontifical court to France, bringing with it a century of brilliance.

The court in Rome had become more or less impossible for the popes, who were incessantly the object of political differences. The Frenchman Bertrand de Got (former archbishop of Bordeaux), elected pope under the name of **Clement V** (1305), decided under pressure from Philip the Fair (who thought that he would make the pope a docile instrument of his wishes) to establish the court in France, where the Holy See possessed (since 1274) the Comtat Venaissin. Clement V solemnly entered Avignon – belonging to the count of Provence – on 9 March 1309. However, he did not reside here permanently as he preferred the calm of Groseau priory, near Malaucène, or Monteux castle, not far from Carpentras. He died in 1314 and the conclave was unable to find a successor. Finally in 1316, the former bishop of Avignon, Jacques Duèse, an old man of 72, was elected. **Pope John XXII** settled in the episcopal place located south of the cathedral; **Benedict XII**, a former Cistercian monk, established the court in a place worthy of it. **Clement VI** purchased Avignon from Queen Joan I of Sicily, countess of Provence, in 1348 for 80 000 florins.

Babylonian captivity – From 1309-77, seven French popes succeeded each other at Avignon: Clement V (1304-14), John XXII (1316-35), Benedict XII (1335-42), Clement VI (1342-52), Innocent VI (1352-62), Urban V (1362-70) and Gregory XI (1370-78).

The pontifical and cardinal courts lived on a grand scale; in their wake evolved a crowd of foreigners, ecclesiastics, artists, pilgrims, litigants and merchants. The university, founded in 1303 by Boniface VIII, numbered thousands of students. The town was transformed: convents, churches and chapels, not to mention the splendid cardinals' palaces, *livrées (see VILLENEUVE-LÈS-AVIGNON)*, sprouted everywhere, while the pontifical palace was constantly being enlarged and embellished. Avignon looked like a vast construction site. The pope wanted to be considered the most powerful ruler in the world. His wealth and munificence shone brilliantly, attracting the notice of the envious, which was why he lived in a fortress and established a line of fortifications to protect the town from mercenary soldiers who pillaged the country where war raged. These soldiers descended upon the city several times; each time the pope had to buy their departure for a very large sum of money: 40 000 *écus* in 1310, 100 000 *écus* in 1365. And yet life in Avignon remained pleasant: liberty and prosperity existed and, a sign that never failed, the population jumped from 5 000 to 40 000. A place of asylum for political refugees like Petrarch, the pontifical city also housed a Jewish community. But this tolerance extended, unfortunately, to adventurers, escaped criminals, smugglers and counterfeiters, who frequented taverns and brothels which cropped up everywhere, and worked their way through itinerant merchants and onlookers alike. The Italians railed against the court at Avignon and declared the pontifical court's years of exile as the Second Babylonian Captivity. The poet **Petrarch** campaigned passionately for the return of the Holy See to Rome and launched violent abuse against Avignon. Tottering under the mass of criticisms and scourges of the time (marauding soldiers, plague), the popes thought of returning to Rome. **Urban V** left for the eternal city in 1367, but hostility in Italy forced him to return to Avignon after three years. **Gregory XI**, convinced by St Catherine of Siena, finally left Avignon in September 1376, to the displeasure of the king of France. The pope's death in 1378 created the Great Schism of the West.

Popes and Schismatic Popes – The cardinals (majority French) of the Sacred College hostile to the reforms of the Italian Pope Urban VI, successor to Gregory XI, elected another pope **Clement VII** (1378-94) who returned to Avignon. The Great Schism divided the Christian world; the Avignon pope was recognised mainly in France, Naples and Spain. Popes and schismatic popes mutually excommunicated each other and attempted by any means possible to bring the other down. They vied with each other for the papacy's great wealth, which included levies on various benefices and tithes, taxes paid by litigants to the pontifical court, sales of positions, bulls etc and finally, on a scale which expanded daily, the traffic of indulgences. **Benedict XIII** (1394-1409) succeeded Clement VII; however, he no longer had the support of the king of France. He fled Avignon in 1403, yet his followers resisted in the palace until 1411. The Great Schism finally ended in 1417 with the election of Martin V. Meanwhile life continued in Avignon as is suggested by the presentation of the *Mystères* (mystery plays enacting an episode of the Scriptures) during Whitsun in 1400, with huge living tableaux and processions which went on for three days and dramatised the Passion of Christ. The modern festivals *(see the Calendar of events at the end of the guide)* which are held in and around Avignon revive this medieval tradition.

The city of penitent brotherhoods – Appearing as early as the 13C, the penitent brotherhoods were at their peak in the 16C and 17C. The brothers were expected to help each other, do public penance and perform good deeds. The brotherhood they belonged to was identified by the colour of their sackcloth and the hood which covered their heads during processions. Avignon was a city where many different brotherhoods – grey, white, blue, black, purple and red – coexisted. The White Penitents were the most aristocratic and included among their members Charles IX and Henri III. Each brotherhood had assets and a chapel: a number of these chapels are still standing (the most interesting are those of the Grey Penitents and Black Penitents). During the Revolution they were disbanded and yet several brotherhoods managed to survive.

Avignon at the time of the legates – Until the Revolution, Avignon was governed by a papal legate and a vice-legate. This friendly, hospitable city remained a centre of art and culture: publishing flourished in the 18C, during the time when the now famous Aubanel dynasty appeared. Tolerance toward the Jews was practised even though some persecution occurred. Confined to a ghetto, which was locked every night, the Jews of the pope had to wear a yellow cap, pay dues, listen to sermons preached to convert them; moreover they were not allowed to mix with Christians, they could only occupy certain positions and they were under constant surveillance.

Avignon society was a society of contrast: the gulf between the wealthy and poor was as great as the confrontation between them from 1652 to 1659. At the Revolution, Avignon was split between the partisans wanting to belong to France and those who wanted the pontifical state maintained. The former won, and on 14 September 1791 the constitutional assembly voted the union of the Comtat Venaissin to France.

STAYING IN AVIGNON

Cafés and Bars – **Cours Jean-Jaurès/Rue de la République:** the main street, bustling with shoppers during the day, and lively with pavement cafés and cinemas in the evening. **Place de l'Horloge:** the town's main square, lined with café and restaurant terraces, including the L'auberge de France wine-bar, and the piano and laser-karaoke bar, the Cyrano. **Rue des Teinturiers:** the Woolloo Moolloo bar at no 16, a former art studio, is popular with young people; at no 22, La Tache d'Encre theatre-restaurant-café holds concerts and bodega evenings. **Other good places:** La Mirande tea-rooms, 4 Place de l'Amirande, holds classical concerts in season, in the hotel of the same name; boat-restaurant Le Mireio, Allée de l'Oulle, offers candle-lit dinners with musical entertainment. In Rue de la Petite-Fusterie the tea room Simple Simon serves English specialities while Les Félibres, another tea shop at nos 14-16 Rue du Limas, has set up a bookstore on its premises. Le Cloître des Arts, erected on the former site of the 17C Collège d'Annecy offers a variety of activities: restaurant, tea room, bookshop, furniture and handicraft store as well as a gallery and art academy (no 83 Rue Joseph-Vernet).

Festival d'Avignon – **Mainstream events:** theatre, dance, lectures, exhibitions, meetings, concerts given in the main courtyard of the Palais des Papes, in the municipal theatre, in the many cloisters and churches of the town, as well as at Villeneuve-lès-Avignon and other outlying areas, such as the Boulbon quarry (Carrière de Boulbon), Montfavet or Châteaublanc. **Fringe events:** in the Place des Palais-des-Papes and dotted around the town.

To receive the programme and reserve apply to the Bureau d'Avignon, 8 bis Rue de Mons ☎ 04 90 27 66 50. Bookings available from the first fortnight in June by telephone ☎ 04 90 14 14 14; by Minitel 3615 Avignon; from FNAC booking offices, St-Louis d'Avignon, Rue Portail-Bocquier in Avignon or at the reception of the charterhouse (Chartreuse) at Villeneuve-lès-Avignon.

To receive a programme of the fringe events, send a stamped envelope (11.50 francs) to Avignon Public Off, B.P.5, 75521 Paris Cedex 11 ☎ 01 48 05 01 19 or consult the minitel 3615 AVIGNONOOF.

★★★PALAIS DES PAPES ⊘ (EY) *1hr*

The palace is a veritable maze of galleries, chambers, chapels and passages, now empty and deserted. That is why the visitor must try to imagine what it was like at the time of the popes...

Picture its luxurious furnishings, sumptuously-painted decoration, the discreet comings and goings of prelates and servants, the changing of the guards in dress uniform, the cardinals, princes and ambassadors arriving and departing, the pilgrims gathered in the courtyard waiting to receive the pope's blessing or to see him leave on his white mule; the litigants and magistrates creating commotion around the pontifical court and myriad other activities.

Construction – This princely residence counts among the largest of its time with an area of 15 000m²/2.6 acres. It is both a fortress and a palace and is made up of two buildings joined together: the Palais Vieux to the north and the Palais Neuf

Palais des Papes

to the south; its construction lasted 30 years. The Cistercian, Benedict XII, brought up in contempt of luxury, had the old episcopal palace razed and entrusted to his compatriot Pierre Poisson, from Mirepoix, the task of building a vast residence which would lend itself to prayer and be well defended: the Palais Vieux thus acquired the appearance of an austere fortress.

Planned around cloisters, its four wings are flanked by towers, the strongest of which, the north tower, Tour de Trouillas was used as a keep and prison. Clement VI, a great prince of the church, artist and prodigy, ordered Jean de Louvres, an architect from the Ile de France to carry out the expansion of the palace. The Tour de la Garde-Robe and two new buildings closed off the main courtyard which preceded Benedict XII's palace.

The exterior was not modified. However, inside, artists directed by Simone Martini and then Matteo Giovanetti sumptuously decorated the different rooms and notably the pope's private apartments. The works continued under Clement VI's successors: Innocent VI had Tour St-Laurent built to the south and Tour de la Gache to the west and the decoration completed (fresco on the vault in the Grande Audience); Urban V had the main courtyard laid out with its well and had buildings constructed linking the palace to the gardens, behind the Tour des Anges.

In 1398 and again from 1410 to 1411, the palace was under siege resulting in the dilapidation of the buildings. Allocated to the legates in 1433, it was restored in 1516 but continued to deteriorate. In a bad state when the Revolution broke out, it was pillaged: furniture dispersed, statues and sculptures broken. In 1791 the Tour des Latrines (or Tour de la Glacière) was the scene of a bloody episode: 60 imprisoned counter-revolutionaries were massacred and their bodies hurled to the bottom of the tower. The palace owes its survival only to its transformation into a prison and barracks (1810). Occupied by military engineers, it was again mistreated: at least the statutory wash on the walls protected some of the mural paintings. Unfortunately, in many places, this safeguard came too late: the soldiers had had time to cut the protective coating off the frescoes and sell the pieces to collectors or antique dealers from Avignon.

Evacuated in 1906 the palace has been under restoration ever since.

Exterior – The palace from the outside has the appearance of a citadel built straight out of the living rock. Its walls, flanked by 10 large square towers, some more than 50m/164ft high, are buttressed by huge depressed arches holding up the machicolations: this is one of the first known examples of such military architecture. Built into the rock, it was naturally protected from sapping and mining.

Take the **Promenade des Papes** for a more striking impression of the height of the building. This follows the pretty little Rue Peyrollerie which leads off from the southwest corner and goes under the enormous buttress supporting the Chapelle Clémentine to emerge on to a square in which there is an attractive 17C townhouse. Go along Rue du Vice-Légat leading to Urban V's orchard, then under a vaulted passageway which opens onto Cour Trouillas. The Escaliers Ste-Anne lead up to the Rocher des Doms, giving a different view of the palace.

Ground Floor (Palais Vieux and Palais Neuf)

Go through the Porte des Champeaux, topped by two turrets (rebuilt in 1933) and the modern coat of arms of Clement VI, and enter the former guard room *(reception and ticket office)*, the walls of which are decorated with 17C paintings (**1**).

Petite Audience (**2**) – A law court consisting of a single judge was held in this Small Audience (or Contradictions) Chamber. Lawyers presented their "contradictions", or cases refuting the testimonies submitted to the Tribunal de la Rota, to this one judge. In the 17C, when this room was in use as an arsenal, the vaulting was decorated with grisaille paintings representing military trophies.

Turn round and go back through the Porte des Champeaux, which is decorated with a pendant archstone.

Main Courtyard – Running along the main courtyard to the north is the machicolated **Conclave Wing** Ⓐ which houses the **Conference Centre**. The Gothic south wing has a number of irregular openings in its façade and the Indulgence window (**15**) on the first floor. It is used during the summer as a backdrop for the theatrical performances of Avignon festival. In the centre of the courtyard there is a well dug by Urban V and the remains of the foundations of John XXII's Audience Chamber.

Enter the Palais Vieux through the small gate in the wall of the east wing of the private apartments, which was once adjacent to the west wing, of which there is now no trace.

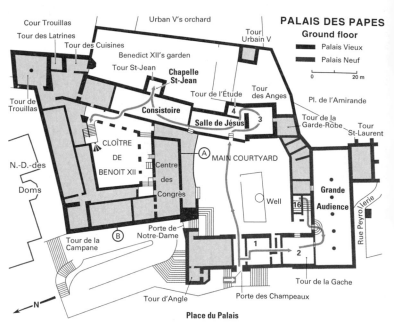

Place du Palais

Treasury (Grande Trésorerie) – This treasury, situated on a lower level with an enormous fireplace decorating the north wall, houses one or two 14C pieces, including glazed earthenware tiles and some alabaster statues. It is next to the **Lower Treasure House** (Trésor Bas), a beautiful vaulted room hollowed out beneath the Tour des Anges. Underneath the flagging were the hidey-holes in which the bags of silver and gold, silverware and valuable ornaments were kept. The cupboards on the walls contained the accounts ledgers and archives.

The wealth of the popes was considerable; ample proof of this is provided by a building such as the Palace at Avignon, which was built in less than 20 years. John XXII, born in Cahors, was able to bequeath 24 million ducats to his heirs after 19 years as pope. The size of the Papal revenue explains why the most important court dignitary was the chamberlain, that is the Minister of Finance. He was closely followed by the Treasurer, another very important figure.

Salle de Jésus – *Enter via the upper floor of the Treasury (staircase).*

Once decorated with monograms of Christ, which accounts for its name, this vast room used to serve as antechamber to the Consistoire.

Chamberlain's Bedchamber (**3**) – Situated just below the Papal Bedchamber, this room is magnificently embellished with a 14C painted beam ceiling and with foliated scrollwork covering parts of the walls. Eight hidey-holes are concealed in the flags on the floor.

Papal Vestiary (**4**) — This small room in the Tour de l'Étude was converted into a chapel in the 17C by the vice-legates. The original timberwork was reinforced by a stone vault. 18C woodwork from the then town hall conceals the walls.

Next to the Tour des Anges which contains the library *(not open to the public)* on the fourth floor is the Tour de la Garde-Robe (Palais Neuf). This was built by Clement VI, who found the austerity of Benedict XII's (his predecessor) apartments not at all to his taste. The bathroom was on the ground floor, and above this the two floors of the Tour de la Garde-Robe *(not open to the public)* contained the wardrobes in which the Pontif's garments were neatly hung.

Gardens planted on the terrace on the east side of the palace enabled the pope to take in air amid colourful flowers and greenery without leaving the palace.

Consistoire — To debate the great theories of Christianity, the pope and his cardinals met in council in this vast rectangular hall which burned down in 1413.

It was here that the pope announced the name of the newly-appointed cardinals and received the sovereigns and their ambassadors in great pomp, that Papal Nuncios reported on their mission, and that cases proposed for canonisation were examined.

Exhibited here are **frescoes** executed by the great artist **Simone Martini** which were brought from the porch of Notre-Dame-des-Doms cathedral (see below). A native of Siena, Martini is considered to be the most illustrious of the 14C Italian painters, together with Giotto.

Chapelle St-Jean or Chapelle du Consistoire — This oratory is adorned with lovely frescoes painted by Matteo Giovanetti from 1346 to 1348 which depicted the lives of the two Saint Johns: Saint John the Baptist and Saint John the Evangelist. From Viterbo in Latium, Matteo Giovanetti can be considered as Clement VI's official court painter.

On leaving the Consistoire, follow the lower gallery of Benedict XII's cloisters and take the staircase to the banqueting hall. There is a fine view of the **Staff Wing** ⑧ — where the staff (persons holding various functions) and the main servants lodged — Tour de la Campane and Benedict XII's chapel.

First Floor (Palais Vieux and Palais Neuf)

Grand Tinel or Banqueting Hall — In this hall, one of the largest in the palace (48m/157ft long and 10.25m/33ft wide), is exhibited a superb series of 18C Gobelins **tapestries**. The immense panelled keel-vaulted roof (in the form of a ship's hull) has been restored.

Continue into the **upper kitchen** (**5**) with its huge chimney in the form of an octagonal pyramid, located on the topmost floor of the Tour des Cuisines. This tower was also used as the pantry and provisions storeroom. Next to it, the Tour des Latrines (or Tour de la Glacière — *not open to the public*) offered on each floor common latrines for the soldiers and staff. It included a 22m/72ft pit where rainwater and used kitchen water were also directed; a main drainpipe took all the waste to a river which flowed into the Rhône. During a siege, the soldiers courageously went up the drainpipe, crossed the pit and appeared suddenly amid the camp of defending soldiers.

In the Latrines tower's pit, the bodies of the 60 political prisoners, who were imprisoned in the castle and killed in 1791, were buried under a blanket of quick-lime for one month. The bodies were pulled out by a crack made at the pit's bottom. As the Consistoire leads into Chapelle St-Jean, here the Banqueting Hall (which is above it) opens into Chapelle St-Martial.

Chapelle du Tinel or Chapelle St-Martial — This oratory is named after the **frescoes** of St Martial (apostle from the Limousin, Clement VI's native region) painted in 1344-45 by Matteo Giovanetti. They recount the life of the saint using a harmony of blues, greys and browns.

Chambre de parement — Next to the pope's bedroom, this antechamber, also known as the Robing Room, was used as a small waiting-room by those who had been accorded a private interview with the pope. Two 18C Gobelins tapestries hang on the walls.

Next to the Robing Room on the first floor of the Tour de l'Étude can be found Benedict XII's study (Studium) (**6**) with its magnificent tiles.

Along the west wall of the Robing Room the pope's private dining room (**7**) called the Petit Tinel was situated, and alongside it was the kitchen (or secret kitchen) (**8**); the rooms in this section of the palace were entirely destroyed in 1810.

Papal Bedchamber (**9**) — The walls of this room were richly painted against a blue background: birds entwined in vines and squirrels climbing oak trees. Designed in the window embrasures were exotic birdcages with open doors. The floor tiles of medieval inspiration have been recently reconstructed. The decoration of this room most probably dates from the reign of Clement VI, replacing the more severe decoration of Benedict XII.

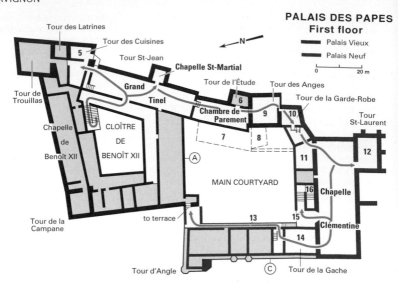

PALAIS DES PAPES
First floor

Palais Vieux
Palais Neuf

0   20 m

Tour des Latrines
Tour des Cuisines
Tour St-Jean
Chapelle St-Martial
5
Grand
Tour de l'Étude
Tour des Anges
Tour de la Garde-Robe
Tour de Trouillas
Tinel
6
Chambre de Parement
9
10
Tour St-Laurent
Chapelle de Benoît XII
CLOÎTRE DE BENOÎT XII
7
8
(A)
11
12
MAIN COURTYARD
16 Chapelle
Tour de la Campane
to terrace
13
15
Clémentine
14
Tour d'Angle
(C)
Tour de la Gache

Chambre du Cerf (10) – This room, known as the Stag Room, is Clement VI's study and is decorated with elegant **frescoes** painted in 1343 probably by Robin de Romans but under the direction of Matteo Giovanetti. The subjects illustrated against a verdant background are profane: hunting, fishing, fruit and flower picking and bathing scenes. The ceiling in larch wood is wonderfully ornate. This intimate and gay room had two windows: one offered a fine view of Avignon and the other overlooked the gardens. Above it was the Oratoire St-Michel *(not open to the public)*, which at one time had been adorned with frescoes by Matteo Giovanetti; only a few traces in red chalk remain.

To get to the Chapelle Clémentine, cross the **north sacristy (11)** comprising two vaulted bays on diagonal ribs and containing plaster casts of characters who figured significantly in the history of the Avignon Papacy. The bridge which was built by Innocent VI to link the pope's private dining room with the chapel led into the east bay.

Grande Chapelle or Chapelle Clémentine – This contains a pontifical altar which was largely restored (a part of it is authentic). The proportions of the flattened nave – 15m/49ft wide, 52m/171ft long and only 20m/66ft high – are due to the fact that the chapel's construction was decided afterwards: the architect had to cover the whole width of the Grande Audience without exceeding the average height of the castle.

South of the pontifical altar, an opening leads into the Cardinals' vestry (**12**) in Tour St-Laurent, where the pope changed vestments when officiating at high mass. It contains casts of recumbent figures of the popes: Clement V, Clement VI, Innocent VI and Urban V.

In this chapel, the Conclave of cardinals came to hear the Mass of the Holy Spirit before returning to the **Conclave Wing** Ⓐ via a narrow passageway called the Conclave gallery (**13**), which has marvellously elegant vaulting. The doors closed behind them and did not open again until they had elected a pope with a two-thirds majority vote.

The **Conclave** was made up of the college of cardinals, who met 10 days after the death of the pope, to elect a successor. The first floor of the Palais Vieux was used to receive the cardinals; and in order to isolate them from the rest of the world all the doors and windows were blocked up 8m/26ft high. Some of the rooms were divided into individual cells for the cardinals, whereas others housed the numerous domestics who assisted them. This tradition goes back to the 13C when at the death of Pope Clement IV in 1268 the cardinals were unable to decide upon a successor. Three years later the pope had still not been elected. The people locked them up in an area reserved for the vote and freed them only after the election of the new pope had taken place. Thus the word *conclave* means under lock and key.

Chamberlain's New Bedchamber (14) – This occupies the far south end of the **High Dignitaries' Wing** Ⓒ, which also houses the bedchamber of the Treasury notaries and the Treasurer's apartment.

Terrasse des Grands Dignitaires – *On the second floor of the High Dignitaries' Wing.* This terrace offers an extensive **view**★★ over the upper storeys of the Palais des Papes, the Tour de l'Horloge, the dome of the cathedral, the Petit Palais and, further in the distance, Pont St-Bénézet and the monuments at Villeneuve-lès-Avignon (Tour Philippe-le-Bel, Fort St-André).

Turn back in the other direction to come across the loggia opposite the doorway of the Chapelle Clémentine. From the window of this loggia the pope would bless the faithful crowds in the courtyard below, which is how the window came to be known as the Indulgence window (**15**).

Ground Floor (Palais Neuf)

Go down the Grand Escalier (**16**); the right-hand flight of stairs is covered with pointed vaulting, proof of bold architectural design for that time.

Grande Audience – This is a magnificent room with two aisles divided by a line of columns supporting the pointed arches of the vaulting. This is also called the Palais des Grandes Causes (Palace of the Great Causes), as it was here that the 13 ecclesiastical judges formed the Tribunal de la Rota – *rota* (wheel) comes from the circular bench on which they were seated and which is located in the room's last east bay. Around the judges sat the lawyers and the papal court's public servants. The rest of the room was for the public; seating ran along the whole of the room's wall. On the vaulting against a dark blue background sprinkled with stars is the fresco of the Prophets painted in 1352 by Matteo Giovanetti.

Cross the Petite Audience (**2**) and the guard room to leave the palace by the Porte des Champeaux.

PLACE DU PALAIS (EY **64**) *2hr*

Hôtel des Monnaies (Mint) (**B**) – This 17C town house (now the Conservatory of Music) is crowned with a balustrade and has an ornately carved **façade★** of dragons, eagles, Borghese coat of arms, cherubs and festoons of fruit.

Cathédrale Notre-Dame-des-Doms – Built in the mid 12C, the cathedral was damaged many times and each time rebuilt and altered. Pillaged during the Revolution, it began services of worship again in 1822.

In the 15C, the large bell tower was rebuilt from the first floor, and it has been crowned since 1859 by a very tall statue of the Virgin. A plain lantern tower crowns the bay preceding the chancel.

The porch was added in the late 12C in the Ancient style and shelters two tympana (a semicircular one surmounted by a triangular one) once magnificently-decorated with frescoes by Simone Martini and now located in the Palais des Papes. On the north side by the entrance, the 15C St John the Baptist Chapel contains a fine 16C Christ (Ecce Homo) in painted stone.

The single nave with five bays is roofed with pointed-barrel vaulting; the Romanesque appearance of the building was tempered by the addition of side chapels (14C-17C), the reconstruction of the apse and the construction of Baroque galleries in the 17C. The Romanesque **dome★** that covers the transept crossing is remarkable: to reduce the area, the master craftsman created a series of projections which supported the dome and its elegant columned lantern.

At the entrance to the chancel, on the left, stands a fine 12C white marble episcopal throne; on its sides are carved animals symbolising St Mark (lion) and St Luke (ox). The chapel adjoining the sacristy contains the Flamboyant Gothic tomb of Pope John XXII; its recumbent figure was lost during the Revolution and replaced by that of a bishop.

★★Rocher des Doms – There is a well-laid out garden planted with different species on this bluff. From the terraces superb **views★★** can be had of the Rhône and Pont St-Bénézet, Villeneuve-lès-Avignon with Tour Phillipe-le-Bel and Fort St-André, the Dentelles de Montmirail, Mont Ventoux, Vaucluse plateau, the Luberon hills and the Alpilles *(viewing table)*.

To follow the Promenade des Papes *(see above)* before rejoining the Place du Palais, take Escaliers Ste-Anne.

★★Petit Palais ⊘ – This was formerly Cardinal Arnaud de Via's livrée before being bought by the pope in 1335 to house the bishopric. The building deteriorated during the different sieges imposed upon the Palais des Papes, and had to be repaired and transformed in the late 15C, especially by Cardinal della Rovere, who subsequently became Pope Julius II.

Famous guests resided here: Cesare Borgia in 1498, François I in 1533, Anne of Austria and the Duke of Orléans in 1660 during Louis XIV's visit to Avignon.

Gallery 1 – This vast broken-barrel vaulted chamber contains **Romanesque and Gothic sculpture** (capitals, statues etc) and has a 15C chimney. On the walls there are parts of 14C **frescoes** originally from a cardinal's palace.

Gallery 2 – This, the former bishops' chapel, with pointed vaulting, presents a sculpture collection which comes from the monumental **tomb of Cardinal de Lagrange** built in the late 14C in the chancel of the Collégiale St-Martial. Note especially the carved figure (at the back of the room) which formed the tomb's base: the realism of the emaciated corpse anticipates the macabre representations of the 15C and 16C.

AVIGNON

Fourbisseurs (R. des) .... **EY** 34
Jaurès (Cours J.) .... **EZ**
Marchands (R. des) .... **EY** 49
République (R. de la) .... **EYZ**
St-Agricol (R.) .... **EY** 94
Vernet (R. J.) .... **EYZ**
Vieux-Sextier (R. du) .... **EFY** 122

Amirande (Pl. de l') .... **EY** 2
Arroussaire (Av. de l') .... **FZ** 3

Aubanel (R. Théodore) .... **EZ** 5
Balance (R. de la) .... **EY** 7
Bancasse (R.) .... **EY** 9
Bertrand (R.) .... **FY** 10
Bon-Martinet (R. du) .... **FZ** 13
Campane (R.) .... **FY** 14
Collège-d'Annecy (R. du) .... **EZ** 18
Collège-du-Roure (R. du) .... **EY** 19
Corps-Saints (Pl. des) .... **EZ** 20
David (R. Félicien) .... **EY** 22
Dorée (R.) .... **EY** 23
Folco-de-Baroncelli (R.) .... **EY** 28
Four (R. du) .... **FY** 33

Four-de-la-Terre (R. du) .... **FZ** 35
Galante (R.) .... **EY** 37
Grande-Fusterie (R. de la) ...... **EY** 39
Grottes (R. des) .... **EY** 41
Italiens (Av. des) .... **GY** 44
Jérusalem (Pl.) .... **EY** 45
Ledru-Rollin (R.) .... **FY** 47
Manivet (R. P.) .... **EFZ** 48
Masse (R. de la) .... **FZ** 52
Molière (R.) .... **EY** 54
Monclar (Av.) .... **EZ** 55
Mons (R. de) .... **EY** 57
Muguet (R.) .... **GY** 62

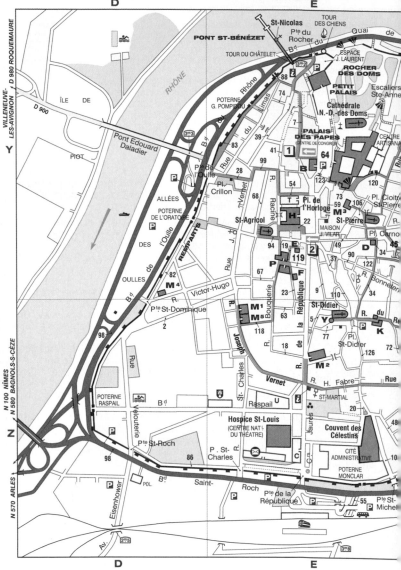

B Hôtel des Monnaies	**H** Hôtel de Ville
D Hôtel de Rascas	**K** Hôtel d'Honorati
E Palais du Roure	**K** Hôtel de Jonquerettes
F Hôtel de Sade	**K** Hôtel Berton de Crillon

K Hôtel de Fortia de Montréal
L Hôtel Salvador
M¹ Musée Calvet

Galleries 3 to 16 house an exceptional group of Italian paintings (13C-16C) which were part of the collection assembled in the 19C by Gian Petro, Marquess Campana di Cavelli, whose interest became an acquisitive obsession which ruined him. The Campana collection was bought by Napoleon III, but then dispersed throughout various French museums after 1870.

Gallery 3 – Tuscany, Rimini, Bologna, Venice 1310-70 – The works of the 13C betray the strong Byzantine influence which still prevailed (fragment of a Crucifix by Berlinghieri and *Last Supper* by the Master of the Madeleine). The intense artistic

Ortolans (R. des) .... **EZ** 63
Palais (Pl. du) .... **EY** 64
Palapharnerie (R.) .... **FY** 66
Petite-Calade (R. de la) .... **EY** 67
Petite-Fusterie (R. de la) .... **EY** 68
Petite-Saunerie
   (R. de la) .... **FY** 70
Pétramale (R.) .... **EZ** 72
Peyrollerie (R.) .... **EY** 73
Pont (R. du) .... **EY** 74
Prés.-Kennedy (Cours) .... **EZ** 76
Prévot (R.) .... **EZ** 77
Rascas (R. de) .... **GY** 79

Rempart-de-l'Oulle (R. du) .... **DY** 82
Rempart-du-Rhône (R. du) .... **EY** 83
Rempart-St-Michel
   (R. du) .... **FZ** 84
Rempart-St-Roch
   (R. du) .... **DEZ** 86
Rhône (Pte du) .... **EY** 88
Rouge (R.) .... **EY** 90
St-Christophe (R.) .... **FZ** 97
St-Dominique (Bd) .... **DZ** 98
St-Étienne (R.) .... **EY** 99
St-Jean-le-Vieux (Pl.) .... **FY** 101
St-Jean-le-Vieux (R.) .... **FY** 102

St-Joseph (R.) .... **FY** 104
St-Michel (R.) .... **EZ** 105
St-Pierre (Pl.) .... **EY** 106
St-Ruf (Av.) .... **FZ** 108
Ste-Catherine (R.) .... **FY** 109
Saraillerie (R. de la) .... **EYZ** 110
Tour (R. de la) .... **GY** 116
Vernet (R. Horace) .... **EZ** 118
Viala (R. Jean) .... **EY** 119
Vice-Légat (R.) .... **EY** 120
Vilar (R. Jean) .... **EY** 123
3-Faucons (R. des) .... **EZ** 126
3-Pilats (R. des) .... **FY** 127

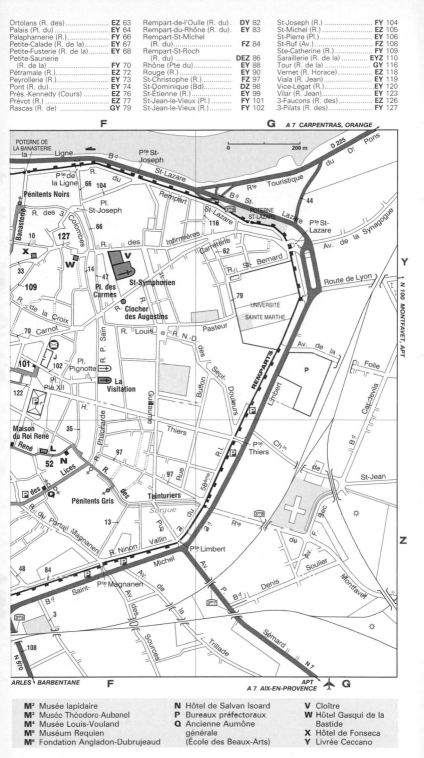

M² Musée lapidaire	**N** Hôtel de Salvan Isoard	**V** Cloître
M³ Musée Théodore-Aubanel	**P** Bureaux préfectoraux	**W** Hôtel Gasqui de la
M⁴ Musée Louis-Vouland	**Q** Ancienne Aumône	Bastide
M⁵ Muséum Requien	générale	**X** Hôtel de Fonseca
M⁶ Fondation Angladon-Dubrujeaud	(École des Beaux-Arts)	**Y** Livrée Ceccano

activity of the 14C is illustrated by the works of the Master of 1310 (a large *Virgin in Majesty* in the centre of the room), the Master of Figline *(God the Father Giving His Blessing)*, Taddeo Gaddi *(Virgin and Child)* and Paolo Veneziano *(Virgin and Child)*. These paintings adorned church altars; the polyptychs were set in a rich gilt Gothic style decoration.

Gallery 4 – Tuscany (Siena, Pisa, Lucca) and Liguria (Genoa) 1350-1420 – The Siennese School (to which Simone Martini, the painter of the Palais des Papes, belonged) shines with the wealth of ornamental decoration, its finely-executed

105

graphics and the beauty of its models, especially visible, for example, in the works of Taddeo di Bartolo *(Virgin and Child)*. It influenced the neighbouring cities, notably Pisa with Cecco di Pietro *(St Peter, St John the Baptist, St Nicholas and St Bartholomew)*.

Galleries 5 and 6 – Florence 1370-1420 – The Florentine School was very prolific and was inspired by Giotto, as is seen in the work of the Master of St-Verdiana (triptych of *the Virgin and Child* between several saints). The international Gothic style, characterised by a certain realistic naturalism, is represented by Lorenzo Monaco and Gherardo Starnina *(Angel and Virgin of the Annunciation)*.

Gallery 7 – Venice 1370-1470 – *Crucifixion* by the Master of the Pesaro Crucifix.

Gallery 8 – 15C Italy: Bologna, Umbria, Marches, Lombardy, Siena – The works of art exhibited in this room offer different facets of the international Gothic style outside Tuscany and Venice: Pietro di Domenico da Montepulciano's *Virgin of Mercy*, Antonio Alberti's *Virgin and Child between St Dominic and St Madeleine* and Giovanni di Paolo's triptych depicting the Nativity.

Gallery 9 – Florence and Tuscany, Perugia 1420-90.

Gallery 10 – Documents on the history of the museum and the Campana collection.

Gallery 11 – Florence, Umbria 1450-1500 – Florence, capital of the Renaissance, concentrated on the form of the drawing in balanced compositions where perspective plays an important role, especially with Bartolomeo della Gatta *(Annunciation)*. Botticelli, the master, introduces, in the late 15C, a new dimension at the same time lyrical and mystical; *Virgin and Child* is a masterpiece.

Gallery 12 – Padua, Venice, Marches 1440-90 – Note the violently expressionist Calvary, attributed to Ludovico Urbani, and the four figures of saints by Carlo Crivelli.

Gallery 13 – Marches, Umbria and Siena mid 15C to early 16C – In this room are works of differing style and inspiration: *Abduction of Helen of Troy* by Liberale da Verona, the altarpiece by Giovanni Massone ordered by Della Rovere, and works by Louis Bréa, the painter from Nice *(Presentation in the Temple, Assumption of the Virgin)*.

Gallery 14 – Florence and Lucca 1470-1500.

Gallery 15 – Florence and its surroundings c 1500 – The Renaissance rediscovers Antiquity, exemplified by the Master of the Cassoni Campana's four panels depicting episodes of Greek mythology.

Gallery 16 – Italy 15C-16C – Of note are: the large Florentine altarpiece of the *Coronation of the Virgin* by Ridolfo Ghirlandaio, a *Holy Conversation* by Vittore Carpaccio, an *Adoration of the Magi* by Johannes Hispanus in which an elaborate landscape of trees and castles appears, and a *Calvary with St Jerome* by Marco Palmezzano.

Galleries 17, 18 and 19 – These galleries are devoted to the painting and sculpture of the Avignon School. The Avignon School, because of the simplicity of its monumental composition, its sculptural force and the importance of light, can be placed midway between the realism of the Flemish School and the stylisation of the Italian Schools. Enguerrand Quarton, painter of the *Coronation of the Virgin* preserved in the Musée Municipal Pierre-de-Luxembourg in Villeneuve-lès-Avignon and the Pietà in the Louvre, is represented here by the significant *Requin Altarpiece* (1450-55). Josse Lieferinxe (panels of the altarpiece of the Virgin) came later, at the end of the 15C. Note the two anonymous works of the early 16C: *Descent from the Cross* from Barbentane and an admirable *Adoration of the Child*. On either side of a remarkable *Virgin of Pity* (1457) stand the works of Jean de la Huerta *(St Lazarus and St Martha)* and Antoine le Moiturier *(Angels)*.

1 QUARTIER DE LA BALANCE (EY) *45min*

The gypsies lived in this area in the 19C; it was renovated in the 1970s and descends as far as the ramparts and the bridge of the French song: *Pont d'Avignon*.

Start at Place du Palais, on a level with the Hôtel des Monnaies, and take Rue de la Balance.

Rue de la Balance (7) – This is the Balance district's main street. On one side are old restored town houses with elegant façades, decorated with mullioned windows; whereas on the other side are modern buildings in Mediterranean style, with small flower-decked patios and shopping arcades at ground level.

★★ Pont St-Bénézet ⊙ – In reality Pont St-Bénézet was a narrow bridge – for people on foot or on horseback; it was never such that one could dance in a ring as in the song: *Sur le pont d'Avignon l'on y danse tous en rond*; it was on the island beneath the arches of the bridge – in other words *sous le pont* – that the people of Avignon did their dancing.

Spanning two arms of the Rhône to Villeneuve-lès-Avignon at the base of the Tour Phillipe-le-Bel, the bridge was 900m/2 953ft long and composed of 22 arches. Another **gatehouse** dating from the 14C and 15C, which guarded the bridge on the Avignon side, has now been restored and gives access to the bridge. On one of the bridge's piers stands the **Chapelle St-Nicolas** consisting of two superimposed sanctuaries, one Romanesque and the other Gothic.

Legend has it that in 1177, a young shepherd boy, Bénézet, was commanded by voices from heaven to build a bridge across the river at a spot indicated by an angel. Everyone thought him crazy until he "proved" that he was inspired by miraculously lifting a huge block of stone. Volunteers appeared and formed themselves into a **Bridge Brotherhood** (*Frères Pontifes*), funds flowed in and in eight years construction was complete. Rebuilt from 1234 to 1237, the bridge was restored in the 15C and then broken by the flooded Rhône in the mid 17C.

On leaving the guards' room at the gatehouse, it is possible to get to Rocher des Doms via the Tour des Chiens in the north section of the ramparts.

★**Remparts** – The actual fortifications (4.3km/2.75mi long) were built in the 14C by the popes. From a military standpoint this is not a first-class work. It was backward in comparison with the defence procedures of the preceding century: the towers were open to the town, part of the walls had no machicolations. In fact the popes had not built an ultimate defence but a preliminary obstacle against attack on the palace. In the 19C, Viollet-le-Duc restored the southern section but unable to re-establish the moats where the River Sorgue branched off. The most interesting part is along the Rue du Rempart-du-Rhône to the pleasant Place Crillon; to the east, note the attractive façade of the 18C theatre (ancienne Comédie).

Return to Place de l'Horloge via Rue St-Étienne bordered by old town houses, Rue Racine to the right and Rue Molière to the left.

② OLD AVIGNON *allow half a day*

From Place de l'Horloge to Place du Palais

This route explores the churches, museums and particularly notable town houses in the part of Old Avignon to the south and to the east of the Palais des Papes.

Place de l'Horloge (**EY**) – The theatre and town hall overlook this vast square shaded by plane trees and in part occupied by open-air cafés.

In the little streets around the Place de l'Horloge there are windows painted with effigies of famous actors which bring to mind the city's theatrical vocation.

Hôtel de Ville (**EY H**) – Built in the 19C, the town hall includes the 14C and 15C **clock tower**. This former belfry, all that remains of the Gothic period, contains a clock with a Jack of the clock.

Take Rue Félicien-David and go around St-Agricol's east end.

Note the Gallo-Roman rampart ruins.

Église St-Agricol ⊘ (**EY**) – 14C-16C – A large staircase leads to the church's parvis overlooked by a finely carved 15C façade. In the tympanum is the Annunciation: the kneeling Virgin receives the angel while God the Father sends her the Holy Spirit. A 15C Virgin is on the pier. Inside there are a number of works of art: a mid-15C white marble stoup, paintings by Nicolas Mignard, Pierre Parrocel and in the south aisle, near the sacristy door, the Doni altarpiece, a work in stone by Boachon (1525) representing the Annunciation.

Rue Viala (**EY 119**) – The street runs between two 18C mansions housing the *Préfecture* (**P**) offices and the general council of the *département* (Conseil Général): to the north is the Hôtel de Forbin de Ste-Croix, once a school (Collège du Roure), and to the south is the Hôtel Desmarez de Montdevergues.

R. Mazin/TOP

Avignon – Place de l'Horloge

Palais du Roure ⊘ (**EY E**) – *No 3 Rue du Collège-du-Roure*. This is the former residence of the Baroncelli-Javon. A decoration of leafy branches frames the doorway. It houses the Flandreysy-Espérandieu Foundation, a centre of Provençal studies.

Hôtel de Sade (**EY F**) – *No 5 Rue Dorée*. This 16C mansion contains the offices of the Vaucluse département. Elegant mullioned windows overlook the street. In the courtyard there is a fine pentagonal turreted staircase.

Take Rue Bouquerie and Rue Horace-Vernet to the Musée Calvet.

★**Musée Calvet** ⊘ (**EZ M¹**) – *Some of the rooms are currently undergoing restoration but should be open to the public by the year 2000.* Set up in the former 18C Hôtel Villeneuve-Martignan, this celebrated museum was named after the physician Esprit Calvet who died in 1810 and who created the foundation that carries his name and that contains a great many works of art. The ground floor is taken up by the Puech bequest: French, Spanish, Flemish and Italian painting, a fine collection of French and Spanish 18C silverware, faience from Moustiers, Montpellier, Marseille and Venice, and in the room with the fireplace a wonderful display of Asian statues and 16C and 17C polychrome wooden statues (large sculpture depicting *St Paul on Horseback on the Road to Damascus*) as well as marble low reliefs from Italy. On the first floor the Galerie Vernet exhibits French paintings: *The Four Seasons* by Nicolas Mignard; large canvases by Joseph Vernet *(Morning by the Sea, Evening by the Sea)*; a strikingly vivid picture by Horace Vernet (*Mazeppa*); a moving *Death of Joseph Bara* by David. The adjoining rooms are devoted to painting from France, Italy and Flanders, spanning several centuries: 16C and 17C (*Saint Antoine Meditating* by Dominique Van Tol), 18C (*The Indiscretion* and *The Letter* by Jean Raoux; *Joséphine Grassini* by Elisabeth Vigée-Lebrun) and 19C (*Nymph Asleep near a Spring* by Théodore Chasseriau; *View of Italy* and *Mountain Landscape* by Corot; *Before Mass* by Victor Leydet).

Muséum Requien ⊘ (**EZ M⁵**) – *Next to the Musée Calvet*. Named after the Avignon naturalist Esprit Requien (1788-1851), this museum contains a very important natural history library, a herbarium with more than 200 000 specimens from all over the world, and a local geological, zoological and botanical collection.

Rue Joseph-Vernet (**EYZ**) – This long street, established on the site of the 13C ramparts (razed after the siege of 1226), is lined with a number of fine 17C and 18C *hôtels* (nos 58, 83 and 87). It opens out across from the Tourist Information Centre and the public gardens and runs into Cours Jean-Jaurès to the south and Rue de la République to the north.

Rue de la République (**EYZ**) – Lively and commercial main street.

The municipality of Avignon has set up a number of circuits throughout the town in order to enlighten visitors on its cultural and historical heritage. The

Morning by the Sea by Joseph Vernet

first one is laid out around the Palais des Papes and features seven explanatory panels (two on Place du Palais and the remaining ones in front of the Pont d'Avignon, before the Rocher des Doms, facing Villeneuve-lès-Avignon, near the Palais gardens and on Place de la Mirande).

★**Musée Lapidaire** ⊘ (**EZ M²**) – Located in the former chapel of the 17C Jesuit College, this building with its unique nave, flanked by side galleries, displays a fine Baroque façade.

It contains sculpture and stone carvings representing the different civilisations which have left their mark on the region: a bestiary in the Celtic tradition, featuring in particular the "Tarasque" of Noves, a man-eating monster; a number of Greek, Greco-Roman (a remarkable copy of Praxiteles' Apollo the Python killer) and local (Gallic warriors from Vachères and Mondragon) statues. Several portraits of emperors (Marcus Aurelius, Tiberius), anonymous people and low reliefs (relief of Cabrières d'Aigues representing a towing scene), sarcophagi and a remarkable series of masks from Vaison are also worth noting.

During the renovation work on the Musée Calvet, the Musée Lapidaire houses a section of the Egyptian display (collection of stelae and statues), the Greek display (Attic stele of a young girl with a doll), and votive and honorific reliefs.

Go back towards the Tourist Information Centre; bear left on Rue Henri-Fabre which goes into Rue des Lices.

In Rue Henri-Fabre stands the Abbaye St-Martial built between 1378 and 1388. The arcades standing in the neighbouring square are all that remain of St-Martial's Cloisters.

Rue des Lices (**EFZ**) – As its name indicates (*lice* means ward or bailey), this street traces the 13C curtain wall. On the left are the 18C buildings of the former almshouse (**FZ Q**) with its façade divided into galleried storeys; it houses the École des Beaux-Arts (School of Fine Arts). Next to it is the Chapelle du Verbe-Incarné by J.-B. Franque which is an evangelical church.

At the end of the street bear right on Rue des Teinturiers.

Rue des Teinturiers (**FGZ**) – The picturesque cobbled street shaded with plane trees follows the course of the River Sorgue, the waters of which were used by the cloth-dyers (after whom the street is named). Several of the large paddle-wheels, which were used by the printed calico manufacturers to make fine shawls until the end of the 19C, can still be seen. On the right is the Franciscans' bell tower, all that remains of a convent where Petrarch's Laura is believed to be buried.

Chapelle des Pénitents Gris ⊘ – *No 8.* A bridge leads to this 16C chapel, restored in the 19C. It contains paintings by Nicolas Mignard, Pierre Parrocel and Simon de Chalons. Above the altar is a 17C gold glory by Péru. A 15C house at no 26 still has its mullioned windows.

Turn around and walk back as far as Rue de la Masse.

Rue de la Masse (**FZ 52**) – At no 36 is the Hôtel de Salvan Isoard (**N**), a 17C mansion with ornately carved window surrounds; and at no 19 Hôtel Salvador (**L**) is an impressive 18C square mansion.

Rue du Roi-René (**EFZ**) – At the corner of Rue Grivolas stands the **Maison du Roi René** (**FZ**), where the king lived during his visits to Avignon; it is currently undergoing restoration work.

Further on four 17C and 18C town houses form a remarkable **group★** (**EZ K**).
The Hôtel d'Honorati de Jonquerettes (nos 10 and 12) is bare of decoration except for its pediments which are triangular or basket-handle.
The Hôtel Berton de Crillon *(no 7)* is emblazoned with portrait medallions, masks, flowers, garlands and adorned with a wrought iron balcony; in the inner courtyard is a grand staircase with a stone balustrade.
Across from it at no 8 is the Hôtel de Fortia de Montréal, less ornate, with pediments and grotesques.

On Place St-Didier, take the second street on the left, Rue Laboureur.

★★Fondation Angladon-Dubrujeaud ⊘ (**EZ M⁶**) – This lovely mansion, once the private residence of the Angladon-Dubrujeaud family, houses the prestigious collection belonging to the famous art lover Jacques Doucet, which his great nephew the painter Jean Angladon-Dubrujeaud subsequently complemented. The ground floor displays works by well-known 19C and 20C artists: Honoré Daumier *(Sancho Pancha)*, Van Gogh *(Train Carriages)*, Cézanne *(Still Life with Stoneware Pot)*, Sisley, Manet, Degas, Derain, Vuillard, Picasso, Modigliani *(The Pink Blouse*, 1919*)*, and two canvases by Japanese artist Foujita *(Self-Portrait* and *Madame Foujita*, 1917*)*. The first floor is furnished and decorated with great style, as befits the house of an art collector. Among the lavish furnishings note the late 16C wardrobe made of two parts, a canopied four-poster bedstead converted into a confessional (18C) and a curule wooden stool (c 1923) sheathed in shagreen, attributed to Pierre Legrain. You may admire a number of paintings and sculptures, in particular the *Portrait of a Gentleman* set in a superb frame enhanced with marble columns and inlaid with mother-of-pearl executed by Corneille de Lyon (c 1500: after 1574), a *Virgin with Child* in sculpted polychrome wood (late 13C), *The Dwarf Mari Barbola* by Vélasquez, a series of red chalk drawings by Lancret, Liotard and Boucher, *Portrait of the Painter Royer* by Jean-Baptiste Charpentier (1783). One room is devoted to the work of Jean Angladon-Dubrujeaud (1906-1979), whose technique was influenced alternately by Fauvism, Cubism and Surrealism, and to that of his wife Paulette Martin (1905-1988). The very last exhibition room presents works of art coming from Asia: late 7C Chinese statuette of a dancer, Chinese porcelain (during the reign of Emperor Kangxi, 1662-1722), Japanese engravings and paintings *(Rooster and Hen)* etc.

Walk back towards Place St-Didier.

Église St-Didier (**EZ**) – This 14C church is in the purest Provençal style with a pentagonal apse and single nave lined with chapels. Located in the first chapel on the south side is the dramatic 15C **altarpiece★** of the Carrying of the Cross by a Dalmatian artist, Francesco Laurana.

The baptismal font chapel at the north end is adorned with a group of **frescoes★** belonging to the second half of the 14C and attributed to Italian artists belonging to the School of Siena. Illustrated are the Deposition of the Cross, the Virgin and the Annunciation, St Gregory, St John the Baptist and the prophets.

Livrée Ceccano (**EZ Y**) – Across from St-Didier's south side rises the powerful tower of the mansion *(livrée)* built by the cardinal of Ceccano in the 14C and later incorporated into the Jesuit College. The building now houses the Avignon **media centre**.

Take Rue des Fourbisseurs and then bear right into Rue du Vieux-Sextier.

Place St-Jean-le-Vieux (**FY 101**) – Set at one corner of the square is a tall square tower (14C), all that remains of the Commandery of the Knights of St John of Jerusalem destroyed in the 19C.

On the small Place Jérusalem (**EY 45**) is the synagogue, which until the 19C was the heart of the Jewish District, also known as the Carrière.

Hôtel de Rascas (**EY D**) – *At the corner of Rue des Marchands and Rue des Fourbisseurs.* A fine 15C corbelled mansion can be seen.

Église St-Pierre (**EY**) – 14C-16C – On the church's west façade open two doors adorned with fine richly-decorated Renaissance **panels★**. Carved in perspective in 1551 by Antoine Valard, the subjects illustrate, on the right, the Virgin and the angel of the Annunciation, and on the left Saints Michael and Jerome.

Inside, in the chancel, there are elegant 17C **woodwork** framed painted panels. North of the chancel, the first chapel contains a 16C altarpiece carved by Boachon, the third chapel a 14C dalmatic (wide-sleeved vestment); south of the chancel the first chapel contains a 15C stone Entombment. A fine late-15C pulpit can also be seen.

Musée Théodore-Aubanel ⊘ (**EY M³**) – This museum is located on the ground floor of the Aubanel family home, a family of printers and publishers since 1744.

In the first room are assembled mementoes belonging to Théodore Aubanel, a founder of the Félibrige as well as paintings by Grivolas, Fromentin and a remarkable sailor's cross. The second room is especially concerned with old printing methods: hand press, font case (boxes containing characters), gilt stamp machine etc. In the display cases are exhibited rare editions and numerous documents relating to life in Avignon (13-20C).

Rue Banasterie (**EFY**) – This street is named for the basket-makers' guild *(banastiers* in Provençal). At no 13 the 17C Hôtel de Madon de Châteaublanc has a façade adorned with garlands of fruit, eagles and masks.

Further along the street there are glimpses of the cathedral's east end and of the Palais des Papes.

Chapelle des Pénitents Noirs ⊘ (**FY**) – On the chapel's façade, remodelled in the 18C, two angels, in the middle of a very large glory surrounded by cherubs, carry St John the Baptist's head (the brotherhood's emblem is the beheading) in a dish. The Baroque interior boasts a handsome group of woodwork and marble, paintings by Levieux, Nicolas Mignard and Pierre Parrocel. In the chancel the roof was painted by Pierre Courtois; note the Apotheosis of St John the Baptist.

Turn around; take Rue du Vice-Légat and Rue Peyrollerie to go back to Place du Palais.

ADDITIONAL SIGHTS

Musée Louis-Vouland ⊘ (**DY M⁴**) – The museum contains a decorative arts collection which concentrates on 18C French **furnishings**: a commode signed by Migeon, an inlaid backgammon table, a money-changer's desk and an amusing travelling table service stamped with the Countess Du Barry's coat of arms.

A fine collection of porcelain and **faience★** is displayed in two rooms; there are many examples of Moustiers and Marseille wares. A number of Flemish and Gobelins *(Pastoral Scene)* tapestries hang on the walls. Among the paintings exhibited is the small canvas of a *Child Eating Cherries* by the school of Joos van Cleve. The Far Eastern Art collection consists of a number of Chinese vases and plates and ivory polychrome statues.

Hospice St-Louis (**EZ**) – The buildings of the hospice date from the 17C and 18C. They surround a pretty **courtyard★** with magnificent plane trees framing a mossy fountain at its centre. Inside the buildings are the offices of the Centre National du Théâtre and a hotel-restaurant. The adjoining Baroque chapel is topped by a dome.

Couvent des Célestins (**EZ**) – 15C – Founded in 1393 on the tomb of Cardinal Pierre of Luxembourg, the convent was built in the Northern Gothic style. Its church with its fine east end and the cloisters have been restored.

Église de la Visitation (**FY**) – This former convent chapel (17C) has a finely carved façade adorned with a pediment.

Place des Carmes (**FY**) – The square is named after the former monastery of the Barefoot Carmelites of which the church and 14C cloisters (**FY V**) still remain. A wrought iron gate by the church's north wall marks the entrance to the cloisters.

Église St-Symphorien (or Église des Carmes) (**FY**) – 15C façade – The first north chapel contains three fine 16C statues in painted wood: Christ, Virgin and St John; in the succeeding chapels hang paintings by Pierre Parrocel *(Holy Family)*, Nicolas Mignard *(St Eligius)* and Guillaume Grève *(Adoration of the Magi)*.

Clocher des Augustins (**FY**) – This is all that remains of the Augustinian convent founded in 1261. Built from 1372 to 1377, the bell tower stands at the corner of the Place des Carmes. The bell cage was added later (16C).

Rue des Trois Pilats (**FY 127**) – At no 16 stands a 17C mansion, (**FY W**), the Hôtel Gasqui de la Bastide, with a triangular pediment.

Rue Ste-Catherine (**FY 109**) – At no 17, the Hôtel de Fonseca (**FY X**) built in 1600 is adorned with mullioned windows. It has a fine courtyard with an old well.

EXCURSIONS

★**Villeneuve-lès-Avignon** – *On the Rhône's south bank. Leave Avignon by Pont E. Daladier. See VILLENEUVE-LÈS-AVIGNON.*

Montfavet – *6km/3.5mi on D 100* (**GY**) *and N 7 to the right.* This small town possesses an imposing **church**, the only vestige of a monastery built in the 14C by Cardinal Bertrand de Montfavet. There remain two crenellated towers. An open-work bell tower caps the church which is framed by massive flying buttresses. Interesting carvings adorn the doorway's lintel. The vast and austere nave is covered by elegant Gothic vaulting and flanked by side chapels.

Parc du Soleil et du Cosmos ⊙ – *6km/3.5mi. Leave Avignon to the southwest on N 100, towards Nîmes. At the large roundabout intersection, take the first road on the right, towards Angles, then turn left towards the quarries.*

Set amid the pines and evergreen oak trees of the Mediterranean *garrigue*, this astronomy park invites visitors on an imaginary journey through space and time. The architecture of the buildings in superimposed terraces is not far removed from the "ziggurats" of ancient Mesopotamia, religious buildings which were believed to symbolise the union between earth and heaven. The planets, stars and asteriods each have a small information booth devoted to them, containing a pedestal bearing a proportionally-sized model of the astronomical body in question (on the scale used by the park, the sun has a diameter of 70cm/27.6in and the earth a diameter of 6mm/0.24in) and an information panel. Following the labyrinthine route among these information booths is an amusing way to get an overview of how human knowledge of the universe has built up over the centuries, from the first observations of classical astronomers to the pioneers of the conquest of space (early instruments, display of the head of a rocket, designs for rockets).

Barbentane – *9.5km/5.75mi on N 570* (**FZ**), *then right on D 35. See BARBENTANE.*

BAGNOLS-SUR-CÈZE

Population 17777
Michelin map 80 folds 10 and 20 or 245 fold 15 or 246 fold 24 – Facilities

To the old town of Bagnols, ringed by boulevards, on the site of the former ramparts, has been added the new city built for the workers of the Marcoule atomic works *(see MARCOULE).*

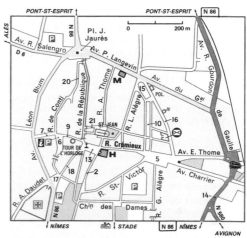

BAGNOLS-SUR-CÈZE

André (R. A.) 2
Boissin (Pl. Bertin) 5
Château (Pl. du) 6
Gentil (R.) 7
Horloge (R. de l') 9
Lacombe (Bd Th.) 10
Mallet (Pl. A.) 13
Mayre (Av. de la) 14
Pasterlon (Pl. du) 15
Perrin (Av. Jean) 16
Richard (Pl. U.) 17
Rivarol (R.) 18
Roc (R. du) 20
Verrerie (R. de la) 21

H Musée d'Art moderne
Albert-André
(Hôtel de ville)
M Musée d'Archéologie
Léon-Alègre

111

★**Musée d'Art Moderne Albert-André** ⊙ (**H**) – The Modern Art Museum shares the same building as the town hall *(second floor)*, a fine 17C mansion. It exhibits contemporary works collected by the painter **Albert André**, curator from 1918 to 1954, with the help of Renoir. In addition there are works by the 19C Lyonnais School, faïence from Moustiers and Marseille and commemorative portrait medals of painters and sculptors. The museum has also been endowed with the private collection of George and Adèle Besson. It is made up of artists' signed works – oils, watercolours, drawings, sculptures (Renoir, Valadon, Bonnard, Matisse, Marquet, Van Dongen).

Musée d'Archéologie Léon-Alègre ⊙ (**M**) – The Archeological Museum's collections originate from the Rhône valley and illustrate the different periods of Antiquity. Two rooms illustrate the Celtic-Ligurian civilisation and Greek influence from the 6C to the 1C BC: pottery, bronze wares, cult objects and sculpture. Along one gallery are assembled various Gallo-Roman remains: ceramics, amphorae, glassware, everyday objects and cinerary urns. Note the fine shop sign of a stone-carver with its mason's level, hammer and two scissors. One room is devoted to the site of the St-Vincent de Gaujac oppidum *(see below)*: reconstructed hypocaust, small pool originally from the baths, pottery and documents (photographs and plans).

Old houses – In **Rue Crémieux**, left of the town hall, note the classical doorways of nos 10, 25 and 29 and the large façade at no 15 adorned with overflowing cornices and huge gargoyles.

LE BAS-VIVARAIS *Round tour of 153km/95mi – allow 1 day*

Leave Bagnols-sur-Ceze on N 86 to the north and turn left onto D 980.

★**La Roque-sur-Cèze** – *2km/1mi on D 166. See La ROQUE-SUR-CÈZE.*

Chartreuse de Valbonne – *5km/3mi on D 23, then take the road to the left. See Chartreuse de VALBONNE.*

Goudargues – The village, ringed by massive plane trees, is dominated by its church. This former abbey church, partly rebuilt in the 17C and 19C, is interesting for its tall Romanesque apse, decorated inside by two storeys of arcading.
Continue along D 980.
Note on the right the old hill-top village of **Cornillon**.

Montclus – At the junction of D 980 and D 901, there is a lovely **view★** of this old village dominated by a tower.
Bear left on D 901 and then right on D 712 and D 417.

★★**Aven d'Orgnac** – *See Aven d'ORGNAC.*
Return to D 901, bear left on D 980 and just before St-André-de-Roquepertuis bear right on D 167.
The road winds through a desolate plateau. Turn right onto D 979 which, as it descends, offers fine views onto the deserted **Cèze gorges★**.
Leave to the right the village of Tharaux and take the road towards Rochegude. Then via D 16 and D 7 go to Brouzet-lès-Alès.

★★**Guidon du Bouquet** – The highest point of the Bouquet range is a beak-shaped rock which dominates the vast horizon extending between the Gard and Ardèche rivers. From the steep approach road the ruins of the Château du Bouquet are visible through the clumps of holm oaks. The **panorama★★** from the summit extends across the Cévennes causses to the west, the irregular crests of the Bas Vivarais range to the north, Mont Ventoux and the Alpilles to the east. From the statue of the Virgin there is a vertiginous view of the immense garrigue surrounding Uzès and to the rear of the television mast a view of the Bouquet range itself.
Return to Brouzet-les-Alès, take D 7 and turn right onto D 37.
The road rises offering a good view of the **ruins★** of Château d'Allègre. It continues through the garrigue to the hill village of **Lussan**.
At Lussan take D 143, then bear right on D 643.

★★**Les Concluses** – *See Les CONCLUSES.*
Once on D 143 turn left. Return to Bagnols-sur-Cèze via St-André-d'Olérargues.

Sabran – This old town is perched on a rock spike. From the foot of the giant statue of the Virgin, in the castle ruins, a vast **panorama★** unfolds over the surrounding countryside.

THE GARRIGUE AND CÔTES DU RHÔNE VINEYARDS
Round tour of 50km/31mi – allow 3hr

Leave Bagnols-sur-Cèze on N 86 southwards to Gaujac, turn right onto D 310 which passes below the village. Take a dirt road (signposted) uphill (unsuitable for cars).

Oppidum de St-Vincent-de-Gaujac – Perched on a height in the middle of a forest, this site was occupied intermittently between the 5C BC and the 6C AD and then again from the 10C to the 14C. During the Gallo-Roman era it was a rural sanctuary with temples and baths. Go through a fortified gate (the vestiges of a curtain wall and peribolus) to discover the ruins of the medieval fortified strong-hold with its cistern and the Gallo-Roman excavations. The latter dates from the Early Empire (1C-3C).

Above are the remains of a fanum, a small Roman temple; below are the **baths**, the arrangement of which can be seen with the remains of the hypocaust and drains. The sanctuary was abandoned in the 3C for an unknown reason.

Return to N 86 and 4km/2.5mi south, after Pouzilhac, turn left onto D 101.

The narrow and winding road crosses a landscape of garrigues and forest; shortly before St-Victor-la-Coste, there is a good view of the ruins of an imposing feudal castle dismantled during the Albigensian Wars.

St-Victor-la-Coste – On the border of the garrigues and vineyards, this picturesque old village *(under restoration)* huddles at the foot of its castle.

Continue along D 101.

On the left a narrow road leads to an isolated chapel. The countryside is now covered by the Côtes du Rhône vineyards. These wines are made from selected grapes and naturally have different names; the most well-known are Lirac and Tavel.

St-Laurent-des-Arbres – In the past this village belonged to the bishops of Avignon. It has preserved some interesting medieval ruins. The Romanesque **church** was fortified in the 14C: the walls were raised and a crenellated parapet was added; inside, the domes on squinches are adorned with symbols of the Evangelists. Near the church stands a rectangular keep from the Lords of the Sabran's castle. The base dates from the late 12C; it was raised in the 14C by a storey set back with crenellated arcades, battlemented turrets at the corners and a small square watch-tower. Not far from the keep, above the village is located another 12C square tower, subsequently remodelled.

Take D 26 to Lirac and Tavel.

These two wine-growing villages have given their names to excellent wines *(see Introduction: Food and wine in Provence).*

Return to St-Laurent-des-Arbres and then take N 580 back to Bagnols-sur-Cèze.

Château de La BARBEN*

Michelin map 84 fold 2 or 245 fold 30 or 246 south of fold 12

Château de La Barben occupies a precipitous site in the small Touloubre valley. The access ramp to the castle offers a plunging view onto the formal French gardens.

★**Château** ⊙ – The present castle was originally a medieval fortress, built before AD 1 000, belonging to the Abbaye St-Victor from Marseille and then to King René, who sold it to the powerful Forbin family. This family owned it for some 500 years and remodelled and enlarged it several times, especially in the 14C and 17C, when it was transformed into a stately home. Its round tower was recently rebuilt after an earthquake. In front of a noble 17C façade is the terrace (Henri IV Staircase with double flight of stairs), from where there is a good view of the gardens designed by Le Nôtre and of the Provençal countryside.

Inside, note the painted ceilings, 16C-17C Aubusson, Flemish and Brussels tapestries, and a fine painting by Largillière. The great drawing room is covered by a Second Empire Aubusson carpet. The reception hall is decorated with **Cordoban leather**★ made near Avignon in 1680. On the second floor the Empire-style bedroom of Pauline Borghese, Napoleon's sister, and her boudoir ornamented with paper painted by Granet and representing the Four Seasons, are also worth noticing.

Vivarium ⊙ – In the castle's former vaulted sheep's pen is a display of reptiles and tropical and European freshwater fish. The aviary contains birds from the five continents.

Parc Zoologique ⊙ – This 30ha/12-acre zoo features a number of enclosures in which over 400 animals roam in relative freedom: big cats, monkeys, elephants, giraffes, bisons, zebras and birds of prey.

Recreational Parks in the Area

Parc Zoologique de La Barben, see above.
OK Corral, see p 95.
El Dorado City, 13220 Chateauneuf-lès-Martigues ☎ 04 42 79 86 90.
La Pyramide (aquatic leisure park), Rue de l'Équerre, 13800 Istres ☎ 04 42 56 99 99.
Aquacity (aquatic leisure park), Plan de Campagne, Route de Septèmes, 13270 Les Pennes Mirabeau ☎ 04 91 96 12 13.
Le Village des Automates, RN 7, 13760 St-Cannat ☎ 04 42 57 30 30.

BARBENTANE

Population 3 273
Michelin map 81 fold 11 or 245 fold 29 or 246 fold 25 - Facilities

Built against the north slope of the Montagnette *(see p 197)*, Barbentane overlooks the plain near the confluence of the Rhône and the Durance, devoted to market gardening. Lying at the foot of the Tour Angelica (1365), the village has retained part of its 14C fortifications (Porte du Séquier, Porte Calendale) as well as the Maison des Chevaliers, a fine Romanesque residence dating back to the 12C.

Château ⓥ – The architecture of this elegant 17C château recalls the stately homes of the Île-de-France. A cornice surmounted by flame ornaments and pediments adorns the finely ordered façades. Terraces lined with stone railings decorated with lions and flower-filled urns open on to the formal gardens.

The interior, which is enhanced by the mementoes belonging to the marquis of Barbentane, features rich 18C **decoration★** of Italian influence. The vaulting, which used a particular stone-carving technique, plasterwork, painted medallions, coloured marble, Louis XV and XVI furnishings, Chinese porcelain and Moustiers faience all add to the charm of this delightful château.

Old village – All that remains from the fortifications are the two entrance gates, Porte Calendale, which opens onto the Cours, and Porte Séquier above the village.

Maison des Chevaliers (House of the Knights) – A lovely Renaissance façade composed of a turret and two basket arches topped by a columned gallery. Across the street is a 12C church, often remodelled, with its 15C bell tower (badly damaged).

Tour Angelica – Overlooking the village, the tower is the keep of the former castle, built in the 14C by the brother of Pope Urban V, Cardinal Anglic de Grimoard. From the terrace there is a good view of Avignon, Châteaurenard and in the distance Mont Ventoux. A short walk through the pines leads to the well-preserved 18C **Moulin de Bretoul** (Bretoul Mill), from where there is a lovely view of the Rhône plain. Near the cemetery, ruins of the old Roman way have been discovered.

Château de Barbentane – Main façade

*The current edition of the annual **Michelin Red Guide France** offers a selection of pleasant and quiet hotels in convenient locations. Their amenities are included (swimming pools, tennis courts, private beaches and gardens...)
as well as their dates of annual closure. The selection also includes establishments which offer excellent cuisine: carefully prepared meals at reasonable prices, Michelin stars for good cooking.
The current annual **Michelin Camping Caravaning France** lists the facilities offered by many campsites (shops, bars, restaurants, laundries, games rooms, tennis courts, miniature golf courses, playgrounds, swimming pools...).*

Les BAUX-DE-PROVENCE★★★

Population 457
Michelin map 83 fold 10 or 245 fold 29 or 246 fold 26
Local map see Les ALPILLES Facilities

Detached from the Alpilles, this bare rock spur – 900m/2 953ft long and 200m/656ft wide – with vertical ravines on either side, a fortified castle lying in ruins, and old desolate houses, compose the spectacular **site★★★** of the village of Les Baux, once a proud fief.

Bauxite – The red bauxite discovered in 1822 on the land of Les Baux, from which it takes its name, is a mineral consisting mainly of aluminium, iron trioxide and water. Extraction of the mineral has given rise to the immense modern aluminium industry. Nowadays bauxite is no longer mined in France: 70% of industrial needs are met by imports from Guinea.

Les Baux Vineyards ⊘ – These surround the village, in the area officially classified as "Coteaux d'Aix-en-Provence – Les Baux", covering the lower slopes of the north and south faces of the Alpilles. The grapes are well-favoured by the microclimate and the geological nature of the soil (calcareous substratum covered by a layer of clay and gravel) in which the vineyards are planted. The vineyards had already won renown in the Provence of Antiquity, and the quality of the wine they produce has since improved further, thanks to the meticulous care taken by the vine growers, some of whom use organic methods, resulting in excellent wines full of character. The vine stocks produce mainly red and rosé wines, but those white wines that are produced, though not numerous, are of high quality.
The 300ha/741 acres of cultivated land yield about 10 000hl/27 500 bushels annually, a proportion of which is exported. There is a signposted wine route (Route des Vins) which can be completed in an afternoon, providing a delightful introduction to the various vine growers' estates.

HISTORICAL NOTES

A warrior line – The lords of Baux were renowned in the Middle Ages, described by Mistral as: "warriors all – vassals never"; they were proud to trace their genealogy back to the Magi king, Balthazar, and, so that no one should ignore the fact, boldly placed the star of Bethlehem on their coat of arms!
From the 11C the lords were among the strongest in the south of France, having in their control 79 towns and villages. From 1145 to 1162 they warred against the House of Barcelona, whose rights to Provence they contested; supported for a while by the German emperor, they finally submitted after succumbing to a siege at Les Baux.
They won titles: members of different branches became variously princes of Orange, viscounts of Marseille, counts of Avellino and dukes of Andria (having followed the Capetian Princes of Anjou who were campaigning in southern Italy).
One of them married Marie of Anjou, sister of Joan I, queen of Sicily and countess of Provence, a lovely woman much loved by the people of Provence. She was destined to lead a tragic existence – three times a widow, she died in 1382, smothered by an ambitious cousin.

Courts of Love – Les Baux was famous as a court of love in the 13C. To become a member the women had to be of noble birth, well read and beautiful. In the company of this court, questions of gallantry and chivalry were raised and discussed.
Troubadours, often great lords, came from all the southern provinces and composed passionate verses in praise of these ladies *(see p 25)*. The prize awarded to the best poet was a crown of peacock feathers and a kiss from the lady in question.

Turenne, the brigand – The house of Turenne, from the Limousin, was a great family: two of its members were popes at Avignon, one of whom was the famous Clement VI. Another of its members was the Viscount Raymond de Turenne, nephew of Gregory XI, who became the guardian of his niece, Alix of Baux, in 1372. His ambitions caused civil war in the region. His pillaging and cruelty terrorised the countryside and he was appropriately named the "Scourge of Provence". His chief delight was to force his unransomed prisoners to jump off the castle walls.
The pope and the lord of Provence hired mercenaries to get rid of the brigands, but the mercenaries themselves ravaged the enemy territories as well as the territories to be protected; as a result their contract was broken and they were given 80 000 livres to leave the area. A truce with Turenne was struck in 1391 costing 30 000 *livres*. Peace was short-lived, and pillaging and fighting broke out quite soon. The king of France joined Turenne's enemies; in 1399 the "scourge" was surrounded at Les Baux; however, he escaped and fled into France.

The end – Alix was Baux's last princess, and on her death in 1426 the domain, incorporated into Provence, became simply a barony. King René granted it to his second wife Jeanne of Laval. Joined with Provence to the French crown, the barony revolted against Louis XI, in 1483, who subsequently had the fortress dismantled. As of 1528 the Constable Anne de Montmorency, who was titular Lord of Les Baux, undertook a large restoration project on the town which once again enjoyed a prosperous period. Les Baux then became a centre of Protestantism under the Manville family who administered it for the crown. In 1632, however, Richelieu, tired of this troublesome fief, had the castle and ramparts demolished and the inhabitants were fined 100 000 *livres* plus the cost of the demolition!

Les Baux was then granted as a marquisate to the Grimaldis, princes of Monaco. But what was once a proud town of 4 000 gradually disintegrated to become a shadow of its former self.

Les Baux-de-Provence

★★★THE VILLAGE *1hr*

D 27 leads to the town and has the advantage of plunging the visitor more quickly into the atmosphere of Les Baux.

Leave the car at the car park ⊘ located at the town's entrance and follow the itinerary marked on the town plan.

Mentioned below are the main sights to be seen on this itinerary, and yet while touring, the visitor will discover others *(signposted)*. Enter through the Porte Mage cut in 1866.

Ancien Hôtel de Ville – This deconsecrated 16C chapel, formerly the town hall still has three rooms with pointed vaulting, which house a **Santon Museum**.

Porte Eyguières – This used to be the town's only entrance gate.

★**Musée Yves-Brayer** ⊘ (**E**) – The 16C **Hôtel des Porcelet** houses a retrospective collection of the works of Yves Brayer (1907-1990), a figurative painter deeply attached to Les Baux (he is buried in the village cemetery). The canvases of his early years take Spain, Morocco then Italy as their theme and are characterised by contrasting shades of black, red and ochre; they include bull-fighting scenes, *German Seminarists in Rome, Start of the Palio in Siena*. But it is the glowing landscapes of Provence which inspired some of his best paintings; his palette lightened in works such as *Les Baux, Herds of Horses in the Marshlands*, or *Field of Almond Trees*. The top floor exhibits watercolours he executed on more recent journeys *Mount Fuji, Cholula Arcades*.

Notice the vaulting of the room opposite the reception, covered with 18C frescoes depicting the Four Seasons.

★**Place St-Vincent** – This is a charming, shaded little square. There is a lovely view of the little Fontaine valley and the Val d'Enfer from the terrace.

Chapelle des Pénitents Blancs – The 17C chapel was restored in 1936; inside, the wall frescoes are by Yves Brayer and depict pastoral Provençal scenes set against the backdrop of the Alpilles or the Val d'Enfer.

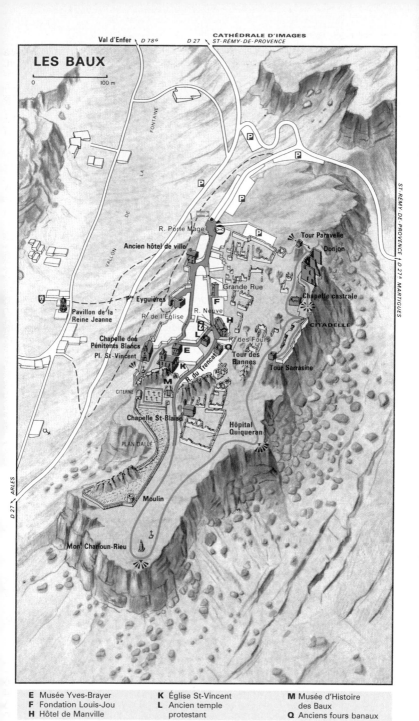

LES BAUX

Val d'Enfer · D 78^G   D 27

0   100 m

R. Porte Mage

Ancien hôtel de ville

Tour Paravelle

Donjon

Chapelle castrale

Grande Rue

P^{te} Eyguières

R. Neuve

R. de l'Église

Pavillon de la
Reine Jeanne

Chapelle des
Pénitents Blancs

Pl. St-Vincent

CITADELLE

R. des Fours

Tour des
Bannes

Tour Sarrasine

R. du Trencat

CITERNE

Chapelle St-Blaise

Hôpital
Quiqueran

PLAN D'ALLÉ

Moulin

Mon^t Charloun-Rieu

E	Musée Yves-Brayer	K	Église St-Vincent	M	Musée d'Histoire
F	Fondation Louis-Jou	L	Ancien temple		des Baux
H	Hôtel de Manville		protestant	Q	Anciens fours banaux

Église St-Vincent (K) – This 12C church is flanked on its north side by a graceful campanile, the so-called lantern of the dead.

Inside, the pointed barrel vaulted nave was enlarged in the 17C by one bay (to the east). On its south side the nave is bordered by a wide aisle covered with rounded vaulting and upon which open three 16C monolithic chapels.

Note the 15C knight's tombstone, a baptismal font carved out of the living rock, stained-glass windows by Max Ingrand and a lamb's cart.

During Christmas Eve and **Midnight Mass**★★ the church hosts the Shepherds' Festival *(Fête des Bergers or Fête du Pastrage)*, an extremely popular celebration which always attracts large crowds. Preceded by musicians playing tambourine and pipe music and draped in their long, sweeping capes, the shepherds lead a newborn lamb to the altar in a small cart drawn by a ram.

Ancien Temple Protestant (**L**) – This former Protestant chapel was once a house dated 1571, part of the Hôtel de Manville *(see below)*. On the lintel of one of its fine windows is the Calvinist motto: "*Post tenebras lux*".

Hôtel de Manville (**H**) – This 16C mansion, donated to the town by the prince of Manville, boasts a beautiful façade decorated with mullioned windows. It houses the town hall. A large room is used to host temporary exhibitions during the summer season.

Go down the main street (Grande Rue) to the Fondation Louis-Jou on the right.

Fondation Louis-Jou ⊙ (**F**) – From 1940 until his death, the engraver, publisher and printer Louis Jou (1881-1968), who devoted his whole life to the art of books, lived in the **Renaissance House Jean de Brion**.

In the midst of incunabula, antique book bindings, Dürer and Goya engravings, Jou's woodcuts and works are on display, underlining more strongly his humanist affiliation with the old masters. Note also the wonderful woodcut series (*Joan of Arc* and *The Life of Jesus)* and the remarkable collection of books, namely *Sonnets for Hélène* by Ronsard, *Psyche* by La Fontaine, *Musicians* by André Suarès, Montaigne's *Essays* and Bossuet's *Funeral Orations*.

There are temporary exhibitions on the first floor *(access from the inside courtyard)*. Across the road, the printing workshop with its manual presses is still operational.

Go back up the Grande Rue.

Anciens Fours Banaux (**Q**) – The townspeople came to bake their bread in these manorial ovens.

★**Rue du Trencat** – The street has been carved into the living rock; note on the right the ridges and cavities created by rain and wind.

★★CHÂTEAU *45min*

Access to the citadel through the Musée d'Histoire des Baux, at the end of Rue du Trencat.

The monumental and archeological heritage of the citadel is currently the subject of an important restoration and development project, expected to last some 20 years.

The most recent excavation work carried out in 1992 allowed three main periods of occupation of the rocky spur prior to the modern era to be determined: the 2C and 1C BC (second Iron Age), the 5C and 6C (construction of a rampart and scattered dwellings), and the medieval period (construction of a keep). At present the work is concentrated on the excavation of the Terras, a large area stretching from the bottom of the castle.

Two viewing tables offer an all-embracing view of the surrounding countryside: to the south an extensive **view**★ towards the Abbaye de Montmajour, Arles, the Crau and the Camargue (on a clear day, Stes-Maries-de-la-Mer and Aigues-Mortes can be seen); to the east, a **view**★ of the patchwork pattern formed by the vineyards, olive groves and orchards which stand out against the Alpilles and Montagne Ste-Victoire.

Musée d'Histoire des Baux ⊙ (**M**). Housed in the old residence of the powerful Tour du Brau family, this History Museum exhibits in a beautiful rib-vaulted room information concerning the most important moments in the history of Les Baux from Antiquity to the present day. In particular, the medieval period is represented by two sculpted heads discovered in the castle embankments in 1992. Two models of the fortress in the 13C and the 16C illustrate the architectural evolution of the site. The final display depicts the period of decline which the town experienced in the 19C, when it became a simple country village described by Mistral, Daudet and Charloun Riéu.

Chapelle St-Blaise – This chapel was the seat of the woollen carders and weavers brotherhood from the 12C. Nowadays it houses a small museum on the olive where the visitor can watch a video entitled "Van Gogh, Gauguin and Cézanne in the country of the olive".

Cemetery – The painter Yves Brayer *(see p 116)* and writer André Suarès (1868-1948), a good friend of Romain Rolland, Gide, Claudel and Péguy, are buried here.

Hôpital Quinqueran – This hospital was built in the 16C by Jehanne de Quinqueran, wife of the governor of Les Baux and was in operation until 1787. Nowadays in ruins, there are plans to rebuild it.

Moulin – The ordinary old mill, the use of which accorded a tax paid to the lord of Les Baux, runs alongside a paved area serving as a catchment for rainwater which then drains into a cistern (1 000m³/35 315cu ft) carved into the rock.

Monument Charloun Riéu – From this monument erected in honour of the poet Charloun Riéu (1846-1924), there is a magnificent **view** ★ over the plain as far as the Berre lagoon.

Citadelle – Towering over the eastern side of the rocky spur, the impressive citadel ruins bear witness to the numerous modifications which have changed the appearance of the citadel itself. The **Tour Sarrasine** (Saracen Tower) (from the top, a good **view** of the village and castle) and the **Tour des Bannes** remain to the south, dominating a group of houses built in the 16C. A beautiful bay of rib vaulting can still be seen in the **Chapelle Castrale** (12C–16C), dedicated to St Catherine.

The **castle** and the **donjon** (keep) *(fairly difficult steps)*, whose walls conceal troglodyte rooms, are the remains of a 13C building constructed on the site of the 10C fortress. From the 13C keep, there is a magnificent **panorama**★★ embracing the Aix countryside, the Luberon, Mont Ventoux and the Cévennes; closer by, the tormented shapes of the Val d'Enfer to the north contrast with the gentle countryside of the Vallon de la Fontaine to the west.

Leaning against the northern rampart, the **Tour Paravelle** affords a pretty **view**★ of the village of Les Baux and the Val d'Enfer.

Retracing your steps, you will skirt the Terras which is currently under excavation.

ADDITIONAL SIGHTS

★★**Panorama** – *Continue along D 27 for about 1km/0.5mi and bear right on a steep road.* This rocky promontory offers the best view of Les Baux and a far-reaching panorama *(signposted, car park, viewing table)*: Arles and Camargue, Rhône valley, Cévennes mountains, Aix-en-Provence, the Luberon and Mont Ventoux.

★**Cathédrale d'Images** ⊘ – *On the side of the road (D 27); 500m/0.3mi north of the village.* The remarkable site of the bauxite quarries, its colossal decoration evoking an Egyptian temple, was "discovered" by journalist Albert Plécy (1914-77), who established a research centre in the quarries. In the semi-darkness the limestone surfaces of the huge rooms and pillars are used as three-dimensional screens for the projection of slides, occupying an area of up to 100m²/1 076sq ft. This giant **audio-visual show**★ changes theme annually.

Val d'Enfer – *Access from D 27 and D 78ᴳ.* A path *(15min return on foot)* crosses this jagged and irregular gorge aptly named Hell Valley. The caves used to be lived in and are still the source of many legends as the place where witches, fairies and sprites reign.

Queen Jeanne's Pavilion (Pavillon de la Reine Jeanne) – *On D 78ᴳ. A path leads down to the pavilion from Porte Eyguières.* The small Renaissance building, built by Jeanne of Les Baux c 1581, was beloved by the Provençal poets of the Félibrige. Mistral had a copy made for his tomb at Maillane.

BEAUCAIRE★

Population 13 400
Michelin map 83 fold 10 or 245 fold 28 or 246 fold 26

At the point where the Domitian Way linked Italy to Spain, Ugernum was an important Gallo-Roman city, where in 455 an assembly of senators from Gaul selected the Emperor Avitus from Arverne. A royal seneschalship in 1229, Beaucaire kept watch over Tarascon, across the river, which was part of the Holy Roman Empire.

The Vallabrègues project in 1970 demonstrates a phase in the hydroelectric works of the Compagnie Nationale du Rhône. The **Beaucaire Power Station** ⊘ (Centrale de Beaucaire – *via* ⑥ *on the town plan*), located on the last branch of the river before flowing into the sea, has an average annual production of more than 1 thousand million kWh. The town's facilities include a river marina, since the Rhône to Sète canal flows through the town, and the Rhône borders it to the east.

Beaucaire Fair – The fair, launched in 1217 by **Raymond VI of Toulouse**, originally lasted one week beginning on 22 July. Throughout the Middle Ages it became one of those great medieval fairs to which people came from everywhere – as many as 300 000, it was said, gathered to do business, roister and celebrate in the town every year in the month of July. Streets were decorated, houses beflagged and crammed with visitors and their merchandise; those who could not get a room on land slept aboard the ships gathered from all corners of the Mediterranean, Brittany and Gascony and moored in the river. Streets specialised in single commodities after which many were named: Beaujolais was a wine street, Bijoutiers – a jewellers' row; the Rue des Marseillais was where oil and soap were sold; elsewhere there were wool, silk, linen, cotton, lace, coloured woven cloth, clothing, weapons, hardware, rope and saddlery shops and harness makers. On the quayside and on board, traders proffered dried fish, sugar, cocoa, coffee, cinnamon, vanilla, lemons, oranges and dates.

The fairground, on the large flat expanse between the castle cliff and the river, was set with stalls offering everything from games to perfume, pipes to pottery. It was of course, also a horse fair. Tumblers and jugglers, acrobats and clowns entertained the crowds; bearded women, giants and dwarfs, monkeys, performing dogs, lions, bears and elephants amazed onlookers. There were even dioramas of Paris, Constantinople and Versailles to be viewed through magnifying lenses.

The advent of industrialisation and rail transport brought about considerable changes in commerce and international exchanges, and, as a result, the Beaucaire Fair ceased to exist. However the riverside quays have remained active and are still engaged in the trading of wine.

★CHATEAU ☉ (Y)

Start at Place du Château; take the steps up to the pine and cypress walk flowered with irises and broom.

Built in the 11C on the site of a Roman camp remodelled in the 13C, the castle was dismantled in the 17C on the orders of Cardinal Richelieu. It stood on the crown of the hill surrounded by ramparts (imposing ruins).

There are **shows of birds of prey in flight** ☉ on the esplanade of Beaucaire castle. Kites, buzzards, eagles and other birds of prey glide to a backgound of evocative music, handled by three falconers clad in medieval costume. After the demonstration, the birds can be seen in their aviary at the bottom of the polygonal tower.

Romanesque Chapel ☉ (**Y B**) – This small chapel (restored in the 19C) has a twin-bayed bell tower and carved tympanum.

Tour polygonale (**Y**) – This extremely unusually shaped tower is also called the triangular tower.

Tour ronde (**Y**) – A fine corner tower.

Curtain wall – A short walk enables the visitor to admire the sheer curtain wall, the barbican defending a castle entrance, and the rocky spur on which the Tour polygonale *(see above)* stands.

Musée Auguste-Jacquet ☉ (**Y M**) – Located within the castle walls, this museum has an archeological section containing exhibits which date from prehistoric to Gallo-Roman times (Celtic-Ligurian funerary column, funerary objects from necropolises, Italic-type ceramics, a white marble statue of Jupiter, sarcophagi lids). On the first floor, documents on the famous Beaucaire Fair, the reconstruction of a typical Beaucaire hall and bedroom, costumes, headdresses, Provençal utensils and ceramics from St-Quentin-la-Poterie can be seen.

ADDITIONAL SIGHTS

Hôtel de Ville (**Z H**) – The town hall is a late-17C mansion by Mansart with a central block flanked by wings outlined by a high, balustraded wall; carved flower garlands surround the windows, and the grand staircase (courtyard) rises behind a double portico of Ionic columns.

Église Notre-Dame-des-Pommiers (**Y**) – Rebuilt (1734-44) in the Jesuit style by the architect Jean-Baptiste Franque, this church presents an elegant façade adorned with two superimposed orders: Ionic and Corinthian; a low relief of the Assumption crowns the great doorway.

BEAUCAIRE

Ledru-Rollin (R.) .... **Z** 17
Nationale (R.) .... **Z**

Barbès (R.) .... **Z** 2
Bijoutiers (R. des) .... **YZ** 3
Charlier (R.) .... **Y** 4
Château (R. du) .... **Y** 5
Clemenceau
  (Pl. Georges) .... **Z** 6
Danton (R.) .... **Y** 7
Denfert-Rochereau (R.) ... **Z** 8
Écluse (R. de l') .... **Z** 9
Foch (Bd Maréchal) .... **YZ** 12
Gambetta (Cours) .... **Z** 13
Hôtel-de-Ville (R. de l') .... **Z** 14
Jaurès (Pl. Jean) .... **Y** 15
Jean-Jacques-
  Rousseau (R.) .... **Y** 16
Pascal (R. Roger) .... **Z** 21
République (Pl. de la) ...... **Z** 22
République (R. de la) ...... **Y** 23
Victor-Hugo (R.) .... **Y** 25

B Chapelle romane
H Hôtel de ville
K Maison des cariatides
M Musée Auguste-Jacquet

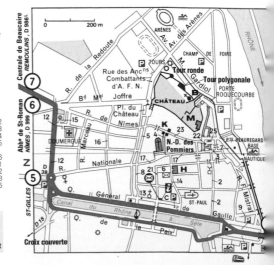

All that remains of the early-Romanesque church is the frieze imbedded in the upper part of the eastern wall which can be seen from Rue Charlier. It depicts the Last Supper, Kiss in the Garden, Flagellation, Carrying of the Cross and Resurrection.

The church's interior is majestic; above the transept crossing is a fine dome on pendentives.

Maison des Cariatides (Y K) – *No 23 Rue de la République.* This 17C house with its lovely carved façade (restored) is known for the caryatids flanking the porch.

Croix couverte – *1.5km/0.75mi southwest at the junction formed by D 15 (Z) and the first road to the right.* This small triangular-shaped oratory (early 15C) is decorated at the top by a delicate openwork railing.

EXCURSIONS

Abbaye de St-Roman ⓥ – *4.5km/2.5mi by ⑤ on the town plan and D 999 and the road to the right, then 30min return on foot. Park the car and take the path to the abbey.*

The ruins of the abbey, dependent in the 12C on the Abbaye de Psalmody near Aigues-Mortes, are located on a limestone peak. They have recently been excavated and developed for tourists.

The abbey was abandoned by the monks in the 16C, gradually transformed into a fortress and then enlarged by the construction of a castle on the upper terrace; stone for both fortress and castle was quarried from the abbey without seriously affecting its original appearance. In 1850 the castle was demolished, and only vestiges of the fortifications can still be seen.

The chapel, built into the rock, contains, at the transept crossing, the tomb of Romanus, a 12C abbot's chair and, on the north side over tombs sunk into the floor, a lantern to the dead with recesses for oil lamps.

The **view★** from the terrace extends to the Rhône and the Vallabrègues dam, Avignon, Mont Ventoux, the Luberon, the Alpilles and, in the foreground, Tarascon and its castle. Note the graves hollowed out of the rock, the basin from which rainwater was channelled to a collecting tank, the monks' cells and a vast hall three storeys high.

Mas Gallo-Romain des Tourelles ⓥ – *4km/2.5mi- to the west. Leave Beaucaire by ④ on the map, towards Bellegarde. After 4km/2.5mi on the right, turn right for the Mas des Tourelles.*

Between the 1C and 3C AD a Gallo-Roman villa covered this area, comprising of a dwelling, a farm and a pottery workshop, and from where its amphora products were easily transported by means of the Rhône or the Domitian Way. Its 17C buildings (sheep barn, present wine-cellar, farm house) containing archeological material found in pottery ovens and information on wine production during the Gallo-Roman period are grouped around an attractive, flowered courtyard.

In the Cella vinaria, a life-size working reconstruction of a Roman wine-cellar, a winepress *(calcatarium)*, vat *(lacus)*, press *(torcula)* and large earthenware jars *(dolia)* are worthy of note. Nowadays the mas produces "archeological" wines such as Muslum, with its honey taste, enhanced with spices, Turriculae, developed according to the Columelle texts, Defrutum (grape juice), as well as the AOC Costières de Nîmes wines. The visit ends with a wine tasting session.

Étang de BERRE★

Michelin map 84 folds 1, 2, 11 and 12 or 245 folds 30 and 43 or 246 folds 13 and 14

The Étang de Berre (Berre Lagoon) 15530ha/60sq mi in extent and nowhere more than 9m/30ft deep, has been France's principal **petroleum port** for the last 70-odd years. The Canal de Caronte, dredged out where there was once a lagoon of the same name, provides a passage to the Mediterranean, as does the underground Rove section of the Marseille-Rhône canal.

The lagoon is fed fresh water by the Arc and Touloubre rivers and the EDF canal (Électricité de France) and is ringed around its 50mile perimeter by limestone hills: the Lançon chain (alt 195m/640ft) to the north, the Vitrolles (alt 271m/890ft) to the east, the Estaque (alt 201m/660ft) to the south, and the St-Mitre (alt 142m/465ft) to the west. The modern installations are but the latest of man's constructions in the area: buildings still above ground and excavations reveal the presence of earlier inhabitants at St-Blaise, Pont Flavian, built by the Romans, the medieval hamlet of Miramas-le-Vieux and the 17C walls of Port-de-Bouc.

The region, nevertheless, was still largely uninhabited when in 1920, under the San Remo Agreement, France obtained the right to purchase the major part of Iraq's annual crude oil production.

Étang de BERRE

The lagoon was transformed into an ideal port for shallow-draught oil tankers; at the same time harbours also began to be developed on the Golfe de Fos – the French BP company set up at Lavéra in 1922-24, Shell-Berre at the Pointe de Berre in 1928 and the Compagnie Française de Raffinage at La Mède in 1934. Esso has had installations in Fos since 1965.

The growth in demand for oil, apparent even in 1938, brought about the transformation, soon after the war, of **Lavéra**, to enable 90 000-ton tankers to dock and pump their cargoes directly into onshore installations. Finally in the 1960s a completely new port was constructed at Martigues.

The installations specialise in the receipt and handling of crude oil and refined products and new equipment has been installed to enable multi-products to be handled simultaneously. They also handle the increasing traffic in liquefied oil gases (400 000 m³ of underground storage space) as well as chemical products, for which a specialized terminal has been built (170 000 m³ of storage, processing and barrelling...).

The lagoon complex is also the terminal of the **South European Oil Pipeline**. This line, inaugurated in 1962, supplies four refineries around the lagoon and 11 in regions as distant as Feyzin, Cressier in Switzerland, Baden and Bavaria in Germany; the total amount of oil piped a year is 68 million metric tons.

Between the Second World War and 1973 the refineries expanded considerably; since then, however, their distillation capacity (27 million metric tons – for the two refineries around the lagoon as well as at Lavéra and Fos) has been reduced. The very modern equipment permits the treatment of crude oil as well as a wide range of oil-related products and lead-free fuels.

Petrochemicals have developed considerably in the last 10 years with Shell's construction of steam cracking facilities, rubber-making and plastics units.

Chemical-petrochemical subsidiaries continue to expand (BP Chimie-Naphtachimie in Lavéra, Albright and Wilson, Ferro), investing on average 1.5 billion francs a year.

Dependent on the docks and refineries which ring the lagoon shore and coast around the Fos gulf are petrochemical factory complexes extending far inland, so that, from the air or from one of the heights overlooking the bay, one sees an irregular mass of silver aluminium storage tanks, tall factory chimneys belching smoke, petroleum gas flares, vast metal warehouses and concrete works and office blocks.

Aviation centre – At the turn of the century the peaceful lagoons and deserted Crau plain were an ideal testing ground for pioneer aviators.

The very first military aerodrome was established in Istres before the First World War and it still operates today. Since then it has expanded considerably and now occupies 2 031 ha/5 017 acres.

Berre was until 1940 the most important hydroplane base of the National Marines with Bizerte. When a civil airport was required for Marseille, the **Marseille-Provence** airport was sited at the east end of the Étang de Berre at **Marignane**.

ROUND TOUR STARTING FROM MARTIGUES
113km/70mi – allow 1 day – local map see below

Martigues – *See MARTIGUES.*

Leave Martigues by ① on the town plan, D 5.

The road winds its way through vineyards, orchards and pinewoods.

St-Mitre-les-Remparts – The old town, encircled by 15C ramparts still pierced by only two gateways, stands just off the road.

Of Falcons and Planes

In 1980, at the Istres air base, a hawk house *(fauconnerie)* was set up in a bid to reduce the number of accidents caused by collisions between birds and aeroplanes. It is a known fact that falcons are fierce birds of prey: they seem to be the only species able to rid the take-off and landing runways of the myriad flying creatures which nestle in Camargue, on the islets and along the Marseille coastline, and which stop over at the Étang de Berre. The falcons' training lasts for about three months: first, the birds' diet is strictly controlled so that hunger will encourage them to go out hunting; then, they are set free and subsequently recaptured to grow familiar with man; finally, they undergo intensive "phonetic sessions" (several hours a day) aimed at getting them accustomed to the human voice.

Different varieties of falcon make it possible to target specific birds: the peregrine falcon, the fastest to swoop down on its prey, feeds on seagulls and pigeons; the gyrfalcon flies at a slower pace and hunts gulls; the goshawk hovers above the ground and pounces on his victims, taking them by surprise. In the first year following the opening of the Istres *fauconnerie*, the number of accidents fell by 70%.

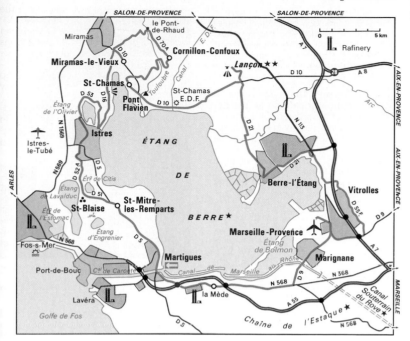

A network of small streets and alleys leads to the church where there is a view of the Étang d'Engrenier.

Leave St-Mitre-les-Remparts by D 51 across D 5.

Good view on the right of the Étang de Berre; the road skirts the Étang de Citis in a cultivated site before passing the foot of the hill on which stands Chapelle St-Blaise, the east end of which is just visible among the pine trees.

St-Blaise Archeological Site – *See Site Archéologique de ST-BLAISE.*

Istres – The town beside the Étang d'Olivier is a military airport base *(see above)*. **Musée Archéologique d'Istres** ⊘ presents local history: paleontology, zoology, prehistory, underwater archeology (collection of amphorae bearing identification marks), economic life of Istres, Fos and Miramas.
To the north lies the Greco-Ligurian town of Castellan also on the banks of the Étang d'Olivier; a surfaced path leads to the edge of the rocky spur from where there is a fine view.

Museums devoted to the sea...

Musée Archéologique d'Istres, see above;
Musée Ciotaden, p 145;
Musée d'Histoire de Marseille, p 179;
Musée des Docks Romains in Marseille, p 179
Musée de la Marine et de l'Économie de Marseille, p 187.

Circle the lagoon by way of D 53 and then turn left onto D 16.
The road offers good views of the Étang de Berre to which it returns.

Miramas-le-Vieux – The small town on a flat ledge of rock is characterised by medieval ramparts, the ruins of the 13C castle and the 15C parish church which replaced the even smaller 12C church still standing in the churchyard. Good view of the Étang de Berre.

Return to D 10 and take D 16 across the way and then D 70⁰.
The road goes through pastureland (sheep farming).

At Le Pont-de-Rhaud bear right onto D 70ᴬ.
The road ascends a height overlooking the Touloubre on the right.

Cornillon-Confoux – At the centre of the hill village stands a small Romanesque church with a bell gable and modern stained glass windows by Frédérique Duran. There are good local **views**★ from the walk which starts at the church and circles the village.

Take D 70 and a tourist road on the right to St-Chamas.

St-Chamas – The town is unique in being dominated by a small, triple-arched aqueduct. The **church**, which is 17C with a Baroque west front, contains a marble high altar and a 16C altarpiece to St Anne (third south chapel).

Pont Flavien – The bridge is named after the patrician who at the beginning of 1C ordered its construction at what is now the south approach to St-Chamas; it crosses the Touloubre in a single span. A civil engineering structure built along a secondary Roman way features at each end ornamental triumphal arches, whose entablatures are surmounted by small sculpted lions.

Continue along D 10 which passes the **St-Chamas Power Station** (Centrale de St-Chamas), the EDF canal's final project which has an annual production capacity of 610 million kWh.

Turn left onto D 21 and left again after 1.7km/1mi onto an unsurfaced road. Park the car.

Pont Flavien (triumphal arch)

★★**Lançon Viewing Table** (Table d'orientation de Lançon) – *15min return on foot*. Steps (48) lead to the top of a rock from where there is a **view**★★ over the lagoon to the surrounding hills.

Turn round and once on D 21 continue to Berre-L'Étang.

Berre-l'Étang – The town lives off fishing and its chemical factories. The chapel, Notre-Dame-de-Caderot, displays at the altar a 16C polychrome wood retable and, in a recess opposite the door, a Roman crystal vessel known as the Caderot vase, said to have contained a lock of the Virgin's hair.

Continue first along D 21, then N 113 on the right; finally turn left for Vitrolles.

Vitrolles – *See VITROLLES*.

Leave Vitrolles by D 55F. At the N 113 crossroads, cross onto D 9 then right onto D 20.

Aéroport de Marseille-Provence – This civil airport of international standing, which can be used by both planes and seaplanes, is ranked second in France for passenger traffic and offers daily connections with 62 cities throughout the world. Spread out over 550ha/235 acres beside the Étang de Berre, Marseille-Provence airport is equipped with two runways respectively 3 500m/11 490ft and 2 400m/7 880ft long as well as a sophisticated landing programme that operates under all weather conditions. The central air terminal now features three satellite buildings connected to the planes by telescopic passageways as well as a new control tower 50m/164ft high.

Marignane – The town is laid out along the Étang de Bolmon, which is linked to the Étang de Berre by a sand bar. In the 17C Marignane acceded to the status of marquisate; from this period there remains the château, which currently houses the town hall *(mairie)*.

Château des Covet ⊘ – Originally built in the 13C by Guillaume des Baux, the château was taken over in the 17C by the Covet, a wealthy family of tradesmen, who applied themselves to extending and embellishing the premises. It is to them that the château owes its present façade, a fine example of classicism, with alternating triangular and curved pediments. Some of the rooms are open to the public: the boudoir, the Louis XV bathroom, the Grand Salon (Salon d'Honneur) and especially the former bedchamber of Jean-Baptiste Covet (Registry Office - Salle des Mariages), presenting a superb **painted ceiling** with a floral decoration attributed to Jean Daret.

Musée d'Arts et Traditions Populaires ⊘ – The museum evokes the traditions, history and activities related to the Marignane area: fisherman's cabin and coot hunting, Provençal interior scenes (a table laid for Christmas dinner), 19C costumes and a room devoted to aeronautics.

Église St-Nicolas – The late 11C church nave has pointed-barrel vaulting with transverse arches set close together and no windows at all. The 16C side aisles feature diagonal rib vaulting. Note the high altar dating from the 16C.

Follow D 9 and turn right on N 568.

The road crosses the Rove or Marseille-Rhône canal and passes through acres of market gardens; fine views of the lagoon and the site of **La Mède** marked by two peculiar rocks at the harbour entrance.

BOLLÈNE

Population 13 907
Michelin map 80 fold 10 or 245 fold 16 or 246 fold 23 – Facilities

The town, which stands on a hillside, has been an agricultural marketing centre since the days of the Avignon popes, when it was one of the popes' richest possessions. A few houses and fine doorways remain as mementoes of the past in what is now a typical Provençal town, with wide shaded boulevards marking the line of the ancient ramparts and a web of narrow streets at the centre.
From the terraces overlooking the Rhône can be seen the Canal du Donzère-Mondragon, the Bollène hydroelectric power station and the vast Tricastin Nuclear Power Station; beyond in the distance are the mountains of the Ardèche and the Bas-Vivarais.

Belvédère Pasteur – From this small public garden, set around the former Romanesque Chapelle des Trois-Croix, there is a pleasant view of the town and its surrounding countryside.
A bust of **Louis Pasteur** commemorates the fact that when the scientist stayed in Bollène in 1882, he discovered an inoculation against swine fever.

Collégiale St-Martin ⊘ – The former parish church (12C-16C) is now used for exhibitions. Its robust bell tower stands atop the hill overlooking the town's rooftops from the east. Go through the lovely Renaissance doorway to admire the size of the nave covered with a vast timberwork saddleback roof.
From the east end, there is a lovely view of old Bollène's rooftops, the Tricastin hills, the Barry site and the Rhône valley.

BOLLÈNE

Chabrières (R. des)	5
Cimetière (Rue Gd)	6
Fabre (R. Henri)	7
Gambetta (Bd)	9
Giono (A. Jean)	10
Louis (R. Auguste)	11
Mistral (R. Frédéric)	12
Paroisse (Montée de la)	13
Puy (R. du)	15
Récollets (Pl. des)	16
République (Cours de la)	17
Reynaud-de-la-Gardette (Pl.)	20
Tour (R. de la)	21
Vietto (Montée René)	22
Zola (R. Émile)	23

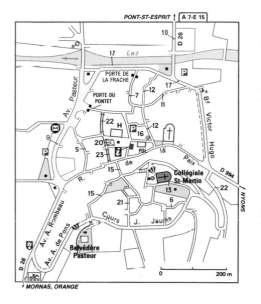

EXCURSION

Mornas – *11km/7mi south via D 26 which cuts through Mondragon, dominated by the castle ruins, then take N 7.*

D 26 crosses Mondragon dominated by the ruins of its castle, and joins N 7. The old village of Mornas clings to the foot of a sheer cliff (137m/449ft) on which lie the ruins of a powerful fortress; the fortified gates and old houses enhance the medieval atmosphere. *Access by a steep alleyway (car park) and path.* Near the cemetery stands the pretty little Romanesque church of Notre-Dame-du-Val-Romigier.

Fortress ⊘ – It features a vast curtain wall, 2km/1mi long, flanked by either semi-circular or square towers. At the top are ruins of the keep and chapel. It belonged to the bishops of Arles, then passed to the count of Toulouse in 1197 and was entirely rebuilt by him.
The castle was also the scene of a terrible episode during the Wars of Religion: it was held by the Catholics and fell into the hands of the sinister **Baron des Adrets**, who in reprisal had all the inhabitants jump off the top of the cliff.

*For a quiet place to stay, consult the annual **Michelin Red Guide France** which offers a selection of pleasant and quiet hotels in convenient locations.*

BONNIEUX★

Population 1 422

Michelin map 81 fold 13 or 114 fold 1 or 245 fold 31 or 246 fold 11

Local map see Montagne du LUBERON – Facilities

This large, attractively-terraced village situated on a Luberon promontory still has vestiges of its ramparts.

BONNIEUX

Ancien-Presbytère (R.de l')......... 2
Aurard (R. J.-B.) 3
Carnot (Pl.) 4
Gare (Av. de la)............................ 5
Hugues (Av. Clovis) 7
Liberté (Pl. de la) 8
Mairie (R. de la) 9
République (R. de la).................. 12
Victor-Hugo (R.) 13
Voltaire (R.) 14
4-Septembre (Pl. du) 16

M Musée de la Boulangerie

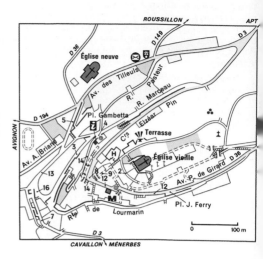

Upper Bonnieux – *Start from Place de la Liberté by the steep vaulted passageway, Rue de la Mairie, to reach the terrace situated below the old church. By car take the road to Cadenet and a steep surfaced path on the left.*

Terrasse – From the terrace there is a lovely **view**★ of the Calavon valley, all the way to the left, of the hilltop village of Lacoste, further to the right of the edge of the Vaucluse plateau to which cling the hilltop village of Gordes and Roussillon blending into its red cliffs. In the background Mont Ventoux stands out.

Église Vieille – From the terrace, take the stairs to the former parish church (12C) remodelled in the 15C and surrounded by fine cedars.

Église Neuve – This vast building dating from the second half of the 19C contains **four paintings**★ belonging to the old church. These 15C Primitives from the German School are brightly painted on wood and illustrate St Veronica wiping Jesus' face, an Ecce Homo, the Crown of Thorns and a Flagellation.

Musée de la Boulangerie ☉ (**M**) – The museum illustrates the work of a baker (utensils, literature on the bakery trade etc).

BRANTES

Population 63

Michelin map 81 southeast fold 3 or 245 fold 18

This picturesque village has an impressive **site**★ at the foot of Mont Ventoux. Wedged on the steep northern face of the Toulourenc valley, it is worth a visit.

Village – The visitor enters this charming hamlet through the upper fortified gate and passes, in succession, the small Chapelle des Pénitents Blancs of the 18C, used for exhibitions, the remains of a Renaissance manor house, with a beautiful sculptured doorway, and the richly-decorated church.

Col des Aires – The road climbing up this pass, D 41, offers splendid **views**★ of the village of Brantes and its site dominated by the ruins of a castle, the Toulourenc valley and the ravined north face of Mont Ventoux.

Michelin on-line gives motorists the freedom to create their own itineraries, to stop and discover tourist attractions. At any time, you can print out your complete route map, as well as the information from the Red Guides and the cost of tolls on the selected itinerary.

Log in at www.michelin-travel.com

CADENET

Population 3 232
Michelin map 84 fold 3 or 114 fold 2 or 245 fold 31 or 246 fold 12
Local map see Basse Vallée de la DURANCE – Facilities

The small town is perched on a spur below the ruins of an 11C castle now half-hidden by pine trees.

Le Tambour d'Arcole – In the main square is a statue of **André Estienne**, born in Cadenet in 1777, the town's famous **drummer boy**. It was he who served in Napoleon's northern Italy campaign of 1796, and in the midst of the battle against the Austrians and Italians for the Arcole Bridge, swam the river and beat such a tattoo that the Austrians mistook it for artillery fire; as they retreated, the French advanced to capture the bridge and win the battle.
It is also the birthplace of **Félicien David** (1810-76), whose travels to the Far-East brought an Oriental touch to his music (*Le Désert*, 1844).

Church (Église) ⊘ – The 14C structure, remodelled in the 16C and 17C, has a fine square bell tower. Inside the church the north aisle contains beautiful **baptismal fonts★** made from a 3C Roman sarcophagus decorated with low reliefs illustrating the Triumph of Ariadne.

Drummer boy

Musée de la Vannerie ⊘ – *Avenue Philippe-de-Girard*. It was the proximity of the River Durance which influenced the development of basket-making in this region; from the beginning of the 19C until the middle of the 20C its beds were harvested for the production of wicker, an industry which mainly benefited local agriculture. The industry reached its zenith between the 1920s and 1930s, after which, as a result of competition from rattan imported from the Far East, production diversified into providing containers, household utensils and various decorative objects. The last business closed down in 1978.
Situated on the site of the former La Glaneuse workshop, the museum contains, in addition to basket-making tools, small articles for daily use, colonial chaise-longues, prams and cradles, demijohns (containers encased in wickerwork), trunks and cases. On the mezzanine, an audio-visual montage evokes life in Cadenet in the olden days, through the experiences of a former basket-maker.

EXCURSION

Lauris – *6.5km/4ml. Leave Cadenet to the west on the Cavaillon road.*
Set against the Luberon, Lauris is a picturesque village whose maze of small streets, lined with houses dating from the 16C, 17C and 18C, are perfect for a stroll. Built at the beginning of the 18C, the church is topped by an attractive rounded bell tower in wrought iron. From the Promenade de la Roque, the visitor is able to explore the terraced gardens of the castle, built at the steepest part of the village and dominating the wide valley of the Durance.

Massif des CALANQUES★★

Michelin map 84 fold 13 or 114 folds 41 and 42 or 245 folds 44 and 45

The Massif des Calanques, with Mont Puget (565m/1 850ft) its highest peak, stretches almost 20km/12.5mi – between Marseille and Cassis *(see illustration p 310)*. With its solid limestone, dazzling whiteness and weather-worn pinnacles, it has long attracted nature lovers for its wild beauty. However, its unique character and exceptional charm stem above all from its deep and narrow indentations, the famous *calanques*, which have been chiselled out along its coastline, creating a majestic union of sea, sky and rocks.

What is a calanque? – The word *calanque* (from the Provençal *cala* or steep slope) describes a narrow and steep-sided coastal valley which has been bored into the solid rock by a river, whose course was usually guided by a fault, during the periods of the sea's retreat, and which has subsequently been submerged by the waves during cycles of flooding. Such fluctuations in sea level result from the alternation of glaciation and deglaciation on the earth's surface over the course of the past two million years. The most recent rise in the water level, an average of 100m/330ft, occurred 10 000 years ago, flooding caves inhabited by prehistoric man *(see Grotte Cosquer below)*. The *calanques* – none of which are longer than 1.5km/1mi – extend towards the open sea via large underwater valleys, and though they can be compared to the abers of Brittany, should not be confused with fjords, which are shaped by glaciers.

Massif des CALANQUES

A fragile, remarkable site – The absence of any form of surface water and the area's dryness can be explained by the permeability of the limestone, the proliferation of faults and low levels of rainfall. The temperature regulation of the sea, the sun's glare on the high, bare rocks, and the area's sheltered position away from the *mistral* all combine to create an exceptionally hot microclimate on the southern slopes of this massif, conditions which occasionally result in winter temperatures 10°C higher than those on its northern side. Aware of this, regular visitors to the *calanques* come here to dip their toes in the water and keep up their tan, while just a stone's throw away, in and around the Vieux Port in Marseille, the inhabitants of Provence's largest city, well wrapped up against the elements, buckle under the harsh gusts of the *mistral*. Some typically tropical and extremely rare species of vegetation have been able to survive the periods of climatic cooling which occurred during the Quaternary period, creating today a botanical reserve of valuable scientific interest, in a paradoxical context in which vegetation continues to suffer; the main culprits of which are the area's dryness, the felling of trees for the local lime kilns, excessive grazing and the repeated forest fires which decimate the range. From the time of the first fire ordered by Julius Caesar in 49BC to the catastrophic blaze on 21 August 1990, the forests of the Massif des Calanques have suffered indescribable damage over the centuries. Increasing protective measures have been introduced in recent years: since 1975 the area has benefited from the protection granted natural monuments and sites; following the 1990 disaster, measures restricting public access during the summer months were stepped up; a large reforestation project through the recycling of purified sludge is also being studied. For some ecosystems, however, the harm already done is irreversible and the threat ever present for those areas still spared.

Flora and fauna – In this semi-arid environment, the best adapted flora includes copses or thickets of green oaks, viburnum, wild olive trees, myrtle and mastic, in addition to woods of Aleppo pine; stony scrub oak, rosemary or heather carpeted *garrigue* also predominate. Ground where vegetation damage is widespread is also home to areas of brachiopods. Samphire (sea-fennel) and sea lavender also grow along the coast, replaced higher up the slopes by a thin cushion of plants including the rare Marseille astralagus or "mother-in-law's cushion" with its fearsome thorns.

Europe's largest lizard and longest snake can also be found in the calanques: the ocellar lizard can grow to 60cm/2ft whereas the Montpellier grass snake can reach 2m-over 6ft in length.

Birds nest mainly on the coastal cliffs and outlying islands. The most common, the herring gull or *gabian*, which feasts on the rubbish left behind by careless visitors, is increasing rapidly in number. The most rare, Bonelli's eagle (about 15 pairs), is a beautiful diurnal bird of prey with white, grey and dark brown plumage.

Rock climbing and deep-sea diving – Breathtaking needle-like rocks and cliff faces overhanging the sea provide excellent rock climbing opportunities; some accessible for experienced climbers only, others ideal for beginners. Several renowned mountaineers, such as Isabelle Patissier, from Cassis, and Gaston Rebuffat, climbed their first peaks in the calanques. Just 30 years ago the sea-bed of the *calanques* was considered to be one of the most unique in the whole of the western Mediterranean. Despite subsequent damage caused by pollutant waste, excessive harpoon fishing which is now posing a particular threat to the region's emblem, the black grouper, and the combing of wrecks for their

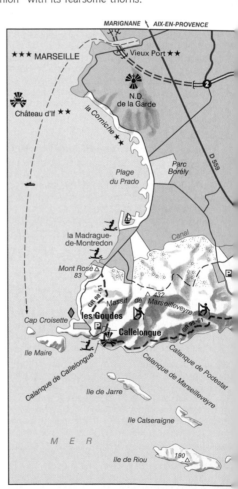

valuable archeological significance, the *calanques* still provide exceptional interest for divers with their abundance of multi-coloured fish, gorgonia, sponge, purple sea urchins, crayfish, mother-of-pearl etc.

PRACTICAL INFORMATION

Caution! With the exception of the direct approaches to the *calanques*, no walking is allowed on the coastal range between 1 July and 30 September. June is probably the best month overall for a visit.

It is strictly forbidden to pick any form of vegetation, stray from marked paths, smoke or light a fire at any time of the year. Make sure you are equipped with walking boots and detailed maps; carry refreshments with you as no watering places exist; take necessary precautions against the harmful effects of the sun.

THE CALANQUES BY BOAT

From Marseille (Vieux Port) ⊘ or Cassis ⊘ – About 4hr. From Marseille most of the calanques are visited though no stops are made for swimming. From Cassis a stop is included for this, though the trip only includes those calanques located in the eastern part of the massif.

An excursion by boat is a practical way of discovering the calanques in summer when access to them by land is strictly controlled *(see Practical information)*. These excursions also enable you to approach the islands of the Riou archipelago, which became separated from the rest of the massif during the last huge rise in the level of the sea: **Maire**, its rocky surface left completely bare by its resident goats; **Jarre** and **Jarron**, to which plague-ridden boats were banished and from where the terrible plague of 1720 spread *(see MARSEILLE)*; and **Riou**, the steepest of the four and renowned until recently for its peregrine falcons (the last was killed in 1971), and still the nesting home for large colonies of birds.

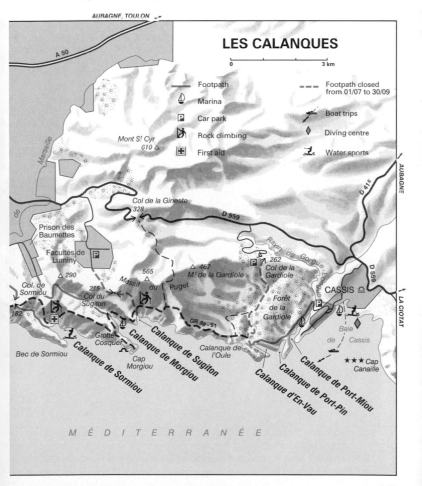

THE CALANQUES ON FOOT

There are no direct approach roads by car to the calanques with the exception of the less attractive coves of Les Goudes, Callelongue and Port-Miou: the only way to reach the others is on foot. Experienced hikers will be tempted to walk the **GR 98-51** footpath from Callelongue to Cassis *(see local map)*, an incomparable 28km/17mi hike *(allow 11-12hr)* along towering cliffs, during the course of which glimpses can be caught of the most secret *calanques*.

Become a true calanque fisherman or "pescadou"...

...by becoming familiar with their local language which is still liberally sprinkled with Provençal terms. Below are a few words currently used to describe their catch (to be pronounced, of course, with the local Provençal accent):

Arrapède: limpet (a shellfish in the shape of a Chinese hat)
Esquinade: spider crab
Favouille: small crab
Fielas: conger eel
Galinette: gurnard
Pourpre: octopus
Supion: squid
Totène: cuttlefish
Violet: sea-squirt (a delicious potato-shaped type of seafood)

Les Goudes – *Leave Marseille by the Promenade de la Plage.* An old fishing village, nestled amid grandiose rocky scenery. No beach.

Continue as far as Callelongue where the tarmac road ends.

Callelongue – This tiny cove, with its attractive **site**, has several *cabanons* or Provençal cabins and provides shelter for a small flotilla of boats.

Sormiou – *Leave Marseille on either Avenue de Hambourg or Chemin de Sormiou. Park in the car park at the entrance to the tarmac road blocked off to vehicles. Walk down to the* calanque *(30min, 45min return).*

This cove has a number of *cabanons*, a small harbour, beach and fish restaurants considered by the local Marseillais population to be the best of all the *calanques*. Sormiou is separated from Morgiou by the Cap Morgiou, a viewpoint affording magnificent views of both *calanques* and the eastern side of the Massif. The opening to the Grotte Cosquer can be found on the north-east side of Sormiou at 37m/121ft below sea-level.

Morgiou – *From Marseille take the same route initially as for Sormiou; turn left at the Intermarché supermarket, then follow "calanque Morgiou" signs, skirting the famous Baumettes prison; park near the "Sens Interdit" (no entry) sign; continue on foot along the paved road (45min, 1hr return).*

A wild setting with an unobtrusive human presence; tiny creeks for swimming, cabanons clustered at the far end of the valley, restaurant, small port.

Calanque d'En-Vau

Sugiton – *From Marseille take the Boulevard Michelet as far as Luminy; park in the car park near the École d'Art et d'Architecture; continue on foot along the forest track (1hr, 1hr 30min return).*

A small *calanque* with turquoise water; well sheltered by its surrounding high cliffs; popular with naturists.

En-Vau – *Access via Col de la Gardiole (Route Gaston-Rebuffat beginning opposite the Carpiagne military camp); leave your car in the Gardiole car park (2hr 30min return) or in Cassis (walk past Port-Miou and Port-Pin* calanques *– 2hr return).*

The best known and most attractive of all the *calanques* with its high white cliffs, emerald water and small stony beach. It is encircled by a forest of rock pinnacles overlooked by the "*Doigt de Dieu*" or Finger of God.

Port-Pin – *Access via Col de la Gardiole (same directions as En-Vau – 3hr return) or Cassis (skirting Port-Miou calanque – 1hr return).*

A more spacious *calanque* with less steep rock walls and a sandy beach surrounded by pine trees.

Port-Miou – *1.5km/1mi to the west of Cassis. Access by car; car park always full in summer.*

The longest of the *calanques*; invaded by pleasure boats and slightly disfigured by an old "Cassis stone" quarry.

The Grotte Cosquer

From 1985 onwards this underwater cave, located near the Cap Morgiou headland, was explored by the Cassis diver, Henri Cosquer. On 3 September 1991 the sensational public disclosure of its Paleolithic paintings and engraving shot it to the rank of the buried cathedral of cave art. Initially, it was feared that this was a huge "Marseille tall story" until scientists quickly proved the authenticity of the representations; the new neutronic activation dating method, able to analyse minuscule quantities of organic matter, has dated the "negative hands" to 25 000 BC and the animal drawings to approximately 17 000 BC, one or two millennium prior to those found at Lascaux which are similar in both style and technique. The unusual discovery of marine fauna such as seals, large penguins and fish adds further originality to this ornate cave.

Due to the fact that it has remained submerged since the last huge rise in sea level it has been able to preserve its treasures. Its inaccessibility makes its highly unlikely that it will ever be put on display to the general public.

Site de CALÈS

Michelin map 84 folds 1 and 2 or 245 fold 30 or 246 fold 12
10km/6mi north of Salon-de-Provence

Nestling on the slopes of the Défends mountain, the Calès site features an impressive cluster of troglodyte dwellings overlooked by a medieval castle and chapels dating from the same period.

Access – *Leave the car on the car park of the fire brigade station. Then walk to the cobbled path behind the church. There are two lanes; one leads to the caves and castle ruins (blue signposts – 1hr 30min return), the other to the chapels (green signposts – 2hr 30min return). Bear in mind that the site is closed in July and August.*

Caves (Grottes) – Carved out of the rock right at the foot of the cliffs to form a natural amphitheatre, the caves were used as quarries during the construction of the castle in the Middle Ages, and subsequently converted into outbuildings and habitations. Visitors may observe the various architectural features of these strange dwellings: holes made for beams, gutters, stairs as well as silos dug out of the rock and used to store food. The caves were inhabited until the castle was destroyed in the late 16C.

Castle – Of the 12C fortress there remain only a few vestiges. From the edge of the terrace, on which a statue of Notre-Dame-de-la-Garde has been erected, there are **views** through the pine forest: northwards, of the Durance valley and the Luberon; eastwards, of these troglodyte dwellings; and southwards, of the Lamanon gap, where the Durance used to flow, the Salon plain, Estaque chain, Crau plain and Berre lagoon.

Go back down towards the cirque and follow the green signposts on the left, leading to the Chapelle St-Denis.

Chapels – First visitors will come across the Chapelle St-Denis, a typical example of rural church architecture in Provence, which was built around the same time as the castle. Turning right into a lane leading to the St-Jean plateau, they will reach the ruins of a double chapel, once an important place of pilgrimage. On the plateau, a viewing table offers pretty views of the surrounding countryside.

La CAMARGUE★★

Camargue, the most original and romantic region of Provence and possibly of France, has been largely preserved in its natural state through its designation in 1927 and 1970 as a botanical and zoological nature reserve. Late spring and early autumn are the best times for a visit: horses and bulls are easily seen and birds abound, the sun shines (but not overpoweringly) and there are the famous pilgrimages to Stes-Maries-de-la-Mer.

Parc Naturel Régional de Camargue – This nature park occupies an area of 85 000ha/328sq mi in the Rhône delta, including the municipalities of Arles and Stes-Maries-de-la-Mer. The main objective of the park, besides its basic policy of protecting nature, is to allow its occupants to live in their natural habitat, while preserving agricultural activity and strictly monitoring both the hydraulic balance of the region and the growing influx of tourists.

A SHORT SURVEY OF CAMARGUE

Information – Centre d'Information de Ginès, Pont de Gau, 13460 Les Stes-Maries-de-la-Mer ☎ 04 90 97 86 32 or Musée Camarguais, Mas du Pont de Rousty, 13200 Arles ☎ 04 90 97 10 40. These two information centres provide a number of leaflets published by the regional park. Information may also be obtained from Tourist Information Centres in Arles, Stes-Maries-de-la-Mer and Salin-de-Giraud as well as from the minitel on 3615 CAMARGUE.

Accommodation – You can find city accommodation at Arles and Les Stes-Maries-de-la-Mer; in the country it is best to choose the hotels set up in *mas* or *cabanes de guardian* or to opt for bed and breakfast accommodation *(gîtes ruraux* and *chambres d'hôtes – see Practical information at the end of the guide).*

Birdwatching – To make sure you get a good chance of seeing the birds, you must leave early in the morning (well before 10am) or at dusk from April to October. You must endeavour to stay still most of the time as birds are wary of people and to remember to bring a pair of binoculars. The best places for bird-watching are the footpaths around La Capelière and the Domaine de la Palissade, the seawall and the Pont de Gau bird sanctuary.

Leisure Activities – Rambling is quite popular in the region since it is the ideal way to observe regional fauna and discover the area's rich vegetation (GR 653 and the footpaths mentioned above). The more adventurous tourists might prefer to go riding astride the famous Camargue horses on the plain, in the marshes or along the beach, accompanied by a *gardian* (Les Chevaux des Lys, Route d'Arles, 13460 Les Stes-Maries-de-la-Mer ☎ 04 90 97 86 27). Mountain biking is also an option along one of the three recommended routes: the first one takes you through countryside peopled with pink flamingoes (from the seawall to the Étang du Fangassier, 22km/14mi), the second one wends its way through the salt marshes *(marais salants)* whereas the third one takes you on a tour of the Camargue rice fields.

Gastronomy – *Tellines* are light brown, small, flat, oblong shellfish which are particularly tasty when seasoned with a touch of parsley and garlic and served with either tomato sauce or aïoli. *Gardiane* is a marinade made with red wine, herbs and spices (thyme, bay laurel, parsley, cayenne pepper, cloves...), orange peel and garlic into which pieces of Camargue bull meat are dipped; it is served with white rice and a good bottle of red Côtes du Rhône.

Useful Tips – Remember to pack a cream to protect yourself against mosquitoes as they swarm everywhere and are especially aggressive between April and November. It is advisable to take drinking water with you as none is available outside of the villages (Le Sambuc, Gageron, Salin-de-Giraud).

GEOGRAPHICAL NOTES

The Rhône Delta – Camargue, an immense alluvial plain of 95 000ha/367sq mi (75 000ha/289sq mi are the delta's island) is the product of the interaction of the Rhône, the Mediterranean and the winds.

During the end of the Tertiary Era and the beginning of the Quaternary Period while the sea was receding, waterways transported huge quantities of shingle which piled up along the shore creating a shingle bar some 10m/33ft wide. On top of this rocky base marine sediment was deposited after the last glacial period (some 10 000 years ago; the sea then extended to the north shore of the Étang de Vaccarès. However, the landscape changed constantly owing to the conflicting forces of the freshwater Rhône and the sea. The powerful Rhône has shifted its course over the centuries – it has occupied the two present arms of its bed only since the 15C – transporting enormous amounts of alluvial deposits: barriers were formed which isolated the marshes; sandbanks created by the coastal currents closed off lagoons. Every year the Grand Rhône, which accounts for 90% of the flow, hollows out from its banks and sweeps towards the sea 20 million m³/26 157cu yd of gravel, sand and mud – enough to cover Paris in a silt blanket 25cm/10.5in thick. A part of the deposit is moved on by currents to the lower Languedoc coast; some comes to form sandbanks across the Golfe de Fos, thus blocking the access to the Étang de Berre.

The construction of the **seawall** ⊘ and the Rhône dikes in the 19C has partially helped to curb these phenomena. And yet the encroachment of the shore line – 10-50m/33-164ft a year – continues in several places (l'Espiguette and Sablon Points); Aigues-Mortes where St Louis embarked is now 5km/3mi inland.

Elsewhere however, owing to continental subsidence, the sea is invading the shore: the Vieux Rhône and Petit Rhône promontories have been swept away by southeasterly storms; **Phare de Faraman**, a lighthouse 700m/0.5mi inland in 1840 was swallowed up by the sea in 1917 so that a new one had to be built; Stes-Maries-de-la-Mer, once an inland town, is now protected by breakwaters.

Different faces of the Camargue – Although Camargue is one vast plain, it is divided into three distinct regions.

The cultivated region – North of the delta and along the two arms of its river bed, the Rhône has created banks of fine alluvium (*lônes*) which make up the best soil and where the *mas* have been built. This area, the upper Camargue, well-drained and tillable, started being improved during the Middle Ages. Man had to battle against water and salt: the level of salt in the soil was increased by intense heat in summer causing evaporation.

Since the Second World War great drainage and irrigation projects have been undertaken and have brought satisfactory results. After the marshes have been drained and the waters dumped into the Étang de Vaccarès, and the salt content, the soil's sterilising element, has been reduced by washing down the soil, the Rhône's beneficial water is pumped through; the used water is then drained into the Étang de Vaccarès. This operation is a very difficult one requiring constant surveillance, because irrigation can cause the water table to rise and thus the problem of evaporation and increased salt content of the soil recurs, and the process begins all over again.

The extent of arable land has considerably increased and large farming units are predominant. Wheat, vineyards, orchards, market gardens, maize, rape and forage are grown in rotation on this productive soil.

After a period of strong expansion in the 1960s, rice cultivation has dropped drastically: the 33 000ha/127sq mi in 1961 have dwindled to about 10 000ha/24 700 acres. Rice is sown directly in perfectly levelled 3ha/7-acre plots separated by banks of earth and submerged from April to September. The harvesting starts in late September to early October and includes the milling, processing and application of a glossy finish; the rice can then be pretreated or parboiled.

Here and there small clumps of trees – white oak, ash, elm, poplar, robinia and willows – appear.

The salt marshes – They extend almost to Salin-de-Giraud (11 000ha/27 181 acres) and west of the Petit Rhône, and appear as a checkerboard of evaporation pans and huge glistening mounds. The production of salt goes back to Antiquity and made, during the Middle Ages, the wealth of the salt abbeys like Ulmet and Psalmody; industrial salt production started in the 19C.

Between March and September a shallow flow of seawater (not more than a foot deep) is pumped across large "tables" for about 20mi until a saturated solution of sodium chloride has been formed. This is then passed into 9ha/22 acre crystallising pans, 12cm/5in deep, divided by dikes *(cairels)*. Between late August and early October, when evaporation is complete, the salt crystals are raked to the edge, washed and piled into huge white glistening mounds *(camelles)*, some 21m/70ft high. After further washing, drying and crushing, the salt crystals are ready for use in industry to feed to animals or for human consumption.

La Compagnie des Salins du Midi is currently the most powerful company involved in salt harvesting.

La CAMARGUE

The natural region – The wild southern delta comprises a sterile plain dotted with lagoons and smaller pools linked to the sea by a number of channels. A desert of sand and marsh with small dunes lining the coast forms a fascinating nature reserve. This wild Camargue perpetuates the tradition of herds (*manades*), sheep, horses and bulls with their herdsmen (*gardians*), and has protected the ecosystem from human encroachment. Roads cross Camargue, but for a better idea of this nature reserve, walk along the paths laid out by the Regional Nature Park or Nature Reserve.

Flora – These flat expanses, cracked by drought and whitened by the efflorescence of salt, are covered with sparse vegetation known as **sansouire**. Halophilous plants (liking salt), sea lavender and glasswort, green in the spring, grey in the summer and red in the winter, proliferate and are used to feed the herds of wild bulls. The only shrubs are tamarisks. The reeds serve to make *sagno*, a screen that protects cultivated land and provides roofing material for the cabins of *gardians* (*see illustration p 55*). The *sagneurs* are the men who find and cut down the reeds: they go about their task in small boats manoeuvered with long poles, winding their way along freshwater canals known as *roubines*. When the bundles of reeds are made, they are placed along the banks, where a lorry comes to pick them up once or twice a week.

The **Îlots des Rièges**, islands which lie at the south end of the Étang de Vaccarès, have a lush vegetation, a kaleidoscope of colour in the spring, of blue thistles, tamarisk, wild daisies and zinerarias, junipers, yellow irises and narcissi etc.

Fauna – *If you are interested in birdwatching or spotting animals bring binoculars and one of the books on the area listed in the books and films section p 296.* The fauna is of exceptional variety and quantity. Besides racoons, otters and beavers, which are difficult to find, birds reign supreme in this vast marshy land. There are some 400 different species, 160 of which are migratory. The bird population changes according to the season due to the migratory birds which come from northern Europe (Finland and Siberia) to spend the winter, such as the teal, or stopping over in spring or autumn, such as the purple heron. Other kinds to be spotted are: the cattle egret, which follows the *manades* so as to feed off the insects which the cattle put to flight; the greater flamingo which feeds on shellfish; the egret,

Black stork

black-headed gull, herring gull, cormorant, lark, tit and so on.

The waters teem with fish: pike, perch, carp, bream and especially eel found in the *roubines* which are fished with long nets *(trabacs)* composed of three pockets sectioned by passages which get narrower. In the past the people lived off their catch. The cistudo (small aquatic tortoise) and common snake are also happy in this watery zone – the perfect natural environment for these two species.

CAMARGUE TRADITIONS

Manades – The *manade* designates livestock and everything that relates to the upkeep of the herd: herdsmen, pastureland, horses etc. It is given the name of its owner *(manadier)*. The *mas*, the large farm of several hundred acres, is managed by a steward *(bayle-gardian)* and numbers an average of 200 horned cattle plus the horses. The *manades*, which contribute to the ecological balance of the Camargue, are tending to decline in favour of agriculture and salt production.

Camargue horses are descended from prehistoric animals, the skeletons of which were discovered in a vast horse cemetery at Solutré (north-northwest of Lyon). Small (not more than 10 hands), they possess stamina, sureness of foot and lively intelligence; the foals are born brown and turn white only in their fourth or fifth year.

The bulls, black, lithe and agile, with horns aloft, are the stars of the Provençal bull-fights or *cocardes*, where the bull survives the fight (as opposed to the Spanish-style bullfight which ends in the bull's death); some Spanish bulls with short horns are also raised. In the spring the round-up *(ferrade)* is a colourful event: the young calves (one-year-old) are separated from the herd for branding by the *gardians*. They are roped, thrown on to their side and branded on their left thigh with the mark of their owner – the excitement, crush of beasts, smell of burning leather all combine to create a very festive occasion.

The flocks of sheep which number 80 000 head graze in Camargue during the winter and go up the Alps over the summer; they too seem to be affected by the encroachment of farmland and salt production.

Gardians – The *gardian* is the soul of the *manades*, the cowboy of Camargue, a man of pride and character, in a large felt hat, carrying a long, three-pronged stick, watching over his herd (checking the sick animals, caring for them, selecting the bulls for the bullfight – *cocarde*). Although the hat and three-pronged stick are kept more and more for traditional fairs, the horse remains the faithful companion of the *gardian* – an excellent horseman.

The *gardian*'s saddle, made especially by a saddle-maker of the region, must offer maximum comfort and security: padding, fenders which fall along the horse's flanks, cage-like stirrups, pommel in front and cantle behind.

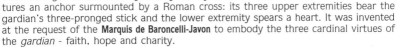

The **Confrérie de Saint-Georges**, a brotherhood founded in 1512, laid down the first statutes regarding the profession of *gardian*. Every year, on 1 May, *gardians* congregate in Arles to take part in a procession to accompany the statue of their saint to the Église Notre-Dame-la-Major. In the church they receive holy blessing and attend High Mass recited in Provençal. The ceremony ends with a banquet, a race followed by a *cocarde* and traditional games played by *gardians*.

The Camargue cross, which you may see by the roadside, features an anchor surmounted by a Roman cross: its three upper extremities bear the gardian's three-pronged stick and the lower extremity spears a heart. It was invented at the request of the **Marquis de Baroncelli-Javon** to embody the three cardinal virtues of the *gardian* - faith, hope and charity.

1 THE RHÔNE DELTA

Round Tour starting from Arles

160km/99mi – allow one day (not including tour of Arles) – local map see below

★★★ **Arles** – *Tour: half a day. See ARLES.*

Leave Arles by ④ on town plan, D 570.

★ **Musée Camarguais** ⊘ – This museum has been set up in the old sheep-fold of the *mas* at Pont de Rousty and retraces the history of the Camargue region since the formation of the Rhône delta (5000 BC). The later periods studied, including Antiquity (Ligurian, Greek and Roman occupation), the Middle Ages (development of the river delta in the 11C by monks reclaiming the land for settlement) and above all the 19C, familiarise the visitor with traditional activities linked with the natural environment of the Camargue. There is a model illustrating the social organisation of a *mas* towards 1850, as well as the animated reconstruction of part of the sheep-fold on the south side.

A footpath of 3.5km/2.2mi through the estate reveals the crops, pasture and marshlands in between the irrigation canals, all of which form a natural part of the grounds of a Camargue *mas*.

Continue along D 570 through a vast cultivated area.

Albaron – Albaron, once a stronghold, as can be seen from its fine 13C-16C tower, is now an important pumping and desalination station.

Continue again along D 570.

Château d'Avignon ⊘ – This vast residence with its classical appearance was part of a huge 18C estate which belonged to Joseph François d'Avignon, from whom the château gets its name. It was modified at the end of the 19C by the industrialist from Marseille, Louis Prat-Noilly, and is a fine illustration of bourgeois tastes from that period. A tour of the interior reveals beautifully-panelled and furnished rooms on the ground floor (testifying to the skill of the Marseille cabinet maker **Auguste Blanqui**) which are decorated with 18C Aubusson or Gobelins tapestries. A grand staircase leads up to the first floor, which houses a suite of bedrooms.

A botanical footpath (500m/just over 500yd) leads visitors past the variety of trees in the gardens.

Centre d'Information de Ginès/François-Hüe ⊘ – The Information Centre of the Parc Naturel Régional de Camargue is located at Pont de Gau, on the edge of the Étang de Ginès. Its aim is to make visitors more aware of the fragility of the environment under the park's protection. A permanent exhibition describes the flora and fauna of the Camargue and the working methods and traditions of those who make a living from its natural resources. Large windows overlook the lagoon and marshlands, also giving visitors a good view of any examples of Camargue birdlife as they fly past. Upstairs, there are audiovisual presentations and video films on the subjects of the saltmarshes and related activities, pink flamingoes or the various projects within the park.

Parc Ornithologique du Pont de Gau 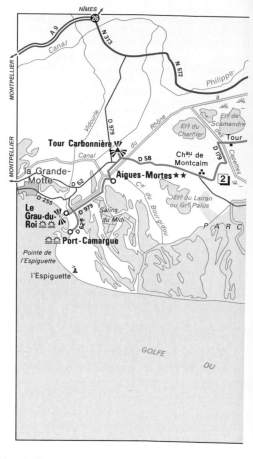 – This bird sanctuary shares a boundary with the information centre and covers 60ha/148 acres of marshland and lagoons. By following a trail marked out with explanatory panels and observation posts visitors can see for themselves most of the bird species which live in or pass through the Camargue in their natural habitat: nocturnal and diurnal birds of prey, such as the marsh-harrier; waders, such as the avocet or the oyster-catcher; grey herons; ducks of all sorts; pink flamingoes and many more. A footpath running alongside Ginès lagoon offers the opportunity of observing, besides birds, a *manade* of bulls grazing on the banks of the lagoon in the right season. Huge aviaries, originally intended for keeping injured animals, are used for stock-raising.

*Les Stes-Maries-de-la-Mer – *See Les STES-MARIES-DE-LA-MER.*

Take D 38 west and after 1km/0.5mi, turn left onto a surfaced road.

On the left is the tomb of Folco de Baroncelli-Javon; it was set up in 1951 on the site of his property, the Mas du Simbeu.

Boat trip on the Petit Rhône 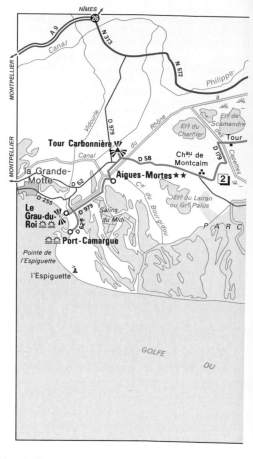 – The trip, which goes upstream to the Petit Sauvage ferry, takes visitors past scenes of the everyday life of the Camargue *manadiers*: wild horses and bulls grazing on the vast plains, and, on the tamarisk-covered river banks, osprey, grey heron, duck and occasionally flamingoes.

Return to Les Stes-Maries-de-la-Mer and take D 85ᴬ.

The road crosses Couvin marsh, a saltwater landscape of stunted plants and swamp. Mas de Cacherel stands to the right; Stes-Maries can be seen to the rear.

At Pioch-Badet, turn right onto D 570; at the entrance to Albaron, turn right again onto D 37 which winds through rice fields. 4.5km/2.5mi further on bear right to Méjanes.

Méjanes 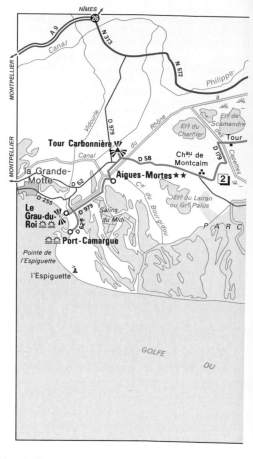 – The amusement centre includes a bull ring, pony trekking and horse-drawn carriages; an electric railway runs 3.5km/2mi along Vaccarès lagoon.

Continue along D 37.

The road crosses an expanse relieved by the occasional clump of trees, reeds and isolated *mas*. On the right there is a small viewpoint which looks out over Vaccarès lagoon towards the Rièges islands.

Return to D 37 where you bear right; in Villeneuve turn right towards Vaccarès lagoon.

To the right there is a lovely view over the lagoon.

La Capelière 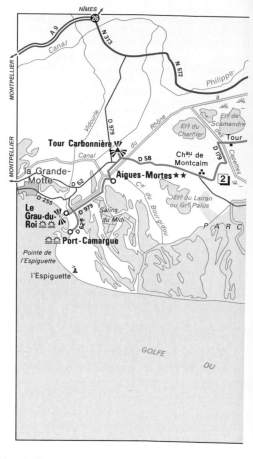 – This is the information centre of the **Réserve Nationale de Camargue**, founded by the national society for the protection of nature.

The reserve covers more than 13 000ha/32 000 acres at the heart of the Rhône delta in the area of the **Étang de Vaccarès**. The species of animal (in particular migratory birds) and plant life which feature in this complex natural environment are protected here. The centre offers a permanent exhibition, footpaths (1.5km/1mi) and two observatories to make visitors better acquainted with the Camargue landscape. To the left, on St-Seren marsh, there is a typical *gardian's* cabin. The road skirts the Étang de Fournelet.

Salin-de-Badon 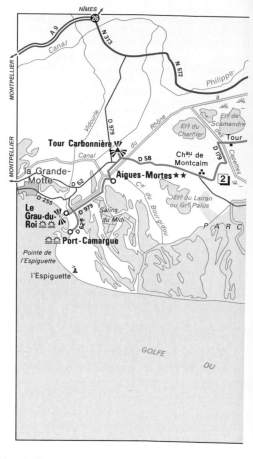 – All year round birds flock to this old royal saltmarsh in their thousands. The Réserve Nationale de Camargue *(see above)* has laid out footpaths, put up explanatory panels and built observatories for the visitors' use.

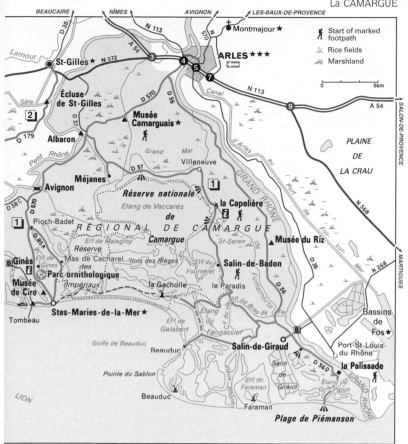

From Le Paradis two excursions *(open to traffic at driver's own risk)* can be under-taken in dry weather, enabling the tourist to discover the birds of the Camargue and particularly the pink flamingoes:
– one goes, via part of the seawall, to **Phare de la Gacholle** (La Gacholle lighthouse) where there is a telescope in a cabin *(traffic prohibited from Perthuis de la Comtesse; do the last half a mile on foot).*
– the other is along the causeway running between two pools, the **Étang Fangassier** and the **Étang Galabert** *(access to cars is forbidden; leave the car at the pumping station)*. Fangassier island is the only nesting site in France for pink flamingoes.
D 36ᶜ and D 36 on the right bring you to Salin-de-Giraud.

Salin-de-Giraud – In salt country, the small town on the south bank of the Rhône, with its grid pattern of streets shaded by plane trees, acacias and catalpas, is a chemical manufacturing centre – every district is named after a firm (Péchiney, Solvay). The surrounding countryside lives from cattle-rearing and mixed farming.
Follow the road which skirts the Grand Rhône.

Viewpoint over the saltmarsh – The viewpoint beside a salt heap looks out over the Giraud pans and workings *(see above and Introduction: Local Economy).*
Continue towards the Palissade estate.
The Rhône and Port-St-Louis can be seen at intervals along the way.

Domaine de la Palissade ⊙ – This estate, the property of the Conservatoire de l'Espace Littoral et des Rivages Lacustres (Society for the Preservation of Coast-lines and River Banks), covers 702ha/1 735 acres and is situated 4km/2.5mi from the mouth of the Grand Rhône. It is the only area of the delta not to have been enclosed by dikes, with the result that the scenery here reflects the original char-acter of the lower Camargue: alluvial deposits from the old course of the Rhône; riparial shrubs on the present banks; dunes or hummocks; a type of marsh sam-phire *(sansouires in Provençal)*, fields of sea lavender used for grazing and beds of reeds and rushes. Footpaths lead visitors round the estate: Baisse Claire *(45min)*; Baisse Sableuse *(2hr 30min)*; and Grande Palun *(3hr 30min)*. In the old hunting pavilion now housing the reception there is an assortment of literature and an audiovisual presentation on the flora and fauna of this protected environment.
Continue towards Plage de Piémanson.

Camargue horses

The road goes along a dike, through a region of lagoons glistening white with salt.

Plage de Piémanson – This beach has a vast sweep of fine sand *(25km/15.5mi)*, bordered by low dunes; to the east can be seen the Estaque mountains, the Marseilleveyre and Etoile massifs, and due north, in the far distance, the Alpilles.
Head towards Arles through Salin-de-Giraud and then along D 36.
The road crosses an area of cultivated fields cut by rows of poplars.

Musée du Riz ⊙ – The Petit Manusclat estate is given over to the cultivation of rice. Its museum describes methods used in the Camargue. Upstairs, there is a pretty *santon* scene displayed in a model of the Roman Theatre at Arles.
D 36 and then D 570, on the right, lead back to Arles.

★★AIGUES-MORTES PLAIN

② From St-Gilles to Port-Camargue
43km/26.5mi – about 5hr – local map see above

★**St-Gilles** – *See ST-GILLES.*
Leave St-Gilles by N 572 going southeast; turn right onto D 179.
Vineyards, pinewoods and fields edged with rushes border the road.

Écluse de St-Gilles – This lock controls the canal between the Petit Rhône and the Rhône-Sète canal – go on to the bridge for a good view of the works.
Continue along D 179.
Rice fields extend to the hills on the horizon where the Puech de Dardaillon towers 146m/479ft high. On the left is an old watchtower.
The road bears left to skirt the Canal des Capettes.
The ruins before the junction with D 58, where you turn right, are those of the early-18C château of the marquess of Montcalm, who lived here before travelling to Canada. The chapel in the vineyards on the right is also 18C.
Continue along D 58, which crosses the Rhône-Sète canal, and shortly afterwards turn right onto D 46.

Tour Carbonnière – A 14C tower, complete with gates, portcullises and battlements, was the advanced barbican of Aigues-Mortes on the old salt road. A small garrison was quartered in the first-floor room which was equipped with a big fireplace and a bread oven.
The platform *(66 steps)* commands a **panorama**★ of Aigues-Mortes and the saltmarshes to the south, the Cévennes foothills to the northwest and Petite Camargue to the east.
Return to D 58 and turn right.

★★ Aigues-Mortes – *See AIGUES-MORTES.*
Take D 979 southwest.
The road passes between the Grande Roubine and the Salins du Midi.

≙≙ **Le Grau-du-Roi** – *See Le GRAU-DU-ROI.*

CARPENTRAS★

Population 24 212

Michelin map 81 folds 12 and 13 or 245 fold 17 or 246 fold 10 – Facilities

Market centre for a Celtic-Ligurian tribe, Gallo-Roman city, bishopric which was temporarily moved to Venasque, Carpentras blossomed when the popes came to Provence. Pope Clement V stayed here frequently from 1309 to 1314, as did the cardinals. A conclave met here in 1314, although it moved to Lyon where it elected John XXII. Capital of the Comtat Venaissin in 1320, the town profited from papal munificence; it expanded and protected itself, under Innocent VI, with powerful ramparts consisting of 32 towers and four gates, demolished in the 19C. With Avignon, Cavaillon and Isle-sur-la-Sorgue it had, until the Revolution, a Jewish ghetto.

The famous sons of Carpentras include the 18C Bishop Malachie d'Inguimbert, benefactor and founder of the hospital (Hôtel-Dieu), who also founded, in 1745, the famous library named after him, the **Bibliothèque Inguimbertine** (**Z B**). The 19C can account for F. Raspail (1794-1878) and A. Naquet (1834-1916), both doctors and republican political figures, while in the 20C E. Daladier (1884-1970) became President of the Council and was one of the signatories of the 1938 Treaty of Munich. Although Carpentras grew prosperous from the expansion of madder, a dye-plant introduced in 1768, the surrounding plain became a fertile garden when a canal, a branch of the Durance, was built in the 19C, enabling the area to be irrigated. At the same time the railway arrived. The town continues to thrive as an active agricultural centre. The old tradi-

Berlingots: a Carpentras speciality

tion of making decoys, which the Provençal hunter uses to attract game, also continues. The local speciality are small pyramid-shaped humbugs called *berlingots*.

Every year Carpentras organises a **festival** with a very varied programme of events, including theatre, opera, dance, folklore and so on *(see the Calendar of events at the end of the guide).*

The weekly Provençal market is held on Fridays.

OLD ST-SIFFREIN CATHEDRAL PRECINCTS *45min*

★**Ancienne Cathédrale St-Siffrein** (**Z**) – The cathedral was started in 1404, on the orders of Pope Benedict XIII of Avignon, and is a good example of the southern Gothic style. It was finished in the early 16C, and its façade was completed in the 17C with the classical doorway. The bell tower dates from the early 20C.

Enter the cathedral by the Flamboyant Gothic south door (late 15C), known as the Porte Juive or Jewish door after the Jewish converts who passed through it to be baptised *(see illustration on p 40 under Art: Architectural Terms).* Inside, the balcony on the nave's end wall connects with the bishop's apartments, and from the small room above the first bay he could follow services. There are paintings in the north chapels by Mignard and Parrocel and sculptures, including a gilded wooden glory, by the Provençal, Bernus, in the chancel; to the left is a late-15C altarpiece depicting the *Coronation of the Virgin.*

★**Treasury (Trésor d'Art sacré)** ⊙ – Displayed in a chapel north of the chancel. Among the exhibits are 14C-16C wooden statues (14C *Virgin with Child*, 15C *Prophet Daniel),* sacerdotal ornaments, gold and silver plate (18C-19C), sculpture by Bernus and a Limoges enamel cross.

Palais de Justice ⊙ (**Z J**) – The former episcopal palace dates from the 17C and now houses the law courts. The interior is decorated with paintings (17C), especially worth noting in the Assize Gallery and Sitting Room.

Arc de triomphe (**Z D**) – The Roman municipal arch behind the Law Courts was built most likely during the same period as the arch in Orange. Its decorations (mutilated) are particularly interesting on the east face, where two prisoners are chained to a tree hung with military trophies.

Amid ruins of the old Romanesque cathedral, located near the present church's east end, is a richly decorated dome.

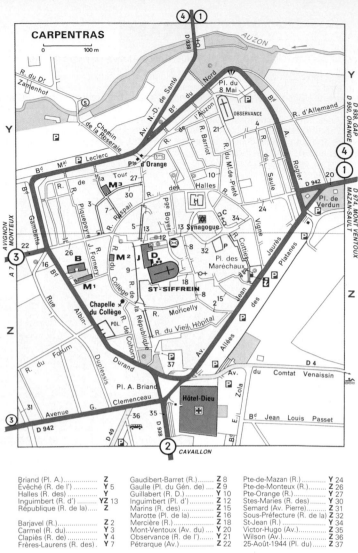

CARPENTRAS

0   100 m

Briand (Pl. A.)	**Z**	Gaudibert-Barret (R.)	**Z** 8	Pte-de-Mazan (R.)	**Y** 24
Évêché (R. de l')	**Y** 5	Gaulle (Pl. du Gén. de)	**Z** 9	Pte-de-Monteux (R.)	**Z** 26
Halles (R. des)	**Y**	Guillabert (R. D.)	**Y** 10	Pte-Orange (R.)	**Y** 27
Inguimbert (R. d')	**YZ** 13	Inguimbert (Pl. d')	**Z** 12	Stes-Maries (R. des)	**Y** 30
République (R. de la)	**Z**	Marins (R. des)	**Z** 15	Semard (Av. Pierre)	**Z** 31
		Marotte (Pl. de la)	**Z** 16	Sous-Préfecture (R. de la)	**Z** 32
Barjavel (R.)	**Z** 2	Mercière (R.)	**Z** 18	St-Jean (R.)	**Y** 34
Carmel (R. du)	**Y** 3	Mont-Ventoux (Av. du)	**Y** 20	Victor-Hugo (Av.)	**Z** 35
Clapiès (R. de)	**Y** 4	Observance (R. de l')	**Y** 21	Wilson (Av.)	**Z** 36
Frères-Laurens (R. des)	**Y** 7	Pétrarque (Av.)	**Z** 22	25-Août-1944 (Pl. du)	**Z** 37

B	Bibliothèque Inguimbertine	**J**	Palais de Justice	**M¹**	Musée Duplessis
D	Arc de Triomphe	**M¹**	Musée Comtadin	**M²**	Musée Sobirats
				M³	Musée lapidaire

ADDITIONAL SIGHTS

Viewpoint – From the terrace on Place du 8-Mai to the north there are fine views of the Dentelles de Montmirail and Mont Ventoux.

Porte d'Orange (**Y**) – This gate dates from the 14C and is the only remaining part of the city wall.

Museums ⊘ – Four museums have assembled collections of essentially regional interest.

Musée Comtadin (**Z M¹**) – *Ground floor.* Regional mementoes from the Comtat Venaissin include coins and seals, local headdresses and bells for cattle and sheep driven through the town to summer and winter pastures.

Musée Duplessis (**Z M¹**) – *First floor.* Paintings by local Primitive artists, Parrocel, Rigaud, the Carpentras artists Duplessis and J. Laurens.

Musée Sobirats (**Z M²**) – Lovely reconstruction of an 18C mansion.

Musée Lapidaire (**Y M³**) – The building used to be the Chapel of the Grey Penitents (once the Convent of the Visitation), consecrated in 1717. In the second south chapel there are several columns and capitals from the cathedral's Romanesque cloisters.

Hôtel-Dieu ⊘ (**Z**) – The building housing the former hospital dates from the 18C. The tour includes a visit to the pharmacy, which contains cabinets painted with landscapes and amusing figures (monkey apothecaries) in which there is a large collection of Moustiers *faïence* (glazed earthenware) jars. The Baroque chapel houses to the left of the chancel the tomb of Monseigneur d'Inguimbert, founder of the hospital, and a beautiful altar screen. The striking grand staircase has an elegant wrought iron banister.

Synagogue ⊘ (**Y**) – The synagogue, dating from the 14C, rebuilt in the 18C and restored in 1929 and 1958, is the oldest in France and the last relic of a Jewish ghetto, which before the Revolution numbered more than 1 500 people. On the first floor is the panelled sanctuary with lamps; on the ground floor are the oven for baking unleavened bread and some annexes; and in the basement the piscina for women's purification rites.

Chapelle du Collège (**Z**) – The chapel was built in the 17C, in Jesuit style, and is now used for contemporary art exhibitions. Note inside the building the baluster chapels which surround the chancel, the finely-decorated central chapel on the left and the dome, with its alternating windows and shell-shaped alcoves.

EXCURSIONS

Monteux – *4.5km/2.5mi on* ③ *on the town plan, D 942.* This small market-garden centre had a moment of glory in the early 14C when Pope Clement V came here to rest; a tower remains from the castle in which he stayed. Also standing are two gates from the old 14C ramparts.
Monteux is also the birthplace of St Gentius, patron saint of Provençal farmers, who reputedly had the ability to bring on rain. A pilgrimage *(see the Calendar of events at the end of the guide)* is held annually in his honour in Le Beaucet.

Mazan – *7km/4mi to the east on D 942.* The small town in the Auzon valley is close to Mormoiron, Europe's largest gypsum deposit and quarry. The village was the birthplace of the Comtat Venaissin's most reputed sculptor, **Jacques Bernus** (1650-1728).
Sixty-two Gallo-Roman sarcophagi, which once lined the Roman road from Carpentras to Sault, now form a wall in the **churchyard** of the 12C Notre-Dame-de-Pareloup, which is half underground. From here there is a fine **view**★ of the Dentelles de Montmirail, Mont Ventoux and Lure mountain.
Near the church, the 17C Chapelle des Pénitents Blancs houses a **local museum** ⊘ (parchments, costumes, furnishings, agricultural implements). Note the vestiges from the Stone Age found during the excavations on the south face of Mont Ventoux, and a carving by Jacques Bernus. In the courtyard is a 14C bread oven.
The Château de Mazan, today an old people's home *(not open to the public)*, once witnessed the extravagant sexual antics of the notorious **Marquis de Sade.** A plaque testifies to his stay in this residence: "The Marquis de Sade, Lord of Mazan (1740-1814) once lived on these premises".

Sarrians – *8km/5mi northwest, taking Avenue Notre-Dame-de-Santé* (**Y**), *then D 950.* The partly-hidden **church** of this small town of the Comtat Venaissin, on a rock bluff, was once a Benedictine priory. The interior has an unusually attractive chancel and is remarkable for its squinch-supported dome (11C).

The main shopping streets are printed in red at the head of the street list accompanying town plans.

CASSIS ⌂

Population 7 967
Michelin map 84 fold 13 or 114 fold 29 or 245 fold 45 or 246 fold M
Local map see Massif des CALANQUES – Facilities

Cassis, a small, bustling fishing port, lies in an attractive **setting**★ at the end of a bay where the valley, between the arid Puget heights (to the west) and the wooded escarpments of Cap Canaille (to the east), comes down to the sea. It is justly reputed for the quality of its fish, shellfish and other seafood; the sea-urchins *(oursins)* with Cassis white wine are a local delicacy. It is also a popular summer resort which has three small beaches, two of sand, one of shingle, each sheltered by rocks with a fairly steep slope.
Cassis became known in 1867 with a mention of the village by **Frédéric Mistral** in his poem *Calendal* and again at the turn of the century, when it became the chosen summer resort of the artists Derain, Vlaminck, Matisse and Dufy.
The quarries not far from the village, notably by the Calanque de Port-Miou, produce a hard white stone which has been used for quaysides and gateways, such as for the Rove Tunnel, the Suez Canal and the Campo Santo in Genoa.

CASSIS

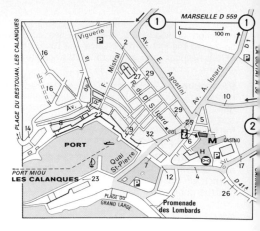

Abbé-Mouton (R.)	2
Arène (R. de l')	4
Autheman (R. V.)	5
Baragnon (Pl.)	6
Barthélemy (Bd)	7
Barthélemy (Quai J.-J.)	8
Baux (Quai des)	9
Ciotat (R. de la)	10
Clemenceau (Pl.)	12
Dardanelles (Av. des)	14
Jaurès (Av. J.)	16
Leriche	
(Av. Professeur)	17
Mirabeau (Pl.)	22
Moulins (Q. des)	23
République (Pl.)	25
Revestel (Av. du)	26
St-Michel (R.)	27
Thiers (R. Adolphe)	29
Victor-Hugo (Av.)	32

Musée d'Arts et Traditions Populaires ⊙ (**M**) – Located in an 18C restored town house, Maison de Cassis, this small museum contains archeological finds from the area, including a 1C cippus, Roman and Greek coins, pottery, amphorae, various manuscripts relating to the town and paintings and sculpture by local artists.

Promenade des Lombards – This pleasant walk along the beach continues round the foot of the rock spike crowned with the **castle** of Les Baux which has been restored.

EXCURSION

★★**Massif des Calanques** – *See Massif des CALANQUES.*

CAVAILLON

Population 23 102
Michelin map 81 fold 12 or 245 fold 30 or 246 fold 11
Local maps see Basse Vallée de la DURANCE and Montagne du LUBERON
Facilities

The name Cavaillon, to the French, conjures up fragrant melons and the early veg-etables of spring. The melons are sweet and rose pink inside; the harvest begins in May; the vegetables come from the mile upon mile of market gardens which surround the town and make it France's largest designated "national market", with an annual turnover of nearly 800 000 metric tons.
Ancient Cabellio was an *oppidum* of the Cavares, a Celtic-Ligurian people, and was located on the hill of St-Jacques. It was under Marseille's jurisdiction until the latter's downfall. The town then left its hilltop site and became a prosperous Roman colony. During the Middle Ages it had two famous bishops: in the 6C St Veranus, patron saint of shepherds, and in the 14C Philippe de Cabassole, friend of Petrarch *(see p 157).*

SIGHTS

Arc romain – *Place François-Tourel.* On the square lie the ruins of a small, deli-cately-carved Roman arch dating from the 1C BC which stood near the cathedral at the intersection of the main streets of the Roman town and was re-erected here in 1880.

Chapelle St-Jacques – *45min on foot. At the end of the square, left of the arch, take the picturesque stepped path.*

Carved into the rock at the second bend is an inscription to Mistral. From the viewing table placed in front of the Calvary, the **view★** embraces the Cavaillon plain, Mont Ventoux, the Coulon valley, the Vaucluse plateau, the Luberon (quite near), the Durance valley and the Alpilles.
Continue to the **Chapelle St-Jacques**, a 12C chapel dedicated to St James, remodelled in the 16C and 17C. It stands among cypresses, pines and almond trees, near a small hermitage occupied from the 14C to the beginning of this century.
It is accessible also by car *(5.5km/3mi)* by way of D 938 going north; just over 50m/50yd beyond the crossroads turn left uphill (views of the Montagnette hills and the Rhône).

Ancienne Cathédrale Notre-Dame-et-St-Véran – To the original Romanesque structure of the cathedral, side chapels were added from the 14C to the 18C. The façade was almost entirely rebuilt in the 18C and the east end holds a fine pen-tagonal apse.
Enter on the south side.

Cross the small Romanesque **cloisters**. Inside, despite the darkness, one can glimpse gilded 17C panelling in the chancel and side chapels (paintings by Pierre and Nicolas Mignard, Parrocel and Daret) and choir stalls which date back to 1585.

Synagogue ⊘ – Rebuilt in 1772-1774, this synagogue has drawn inspiration from Baroque Provençal architecture. It features two superimposed ensembles connected by an outside staircase. The interior is ornamented with delightful wood panelling painted grey and decorated with blue and yellow touches, shell motifs, flowers and scrolls. A superb wrought iron balustrade, echoing the one at the town hall, encircles the gallery of the officiating rabbi and the tabernacle.

Jewish Comtat Venaissin Museum – It is located in the lower part of the building, traditionally occupied by women, and also served as a bakery, a fact evidenced by the oven and grey marble tablet used for making unleavened bread. The Jewish community is evoked through a miscellaneous collection of objects and documents: manuscripts, prayer books, sacred articles, Torahic ornaments and relics of the original 14C synagogue built on the same site.

Musée de l'Hôtel-Dieu ⊘ **(M)** – The museum is housed in the chapel (1755) and main building of an old hospital. The chapel contains a lapidary section: Gallo-Grecian and Gallo-Roman tombstones, statues (head of Agrippine from 1C AD), early medieval altar taken from the cathedral.

On the ground floor, one room is devoted to Neolithic settlements in western Luberon, whereas another room houses a presentation of the former hospital: note the oitment jars made of glass and earthenware, a 1773 mortar, reliquaries...

The first floor displays an important **archeological collection★** of objects discovered for the most part on the hill of St-Jacques or in wells or ditches dating back to 2C and 1C BC: a great many ceramic pieces made between 5C BC and 6C AD, coins, funarary urns, everyday objects and even remains of food.

CAVAILLON

Bournissac (Cours)	3
Castil-Blaze (Pl.)	5
Clus (Pl. du)	7
République (R. de la)	37
Victor-Hugo (Cours)	43

Berthelot (Av.)	2
Clemenceau (Av. G.)	6
Coty (Av. R.)	9
Crillon (Bd)	10
Diderot (R.)	12
Donné (Chemin)	13
Doumer (Av. P.)	14
Dublé (Av. Véran)	15
Durance (R. de la)	17
Gambetta (Cours L.)	18
Gambetta (Pl. L.)	19
Gaulle (Av. Gén. de)	22
Grand-Rue	23
Jaurès (Av. Jean)	24
Joffre (Av. Mar.)	26
Kennedy (Av. J.-F.)	27
Lattre-de-Tassigny (R.P.J. de)	29
Pasteur (R.)	30
Péri (Av. Gabriel)	31
Pertuis (Rte de)	32
Raspail (R.)	34
Renan (Cours E.)	35
Sarnette (Av. Abel)	38
Saunerie (R.)	40
Semard (Av. Pierre)	41
Tourel (Pl. F.)	42

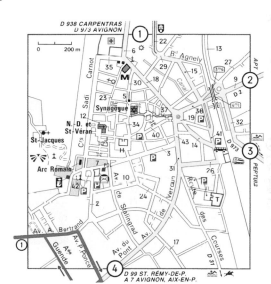

CHÂTEAU-BAS

Michelin map 84 fold 2 or 245 fold 30 or 246 fold 12
8km/5mi northwest of Lambesc

The fascinating ruins of a Roman temple and chapel stand in a charming site at the far end of the castle (16C-18C) estate.

Barely 1km/0.5mi southwest of Cazan a road (marked) leaves D 22 in the direction of Pélissanne; car park at the end.

Temple Romain ⊘ – The Roman temple probably dates from the late 1C BC, a period characterised by many impressive buildings such as the Commemorative Arch at St-Rémy-de-Provence or the Maison Carrée in Nîmes. The remains include part of the foundations, the left side wall, a wall ending in a square pilaster, surmounted by a beautiful Corinthian capital, and a 7m/23ft fluted column still standing intact. Among the surrounding ruins are a second temple and a semicircular precinct (Roman), probably the ruins of a sanctuary.

Chapelle St-Césaire – The 12C chapel, abutting the left wall of the temple, is barrel vaulted, with an oven-vaulted apse and a 16C doorway and niche.

CHÂTEAUNEUF-DU-PAPE

Population 2 062
Michelin map 81 fold 12 or 245 fold 16 or 246 fold 24 – Facilities

The town has given its name to the most heady of all the Rhône wines. The original vineyard was planted in the 14C on land belonging to the Avignon popes, who summered here, and the wine was consumed locally until the mid 18C when its renown began to spread.

For a long time the wine was sent in barrels to Burgundy for improvement. In c 1880 phylloxera ravaged the vineyard, resulting in its ruin; the vineyard was then replanted. In 1923 the winegrowers' association laid down strict rules defining the area, the management of the vineyards, harvest dates, the selection of grapes, the 13 acceptable wine types, vinification and vintage labelling. The strict control has brought about a highly refined and often superb product: a wine known for its finesse and nose – Châteauneuf-du-Pape.

Château des Papes – All that remains of the fortress built by the Avignon popes in the 14C and burned down during the Wars of Religion is the keep and a stretch of wall. The ruins, however, still command a splendid **view★★**: the valley of the Rhône, Roquemaure and the ruins of Château de l'Hers, Avignon with Notre-Dame-des-Doms and the Palais des Papes clearly outlined against the more distant Alpilles, the Luberon and the Vaucluse plateau, the Dentelles de Montmirail and, further off, Mont Ventoux, the Baronnies and Lance mountain.

Musée des Outils de Vigneron ⊘ – Located in Père Anselme's wine cellar, this museum is devoted to the world of wine. The tour is conducted in the order that wine is produced: from work in the vineyard (plough, hoes, pruning clippers), its treatment (copper sulphate spraying-machines), harvesting (baskets, wine press), work in the cellar (funnel, 16C press, huge 14C barrel) and related subjects such as cooperage, grafting, weights and measures, phylloxera, bottling, corking etc. In one room an exhibition describes the vineyard, which extends nowadays over 3 300ha/8 151 acres and involves 300 winegrowers. In the courtyard is a display of old ploughs.

EXCURSION

Roquemaure – *Drive for around 10km/6mi along D 17 and D 976.*

The road runs through beautifully-kept vineyards. On the left, some 2km/1mi further on, appear the ruins of Château de l'Hers. Its machicolated tower seems to hover protectively over its precious vineyard. Opposite it, on the far bank of the Rhône, is Château de Roquemaure where Pope Clement V died on 20 April 1314. Cross the Rhône, which the road borders for a couple of miles, and continue to Roquemaure which has preserved several old houses (notably the one belonging to Cardinal Bertrand, near the church). The 13C church has a fine 17C organ.

*The chapter on art and architecture in this guide gives
an outline of artistic creation in the region, providing
the context of the buildings and works of art described
in the Sights section.
This chapter may also provide ideas for touring.
It is advisable to read it at leisure before setting out.*

CHÂTEAURENARD

Population 11 790
Michelin map 81 fold 12 or 245 fold 29 or 246 fold 25
Local map see Basse Vallée de la DURANCE – Facilities

The town, at the foot of a hill beneath medieval twin towers, has become a national market with a designated site of 150 000m²/35 acres, handling the produce (350 000 to 400 000 metric tons annually) harvested from the market gardens and fruit farms in the neighbouring plain.

In Mistral's work *Nerte*, a 15C lord from Châteaurenard sold his daughter's soul to the devil.

Château Féodal ⊘ – *Access: on foot by taking the staircase to the right of the church, by car 1km/0.5mi via Avenue Marx-Dormoy and a signposted road on the right.*

Of the feudal castle, ruined during the Revolution, there remain only two towers connected by a covered walk. The interior of these towers houses a Regional History Museum. From the top of one, the Tour du Griffon, a fine **panorama★** can be had of the town and surrounding countryside, the Montagnette hills, Avignon and Villeneuve-lès-Avignon, the Dentelles de Montmirail, Mont Ventoux and the Alpilles.

La CIOTAT ⚐⚐

Population 30 620
Michelin map 84 fold 14 or 114 folds 42 and 43 or 245 fold 45
or 246 fold M Facilities

La Ciotat, where the houses rise in tiers above the bay of the same name, has been a port since ancient times when, as Citharista, it was an outpost of Marseille. Roman occupation, barbarian invasion and devastation were followed by a revival in the Middle Ages, and from the 16C the provision of a merchant fleet in the eastern Mediterranean.

The city continues to fulfil its maritime vocation, particularly by running large ship-building yards specialising in oil and methane tankers. However, the worldwide crisis in the shipbuilding industry has scored a direct hit here, and the city is having to adapt to different technologies and seek new areas of commercial activity.

Auguste and **Louis Lumière**, two brothers who invented the *cinématographe*, brought fame to the town when, on 21 September 1895, the first private viewing of a short motion picture was held, two months before being shown in Paris.

SIGHTS

Vieux Port – This old harbour has all the charm of a small fishing port.

Notre-Dame-de-l'Assomption (**B**) – This 17C church's lovely pink Baroque façade overlooks the harbour. Inside, the modern-looking interior is notable for a *Descent from the Cross* by André Gaudion painted in 1616 (south aisle) and a modern frieze (22m/72ft long) by Gilbert Ganteaume of scenes from the Gospels. At the end of the nave are paintings by Tony Roux representing Man and Woman.

Musée Ciotaden ⊘ (**M**) – Inside are mementoes and documents about this seafaring town and its past.

Clos des Plages – The district has been developed just north of the new harbour (Nouveau Port: 850 berths) as a resort with hotels and seaside villas lining the beach. A thalassotherapy centre has been established. Marking one of the squares open to the sea is a monument to the Lumière brothers *(see above)*.

Parc du Mugel ⊘ – *Access by Quai de Roumanie, south of the town plan.* Located at the tip of Cap de l'Aigle, this natural protected area with pudding-stone soil (reddish conglomerate of shingles and sand) favours abundant and varied vegetation (cork trees,

LA CIOTAT

Foch (R. Mar.)	16
Poilus (R. des)	
Anatole-France (Bd)	2
Bartolucci (Bd)	6
Clemenceau (Bd G.)	13
Gallieni (Av. Mar.)	18
Ganteaume (Quai)	19
Gaulle (Quai Gén. de)	21
Kennedy (Av. J.-F.)	23
Lamartine (Bd)	24
Prés.-Wilson (Av.)	31

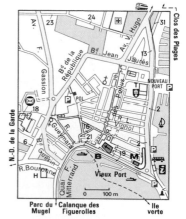

B Église Notre-Dame-de-l'Assomption
M Musée ciotaden

mimosa, arbutus etc). A marked trail amid the identified plants makes the walk instructive as well as enjoyable. At the top *(steep path)*, some 155m/509ft, there is a lovely view of La Ciotat and its surroundings.

★**Île Verte** ⊙ – *30min return by boat.* The rock at Cap de l'Aigle, so clearly a bird of prey *(aigle means eagle)* when seen from the small fort on Ile Verte, is what gave the point its name.

Chapelle Notre-Dame-de-la-Garde – *2.5km/1.5mi – plus 15min return on foot. Leave La Ciotat by Boulevards Bertolucci and Narvik, Rue du Cardinal-Maurin and Chemin de la Garde, on the right; after 500m/0.3mi turn left towards a built-up area and park the car.*

At the chapel, bear right onto a path which leads to a terrace above the chapel *(85 steps cut out of the rock)*. The **view**★★ embraces the full extent of La Ciotat bay.

LES CALANQUES

1.5km/1mi. Leave La Ciotat along Quai de Roumanie, Avenue des Calanques and turn left into Avenue du Mugel. These rocky inlets known as calanques *can also be visited on board a catamaran-type boat with a cabin affording underwater views (see the section on Sport and recreation at the end of the guide).*

Calanque du Mugel – The inlet is dominated by the rock of Cap de l'Aigle. There is a good view of Île Verte from here.

Take Avenue des Calanques and bear left into Avenue de Figuerolles.

★**Calanque de Figuerolles** – *15min return on foot.*

A short green valley leads to the small clear-water inlet. This curious site is characterised by strangely eroded rocks, including the "Capucin", an isolated crag projecting forward on the right, and cliffs featuring cavities with sharp edges and a smooth, polished interior.

The Baie de La Ciotat has been made into a Regional Marine Park. It is now a preserved area where fishing and other leisure activities are strictly regulated. For further details, see the section on Practical information at the end of the guide.

Grotte de la COCALIÈRE★

Michelin map 80 fold 8 or 240 fold 7

This cave, northwest of St-Ambroix on the Gard plateau, contains a network of explored galleries running 46km/29mi underground. In addition the site of La Cocalière has revealed a very populated prehistoric settlement which was occupied from the Mousterian period (45 000 BC) to the Iron Age (400 BC).

From Les Vans bear left on a road which branches off D 904 on the left; not far after, the road to the right goes off to Courry.

TOUR ⊙ *1hr 15min*

At the bottom of the tunnel, a path follows along (about 1 200m/1 312yd) the bottom of a horizontal gallery which communicates with each of the other galleries. The cave (inside temperature: 14°C/57°F) is rich in its variety of concretions, reflected in the pools of water fed by small waterfalls. As you travel underground you will see discs – huge concretions with a wide diameter which specialists have not yet been able to explain; delicate stalactites: white (if charged with calcite) or multi-coloured (if charged with metallic oxide); and gours (natural dams). After the speleologists' camp site, walk through the Chaos chamber, where the roof is covered with stalactites and other forms of erosion, to the gallery of frozen falls and eccentrics which overlooks an imposing sparkling **waterfall** and wells linked to the lower stages where underground rivers flow. Pass through a prehistoric deposit before returning to the entrance area on a small train.

Outside, the cave's immediate surroundings are: a dolmen, tumuli, small constructions of dried stones much like the *bories* from Provence, prehistoric shelters and varied karstic phenomena (caves, sinkholes, faults).

In this guide town plans show the main streets and the way to the sights; local maps show the main roads and the roads of the recommended tour.

COMTAT VENAISSIN

Michelin map 81 folds 2, 3, 12 and 13 or 245 folds 16-18 and 30-31
or 246 folds 9-11

Located between the Rhône and Durance rivers and Mont Ventoux, the territory comprising this old county owes its name to its first capital, Venasque. It was given the name Comtat Venaissin when it was annexed by the Holy See in 1274. The Comtat Venaissin is an important territory in the history of the French nation. It had previously been included in the marquisate of Provence and was under the county of Toulouse's rule; and like all the county's other possessions it was affected by the Albigensian heresy and the 1229 Treaty of Paris *(see Michelin Green Guide Pyrénées Roussillon Albigeois).*

United under the crown in 1271, it was ceded three years later to Pope Gregory X by Philip III, the Bold, and remained under papal authority until 1791 when it once again became part of France. This enclave had its own administration; its law courts were located at Carpentras, capital of the Comtat, having superseded Pernes-les-Fontaines in 1320. Made up of the rich Vaucluse Plain, Comtat Venaissin occupies the largest and most southerly basin of the Rhône Valley. Its rich calcareous soil, benefiting from irrigation, has brought about the creation of vast gardens specialising in the production of market garden vegetables and fruit which are distributed nationwide *(see Introduction: Local economy).* Cultivation occurs within a framework of scattered habitats and a mosaic of scientifically-managed small farms.

Based on a July 1745 map

The Ouvèze, Sorgue and Durance rivers have created vast, fertile alluvial plains which have brought prosperity to market towns such as Orange, Avignon, Cavaillon and Carpentras; some of these same towns have become very large dispatching centres.

Les CONCLUSES★★

Michelin map 80 south of fold 9 or 245 fold 14 or 246 fold 24
8km/5mi northeast of Lussan

D 643, lined with clipped boxwood, crosses a *garrigue* of holm oak to the Gorges de l'Aiguillon, also known as Les Concluses.
The **Aiguillon** torrent, dry in summer, has hollowed out of the calcareous grey-white rock a rocky defile some 1km/0.5mi long and opened upstream by a fine natural phenomenon: the Portail (Gateway).

TOUR *1hr return on foot*

Leave the car at the road's end, preferably in the second of the two car parks, in a lay-by halfway down. From here there is a **view★** upstream of the giant holes in the riverbed.
Take the path on the right signposted: Portail.
As you descend you see the caves on the opposite bank, most notably the Baume de Biou or Bulls' Cave, and come to the promontory and Beauquier pool, a widening of the stream fringed by trees at the feet of majestic rock escarpments. Note on the cliff face three abandoned eagles' eyries. The path ends at the gateway where the rock overhang finally meets above the river's course; the bottom forms a narrow gorge through which the Aiguillon flows when in spate. Pass under the gateway, then walk through the rocky **straits** following the riverbed for about 200m/219yd. *(This walk is possible only in summer.)*
On the way back, experienced walkers may enjoy returning to the car park by way of the riverbed upstream as far as Baume de Biou and from there a very rough path *(allow an extra 15min).*

CORNICHE DES CRÊTES★★

Michelin map 84 folds 13, 14 or 114 folds 42 and 43 or 246 fold M

The stretch of coast road between Cassis and La Ciotat skirts the crests of the Canaille, a short limestone range which rises from the sea in towering white cliffs, some of the tallest in France – 362m/1 188ft at Cap Canaille, 399m/1 310ft at the Grande Tête. The tourist road and its viewpoints offer superb and dizzying views.

FROM CASSIS TO LA CIOTAT *19km/11.5mi – allow 4hr*

⌂ **Cassis** – *See CASSIS.*

Leave Cassis by ② on the town plan, the road to Toulon, and during the ascent take a signposted road to the right. At Pas de la Colle turn left.

Mont de la Saoupe – The **panorama**★★ from the television mast at the top of this mountain includes Cassis, the Île de Riou, Massif de Marseilleveyre and Chaîne St-Cyr to the west, the Chaîne de l'Étoile, Mont Garlaban and Massif de la Ste-Baume to the north, La Ciotat and Caps de l'Aigle et de Sicié to the southeast.

Return to Pas de la Colle and continue uphill.

Bends and viewpoints reveal an ever-wider view of Cassis and La Ciotat.

★★★**Cap Canaille** – From the guard rail on the cape there is an outstanding **view**★★★ of the cliff face, Massif de Puget and the *calanques* and Massif de Marseilleveyre.

Beyond Grande Tête, turn right to the semaphore.

Semaphore – The **view**★★★ embraces La Ciotat and its shipyards, Aigle point, the Embiez islands, and capes Sicié and Canaille *(telescope)*.

Return to the crest road; bear right for La Ciotat.

The descent into town passes quarries, recently planted pinewoods and the *"pont naturel"*, a natural limestone arch standing on a pudding-stone base.

⌂ **La Ciotat** – *See La CIOTAT.*

Plaine de la CRAU

Michelin maps 83 fold 10 and 84 fold 1 or 245 folds 29 and 42 or 246 folds 12, 13, 26 and 27

The Crau plain, which extends over 50 000ha/200sq mi between the Rhône, the Alpilles, St-Mitre hills and the sea, is a grey-white desert of shingle and gravel which, in places, reaches a depth of 15m/50ft. For centuries the only signs of man's existence were the roads going north up the Rhône valley towards Lyon.

A museum called l'**Écomusée de la Crau** ⊘ at St-Martin-de-Crau contains an exhibition on this unique region which can also be explored through guided tours around the nature reserve at Peau de Meau.

Since the construction of the Canal de Craponne in 1554 which brought the waters of the Durance to their original delta on the Étang de Berre, and the subsequent development of a network of irrigation channels, the cultivation of the **Petite Crau** in the north has steadily extended until it now covers half the plain. From Arles in the west to Salon in the east, windbreaks of poplar and cypress shelter fields of fruit and vegetables *(follow N 113)*. There are four crops a year of the famous Crau hay (annual crop approximately 100 000 metric tons) – the last of which is grazed in the fields by sheep wintering in the plain.

The **Grande Crau** to the south remains the symbolic Provençal desert, a sea of stones explained imaginatively by a Greek legend: Heracles, his way to Spain barred by the Ligurians, and having exhausted his stock of arrows against them, called on Zeus for help; the god sent down a hail of stones and rocks which became the plain. More prosaically, geologists attribute the presence of the stones to the Durance, which originally flowed directly into the sea through the Lamanon gap. The rocks and stones brought down by the stream accumulated into a vast delta which eventually dried out when the river changed course and became a tributary of the Rhône.

The Grande Crau, resembling a huge steppe, is devoted to **sheep farming**. The traditional breed is the fine-wooled Merino, a cross between the Crau country breed and the Spanish Merino introduced into France around the early 19C. About 100 000 head graze on **coussous** (tufts of fine grass growing between the stones) between mid-October and early June. The shepherds (belonging to the Union of Arles Breeders) own but their personal flock; in the spring they settle on the grazing land (which they rent) which includes a sheepfold and a well. All the sheepfolds, which amount to forty, were built from 1830 to 1880 on an identical plan: a rectangle (40m x 10m/131ft x 33ft) open on two sides and covered by stones placed like fish scales. Sometimes the shepherd lives nearby in a one-room hut. The wellhead is made up of Alpilles stone carved in one piece. During the autumn and winter, the flock grazes on *coussous*, hay, and the second growth of the irrigated plain; at the end of the winter some of the sheep eat the grass (lucerne, sainfoin) bought by the shepherd whereas the remaining animals are once again fed on *coussous*. The flock is moved by truck from its much higher altitude summer pastures to its winter ones (and vice versa). The sheep, although well integrated into the local rural economy, pose a number of problems: the Merino is not sufficiently profitable, shepherds are hard to find, and the area of sheep-grazing land is diminishing.

DISCOVERING THE PLAINE DE CRAU

The route from St-Hippolyte *(12km/7.5mi southeast of Arles on N 453)* south-east along N 568 gives a good idea of the special atmosphere of the Grande Crau. Green countryside gives way to a progressively more barren landscape, devoid of artefacts, of man and beast, apart from the very occasional sheepfold and cabin near a well, reflecting the decline of such pastoral activities as sheep farming.

In addition to the encroachment of agriculture from the north, the continued expansion of the Bassins de Fos implies incursion from the south for industrial development; but for the moment the heart of one of France's most fertile regions remains a semi-desert, the Plaine de la Crau.

DENTELLES DE MONTMIRAIL★

Michelin map 81 folds 2, 3 and 12 or 245 fold 17 or 246 folds 9 and 10

The pine and oak-clad heights, sometimes blanketed with vines, are the final foothills of Mont Ventoux overlooking the Rhône and owe their name (*dentelle* means lace) to the unique outline of the peaks. The geological cause of these sharp peaks lies in the upper strata of Jurassic limestone having been forced upright by the folding of the earth's crust and then eroded by wind and weather into needle-thin spikes and ridges. Although not very high in altitude (St-Amand: 734m/2409ft), the Dentelles have a more alpine appearance than their taller neighbour (Mont Ventoux: 1909m/6263ft). The hills, broom-covered in May and June, attract painters and naturalists as well as walkers, who come either for a short stroll or for a long hike.

ROUND TOUR FROM VAISON-LA-ROMAINE

60km/37mi – about half a day – local map see overleaf

★★**Vaison-la-Romaine** – *See VAISON-LA-ROMAINE.*

Leave Vaison-la-Romaine on D 977, the road towards Avignon; turn left after 5.5km/3.75mi onto D 88.

The road climbs into the mountains, disclosing views of the Ouvèze valley to the west.

★**Séguret** – The picturesque village, built against the side of a steep hill, is worth a visit. At the village entrance walk through the covered passage into the main street and continue past the 15C Mascarons fountain and the 14C belfry to the 12C Église St-Denis. From the square *(viewing-table)* the **view** embraces the Dentelles, the Comtat Venaissin and, to the far north, the line of the Massif Central. A ruined castle and a network of steep streets, lined with old houses, all add character.

On leaving Séguret turn left onto D 23 for Sablet and then take D 7 and D 79 for Gigondas.

Dentelles de Montmirail

Gigondas – The village has given its name to the local red Grenache wine.

By way of Les Florets, where there is an alpine club hut, drive to the Col de Cayron.

Col de Cayron – Alt 396m/1 299ft. This pass is at the centre of the Dentelles' principal peaks which, with faces rearing nearly 100m/300ft high, offer all the complexity of feature relished by rock climbers.

Park the car and bear right (1hr return on foot) on the unsurfaced road which winds through the Dentelles.

There are splendid **views★** of the Rhône plain blocked by the Cévennes, Vaucluse plateau and Mont Ventoux. The road passes below a ruined Saracen tower (Tour Sarrazine).

Return to the car and take D 7, then turn left towards Vacqueyras.

Chapelle Notre-Dame d'Aubune – Near Fontenouilles farm. The Romanesque chapel at the foot of the mountain stands on a small terrace from which there is a good view of the Comtat plain. It is surmounted by an elegant **bell tower★** ornamented on each of its four sides by tall Antique-style pilasters and rounded bays between larger and smaller pillars – note the decoration on the columns and capitals (straight or twisted fluting, grapes, acanthus leaves – *see Art: Architectural Terms*).

Continue left along D 81.

The road winds through vineyards and olive groves.

Beaumes-de-Venise – A terraced village, on the southernmost foothills of the Dentelles, which produces a delicious fortified sweet white wine from the Muscat grape.

Leave Beaumes-de-Venise eastwards on D 21, bear left on D 938 and left again on D 78.

Le Barroux – *Car park at entrance to village.* The picturesque village, with sloping streets, is dominated by the lofty silhouette of its **castle** ⊙.

This huge quadrilateral construction, flanked by round towers, originally (12C) guarded the Comtat Venaisson plain. Remodelled in the Renaissance, burnt down during the Second World War, then restored once more, the castle was, until the 18C, the seat of several lordships, including that of Rovigliasc (note the coats of arms above the square tower doorway). After visiting the chapel, the lower rooms and the Guard room, walk through the different floors, where contemporary exhibitions are on display in several of the rooms (Salles des Audiences, Salle de la Garenne, Salle du Parlement, among others).

From the front of the castle *(access through the lower rooms)* the **view★** extends towards the Dentelles de Montmirail.

Leave Le Barroux northwards towards Suzette and meet up with D 90.

After Suzette the road enters the vertical-walled Cirque de St-Amand.

The road rises to a small pass from which there is a good **view★** on one side of the Dentelles and on the other of Mont Ventoux, Ouvèze valley and the Baronnies.

Malaucène – Facilities. This large Provençal town is for the most part surrounded by a large avenue shaded by huge plane trees.

Rebuilt in the 14C, on the site of the former Romanesque church, once a part of the ramparts, which explains its fortified appearance: the façade is surmounted by corbelled machicolations. Inside, the Provençal Romanesque nave is covered with splendid pointed-barrel vaulting, the south side chapels with pointed vaulting and the apse with a dome of flat ribs. Note the 18C organ loft with beautifully-carved musical instruments and a pulpit carved out of oak.

Go through Porte Soubeyran, the gate beside the church, into the old village of small streets, old houses, fountains, washhouses and oratories, with

an old belfry crowned by a wrought iron bell cage at its centre. Take the path along the church's north wall to the Calvary for a view of the Drôme mountains and Mont Ventoux.

D 938 northwest climbs the fertile Groseau valley.

Turn left onto D 76.

Crestet – Leave the car in the castle car park. The village is one of the most typical of Vaucluse, with the 14C church standing in a minute square lined by an arcade and decorated at the centre with a fountain. Narrow streets between Renaissance houses climb the hill crowned by a 12C **castle**, from where there is a good view of the village, the Ouvèze, Mont Ventoux and the Baronnies.

Return to D 938 and turn left for Vaison-la-Romaine.

Basse Vallée de la DURANCE

Michelin map 84 folds 1-4 or 245 folds 29-32 or 246 folds 11, 12 and 25

The Durance, the great fluctuating river of the southern Alps, known for its bursting, unheralded floodwaters and long periods of low ebb, has, at last, been harnessed to serve the local economy; it supplies hydraulic power and a constant flow of water for irrigation for most of the fruit and vegetable growing area.

The Durance's hydraulic structure – The river rises close to the Italian border (Mont Genèvre, near Briançon), pours through a wide gap which it has cut in the mountains and continues on an irregular 32km/201mi course to join the Rhône as its final east tributary, at Avignon.

Upstream of Sisteron – *See Michelin Green Guide Alpes du Sud in French.* A number of small mountain streams, such as the Ubaye, give the river its torrential, alpine appearance, with shallows in winter.

The Serre-Ponçon reservoir, with a capacity of 1 030 million m³/36 373 million cubic ft collected when the river is in spate, maintains regular irrigation (It can hold 200 million m³/7 074 million cubic ft when the river is low).

From Sisteron to Manosque – *See Michelin Green Guide Alpes du Sud in French.* The river enters the Mediterranean basin: the slope of its bed, which is less steep, reaches 0.3% between Mées and Manosque; yet the river widens and flows between pebbly shores which are rarely flooded. The flow stays irregular.

At Cardache, 175km/109mi from the sea, the Durance remains at an altitude of 256m/840ft. To reach the same altitude as the Rhône, the river flows 490km/304.5mi inland (at Génissiat dam). These two figures clearly reveal the hydroelectric potential of the Durance.

Downstream of Manosque – The river runs approximately parallel to the coast until it enters the Rhône, but once, when the ice cap melted at the end of the last Ice Age, the swollen waters burst through the Lamanon gap on a more direct route to the sea, depositing a huge mass of rock and stone over the wide expanse of what is now the Plaine de la Crau. The violence of rain storms provokes floodwaters, the power of which bears no relationship to that of the Durance's average flow.

Upstream of the River Verdon (last great tributary of the Durance) at Pont-Mirabeau, the flow is reduced in August to less than 45m³/9 900 gallons per second – in November 1886 the river in spate flowed at 6 000m³/1 320 000 gallons per second. This flooding raises the water level only slightly – it sprawls over a vast pebbly bed which slows the speed of the flow before being absorbed, for the most part, by sandy soil.

Lower Provence's canal network – It is rare for any one region to be as well served by canals as Provence is between the Durance and the sea. Each was constructed for one of three purposes: irrigation, the provision of town and factory water and the production of electricity.

Canal de Craponne – The 16C course, one of the oldest in Provence, which is now decaying in its upper reaches, has contributed most, through irrigation, to the transformation of the Plaine de la Crau.

Canal de Marseille and Canal du Verdon – Each in its time – both date from the 19C – has increased the fertility of the countryside around Aix and Marseille, but with the immense development in market gardening neither is now sufficient. The Canal de Marseille 90km/60mi long, begins at St-Estève-Janson and on its course serves the St-Christophe and Réaltor reservoirs and crosses the Arc valley by means of the Aqueduc de Roquefavour. It supplies a branch of the Canal de Provence *(see below)*, which serves the industrial zone of the Étang de Berre.

The Canal du Verdon has been disused since 1991; part of it has been rebuilt in the renovation work of the Canal de Provence.

Canal EDF (Électricité de France) – This canal begins at Cadarache dam and runs parallel to the Durance before following the river's original course through the Lamanon gap to the Étang de Berre. Five major power stations (Jouques, St-Estève-Janson,

Basse Vallée de la DURANCE

Mallemort, Salon and St-Chamas) are served by the canal, supplying 15 other channels which irrigate some 75 000ha/185 000 acres of lower Provence including the Plaine de la Crau.

Canal de Provence – The completion of the Serre-Ponçon dam and the construction of the EDF canal have removed the need for the Verdon canal to act as a regulator of the Durance.

Its waters have, therefore, been diverted into the new Canal de Provence, which was built between 1964 and 1989. The canal has an annual flow of 700 million m³/154 000 million gallons drawn from a 4 000km/2 500mi network of tunnels, canals, and underground pipes. It supplies town water to Aix, Marseille and Toulon and irrigates some 60 000ha/148 000 acres in the Bouches-du-Rhône and Var *départements* as well as topping up a number of dams and reservoirs, such as the Bimont dam.

FROM LA TOUR-D'AIGUES TO AVIGNON
150km/93mi – allow half a day (not including tour of Avignon)

La Tour-d'Aigues – See La TOUR-D'AIGUES.
Take D 135 eastwards and proceed towards Mirabeau.

Défilé de Mirabeau – The river bends sharply to the west and emerges from upper Provence through this dramatic narrow channel cut out by the action of the water.

Pont Mirabeau – This bridge spans the Durance at the Défilé de Mirabeau.
Turn left onto D 952 which leads to the Research Centre for Atomic Energy.

Centre d'Études (C.E.A. – Atomic Energy Commission) – Set at a distance from the villages, this research centre for the Atomic Energy Commission lies on the north bank of the Durance in a large valley which opens onto a plateau wooded with oak. The centre produces experimental prototype reactors for power stations and carries out research into controlled fusion, radio ecology, radio agronomy, biotechnology etc.

Barrage de Cadarache – This small dam spanning the waters of both the Durance and its tributary the Verdon, feeds the Jouques Power Station (a couple of miles south) by means of a canal.

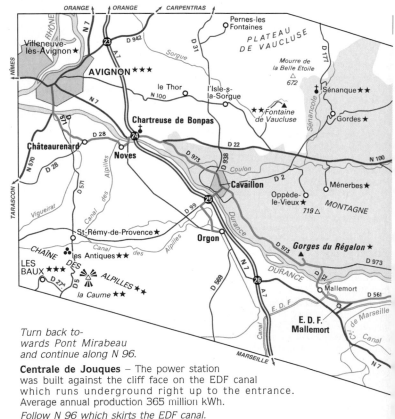

Turn back towards Pont Mirabeau and continue along N 96.

Centrale de Jouques – The power station was built against the cliff face on the EDF canal which runs underground right up to the entrance. Average annual production 365 million kWh.
Follow N 96 which skirts the EDF canal.

Peyrolles-en-Provence – See PEYROLLES-EN-PROVENCE.

Meyrargues – Facilities. The town is dominated by its château (now a hotel) rebuilt in the 17C. A pleasant walk leads to the remains of a Roman aqueduct (below the castle) which brought water to Aix-en-Provence and continues to the wild Étroit gorges.

On leaving, take D 561 and after 3km/2mi D 556, on the right.

Pertuis – Facilities. Capital of Aigues country and birthplace of Mirabeau's father, the town retains, as reminders of its past, a 14C battlemented tower – St-Jacques – 13C clock tower, a castle ruin and the **Église St-Nicolas**. This church, rebuilt in the 16C, contains a 16C triptych and two 17C marble statues given to the monks of the town by Cardinal Barberini.

Take the westward-bound D 973 to Cadenet.

Cadenet – *See CADENET.*

D 943 goes south to cross the Durance; turn left onto D 561 and after 2.7km/1.5mi, right towards the power station.

Centrale de St-Estève-Janson – Balcony and explanatory panel *(in French)* at the base of the power station building. Annual production 635 million kWh.

EDF power stations to be visited in the Lower Valley of the Durance:
Centrale de Jouques ☎ 04 42 61 90 22
Centrale de St-Estève-Janson ☎ 04 42 61 90 22
Centrale de Mallemort ☎ 04 90 59 40 58
Centrale de Salon ☎ 04 90 42 18 47
Centrale de St-Chamas ☎ 04 90 42 18 47

Bassin de St-Christophe – The reservoir waters, covering 22ha/54 acres at the foot of the Côtes chain, derive from the Durance and its tributary, the EDF canal, and are destined to supply Marseille.

Rognes – Rognes is located on the north face of the Chaîne de la Trévaresse. The well-known Rognes stone is extracted from quarries found on D 15 going to Lambesc.
The **church** ⊙ built in the early 17C is decorated with a remarkable group of **ten altarpieces★** (17C-18C). Note especially the one at the high altar and another along the chancel's north side which is decorated with three people in low relief.

Return to the reservoir: skirt it to the left until you come to D 561.

★★**Abbaye de Silvacane** – *See Abbaye de SILVACANE.*

La Roque-d'Anthéron – At the centre of the town stands the 17C Château de Florans flanked by round towers. This acts as a backdrop to the prestigious International Piano Festival *(see the Calendar*

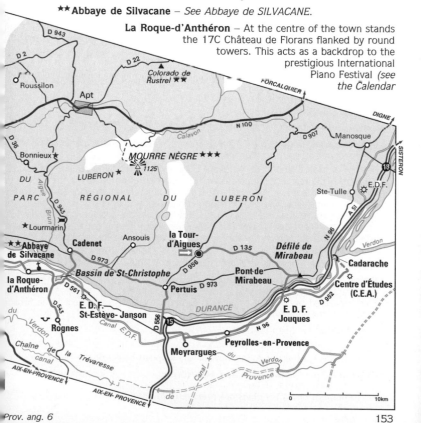

of events at the end of the guide). The **Musée de Géologie Provençale** ⊘, which houses paleontological and mineralogical collections, is situated on Place Paul-Cézanne.

Continue along D 561 to D 23c on the right.

Centrale de Mallemort – The power station, on the left, produces an average 450 million kWh annually.

Beyond the town of Mallemort turn onto D 32 to cross the river; turn left onto D 973. Continue for 2km/1mi and just before a bridge, bear right onto a small road which skirts a quarry.

★**Gorges du Régalon** – *1hr 15min return on foot. Some yards further on bear right, ignoring the uphill road on the left. Leave the car in the parking area; take the path opposite which skirts the stream; cross the olive grove on your left and go through a narrow gap to enter the gorges. Note: (a) it will be colder, (b) the*

Gorges du Régalon

rocks are often wet and slippery – therefore go suitably clad and shod; (c) on showery, rainy days the stream becomes a rushing torrent and the expedition should not be ventured.

The route follows the bed of the stream, runs beneath a huge rock caught fast between the sides of the gorges, and over a rocky and sometimes slippery section before coming to a cave. The tunnel bends sharply into a passage 100m/328ft long and 30m/98ft high but only 80cm/30in wide in places. The cave and passage are the most remarkable parts of the gorges.

At the end retrace your steps.

Continue once more along D 973 as it skirts the Montagne du Luberon.

Cavaillon – *See CAVAILLON.*

Orgon – *See ORGON.*

Leave Cavaillon by ① on the town plan, D 938; turn left onto D 973.

Chartreuse de Bonpas ⊘ – *Enter through a fortified gate; the porter's lodge opens (under a vault) on the right.*

Next to a small chapel, the Templars built a church and monastery in the 13C which took the name of Bonpas. It enjoyed a period of prosperity in the 17C when the chapterhouse was constructed. At the Revolution it was abandoned and it gradually fell into ruins. The charterhouse has recently been restored, whereas the remaining conventual buildings have been converted into a house. The old Romanesque chapel has an elevated altar. The formal French gardens are well kept. From the terrace there is a clear view of the Alpilles, which stand out in the distance, and the Durance spanned by a 500m/0.3mi long bridge.

Pass under the motorway and turn right onto N 7 and right again onto D 28.

Noves – Noves is an old town with a network of narrow winding streets, two medieval gateways (Porte d'Agel and Porte Aurose) and a 12C stone-roofed **church**. This is covered by a dome on squinches and its apse is enhanced by an arcade (restored); the aisles were added in the 14C.

Châteaurenard – *See CHÂTEAURENARD.*

D 571 and N 570 continue to Avignon.

From the bridge there is a fine view of the wooded banks of the Durance.

★★★**Avignon** – *Tour: allow 1 day. See AVIGNON.*

Michelin maps and town plans are oriented with north at the top of the page.

Chaîne de l'ESTAQUE★

Michelin map 84 fold 12 or 246 folds P and Q

The Chaîne de l'Estaque, which divides the Étang de Berre from the Mediterranean, is an unusual limestone formation, arid in appearance and almost uninhabited. Deep inlets *(calanques)* in the steep coastline shelter a few small fishing villages, which scrape a meagre living from the poor fish stocks of the Mediterranean but now hope to profit from the expansion of the port of Marseille, the increasing industrialisation of the area and the tourist trade.

FROM PORT-DE-BOUC TO MARSEILLE

74km/46mi – about 4hr (not including tour of Marseille)

Port-de-Bouc – The port is protected by a fort erected by Vauban in 1664 on the southern bank of the passage. The 12C tower, part of these fortifications, is now a lighthouse *(see illustration on p 42 under Art: Architectural Terms)*. Situated at the western exit of the town, along N 568, the **Musée Morales** ⊙ offers an unusual walk through a veritable forest of gigantic creatures in the form of metal sculptures following themes which are in turn amusing, puzzling and even occasionally disturbing.

Martigues – *See MARTIGUES.*

Leave Martigues by D 5.

On the left are views of the Étang de Berre and Martigues.

After Les Ventrons continue along D 5 to St-Julien.

St-Julien – A path *(on the left)* from the village leads to a chapel where embedded in the north wall there is a Gallo-Roman relief (1C) of a group of eight people in a funeral scene.

From St-Julien, return to Les Ventrons and turn left onto D 49.

The road climbs through an arid landscape of dark pines against the white limestone and, at 120m/394ft, looks back *(observation tower)* over the industrial harbour complex of Lavéra, Port-de-Bouc and Fos.

4km/2.5mi further on, bear right for Carro.

Carro – The attractive small fishing village and resort lies well protected at the back of a rock-strewn bay.

Make for La Couronne by way of D 49B; turn right before the church.

Cap Couronne – From the lighthouse on the point there is a view right round to Marseille, with the Chaîne de l'Estaque in the foreground, the Chaîne de l'Étoile and the Marseilleveyre. The huge beach of La Couronne is very popular and is a favourite spot among the youth of Marseille.

On leaving the point, turn right onto D 49.

The road winds through the hills before dropping down to follow the coastline.

Sausset-les-Pins – Facilities. The fishing village and seaside resort has a fine promenade from where one can look across the sea to Marseille.

Carry-le-Rouet – Facilities. The one time fishing village is now a seaside resort. Summer residences can be seen in the woods which line the bay.

Le Rouet-Plage – An attractive creek with a beach and small harbour, and, half-hidden among the pine trees, some elegant houses.

The road up the **Vallon de l'Aigle** is bordered by pines and holm oaks.

Ensuès-la-Redonne – A village amid vineyards and olive groves.

On leaving Ensuès, turn right onto D 48.

A rapid descent, through a pinewood, goes to La Madrague-de-Gignac.

La Madrague-de-Gignac – The village, set in a lovely site, lines a *calanque*, which faces Marseille across the water.

Return to D 5 and turn right.

The road crosses an arid, treeless stretch of countryside.

Bear right on D 48 to Niolon.

The section of coastland stretching between Sausset-les-Pins and Niolon is a preserved area called the Parc Régional Marin de la Côte Bleue. For further details, see the chapter on Practical information at the end of the guide on p 292.

The road plunges into bleak countryside where only a few pines resist the wind.

Niolon – The village clings to the hillside above a *calanque* of the same name. It is a good spot for deep-sea diving.

From D 5, there is a clear view of the Étoile and Estaque ranges.

Turn right onto N 568.

The road goes under the railway bridge and over the entrance to the Canal du Rove.

Niolon

★ **Canal Souterrain du Rove** – *Access: take the Carrière Chagnaud road – pass under the railway before turning down the slope to the entrance.*

The tunnel was cut in the 1920s beneath the Chaîne de l'Estaque to link the Marseille docks and the Étang de Berre, and was used regularly by 1 200 metric ton barges until it was obstructed by a rockfall in 1963. It is more than 7km/4mi long and dead straight – one can still see daylight at the far end. Height, width and water depth respectively are 15.4, 22 and 4.5m (50, 72 and 14ft).

L'Estaque – *See MARSEILLE: Excursions.*

The road continues through the industrial suburbs to the tunnel beneath the Vieux Port into the heart of Marseille.

★★★ **Marseille** – *Tour: allow 1 day. See MARSEILLE.*

"A Small House by the Sea"

Faithful to a tradition which dates back to the 16C, no effort is spared on the part of the town dweller to purchase his *cabanon*, which was, until recently, a modest building "no bigger than a pocket handkerchief", a fisherman's hut, a cabin in the hills or a small village house, where Sundays and summer holidays were spent. Although nowadays the hut is more likely to be a comfortable villa, and the stay lengthened to week-ends and school holidays, a typical day in the *cabanon* is not so far removed from the picture painted in the operettas of Vincent Scotto: on the return of the early-risers who have been out hunting, fishing or simply to the market, the household gathers in the shade of the terrace to sip an iced *pastis*, an ideal moment to exchange tall stories and tell jokes. The delicious *aïoli* served with the midday meal inevitably ends with a restorative after-lunch siesta, lulled by the shrilling of the cicadas. Everyone has to be up and about, however, before the angelus, so as not to miss the ritual game of *pétanque*, punctuated by impassioned cries in the local dialect. The wise decision will have been made to have a light dinner, in other words to refuse second helpings of the delicious *pistou*, in order to be at one's best for the *belote* card game, a last chance for amicable dispute before turning in for a sound sleep, with all the cares in the world having been left in the noise and pollution of the city.

Discover the suggested Touring Programmes at the beginning of the guide.
Plan a trip with the help of the Map of Principal Sights.

Chaîne de l'ÉTOILE★

Michelin map 84 fold 13 or 114 folds 16, 29 and 30 or 246 folds K and L

This chain of mountains, which belongs to the small Alps of Provence and is a result of the Pyrenean fold, separates the Arc basin to the north from that of the Huveaune to the east; it extends, beyond the shelf of St-Antoine, the Chaîne de l'Estaque. In spite of the low altitude of its mountain tops, the chain rises spectacularly above the Marseille plain. Its central crest, which spreads out like a fan, ends at 781m/2 562ft at the Tête du Grand Puche. Mont Julien, the Pilon du Roi and Étoile peak also dominate the landscape, which is bare to the south.

FROM GARDANNE TO AUBAGNE

61km/38mi – about 3hr 30min (not including the climb to Étoile peak)

Gardanne – This important industrial town with its bauxite and cement works and coal mining lies between the Étoile chain and Montagne Ste-Victoire.

Leave Gardanne on D 58 going south which becomes D 8. After 7km/4mi turn right to Mimet.

Mimet – This small hill-top village is undergoing considerable expansion. From its terrace there is a fine **view**★ of the Luynes valley, Gardanne and its furnaces.

Return to D 8 and bear right.

The picturesque D 7 and D 908 skirt the Étoile chain.

At Le Logis-Neuf turn left to Allauch.

Allauch – *See ALLAUCH.*

Take D 44ᶠ northwest of Allauch.

Musée des Arts et Traditions Populaires du Terroir Marseillais (at Château-Gombert) – *See MARSEILLE: Excursions.*

Leave Château-Gombert towards Marseille and turn right into Traverse de la Baume-Loubière. Park the car at the Grottes Loubière; continue uphill (4hr return on foot). Bear right before the intersection of surfaced roads.

After a winding trail through a rocky passage you reach the **Grande Étoile** (alt 590m/1 936ft), where a telecommunications tower stands, and then **Étoile peak** (alt 651m/2 136ft). From the shelf separating these last two summits there is a splendid **panorama**★★ over the Gardanne basin to the north and the thresholds which cut the chain's southern slopes.

Return to Allauch by the same way you came. Continue south on D 4ᴬ; at Les 4-Saisons bear left and soon after left again.

Camoins-les-Bains – This small spa enjoys picturesque greenery.

La Treille – **Marcel Pagnol** (1895-1974), writer and film director who was born in Aubagne *(see p 94)*, is buried in La Treille cemetery at the town's entrance.

Return to Camoins-les-Bains and take D 44ᴬ to Aubagne.

Aubagne – *See AUBAGNE.*

FONTAINE-DE-VAUCLUSE

Population 580
Michelin map 81 fold 13 or 245 south of fold 17 or 246 fold 11 – Facilities

Vallis clausa (the "enclosed valley"), from which this *département* gets its name, is best known for its fountain, the famous resurgent spring which rises in a picturesque site dear to Petrarch and is the source of the River Sorgue. It is in winter or spring, during the floods, that the stream is at its most dramatic, when the water level rises 150m³/32 985 gallons per second, while in the summer or autumn the flow is reduced to a mere 4.5m³/159cu ft per second.

Petrarch – On 6 April 1327 in an Avignon church the great poet and humanist, who was a familiar member of the pontifical court in Avignon, met the lovely **Laura**, with whom he fell passionately in love. However this love remained platonic – Laura was married and virtuous – inspiring many of the poet's works throughout his life, and indeed his best works. Ten years after his first meeting with her, Petrarch, who was only 33 years old, retired to Vaucluse. He remained here for 16 years seeking peace in the tranquil Sorgue valley; during his stay Laura died of the plague in Avignon in 1348. The poet was to die 20 years later in Arquà Petrarca near Padua, never having forgotten her.

★★FONTAINE DE VAUCLUSE *30min return on foot*

Leave the car in the car park (fee charged). From Place de la Colonne, where there stands a commemorative column of the fifth centenary (1304-1804) of Petrarch's birth, take Chemin de la Fontaine.

Fontaine de Vaucluse

The Fontaine de Vaucluse is one of the most powerful resurgent springs in the world; it is the outlet of an important underwater river fed by rainwater draining through the Vaucluse plateau pitted with numerous chasms *(avens)*, through which the speleologists have searched in vain for the underground Sorgue. The exploration of the fountain's chasm began as early as the 19C (in 1878 a diver descended 23m/75ft) and continues actively. The last record was 315m/1 033ft deep and was achieved in August 1985 with the help of a small remote-controlled submarine equipped with cameras.

A *son et lumière* show is organised in summer.

The cave from which the River Sorgue emerges is at the foot of a rocky cirque formed by high cliffs. In front of it stands a pile of rocks through which the waters usually filter.

During heavy flooding the water reaches the level of the fig trees growing in the rock above the cave mouth, before racing away over the rocks in a vivid green fury of tumbling foaming water. It is a magnificent spectacle.

ADDITIONAL SIGHTS

★**Musée d'Histoire (1939-1945)** ⊘ – *On Chemin de la Fontaine*. This museum houses the exhibits and documents from the old Musée des Restrictions in a plain and functional building, offering a historical, literary and artistic view of the years 1939-1945 within a modern framework. There are three sections to the exhibition: the first describes daily life in occupied France; the second, the activity of the Resistance in the Vaucluse *département*, through the testimonies of those involved in or observing events during the "dark years". An audiovisual support helps to situate local history within the national context. The final section of the exhibition called "La Liberté de l'Esprit" (Freedom of Spirit), is devoted to the works of activists – writings by René Char, or paintings by Matisse, for example – which provide a deeper insight into the ideals of the Resistance movement.

Le Monde Souterrain de Norbert Casteret ⊘ – *On Chemin de la Fontaine*. The underground museum presents the **Casteret collection★** of limestone concretions (calcite, gypsum, aragonite) assembled over 30 years of underground exploration by the speleologist. Different sites have been reconstructed: stalactite and stalagmite caves, chasm and rubble, rivers, waterfalls, natural dams and caves with human imprints. A detailed documentation introduces the visitor to Vaucluse speleology; a permanent display (documents, photos, models) explains the discoveries made on Fontaine-de-Vaucluse through the years.

Vallis Clausa – *Near the underground museum*. In this craft centre is a **paper mill** fed by the waters of the Sorgue, where paper is made according to traditional methods. A little further along, a **Santon Museum** ⊘ houses a pretty collection of cribs and figurines made by local artisans both recently and in the past.

Musée-Bibliothèque Pétrarque ⊘ – *In the village on the south bank of the Sorgue: go through a covered passageway.* This library-museum is located at the heart of the village in a house said to be built on the site of the house where Petrarch once lived. Upstairs, there is an exhibition of drawings and prints (16C-19C) on the subjects of Petrarch, Laura, Avignon and the Fontaine-de-Vaucluse, as well as a collection of old editions of the writings of the poet and his followers. On the ground floor there is a rotating display of works by artists linked with the site of the Fontaine-de-Vaucluse; also of writings by René Char illustrated by Zao Wou Ki, Braque or Vieira da Silva.

Église St-Véran – This small Romanesque church has rounded vaulting over its nave and an oven-vaulted apse flanked by antique fluted columns. To the right of the chancel opens the crypt containing the sarcophagus of St Veranus, 6C bishop of Cavaillon, credited with having dispatched Coulobre, a monster which terrorised the region.

Castle (Château) – *30min return on foot.* Set on a rock overlooking the village, the castle, now in ruins, belonged to the bishop of Cavaillon, a friend of Petrarch's. It commands a lovely view of the Fontaine-de-Vaucluse and its site.

EXCURSION

Saumane-de-Vaucluse – *4km/2.5mi northwest. Leave Fontaine-de-Vaucluse on D 25, then turn right onto D 57.*

The road follows the hillside across the limestone slopes of the Vaucluse mountains, before arriving at this attractive village perched above the Sorgue valley. Here stands the old 15C castle belonging to the family of the **Marquis de Sade** (now a training centre – *not open to the public*): it was in this residence that the young Donatien Alphonse François, later nicknamed the Divine Marquis, was to spend his childhood. St-Trophime church, dating from the 12C but modified several times since, is crowned by an arcaded belfry. From the square, which contains a 16C stone cross, there is a broad **view** across the Sorgue valley, the Luberon and the Alpilles.

Bassins de FOS★

Michelin map 84 fold 11 or 245 folds 42 and 43 or 246 folds 13, 14, 27 and 28

The development of the new complex, the largest in southern Europe and which complements the port of Marseille, was begun in 1965 on the Golfe de Fos. The advantages of the site, some 10 000ha/24 700 acres, are a deep water channel, a low tidal range and the extensive stony surface of the Plaine de la Crau which makes an ideal foundation on which to build an industrial estate.

The port – With over 90 million metric tons of traffic per year, of which Fos handles two-thirds, the combined Marseille-Fos complex is the largest port in France and third in Europe.

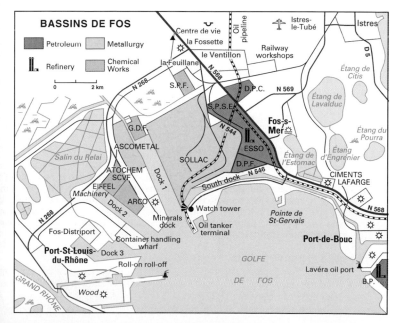

Fos is equipped to handle two types of traffic: Dock 1 with its two basins can accommodate vessels up to 400 000 metric tons carrying bulk cargoes such as oil, coal, minerals and natural liquefied gas; Docks 2 and 3 (Gloria basin) handle commercial traffic such as containers, vehicles and wood. The container terminal has a capacity of 500 000 units. A distribution platform, "Fos Distriport", is to adjoin the service area and is to be a free zone for manufacturers worldwide. The South Dock is reserved for steel and petrol exports.

Dock 1 was linked to the Rhône and the Étang de Berre by a canal built to European standards and capable of carrying 4 400 metric ton-barge convoys.

Centre d'Information du Port Autonome de Marseille (CIPAM) ⊙ – Laid out in the La Fossette zone, the CIPAM houses an exhibition on the installations and activites of the Autonomous Port of Marseille (including a model of the industrial port area), as well as offering films and a tour of the port.

Tour of the port ⊙ – The bus tour visits the Graveleau jetty, the ore terminal and the Fos oil port.

The industrial zone – More than 60% of the available land is given over to factories, some with their own quays, accommodating basic processing and first-stage industries such as steel (Soolac-Fos – sheet and laminates: 4 million tons per year, Ascometal – production and lamination of special steels: 200 000 metric tons); metal construction; petrol (Esso: 8 million metric tons); chemicals and petrochemicals (Atochem: 590 000 metric tons of chloride, 645 000 metric tons of soda; SPF: 100 000 metric tons of polyethylene; L'Air Liquide: 1 500 000 metric tons of industrial gas; SCVF: 350 000 metric tons of MVC; Arco Chimie France: 550 000 metric tons of MTBE (leaded fuel additives), 200 000 metric tons of propylene oxide).

Approximately 3 billion m³/105 942 thousand million cubic ft of liquid natural gas are treated each year by Gaz de France and distributed after conversion. Crude oil and refined products supply the South European Oil Pipeline and the Mediterranean-Rhône Oil Pipeline respectively.

The Ventillon and Feuillane industrial estates are home to chemical and other specialised industries as well as to a special zone for products classified as dangerous. These zones are located adjacent to an area set aside for small and medium-sized businesses.

Fos-sur-Mer – *To the northeast.* The town is named after the Fosses Mariennes, a canal dug at the mouth of the Rhône by Marius' legions in 102 BC (*fosse*: hole, pit, canal). Medieval rather than Roman remains are evident in sections of the 14C ramparts and castle ruins. The chief attraction, however, lies in the **views** from the terrace and rampart garden of the new town of Fos, the harbour, Port-de-Bouc, Étang de Lavalduc and the St-Blaise heights.

EXCURSIONS

Port-St-Louis-du-Rhône – *15km/10mi southwest.* A town and port have developed around the St-Louis tower, built to defend the mouth of the Grand Rhône in the 18C. The dock, constructed in 1863 and now part of the Marseille complex, is used both by seagoing ships and Rhône barges; its lock and the large Fos-Rhône canal make it the key point for river and maritime-river traffic between Europe and the Mediterranean. It handles products as diverse as hydrocarbons, liquid chemicals, timber and wine.

Port-de-Bouc – *See p 155.*

Les GARRIGUES

Michelin map 80 fold 19 or 245 folds 14 and 15 or 246 fold 25

The *garrigues* are a limestone formation which sweeps along the foot of the more ancient Massif Central. The low hills rise 200m-300m/656ft-984ft in the area which is covered by this guide. This region was once covered with holm oaks and Aleppo pines but the forest has been almost completely razed by man. Rain, frost, drought and wind have in many places weathered and carried away the thin layer of soil. In areas where the rock has not been completely uncovered scrub oak, cistus, gorse, asphodel and wild aromatic plants carpet the ground. Rivers have sometimes carved picturesque gorges through these arid, scorched hills.

FROM UZÈS TO REMOULINS 51km/31mi – about 6hr

★★ **Uzès** – *See UZÈS.*

Leave Uzès by ② *on the map, D 979.*

The road winds through the countryside offering views of Uzès and its environs.

Pont St-Nicolas – The nine-arched bridge, built in the 13C by the Bridge Brotherhood, spans the River Gardon in a particularly beautiful spot. D 979 cuts into the overhanging rocks as it climbs, affording good views of the Gardon; the right-hand bend at the top *(car park)* affords a spectacular **view**★ along the course of the Gardon gorges.

Turn left onto D 135 and, just before Poulx, left again onto D 127.

★**Gorges du Gardon** – *Poorly-surfaced road, passing difficult, sometimes impossible except in lay-bys hewn out of the rock: at the final bend, park the car.* A path *(1hr return on foot)* ends at the bottom of the gorges in a picturesque spot, facing the opening of the Baume cave in the cliff on the far bank of the river.

Poulx – Village with a small, single-aisled, Romanesque church.

Continue along D 427.

The road crosses the *garrigues* interspersed with vineyards and orchards.

In Cabrières turn left onto D 3.

Fine views open out onto the Rhône plain and the Alpilles; the road rises precipitously at the end of the run before descending into the Gardon valley.

On entering Collias bear right on D 3, which climbs the large and cultivated Alzon valley; bear right again onto D 981.

Château de Castille – *(Not open to the public).* A small Romanesque chapel and a funerary chapel surrounded by columns stand to the right of the avenue of yew trees leading to the château which was built in the 16C and remodelled in the 18C. Two low wings on either side, surrounded by a colonnade, are preceded by a vast balustered, horseshoe-shaped peristyle. The château itself is also columned and balustered.

Continue along D 981

★★★**Pont du Gard** – *See PONT DU GARD.*

Remoulins – Facilities. The village set amid cherry and other fruit orchards is protected in places by its medieval wall. A small Romanesque church with a bell gable houses the town hall.

GORDES★

Population 2 031
Michelin map 81 fold 13 or 245 south of fold 17 or 246 fold 11 – Facilities

The houses of Gordes rise in picturesque tiers above the Imergue valley on the edge of the Vaucluse plateau *(see p 11)*, facing the Luberon. The site was already occupied by man as early back as the Neolithic era. The very first inhabitants, the *Vordeuses*, a tribe of Celtic Ligurian descent, named the city Vorda; over the centuries this appellation underwent a number of phonetic changes to finally become Gordes.

The village – It is pleasant to walk through this charming town along the *calades* – small paved, sometimes stepped alleyways lined with gutters defined by two rows of stone – with vaulted passageways, arcades of old, tall houses and rampart ruins; the shops, craftshops and lively market add to the bustle.

Viewpoint – The **site**★ can best be seen from a rock platform *(no barrier)* about 1km/0.5mi from the village on the Cavaillon road, D 15.

Château ⊙ – The Renaissance château stands on the village's highest point. It was rebuilt by Bertrand de Simiane on the site of a 12C fortress. The north face flanked by round machicolated towers is austere, the south monumental, relieved by mullioned windows and small turrets. In the courtyard note the fine Renaissance door (the soft limestone has been worn away by erosion). Inside, in the great hall *(first floor)* two flanking doorways show off a splendid **chimneypiece**★ (1541) with ornate pediments and pilasters, shells and flowers.
The three top floors of the château present a standing **exhibition** of works by the contemporary Flemish artist Pol Mara.

EXCURSIONS

★**Village des Bories: St-Pantaléon** – *Round tour of 12km/7.5mi – allow 2hr. Leave Gordes on D 15 towards Cavaillon; just beyond the fork with D 2 turn right onto a tarred road and enter the village.*

★**Village des Bories** ⊙ – This village is now a **Museum of Rural Life.** Twenty restored *bories* (see text and photograph under Montagne du Luberon), between 200 and 500 years old, are grouped around a communal bread oven. The larger *bories* served as dwellings, the others were either sheep-folds or various outbuildings. They were inhabited until the early 19C but their origin remains a mystery.

Gordes

Return to D 2 and bear right; turn left on D 103 towards Beaumettes and left again onto D 148 towards St-Pantaléon; continue along this road about 110yd to the place called Moulin des Bouillons.

Musée de l'Histoire du Verre et du Vitrail – The modern museum building houses an exhibition on the history of stained-glass making (tools and documents) and displays reconstructed ovens, Middle Eastern glassware, period stained glass and works by Frédérique Duran, contemporary painter and glassmaker, with her own distinctive technique for obtaining jewelled results.

Located in the same park as the Musée de l'Histoire du Verre et du Vitrail, the bastide known as the **Moulin des Bouillons** (16C-18C), has a remarkably large **olive press★** made from a whole oak tree trunk weighing 7 tons! It is Gallo-Roman in appearance, and it is the oldest and the only one preserved with its tools.

St-Pantaléon – The small village occupies a dominant position in the countryside. Its small Romanesque **church** is built out of the living rock and consists of three naves; the central part dates back to the 5C.
Surrounding the church is a rock necropolis, most of the tombs of which are child-size. This necropolis was most likely a sanctuary of grace; there are other examples like it in Provence. Children who died before they were baptised were brought here by their parents; they revived – according to the beliefs of the period – for the duration of a mass during which they were baptised, they then died again and were buried here.

Leave St-Pantaléon from the north and join D 104ᴬ, then D 2 which returns to Gordes.

Le GRAU-DU-ROI⚓⚓

Population 5 253
Michelin map 83 fold 8 or 240 fold 23 – Local map see La CAMARGUE

This seaside resort was part of the town of Aigues-Mortes until 1879; it grew up around a pretty little port. This extends in part from an inland estuary or "grau" formed by a spate in the Rhône during the 16C (in Languedoc, *grau* designates an open breach in the offshore bar separating the lagoon from the sea). In the 18C the *grau* was enlarged, and lengthened by a sea channel which connects it with the Aigues-Mortes saltmarshes. From the far end of the pier there is a **view** of the Grande-Motte pyramids, Boucanet beach and Port-Camargue.
An 18km/11mi stretch of fine sandy beach runs past the resorts of Le Grau-du-Roi and Port-Camargue, which are equipped with a variety of sports facilities and attract many holiday-makers in the summer.

★PORT-CAMARGUE

Via D 62B

Located between the fishing harbour and Point de l'Espiguette, the resort of Port-Camargue represents the furthermost eastern resort created in the development of the Languedoc-Roussillon coast.

It is a good departure point for cruising along this coastline.

Port – This project began in 1969 and was entirely man-made; it covers 150ha/371 acres, of which more than half is taken up by water. It provides mooring for more than 4300 pleasure craft and includes short-term mooring facilities, winter berths, a harbour master's office, shipyard, depots, and water-sports facilities.

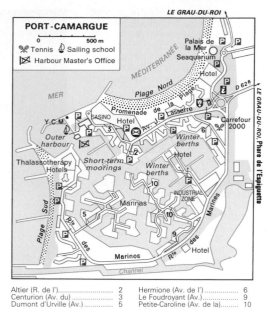

PORT-CAMARGUE

0   500 m

✂ Tennis   ⚓ Sailing school
◳ Harbour Master's Office

Altier (R. de l')	2
Centurion (Av. du)	3
Dumont d'Urville (Av.)	5
Hermione (Av. de l')	6
Le Foudroyant (Av.)	9
Petite-Caroline (Av. de la)	10

Resort – The buildings, never exceeding two storeys with smooth-stepped façades interspersed with gardens, advance into the harbour on crooked finger-like promontories.

Phare de l'Espiguette – *6km/3.5mi south by a road off the intersection (carrefour) leading into Port-Camargue, opposite the direct road to Le Grau-du-Roi.*

This lighthouse which overlooks Point de l'Espiguette stands amid a typical Camargue landscape where on windswept dunes tamarisk, thistles, sea rockets and cakiles grow. From the beach the view embraces the Sète coastline.

EXCURSIONS

★★**Aigues-Mortes Plain** – *Follow the itinerary described under Camargue* ② *in reverse, starting from Port-Camargue*

Salins du Midi ⊙ **and Caves du Listel** ⊙ – *4km/2.5mi northeast on D 979. See AIGUES-MORTES: Excursions.*

GRIGNAN★

Population 1 300
Michelin map 81 fold 2 or 245 fold 3 or 246 folds 8 and 22 – Facilities

Located on an isolated rocky hillock, the imposing château belonging to Adhémar de Monteil overlooks the old town of Tricastin and owes its fame to the delightful letters written in the late 17C by **Mme de Sévigné** to her daughter, Mme de Grignan, wherein she recounts with a keen eye and nice turn of phrase, life at the court of Louis XIV, Paris society, visits to the country and day-to-day domestic matters.

A good marriage – When Mme de Sévigné's daughter married the count of Grignan, Lieutenant-General of Provence in 1669, the girl's mother commented: "the prettiest girl in France is marrying not the most handsome of young men (the count was very ugly!) but one of the most honest in the kingdom".

The good life in Provence – Mme de Sévigné spent several long stays at the château. She enjoyed her visits and described the château as "very fine and magnificent", adding characteristically "one eats well and there are masses of visitors". She gives a mouthwatering description of how the partridges were fed on thyme, marjoram and other herbs to give them flavour, how the quail had fat and tender legs, the doves were succulent and the melons, figs and muscat grapes perfect. Although she admired the view from the terrace, she preferred the cool fragrance of the nearby grotto to write in; her only complaint was the mistral, which she viewed as a personal enemy, describing it as "that bitter, freezing and cutting wind".

The misplaced curiosity of 18C phrenologists – Mme de Sévigné died at the château in 1696 aged 69 from over-fatigue after nursing her sick daughter. She was buried in the château's chapel, but during the Revolution her head was dispatched to Paris for examination by avid phrenologists. It has since disappeared.

Literary pilgrims – "I am so proud to be here that I feel inclined to sit up all night and write letters if for no other reason than that they might bear the château's address. My imagination is so filled with Mme de Sévigné that at every moment I expect to see her before me!" So wrote an English noblewoman in 1770, just one of many who come on a literary pilgrimage inspired by the letters.

SIGHTS

★★**Château** ⊘ – The medieval castle was remodelled from 1545 to 1558 by Louis Adhémar, governor of the Galleys of Provence,

Mme de Sévigné by C. Lefebvre
(Musée Carnavalet, Paris)

and from 1668 to 1690 by François de Castellane-Adhémar.

The Renaissance south façade (restored in 1913) overlooks the garden in the lower courtyard. Well Court opens onto a terrace enclosed by a transitional Gothic gallery on the left and by Renaissance wings on the right and at the far end.

The great staircase, the drawing-rooms, the audience chamber, the Count of Grignan's apartments, Mme de Sévigné's bedroom and dressing room, the chapel, the Gothic staircase and the panelled Adhémar gallery are also open.

The **furnishings**★ recreate past settings: Louis XIII furniture, Italian writing desk in the audience chamber; Régence style and Louis XV period furnishings in the Grignans' apartments where the parquet flooring is lovely. The walls are hung with Aubusson **tapestries** (17C mythological scene).

From the terrace, constructed over Église St-Sauveur *(see below)*, is a vast **panorama**★ including Montagne de Rachas and the long ridge of the Lance (northeast), Mont Ventoux and the Dentelles de Montmirail heights (southeast), the Comtat Venaissin plain, the Alpilles, Suze-la-Rousse and the Chamaret belfry (southwest), Grignan woods and the Vivarais mountains beyond the Rhône (northwest).

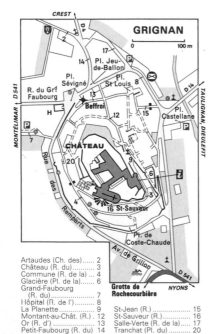

Église St-Sauveur ⊘ – 16C. The church's west front, the portico of which was destroyed by the Protestants and subsequently rebuilt in 1554, is lit through a Flamboyant Gothic rose window.

Inside, the features of interest are the small gallery beneath the roof which communicated directly with the castle until the Revolution, when the door was bricked up; 17C **organ loft**, 17C altarpiece and fine chancel panelling. On the north side is the marble funerary stone to Mme de Sévigné.

Beffroi – The belfry, the 12C town gateway, was transformed in the 17C.

Grotte de Rochecourbière – *1km/0.5mi. Take D 541 south out of Grignan, at a Calvary take the road that branches off; after about 1km/0.5mi from D 541 park the car and walk back to the stone steps on the right.*

This grotto was one of Mme de Sévigné's favourite places, where she loved to sit and write.

Artaudes (Ch. des)...... 2
Château (R. du)........... 3
Commune (R. de la) ... 4
Glacière (Pl. de la)...... 6
Grand-Faubourg
   (R. du).................... 7
Hôpital (R. de l')......... 8
La Planette................. 9
Montant-au-Chât. (R.) . 12
Or (R. d') 13
Petit-Faubourg (R. du) 14
St-Jean (R.) 15
St-Sauveur (R.)........... 16
Salle-Verte (R. de la)..... 17
Tranchat (Pl. du) 20

EXCURSION

Taulignan – *7km/4mi northeast on D 14 and D 24*. On the boundary between Dauphiné and Provence, this old agricultural town remains ensconced within its medieval fortifications. An almost uninterrupted circle, it has preserved 11 towers (nine round and two square) joined by a curtain wall (machicolations remain in several places), into which dwellings are integrated.

Walk along the old streets and admire the ancient façades with their ogee-arched doorways and mullioned windows (Rue des Fontaines) and go through (to the northeast) Porte d'Anguille, the only fortified gate flanked by two towers still standing. The Romanesque church was disfigured in the 19C.

On the edge of town on D 14, stands a small Protestant church built in 1868.

L'ISLE-SUR-LA-SORGUE

Population 15 564

Michelin map 81 fold 12 or 245 folds 17 and 30 or 246 fold 11

Local map see Basse Vallée de la Durance – Facilities

L'Isle-sur-la-Sorgue is set at the foot of the Plateau de Vaucluse. The arms of the River Sorgue and the avenues lined with plane trees add freshness to this charming site.

For a long time the town was a very active industrial centre: weaving, dyeing, tanning as well as paper, grain and oil mills flourished; some 10 wheels set the beat of this bustling town.

The town is also the birthplace of the poet **René Char** (1907-1988).

Église Notre-Dame-des-Anges ⊙ – The church was rebuilt in the 17C, and has a lovely façade made up of two superimposed orders, Doric on the ground floor, Ionic above.

The fascinating interior catches the attention due to the ornate 17C **decoration**★, recalling Italian church interiors. The single nave is adorned on the back of the west face with an immense gilded wooden glory attributed to Jean Péru, as are the figures of the Virtues placed In the spandrels underneath the balustrades. The side chapels are decorated with fine woodwork and paintings by Mignard, Sauvan, Simon Vouet and Parrocel. In the chancel a large altarpiece frames a work by Reynaud Levieux representing the Assumption; there is also a 17C organ.

Hôtel Donadeï de Campredon (Centre Xavier-Battini) ⊙ (**B**) – This lovely 18C mansion is a good example of the French classical style. Its renovated rooms are used for cultural events and are well-suited for housing interesting temporary exhibitions.

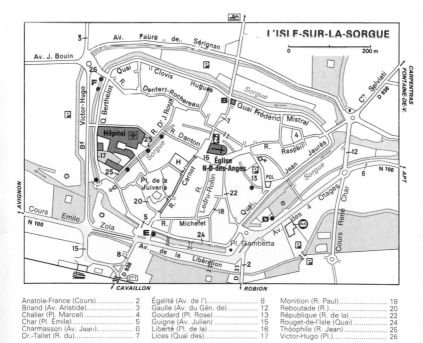

Anatole-France (Cours) 2	Égalité (Av. de l') 8	Monition (R. Paul) 18
Briand (Av. Aristide) 3	Gaulle (Av. du Gén. de) 12	Reboutade (R.) 20
Chalier (Pl. Marcel) 4	Goudard (Pl. Rose) 13	République (R. de la) 22
Char (Pl. Émile) 5	Guigne (Av. Julien) 15	Rouget-de-l'Isle (Quai) 24
Charmasson (Av. Jean) 6	Liberté (Pl. de la) 16	Théophile (R. Jean) 25
Dr.-Tallet (R. du) 7	Lices (Quai des) 17	Victor-Hugo (Pl.) 26

B Hôtel Donadeï de Campredon	**D, E, F** Roues à eau

Hôpital ⊘ – The hospital's entrance is on Rue Jean-Théophile parallel to a branch of the River Sorgue. Admire in the hall the gilded wooden Virgin, the grand staircase, embellished by an 18C wrought iron banister, a chapel with 18C woodwork, and pharmacy with Moustiers faience pottery jars and a huge 17C mortar. An additional attraction is the peaceful garden, ornamented by an 18C fountain.

Roues à eau – Near the Place Gambetta at the corner of the Caisse d'Épargne's garden is a **wheel** (**D**), similar to those which worked the silk factories and oil mills. Seven other old water wheels still exist: one (**E**) in Place Émile-Char, two others (**F**) in Boulevard Victor-Hugo, three in Rue Jean-Théophile and one in Quai des Lices.

LABEAUME★

Population 455
Michelin map 80 east of fold 8 or 245 south of fold 1

The old village situated on the bank of the gorges of the Beaume, a tributary of the Ardèche, merges almost totally into the rock face. At the village's foot, a low level bridge, with no parapet walls but stout piers protected by cutwaters, spans the river, a perfect feature in such surroundings.

Leave the car on the large square at the village's entrance.

Church (Église) – The very high belfry-porch (19C) rests on two large round columns.

Take, to the left of the church, an alleyway which ends at the river bank and a shaded esplanade. For a better overall view of the village cross the bridge and follow the uphill path for a couple of hundred yards.

★**Gorges de la Beaume** – The walk upstream along the river's north bank, beside the clear waters, across from the fascinating eroded limestone cliff, is worthwhile.

Village – As you return to the car stroll along the uphill streets admiring the covered passageways and balconied houses along them.

EXCURSIONS AROUND RUOMS *11km/7mi*

Leave Labeaume on D 245, then turn left onto D 4.

The road goes through picturesque rock tunnels and affords plunging views of the river with its clear green waters.

★**Défilé de Ruoms** – Following the Ruoms defile are the Ligne gorges; from the confluence of the two rivers (Ardèche and Ligne), framed by 100m/329ft high cliffs striped by the rock strata, is revealed a good **view** upstream. On the return trip, at the end of the tunnels, the silhouette of Rocher de Sampzon *(see below)* appears at the end of the valley.

Cross the Ardèche towards Ruoms.

Ruoms – Facilities. The old walled centre of the small commercial town is unexpected – a quadrilateral of ramparts flanked by seven round towers. At the heart of the old town is a small Romanesque church with an unusual arcaded belfry faced with motifs worked in volcanic rock. The view is best from Ruelle St-Roch opening onto the parvis.

Leave Ruoms on D 579 towards Vallon.

★**Rocher de Sampzon** – *On the Ardèche's south bank via a narrow road which climbs steeply through many bends. Park below Sampzon church and walk to the top (45min return), first by the tarred path and then by the path level with the turning place.*

From the top (television relay mast) there is a **panorama**★★ including the Vallon basin, the Orgnac plateau and the meanders of the Ardèche.

MICHELIN GREEN TOURIST GUIDES

Landscapes
Monuments
Scenic routes, touring programmes
Geography
History, Art
Places to stay
Town and site plans
Practical information

A collection of guides for your travels in France and around the world.

LOURMARIN

Population 1 108
Michelin map 84 fold 3 or 114 fold 2 or 245 fold 31 or 246 fold 12
Local map see Montagne du LUBERON

The village at the foot of the Montagne du Luberon and at the south end of the coomb of the same name, is dominated by its château built high on a rock bluff.
Albert Camus (1913-60), the author of *L'Étranger (The Stranger)* and *La Peste (The Plague)*, is buried in the cemetery, together with the author **Henri Bosco** (1888-1976).

★**Château** ⊘ – The château includes a 15C part, the old château, and a Renaissance part, the new château. It was restored by Robert Laurent-Vibert, who bequeathed it to the Aix-en-Provence Education Academy when he died in 1925.
The Renaissance wing has remarkable stylistic unity and contains large chimney-pieces ornamented with caryatids or Corinthian columns. The grand staircase ends dramatically with a slender pillar supporting a stone cupola. The château offers a lovely view of the Durance valley and the olive grove lying within the grounds. The 15C wing, which now houses the library and students' quarters, overlooks pretty stone or wood arcades.

Château de Lourmarin

C. Moirenc/DIAF

Montagne du LUBERON★

Michelin map 81 folds 12-15 or 114 folds 1-3 or 245 folds 30-32

Midway between the Alps and the Mediterranean lies the mountainous Luberon range. This region is full of charm: striking solitary woods and rocky countryside and picturesque, old hill-top villages and drystone huts.
During the 16C the area was the backdrop to bloody attacks on the Vaudois community *(see Introduction: Historical table and notes)*. Numerous place and family names bear witness to their passage through the region, and a historical tour – "**Route Historique des Vaudois en Luberon**" – through 28 towns and villages, illustrating all the various manifestations of the Vaudois heritage *(see Thematic trips at the end of the guide)*.

Parc Naturel Régional du Luberon – Founded in 1977, the regional nature park includes 60 communes covering 140 000ha/ 297 000 acres including the *départements* of Vaucluse and Alpes-de-Haute-Provence (that is, from Manosque to Cavaillon and the Coulon – or Calavon – valley to the Durance valley). Its goal is to preserve the natural balance of the region with the aim of improving the living conditions of the village folk, the promotion of agricultural activity through irrigation, mechanisation and the reorganisation of the holdings. The main developments in the tourist industry are the opening of Tourist Information Centres and museums at Apt, Buoux and La Tour-d'Aigues, and the creation of nature trails (through the cedar forest at Bonnieux, the ochre cliffs of Roussillon, the Viens *bories* and the cultivation terraces at Goult).

Natural habitat and man's imprint – The Montagne du Luberon is a gigantic anticlinal fold of calcareous rock of the Tertiary Era running east-west. The range is divided from north to south by the Lourmarin coomb into two unequal parts: to the west the Petit Luberon forms a plateau carved by gorges and ravines where the altitude rarely exceeds 700m/2 297ft; whereas to the east, the massive summits of the Grand Luberon rise up to 1 125m/3 691ft at Mourre Nègre.

The contrast between the north and south slopes is no less great. The northern face, steep and ravined, is cooler, more humid and wears a fine forest of downy oaks. The southern face, turned towards Aix, is more Mediterranean in its vegetation (oak groves, rosemary-filled *garrigues*), and with its sunny slopes, crops and cypresses, announces the delightful countryside along the River Durance.

The diversity of the vegetation is a delight to nature lovers: oak forests, Atlas cedar (planted in 1862) on the heights of the Petit Luberon, beech, Scots pine, moors of broom and box-wood, *garrigues*, an extraordinary variety of aromatic plants (herbs of Provence) clinging here and there to the rocky slopes. The *mistral* contributes, provoking unusual local changes: holm oaks are blown onto the northern exposed slopes and downy oaks onto the southern exposed slopes. In winter the contrast between the evergreens and deciduous trees is striking. The fauna is equally rich: snakes (seven different varieties), lizards, warblers, blue rock thrushes, owls, eagles etc. The Luberon has always been inhabited by man. Since prehistoric times, it has served as a hiding-place during periods of insecurity and political and religious persecutions: the memory of the Vaudois massacres still lingers. Villages appeared during the Middle Ages, clinging to the rock face near a water hole. The tall houses with their imposing walls huddled close together at the foot of a castle or church; most of them had rooms cut out of the rock. The men left their homes to work in the surrounding countryside and when necessary they lived in drystone huts called *bories (see below)*. Their livelihood was obtained mostly from sheep, olives, grain and vineyards as well as lavender and silkworms. Each parcel of cultivated land was carefully cleared of stones – the stones were grouped into piles called *clapiers* – and bordered by low walls which served to protect the land from soil erosion. The flocks were also contained within a close of drystone. Traces of these arrangements are still visible in the rural landscape. This traditional economy was swept away by the agricultural improvements of the 19C and 20C: villages lost their inhabitants and fell into ruins. Nowadays, the trend is reversing itself; village populations are increasing at an almost constant rate, and the villages themselves have been well restored. However, the villages on the southern slopes, which have always been better off because of their rich land, have adapted to the requirements of the modern rural economy: market gardening, fruit growing and vineyards from Aigues have enabled the native population to survive.

A BRIEF SURVEY OF THE LUBERON

Information – All details regarding leisure activities and accommodation can be obtained from La Maison du Parc, 60 Place Jean-Jaurès, B.P. 122, 84404 Apt ☎ 04 90 04 42 00 or by minitel 3615 LUBERON. You can also apply to local Tourist Information Centres.

Leisure Activities – Rambling or cycling through the park provides an excellent opportunity to study local flora and fauna and to discover the region's natural and architectural heritage. The best seasons in which to do so are spring and autumn. The French National Rambling Federation issues two guides called *Tour du Luberon, GR 9* and *20 Ballades dans le Parc Naturel Régional du Luberon*. The Maison du Parc will give you information about guided walks *(free of charge)* as well as bed and breakfast accommodation. It has also mapped out a tourist route especially for cyclists, stretching from Cavaillon to Forcalquier (around 100km/62mi): signposts have been set up at all main crossraods (white heading from Cavaillon towards Forcalquier, ochre in the opposite direction); additional road signs with further information are to be found in 25 nearby villages.

The bories – On the slopes of the Luberon and the Vaucluse plateau stand these curious drystone huts, one or two floors high, called *bories*. They are either alone or in groups forming a very picturesque unit; there are about 3 000 of them. They were sometimes just tool sheds or sheep pens but many were inhabited over the different periods from the Iron Age until the 18C for the most recent, which in fact are better constructed.

The *bories* were built with materials found on the spot: thin slabs of limestone which have become detached from the rock, or slabs picked when clearing the fields. These stones called *lauzes* are on average 10cm/3.75in thick. Specialised masons knew how to select the *lauzes* and assemble them without either mortar or water. The thickness of the walls obtained by the juxtaposition of several rows of slabs varied from 0.80m/31.5in to 1.60m/4.5ft; it was always reinforced at the base. The bonding whether from the outside or inside was remarkably regular. The technique used for the roofing of the *borie* consisted of a type of false corbelled vaulting: as the walls were raised each stone course was carefully made to overhang the preceding one, so that at a height of 3 or 4m/10 to 13ft – the diameter diminished to the point of being reduced to a small opening which could be closed simply by placing one slab. To avoid the infiltration of water the different layers of stone were slightly inclined towards the exterior. Inside, the vaulting appeared as a hemispheric dome on pendentives which allowed the plan to pass from a square or a circle or a cone.

Bories

The *bories* offered a variety of forms. The simplest, round, ovoid or square, consisted of one room (1-8m/3-26ft in diameter) and one opening set east or southeast. The interior arrangement was rudimentary, limited to hollow niches used for storage. The temperature of the *borie* remained constant whatever the season. Larger dwellings exist, especially at Gordes. They are rectangular, with a few narrow openings, and the roof had double or quadruple pitch using the technique of false vaulting either rounded, pointed barrel or an inverted ship's hull (Gordes). Their organisation was similar to that of a traditional farm: disposed around a courtyard encircled by a high wall were the living quarters (tiled floors, benches, and chimney for the most comfortable ones), bread oven and outbuildings.

These villages of *bories* produce numerous suppositions: were these places of refuge during troubled times, and if so occupied permanently? But then why has neither a burial place nor a place of worship been discovered near them? Were they then perhaps just temporary, seasonal places to live in?

★★ GRAND LUBERON

① Round Tour from Apt

119km/74mi – allow half a day (not including climb to Mourre Nègre)

Apt – *See APT.*

Leave Apt on D 48 going southeast on Avenue de Saignon.

As the road climbs, the hill-top site of Saignon, Apt basin, Vaucluse plateau and Mont Ventoux come into view.

Saignon – The village, close to a tall rock, contains a Romanesque church with a west front rebuilt in the 16C to include beautiful, trilobed blind arcading.

Continue along D 48.

The road skirts Claparèdes plateau with its scattered *bories*.

Leave the car at Auribeau; exit from town northwards and bear left on the unsurfaced road towards Mourre Nègre. The GR 92 leads to the summit.

★★★ **Mourre Nègre** – *Half a day return on foot.* Mourre Nègre at 1 125m/3 691ft is the highest point of the Montagne du Luberon and the site of the Paris-Nice television relay mast. The **panorama**★★★ embraces four points of the compass: the Montagne de Lure and Digne pre-Alps (northeast), the Durance valley with Montagne Ste-Victoire in the background (southeast), Étang de Berre and the Alpilles (southwest), Apt basin, Vaucluse plateau and Mont Ventoux (northwest).

Return to D 48 and continue through Auribeau.

Castellet – The tiny terraced hamlet is now a lavender distillery centre. The road crosses a *garrigues* landscape before reaching the Calavon valley.

Turn right on N 100.

After 2km/1mi – take a small road on the right after crossing the River Calavon.

Tour d'Embarbe – This tower dates from the 12C and presents a practically blind façade with only a few arrow slits along its spiral staircase.

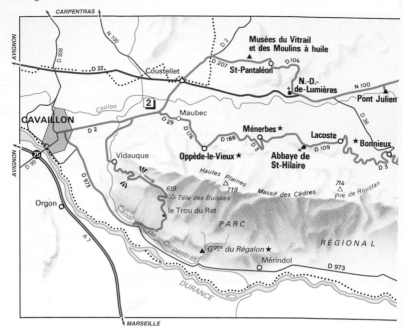

Céreste – This old Roman village was on the Domitian Way, which linked Italy to the Rhône delta at the time of the Romans, and became an important centre for Christianity because of the Carluc priory.

The village still has some of its fortifications and constitutes a lovely architectural unit. The surrounding earth is rich in marvellous fossils (fish, plants) which have formed in the calcareous strata.

Leave Céreste towards Forcalquier and turn left into Avenue du Pont-Romain.

The so-called Roman bridge, which is in fact medieval, can be seen on the right, spanning the River Encrmè. The Nid d'amour or Love nest *(below the village near to the Encrème)* is a curious fountain-tank beneath a stone vault, fed by two streams gushing from the rock and extended by a pool corbelled into the rock.

Follow the small road, keeping closely to the right, as it crosses the first foothills of the Vaucluse plateau. After 3.5km/2.2mi, turn left into a road downhill.

Prieuré de Carluc ⊙ – The remains of the 12C priory of Carluc, dependent on the Abbaye de Montmajour, are tucked at the bottom of a peaceful little valley. The church is modest in size and features a five-sided apse decorated with colonettes and a frieze of billet moulding.

A gallery cut into the rock opens from the north side of the church; it has a very old roof, consisting partly of groined vaulting. Tombs in the shape of human figures and benches are visible on the ground. This gallery once led to a second church, however, the part hollowed out of the rock is all that now remains of this.

Return to Céreste and take D 31 to the left.

The road winds up the north slope of the Grand Luberon from where one can see over the Calavon valley to the Vaucluse plateau. The road then descends the southern slope passing through Vitrolles down onto the plain; turn right into D 42; continue along D 27, which skirts the Étang de la Bonde.

Cucuron – Inside the **church**, which has a Romanesque nave and Gothic apse and chapels, are an early-18C marble altarpiece, a multicoloured marble pulpit and a 16C painted wood *Christ Seated and Chained* in the baptismal chapel.

Opposite the church, on the first floor of the 17C Hôtel de Bouliers is a small **museum** ⊙: local prehistory, Gallo-Roman period, and later local traditions.

From the terrace below the keep, there is a fine view over the Cucuron basin to Montagne Ste-Victoire on the horizon. The belfry was once a gateway in the old walls.

Ansouis – 4.5km/2.5mi from Cucuron on D 56 going southeast. See ANSOUIS.

Lourmarin – See LOURMARIN.

D 943 travels northwest up the Lourmarin coomb.

The River Aigue Brun has cut narrow gorges through the rock. The road goes through a children's holiday camp (old 16C-18C château) before crossing a bridge and reaching a group of houses.

Just before these houses turn right onto the narrow path (car park).

Fort de Buoux ⊙ – 30min return on foot, plus 45min tour. Go through the gate and follow the path beneath a vertical rock wall to the porter's lodge.

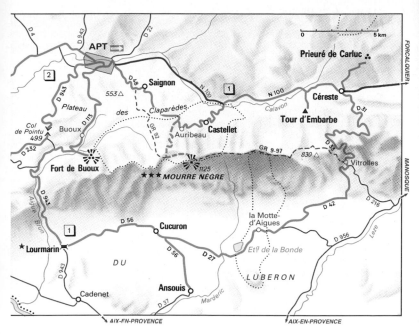

The rock spur on which the fort stands is a natural defence which has, in succession, been occupied by Ligurians, Romans, Catholics and Protestants. Louis XIV ordered its demolition in 1660 – there nevertheless remain three defensive walls, a Romanesque chapel, houses, silos hewn out of the rock, a keep, a Ligurian sacrificial altar and a concealed staircase.

From the rock spur, there is a fine view of the Upper Aigue Brun valley.

Return to the holiday camp and turn right onto D 113.

Beyond Buoux village the road returns to Apt along a picturesque route.

The mountain flora found in the Luberon area features several characteristic species such as leuzea (easily recognisable by its resinous cones), rockrose with its soft green, furry leaves and sweet-smelling honeysuckle.

★PETIT LUBERON

② Round Tour from Apt *101km/62.5mi – about 6hr*

Apt – *See APT.*

Leave Apt by ② on the map, D 943. After the Col de Pointu pass, turn right onto D 232.

The road crosses the Claparèdes plateau, studded with *bories* among oak trees and truffle beds.

Bear right onto D 36.

★**Bonnieux** – *See BONNIEUX.*

Leave Bonnieux south on D 3 then bear right on D 109.

The road winds along the slope of the Petit Luberon; fine view of Bonnieux.

Lacoste – This hill-top village has a small elegant 17C belfry and is dominated by the imposing ruins (partially rebuilt) of a château which belonged to the Sade family and included 42 rooms. The **Marquis de Sade** (1740-1814), author of erotic works *(Justine ou les Malheurs de la Vertu, etc.)*, was the lord of Lacoste for some 30 years. He was extremely fond of the stage and gave orders to build an extravagant, luxurious theatre that could accommodate over 100 people. Condemned several times, he escaped and hid here; but in 1778 he was caught and imprisoned – mainly in the Bastille. His château was wrecked during the Revolution.

Continue to Ménerbes via D 109; note the quarries which extract a well-known freestone in the area near Lacoste.

Improve your knowledge of the Divine Marquis by visiting... the Château de Lacoste, where Sade indulged in several nights of orgy, the Château de Saumane (see p 159) where he spent his childhood and was brought up by his uncle, a learned and libertine clergyman, and, finally, the Château de Mazan (see p 141), where the notorious marquis was said to be a frequent visitor.

Abbaye de St-Hilaire ⊘ – *Currently under restoration*. Located in a pretty site facing the Luberon, this former monastery (nowadays in private hands) was occupied by the Carmelites from the 13C to the 18C. It retains three chapels, from the 12C, 13C (broken barrel vault) and 14C respectively, in addition to the monastic buildings from the 17C.

★**Ménerbes** – *See MÉNERBES*.

Go south along D 3 and then take D 188.

The road offers attractive views of the Vaucluse plateau and Mont Ventoux.

★**Oppède-le-Vieux** – The terraced **site**★ of the village on its picturesque rocky spur, once partially abandoned, has come to life again through its restoration.

The old village square is surrounded by restored houses. An old gateway in the walls leads to the upper village crowned by its 13C collegiate church (remodelled in the 16C and 19C) and ruined castle (founded by the counts of Toulouse and rebuilt in the 15C and 16C).

The fine **view**★ from the church terrace is of the Coulon valley and Vaucluse plateau, Ménerbes and, from the rear of the castle, of the ravined north face of the Luberon.

Cross the Maubec wine region (D 176, D 29) and bear left on D 2.

On leaving Robion bear left on D 31 to the intersection with the Vidauque road, which you take to the left.

This very steep winding road *(one-way road; speed limit 30kph/20mph)*, skirts the wild Vidauque coomb and offers magnificent plunging **views**★★ of the surrounding countryside: tip of Vaucluse plateau and Coulon valley (north), Alpilles and Durance valley (south and west), and below, Cavaillon plain with its market-gardens hemmed in by cypresses and reeds.

Level with the television relay mast the road branches off to the right on the so-called Trou-du-Rat road leading to D 973 which you take to the right.

Cavaillon – *See CAVAILLON*.

Leave the town by ② on the town plan.

D 2 climbs the fertile Coulon valley.

Coustellet – The **Musée de la Lavande** ⊘ *(on the right on the Gordes road)* has a collection of old red copper stills (for use over an open fire, with steam, in a bain-marie, for concretes – waxes and perfume oil – and for absolutes – concentrated flower oil) which illustrate the different distillation processes for lavender, which grows at an altitude of between 1 000 and 1 200m/3 280 and 3 937ft. Products on sale are made from lavender grown at the Château du Bois in the Lagarde d'Apt commune (Albion plateau).

3km/2mi after Coustellet bear right on D 207 towards Moulin des Bouillons.

Musée de l'Histoire du Verre et du Vitrail and Musée du Moulin des Bouillons – *See GORDES: Excursions*.

St-Pantaléon – *See GORDES: Excursions*.

D 104 and D 60 to the right lead to Notre-Dame-de-Lumières.

Notre-Dame-de-Lumières – The statue of Our Lady in the crypt of this 17C sanctuary is the object of a popular Provençal pilgrimage; in the chapel above, on the third south altar is a 17C Pietà in carved and gilded wood. A large ex-voto collection is on display. The conventual buildings stand in a fine park.

N 100 climbs the Coulon valley. On the left is ochre country.

Pont Julien – *See APT: Excursions*.

N 100 returns to Apt.

Grotte de la MADELEINE★

Michelin map 80 fold 9 or 245 north of fold 15 or 246 fold 23
Local map see Gorges de l'ARDÈCHE

This cave opens onto the north face of the cliff, hollowed out by the Gorges de l'Ardèche.

The downhill road to the cave branches onto D 290, the road of the Gorges de l'Ardèche, and leads to the entrance (car park).

TOUR ⊘ *45min*

The cave discovered in 1887 was formed by an underground river which once drained part of Gras plateau. Enter through the Grotte Obscure, then follow a tunnel hewn out of the rock *(steep staircase)* to the Salle du Chaos or Chaos Cave.

Beyond this chamber, divided into two parts by a mass of columns detached from the vault, extends a vast gallery full of richly-decorated concretions: draperies, organs 30m/98ft high, eccentrics in the shape of horns etc. Note in particular a magnificent white flow, between two formations of red draperies evoking frozen falls by their fluidity, and concretions in the form of gypsum flowers. The sides of the chamber are covered with small crystallisations resembling coral.

MAILLANE

Population 1 664
Michelin map 81 folds 11 and 12 or 245 fold 29 or 246 fold 25
16km/10mi south of Avignon

In the fertile countryside named Petite Crau de St-Rémy, Maillane offers the charm typical of a Provençal town with its small squares shaded with plane trees and white houses roofed with tiles. Its renown is due largely to the fame of **Frédéric Mistral**, the Provençal poet and one of the founders of the Félibrige movement.

Frédéric Mistral – Mistral was born on 8 September 1830 (d 1914) and spent his childhood at the Mas du Juge on the road to Graveson. From schooling in Maillane he went to boarding school at St-Michel-de-Frigolet, then studied at the Collège Royal in Avignon where he met Roumanille. After having studied law at Aix (in 1851), he returned to the family home more attracted to the charm of the Provençal language than the complexities of the *Code Napoléon*. At the death of his father, he had to leave the Mas du Juge for the Maison du Lézard *(house facing the museum)*, a small family home at the village's entrance, where he lived with his mother and finished writing *Mirèio* (1859). He married in 1876 and moved to a new house which has religiously safeguarded his memory *(see below)*. In 1904 he was awarded the Nobel Prize for Literature.
In the cemetery, down the main path, level with the war memorial stands, on the left, Mistral's mausoleum which he copied from Queen Jeanne's pavilion near Les Baux.

Frédéric Mistral

Museon Mistral ⊙ – The museum is located in the house which Mistral had built and then lived in from 1876 to 1914. Mistral's memory is evoked throughout the various rooms – office, living room, dining room, bedroom – which have been kept as they were at his death.

MARCOULE

Michelin map 80 north of fold 20 or 246 fold 24

The nuclear power station, identified from afar by its two 80 and 100m/262 and 328ft tall chimneys, is surrounded by vineyards and *garrigue*. Three organisations are active here: COGEMA (Compagnie Générale des Matières Premières – Raw Materials Company), CEA (Commissariat à l'Energie Atomique – Atomic Energy Commission) and MELOX. The main purpose of COGEMA is the industrial processing of nuclear waste (natural uranium-graphite-gas) derived from nuclear reactors. An industrial workshop, complementary to the chemical factory, started in 1978 the French process of vitrification of radioactive waste. The CEA, more a centre of research than a producer of energy, works on different aspects of research and development in the processing of irradiated fuels and waste containment and for this purpose operates the Phénix fast reactor. Situated alongside the River Rhône and bordering the Marcoule site, the MELOX factory produces MOX fuel (a mixture of uranium and plutonium oxides), which supplies some of the French electronuclear park reactors.

★★Viewing platform (Belvédère) – *Access via D 138 east of Chusclan.*

View – A panel on the raised area between the two exhibition halls identifies the main installations. From the platform there is also an extensive scenic view of the Rhône, Orange and its Roman theatre, Mont Ventoux, the Comtat plain, the Alpilles, the Ardoise iron and metalworks and the Lower Gard valley.

Exhibition ⊙ – Two galleries exhibit information pertaining to nuclear energy: the activities of the plant are presented, the nuclear fuel cycle explained, and different types of energy and the various ways of protecting the environment are evoked.

This guide, which is revised regularly, incorporates tourist information provided at the time of going to press. Changes are however inevitable owing to improved facilities and fluctuations in the cost of living.

MARSEILLE★★★

Pop 800 550

Michelin map 84 fold 13 or 114 fold 28 or 245 fold 44 or 246 folds K, L and M

Twenty-six centuries of history have contributed to making Marseille the oldest of the great French cities. Jealous of its independence, the city has always struck out on its own, resulting in its isolation from the regional and national community until the 19C. Even nowadays, although proud of being the second most populated city in France, it has retained its own distinct character: a combination of authenticity and hardworn clichés (tall stories about Marius and César, the cries of the fishmongers on the Vieux Port or of the *boule* players, or shady judicial proceedings).

And yet Marseille does not survive on its folklore, it is a city which has progressed with the times: modernising constantly and developing ambitious projects, especially cultural ones (a dozen museums to which have been added the Vieille Charité cultural centre, the Opera, the Criée theatre, the dynamic Luminy School of Art, a group of young artists etc).

★★★**Site** – As an introduction to the bustling and picturesque city, visitors are advised to take the time to admire the unique site on which the city was built. Notre-Dame-de-la-Garde is the best viewpoint and from the parvis and the area near the basilica a splendid **panorama★★★** extends over the roofs of the city, the harbour and the surrounding mountains. On the left rise Pomègues and Ratonneau islands, Château d'If and in the distance the Massif de Marseilleveyre; opposite is the port overlooked by Fort St-Jean (14C-17C) and Parc du Pharo in the foreground, further to the right the city and in the background the Chaîne de l'Estaque with the Chaîne de l'Étoile in the distance. By the Vieux Port, from the terrace near Palais du Pharo and the parvis of St-Laurent church there are fine **views★** of the old port with its boats, the beginning of the Canebière and the town.

HISTORICAL NOTES

The founding of Massalia – Before the official founding of the city there was probably a settlement on the site, a sort of trading-post, which was used by the Greeks. Around 600 BC a few galleys manned by Phocaeans (Greeks from Asia Minor) hoping to expand their commercial activity landed on the coast in Lacydon creek, which is now the Vieux Port.

According to legend, their leader, Protis, visited the Ligurian tribe which occupied the country. It was the day on which the king was giving a great banquet for the warriors seeking the hand of his daughter, **Gyptis**. According to Ligurian custom, at the end of the meal, the young girl was to enter with a cup full of wine which she would present to the man of her choice. **Protis**, invited to the banquet, mixed with the crowd of suitors: Gyptis entered. She stopped in front of the handsome Greek and offered him the ritual cup. The marriage was celebrated and the young woman brought as her dowry the hill which dominated the north bank of Lacydon creek and the land around it. Soon, a little town grew up. This was Massalia (or Massilia), the mother of Marseille.

After the destruction of Phocaea by the Persians (540 BC) Massalia was at the forefront of a number of new territorial acquisitions. The Greeks, who were expert traders, quickly made the city prosperous. They set up busy trading-posts at Arles, Nice, Antibes, Agde, Le Brusc, the Hyères islands, and inland at Glanon, Cavaillon, Avignon and perhaps St-Blaise on Étang de Berre.

With the Celtic-Ligurians, intense trade concentrated on arms, bronze objects, oil, wine, salt, most likely slaves and ceramics. Masters of the sea between the straits of Messina and the Iberian coast, and dominant in the Rhone valley having overcome their Etruscan and Punic rivals, the Massalians controlled international trade in amber and raw metals in particular: silver and pewter from Spain or Brittany, copper from Etruria. After a period of eclipse, the city regained its splendour in the 4C. The coastal region was developed and planted with fruit and olive trees and vines.

Greek sailors pushed further south as far as Senegal and to the north explored the Baltic coast as far as Iceland. Massalia was administered as a republic, famous for the wisdom of its laws, and widely recognised as a cultural centre.

In 1995 excavations carried out on the Place des Pistoles have uncovered vestiges of human dwellings dating back to the second quarter of the 4C BC: household furnishings (vestibules, window seats), local and foreign ceramic pieces, and a plan of the city indicating that even in those days Marseille was a highly active centre. The ceramics imported from other countries confirm that the area had developed commercial exchanges with Mediterranean Greece (Ionian bowls, Corinthian ceramics and black, shiny Etruscan baked clay known as *bucchero nero*). The excavations around the Vieux Port and the Bourse commercial district have enabled historians to establish the layout of the town: it covered 50ha/124 acres and was built facing the sea on the hills of St-Laurent, Moulins and Carmes. It was surrounded by ramparts, aimed at protecting the town, and featured two temples (one celebrating Artemis and the other Apollo), a theatre as well as several other monuments.

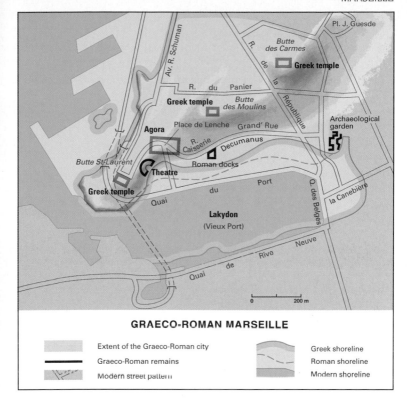

GRAECO-ROMAN MARSEILLE

Extent of the Graeco-Roman city

Graeco-Roman remains

Modern street pattern

Greek shoreline

Roman shoreline

Modern shoreline

Rome comes to Massalia's aid – An ally of Rome during the Second Punic War (154 BC), Massalia asked for its help against the Salian Franks (a tribe which comprised the majority of the local peoples) less than 30 years later. The Romans took this event as an occasion to acquire more influence, and entered Provence in 125 BC, rescuing Massalia and beginning their conquest of the area.

For three years battles raged as the Salian Frankish tribe harassed the land from entrenched camps. But Roman tenacity triumphed. Transalpine Gaul was founded with Aix and Narbonne as colonies. Massalia remained an independent republic allied to Rome, it kept a strip of territory along the coast.

Roman Marseille – At the moment when the rivalry between Caesar and Pompey was at its height, Marseille was forced to decide for one or the other of the two Roman generals. It backed Pompey, making the wrong choice. Besieged for six months, the town at last fell in 49 BC; Caesar stripped it of its fleet, its treasures and its trade. Arles, Narbonne and Fréjus were enriched with its spoils. Nevertheless, Marseille remained a free city and maintained a brilliant university, the last refuge of Greek teaching in the West.

The excavations of the old district have uncovered maritime warehouses (Roman dockyards) from 1C, proving that the town stayed commercially active in spite of the fact that most of the trade with the Far East and Italy was with Arles. In the 3C Marseille lost its municipal autonomy and became a town like all the others. A period of stagnation seemed to set in. However, Christianity came early to the town, as is shown by: the catacombs on the slopes of La Garde hill, the martyrdom of a Roman officer c 290, the two monasteries (among the first in the West) founded in the 5C and the treatises (c 450) written by a priest.

After the invasions, Marseille seemed to remain an active port which continued to trade with the Far East; it was the object of violent rivalry between the barbarian leaders. In 543 the plague arrived in Gaul for the first time. Definite decline began in the 7C. Pillaging by the Saracens, the Greeks and Charles Martel pushed the town back behind the fortifications of the bishopric on St-Laurent hill.

Maritime development – As early as the 11C the old Phocaean city mobilised all its shipping resources and put its shipyards to work.

In 1214 Marseille became an independent republic, but only for a short time, as in 1252 it had to submit to the rule of Charles of Anjou. During this prosperous period (12C-14C), which was marked by the Crusades, Marseille competed with Genoa for the rich supply trade in war material and food to the Crusaders. Not only did the city reap great profit from this, but it was granted ownership of a section of Jerusalem with its own church.

Marseille, now rich again, sought new outlets. Its sailors began to trade along the Catalan coast, competed in their own waters with the men of Pisa and Genoa, and often sailed as far as the Levant, Egypt and North Africa. In the early 15C prosperity was undermined by crises and recession which came to a head in 1423 when the fleet from Aragon pillaged the city. But this was just temporary because under the influence of two clever merchants, the Forbin brothers, trade started up again.

Good King René also discovered this world of trade and commerce during his long stay in the city during the summer of 1447.

In 1481 the town was united under the French crown at the same time as Provence. But there was hardly a reign in which the turbulent people of Marseille were not in rebellion, especially during the Wars of Religion.

STAYING IN MARSEILLE

Transport – The most convenient means of public transport is the metro; the two lines run from 5am to 9pm and are replaced between 9pm and 1am by *fluobus*, buses which operate along the same route. Tickets are sold in the form of magnetic cards valid for a single trip *(carte solo)*, a whole day *(carte journée)* or for several trips *(carte liberté*: each card is credited with the number of journeys you want to make*)*. Free network maps are available from ticket offices.

City Tours – The tourist office organises walking tours *(see Admission times and charges)* as well as tours by bus, boat or taxi; information and booking at tourist office.

Markets – Fish market every morning along the Quai des Belges; food markets every morning except Sunday, in Cours Pierre-Puget, on Place Jean-Jaurès (La Plaine), on Place du Marché-des-Capucins and in Avenue du Prado. A flower market is held on Tuesday and Saturday mornings along the Canebière and a book market takes place on the second Saturday of the month in Cours Julien. A flea market is held in Avenue du Cap-Pinède on Sunday mornings.

Arts and Crafts – The Carbonel and Aillaud *santon* workshops are open to the public (47 Rue Neuve-Ste-Catherine and 81 Rue d'Aubagne respectively), *santon* fair on Allées Léon-Gambetta from the end of November to mid-January; Provençal fabrics and other products at Souleido, 101 Rue Paradis; household soap *(savon de Marseille)* available from La Compagnie de Provence, 1 Rue

The "Four des Navettes" bakery

Caisserie; rape seed loaves of bread *(navettes)* from Le Four des Navettes, said to be the oldest bakery in town, 136 Rue Sainte (at the corner of Rue Sainte and Place St-Victor).

Football – Olympique de Marseille matches at the Stade Vélodrome, Boulevard Michelet and club shop at 100 La Canebière.

Entertainment – Pastorals (in December and January) at Théâtres Mazenod, 88 Rue d'Aubagne and Nau, 9 Rue Nau; classical music concerts and opera at the Opéra Municipal, 2 Rue Molière; ballet performances at the Ballet National de Marseille Roland-Petit, 1 Place Auguste-Carli; varied musical programmes at the Cité de la Musique, 4 Rue Bernard-du-Bois; classical or contemporary plays at the Théâtre National de Marseille-La-Criée, 30 Quai de Rive-Neuve, at Théâtres du Gymnase, 4 Rue du Théâtre-Français, Toursky (poetry), 16 Passage du Théâtre, and Lenche, 4 Place de Lenche; avant-garde performances at the Théâtre du Merlan-Scène nationale, Avenue Raimu, Théâtre des Bernadines, 17 Boulevard Garibaldi, and at the Chocolat-Théâtre, 59 Cours Julien; rock, jazz and reggae concerts at Espace Julien, 39 Cours Julien; various shows at Dôme-Nouvel Alcazar, at St-Just *(see p 193)*.

Music – La Samaritaine (jazz; 2 Quai du port), La Scala (karaoke; 53 Promenade Georges-Pompidou), L'Intermédiaire (rock and pop; 6 Place Jean-Jaurès), the Montana Blues Station (blues, rhythm and blues; 16 Place Jean-Jaurès).

The Great Plague – In the early 18C Marseille's population was about 90 000. It was a great port which had profited from an edict of franchise since 1669 and from a monopoly of trade with the Levant. It subsequently became a huge warehouse of imported products (textiles, food products, drugs and miscellaneous items); and was preparing to launch into trade with the West Indies and the New World, when in May 1720 it fell victim to a dreadful curse. A ship coming from Syria, the *Grand St-Antoine*, was stricken with several cases of the plague during its journey. When it arrived in Marseille, it was put under quarantine at the Île de Jarre *(see Massif des CALANQUES: The Calanques by Boat)*. Despite the precautions taken, the epidemic struck the town in circumstances which are still unclear, exacting a terrible toll. Did some of the sailors from the *Grand St-Antoine* arrange secret meetings with members of their families? Was the cargo of cloth from the East taken to the fair at Beaucaire by smugglers? Whatever happened, the hospitals were soon full of people suffering from the plague; the sick, often driven from their homes by their families, died in the streets; thousands of corpses lay on the ground, for there were not enough galley slaves to carry the bodies to the mass graves.

Three celebrities distinguished themselves by their unselfish devotion during this dark period: Xavier of Belsunce, bishop of Marseille, the Chevalier Rose, a French merchant who had formerly served as ambassador at Modon, in the Peloponnesus, and Squadron Commander Langeron.

The Parliament at Aix forbade all communication between Marseille and the rest of Provence under penalty of death. But this did not stop the plague from spreading to Aix, Apt, Arles and Toulon. Despite the construction of a "Plague wall" 28km/17.5mi long, ordered by the Papal vice-legate, neither was the Comtat Venaissin spared.

In two years 100 000 people died, 50 000 of whom came from Marseille.

In 1994, a mass grave dating from the end of the epidemic was discovered during the excavation of the Couvent de l'Observance gardens, near the Vieille-Charité. The 150 victims had been covered with quicklime.

Marseille recovered rapidly: in only a couple of years the city had re-established its incredible demographic and economic energy. By 1765 the city had returned to the demographic level it was at in 1720 with 85-90 000 inhabitants. Trade found new openings with Latin America and the West Indies; Marseille began importing sugar, coffee and cacao. Industrialisation began: soap and glass making, sugar refining, glazed earthenware *(faïence)* and textiles etc. Huge fortunes were made: ship owners and merchants, whose number doubled in the century, displayed their wealth amid the artisans and workers who lived directly from the cargo brought off the docks.

From the Revolution to the Second Empire – The city welcomed the Revolution with enthusiasm. It elected Mirabeau as representative to the States-General. The Tribune, however, opted for Aix, which had also chosen him.

In 1792, volunteers from Marseille popularised the *Chant de Guerre de l'Armée du Rhin*, composed by Rouget de Lisle and soon baptised the "Marseillaise" *(see box below)*. Marseille was also the first town to demand the abolition of the monarchy. The heavy hand of the Convention, however, soon became unbearable for Marseille, federalist at heart. It rebelled. Taken by assault, Marseille became "the city without a name". The **Porte d'Aix** (**ES V**) is a triumphal arch erected in 1833 to commemorate the Revolutionary and First Empire Wars.

The Marseillaise

On 20 April 1792, Revolutionary France declared war against Austria. In Strasbourg, General Kellerman asked **Claude Joseph Rouget de Lisle,** a talented captain and a composer-songwriter in his spare time, to write "a new piece to celebrate the departure of the volunteers"; the *Chant de Guerre pour l'Armée du Rhin (War Song for the Rhine Army)* was written on the night of 25 to 26 April. Soon adopted by a batallion from Rhône-et-Loire and carried south by commercial travellers, the *Chant* was heard in Montpellier on 17 June. On 20 June, a young patriot from Montpellier on assignment in Marseille, François Mireur, sang it during a banquet offered by the Marseille Jacobin club, located at Rue Thubaneau. Enthusiasm was such that the text of the song was distributed to 500 national guards from Marseille, who had been called to arms for the defence of Paris. Re-named *Chant de Guerre aux Armées des Frontières (War Song for the Border Armies)*, the anthem was sung at each of the 28 stages of the journey towards the capital, with increasing success and virtuosity. On 30 July, the impassioned verses sung by these warm southern voices, ringing out across the St-Antoine district, was referred to by the electrified crowd as the *Chant des Marseillais (Song of the Marseillais)*. A few days later, on the storming of the Tuileries, was given its definitive name. *The Marseillaise* became the national anthem on *26 Messidor an III* (14 July 1795) and once again, after a long period of eclipse, on 14 February 1879.

MARSEILLE

Under the Empire, Marseille became royalist, the city's trade having been hard hit by the British fleet and the continental blockade. When Napoleon returned from Elba, the authorities of Marseille pursued him and he only just escaped arrest. The city supported the Bourbons against the Orléans family. Blood ran in 1848. Under the Second Empire, Marseille became Republican; extensive urban projects were undertaken (the opening of the present Rue de la République, construction of Palais Longchamp, Notre-Dame-de-la-Garde, the cathedral, Pharo palace and park etc). The conquest of Algeria put an end to the Barbary pirates and stimulated the economic activity of Marseille.
The opening of the Suez Canal in 1869 was another step forward in its development.

The events of 1940-44 and the post-war period – The German-Italian bombing of 1940 and that of the Allies in 1943-44 to prepare for their landing in Provence caused widespread damage and resulted in many victims. In January 1943, under the pretext of public health, the Germans evacuated 40 000 inhabitants from the old district in order to raze the streets between Rue Caisserie and the Vieux Port *(see below)*.
Like most cities damaged by the war, after the Liberation Marseille threw all its energy into reconstruction programmes. The most striking project of this period was the **Cité Radieuse**, built between 1947 and 1952 on Boulevard Michelet. Nicknamed from the outset the "Maison de Fada" or crazy house, this first housing complex by Le Corbusier is still striking today for its bold and innovative design. The result of research by the architect on housing and its role in society, it brings together in one area features of a small town including local services, and leisure and community areas. It is now much studied by architects worldwide and is open to the public.

★★VIEUX PORT (DETU) *illustration p 8*

In this creek the Phocaeans landed in the year 600 BC. It was here that, until the 19C, all Marseille's maritime life was concentrated. The quays were constructed under Louis XII and Louis XIII. In the 19C, the depth of two fathoms was found to be insufficient for steamships of large tonnage; new docks were built at this time *(see The Port p 191)*.

The hub of Marseille – All streets lead to the old port where visitors tend to congregate. Here the many cafés and restaurants offer *bouillabaisse* and other fish specialities. The water of the port almost disappears under the forest of masts belonging to the pleasure boats; occasionally warships tower above the **Quai des Belges** (**ET 5**), the liveliest of the quays, where a small **fish market** is held every morning, a scene enhanced by the thick Marseille accent of the locals. Excursion boats leave from here and the picturesque **ferry-boat** ⊘ (**ETU**) described by Pagnol in his novel *César* still plies across the harbour between Quai du Port and Quai de Rive-Neuve.

Jardin des Vestiges (Archeological garden) (**ET K**) – The fortifications of the Greek town, the horn shape of the ancient port surrounded by its 1C quays and an entrance way into the town dating from the 4C make up this archeological garden. During the Phoceaen period, this site was located beside a swamp which slowly dried up in the 3C and 2C BC.

Vieux Port – Harbour channel

In the second half of the 2C BC a new wall was built, from which interesting ruins remain: square towers, bastions and stepped curtain walls. Note the construction of the stone blocks hewn out of pink limestone from the cape of Couronne. A road dating from the Roman period enters the town through an older gate (2C BC), one of the flanking towers of which is still identifiable. An underground aqueduct carried spring water from the east; a canal brought water to a square tank situated close to the horn-shaped port. In order to have a good idea of the plan, opposite the ancient town, stand in front of the Musée d'Histoire de Marseille which is at the end of the Roman road.

Musée d'Histoire de Marseille ⊘ (**ET M¹**) – The museum is located at the end of the Jardin des Vestiges, on the ground floor of the Centre Bourse shopping centre. It traces the history of Marseille in its Provençal context from prehistoric to Gallo-Roman times through archeological finds, documents and models.

The model of Greek Marseille in the 3C and 2C BC shows that the horn shape of the ancient port preserved in the Jardin des Vestiges acted as an annex to Lacydon, whose northern bank, the main berthing-point for ships, was fitted with slipways. Celtic-Ligurian customs are evoked through the reconstruction of the Roqueper-tuse sanctuary portico (2C BC), complete with its "broken heads". The Greek town, funerary customs, metallurgy etc are all dealt with clearly and accurately. The transport and storage of food is explained by means of the cross-section of a *dolium* (large urn), and the exhibition of various types of amphorae which once contained wine, oil or different types of fish dressing.

A Roman merchant vessel dating from the 3C, preserved through freeze-drying, shows the wide range of wood used in naval construction of the time: the keel is made of cypress, the stem of umbrella pine, the keys and plugs of olive or ilex, and the planking and interior covering of larch and Aleppo pine!

A new exhibition "**Le Temps des découvertes de Protis à la Reine Jeanne**" (Discoveries from Protis to Queen Jeanne), is dedicated to the spectacular result of the most recent excavations: the discovery, in Place Jules-Verne, of Greek wrecks dating from the 6C BC, abandoned in the mud of the port and which will be exhibited once the wood has been treated; the major revelation of a necropolis containing 548 graves which date from the end of 5C BC to 2C AD in the basement of Ste-Barbe islet outside the Greek ramparts; identification of the Olliers craft area (13C), the oldest known *faïencerie* or earthenware factory in France, with a reconstruction of a workshop.

Église St-Ferréol (**ET**) – Facing the old port stands St-Ferréol or the Church of the Augustinians with its Renaissance façade, rebuilt in 1804. Features of particular interest inside the church include a Gothic nave and an 18C marble altar.

The Corps-de-Ville, a district symbolic of old Marseille, bordering Quai du Port, was dynamited by the Germans in 1943. Only a few buildings of interest were spared, one of which is the Hôtel de Ville, surrounded nowadays by post-war constructions, built to plans by Jean Pouillon (1912-1986).

Hôtel de Ville (**ET H**) – A town hall has existed on this site since the 13C. The present building and its interesting façade, an example of Provençal Baroque architecture, date from the middle of the 17C. The king's coat of arms above the main entrance is a copy of a work by **Pierre Puget** exhibited in the Musée des Beaux-Arts.

Musée du Vieux Marseille ⊘ (**DET M²**) – The Museum of Old Marseille is in the 16C Maison Diamantée (*diamant* means diamond), so-called because of the faceted stones used in its construction.

The ground floor contains 18C Provençal furniture and domestic objects.

The fine staircase with its coffered ceiling goes up to the first floor where a number of 18C cribs in spun glass or resin-and-breadcrumbs and a large collection of *santons* (1830-early 1900s) are exhibited. Another room is devoted to Marseille's old district, with a relief model of the town in 1848, while another room contains miscellaneous items concerning the great plague of 1720.

On the second floor, displays of costumes, engravings and paintings illustrate 19C Marseille life. Also worth noting is the large Camoin (Marseille cardmakers since the 18C) donation, which includes the appropriate material needed for the making of playing cards and the different techniques used *(see p 35)*.

Musée des Docks Romains (**DT M³**) – During reconstruction work in 1947 the remains of some commercial Roman warehouses used for storing *dolia* (large earthenware jars) were uncovered. They date from the 1C to the 3C.

The museum contains some *dolia* and other objects found on the site, which date from the Greek period to the Middle Ages. A model reconstruction illustrates the site and its surroundings. The warehouse complex consisted of a ground floor level opening out onto the quay and a first floor level which was probably connected by a gateway to the main street of the city, the *decumanus*, which is now Rue Caisserie. The ground floor housed the *dolia* for grain, wine and oil.

The history of trade in Marseille is retraced in the museum with the help of ceramic and metal ware and amphorae, retrieved from shipwrecks, and coins and measures. A potter's kiln demonstrates how amphorae were made.

Exhibits and literature on maritime techniques and professions linked with the sea are also on display.

MARSEILLE

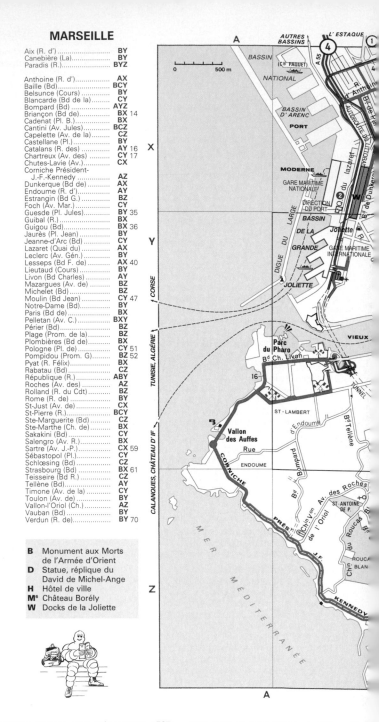

Aix (R. d')		BY
Canebière (La)		BY
Paradis (R.)		BYZ
Anthoine (R. d')		AX
Baille (Bd)		BCY
Belsunce (Cours)		BY
Blancarde (Bd de la)		CY
Bompard (Bd)		AYZ
Briançon (Bd de)		BX 14
Cadenat (Pl. B.)		BX
Cantini (Av. Jules)		BCZ
Capelette (Av. de la)		CZ
Castellane (Pl.)		BY
Catalans (R. des)		AY 16
Chartreux (Av. des)		CY 17
Chutes-Lavie (Av.)		CX
Corniche Président- J.-F.-Kennedy		AZ
Dunkerque (Bd de)		AX
Endoume (R. d')		AY
Estrangin (Bd G.)		BZ
Foch (Av. Mar.)		CY
Guesde (Pl. Jules)		BY 35
Guibal (R.)		BX
Guigou (Bd)		BX 36
Jaurès (Pl. Jean)		BY
Jeanne-d'Arc (Bd)		CY
Lazaret (Quai du)		AX
Leclerc (Av. Gén.)		BY
Lesseps (Bd F. de)		AX 40
Lieutaud (Cours)		BY
Livon (Bd Charles)		AY
Mazargues (Av. de)		BZ
Michelet (Bd)		BZ
Moulin (Bd Jean)		CY 47
Notre-Dame (Bd)		BY
Paris (Bd de)		BX
Pelletan (Av. C.)		BXY
Périer (Bd)		BZ
Plage (Prom. de la)		BZ
Plombières (Bd de)		BX
Pologne (Pl. de)		CY 51
Pompidou (Prom. G.)		BZ 52
Pyat (R. Félix)		BX
Rabatau (Bd)		CZ
République (R.)		ABY
Roches (Av. des)		AZ
Rolland (R. du Cdt)		BZ
Rome (R. de)		BY
St-Just (Av. de)		CX
St-Pierre (R.)		BCY
Ste-Marguerite (Bd)		CZ
Ste-Marthe (Ch. de)		BX
Sakakini (Bd)		CY
Salengro (Av. R.)		BX
Sartre (Av. J.-P.)		CX 59
Sébastopol (Pl.)		CY
Schlœsing (Bd)		CZ
Strasbourg (Bd)		BX 61
Teisseire (Bd R.)		CZ
Tellène (Bd)		AY
Timone (Av. de la)		CY
Toulon (Av. de)		BY
Vallon-l'Oriol (Ch.)		AZ
Vauban (Bd)		BY
Verdun (R. de)		BY 70

B   Monument aux Morts
de l'Armée d'Orient
D   Statue, réplique du
David de Michel-Ange
H   Hôtel de ville
Mᵉ   Château Borély
W   Docks de la Joliette

Pavillon Daviel and Hôtel-Dieu (EST) – The former Law Courts building, the **Pavillon Daviel** (mid 18C), has a beautiful wrought iron balcony decorated in the style typical of Marseille known as *à la marguerite* or daisy style, and a harmonious façade of pilasters.

The imposing **Hôtel-Dieu** which dominates the port is typical of hospital architecture of the second half of the 18C; note the arrangement of space and the superimposing of its arcaded galleries.

Take a few steps into Grand-Rue; no 27 bis is the Hôtel de Cabre (now a branch of the Crédit Agricole bank).

Hôtel de Cabre (ET S) – Built in 1535 and spared when much of the district was destroyed in 1943, this is one of the oldest houses in the city. Its composite style bears witness to the long-lasting influence of the Gothic style on civil Marseille architecture.

Return to Place Daviel and enter the Panier district by Montée des Accoules.

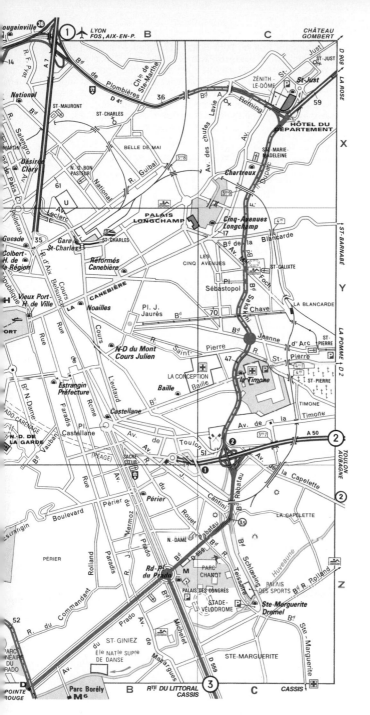

QUARTIER DU PANIER AND CATHEDRAL (DST)

Built on the Moulins hill on the site of ancient Massalia, the Panier district is, since the Liberation, all that remains of old Marseille. In the past its inhabitants, the majority of whom were of modest means and lived mainly from the sea, made the most of their tiny plots of land by constructing tall buildings. Just at the time when it was gradually becoming something of a ghetto, Le Panier reaped the benefits of a large renovation and development programme to turn the restored Vieille Charité into a museum *(see below)*. The area, with its narrow streets dissected here and there by flights of steps and where the tall façades are gradually regaining their former colours, is best explored on foot, preferably between shopping and lunch time, at the end of the morning: the **Montée des Accoules**, symbol of the area, but also **Rue du Panier**, Rue Fontaine-de-Caylus,

181

MARSEILLE

Rue Porte-Baussenque, Rue du Petit-Puits, Rue Sainte-Françoise, Rue du Poirier, and Rue des Moulins which leads to Place des Moulins... This charming and highly picturesque quarter of Marseille can be seen as a melting pot where Naples, Catalonia and the Mediterranean coast mingle with the French West Indies, Vietnam or the Comoro Islands to produce scenes which delight the senses: washing hangs from windows, the air is full of the scents of basil and *ratatouille*, locals in characteristic blue overalls browse through the papers on the doorsteps and bursts of Marseille French, and its inimitable turns of phrase, can be heard everywhere.

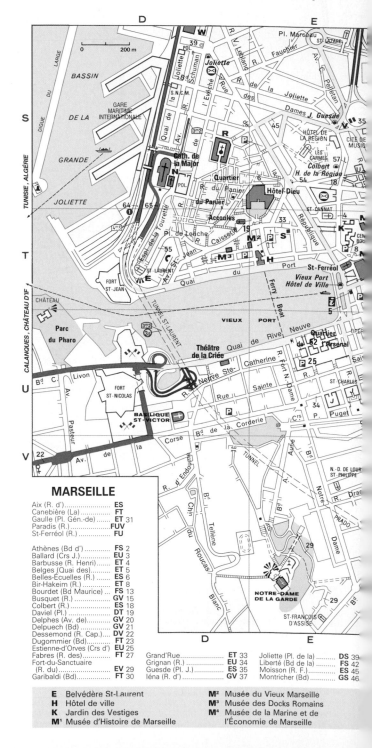

MARSEILLE

Aix (R. d')	**ES**
Canebière (La)	**FT**
Gaulle (Pl. Gén.-de)	**ET** 31
Paradis (R.)	**FUV**
St-Ferréol (R.)	**FU**
Athènes (Bd d')	**FS** 2
Ballard (Crs J.)	**EU** 3
Barbusse (R. Henri)	**ET** 4
Belges (Quai des)	**ET** 5
Belles-Écuelles (R.)	**ES** 6
Bir-Hakeim (R.)	**ET** 8
Bourdet (Bd Maurice)	**FS** 13
Busquet (R.)	**GV** 15
Colbert (R.)	**ES** 18
Daviel (Pl.)	**DT** 19
Delphes (Av. de)	**GV** 20
Delpuech (Bd)	**GV** 21
Dessemond (R. Cap.)	**DV** 22
Dugommier (Bd)	**FT** 23
Estienne-d'Orves (Crs d')	**EU** 25
Fabres (R. des)	**FT** 27
Fort-du-Sanctuaire (R. du)	**EV** 29
Garibaldi (Bd)	**FT** 30

Grand'Rue	**ET** 33	Joliette (Pl. de la)	**DS** 39
Grignan (R.)	**EU** 34	Liberté (Bd de la)	**FS** 42
Guesde (Pl. J.)	**ES** 35	Moisson (R. F.)	**ES** 45
Iéna (R. d')	**GV** 37	Montricher (Bd)	**GS** 46

E	Belvédère St-Laurent	**M²**	Musée du Vieux Marseille
H	Hôtel de ville	**M³**	Musée des Docks Romains
K	Jardin des Vestiges	**M⁴**	Musée de la Marine et de
M¹	Musée d'Histoire de Marseille		l'Économie de Marseille

Clocher des Accoules (**DT**) – This 11C bell tower is all that remains of one of Marseille's oldest churches.

★★ Centre de la Vieille Charité (**DS R**) – *See below.*

Cathédrale de la Major ⊘ (**DS**) – A huge and sumptuous construction started in 1852 in Roman-Byzantine style. It was originally built at the instigation of the future Napoleon III who wished to conciliate both the Church and the people of Marseille.

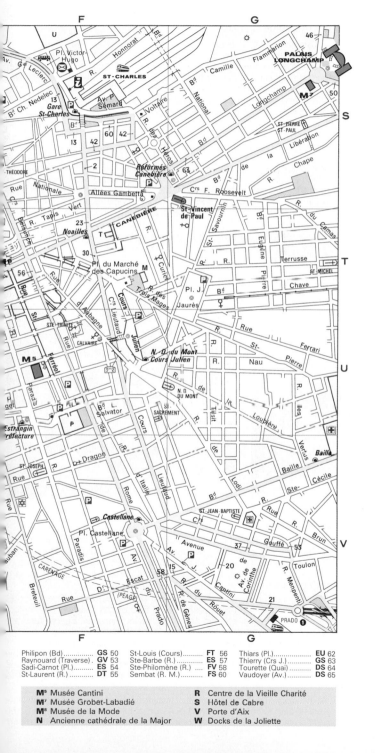

Philipon (Bd)	**GS** 50	St-Louis (Cours)	**FT** 56	Thiars (Pl.)	**EU** 62
Raynouard (Traverse)	**GV** 53	Ste-Barbe (R.)	**ES** 57	Thierry (Crs J.)	**GS** 63
Sadi-Carnot (Pl.)	**ES** 54	Ste-Philomène (R.)	**FV** 58	Tourette (Quai)	**DS** 64
St-Laurent (R.)	**DT** 55	Sembat (R. M.)	**FS** 60	Vaudoyer (Av.)	**DS** 65

M⁵	Musée Cantini	**R**	Centre de la Vieille Charité
M′	Musée Grobet-Labadié	**S**	Hôtel de Cabre
M⁶	Musée de la Mode	**V**	Porte d'Aix
N	Ancienne cathédrale de la Major	**W**	Docks de la Joliette

Ancienne Cathédrale de la Major ⊘ **(DS N)** – The "Old Major" in stout contrast is a fine example of mid–11C Romanesque, truncated in the 19C to make space for the building of the new cathedral. Only the chancel, transept and one bay of the nave and side aisles remain.

The contents include, most notably, a reliquary altar dating from 1073, a ceramic relief of the Deposition by Luca della Robbia and a 15C altar to St Lazarus by Francesco Laurana.

Place de Lenche (DT) – This lively square with façades embellished with wrought-iron balconies is located on the presumed site of the agora of the Greek town; from one of the café terraces there is an interesting view of Notre-Dame-de-la-Garde and the Théâtre de la Criée.

Belvédère St-Laurent (DT E) – Located on the parvis of St-Laurent church *(currently undergoing restoration)*, the old fishermen's parish of the St-Jean district, the viewpoint offers a fine **view★** of the Vieux Port, the entrance to the Canebière, the Étoile chain, Notre-Dame-de-la-Garde basilica and the **Forts St-Jean and St-Nicolas**, built by Louis XIV in an attempt to control the town; Fort St-Nicolas was stormed on 30 April 1790 and members of the Royal Familly were imprisoned in Fort St-Jean. The latter includes earlier constructions such as the Tour du Fanal or Tourette which resembles a minaret.

★★CENTRE DE LA VIEILLE CHARITÉ ⊘ (DS R)

This well-restored former hospice is a fine architectural unit built from 1671 to 1749 based on the plans of Pierre and Jean Puget. The buildings, created originally to shelter the deprived, stand around the central **chapel★**, a fine Baroque building with an ovoid dome by Pierre Puget. The courtyard façades present three storeys of arcaded galleries in elegant pink and yellow-tinted Couronne stone.

Centre de la Vieille Charité

Oriental and Classical Antiquities – *First floor, north wing.* The rich and varied collection of the Musée d'Archéologie de Marseille, bringing together some 900 artefacts from the Near East, Greece, Etruria and Rome, constitutes one of the few provincial museums able to offer an almost complete picture of ancient Mediterranean civilisations.

Egypt – Spanning the beginning of the Old Kingdom (2 700 BC) to the Coptic Period (3C and 4C AD), this collection of approximately 1 600 pieces provides a complete overview of art, funerary rites, religion and daily life in Pharaonic Egypt: funerary statuettes, known as *ouchtebis*, two masks of Osiris in beaten gold leaf, a large ibis in silver and gilded wood from the Ptolemaic Period, a black granite staue of the goddess Neith (New Kingdom, 18th dynasty) as well as an offering table bearing 34 royal cartouches (New Kingdom, 19th dynasty). Note the four slanted steles from the tomb of Kasa, a royal scribe and army general under the 19th dynasty and the papyrus Book of the Dead (26th dynasty).

Near East – Apart from the Assyrian pieces from the palace of Sargon II at Dur-Sharukin (present-day Khorsabad) and the Assurbanipal Palace at Nineveh, the Marseille collection of oriental antiquities focuses on Susiane territory (western part of the Iranian plateau) as well as the **Susa** civilization, covering a period which stretches from the fourth millenium BC to 7C AD: two ceramics of exceptional elegance and delicacy (fourth millenium), a brick stele dedicated to the God of Susa Inshushinak dating from the Middle Elamite period (1500-1100 BC), with palmettes motifs (4C BC).

Cyprus – With as many as 185 artefacts, the collection of Cypriot antiquities is the largest to be found in any provincial museum. Spanning almost two millenium (from the Bronze Age to the Roman Period), the collection is representative of the original art developed on this island situated at the crossroads of several civilizations (Aegean countries, the East, Egypt and Anatolia): pieces of pottery with a shiny red surface bearing incised or light relief decoration dating from the Early Cypriot Bronze Age (2300-2000 BC), Mycenaen-type funerary objects crafted in the Late Cypriot Bronze Age (1600-750 BC) and turned ceramic pieces decorated with concentric circles from the Cypriot Geometric period (1050-750 BC). As for the Cypriot Archaic style, it is represented by the head of a young man in limestone, his hair caught in a roll around his head (510 BC).

Greece, Magna Grecia – The main trends of the minor arts in **Greece** from the Bronze Age to the Hellenistic Period are well represented. Statues of marble Cycladic idols precede an exhibit dating from the Minoan civilisation. Ceramics decorated with geometrical motif friezes are characteristic of the 9C and 8C BC. Ceramic art from the **Archaic Period** (620-480 BC) is illustrated by a Boeotian clay vase depicting the mother-goddess, Corinthian works influenced by Eastern art (aruballos and alabaster: perfume vases ornamented with animal or floral motifs), black-figure ceramics, red-figure ceramics and sculptures of a naked young man *(couros)* or a clothed young woman *(koré)*. **Classical Greece** (5C-4C) produced lekythos with a white background and funerary steles. The **Hellenistic Period** (4C-2C BC) is represented by clay statuettes from Boeotia (Tanagra), Cyrenaica, Alexandria and Asia Minor **Magna Grecia** (the territories conquered in southern Italy from the 8C BC) is also present with sculptures, terracotta and ceramics exhibits from Taranto, Canosa, Ruvo and Gnathia.

Etruria, Rome – Etruria, which reached its zenith in the 7C and 6C BC, developed a civilisation with a strong Greco-Eastern influence; its evolution can be roughly divided into three phases. **Villanovan Period** (9C-mid 8C): funerary furnishings (metallurgy). **Orientalising Period** (from the second half of the 8C): ceramics in **bucchero nero**, where the carefully-smoothed black paste rivals the shine of the silver pieces (amphora, hydria, cist feet in the shape of a Gorgon, chalice with caryatids). **Archaic Period**: funerary painting from Chiusi and Tarquinia, Vulci in stone sculpture, Cerveteri and Veii (sculpture of *koré*, clothed young women).

Roquepertuse and the Celtic-Ligurians – Roquepertuse is situated in the commune of Velaux (north of Vitrolles, in the *département* of the Bouches-du-Rhône) where various excavation projects have unearthed a remarkable archeological collection. These include a collection of lapidary pieces from the 3C DC, painted, sculpted and engraved fragments, statues of warriors sitting cross-legged, huge birds and the **bicephalous Hermes★**, a magnificent sculpture of two heads attached by a mortice and tenon joint. The "broken heads" portico consists of three monolithic pillars, the upper part of which is hollowed out with cephaliform cavities which were intended to hold skulls.

Musée des Arts Africains, Océaniens et Amérindiens

(MAAOA) – *Second floor, north and east wings.* After the Musée de l'Homme in Paris, this museum has the richest collection of artefacts from Africa, Oceania and the Americas of any provincial museum in France. It also features a remarkable research centre unrivalled in the south of France. The layout of the museum offers an ideal setting for contemplation: the works are exhibited on one side against a black background, illuminated by indirect lighting, whereas opposite the exhibit is the corresponding explanatory text.

To the left of the entrance, accessories used in the *namangui* dance, performed in traditional festivals in Spiritu Santo (Vanuatu), are on display.

Musées de Marseille

Wooden Tsimshian mask
(Indians of the North Pacific coast, North America)

Salle Pierre-Guerre – In this room are housed objects donated by Pierre Guerre, those given by the Chambre de Commerce et d'Industrie de Marseille, as well as other recent gifts and acquisitions. Among the masks, sculptures, reliquaries and other daily objects mainly from West Africa, note in particular: a rare wooden Batcham mask from Cameroon, a Yoruba vase from the ancient Kingdom of Benin in clay decorated with small figures, masks of the Numuma people of Burkina-Faso, a wood and brass Marka mask from Mali, a royal clay pipe from Cameroon, magical statuettes from Zaire and the Congo.

Salle Antonin-Artaud – The objects in this room recall the civilisations of Oceania and the Americas: ceremonial paddles, a headdress mask from Wayana (Brazil), shrunken human heads (*tsantsas* of the Jivaros Indians, Ecuador) and other cult objects.

The Gastaut collection brings together a unique set of sculptured, engraved and shaped human skulls, illustrating the ancient civilisations of Oceania and Amazonia, including trophy heads from Mundurucu (Amazonia) and Nazca (Peru).

The MAAOA also houses a research centre, the only one of its kind in the south of France.

François Reichenbach Collection – A collection of popular *objets d'art* from Mexico.

RIVE NEUVE DU VIEUX PORT
AND NOTRE-DAME-DE-LA-GARDE

Quartier de l'Arsenal (EU) – At the end of the 17C Marseille was able to arm 40 000 galleys using 18 000 men to maintain and work them; two thirds of this number were employed as galley slaves. The entire south-eastern corner of the port was at that time occupied by the main galley shipyard, comprising ship repair and construction yards, gunsmiths and a galley slave hospital. Following the abolition of galley crews, at which time the galley slaves were sent to the Toulon penal colony (1749), the abandoned shipyard was occupied by artisans, then by artists and bohemians, and was gradually demolished.

Cours Honoré-d'Estienne-d'Orves is laid out in the form of an Italian style square and follows the course of a canal dug in 1787; it is a pleasant area to enjoy a drink or a meal in one of its many terrace restaurants. The façade of the hôtel *La Capitainerie des Galères* at no 23 and the *Cour des Arcenaulx (shops, including a bookshop specializing in books about the region, open until midnight)* at no 25 are the last visible remains of the shipyard buildings.

Place Thiars – This pleasant square, dating from the end of the 18C, is full of restaurants and bars where *bagna freda* (anchovy paste and small raw vegetables) is often served with your apéritif; it is situated on the former naval construction site of the shipyard. In the streets nearby, particularly in Rue St-Saens and Rue Fortia, a number of restaurants serve *bouillabaisse*.

Quai de Rive-Neuve (DEU) – It was only relatively recently that the shallows blocking this part of the port were removed and the bank converted. Surrounded by beautiful buildings in Neo-classical style, the Quai de Rive-Neuve is nowadays livelier than its opposite bank. Opposite no 12, the bust of Vincent Scotto stands at the Ferryboat pier *(see above)*. Further along, the **Théâtre National de Marseille-La Criée (DU)**, whose reputation has been made by the Marcel Maréchal company, is located in the former fish auction house *(criée)*, which was moved near to the Estaque in 1975.

★**Basilique St-Victor (DU)** – This church is the last relic of the famous abbey known as the "key to Marseille harbour" founded in the early 5C by St John Cassian, a monk from the Far East, in honour of St Victor, patron of sailors and millers, who suffered martyrdom in the 3C by being slowly ground between two millstones. The sanctuary, destroyed in a Saracen raid, was rebuilt in c 1040 and subsequently remodelled and strongly fortified.

From the outside it is truly a fortress. The porch which opens into the Tour d'Isarn is roofed with heavy pointed vaulting (1140) which is among the oldest in Provence. The interior presents two very distinct parts: the nave and aisles, with the 13C vaulting, are a good example of the Primitive Gothic style; the chancel and transept are 14C. The high altar dates from 1966.

★★**Crypt** – The most interesting part is the 5C basilica, erected by St Cassian, which was submerged when the 11C church was built. Near it are the cave of St Victor and the entrance to the catacombs where, since the Middle Ages, St Lazarus and St Mary Magdalene *(see below)* have been venerated.

In the neighbouring crypts a remarkable series of ancient, pagan and Christian sarcophagi can be seen.

In the central chapel, near the so-called St-Cassian sarcophagus is a shrine (3C) discovered in 1965, which contained the remains of town martyrs on the tomb of which the abbey was built.

Every year on 2 February the people of Marseille, led by the local fishmongers, flock to St-Victor for the Candlemas procession. Small cakes, known as *navettes*, in the shape of a boat and hollowed out in the middle are sold to commemorate the legendary arrival of St Lazarus and Saints Mary Magdalene and Martha on Provençal soil. The *Four des Navettes*, said to be the oldest bakery in Marseille, situated on the corner of Place St-Victor and Rue Sainte, specializes in these cakes. From Place St-Victor, the **view**, counterpoint to that of Belvédère St-Laurent, extends across the northern part of town, as far as the Chaîne de l'Estaque.

Basilique de Notre-Dame-de-la-Garde ⊘ – *Leave the car on "Plateau de la Croix" (car parks). Bus no 60 runs from Cours Ballard near the Vieux Port to the basilica.*

The basilica was built by Espérandieu in the mid 19C in the then fashionable Romano-Byzantine style. It stands on a limestone spike (alt 162m/532ft) on the site of a 13C chapel also dedicated to Our Lady. Surmounting the belfry (60m/197ft high) is a huge gilded statue of the Virgin.

The interior is faced with multicoloured marble, mosaics and mural paintings by the Düsseldorf School. Numerous ex-votos cover the walls, whereas in the crypt is the lovely Mater Dolorosa in marble carved by Carpeaux.

A popular pilgrimage to Notre-Dame takes place annually on 15 August.

A magnificent **panorama**★★★ can be enjoyed from the parvis of the basilica.

THE CANEBIÈRE (EFT)

Built as Marseille expanded in the 17C, this avenue, the most famous in the city, derives its name from a hemp rope factory (hemp: *canèbe* in Provençal) which once existed here. Its fame has spread worldwide as sailors of all nationalities who visited the great Mediterranean port spread the word.

Operettas and popular songs have also contributed to making this avenue the symbol of the bustling city. The street's real period of glory lasted for three-quarters of a century, until the Occupation, when it was the junction point for the whole public transport system and where all the city's fashionable cafés, cinemas and department stores were gathered.

Musée de la Marine et de l'Économie de Marseille ⊘ **(ET M¹)** – This maritime and commercial museum is located on the ground floor of the stock exchange, which also houses the chamber of commerce, the first to be created in France (beginning of the 16C).

Several models of sailboats and steamships, paintings, water-colours, engravings and plans illustrate marine history and the history of the port of Marseille, concentrating on the 17C to the present.

Musée de la Mode ⊘ **(EFT M⁸)** – *No 11.* This museum has temporary exhibitions on costume and fashion themes.

Walking up the Canebière, several buildings are noticeable for their architectural quality, particularly on the right: between Rue St-Ferréol and Cours St-Louis, rocaille-style façades from the middle of the 18C; at the corner of Cours St-Louis *(nos 1-3 of the Cours)*, a Baroque style construction, built in 1671-72, which was

---

The Alcazar Music-Hall of Marseille

Long since closed down, the renowned Alcazar music-hall is still cherished by the people of Marseille and has become something of a legend.

The Alcazar opened its doors in 1857 on the present Cours Belsunce and for over a century was the temple of variety shows in Marseille. Here, against a backdrop of Moorish-inspired decor, mime artists, pastoral players, "Marseille review" entertainers, music-hall celebrities, fortune-tellers, bawdy comedians, local eccentrics and, in later years, rock and roll pop stars all performed. The operettas of Vincent Scotto and Sarvil, performed by well-known French singers such as Alibert, Rellys or Chargrin, developed their own style here, while at the same time the spirit of the Alcazar carried more than a hint of Marcel Pagnol. The music-hall reached its zenith between 1920 and 1950, with such artists as Mayol, Mistinguett, Rina Ketty and Maurice Chevalier, a regular performer here since his very first appearance at the age of 16. Raimu, Fernandel, Tino Rossi and Yves Montand all made their débuts at the Alcazar, the latter in a western-style repertoire which dubbed him the "young swing star of 1941".

Performing at this mythical venue was indeed a test: the audience here, as in the nearby Opéra, were merciless and would not tolerate a single note out of key or any vocal weakness, seizing the first opportunity to heckle, shout jibes or burst into raucous laughter. The performers nonetheless appreciated the skill and generosity of the theatre: stars tried out their shows at the Alcazar before heading up to Paris. First-time performers who rose above the uproar and were not bombarded by missiles were rewarded by a passport to glory. The Alcazar closed down in 1964: one of the last personalities to triumph there was the French pop singer Johnny Hallyday.

intended to form one of the sides of the Place Royale designed by Pierre Puget and was never finished; at nos 53 (C&A department store) and 62 (Hotel Noailles), buildings characteristic of the Second Empire.

The upper section of the Canebière is coupled with Allée Léon-Gambetta, where the *santon* fair is held every year.

Église St-Vincent-de-Paul, also called des Réformés (GS) – The top of this Neo-Gothic style church offers a view over the Canebière.

The walk described below combines a stroll through the lively and commercial district immediately south of the Canebière with a visit to the Cantini Museum.

Rue St-Ferréol (FTU) – This, the main pedestrian street, is a pleasant area for strolling and socialising. There are a number of shops selling shoes, clothes and leather, ice-cream parlours and department stores, including Galeries Lafayette, Marks & Spencer, Virgin Megastore…

★**Musée Cantini** ⊘ **(FU M⁵)** – The sculptor Jules Cantini donated his collection and the 17C Hôtel de la Compagnie du Cap Nègre to the city.

The museum decided to specialise in 20C art after the Second World War. Most of the works dating from post-1960 can now be found in the Musée d'Art Contemporain *(see below)* and the Musée Cantini is now essentially devoted to modern art. From 1985 its collection of Fauvist, early Cubist, Expressionist and Abstract art was greatly enhanced by works by Matisse, André Derain *(Pine Forest, Cassis)*, Raoul Dufy *(Factory in the Estaque)*, Alberto Magnelli *(Stones no 2, 1932)*, Dubuffet *(Striking Woman)*, Kandinsky, Chagall, Jean Hélion and Picasso.

The presence of a number of Surrealist artists in Marseille during the last war, gathered around André Breton at the Villa Air-Bel, explains a selection of paintings from this movement at the Cantini Museum; paintings by André Masson *(Antille, 1943)*, Max Ernst *(Monument to the Birds, 1927)*, Wilfredo Lam, Victor Brauner, Jacques Hérold, Joan Miró and rare drawings by the Marseille artist Antonin Artaud.

The port of Marseille, a local subject of inspiration along with the Estaque, is represented on canvases by Marquet, Signac and the Marseille specialist in this subject, Louis Mathieu Verdilhan (1875-1928).

Finally, the collection features a few works by 20C artists who defy classification: Baltus *(The Bather)*, Giacometti *(Portrait of Diego)* and Francis Bacon *(Self-Portrait)*.

Retrace your steps to Rue St-Ferréol.

Rue Vacon leads to the heart of Marseille, which plays a less important economic role now that some of the city's commercial activites have moved to the outskirts; it has retained its picturesque character nonetheless.

From Rue Longue to Cours Julien (FTU) – Rue Vacon *(Provençal fabric on display)* leads into Rue des Halles-Charles-Delacroix, which is, in fact, a square (former fish market, demolished) lined with grocery stores and shops selling exotic wares. In the narrow **Rue Longue-des-Capucins** the atmosphere of which is part souk, part flea market, the air is full of different scents: spices mingled with coffee, pitted or marinated olives, anchovies, herbs, dried fruit etc.

Marseille – Market stalls in the Rue Longue-des-Capucins

Place du Marché des Capucins, opposite Noailles metro station, is the kingdom of the local stall-holders or *partisanes*. The air rings with their loud cries, urging passers-by to purchase their lemons and beans.

Rue du Musée and Rue Rodolph-Pollack specialize in exotic and afro-cosmetic hairdressers.

Take Rue Aubagne, which also has its share of unusual establishments *(for example, the grocery shop at no 34)*, and the footbridge spanning Cours Lieutard, to reach **Cours Julien**, which was until 1972 the Marseille wholesale market for market garden produce. It has now been renovated and here you will find specialist restaurants and antique or clothes shops *(Madame Zaza of Marseille, Fille de Lune etc)*; it is a pleasant area for a relaxing stroll. The roads leading off to the east of the Cours, such as Rue de Bussy-l'Indien, Rue Pastoret, Rue Crudère, Rue Vian, are slightly on the "fringe", their façades covered with occasional artists' graffiti *(note the front of La Maison Hantée, Rue Vian)* and the clubs and cafés which come to life as night falls.

Head back to La Canebière by Cours Lieutard. In front of the Palais des Arts, seat of the National Conservatory of Music, there are second-hand book and record stalls.

LONGCHAMP DISTRICT (GS) *2hr*

★★ **Musée Grobet-Labadié** ⊙ **(GS M')** – This town house built in 1873 for Alexandre Labadié, a Marseille merchant, was donated to Marseille in 1919 by his daughter Marie-Louise, wife to Louis Grobet, a music lover and art collector. She considerably varied and enriched the collection with her own personal acquisitions.

The bourgeois interior has been kept with its fine Flemish and French (16C-18C) tapestries, furniture, 18C Marseille and Moustiers *faïence* ware, religious gold and silver plate, wrought iron work and old musical instruments. Fine paintings hang on the walls: Flemish, German and Italian Primitives, French School covering the 17C-19C. The museum is further enriched by a collection of drawings by European schools from the 15C to the 19C.

★ **Palais Longchamp** (GS) – This imposing building was constructed by the Nîmes architect Henri Espérandieu (he also built the Notre-Dame-de-la-Garde basilica) from 1862 to 1869.

In its centre stands a well-disguised water tower animated by fountains *(see illustration on p 43 under Art: Architectural Terms)*; it

Fountain, Palais Longchamp

is linked by colonnades to the Musée des Beaux-Arts (on the left) and the Muséum d'Histoire Naturelle (on the right).

★ **Musée des Beaux-Arts** ⊙ – On the first floor there is a large gallery devoted to **16C and 17C painting**. There are works from the French School: Vouet *(Madonna with Rose)*, Le Sueur, Champaigne, Rigaud, Largillière; the Italian School: Perugino, Cariani, Carracci, Lanfranco, Guercino; the Flemish School: Snijders, Jordaens, several Rubens (portrait assumed to be of Hélène Froment) and Gaspard de Crayer. Provençal artists are represented by Michel Serre, Jean Daret, Finson and Meiffren Comte.

On the ground floor, a large room exhibits the works of **Pierre Puget** (1620-94), native of Marseille, sculptor, painter and architect. In the centre are castings of monumental sculptures found either in the Louvre or in Genoa. On either side of the room are the **original works★**: drawings, paintings – of remarkable imagination *(Infant Jesus Sleeping)*, statues *(The Faun)* and low reliefs *(The Plague at Milan, Louis XIV Riding)*. In the stairwell are two murals by Puvis de Chavannes: Marseille as a Greek Colony and as the *Gateway to the Levant*.

On the second floor a sequence of rooms is devoted to **French painting of the 18C and 19C**. The 18C is represented by beautiful canvases by Nattier, Verdussen, Watteau de Lille, Carle Van Loo, Françoise Duparc, Greuze, Joseph Vernet *(Storm)*, Mme Vigée-Lebrun *(The Duchess of Orleans)* and sculpture by Chastel. Among the 19C works, those by Courbet *(Deer at Water's Edge)*, Millet, Corot, Girodet, Gros, Gérard, Ingres, David, and the Provençal painters Guigou and Casile compete for the viewer's attention. Notice also the sculptures by **Daumier** (famous caricaturist born in Marseille in 1808).

The **Drawings Room** contains Italian (Pontormo, Guercino, Bandinelli, Lorenzo Lippi and Tiepolo) and French works (Le Sueur, Poussin, Claude Lorrain, Puget, Mignard, Daret) displayed as temporary exhibitions.

★**Musée d'Histoire Naturelle** ⊙ – Rich zoological, geological and prehistorical collections are exhibited. Four hundred million years of history of the Provence-French Riviera region are retraced, and a safari museum illustrates the diversity of the animal kingdom throughout the world. A gallery is devoted to Provençal flora and fauna. The various **aquariums** present a standing exhibition on white waters in Provence under the title "Eaux vives, du Verdon aux Calanques".

SOUTHERN DISTRICTS

Parc du Pharo (**DU**) – This park is situated on a promontory dominating the entrance to the Vieux Port, of which there is an attractive **view** from the terrace near the Pharo palace, built for Napoleon III. From the top of this viewpoint Joseph Vernet painted *The Entrance to the Port of Marseille* in 1754, a famous painting displayed in the Louvre Museum.

★★**Corniche Président-J.-F.-Kennedy** (**AYZ**) – This corniche runs for nearly 5km/3mi – almost entirely along the sea-front. It is dominated by elegant villas built at the end of the 19C.

Level with the **Monument aux Morts de l'Armée d'Orient** (**AY B**), attractive views open out towards the coast and the islands, the latter appearing extremely close when the *mistral* wind is blowing. A viaduct crosses the picturesque Auffes valley.

Vallon des Auffes – *Access through Boulevard des Dardanelles, just before the viaduct.* This tiny fishing port, crowded with traditional boats and ringed with *cabanons*, inspired Vincent Scotto. To eat out in this Marseille operetta scene, in the constantly changing light of the setting sun, is to soak up the best of this Phocaean city's atmosphere.

Promenade de la Plage (**BZ**) – This is the extension of the Corniche to the south, running alongside the **Parc Balnéaire du Prado**, a leisure area bordered by gardens with children's playgrounds which contains a number of pleasure pools and artificial beaches. On the other side of the road there are several restaurants.

The Pointe Rouge, on the opposite side of the Prado roundabout, with its replica of Michelangelo's *David* (**BZ D**), is an important sailing centre.

Château et Parc Borély (**BZ M⁶**) – Built between 1767 and 1778 by the Borély, a family of wealthy merchants, the **château** will house the town's Museum of Decorative Arts once restoration work is complete.

The **park**, which has a network of paths and extends to the east with beautiful **botanical gardens**, is the venue every year for the extremely popular Provençal and Marseille *boules* competition, so typical of Marseille life.

Vallon des Auffes

Musée d'Art Contemporain ⊘ *(not on town plan) – Return to the Promenade de la Plage. Once level with the Escale Borély, turn into Avenue de Bonneveine and continue to the intersection with Avenue Haifa, where a large metal thumb sculpted by César can be seen.*

The MAC, as it is already referred to by the people of Marseille, was opened in 1994. This single-storey museum has been constructed via the juxtaposition of identical modules. The permanent collection, which concentrates on French artists and gives pride of place to artists either born or living in Marseille, brings together the different trends in contemporary art from the 1960s to the present day: structured movements, such as New Realism, the Support-Surface or Arte Povera group, but also eclectic work from the 1980s and maverick art which resists all attempts at classification. This rewarding collection includes: *Compressions and Expansions* by César, work by Richard Baquié (*Amore Mio*, 1985), Jean-Luc Parent (*Viewing Machines*, 1993), Daniel Burren *(Cabane éclatée no 2)*, the complex creative approach of Martial Raysse, (*Bird of Paradise*, 1960), Arman, Jean-Pierre Raynaud, the *Rotazaza* machine by Tinguely, an *Anthropometry* by Yves Klein, contributions by Robert Combas and Jean-Michel Basquiat as well as exhibits of the sometimes underrated art of our culture: cartoons, graffiti etc.

*★**Musée de la Faïence** ⊘ (not on town plan) – Walk past the Parc Borély and proceed towards Pointe Rouge. The museum is situated at the far end of the Parc de Montredon. A small train will take you up to the entrance.*

Set up in the Château Pastré, a fine 19C mansion built at the foot of the Marseilleveyre massif, this museum is devoted to the art of ceramics, from the early Neolithic Era up to the present day. A great many of the collections feature exhibits coming from Provence, and particularly Marseille, where the manufacturing of faience pottery was considerable in the late 17C and the 18C. Laid out over three levels, the visit takes you through a series of lovely rooms with 18C decoration, retracing the development of faience in the Marseille region.

Visitors can feast their eyes on a series of superb exhibits turned out by the Clérissy workshops, which played a key role in reviving the art of faience in the late 17C (sharp firing technique for enamelling blue and manganese pieces), as well as three other manufactures - Madeleine Héraud, Louis Leroy and Fauchier (*rocaille* ornamentation and yellow enamels). Four well-known factories used the mild firing technique for vitreous glazes during the 18C: La Veuve Perrin (fish motifs, Chinese scenes, large flowers with insect), Gaspard Robert, Honoré Savy (mild firing applied to green pieces) and Antoine Bonnefoy.

The tour then moves on to Provençal collections: Moustiers faience manufactured by Clérissy, Ferrat, Fouque and Olérys, ceramics from La Tour-d'Aigues and Aubagne (glazed green and yellow pottery), Apt and Le Castellet (glazed pieces featuring different types of clay). One room is taken up by industrial production: Sèvres, Wedgwood, Creil (black fine stoneware), Rubelles (fine faience with *ombrant* enamelling that produces darker hues). The display devoted to the late 19C contains several splendid examples: glazed pottery from Avisseau in the tradition of Bernard Palissy, enamelled stoneware by Ernest Chaplet, Art Nouveau vases by Théodore Deck. Contemporary creations are also represented with the work of Émile Decouer (1930s), Georges Jouve (after 1954) and Claude Varlan (1990).

★★THE PORT (AXY)

Marseille, standing on the shores of the Mediterranean, has always relied on international trade. As the traditional gate to the Orient, its wealth was derived from France's 19C colonies, whose agricultural products and raw materials were processed and then, for the most part, re-exported. However, the two World Wars, the fact that larger ships which could no longer use the Suez canal and decolonization dealt Marseille a heavy blow. Reconversion and modernization, mainly in the oil and chemical sectors, have brought about a shift in the main industrial activities to the area around the Étang de Berre and the Golfe de Fos. The new installations, administered by the Port Autonome de Marseille, place the Phocaean city among the three main European ports.

The city has nevertheless retained some traditional Marseille activites, based on maritime trade industries: oil pressing, soap making (household or Marseille soap represents 20% of the French market in laundry products), flour milling, semolina production and metalworking.

Origins and development – The old port had become inadequate – ships were crowded four or five rows deep; in 1844 a law authorised the construction of a dock at La Joliette; later the docks of Lazaret and Arenc were built and the port area was enlarged through the addition of further docks to the north.

Although destroyed in 1944, by the end of the war the port was again able to play a major role in the French economy, benefiting from expansion and modernization projects.

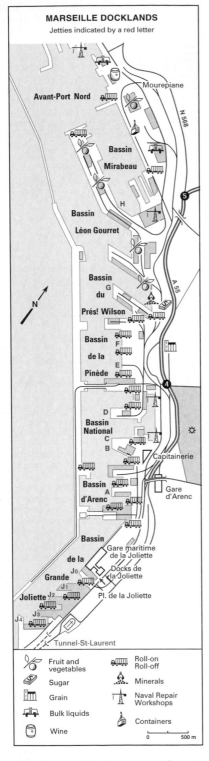

MARSEILLE DOCKLANDS
Jetties indicated by a red letter

Avant-Port Nord

Mourepiane

Bassin Mirabeau

Bassin Léon Gourret

H

Bassin du Prés! Wilson

G

Bassin de la Pinède

F
E

D
Bassin National
C
B

Bassin d'Arenc
A

Bassin de la Grande Joliette

J0
J1
J2
J3
J4

Gare maritime de la Joliette
Docks de la Joliette
Pl. de la Joliette

Tunnel-St-Laurent

Capitainerie

Gare d'Arenc

N 568
A 55
5
4

N

Fruit and vegetables
Sugar
Grain
Bulk liquids
Wine

Roll-on Roll-off
Minerals
Naval Repair Workshops
Containers

0   500 m

Port activity – Most of the facilities specialize in roll-on/roll-off operations (the ship's hold being directly accessible to lorries). Marseille is one of the world's largest ports in this sector. The two terminals of Mourepiane and La Pinède are used for coastal shipping, which is container-operated, and commercial traffic with Africa.

Bulk foodstuffs have retained their important position as Marseille redistributes imported fruit and vegetables throughout Europe, as well as having commercial interests in both sugar and grain. A variety of industrial bulk cargo is handled: aluminia, clinkers (elements used in cement-making) etc.

More than a million passengers and more than 300 000 vehicles pass through the port of Marseille each year, using the regular shipping lines of Corsica and North Africa (La Joliette Passenger Ship Terminal), together with cruise ships (North Passenger Ship Terminal). A new harbour complex became operational in 1995.

Half of France's ship repairs are also carried out in Marseille. The number 10 dry dock (465 m x 85 m/1 526ft x 279ft) is able to handle the largest ships in the world.

TOUR

La Joliette Docks (**DS W**) – *Access: Joliette metro station . Entrance at Place de la Joliette, through the administrative buildings.* Built from 1858 to 1863, based on an English docks design, this huge row of warehouses, almost 400m/1 312ft long, is the embodiment of Marseille's economic peak as the Gateway to the Orient. Situated between the new port of La Joliette and the railway line, the docks receive raw goods, package or sometimes process them, then ship them by sea or rail. The most modern techniques were installed for these activities, such as hydraulic lifts, the first to be used in Marseille.

The exclusive use of stone, brick and cast iron in the construction, which nowadays is a specific feature of this type of architecture, was intended to prevent the risk of fire. Various other installations connected to the activities of the docks, which were renovated in 1991, now hold plays and exhibitions, enabling the visitor to admire the remarkable vaulted cellars.

The Docks ⊙ – *The Traverse and the Pont d'Arenc lead to the Digue du Large (outer breakwater).* Do not stay on the vehicle roadway but walk through either its upper section, paved and lined with benches (good general view of the port installations, the ships, the roadstead and the offshore islands), or its outer section, a few metres higher than the protecting blocks, which is popular with fishermen.

The coastal motorway also offers a good general view of the installations and of port traffic.

View of the Port

EXCURSIONS

★★**Château d'If** ⊘ – *About 1hr 30min including boat trip and a tour of the castle; embarkation Quai des Belges.* **Alexandre Dumas** (1802-70), the popular 19C French author of *The Three Musketeers*, gave this castle literary fame by imprisoning two of his fictional heroes (in *The Count of Monte Cristo*) here: The Count of Monte Cristo and Abbé Faria. Built rapidly from 1524 to 1528, Château d'If was an outpost destined to protect the port of Marseille. In the late 16C the castle was encircled by a bastioned curtain wall. The castle, which had fallen into disuse, then became a state prison where Huguenots, the Man in the Iron Mask, and various political prisoners were held; their cells can be visited.

The **panorama**★★★ from the old chapel terrace is remarkable: note the roadstead, city and the Ratonneau and Pomègues islands linked by the new port of Frioul.

★★**Massif des Calanques** – *See Massif des CALANQUES.*

★**Hôtel du Département and Dôme-Nouvel Alcazar** (**CX**) – *St-Just metro station.* This new office building, which handles departmental affairs for the Bouches-du-Rhône, is a futurist work in "high-tech" style by the English architect Will Alsop and has established itself as the most innovative and remarkable contemporary architectural work in Provence, a kind of Marseille Pompidou Centre. It consists of two sections linked by a suspended gallery and walkway. The first section houses the administrative departments and is a huge parallelepiped; its inside has been hollowed out into a huge covered piazza and is filled by an elliptic vessel and crossed with light footbridges. The second area, used for departmental council meetings, is an aerodynamically lined building, which suggests a large insect standing on a series of legs. Among a real explosion of colours – geranium red, cadmium orange, purple – the blue known as Bristol blue, symbol of the Mediterranean soul of Marseille, dominates. Next door, the Dôme-Nouvel Alcazar de Marseille, an extraordinary "flying saucer" encompassed by a pastel green arch halo, is a theatre of 8 000 seats; its name recalls the legendary Marseille music-hall, the Alcazar *(see box p 187)*.

Musée des Arts et Traditions Populaires du Terroir Marseillais ⊘ – *11km/7mi northeast, at Château-Gombert. Take Avenue de St-Just* (**CX**) *and Avenue de Château-Gombert, following the signs for Château-Gombert Technopole.*

The museum is situated in the main square shaded by plane trees. The first part of the museum, dedicated to local arts and traditions, is set out as a traditional interior of an old provençal dwelling. The kitchen, with its fireplace hood and typical *pile* (sink), is full of ceramics from Marseille and Moustiers, pewter, *terrailho* (culinary pottery) and utensils which demonstrate local customs: baskets in which snails were left to fast, the big clay *tian* (bowl), mortars for *aïoli* (garlic mayonnaise), Marseille filters...The middle class living room and bedroom are arrayed with beautiful furniture from the region; note the radassié, a long couch which used to be found in country farmhouses. In the Marseille and Arlesian costume section, it is pointed out that the "typically Provençal" calico was actually made in Jouy-en-Josas and Mulhouse in northeastern France; it was distributed in the region through the Beaucaire fair.

After the section dedicated to the St-Eloi cavalcade, a popular festival still celebrated in Château-Gombert and eastern Marseille, and the *santon* workshop, admire the interesting re-creation of a seaside *cabanon* (hut), with its pairs of Provençal *boule* sets of venerable age.

L'Estaque by Georges Braque

Musée de l'Annonciade, St-Tropez/LAUROS GIRAUDON © ADAGP 1995

L'Estaque – *9km/5.5mi to the north. Leave Marseille by ④ on the plan, along the coastal motorway.*

"Just like a playing card – red roofs on a blue sea" is how Paul Cézanne described the charms of this fishing village dotted with factories to Camille Pisarro in July 1876. The village was made famous by a number of avant-garde painters between 1870 and the First World War. It was partly here that the foundations of modern art were laid by Cézanne, Renoir, Braque, Dufy, Derain, Marquet, Othon Friesz, with, in particular, the birth of Cubism between 1908 and 1910.

The Estaque no longer holds the same attraction for visitors. Inhabitants of Marseille are attracted by the fishmonger shops (the Marseille fish auction house is now located in the nearby Saumaty cove) the restaurants, as well as by the odd stall which continues to make *chichi frégi* – long fried doughnuts which are a little difficult to digest, but delicious.

L'Estaque was the setting for *Marius et Jeannette*, a hugely popular French film released in 1996, which focused on the life of this humble yet picturesque neighborhood close to Marseille *(see films p 296)*.

MARTIGUES

Population 72 375
Michelin map 84 folds 11 and 12 or 245 fold 43 or 246 folds 13 and 14
Local map see Étang de BERRE – Facilities

Martigues took its name in 1581 after the union of the three villages of Jonquières, Ile and Ferrières established here since the Middle Ages.

Set on the banks of the Étang de Berre and linked to the sea by the Canal de Caronte, Martigues, once a small fishing village, has been transformed and enlarged as a result of the expansion of the oil industry and its subsidiaries around Lavéra-Étang de Berre. Both painters (Corot, Ziem) and writers (Charles Maurras) were captivated by the luminosity and charm of this typical Provençal port; and thus Martigues acquired great renown in literary and artistic circles.

SIGHTS

Pont St-Sébastien (Z B) – The bridge on Île Brescon affords a **view**★ of the brightly-coloured pleasure craft along Canal St-Sébastien and Quai Brescon. Popular with painters, this spot is known as the Birds' Looking Glass *(see photograph below)*.

Église Ste-Madeleine-de-l'Île (YZ D) – The 17C church on Canal St-Sébastien has a Corinthian style front and pilasters, cornices and an imposing organ loft inside.

Musée Ziem ⊙ **(Y M¹)** – Grouped around the works of **Félix Ziem** (1821-1911), painter of landscapes and oriental scenes, whose granddaughter recently bequeathed his paintings, sketches and travel notebooks to the city, are works by Provençal artists from the 19C and 20C. Also exhibited in the museum are collections of local ethnology and archeology and an exhibition of contemporary art.

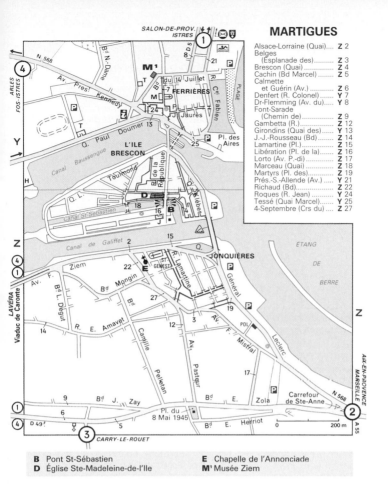

MARTIGUES

Alsace-Lorraine (Quai)....	**Z** 2
Belges (Esplanade des).........	**Z** 3
Brescon (Quai)................	**Z** 4
Cachin (Bd Marcel)	**Z** 5
Calmette et Guérin (Av.)	**Z** 6
Denfert (R. Colonel)	**Y** 7
Dr-Flemming (Av. du)....	**Y** 8
Font-Sarade (Chemin de)................	**Z** 9
Gambetta (R.)................	**Z** 12
Girondins (Quai des)......	**Y** 13
J.-J.-Rousseau (Bd)	**Z** 14
Lamartine (Pl.)................	**Z** 15
Libération (Pl. de la)......	**Z** 16
Lorto (Av. P.-di)	**Z** 17
Marceau (Quai)	**Z** 18
Martyrs (Pl. des).............	**Z** 19
Prés.-S.-Allende (Av.)	**Y** 21
Richaud (Bd).................	**Z** 22
Roques (R. Jean)	**Z** 24
Tessé (Quai Marcel)......	**Y** 25
4-Septembre (Crs du)	**Z** 27

B Pont St-Sébastien **E** Chapelle de l'Annonciade
D Église Ste-Madeleine-de-l'Ile **M¹** Musée Ziem

Chapelle de l'Annonciade ⊘ (**Z E**) – Built at the beginning of the 17C for the Brothers of the White Penitents, this chapel is richly decorated in Baroque style.

★**Viaduc Autoroutier de Caronte** – *By Avenue F.-Ziem* (**Z**). The Canal de Caronte, from the lagoon to the sea, has been spanned since 1972 by a spectacular 300m-984ft long road bridge. This metal deck suspended 50m/164ft above the water between inclined supports gives a good bird's-eye **view** of the town.

The Birds' Looking-Glass, Martigues

Meissonnier/CAMPAGNE CAMPAGNE

EXCURSIONS

★**Étang de Berre** – *Round tour of 113km/70mi by* ① *on the town plan, D 5. See Étang de BERRE.*

Chapelle Notre-Dame-des-Marins – *3.5km/2.25mi. Leave Martigues by* ④ *on the town plan, N 568; after 1.5km/0.75mi from the centre bear right at the main crossroads onto D 50 (towards the hospital); 1.2km/0.5mi further, just before the top of the hill, turn right onto a surfaced path to the chapel (car park).*

From the precincts of this chapel, the **panorama★** sweeps around Port-de-Bouc, Fos, Port-St-Louis, Lavéra complex, the Caronte railway and road bridges, the Chaîne de l'Estaque, Martigues, Étang de Berre with the Arles canal linking it to Fos-sur-Mer, the Étoile and Vitrolles chains, Montagne Ste-Victoire and on clear days Mont Ventoux, Marseille-Provence airport, the towns of Berre and St-Mitre-des-Remparts.

★**Bassins de Fos** – *9km/5.5mi by* ④ *on the town plan, N 568. See Bassins de FOS.*

Aven de MARZAL★

Michelin map **80** fold 9 or **245** folds 2 and 15 or **246** fold 23
Local map see Gorges de l'ARDÈCHE

Buried under the Gras plateau, this chasm *(photograph p 315)* is remarkable for the wealth of limestone formations which range in their oxide colouring from brown ochre to snow white.

The discovery – The local word *marzal* identifies a wild grass. The name *marzal* was given in c 1810 to the forester Dechame, from St-Remèze, after he had fined his wife who had picked some for her rabbits. A little later Marzal was murdered and thrown into a well, the so-called Trou de la Barthe, with his dog. The crime was discovered and the local people began calling the well Marzal.

The chasm was actually discovered in 1892 when the speleologist **Édouard-Alfred Martel** (1859-1938) explored it for the first time, but its exact location was lost through incorrect signposting and it was not rediscovered until 1949.

Musée du Monde Souterrain ⊘ – This museum recalls the great names and great moments of French speleology: Martel's "Berthon" boat (1890) and ladder; a speleologist's equipment (1892); outfit of **Robert de Joly** (inventor of equipment adapted for the underground world's demands); Elisabeth and Norbert Casteret's helmet, electrical material and waterproof bag; Guy de Lavaur's diving suit (1946).

Chasm (Aven) ⊘ – *Inside temperature: 14°C/57°F.* A metal staircase *(743 steps)* leads to the natural opening in the Gras plateau. The chasm opens into the Salle du Tombeau or Tomb Gallery; nearby are bones of animals (bear, stag, bison) that fell into the cave.

Cave (Grotte) ⊘ – The Salle du Chien (Dog Gallery) (**1**), whose entrance is surmounted by a flow of white draperies, contains a large variety of concretions, eccentrics, brightly-coloured organs, disc-like formations and shapes resembling bunches of grapes. Salle de la Pomme de Pin (Pine Cone Gallery) (**2**) is interesting for the wealth of its colours. The Salle des Colonnes was the bed into which an underground river (since disappeared) cascaded. The Salle des Diamants

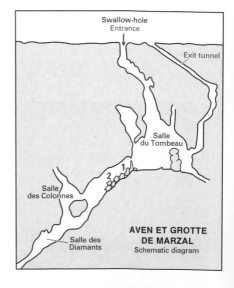

Swallow-hole
Entrance

Exit tunnel

Salle
du Tombeau

Salle
des Colonnes

Salle des
Diamants

**AVEN ET GROTTE
DE MARZAL**
Schematic diagram

(130m/426ft below ground) ends the visit; it presents a sparkling scene of fairy-like colours reflected in the glinting crystals which line the walls.

Prehistoric Zoo ⊘ – Displayed along a shaded path (800m/0.5mi) are life-sized reproductions of animals from the Primary (Dimetrodon, Moschops) and Secondary Eras (Stegosaurus, Tyrannosaurus) through to the mammoth of the Quaternary Era.

MÉNERBES★

Population 1 118
Michelin map 81 fold 13 or 245 fold 13 or 246 fold 11
Local map see Montagne du LUBERON

This old village occupies a picturesque site on a promontory of the Luberon's north face. In 1573 the Calvinists captured the stronghold by a ruse, and it took five years and a large ransom to dislodge them.

Place de l'Horloge – The square is overlooked by the town hall's bell tower with its simple wrought iron bell cage. In one corner of the square stands a noble Renaissance mansion with a round-arched doorway.

Church – The church stands at the end of the village and dates back to the 14C when it was a priory dependent on St-Agricol of Avignon. Behind the east end there is a fine **view★** of Coulon valley, the villages of Gordes and Roussillon (with its ochre cliffs), Mont Ventoux, the Vaucluse plateau and the Luberon.

Citadelle – This 13C fortress (rebuilt in the 16C and 19C) has preserved part of its defence system with its corner towers and machicolations. Owing to its strategic position it played an important part during the Wars of Religion.

An Artist's Village

Ever since the English writer Peter Mayle published *A Year in Provence*, Ménerbes has become famous throughout the world and it is even said that coachloads of Japanese and American tourists turn up to visit the small Provençal village. However, before Peter Mayle, other artists had already discovered this charming spot in the Luberon: the French author and literary critic François Nourissier has lived here for around 15 years, Picasso stayed here in 1946 and the place has often been frequented by celebrities, including the famous novelist Albert Camus, and the painter Nicolas de Staël, who in 1953 bought the small castle west of the town (once a medieval fortress) and had it converted into a private residence.

Musée du Tire-Bouchon ⊙ – *Take the western exit "sortie ouest" at Ménerbes on the road to Cavaillon (D 3).* Nestling in the wine-producing estate of La Citadelle, this museum displays a fine collection of corkscrews carved in different materials (horn, ivory, gold, silver...) and presenting a variety of shapes (the letter T, animals, an effigy of Senator Volstead, who promoted the laws on Prohibition in the United States in the 1920-1930s) from the 17C up to today. The different methods used for uncorking wine are well illustrated through a remarkable display of models – wing-nut, narrow-rack, rack-and-pinion, Thomason etc, as well as some outstanding collector's pieces: one combining the functions of corkscrew and nutmeg grater, the very first French corkscrew (17C) and a compressed sculpture by the artist César. Visitors may also be taken on a tour of the wine cellars.

La MONTAGNETTE

Michelin map 81 fold 11 or 245 folds 28 and 29 or 246 folds 25 and 26

Between the River Durance and Tarascon, the Montagnette is a range of hills, none of which tops 200m/656ft, which parallels the Rhône as it flows southwest below Avignon. On a small scale it offers a typical Provençal landscape of rock escarpments, hillsides fragrant with wild flowers and aromatic herbs, quiet hollows sheltering olive, almond and apricot trees, pines, poplars and cypresses.

ROUND TOUR LEAVING FROM BEAUCAIRE *33km/20mi*

★**Beaucaire** – *See BEAUCAIRE.*

★**Tarascon** – *See TARASCON.*

Take the westbound D 80 leading to Maillane.

Musée des Arômes et du Parfum ⊙ – Located south of Graveson, this Fragrance and Perfume Museum occupies a site that once belonged to the monks of St-Michel-de-Frigolet. Traditional techniques related to the making of aromatic scent are presented and explained by a fascinating exhibition: copper stills, collection of old flasks, semicircular racks displaying all types of essences *(orgues de parfumeur)* and receptacles used for catching the essential oils and floral water after distillation *(essenciers)*.

Proceed along D 80 until you reach Graveson.

Graveson – Standing amid orchards, the church has a Romanesque oven-vaulted apse with a low, delicately-carved blind arcade.

At the end of the Cours National is the **Musée Auguste-Chabaud** ⊘★ which houses a collection of paintings by this painter, sculpter and poet, who was born in Nîmes in 1882 and died in Graveson in 1955. Following periods of residence in Paris, the artist moved to the Mas de Martin at the foot of the Montagnette hills, where he found inspiration in the countryside, rural scenes and festivals of Provence in the Rhône valley. His technique of using smooth lines of pure colour outlined with black has obviously drawn comparisons with the Fauvist School yet the keen expression and fervour shown in his work classifies him more as an Expressionist painter. Note: *Barbentane, Village with Tower, Old Provençal Women, Shepherd Leaning on a Stick, Girls in the Wind, The Olive Harvest.*

Head back down towards Tarascon along D 970 and turn left onto D 81 leading to the Abbaye de St-Michel-de-Frigolet (the road crosses over D 970).

Abbaye de St-Michel-de-Frigolet – *See Abbaye de ST-MICHEL-DE-FRIGOLET.*

You will reach Barbentane by the northbound D 80, then D 35ᴱ.

Barbentane – *See BARBENTANE.*

Moulin de Bretoul – Set in pine woods, south of Barbentane, this mill is the only well-preserved windmill left of the many which at one time were scattered across the countryside.

D 35 south of Barbentane leads to Boulbon.

Boulbon – An impressive fort marks the site of the town laid out like an amphitheatre against the Montagnette hillside. The local Romanesque St-Marcellin **chapel** contains a number of statues, particularly the 14C recessed tomb with a recumbent figure and mourners. On 1 June each year a picturesque Bottle Procession makes its way to the chapel for the blessing of the local wine *(see the Calendar of events at the end of the guide).*

Go back to D 35, which will take you back to Tarascon.

Abbaye de MONTMAJOUR★

Michelin map 83 fold 10 or 245 fold 28 or 246 fold 26

On a hill overlooking the Arles plain lie the ruins of Abbaye de Montmajour, the buildings of which represent two different periods: medieval and 18C.

The struggle against the marshes – The hill was, for a long time, surrounded by marshes. A Christian cemetery was established here and a group of hermits, who looked after the burial ground, were at the origin of the abbey, founded in the 10C under Benedictine rule. In spite of the fact that the monk population was not large, the abbey possessed a number of priories. The main occupation of these people was the drainage of the marshland: between the Alpilles and the Rhône, firm land was reclaimed little by little. To finance these projects a pardon was created in the 11C; at one time 150 000 pilgrims were counted.

Decadence – In the 17C the abbey consisted of about 20 monks and "religious" laymen, officers of the crown, to whom the king granted a position in the community and more significantly part of the revenues. One could see, mingling in the processions with the monks in sackcloth, these young colourfully-dressed men strutting and flirting with the lovely women of Arles.

The congregation of reformed monks of St-Maur, in charge of restoring discipline, sent new monks to the abbey in 1639; the monks who had been expelled by force pillaged the abbey.

In the 18C part of the buildings collapsed and were replaced by magnificent new constructions. The last abbot, the cardinal of Rohan, was implicated in the affair of the queen's necklace, with the result that in 1786 Louis XVI proclaimed the suppression of the abbey as retribution.

The misfortunes of a national property – In 1791, Montmajour was sold as a national property. It was bought by a second-hand dealer for 62 000 *livres*, payable over 12 years. To help repay the debt this woman broke up the buildings: furniture, panelling, lead, timberwork and marble were loaded on carts and sold. In spite of that, the woman was late in her payments and in 1793 the sale was annulled. The abbey was sold for 23 000 *livres* to an estate agent. He broke up the fine stonework and sold the old buildings to people who converted them into lodgings.

During the last century, the people of Arles, friends of old monuments, and the town itself recovered the buildings little by little: 6 000 francs for the tower, 2 000 francs for the church. In 1872 the restoration of the medieval buildings was started; the 18C buildings remained in ruins. The abbey is now state property.

TOUR ⊘ 45min

★**Église Notre-Dame** – The 12C building in the main part includes an upper church and a crypt or lower church.

Upper church – The upper church was never completed and consists of a chancel, a transept and a nave with two bays; the transept crossing was covered with pointed vaulting in the 13C.

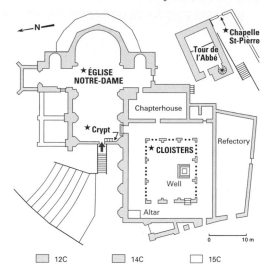

★ Crypt – Due to the incline of the land, the crypt was in part built into the sloping rock and in part raised. Its design was different from that of the upper church: on a cruciform plan with a central chapel and two chapels at either end of the arm of the transept. It is remarkable for the size of its vaulting and the fine dome which crowns the chancel. Five apsidal chapels open onto the ambulatory.

★ Cloisters – The cloisters were built at the end of the 12C but three of the galleries were rebuilt at different periods: north gallery in the 19C, west gallery in the 18C,

south gallery in the 14C. Only the eastern gallery has preserved its Romanesque characteristics. These galleries of three bays nevertheless contain some fascinating sculpture.

The capitals feature remarkable historiated decoration which has been associated with that of St-Trophime in Arles. The base of the columns is also carved at the four corners. Under the galleries are Gothic recessed tombs; in the courtyard there are laurel bushes and an ancient well.

Monastic buildings – The remaining buildings include the chapterhouse with rounded barrel vaulting, the refectory with its interesting pointed barrel vaulting *(access from the exterior)* and the dormitory, on the first floor above the refectory.

Tour de l'Abbé – This fine keep (1369), the machicolations of which have been rebuilt, was the abbey's main defence.

From the platform *(124 steps)* a fine **panorama★** embraces the Alpilles, Crau plain, Arles, Cévennes, Beaucaire and Tarascon.

★ Chapelle St-Pierre – When the abbey was founded, this tiny church was built and half-carved out of the hillside. It includes a church with two naves (capitals carved with geometric designs) and, extending it, a hermitage formed from natural caves.

★ Chapelle Ste-Croix ⊙ – *See illustration on p 40 under Art: Architectural Terms.* This charming 12C building is located outside the abbey precincts *(200m/218yd to the right towards Fontvieille)*. It is built in the form of a Greek cross: a square surmounted by a dome with triangular pediments and a bell tower surrounded by four apsidal chapels with oven vaulting. This was the funerary chapel for the Mont-majour cemetery.

Note the ancient tombs hewn out of the rock and stretched out over the rocky platform.

MOULIN DE DAUDET

Michelin map 83 fold 10 or 245 fold 29 or 246 fold 26 – Local map see Les ALPILLES

Between Arles and Les Baux-de-Provence, the admirers of Alphonse Daudet's works can make a literary pilgrimage to his **mill** ⊙, the inspiration for his famous *Lettres de mon Moulin* (Letters from My Mill). A lovely avenue of pines leads from Fontvieille to the mill.

Alphonse Daudet, the son of a silk manufacturer, was born at Nîmes on 13 May 1840 (d 1897). An outstanding author of tales of Provençal life and member of the Académie Goncourt, Daudet was also a contemporary of such important 19C literary figures as Zola and Mistral. He often stayed with friends at the Château de Montauban at the foot of the hill, but it was in Paris that he wrote. And yet he enjoyed strolling through the countryside, seeking inspiration, listening to the miller's tales or day-dreaming. The **view★** embraces the Alpilles, Beaucaire and Tarascon castles, the vast Rhône valley and the Abbaye de Montmajour.

Daudet's Mill

TOUR ⊙

Inside the mill, the first floor displays different kinds of millstones used in the grinding of grain. Note at roof level the names of the local winds, positioned according to their source.

The small **museum** contains memorabilia of the author remembered for the humour and sentiment with which he described the life and characters of Provence *(Lettres de mon Moulin*, 1869; *Tartarin de Tarascon*, 1872, the first of his *Tartarin* burlesques; *Fromont Jeune et Risler Aîné*, 1874, which won an award from the Académie Française; *Sapho*, 1884; *Notes sur la Vie*, 1899).

Oppidum de NAGES

Michelin map 83 fold 8 or 245 fold 27 – 10km/6mi southeast of Nîmes

On Les Castels hill, overlooking the Vaunage plain, the Nages-et-Solorgues **oppidum**, a fortified township, is a fascinating archeological site. A rocky path climbs up the hill *(signposted)* to the site.

Oppidum – Nages was one of the five *oppida* of the Iron Age (800-50 BC) that housed the Vaunage population. The islands of living quarters, arranged on the slope's incline and separated by parallel streets 5m/16.5ft wide, suggest an early urban plan and give an insight into the characteristics of the Gauls' living arrangements.

The rows of small uniform houses with drystone walls, sometimes quite high, are clearly visible. They were all covered with roofs made of cobwork applied to branches supported by beams which themselves were retained by posts.

To begin with, these dwellings were on a one-room plan with a hearth at its centre; in the 2C BC they were enlarged and subdivided but the comfort remained rudimentary. The settlement was surrounded by fortifications (there were four successive ones from 300 BC to 150 BC) interspersed with round towers (one of them from the 3C BC was 11m/36ft in diameter) and gates (a part of which has been successfully excavated). No public monument has been uncovered except for a *fanum*, a small native temple (70 BC). Roman infiltration did not hinder the *oppidum's* development which was at its greatest between 70 and 30 BC, the period in which appears the beginning of economic specialisation (presence of a forge).

On the return trip down, at the village's entrance, take the first street to the left leading to the Roman cistern, which still feeds several of the village's fountains.

Musée Archéologique ⊙ – Located in the town hall, on the first floor, the Archeological Museum displays pottery and various items excavated from Les Castels site. Different aspects of the successive inhabitants' daily life are evoked: food-related activities (agriculture, husbandry, hunting), crafts (metalwork, pottery making, weaving), arms, toilet requisites and funerary objects.

Book well in advance as vacant hotel rooms are often scarce in high season.

Gorges de la NESQUE★★

Michelin map 81 folds 13 and 14 or 245 folds 17 and 18

The River Nesque rises on the east face of Mont Ventoux and after some 70km/45mi flows into a tributary of the Sorgue, west of Pernes-les-Fontaines. In its upper reaches, the most attractive part of its course, the river has cut a spectacular gorge through the calcareous rock of the Vaucluse plateau.

FROM SAULT TO FLASSAN *52km/32mi – about 2hr*

The road has been widened in places to allow parking and good views of the gorges.

Sault – *See SAULT.*

Leave Sault to the southeast along D 942.

This corniche road follows the right riverbank through the gorge.

Monieux – This picturesque old village perched above the Nesque is overlooked by a high 12C tower connected to the village by what remains of a defensive wall. Some of the village's medieval houses have retained their old doors.

The gorges begin to form a few kilometres after leaving Monieux.

★★**Viewpoint (Belvédère)** – Alt 734m/2 408ft. The viewpoint *(left of the road)*, signalled by a stele bearing verses from Mistral's *Calendal*, overlooks the gorges and the jagged Cire rock (872m/2 860ft high). The descent begins with a passage through three tunnels, between which the road affords beautiful views of the site. At this point the Nesque runs in a cleft buried so deep in lush vegetation that only the murmuring of the fast flowing crystal-clear waters over its pebble-strewn bed can be heard.

D 942 moves slightly away from the gorge to cross the Coste Chaude coomb. At the exit to the fourth tunnel there is a good **view** back along the gorge to the **Rocher du Cire**. The road runs below the ruined hamlet of Fayol, buried beneath luxuriant Provençal vegetation (note the large-scale reforestation on the left bank) before the landscape changes suddenly as the river emerges into the Comtat Venaissin plain, and the horizon expands to include Mont Ventoux to the east and Carpentras and its countryside straight ahead. The beautiful Hermitage coomb precedes the next village.

Villes-sur-Auzon – Three-quarters of the district of Villes-sur-Auzon is covered by the wooded slopes of Mont Ventoux. The village itself, an important agricultural centre, is centred on a large square overlooked by old houses and is ringed by a street of plane trees and splashing fountains.

Take D 1 towards La Gabelle.

As the road crosses the plateau, Mont Ventoux (north), the Dentelles de Montmirail (northwest) and the Carpentras basin (west) fill the horizon. At the entrance to La Gabelle the **view** extends to the opposite slope, with the Nesque gorges in the foreground and the Luberon mountains in the background (south).

From La Gabelle continue north, cross D 1 and head towards Flassan.

The road descends into a cool valley studded with pines and spruce.

Flassan – The minute village has ochre walled houses and a typically picturesque Provençal square.

NÎMES ★★★

Population 128 471

Michelin map 83 fold 9 or 245 fold 27 or 246 folds 25 and 26

Situated on the edge of the *garrigue* limestone hills and the Petite Camargue plain, Nîmes exudes the air of a great city of the arts, proud of its prestigious Gallo-Roman past, yet nonetheless anxious to open itself up to new ideas. Deeply-marked by its Huguenot past, Nîmes is a city of old traditional industries, particularly textiles and the processing of local agricultural products (canning of fruit, wine production). It is also an administrative capital (*préfecture* of the Gard) and a garrison town (artilleryman Guillaume Apollinaire passed through the city in 1914-1915 and his romance here with Louise de Coligny has been frequently penned in French literature), one which only recently has endeavoured to embrace the advancement of high technology with the opening of a computing college and the Georges Besse industrial estate.

Among the city's gastronomic specialities note: *brandade de morue (see below)*, marinated olives, *caladons*, almond biscuits, and the *Croquant Villaret*, baked in the same ovens for two centuries; in the past few years the local *Costières de Nîmes* wines (red, rosé and white) have gained an excellent reputation.

Nîmes is also the centre for tauromachy. The *corridas* or bullfights, with their set rules, which take place in the amphitheatre, Camargue races and the setting loose of bulls through the streets have brought immense popularity and fame to the city.

OVER TWENTY CENTURIES OF HISTORY

The chained crocodile – Capital of Volcae Arecomici, Nemausus (Nîmes' ancient name originated from a sacred spring around which the town settled) was at the head of a vast territory of 24 settlements between the sea the Cévennes and from the River Rhône to the Sète mountains, when it accepted Roman domination. The date of Roman colonisation, its founder and the ethnic origin of its colonists are now matters of controversy. Two theories have been put forward: the founder was either Augustus, who settled here in 31 BC with a Roman colony of veterans of the Egyptian campaign (evidence of this settlement is the famous coin stamped with the chained crocodile), or Caesar with a Latin colony in 44 BC.

Regardless of the issue as to who founded Nîmes, Augustus was the one who heaped privileges on the town and allowed it to surround 200ha/494 acres with fortifications. The town, situated on the Domitian Way, then proceeded to embellish itself with splendid buildings: a

---

A Tale of Barter

The renown of *brandade de morue* (the verb *brandar* in Provençal means "to stir") as a gastronomic speciality of Nîmes owes its origin to a barter in the Middle Ages between Breton fisherman who paid for salt from the marshes around Aigues-Mortes with quantities of dried cod. Once the bones have been removed (the skin is kept), the warm cod is ground in a mortar with olive oil and milk. The *brandade* is considered ready to eat once it has reached a creamy consistency. This traditional dish, which appears on the menus of all the best restaurants in the region, is best served either in *vol-au-vent* or with fried croutons.

---

forum with the Maison Carrée to the south, an amphitheatre able to hold 24 000 people, a circus, baths and fountains fed by an imposing aqueduct, the Pont du Gard which yielded $20\,000\text{m}^3/7\,063$cu ft of water a day. In the 2C the city received privileges from the Emperors Hadrian and Antoninus Pius (whose in-laws came from Nîmes) and continued to flourish and build (Plotinius' basilica, arrangement of the Fountaine district etc), reaching its zenith with a population of 20 000 to 25 000 inhabitants. The surrounding countryside also benefited: the land was surveyed and improved and large agricultural settlements, seeking to recreate the pattern of urban life, fed this brilliant metropolis.

The centuries of Roman occupation have left vivid memories: first names like Numa, Flavien, Adrien and Antoninus are still very popular. In the city's coat of arms appears the chained crocodile, the symbol of the conquest of Egypt and the Nile by Roman legionaries, who subsequently became citizens of Nîmes.

Religious struggles – The most significant period of Nîmes history, together with that of the Roman occupation, is the period of bitterly-disputed religious differences.

In the 5C the Visigoths, who ruled the country (from Toulouse to the River Rhône), clashed with the Catholic population when they tried to impose their beliefs: churches were closed and the Catholics were persecuted well into the 6C.

In the 13C the people of Nîmes sided with the Albigensians (a heretical Christian sect that believed in the separation of Good and Evil – Good was symbolised by God who ruled over a spiritual world of light and beauty; Evil was the material world ruled by the Devil). Simon de Montfort headed the terrible crusade against these heretics, and the city surrendered without resistance in 1213.

In the 14C a wave of intolerance fell upon the Jews; they were expelled from the city and their possessions confiscated. In the 16C Nîmes became a Huguenot city. It was the Geneva of France: three quarters of its population believed in the Reform.

On 29 September 1567 the Michelade tragedy occurred: 200 Catholics, most of whom were priests, were massacred. There ensued a long dark period of persecution and war in which both sides suffered in turn: the active participation of Nîmes in the War of the Camisards (1700-1704) following the Revocation of the Edict of Nantes was followed later the same century by Protestant revenge at the time of the Revolution; the Restoration of the Bourbon monarchy (1814-1830) was marked by the White Terror perpetrated by the Catholics.

Académie de Nîmes – The Nîmes Academy is more than 300 years old. In 1682 Louis XIV conferred upon the Academy the same privileges as the French Academy in Paris. Concerned for the most part with historical and archeological subjects, the Nîmes Academy also concentrates on the fields of literature, art and music.

The city has also given rise to several famous writers: **Alphonse Daudet** (the birthplace of the author of *Les Lettres de mon Moulin* is at no 20 Boulevard Gambetta), **André Chamson**, **Jean Paulhan**, the Editor-in-Chief of the *Nouvelle Revue Française* from 1925 to 1940, and **Marc Bernard**, who illustrated the lives of the Nîmes working classes in his works. Among Occitan writers stand out the fervent 19C Catholic poet and baker **Reboul**, his Protestant rival **Bigot**, and the contemporary author **Robert Laffont**.

The Conquest of the West – From the Middle Ages local serge was well known throughout Europe for its hard-wearing quality. Legend has it that Christopher Columbus used it to manufacture the sails of his caravels; this same cloth, which was exported via Genoa, was also used to make sailors' trousers. In 1873, a Bavarian emigrant in the United States called Lévy-Strauss had the idea of capitalizing on its robust qualities to make trousers for gold-diggers and migrants setting out to discover the West. The name *"bleu de Gênes"* or *"blue from Genoa"* became "blue jeans" and the brand name "denim" (literally "from Nîmes") still bears testimony today to the contribution made by the city in the conquest of the West.

The golden age of textiles – Several times in Nîmes history, the city has known periods of decline followed by periods of revival. In the early 15C, the wars, road bandits, earthquakes and the plague had made of the flourishing ancient city of Nemausus but a small village under the Vivarais bailiwick. At the end of the 15C the town prospered: wood, leather, silk and glass were manufactured. Louis XI (1461-83) ordered the founding of a textile manufacture workshop. But it was mostly during the reign of François I (1515-1547) that Nîmes developed; the textile industry prospered and progressed constantly. In the 18C the textile mills (silk and serge) employed 10 000 people and 300 looms. The textile industry was handled by the Protestant middle class.

In the 19C the arrival of the railway favoured the industrial activities and the extension of the Gard vineyards. Nowadays Nîmes is a city dominated by tertiary industries. It is trying to attract high-tech companies and is undertaking a programme of architectural and urban development projects which have been entrusted to some of the most famous names in the Arts: Jean Nouvel (architect of the Nemausus housing complex to the south of the city – **BZ**), Norman Foster, Jean-Michel Vilmotte and Kurokawa; the choice of Philippe Stark to redesign the city's arms symbolizes Nîmes' willingness to open itself out to the contemporary world at large.

STAYING IN NÎMES

Cafés and Bars – Le Shaker piano bar with live music after 9pm. (except Sundays and Mondays); Le Haddock Café, with its young atmosphere and music. Boulevard Victor-Hugo: the outside tables of three popular cafés, Le Cygne, Le Parisien and Le Napoléon, near the Maison Carrée. Around the amphitheatre: Café de la Bourse, Les Vendanges wine bar, 1 Rue Violette, Bar des Trois Maures, the headquarters of the Bullfighting Club, as well as the favoured meeting-place of football and rugby fans. San Francisco Steak House, 33 Rue Roussy, La Movida tapas bar, Place de la Placette with its flamenco shows, and numerous bars and brasseries along Boulevard de la Libération and Boulevard Amiral-Courbet.

The Ferias – The Whitsun Feria is held in May, the Grape-Harvesting Feria (Vendanges) in September while the Primavera Feria takes place in February (it is characterised by its *novilladas*, fights between novice toreros and bulls under four years of age). Seats for the corridas may be booked 15 days before the event at the Bureau de Location des Arènes, Rue Alexandre-Ducros, 30000 Nîmes ☎ 04 66 67 28 02. The price of the tickets range from 100F to 500F for a corrida and from 50F to 300F for a *novillada*.

ROMAN PUBLIC BUILDINGS *allow 3hr*

★★★**Amphitheatre (Arènes)** ⊘ **(CV)** – *See p 46.* This beautifully preserved amphitheatre is twin to the one at Arles; most likely from the same period (late 1C-early 2C), with the same layout, similar dimensions and capacity (133m x 101m/436ft x 331ft; seating capacity 24 000). Its differences are slight architectural ones such as the galleries with barrel vaulting of Roman construction which are replaced by the Greek trabeated form. The Nîmes amphitheatre because of its axial dimensions is ranked ninth out of the 20 important amphitheatres discovered in Gaul; however, it is the best preserved of the Roman ones especially in its upper storey where, in several places, sockets remain that held posts carrying a huge adjustable awning, the *velarium*, to shelter the spectators from the sun and rain. From the exterior, the building presents two storeys each of 60 arcades (total height: 21m/65.5ft) crowned with an attic. The building material in hard limestone from Barutel did not require detailed ornamentation: pilasters on the lower register and engaged Doric columns above. Four axial doorways correspond to the four entrances. The main northern gateway has kept its pediment, adorned with bulls. Note in front of the amphitheatre traces (tower and curtain wall) of the Augustinian fortifications.

Inside (climb to the topmost tiers to have a view of the whole), the *cavea* (all of the tiers) was divided into 34 tiers of seats grouped into four independent *maeniae* (a group of 4 tiers below then 3 times 10 tiers rising to the top); the spectators were seated according to their social station. An ingenious system of corridors, stairways, galleries and *vomitaria* (sloping corridors) made it possible for all the spectators to reach their seats quickly without crowding and without any mingling of the classes. Under the arena itself a substructure (68 x 37m/223 x 121ft) made of two vast galleries served as backstage.

The Games – The games included fighting of three kinds (between animals, between gladiators and animals, and between gladiators), Olympic games and chariot races. Performances were announced in advance by painted posters, giving the names of the performers and details of the programmes in sensational terms. Long before opening time the crowd, who loved to see bloodshed and prowess in the arena, waited at the doors. As soon as these were opened they invaded the upper tiers of seats. Distinguished spectators arrived on litters or in sedan-chairs.

To neutralise the smell of animals and stables incense-burners were set up in the arena and slaves armed with scent sprays aimed clouds of perfume *(sparsiones)* at the notables. An orchestra punctuated the games with gay music. Friends met in the promenades during the intervals, and food and drinks were sold in the galleries.

Bullfight at Nîmes

Carnivorous and exotic beasts – lions, tigers, panthers, elephants and rhinoceroses, brought over in small numbers from the African provinces - were reserved for Rome or for games in the provinces attended by the Emperor; but more frequently bulls, bears, wild boar and trained mastiffs were used. To whet the appetite of the spectators before sensational contests, birds of prey were released against hares, rabbits and pigeons, while dogs got bloody muzzles by attacking porcupines. Performing animals were also on show.

Most gladiators were slaves or prisoners but among them, also, were free Barbarians: Germans, Syrians or Berbers who had entered this dangerous profession for sheer love of fighting. These combatants had barracks to themselves; they formed teams carefully trained by impresarios who hired them out, for large fees, to rich citizens, usually candidates for high office.

In principle, a duel between gladiators had always to end in the death of one of the contestants. A man who could fight no more would raise his finger to ask for quarter. If he had pleased the public, the President of the Games would turn up his thumb, and the man would be reprieved; if he turned down his thumb, the winner would cut the loser's throat.

Executions also took place in the amphitheatre: the condemned, not Roman citizens, were delivered to the beasts or the executioner: the first Christians were more than once the victims of this procedure. Furthermore, it was under the influence of Christianity that the gladiator combats were forbidden in 404.

Ferias and Bullfighting

The focus of the **Whitsun Feria** (Feria de Pentecôte), created in 1952 in imitation of Spanish bullfighting festivals, is on the amphitheatre *(arènes)* and the *corridas* and *novilladas* (bullfights with young bulls and novice matadors) held inside it during the late mornings and afternoons and occasionally in the evenings. Although the bull reigns supreme, the whole town becomes enveloped in its traditions: running of the bulls along the boulevards, bullfights for eager amateurs in smaller bullrings nearby, concerts, exhibitions, folklore parades, dances and impromptu events, all of which attract large crowds from far and wide. In the narrow streets local associations open up **bodegas** (informal bars or restaurants) in which pride of place is given to Spanish food (**tapas** and **paella**) and sherries (the dry *fino*, in particular). Since 1978, a second feria, centred around the Corrida des Vendanges, a bullfight to celebrate the grape harvest, has taken place every September. A third feria, the February Feria de Primavera, allows young, aspiring bullfighters to compete under the "bubble" which covers the amphitheatre during the winter months.

Although the amphitheatre is a must at any time, it is during the important *corridas* which fill it to its seams with multicoloured crowds that it undoubtedly most resembles its former self.

The amphitheatre's role through the centuries – Having lost its main purpose, the amphitheatre was transformed into a fortress by the Visigoths; arcades were boarded up and towers added, a deep moat was dug around the arena itself and perhaps backed up by a small rampart wall (ruins can be seen in the basement of the Law Courts). In the eastern part of the building, the castle of the Viscounts of Nîmes was later built (two walled arcades lit by small Romanesque windows were preserved). The watch was undertaken by a group of knights, members of a feudal aristocracy who aided the viscount. This cavalry of knights declined in the 12C and disappeared when the king established his rule in Nîmes in 1226.

The amphitheatre was, like the one at Arles, overtaken by houses, streets and two chapels; a village was established and numbered 700 inhabitants in the 18C.

The demolition of these buildings started in 1809 and restoration began. The first *corrida* was performed in 1853.

Since 1988 the amphitheatre has been covered between October and April with an inflatable canvas dome fastened to an elliptical beam, which is itself supported on posts fixed to the modern parts of the monument. This structure means that its potential as a magnificent entertainments venue with a seating capacity of 7 000 people can be exploited to the full.

★★ **Maison Carrée** ⊙ **(CU)** – *See illustration on p 38 under Art: Architectural Terms.* This magnificent temple, known as the Square House, is the best preserved of the Roman temples still standing. It was built under Augustus' (late 1C BC) reign by an architect from the Narbonensis who was inspired by the Temple of Apollo in Rome. It is built on a rectangle 26m/85ft long and 15m/49ft wide and stands 17m/55.5ft high; it rests on a podium which is reached up a stairway of 15 steps (the uneven number of steps was calculated so that by starting to mount the steps on the right foot, one arrived on the podium on the same foot one started with).

J.-P. Lescouret/EXPLORER

Nîmes – Maison Carrée

Like all the Classical temples, the Maison Carrée's layout consisted of a *pronaos* (vestibule) lined by a colonnade, and a *cella* (the room which contained the statue of the divinity). Consecrated to the Imperial cult and dedicated to Augustus' grandsons, the temple faced the forum and was surrounded by a portico of finely carved columns.

The purity of line of the building, its harmonious proportions and the elegance of its fluted columns denote Greek influence, which is also found in the temple's ornamentation: Corinthian columns, architrave divided by lines of pearls, a scrolled frieze, a modillioned cornice with rosettes, lions' heads... The entrance façade and the façade at the opposite end are each surmounted by a triangular pediment. The 10 columns of the *pronaos* stand alone with an ease rarely seen elsewhere, whereas the other 20 columns are engaged in the *cella* wall. Under the podium, rooms were set up for the sanctuary's archives and the treasury.

Like the amphitheatre, the Maison Carrée's fortunes have varied: it has served as a public building (early Middle Ages), a canon's house (c 1015), a consuls' house (until 1540), a private house, stables and a church belonging to the Augustinian order (in 1670). Sold as public property during the Revolution, it subsequently housed the *département* archives, then, from 1823, the collections of the city's first museum. The interior was restored in 1988 and now houses temporary exhibitions of contemporary art.

★Carré d'Art ⊘ **(CU)** – This large building, designed by the British architect Norman Foster to house both the city's Museum of Contemporary Art and its media library, stands opposite the Maison Carrée, from which it has adopted its sobriety of line and copied several of its architectural features: podium evoking the dressed stone, columned portico on the main façade, rectangular plan, sober colour range in light beige, grey and white. Over 250 works are on permanent exhibition inside, including paintings, sculptures and drawings from 1960 onwards, spread out on two levels, and with three main themes: French art from 1960 to the present day, Anglo-Saxon and Germanic artists and Mediterranean identity.

The museum has several main objectives: to give precedence to certain key movements in contemporary art such as New Realism, Supports/Surfaces, the BMPT group (Buren, Mosset, Parmentier, Toroni), Figuration Libre (Free Figuration), New Figuration; to attempt to bring together entire collections of works by artists such as Martial Raysse, Claude Viallat and Arman; it has also shown interest in Avant-Garde movements in neighbouring countries (Arte Povera, Transavangarde). The museum's collection of canvases is displayed on a rotation system which may result in some works being temporarily withdrawn to provide space for exhibitions. Some of these may focus on famous names such as Jean Tinguely (*Baluba*, 1962), Martial Raysse (*Tribute to Los Angeles*, 1962), Yves Klein, Gerhard Richter, Sigmar Polke, Christian Boltanski, Gérard Garouste, Jean-Claude Blais etc.

★★Jardin de la Fontaine (AX) – This garden is the unexpected creation of an 18C army engineer, J.-P. Mareschal. Planted with tall densely-foliated trees, pines and cedars, shading lawns, terraces and stone balustraded paths, and filled with flowers, the gardens extend from the famous Nemausus spring up the slopes of Mont Cavalier to the white octagonal form of the Tour Magne.

Since the creation of the garden in the 18C, the spring water has been collected in a mirror-like pool surrounded by balustraded walks, before flowing through pools to the canal. The fountain is in fact the karstic resurgence of a rainwater spring which infiltrates the limestone *garrigues* to the northwest of the city.

NÎMES

Gambetta (Bd) .... **ABX**
République (R. de la) .... **AYZ**

Briçonnet (R.) .... **BY** 8
Cirque-Romain (R. du) .... **AY** 13

Fontaine (Q. de la) .... **AX** 20
Gamel (Av. P.) .... **BZ** 22
Générac (R. de) ....**AYZ** 23
Mallarmé (R. Steph.) .... **AX** 34
Martyrs-de-la-R.
 (Pl.) .... **AZ** 36
Mendès-France
 (Av. P.) .... **BZ** 39

Ste-Anne (R.) .... **AY** 46
Verdun (R. de) .... **AY** 47

M² Musée des Beaux-Arts

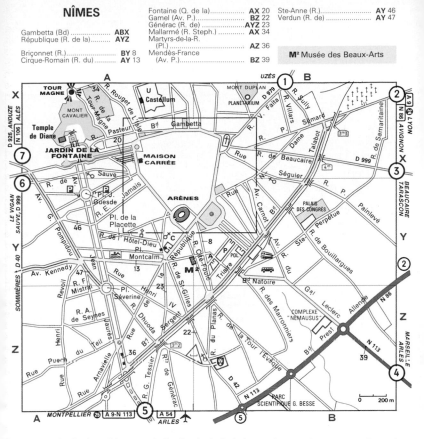

During Antiquity, this sacred district included the spring, a theatre, temple and baths. Recent excavations have uncovered some of the surrounding area: to the east on Rue Pasteur an opulent 2C *domus*; to the west behind the Temple of Diana, a district for local people (razed in the 2C most likely because it did not fit into Antoninus Pius' projects of architectural splendour); to the south at the crossroads of Boulevard Jaurès and Rue de Sauve, a sumptuous public building (2C), whose function still arouses speculation. Discovered at the same time were lovely mosaics, fragments of mural paintings, a marble head of a man etc.

Temple de Diane (AX) – This building which dates from the first half of the 2C is known as the Temple of Diana but its true function is unknown. It was most likely part of a vast architectural ensemble, still buried, made up of several different levels (traces of stairs). It was occupied by the Benedictine nuns in the Middle Ages, who converted it into a church without too many modifications, and was destroyed during the Wars of Religion.

There appears to be a large room (possibly the *cella*) flanked by aisles and covered with barrel vaulting. Niches with pediments (alternately triangular and rounded) are carved into the side walls and most probably contained statues.

★**Tour Magne** ⊘ **(AX)** – Located at the top of Mont Cavalier, the city's highest point, the tower is the most remarkable vestige of the massive defences built in 15 BC. The line of fortifications and some 30 towers have been identified.

Originally the tower was part of a pre-Roman rampart and was simply reinforced and raised during Augustus' reign. It is a three-storey polygonal tower standing 34m/112ft since the excavations in 1601 by a certain Traucat, a gardener and would-be archeologist who was convinced that under the tower was a hidden treasure left by the Romans; he was authorised by Henri IV to keep digging – two-thirds of the treasure was to go to the crown – but the digging was stopped when it was discovered that the tower was falling down.

There is a good **view**★ *(140 steps via an inside staircase to the platform)* of Mont Ventoux, the Alpilles, Nîmes, Vistre plain and the *garrigues*.

From the Rue Stéphane-Mallarmé there is a fine view of the tower.

Castellum (AX) – A unique ruin of its kind, this was the Roman distribution tank to which water, from Uzès, was brought by the Pont du Gard aqueduct, stored in a circular basin and then distributed in the town by means of 10 lead canal ducts (40cm/15.5in in diameter). Above it stands the citadel built in 1687 to watch over Protestant Nîmes.

NÎMES

Aspic (R. de l') .... **CUV**
Courbet (Bd Amiral).......... **DUV** 14
Crémieux (R.) .... **DU** 16
Curaterie (R.) .... **DU** 17
Daudet (Bd A.) .... **CU** 18
Gambetta (Bd) .... **CDU**
Grand'Rue .... **DU** 24

Guizot (R.) .... **CU** 26
Madeleine (R. de la) .... **CU** 32
Nationale (R.) .... **CDU**
Perrier (R. Gén.) .... **CU**
République (R. de la) .... **CV** 43
Victor-Hugo (Bd) .... **CUV**

Arènes (Bd des) .... **CV** 2
Auguste (R.) .... **CU** 4
Bernis (R. de) .... **CV** 6

Chapitre (R. du)................. **CDU** 12
Fontaine (Q. de la)............. **CU** 20
Halles (R. des)................... **CU** 27
Horloge (R. de l')............... **CU** 28
Libération (Bd de la).......... **DV** 30
Maison-Carrée (Pl. de la).. **CU** 33
Marchands (R. des) .... **CU** 35
Prague (Bd de)................... **DV** 42
Saintenac (Bd E.) .... **DU** 45
Violette (R.) .... **CV** 49

B   Chapelle des Jésuites
E   Maison Natale
    d'Alphonse Daudet
L   Hôtel de Régis

M¹ Musée Archéologique
    Museum d'Histoire Naturelle
M³ Musée du Vieux Nîmes
M⁴ Galerie Taurine

N   Façade Romane
S   Hôtel Meynier de Salinelles
V   Hôtel Fontfroide
Z   Hôtel de Bernis

Porte d'Auguste (**DU**) – This gate, a ruin of the Augustinian fortified wall on the Domitian Way, was flanked originally by two semicircular towers enclosing an interior courtyard, an effective defensive procedure. It still has the two wide passages for chariots and two narrower passages for pedestrians. There is also a bronze copy of the statue of Augustus.

THE OLD QUARTER

This preserved area is clustered around the ancient cathedral and presents a great many narrow streets featuring quaint covered passageways.

Leave from Place aux Herbes.

Cathédrale Notre-Dame-et-St-Castor (**CDU**) – Built in 1096 and remodelled frequently over the centuries, the cathedral was finally almost entirely rebuilt in the 19C. The west front, surmounted by a classical pediment, still has a partly Romanesque frieze depicting scenes of the Old Testament (Adam and Eve, Cain and Abel). Inside in the third south chapel is a Christian sarcophagus.

Take Rue de la Poissonnerie right of the cathedral then, when you reach Place du Chapitre, turn into Rue de la Prévôté which gives onto Rue du Chapitre.

Rue du Chapitre (**CDU** 12) – No 14 (**L**). The Hôtel de Regis displays an 18C façade and a lovely 16C paved courtyard.

★**Musée du Vieux Nîmes** ⊘ (**CU M³**) – This museum is located in what used to be the episcopal palace (17C) at the heart of the old town. It was founded in 1920 by a rival of Frédéric Mistral and contains numerous local exhibits in a remarkably well-restored historical setting. The city of Nîmes actually reflects characteristics of both Languedoc and Provence, and there are some pieces of furniture typical of both these regions on display here; notice in particular a **dining hall** and a **billiard room**.

The museum also houses temporary exhibitions on various themes.

Retrace your steps and go back to Grand'Rue on the right.

Chapelle des Jésuites (DU B) – The 18C Jesuit college chapel has surprisingly harmonious proportions. The striking two-storey façade is topped by a triangular pediment and has a regular pattern of alternating pilasters, engaged columns and alcoves. The **interior★** is lit through skylights and consists of a short single-aisle nave with balustraded galleries running along its sides, a transept crowned by a flattened dome above the crossing, and a chancel with a semi-circular vault and prominent ribbing. The richness of the sculpted ornamentation (pilasters, capitals, entablatures) puts the finishing touches to the balance of the building, which houses temporary exhibitions.

Musée d'Histoire Naturelle ⊘ **(DU M¹)** – *Located on the first floor of the former Jesuit College.* The museum houses an ethnographic section (arms, headdresses from Africa, Asia, Oceania and Madagascar) and a natural history section (a local prehistoric collection; mammals and reptiles from all over the world).

★Musée Archéologique ⊘ **(DU M¹)** – *The Archeological Museum is located in the former Jesuit College.* In the ground-floor gallery, numerous carvings displayed are pre-Roman: busts of Gaul warriors, steles and friezes and contemporary artefacts (arms, ceramics) as well as a large collection of Roman inscriptions. Also on the ground floor are two lifesize human dwellings, reconstructed with great care and attention to detail: a Gallic house dating from the second half of the 5C BC and the bedroom *(cubiculum)* of a Roman residence in the years 40-30 BC.

Upstairs the first gallery contains Gallo-Roman items used daily (toilet articles, head-dresses, kitchen utensils, tools), funerary steles, oil lamps; the second gallery contains glassware (flasks, funerary vases, bone and bronze objects); the third gallery exhibits pottery (Archaic Greek, black and red figure, Far Eastern influenced, Etruscan and Punic). A coin collection is displayed in the last room.

At the corner of the museum take Rue des Greffes then turn right into Rue de l'Aspic.

Hôtel Fontfroide ⊘ **(V)** – *No 14.* Note the superb double spiral grand staircase dating from the 17C.

Turn left into Rue de Bernis.

Rue de Bernis (CV 6) – *No 3* **(Z)**. The Hôtel de Bernis has a fine 15C façade with mullioned windows. The antique style inside courtyard has a well.

Go back to Rue de l'Aspic.

Rue de l'Aspic (CUV) – *No 8* **(S)**. The porch of the Hôtel Meynier de Salinelles is adorned with three paleochristian sarcophagi imbedded in the wall, and a cippus; lovely Renaissance stairway door.

Turn right at the end of the street.

Rue de la Madeleine (CU 32) – *No 1* **(N)**. The house displays a finely-carved Romanesque façade.

ADDITIONAL SIGHTS

★Musée des Beaux-Arts ⊘ **(ABY M²)** – The Fine Arts Museum was remodelled in 1986 by the architect J-M. Wilmotte. On the ground floor there is a large Roman mosaic depicting the marriage of Admetus; it was discovered in Nîmes in the 19C. On the first floor are displayed works of art from the French, Italian, Flemish and Dutch Schools (15C-19C) including paintings by Giambono *(The Mystic Marriage of St Catherine)*, Bassano *(Susanna and the Elders)*, Rubens *(Portrait of a Monk)*, Seghers *(Christ Taking Leave of his Mother)*, Troy *(The Sleeping Reaper)*, Natoire *(Venus and Adonis)* and Delaroche *(Cromwell and Charles I's Coffin)*. The adjoining rooms are devoted to the Naples and Genoa Schools, both from the 17C. Note the group of sculptures signed by the 19C artist **James Pradier**.

Maison Natale d'Alphonse Daudet (CU E) – *No 20 Boulevard Gambetta.* This bourgeois townhouse, with columns flanking its entrance, is the birthplace of Alphonse Daudet.

Fontaine Pradier (DV) – Built in 1848. The statue, which symbolises Nîmes, had as a model Juliette Drouet, friend of Pradier and Victor Hugo.

Galerie Taurine (CV M⁴) - Located close to the amphitheatre, this small museum displays miscellaneous documents (posters, programmes), paintings and bullfighters' costumes illustrating the city's tauromachian traditions during temporary exhibitions.

EXCURSIONS

Les Garrigues – *11km/7mi by* ① *on the map, D 979, to join the itinerary described under Les GARRIGUES.*

The country around Nîmes – *Round tour of 44km/27mi – about 2hr 30min Leave Nîmes by Rue Arnavielle* **(AZ)** *which becomes D 40, the road to Sommières.*

Caveirac – An imposing 17C horseshoe-shaped château houses the town hall. Two corner towers roofed with glazed tiles, the mullioned windows, some amusing gargoyles and a fine staircase with a wrought iron balustrade enhance the building. The porch is so big that it straddles the road (D 103).

Calvisson – This village lies amid vines in the centre of Vaunage plain.

In the centre of town take CD 107 in the direction of Fontanès; leave the village and bear left on the signposted road indicating Roc de Gachonne.

From the viewing table located at the top of a tower, there is a picturesque **view** of the red tile-roofed village, Vidourle valley (southwest), St-Loup peak (west) and on the horizon the Mediterranean and the Pyrenees.

Aire de Caissargues

This motorway rest stop, situated between the Nîmes-Centre and Garon interchanges on motorway A 54, is spread out over an area of approximately 30ha. Here, the fine Neo-classical style colonnade of Nîmes' former theatre has been rebuilt at the end of an avenue lined with lotus trees, and from the Tour de Magne-inspired viewpoint there is a fine, overall panorama of the whole site, Nîmes and the Vistre plain.

The exterior of the exhibition building *(open all year round)* is decorated with a enamelled lava fresco by Francesca Guerrier, while the inside houses remains (moulds) discovered on this motorway site, including the "Dame de Caissargues", the skeleton of a 25-30 year-old-woman, dating from 5 000 BC, buried in a contracted foetal position and wearing a shell necklace. The remaining area recalls daily life in the Languedoc region during the Copper Age (3 000 BC) and show examples of the habitat, working tools and funerary rituals of the period.

Oppidum de Nages – *See Oppidum de NAGES.*

Continue on D 345 through Boissières, overlooked by an extensively-restored medieval castle, to D 107, bear right on N 113 then left on D 139.

Source Perrier ⊙ – The Perrier spring forms an underground lake 15°C/50°F; the abundant natural gas which escapes is captured and reinserted in the water under pressure. The tour includes a visit to the various plants for bottle making, bottling, labelling etc.

Annual production now exceeds 800 million bottles thanks to automated bottling procedures. Major markets for Perrier are France, Great Britain and the other members of the European Community, the United States, Canada, Switzerland, Australia and Saudi Arabia.

NYONS

Population 6 353

Michelin map 81 fold 3 or 245 folds 4 and 17 or 246 fold 9 – Facilities

Situated within a protective ring of mountains *(see Introduction: Legends and tales for the legend of St Caesarius and Nyons)*, astride the River Eygues, where it emerges from a gorge into the Tricastin plain, Nyons basks in a pleasant climate in which exotic flora flourishes out of doors; this warm winter climate attracts many visitors.

The olive groves surrounding Nyons (olives and oil are marketed by the town) give it a very Provençal look. The town has a truffle market, and on Thursday mornings a colourful weekly market takes place.

OIL MILLS

The mills are fully operational between November and February.

Moulin Ramade ⊙ – *Access to the west via ③ on the plan and the fourth street on the left.* The first gallery houses millstones and presses used in the production of olive oil. The second gallery is specialised in refining and stocking the produce. It is here that the *tanche*, a local variety of black olive, is processed.

Vieux Moulins ⊙ – *Access via Avenue de la Digue.* Old 18C and 19C oil mills can be seen, in which the oil is produced using traditional methods. You may also visit an old soap factory.

Coopérative Oléicole et Viticole ⊙ – *Place Olivier-de-Serres. Access to the west via ③ on the plan.* In this wine and oil cooperative, two adjoining rooms are devoted to the production of virgin olive oil (70% of production), obtained by only one mechanical pressing without further treatment. The remaining olives, the *tanche* variety, or Nyons black olives, are subsequently processed for canning.

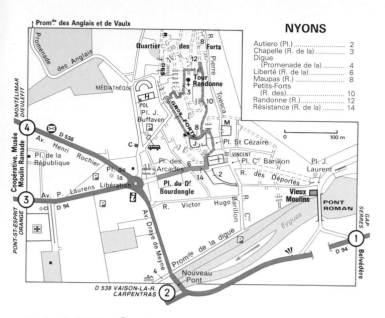

NYONS

Autiero (Pl.) 2
Chapelle (R. de la) 3
Digue
    (Promenade de la) 4
Liberté (R. de la) 6
Maupas (R.) 8
Petits-Forts
    (R. des) 10
Randonne (R.) 12
Résistance (R. de la) 14

0   100 m

Musée de l'Olivier ⊘ – *Avenue des Tilleuls. Access to the west via* ③, *on the plan, then northwest of Place Olivier-de-Serres.* This Olive Museum includes a wide variety of utensils, presses, tools and so on used in the production of olives and olive oil; there is also a group of items, such as lamps, showing how oil can be used. Documents enhance the collection. Note as well the giant fossil weighing 148kg/326lb.

ADDITIONAL SIGHTS

Quartier des Forts – This old district is built on a hill overlooking the town. Start from the arcaded **Place du Dr-Bourdongle**.

Take Rue de la Résistance and Rue de la Mairie to Rue des Petits-Forts.

This is a narrow alley lined with low-roofed houses (early 14C).

Tour Randonne – The 13C tower houses the tiny chapel of Notre-Dame-de-Bon-Secours.

Bear left on Rue de la Chapelle.

★**Rue des Grands-Forts** – This is a long covered gallery where the thick walls have been pierced with windows to allow the light to filter through.
Go under the tall vaulted gateway, the ruins of a feudal castle, and bear left into Rue Maupas, a stepped street which leads back to Rue de la Mairie.

Millenarian olive tree in Nyons

★Pont Roman – This 13C-14C humpbacked bridge spans the Eygues with a single 40m/131ft arch, one of the boldest in the Midi.

Viewpoint (Belvédère) – *Cross the Eygues over the Nouveau Pont, bear left on D 94, leaving the Pont Roman on the left; pass under the tunnel and turn right.*

From the rocky spike *(bench)* the **view** embraces old Nyons overlooked by Angèle mountain (alt 1 606m/5 268ft), and the deep, narrow Eygues valley to the right contrasting with the wide basin, to the left, where the new town has spread.

EXCURSION

Promenade des Anglais et de Vaulx – *Round tour of 8km/5mi. Leave Nyons Promenade des Anglais (northwest of town plan) and after 300m/328yd turn right.*

The narrow, winding but nicely laid out road runs along the hillside through olive groves. It offers good views of Nyons, Eygues valley and the Baronnies massif. *On the descent to D 538, leave the road on the right to Venterol and return to Nyons via D 538.*

ORANGE★★

Population 26 964
Michelin map 81 folds 11 and 12 or 245 fold 16 or 246 fold 24

Gateway to the Midi, at the crossroads of two motorways, Orange is famous for its prestigious Roman public buildings which include the triumphal arch and the Roman theatre. These monuments serve as the stage for the international music festival created in 1869 called **Chorégies**.

An important market centre for fruit and early produce, Orange also has industrial (canning, chemicals) and military (air base, Foreign Legion) activities.

Roman Orange – Ancient Arausio was a Celtic settlement, when in 105 BC a terrible battle erupted between the Roman legions and the army of the Cimbrians and Teutons. The Romans were caught off guard by the size and brutality of the invaders and suffered a resounding defeat which threatened to compromise their recent conquest of Gaul. However, they recovered quickly, returning three years later under the command of the brilliant **General Marius** to win a convincing victory over the Barbarians. The battle took place near Aix. Established in 35 BC, the Roman colony of Orange welcomed the veterans of the Second Gallica. The town had a well-ordered urban plan, enhanced by public buildings and surrounded by fortifications which protected some 70ha/173 acres. It was at the head of a vast territory, which the Roman land surveyors laid out with precision. Lots were attributed with priority to the veterans, the next more mediocre lots were rented out to the highest bidders and the remaining lots belonged to the collectivity. In this way the Roman state encouraged colonisation and the development of land at the natives' expense. The land survey, revised several times, was posted publicly; several parts of it (in good condition) can be seen in the Musée Municipal *(see below)*. Until 412, the date the town was ransacked by the Visigoths, Orange prospered. Because it was a bishopric two synods took place here, one in 441 and the other in 529.

Dutch Orange – In the second half of the 12C, the town became the seat of a small principality in Comtat Venaissin. Through marriage and inheritance Orange ended up belonging to a branch of the Baux family, heir also to the German principality of Nassau. In the 16C the then prince of Orange and Nassau, William the Silent, transformed his fief into the United Provinces with himself as first stadtholder. At the same time, the town became Protestant and fell victim to the ravages of the Wars of Religion, but it succeeded in preserving its autonomy.

Orange is justly proud of the fact that the preferred title of the glorious royal dynasty of Holland is Prince or Princess of Orange; and its name has been given to a state, cities, rivers etc in South Africa and the USA.

While governing the Low Countries and even England, the House of Orange-Nassau did not forget its tiny enclave in France.

In 1622 Maurice of Nassau surrounded the town with strong ramparts and built a large castle. Unfortunately, for economic reasons as well as through lack of time, he took the stones necessary for his fortifications from the Roman ruins which had not been destroyed by the Barbarian invasions. This time nothing was left standing except the theatre, part of the ramparts and the triumphal arch which had been transformed into a fortress.

French Orange – During the war against Holland, Louis XIV coveted the Principality of Orange. It was the count of Grignan, lieutenant-general to the king in Provence and Mme de Sévigné's son-in-law, who captured the town. The ramparts were razed and the castle demolished. In 1713 the Treaty of Utrecht ceded Orange to France. At the Revolution, Orange was joined to the Drôme *département*, then to Bouches-du-Rhône and finally to Vaucluse.

The prosperous Roman town of Arausio became the main town of a canton.

ORANGE

République
  (R. de la) .... **BY** 9
St-Martin (R.) .... **AY** 13

Arc-de-Triomphe
  (Av. de l') .... **AY**
Artaud (Av. A.) .... **ABY**
Blanc (R. A.) .... **BZ**
Briand (Cours A.) .... **AYZ**
Caristie (R.) .... **BY** 2
Châteauneuf (R. de) .... **BZ** 4
Clemenceau (Pl. G.) .... **BY** 3
Concorde (R. de la) .... **BY**
Contrescarpe
  (R. de la) .... **BY**
Daladier (Bd E.) .... **ABY**
Fabre (Av. H.) .... **BY**
Frères-Mounet
  (Pl. des) .... **BY** 5
Guillaume-le-
  Taciturne (Av.) .... **BY**
Lacour (R.) .... **AY**
Leclerc (Av. Gén.) .... **BZ**
Levade (R. de la) .... **BY**
Mistral (Av. F.) .... **BY** 6
Noble (R. du.) .... **ABY**
Pourtoules (Cours) .... **BZ**
Pourtoules (R.) .... **BZ** 7
Princes-d'Orange-
  Nassau (Mtée des) .... **AZ**
République (Pl. de la) .... **BY** 8
Roch (R. Madeleine) .... **BZ** 10
St-Clément (R.) .... **AZ**
St-Florent (R.) .... **BY** 12
St-Jean (R.) .... **AY**
Tanneurs (R. des) .... **AY** 16
Thermes (Av. des) .... **AZ**
Tourre (R. de) .... **AZ** 20
Victor-Hugo (R.) .... **AY**

M   Musée municipal

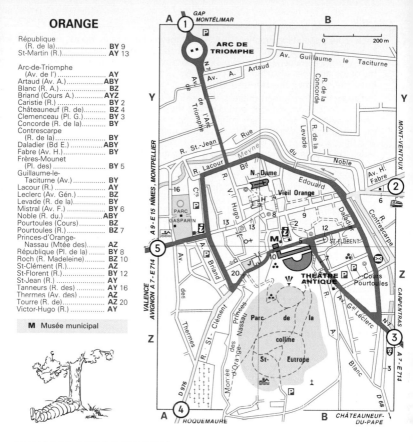

ROMAN MONUMENTS *2hr*

★★★ **Roman Theatre (Théâtre antique)** ⊙ (BZ) – The theatre has, justly so, been the pride
de of the city, as it is the best preserved not only in Provence but in the whole of
the Roman empire.

Each summer, within these walls, the Chorégies takes place. This is a high-quality
festival of music where notably great operas are performed.

Exterior – Built during Augustus' reign, the theatre has the same dimensions as the
theatre in Arles; the *cavea* (all of the tiers) was built onto a natural height which
allowed for a quicker and more economical construction. The formidable stage wall
(103m/338ft long and 36m/118ft high), which Louis XIV had qualified as the finest
wall of the kingdom, is the theatre's external façade.

Its upper storey was made up of two rows of corbels pierced with holes to hold
up the poles for the *velarium*, which shaded the spectators from the sun. Below,
19 blind arcades corresponded with rooms inside, corridors and staircases. In front
of it stood a portico 8m/26ft wide, the foundations of which can be seen.

The present-day square in front of the theatre was most probably occupied by a
garden encircled by a vast portico; the portico mentioned above was one of its
side walls.

Interior – *See illustration on p 38 under Art: Architectural Terms.* The building is
almost complete; however, the portico which crowned the top of the tiers, the
roof sheltering the stage and of course its decoration are missing.

The semicircle, the *cavea*, held up to 8-9000 spectators seated according to their
social station. It was divided into three sections of 37 tiers of seats and separated
by walls. Below, the orchestra was in the shape of a half circle; along it were three
low tiers of seats where movable seats were set up for the high-ranking citizens.
On either side of the stage, large rooms, one on top of the other (entrance is now
from the lower room, west side), were for receiving the public, and housed the
backstage.

The stage, with wooden flooring, under which the machinery was kept, measured
61m/200ft long and 9m/30ft wide of performing area; it was raised above the
orchestra by about 1.10m/3.5ft. It was held up by a low wall, *pulpitum*. Behind
was the curtain slot (the curtain was dropped during the performances).

The stage wall was as high as the topmost tier, and displayed a richly ornate decoration of marble facing, stucco, mosaics, several tiers of columns, and niches for
statues, including the imperial one of Augustus (3.55m/11ft) which was brought

back to its original location in 1951. The stage wall had three doors, each of which had a particular function. The main door in the centre was used by the actors for their entrances, whereas the two side doors were for the hosts. A roof protected the stage and was also useful acoustically.

From the top row one can hear someone speaking in the semicircle.

Performances – The Roman theatre was used as a hall for political meetings, lectures and concerts. Competitions and distribution of bread or money took place here. The shows were very varied: conjurors, bear-leaders, tight-rope walkers, illusionists, sword-swallowers, jugglers, acrobats, mimes and marionettes could be seen, and there were already cock fights.

When they became more elaborate – thus more costly – shows often included scenery and a number of walk-on parts. But the chief function of the theatre was the performance of comedies and tragedies.

And yet neither the plays nor their authors are known; it is believed that Greek plays were frequently performed but it seems they did not have much success with the Gallo-Roman audience. The more popular Roman comedies attracted large crowds, especially when a lot of scenery, accessories and actors were used.

There were also the performances inspired by mythology, in relation to the religious calendar.

In fact theatrical performances became licentious and in the 5C they were abolished under the influence of Christianity.

The actors, grouped in a troop financed by wealthy citizens, wore pasteboard masks. Each type of character: father, mother, daughter, young man, parasite, slave, tyrant etc had a distinctive mask; as soon as the masked actor entered, one knew what role he or she played. The tragic actors, to appear even more awesome, wore sandals with a thick cork sole.

All sorts of means were used to obtain perfect acoustics. The actors' masks amplified the voice; the large sloping roof over the stage threw the sound downwards, the upward curve of the seats received it smoothly, the colonnades broke up the echo and carefully graduated sounding-boards under the seats acted as loudspeakers. One detail will show how far these refinements were carried: the doors on the stage were hollow and made like violins inside. When an actor wished to amplify his voice he would stand against one of these sound-boxes.

Theatre district – Near the theatre, the excavations undertaken by Jules Formigé have uncovered the substructures of a temple and a mysterious building which ended in a semicircle parallel to the theatre *(access via the theatre)*.

In the centre of this semicircle, raised on a platform, stood a large temple, probably built under Hadrian (2C) on the site of a sacred spring; the podium and some vestiges remain.

A double staircase climbed 28m/92ft higher to a smaller second temple, which with its annexes occupied what is now the site of the city's reservoir. Overlooking the whole, it seems that an immense group of three temples (60m/197ft wide) stood on a rectangular platform extending east to west and supported on the north and west side by powerful buttresses. The magnificent perspective created in this way is not difficult to imagine.

Roman Theatre – Performance during Les Chorégies Festival

North Face

1) Fighting between Gauls and legionaries. Prisoners.
2) Naval accessories: prows, beaks of galleys, anchors, ropes, tridents.
3) Trophies: helmets, armour, javelins, military banners, flags.
4) Fruit, flowers, ancient ornamentation.
5) Coffered vaulting adorned with rosettes and various designs.

East Face

6) Trophies
7) Chained prisoners.

Arc de Triomphe, Orange

★★Arc de Triomphe (AY) – The arch stands on the north side of the city on the old Via Agrippa which linked Lyon to Arles. It ranks third among the Roman constructions of this type owing to its dimensions: 22m/72ft high, 21m/69ft wide and 8m/26ft deep. It is one of the best preserved, particularly the north face (the west has been restored). Built c 20 BC and dedicated later to Tiberius, the arch commemorated the campaigns of the II Legion.

It has three openings flanked by columns and displays two unusual architectural features: a pediment above the central opening and two attic storeys. It was surmounted at the time of its construction by a bronze quadriga (a chariot drawn by four horses harnessed abreast) flanked by two trophies.

Its exuberant decoration is linked to Roman classicism and the plastic beauty of the Hellenistic style. Note the scenes of battles and arms captured (**1, 3, 6, 7**), which recall the conquering of Gaul, and naval accessories (**2**) pertaining to Augustus' victory over Actium rather than to the fall of Marseille under Caesar.

ADDITIONAL SIGHTS

Colline St-Eutrope (St Eutrope Hill) (**BZ**) – *Drive up Montée des Princes-d'Orange-Nassau. Leave the car in the car park in front of the public gardens.*

The main avenue crosses the moat of the former castle of the Princes of Orange; the excavations (left of Square Reine-Juliana) have uncovered important ruins. At the far north end of the park, near a statue to the Virgin, there is a viewing table offering a beautiful view★ of the Roman theatre in the foreground, the city of Orange, the Marcoule nuclear power centre and the Rhône plain enclosed by mountains. On the left are ruins of the Roman capitol.

Musée Municipal ⊙ (**BYZ M**) – This museum displays in the courtyard and ground floor lapidary vestiges from the Roman monuments (no longer standing) and the castle of the Princes of Orange.

One gallery contains fragments (meticulously reconstructed) of the renowned Roman **land survey** of Orange *(see above)*, unique in France. On these marble tablets, the historians have identified the well-planned grid pattern (with its *cardo* and *decumanus*), the administrative subdivisions and topographical references (roads, mountains, rivers, swamps) and finally written information on the judicial and fiscal status of the land. The pieces found belong to three successive surveys: the first one dates from 77, the second from Trajan's reign (2C), the third is of a later date. The historians have been able to locate the site of the second survey: south of Montélimar to north of Orange, bounded to the west by the River Rhône and extending to the east probably as far as Vaison, and covering 836km²/323sq mi. Some of the land around Orange still clearly shows the influence of the Roman subdivisions.

The museum's other rooms are devoted to the history of Orange, local traditions, painting, and the making of printed fabrics in 18C Orange.

Ancienne Cathédrale Notre-Dame (**ABY**) – This Romanesque building was very badly damaged during the Wars of Religion and the majority of it had to be rebuilt. Carvings of Antique influence decorate the southern porch.

Vieil Orange (**ABY**) – The streets of the old town centre are very animated and pleasant to stroll along. Start at the Roman theatre, taking Rue Caristie and the streets around the town hall (17C belfry) and cathedral, which end in lovely Provençal squares with their café terraces shaded by plane trees.

EXCURSIONS

Caderousse – *6km/3.5mi by* ⑤ *on the map,D 17*. This village is located on the banks of the Rhône and has often been subject to flooding. On the town hall's façade left of the door, four plaques indicate the level reached by the rise of the floodwaters.

Since 1856 a dike has protected the village from the floodwaters; ramparts encircle the whole village and only two doors open at the cardinal points.

Église St-Michel – The church is in the Provençal Romanesque style. Inside, south of the chancel, Chapelle St-Claude in the Flamboyant style was added in the 16C; its vaulting is lovely.

Harmas Jean-Henri-Fabre ⊙ – *8km/5mi by* ⑤ *on the map, N 7 and D 576*. At the entrance of **Sérignan-du-Comtat** stands the house of **Jean-Henri Fabre**, the famous entomologist (1823-1915) who lived here for the last 36 years of his life. The visit includes the scientist's office, where display cases contain his own collections: insects, shells, fossils, minerals, and a gallery in which his watercolours (mushrooms of the region) are hung. A tour of the land around his house, which was his main field of observation and has become a botanical garden, ends the visit.

Aven d'ORGNAC★★

Michelin map 80 fold 9 or 245 fold 14 or 246 fold 23
Local map see Gorges de l'ARDÈCHE

The great hole in the ground was known to the local people, who paid little attention to it until 19 August 1935, when the speleologist **Robert de Joly** (1887-1968) made an initial exploration. The engineer and speleologist, who explored his native Cévennes, also played an important role in improving the equipment and techniques used in underground exploration *(see Aven de MARZAL)*.

This cave is fascinating because of the natural development of underground streams, fed by infiltration and through fissures in the calcareous rock *(see p 11)*. The first concretions, which were at times 10m/33ft in diameter, were broken by a major earthquake at the end of the Tertiary Era. These columns, broken or turned upside down, served as a base for more recent stalagmites.

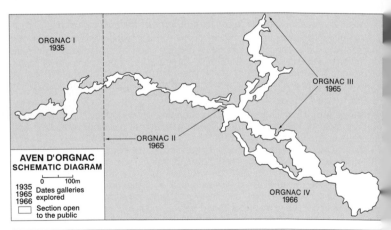

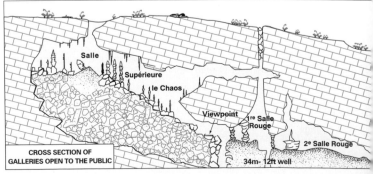

Aven d'Orgnac – Stalagmites in the Salle Supérieure

TOUR ⊙ *allow 1hr (788 steps) – Interior temperature 13°C/55°F*

The **Salle Supérieure** (Upper Chamber), in which there is a vast cone of rubble, is astonishing in its dimensions and perspectives. The dim light which comes from the cave's natural opening illuminates the chamber with a strange bluish light: 17-40m/58-131ft high, 250m/820ft long and 125m/410ft wide, this chamber contains magnificent stalagmites. The largest are in the middle: a number of growths give them the shape of pine cones. Unable, due to the height of the vault, to join the stalactites to form pillars, the stalagmites have thickened at the base and become quite large; other more recent and thinner stalagmites have piled on top of them like a stack of plates. Along the walls of the chamber, note the delicate columns which came after the earthquake; some are very tall, either in bayonet-shape or standing very straight. In the niche of a concretion shaped like a cupboard is an urn containing the heart of Robert de Joly. In **Le Chaos** (Chaos Chamber), encumbered by concretions which have fallen in from the Salle Supérieure, magnificent curtains of varied colours can be glimpsed from a fissure in the vault.

On a level with the viewpoint of the **Première Salle Rouge** (First Red Chamber), the water filtering in, enriched with carbonate of lime through the calcareous layer, has encouraged the formation of a mass of concretions. Nearby is the well, the deepest in the cave at 34m/112ft which leads into another chamber 180m/591ft deep.

Musée de Préhistoire ⊙ – Rooms arranged around a patio contain the discoveries of excavations carried out in the Ardèche and the north of the Gard regions. The exhibits date from the Lower Paleolithic Age to the Iron Age, that is from 350 000 to 750 BC. Reconstructions (Acheulean hut from Orgnac III, flint knapping workshop, Lion's Head decorated cave) introduce visitors to the way of life of prehistoric man.

On a town plan, the sights are indicated in orange. Some names appear on the map, others can be found by using the co-ordinates given in the caption below.

ORGON

Population 2 453

Michelin map 81 fold 12 or 245 fold 30 or 246 fold 12

7km/4mi south of Cavaillon – Local map see Les ALPILLES

Orgon, crossed by N 7, lies in the Durance plain. It overlooks the ridge which separates the Alpilles to the west and the Montagne du Luberon to the east.

Napoleon's woes – Fleeing Avignon in April 1814, **Napoleon Bonaparte**, on his way to exile on the island of Elba, stopped at an inn in Orgon. A hostile crowd, alerted by the Royalist drummers, gathered. The excited mob wanted to lynch him but he was saved by the mayor of Orgon and fled. He was able to reach the Auberge de La Calade near Aix.

Church (Église) – 14C. The choir and nave are slightly out of alignment; the chapels were added in the 17C. On the nave's north side hang fine 14C painted panels.

Chapelle Notre-Dame-de-Beauregard – Crowning the hill overlooking the town to the south *(road subject to restrictions)*, the chapel's terrace presents a fine view of the Durance valley, Luberon mountains, and Côtes chain.

Bois de PAÏOLIVE★

Michelin map 80 fold 8 or 240 fold 7

This limestone area of Bas Vivarais stretches over about 16km²/6sq mi southeast of Les Vans on either side of the Chassezac. The ground consists of grey Jurassic limestone (Secondary Era), which is both hard and permeable, making it resistant to wind and weather erosion but susceptible to rain water, full of carbonic acid, which has enlarged the fissures into deep defiles and remoulded the rocks into strange forms. Elsewhere residual rock has turned to clay and encouraged the growth of vegetation (especially the common oak).

Jalès and the Royalists – The basin stretching southeast of Vans, on either side of the village of Jalès, is closely linked to a dramatic period in France's counter-revolutionary history. Between 1790 and 1792, nostalgic followers of the Ancien Régime would congregate at the Château de Jalès. At the time the Civil Constitution of the Clergy was being implemented and this served to accentuate the divide as many nonjuring bishops ended up supporting the Royalists. On 21 June 1792, the revolutionary cockade was trampled underfoot at Berrias. Hailed as the leader of the Royalist movement in the area, the **Comte de Saillans**, whose family originally came from the Dauphiné, precipitated the date of the uprising. However, his plot was exposed. A troup of soldiers sent to defeat Saillans' men overcame them not far from Courry *(18km/11mi south of Vans)* on 11 July. Saillans took refuge at the Château de Banne, then decided to flee the area with a group of his comrades-in-arms. They were arrested on the road to Villefort and taken to Vans: the crowds, who blamed Saillans for the execution of several "patriots", murdered him and his friends in the street. It is said that a few Royalists succeeded in escaping to the Bois de Païolive, where they probably died of hunger.

TOUR *allow 2hr*

D 252 crosses the woods west to east.

About 300m/328yd from D 901 and some 20m/21yd off to the right coming from Les Vans stand the rocks known locally as L'Ours (The Bear) and Le Lion (The Lion).

★**Clairière** – A clearing is accessible to cars near D 252 in a right hand bend coming from Les Vans, up an unsurfaced ramp. It is established on a *doline* or sinkhole (picnic area).

★★**Corniche du Chassezac** – *45min return on foot. Take the trail to the left, which is an extension of D 252 coming from Les Vans and passes under a telephone wire (leave on the left another trail also passing underneath the telephone wire).*

A short walk away, Casteljau Manor-house, flanked by two corner towers of the same height, can be seen in the distance. Continue along the trail using the manor-house as a guide, the silhouette of which becomes more defined.

After a couple of hundred feet the trail branches slightly off to the left, heading still towards the manor house. After less than 10 minutes' walk you suddenly come upon the

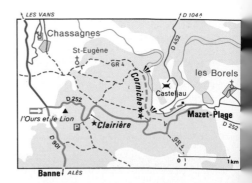

grandiose Chassezac gorge winding past below, at the foot of the cave-pitted cliffs. The footpath, a sheer drop of 80m/262ft above the water, leads to the left, opposite the manor-house, to a viewpoint located upstream.

Return by the way you came or, for those who like to walk, by the trails marked on the map right.

Mazet-Plage – *A surfaced path off D 252 leads 300m/328yd to a couple of houses along the river bank.*

Walk along the Chassezac, going towards the left for about 500m/0.3mi along the shingle beach with its small willows opposite the unusual cave-pitted cliffs *(15 return on foot).*

Banne – *6km/3.5mi from the crossroads of D 901 and D 252. Leave the car in the square; climb up the slope behind the Calvary.*

The path leads to a platform overlooking the Jalès depression. From the top, where the ruins of Banne's old citadel lie, there is a vast **panorama**★ extending from the River Gard to the lower Ardèche. Half-buried in the platform's southwest side a long vaulted gallery can be seen, which served as Banne castle's stables.

PERNES-LES-FONTAINES

Population 8 304
Michelin map 81 folds 12 and 13 or 245 fold 17 or 246 fold 11

The town located on the border of the Vaucluse plateau was once the capital of Comtat Venaissin (968-1320) before Carpentras. It was the home town of **Fléchier** (1632-1710), one of the best orators of the late 17C; his funeral orations included those for Turenne and Marie-Thérèse of Austria.
The town gets its name from the 36 or so fountains, in which it takes great pride. These decorate the numerous squares of its urban districts. Most of them were built in the middle of the 18C, following the discovery of a large spring near Chapelle St-Roch. The older fountains have thus since been restored.
Like most of the towns on the Vaucluse plateau, Pernes les Fontaines has canning factories. Fruit – cherries, strawberries, melons, grapes – is especially abundant in the region.

OLD TOWN *1hr*

Leave the car in front of the Tourist Information Centre or on Cours Frizet.
This walk includes the main sights in Pernes, but the network of pretty little streets offers ample opportunity for a longer stroll.

Porte de Villeneuve – This gate is a remnant of the 16C fortifications and is flanked by two round, machicolated towers.
On the corner of Rue Gambetta and Rue de la République, notice the 16C **Hôtel de Vichet** (**V**) with its doorway surmounted by an elegant wrought iron balcony. The nuns of Christian retreat, who occupy the mansion, make the eucharistic host which is then sent all over France and the French-speaking countries of Africa.

Tour Ferrande ⊘ (**F**) – This square crenellated 13C tower, hemmed in between the houses, overlooks a small square which contains the Guilhaumin, or "Gigot", fountain. The origin of the tower is subject to speculation; it may have once belonged to a military religious order.
Go up a narrow staircase to the third floor, which is decorated with beautiful 13C frescoes depicting the Virgin and Child, St Christopher, and retracing the epic adventures of Charles of Anjou in southern Italy.

Tour de l'Horloge ⊘ (**D**) – This keep was once part of the fortified wall which protected the castle of the Counts of Toulouse, of which nothing now remains. In the 18C this tower had an elegant wrought-iron bell cage added to the top of it. From the top of the clock tower there is a **sweeping panorama** to the west over the Comtat plain and the countryside around Avignon; in the background, to the north and east, the Dentelles de Montmirail, Mont Ventoux and the Vaucluse mountains can be seen against the skyline.

★**Porte Notre-Dame** – This 16C gate precedes an old corbelled bridge spanning the River Nesque. On one of the bridge's piles is the small 16C chapel of Notre-Dame-des-Grâces (**B**). On the left is the 17C covered market.

Fontaine du Cormoran (**E**) – This, the most interesting of the fountains in Pernes, owes its name to the cormorant with outspread wings which is perched on top of it. The base is decorated with low reliefs and masks.

Notre-Dame-de-Nazareth – The oldest parts of the church date from the late 11C. The south porch opens through a lovely door (in bad condition) inspired by Antiquity. Inside, the pointed barrel vaulted nave is adorned with a cornice, and there are Gothic chapels.

PERNES-LES-FONTAINES

Barreau (R.)	2
Brancas (R. de)	3
Briand (Pl. Aristide)	4
Corti (Pl. et Square D.)	5
Gambetta (R.)	6
Giraud (Pl. L.)	7
Mistral (Pl. F.)	8
Neuve (R.)	9
Notre-Dame (Pont)	10
Notre-Dame (R. Porte)	12
Raspail (R.)	13
République (R. de la)	15
Victor-Hugo (R.)	16
Zola (R. E.)	19

B	Chapelle Notre-Dame-des-Grâces
D	Tour de l'Horloge
E	Fontaine du Cormoran
F	Tour Ferrande
H	Hôtel de ville
L	Fontaine Reboul
N	Hôtel de Jocas
R	Fontaine de l'Hôpital
S	Hôtel de Villefranche
V	Hôtel de Vichet

Seen from the church parvis, Notre-Dame gate, the chapel, the bridge and the clock tower, to the right, make a charming picture.

Cross the River Nesque once more through Porte Notre-Dame and go up Rue Raspail. On the way, notice the **Fontaine Reboul (L)**, dating from the end of the 17C and also known as the "Grand' Font" (Big Fount), with its fish-scale ornamentation. Further along, set back on the right, there is the **Hôtel de Jocas (N)** with its beautiful Louis XV doorway.

Porte de St-Gilles – This square tower was part of the 14C fortifications. It still has its machicolations.

Go into the courtyard of the Hôtel de Ville (town hall) via Place Aristide-Briand.

Hôtel de Ville (H) – This 17C mansion once belonged to the Dukes of Brancas, one of whom was Maréchal de France and the ambassador of Louis XIV in Spain. The courtyard is further enhanced by a striking fountain and its vast portico (1750), set against a wall.

Come out of the town hall on the side of Rue de Brancas and turn left into Place Louis-Giraud. On one side of this square the 19C Augustine church, now a cultural centre, can be seen. Carry on along Rue Barreau, which leads into Place de la République.

Fontaine de l'Hôpital (R) – This fountain dates from 1760 and draws its name from its position opposite the Hôtel des Ducs de Berton, seigneurs of Crillon (17C), which was once a hospital.

Rue de la République, with the 17C **Hôtel de Villefranche (S)** set back to the left, leads back to the start of the walk.

ADDITIONAL SIGHT

Croix Couverte – This elegant quadrangular monument, pierced by four ogival openings, is thought to have been built in the 15C by Pierre de Boët of Pernes.

PEYROLLES-EN-PROVENCE

Population 2 918

Michelin map 84 folds 3 and 4 or 114 fold 16 or 245 fold 32

Local map see Basse Vallée de la DURANCE

Located in the valley, Peyrolles extends along the EDF Canal which drains part of the River Durance. All that is left of the medieval fortifications are a belfry crowned by a wrought-iron bell cage and a round tower (in ruins) near the church.

Château – *To visit the château and chapel, contact the town hall.* This former residence of King René was converted into a lofty mansion during the late 17C. The main building is approached by a courtyard of honour and currently houses the town hall. The interior features a somewhat grand sweeping staircase and 18C gypsum furnishings. From the east terrace, overlooking the main building and decorated with a fountain portraying a gladiator, there is a pretty view of the Durance valley.

Église St-Pierre ⊘ – Despite having been remodelled many times in the 15C and 17C, this church still has its original Romanesque pointed barrel-vaulted nave.

Chapelle du St-Sépulcre – This 12C chapel can be found nestling on a rocky spur, its plan is based on a Greek cross with a touch of Oriental influence. Four oven-vaulted apsidal chapels frame a square surmounted by a small bell gable. The wall frescoes depict the *Creation of Adam and Eve* (above the doorway) and a procession of saints with haloes (left apsidal chapel). Sketches of sailing boats, thought to be ex-votos dating from the Middle Ages, adorn the inside walls.

PONT DU GARD★★★

This aqueduct, one of the wonders of the Ancient world, is certainly worth a journey. It is part of a system which brought spring water from a catchment area near Uzès to Nîmes; it was built c 19 BC and in spite of its 2 000 years is in very good condition.

Aqueduct – The Romans attached a great deal of importance to the quality of the water which they required for even the smallest town. The water was collected prefer- ably on the north slope so that it did not heat up in the reservoirs. The water channel was made entirely of stone, either vaulted or tiled and pierced with openings only for ventilation and maintenance. Some aqueducts were equipped with settling tanks. The contours of the land were crossed with exceptional engineering skill – the aqueduct followed its course via bridges, ditches, tunnels and siphons. The aqueduct of Nîmes, some 50km/31mi long, had an average incline of 34cm per km or 1:300, falling more steeply just before the valley to reduce the height of the bridge. Its daily flow was about 20 000 m³/44 million gallons.

Whenever Nîmes was besieged - a common occurrence - the aqueduct was breached. From the 4C it ceased to be maintained, so that lime deposits built up, until finally by the 9C the course had become blocked and it had fallen into disuse. Land holders along the course thereupon began to remove the dressed stones for their own use. In 1743 a road bridge was added downstream of the aqueduct.

★**Bridge (Pont)** – The aqueduct spans the Gardon valley. The golden coloured tone of the old stones harmonises beautifully with the surrounding countryside.

It is composed of colossal dressed blocks of masonry, some weighing as much as 6t, which were laid without mortar, the courses being held together with iron clamps. The stone was lifted into position by block and tackle with goats as auxiliaries and a winch worked by a massive human treadmill.

In order to break the sense of monotony the three levels of arches are recessed, the piers in line one above another. Statistical details are: height above the Gardon at low water: 49m/160ft; lowest level: 6 arches, 142m long, piers 6m thick, arches 22m high (465ft, 20ft, 72ft); middle level: 11 arches, 242 m long, piers 4m thick, arches 20m high (792ft, 13ft, 65ft); top level, the one carrying the canal: 35 arches, 275m long, piers 3m thick, arches 7m high (900ft, 10ft, 23ft). The bridge was restored under Napoleon III. The architect varied the span of the arches very slightly within each range; each arch was constructed independently to give flexibility in the event of subsidence. The stones obtruding from the face were scaffolding supports, and were left not only to facilitate maintenance work but to add interest to the surface, as do the ridges on the piers which held the semicircular wooden frames on which the arches were constructed.

TOUR ⊙

Cars are not allowed on the aqueduct during July and August. During the rest of the year the traffic flows one way from the north bank to the south bank. There is a path across the bridge for pedestrians.

Pont du Gard

Access ⓥ – *Either via the south bank, leaving the car in the municipal car park alongside D 981 downstream of the bridge, or via the north bank, leaving the car in the private car park. Be careful not to take any valuables with you – do not leave them unattended in your car. The walk (1hr) described below begins from the south bank, however, it is possible to begin it from the north bank.*

Passing a shelter beneath a rock, follow the little path which leads under the bridge. The aqueduct can be seen from the banks of the Gardon. After the St-Privat domain *(nature reserve not open to the public)* retrace your steps to take a zigzag path on the right. From a bend there is a superb **view★★** of the aqueduct, with the village of Castillon framed in one of its arches. Continue along this path until you are level with the top of the bridge *(temporarily closed to the public)*. Under normal circumstances it is possible to walk across the bridge itself, either in one of the channels (which chalk deposits have blocked in places) – a perfectly safe crossing, but one which has no view, or preferably across the flagstones which cover the channel – a much more pleasant crossing, but one which is not recommended to those who suffer from vertigo.

Continue along the footpath which leads under the final span to join D 981 downstream of the bridge.

Along the river – *Hire of canoe or kayak for trips to the Pont du Gard (30min or 1hr) or the Gardon gorges (a half or a whole day – see description under Les GARRIGUES). It is essential to be a good swimmer.*

PONT-ST-ESPRIT

Population 9 277
Michelin map 80 fold 10 or 245 fold 15 or 246 fold 23
Local map see Gorges de l'ARDÈCHE

The town owes its existence and name to the bridge built in 1265-1309 by the Bridge Brotherhood under the protection of the Holy Spirit (Saint Esprit); it subsequently became an important halting-place on the Rhône.

SIGHTS

Park the car at the end of Allées Jean-Jaurès

Take **Rue St-Jacques** (**25**), lined with old houses: the 17C Hôtel de Roubin (**B**) at no 10 and especially the **Maison des Chevaliers** (Knights' Mansion – **M²**) at no 2, a former private residence belonging to the Piolenc, a renowned family of merchants from the Rhône valley, who lived on the premises between the 12C and 1988. This townhouse, enhanced by a pretty gemelled bay window in the Romanesque style, is home to the Musée d'Art Sacré du Gard.

Musée d'Art Sacré du Gard ⓥ (**M²**) – The Museum of Sacred Art is set up in the Maison des Chevaliers (Knights' Mansion), whose splendid rooms are laid out around an inner courtyard. The two superimposed ceremonial chambers of **Guillaume de Piolenc** feature lavish ornamentation consisting of French-style ceilings painted with crested escutcheons. The ground floor room presents a fine collection of religious paintings from the 16C and 17C. On the first floor, in a room whose walls are decorated with diamond motifs, note *The Adoration of the Magi* by Nicolas Dipre (c 1495). The **Royal Court of Justice★** on the first floor, whose vaulting rests on a 14C rafter in painted wood, houses a retable by the Provençal Primitive painter **Raymond Boterie**, illustrating *The Fall of the Angels* (1509-10). Visitors may also admire a former apothecary's surgery and the pharmacy of the St-Esprit Hospital (jars coming from early 18C pottery workshops in Montpellier, including an outstanding collection of medieval ceramic pieces of Hispano-Moorish inspiration).

The purpose of this **Museum of Sacred Art** is to enlighten the general public on France's religious heritage by presenting and explaining sacred rites and by commenting on the representation of religion in art, while at the same time adopting a secular approach. As soon as you enter the courtyard, you can admire a poignant polychrome sculpture from the 17C, *Christ in Agony*. On the ground floor, a sacristy displaying various sacred articles for celebrating Mass (a vermeil chalice and patera from the Languedoc area, 1650) stands alongside a collection of clerical garments (interactive terminal showing a priest donning his robes before celebrating Mass; explanations are then given about the actual proceedings of a religious service). The rooms at garden level encourage visitors to reflect on the meaning of sacred issues, which contribute to reinforcing social cohesion, and on the role of the Bible today in a world characterised by scientific progress. On the first floor, an educational area with interactive terminals presents a brief architectural history of the Maison des Chevaliers and touches on the subject of religious art collections. The old tower dominating the garden is devoted to 18C-19C *santons* and cribs. The visits ends with a display of household reliquaries, including a few *paperolles* – paintings consisting of rolled sheets of paper that form a decor framing the relics.

PONT-ST-ESPRIT

Haut-Mazeau (R.)	9
Joliot-Curie (R.)	
Minimes (R. des)	
Mistral (Allées F.)	15
République (Pl. de la)	21
St-Jacques (R.)	25
Allègre-Chemin (Bd)	2
Ancienne mairie (Pl. de)	3
Bas-Mazeau (R.)	4
Bruguier-Roure (R. L.)	5
Couvent (R. du)	6
Doumergue (Av. G.)	7
Gaulle (Av. du Gén.-de-)	8
Jaurès (Allées J.)	10
Jemmapes (R.)	12
Paroisse (R. de la)	17
Plan (Pl. du)	18
St-Pierre (Pl.)	26
Ville (Pl. Georges)	27
19-Mars-1962 (R. du)	28

B Hôtel de Roubin
K Maison du Roy
M¹ Musée Paul-Raymond
M² Maison des Chevaliers
(Musée d'art sacré
du Gard)
N Ancienne collégiale
du Plan

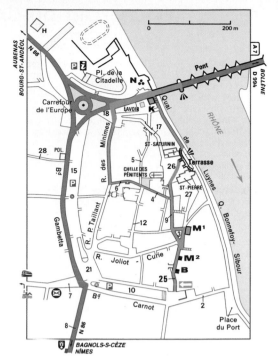

Musée Paul-Raymond ⊙ (**M¹**) – Set up in the former town hall, this museum is laid out over two levels and presents the work of the painter Benn (1905-1989), dedicated to a number of religious themes. It forms a perfect complement to the Museum of Sacred Art mentioned above. In the basement lies the town's former ice-house (1780).

Take Rue Haut-Mazeau to reach Place St-Pierre.

Terrasse – This terrace lies on the east side of Place St-Pierre and is bounded to the north by the 15C parish church, to the southwest by the Baroque façade of the Chapelle des Pénitents and to the southeast by the former 17C Église St-Pierre (now deconsecrated) topped by a dome. From the terrace there is a good overall view of the bridge.

A monumental double flight of stairs leads to Quai de Luynes. Left, almost at the foot of the bridge, the Maison du Roy (**K**) is pierced by Renaissance windows.

Pont – The bridge, nearly 1 000m/3 281ft long, is slightly curved upstream against the current; 19 of the 25 arches are old. It used to be defended at either end with bastions and two towers in the middle – this whole defensive system has been destroyed.

To facilitate navigation – the passage through the bridge had, over the centuries, always been feared by sailors – the bridge's first two arches were replaced by one arch (it was subsequently destroyed during the Second World War and rebuilt in reinforced concrete).

From the bridge there is a fine view of the Rhône and the town. North of the bridge, where there is now a vast terrace, the citadel once stood; it was built in 1595 and fortified by Vauban in the 17C. From the centre of the terrace the view extends to the 15C Flamboyant doorway of the former Plan collegiate church (**N**). Take the stairs for a better look at the door's details (partly uncovered).

Cross the intersection and then take old Rue des Minimes and turn left on Rue du Couvent; continue along Rue Bas-Mazeau, Rue Haut-Mazeau and Rue St-Jacques to the car.

*The current edition of the annual **Michelin Red Guide France** offers a selection of pleasant and quiet hotels in convenient locations. Their amenities are included (swimming pools, tennis courts, private beaches and gardens...) as well as their dates of annual closure. The selection also includes establishments which offer excellent cuisine: carefully prepared meals at reasonable prices, **Michelin stars** for good cooking.*
*The current annual **Michelin Camping Caravaning France** lists the facilities offered by many camp sites (shops, bars, restaurants, laundries, games rooms, tennis courts, miniature golf courses, playgrounds, swimming pools...).*

ROCHEFORT-DU-GARD

Population 4 107
Michelin maps 80 fold 20 or 245 folds 15 and 16 or 246 fold 25

This hanging village with its steep little streets and small shaded squares is a lovely place for a stroll. In 1825 the town hall was set up in St-Joseph's chapel, which was built in 1733. The 19C fountain opposite is surmounted by a triangular pediment and decorated with geometric designs.

All that remains of the "castellas" originally to the east of the village is the looming white silhouette of the Romanesque chapel. The **view★** from the platform stretches over Notre-Dame-de-Grâce sanctuary, the dried-up lake of Pujaut and the mountains in the background.

EXCURSION

Sanctuaire Notre-Dame-de-Grâce ⊙ – *2km-just over a mile northeast. Leave Rochefort on D 976 towards Roquemaure. After 700m/765yd take a small road uphill on the left.*

On a hillock at the edge of Rochefort forest stands Notre-Dame-de-Grâce sanctuary. Built on the site of a Benedictine priory founded in 798, ravaged in the 18C and restored in the 19C by the Marist Fathers, the sanctuary has housed an almshouse since 1964.

In the sparsely-decorated chapel note the lovely wrought-iron grille closing off the chancel; the altar in polychrome marble is surmounted by a statue of Our Lady of Grace.

By the entrance to the chancel, on the south pillar, hangs an ex-voto (1666), which was offered by Anne of Austria for the birth in 1638 of the future Louis XIV, after 23 years of childless marriage. In a room off the chapel more than 100 ex-votos (naïve religious paintings) from the 17C-20C are exhibited. In the cloisters the echo chamber enabled the priest to hear the confessions of lepers: two people stand in opposite corners facing the wall; when they speak quietly, they can hear each other distinctly.

Go around the reception office on the south side and take the Way of the Cross.

From the terrace there is a lovely **view★** of the Lance mountains, Mont Ventoux, the Vaucluse plateau, the Montagnette and the Alpilles, and the Rhône valley.

Ex-votos can be seen in the following churches and basilicas: Notre-Dame-de-la-Garde in Marseille *(p 187)*, Chapelle St-Jean-de-Garguier *(p 95)*, Notre-Dame-de-Lumières *(p 172)* and Notre-Dame-de-Grâce in Rochefort-du-Gard *(see above)*.

Ex-Votos in Provence

A common occurrence in Provence, ex-votos are naïve religious paintings found in churches or other places of worship: they are seen as an act of thanksgiving or an offering for a wish to be fulfilled. During the 17C, the production of ex-votos increased quite considerably: they were often gifts made by noblemen, bourgeois or penitents, a gesture strongly motivated by Counter-Reformation views. Indeed, this is evidenced by the graphics: human prayers feature prominently and representations of the Virgin are scarce. Although most Provençal ex-votos are painted, on the coast they usually take the shape of a miniature ship.

La ROQUE-SUR-CÈZE★

Population 153
Michelin map 80 fold 9 or 245 fold 15 or 246 fold 24

The village appears grouped around its Romanesque chapel on a hilltop darkly plumed by cypresses. An old arched bridge with pointed cutwaters spans the River Cèze. To those approaching from the north on D 980 the **site★** is a true feast for the eyes.

★Cascade du Sautadet – This waterfall is unique in the way it cuts deeply into the river bed and for the complicated network of crevasses in which the Cèze runs.

Arriving at La Roque-sur-Cèze via D 980 and D 166, cross the bridge and take the path on the north bank.

Blocking the river's route, the limestone rock was attacked by the water, which carved rifts and potholes into it. This unique amalgam of natural features (potholes, small falls, pools) is the Sautadet.

Continue beyond the abandoned mill-race to the deeper ravines plumbed by the River Cèze; from the southern end there is a lovely view.

ROUSSILLON ★

Population 1 165
Michelin map 81 fold 13 or 245 folds 18 and 31 or 246 fold 11
Local map see APT: Ochre Tour – Facilities

The village stands on an unusual **site★** on the highest of the hills between Coulon valley and Vaucluse plateau. These striking hills, composed of ochre rock of 16 or 17 different shades featured in the local houses, enhance the village and the surrounding countryside. *For information on ochre see p 15.*

ROUSSILLON

Abbé-Avon (Pl. de l')	2
Burlière (Av. de la)	3
Casteau (R.)	4
Église (R. de l')	5
Eynard (Pl. J.)	6
Forge (Pl. de la)	7
Lauriers (R. des)	8
Mairie (Pl. de la)	9
Mathieu (Pl. C.)	12
Pignotte (Pl.)	14

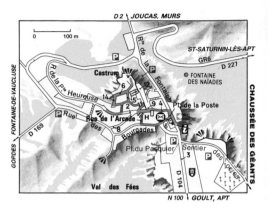

★THE VILLAGE

Start from the Tourist Information Centre and turn left into Rue Casteau, a shopping street. Go past the tower of the belfry to reach Rue de l'Église and then the Castrum.

Castrum – *Viewing-table.* From this platform the view extends northwards to Vaucluse plateau and the white crest of Mont Ventoux, southwards to the Coulon valley and Grand Luberon.

Go via Place Pignotte to reach the far end of the watchpath, from where there is a lovely view of the **Aiguilles du Val des Fées** (Needles of Fairies' Valley), vertical clefts in an ochre cliff-face. Turn back past the belfry and take Rue de l'Arcade, a pretty, narrow stepped street which is partially covered.

Rue des Bourgades leads back to the start of the walk.

★★CHAUSSÉE DES GÉANTS

45min return on foot. Start from the Chaussée des Géants car park and turn left on the first surfaced path.

From the first platform a lovely view of the village and its site opens out. Continue on the path, passing a cemetery on the left to the cliff's edge for a view onto the Giants' Causeway, jagged rust-red cliffs, relieved by a scattering of pines and evergreen oaks.

Site Archéologique de ST-BLAISE

Michelin map 84 fold 11 or 245 fold 43 or 246 fold 13

With the sea, the River Rhône, the Étang de Berre as well as other small lagoons and the vast Crau plain not far away, the *oppidum* of St-Blaise (in the *commune* of St-Mitre-les-Remparts) is a historic site, the wealth of which depended, during the Hellenic occupation, on the working and trading of salt. After being abandoned for some 400 years, it was reoccupied between the 4C and the 14C.

TOUR ⏱ *45min*

Leave the car in the car park and climb a path on the left to the medieval wall surrounding the excavations.

On the left stands the small chapel of St-Blaise (12C-13C) and adjacent to it a 17C hermitage.

Ancient St-Blaise – The settlement of St-Blaise (its ancient name has not been identified; it could be Heraclea or Mastramellè) takes the form of a fortified spur, the natural defences of which, huge vertical cliffs, are reinforced by ramparts from the Hellenistic period; these were built on the most accessible side which overlooks Lavalduc valley.

The oldest traces of human existence date back to early 5 000 BC. The group of small lagoons which link the east arm of the River Rhône to Berre lagoon most probably contributed to the discovery of the site by Etruscan sailors in the 7C BC.

225

They established a trading post and began a successful trade: exchanging salt collected here for wine from Etruria. The settling of the Phocaeans at Marseille in c 600 BC brought about serious competition between St-Blaise and Marseille; nevertheless the discovery of Etruscan, Corinthian and Ionian pottery has proved that the settlement progressed.

In the second half of the 7C, the settlement formed a proto-urban town surrounded by a wall. Like Entremont, a lower and an upper town were established. The dwellings were built of stone on a square plan; one in the lower town still has its walls at a height of 0.9m/35in.

A long period of transition (475-200 BC) then took place, after a fire, marked by the departure of the Etruscans from the trading post, and Marseille took over. It has been suggested that there was a possible period of withdrawal judging from the absence of human dwellings.

From the late 3C to the mid 1C BC the settlement reached its apex: commerce picked up under the influence of Marseille which held St-Blaise without, however, making it a colony.

Large projects for levelling of the terrain preceded the establishment of an urban plan and a strong fortified wall. The lower town was built on a regular grid plan where the squaring off formed island-like units; the façades were all lined up, the streets rectilinear (sometimes with a pavement) and the small dwellings were made up of two, three or four rooms. The commercial and small-scale production-related activities have left a great number of vestiges: cellars full of urns, metal-founder's workshop etc. St-Blaise, thus, played the role of store-house.

The very high **Hellenistic ramparts**★ were raised under the direction of Greek craftsmen between 175 and 140 BC; they are more than 1km/0.5mi long and cut by towers and bastions, equipped with three posterns and a gateway and crowned at the top with merlons. The wall was equipped with a system of water evacuation via channels. It had hardly been finished when the settlement underwent a violent siege (dozens of cannonballs have been discovered) which the historians are seeking to date. According to a recent theory, St-Blaise, a salt trade centre, having escaped the control of Marseille a short time after the ramparts were completed, may have been taken over by the Romans during their conquest from 125 to 123 BC. After this event, St-Blaise went through a period of total decline; after its brief reoccupation in the mid 1C BC the site was totally abandoned for four centuries. Besides the Hellenistic constructions, St-Blaise has also revealed the presence of a native sanctuary similar to the ones found at Roquepertuse, Entremont and Glanum: a building in the form of a portico with skulls, votive steles and so on.

Paleochristian and Medieval St-Blaise – Before the rise of insecurity at the end of the Roman empire, the old settlement was once again inhabited. The Hellenistic fortifications were reused: in the 5C the wall was surmounted by an ornamentation of irregular blocks of stone. Two churches were built: St-Vincent (the apse of which is near the ancient main gate) and St-Pierre (destroyed in the 9C). A necropolis (tombs carved into the living rock) extended to the south. The living quarters of this settlement were unfortunately difficult to identify among the other ruins. In 874, Ugium (the name of the settlement at that time) was destroyed by the Saracens. It recovered slowly, St-Pierre was rebuilt in the 10C, then burned down, then reconstructed again in the 11C (substructures have been found near the chapel of St-Blaise). In 1231, at the plateau's northernmost point a new wall was built to protect the town of Castelveyre (its new name) with its new church Notre-Dame-et-St-Blaise around which the dwellings nestled.

In 1390 Raymond de Turenne's band of brigands pillaged the town. The site was never to be resettled; the last inhabitants settled at St-Mitre. At the end of the spur, a fine view of the Étang de Lavalduc and the Bassins de Fos opens out *(see Bassins de FOS)*.

ST-GILLES ★

Population 11 304
Michelin map 83 fold 9 or 245 fold 28 or 246 fold 26
Local map see La CAMARGUE– Facilities

Gateway to Camargue, and of agricultural importance (fruit, Costières wines), St-Gilles' claim to fame is the old abbey church, the west front of which considerably influenced Romanesque sculpture in Provence *(see Introduction: Art)* and in the Rhône valley.

St Giles and the hind – Legend has it that in the 8C St Giles, who lived in Greece, was touched by the grace of God and gave all his money to the poor. He set out from Greece aboard a raft which was borne by the sea to Provence. The hermit was befriended by a hind which he later saved from a huntsman, miraculously snatching the arrow in mid-flight, and so amazing the bowman that he, being of a rich and noble family, founded an abbey on the site in commemoration of the event. St Giles journeyed to Rome to obtain recognition for the new foundation and was presented by the pope with two doors for the abbey, which he promptly launched on the Tiber and which, after being carried out to sea, landed on the Provençal shore at the same time and place as the saint on his return.

The influence of St Giles (11C-12C) – On the site of St Giles' tomb, a sanctuary was raised which became the object of a fervent cult and a place of pilgrimage, even more frequented because of its location on one of the four major roads to Santiago de Compostela *(see Michelin Green Guide Spain)*. Popes and the counts of Toulouse protected and enriched the Benedictine monastery which since 1066 had been affiliated to the Cluny order.

In the 11C the powerful Count **Raymond IV** built up a vast domain extending from Cahors to the Îles de Lérins. In 1096 he received Pope Urban II, who consecrated the altar of the new abbey church; the count vowed never to return to his land so as to devote himself entirely to the conquest of the Holy Land; this he did, founding the county of Tripoli, where he died.

In the 12C the monastery reached its peak: the town surrounding it had nine parishes and was extraordinarily prosperous. It owed part of its success to the Crusades: a large amount of Far Eastern goods passed through its port; the crusading pilgrims embarked from here and the people of St-Gilles had trading posts with privileges in the Latin States of Jerusalem. The St-Gilles Fair held in September was in full expansion; it was one of the great trading centres between the Mediterranean and northern countries. This prosperity diminished in the 13C owing to the competition of the royal port of Aigues-Mortes.

Excommunication – Before the progress of the Albigensian heresy, the count of Toulouse, **Raymond VI**, was ordered by Pope Innocent III to fight against his heretical subjects. It was at St-Gilles, the extreme limit of the county, that the Papal Legate was received; the next day, 15 January 1208, he was assassinated. The pope immediately excommunicated Raymond VI and preached the Crusades. The count submitted and did penance in St-Gilles on 12 June 1209. However, he soon revolted again, fighting a losing battle against **Simon de Montfort**, and was killed at Muret in 1213.

ST-GILLES ⊘ *45min*

In order to grasp the abbey's great size at the end of the 11C and during the 12C, try to imagine the chancel of the former abbey church extending beyond the present chancel and, on the church's south side, the cloisters with their courtyard surrounded by the chapterhouse, refectory, kitchens and basement storeroom, not to mention the other monastic buildings which stretched as far as the present Rue de la République and Rue Victor-Hugo.

In the 12C, therefore, a vast abbey church stood on the site of an old sanctuary which had housed the tomb of St Giles; but owing to

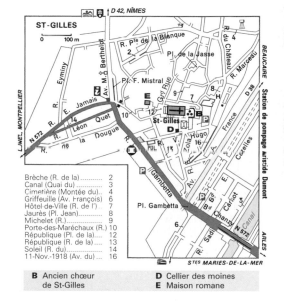

Brèche (R. de la) 2
Canal (Quai du) 3
Cimetière (Montée du).. 4
Griffeuille (Av. François) 6
Hôtel-de-Ville (R. de l') 7
Jaurès (Pl. Jean)........... 8
Michelet (R.)................. 9
Porte-des-Maréchaux (R.) 10
République (Pl. de la)..... 12
République (R. de la) ... 13
Soleil (R. du)............... 14
11-Nov.-1918 (Av. du) ... 16

B Ancien chœur de St-Gilles
D Cellier des moines
E Maison romane

lack of funds the church had still not been completed the following century.

Its plan, influenced by its Burgundian counterparts *(see Michelin Green Guide Burgundy)*, took the form of three naves separated by cruciform pillars, an extended transept and an ambulatory with radiating chapels; underneath the nave was the large crypt.

Secularised and established as a collegiate church in 1538, it suffered irrevocable destruction in 1562 during the Wars of Religion. The Huguenots threw the monks into the crypt's well and set the monastery on fire: the church's vaulting collapsed; in 1622 the great belfry was destroyed. In the 17C the church was shortened by half and its vaulting lowered so that in the future there would be less upkeep. Thus all that is left of a magnificent medieval building are the fine west face, remains of the chancel and the crypt.

★★Façade – The façade which dates from the mid 12C is thought to be one of the finest examples of Romanesque sculpture in the south of France.

Its architectural ordonnance recalls a Roman triumphal arch and is made up of three doorways with pilasters and porticoes. The upper part was badly damaged when the building was lowered in the 17C; much of the sculpture was mutilated during the Wars of Religion and especially the Revolution; several columns and capitals were restored in the 19C. The work was carved in a single time span, according to an initial project which was modified during its carving by several different schools of sculpture. The story told is that of Salvation through the different stages in the life of Christ.

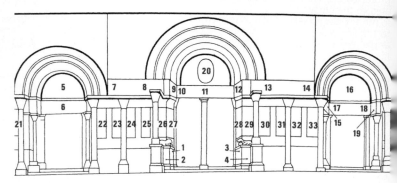

The sculptors were inspired by the Antique style, notably from the paleochristian sarcophagi, as is shown by their use of high relief and the representations of volumes (anatomical proportions) and forms (pleated clothing).

1 – From right to left: Cain offers a grain of wheat to the Lord. Abel sacrifices a lamb.

2 – Murder of Abel by Cain.

3 – A centaur shoots a stag with a bow and arrow.

4 – Balaam and his ass.

5 – Adoration of the Magi.

The great frieze reads from left to right and recounts all the events of Holy Week from Palm Sunday to the morning of Paschal Resurrection and the discovery of the empty tomb by the Holy Women.

6 – Christ's entry into Jerusalem (note the realism of the staggering procession).

7 – Judas returning the thirty pieces of silver.

8 – Christ driving out the merchants from the temple.

9 – Christ announcing the prophecy of Peter's denial.

10 – The Washing of the Feet.

11 – The Last Supper.

12 – The Kiss of Judas.

13 – Flagellation.

14 – The Carrying of the Cross.

15 – Mary Magdalene prostrate before Jesus.

16 – The Crucifixion (note the realistic anatomical details of death by suffocation of the crucified who leans on the steps of the cross to catch his breath).

17 – The Holy Women buying spices.

18 – The Holy Women at the Sepulchre of Christ.

19 – Christ appearing before his disciples.

20 – Christ in Majesty surrounded by the symbols of the four Evangelists.

Art historians identify five stylistic groups with the name of only one master known that of Brunus.

– Brunus: Matthew (**22**), Bartholomew (**23**), John the Evangelist (**26**), James the Greater (**28**), Paul (**29**); characteristics: Antique style, heavy, plain.

– Master "of St Thoma": Thomas (**24**), James the Less (**25**), Peter (**27**), low reliefs of the centre door (**1-2-3-4**); this sculptor is thought to have worked in the west of France; characteristics: linear quality and typically Romanesque treatment.

– "Soft" Master: apostles (**30-31**), left splay of the centre door (**9-10**), tympanum (**5**) and lintel (**6**) of the north door; characteristics: supple drapery modelling the folds around the arms and legs.

– "Hard" Master: apostles (**32-33**), south door (**15-16-17-18-19**); characteristics: long enveloping drapery with voluminous and hard folds sometimes represented in a spiral form, contrasts accentuated by light and shade.

– Master "of St Michael": entablatures on either side of the centre door (**7-8** and **13-14**), St Michael slaying the dragon (**21**); characteristic: very expressive style.

Ancien Chœur de St-Gilles ⊘ (**B**) – This is outside the actual church and corresponds to the part which was devastated in the 17C and razed during the Revolution. The bases of the pillars and the walls indicate precisely the former chancel's layout with its ambulatory and radiating chapels. On either side of the ambulatory, two small bell towers were served by spiral staircases; the one on the left remains: the Vis de St-Gilles.

★**Crypte** ⊘ – This low church (50m/164ft long, 25m/82ft wide) was the scene of one of the West's most important pilgrimages. It lasted three days and some 50 000 people walked past the venerated tomb of St Giles. It was once covered with groined vaulting, which remains in several bays to the right of the entrance. Pointed vaulting from the mid 12C is what remains in the crypt; this vaulting is among the oldest known in France. The decoration of certain arches adorned with a plain band contrasts with that of the others elegantly ornamented with ribbons and ovolo moulding in the bay preceding the tomb (11C); there is a lovely keystone of Christ Blessing and Smiling. An almost Antique influence can be detected; this same influence is seen in the pillars' fluting.

Note the staircase and ramp the monks used to reach the upper church. Sarcophagi, ancient altars and Romanesque capitals are also worth admiring.

★**Vis de St-Gilles** ⊘ – This spiral staircase served the abbey church's north bell tower. Completed in 1142 it has always been admired by the Brotherhood of Stonemasons who during their habitual tour of France stopped to study it (they left graffiti); the stonemasons built scale models to show their skill. Climb to the top (50 steps) to appreciate the rare quality of the cutting and joining of the stone. The steps rest on the central core and the cylindrical walls. The perfection of the interlocking stone composes a spiral vault of nine voussoirs. The art of the stonemason appears in the double concavity and convexity of each voussoir.

ADDITIONAL SIGHTS

Cellier des Moines ⊘ (**D**) – The monks' storeroom has three 11C bays resting on pointed arches.

Maison Romane ⊘ (**E**) – This Romanesque house is the birthplace of **Guy Foulque**, elected pope in 1265 under the name of Clement IV. It houses, on the ground floor, a small lapidary museum containing the ruins of the former abbey church: tympanum, capitals, keystone, 12C low reliefs where the apostles can be identified, 3C sarcophagi in white marble. The first floor is devoted to local fauna (ornithology). From the second floor, which has preserved its chimney with a conical canopy (12C), there is a view of the town's red-tiled roofs. A room, known as Old St Giles' Chamber, presents tools and objects relating to the old trades: the shepherd, coopery, life in the fields, the vineyards, olive groves and domestic life.

Station de Pompage Aristide-Dumont – 5km/3mi northeast on D 38 to a municipality called Pichegu. This is one of Europe's largest pumping stations: it is the heart of the hydraulic system for the lower Rhône and Languedoc regions.

The station is located at the intersection of two canals; one is the main irrigation canal which starts at a distance of 12km/7.5mi in the Rhône, north of Arles, to reach the Montpellier region, and the Canal des Costières which goes north. The station raises the water to a level where it can flow by gravity through the Languedoc plain in order to irrigate it.

ST-JULIEN-LE-MONTAGNIER

Population 1 149
Michelin map 84 west of fold 5 or 114 folds 5 and 6 or 245 fold 33
14km/8.5mi south of Gréoux-les-Bains

The village overlooks the Provence plateau sparsely clad with scrub and the occasional well-tended plot of cereals, vines and olive trees growing on the outskirts of small villages.

From the old threshing floor high up in the village (alt 579m/1 900ft) the **view**★ extends over Haute-Provence: the Durance valley, Valensole plateau, the pre-Alps, Massif de la Ste-Baume and Montagne Ste-Victoire.

Church (Église) – This 11C church is typical of Haute-Provence and contains a 17C high altar in gilded wood and a well-preserved rood-beam. The chancel is lit by a square lantern-belfry.

Ramparts – From the road leading to the entrance to the town, take the road heading northwest to a fortified gate to enjoy another fine **view** of the region. The ruined walls (13C) are all that remain of the ancient fortress.

Michelin Green Guides are regularly revised.
Use the most recent edition to ensure a successful holiday.

Grotte de ST-MARCEL★

Michelin map 80 fold 9 or 245 fold 15 or 246 fold 23
Local map see Gorges de l'ARDÈCHE

The opening to this cave, which was discovered in 1835 by a hunter from Aiguèze, is through a natural shelter cut into the side of the rock faces of the Gorges de l'Ardèche. The cave was formed by a subterranean river which has now dried up but which used to flow beneath the Gras karstic plateau. It hollowed out a 32km/20mi network of chambers, which were for a long time accessible only to scientific experts. A section of these is now open to the public. (Reception is to the north of D 290, 200m/219yd downstream of the Grand Belvédère.)

TOUR ⏱ 1hr

Take a tunnel hollowed out of the rock which leads through striking passages in which stalactites, stalagmites, draperies and tubular and other kinds of eccentrics can be seen. There are various interesting stopping places along the route, where the nature of the concretions in evidence is reflected by the name given to that particular part of the cave: Chamber of the Virgin's Fountain; Painters' Gallery, with different coloured stripes in white (calcite), red (iron oxide) and black (manganese); Chamber of Kings; Cathedral etc. The most interesting feature of the cave is the **cascades of natural dams** (gours) called "pools of lace" (bassins de dentelles), formed by the calcite-bearing water. Special lighting effects show these off to particular advantage (notice the transparency of the rock walls).

A footpath laid out on the site offers a good opportunity of discovering local flora (holmoak, boxwood, cistus etc) and two megalithic monuments (Information leaflet available at ticket office).

ST-MAXIMIN-LA-STE-BAUME★★

Population 9 594
Michelin map 84 folds 4 and 5 or 114 fold 18 or 245 fold 33

St-Maximin lies at the centre of a small basin, once the bottom of a lake, not far from the source of the Argens in a region of flat depressions; the village is flanked to the north by wooded hills and vineyards and to the south by the mountainous foundations of the Massif de la Ste-Baume.

A former new town – the grid pattern has a few irregularities – St-Maximin is enlivened by small shaded squares and fountains, with its houses grouped around the admirable basilica.

The church stands on the spot where according to legend Mary Magdalene (see Massif de la STE-BAUME) and later St Maximinus were buried.

When St Maximinus died, the village, of Gallo-Roman origin, took his name and acquired fame during the 13C when the tombs of the two saints were discovered. (Mary Magdalene, having lived many years of penitence in the Ste-Baume cave, is said to have been buried in the crypt of St Maximinus.) The sarcophagus contained the relics of the saint which were hidden in 716 for fear of the Saracens who were devastating the region, and uncovered in 1279 by Charles of Anjou, brother to St Louis. The spot was indicated by the saint herself in a dream. In 1295 Pope Bonifacio VIII acknowledged the relics and on the site of the crypt Charles of Anjou had a basilica and monastery built.

The monastery was a vast U-shaped three-storey building built on to the basilica. Charles installed the Dominican friars who were in charge of guarding the relics and supervised what soon became a major pilgrimage. During the Revolution the Dominicans were expelled but by great good fortune the basilica and monastery housed **Lucien Bonaparte**, Napoleon's youngest brother, then officer in charge of military stores. He turned the cathedral into a food depot and saved the organ from harm by having the Marseillaise played regularly upon it. The young officer, with an intelligence second only to Napoleon's, became a well-known figure in the town, as he developed into a rousing speaker and was elected president of the local Jacobin club.

In 1858 the Royal Convent of St-Maximinus was reoccupied by Père Lacordaire and became a school of theology.

In 1957 the Dominicans left the convent; it was bought in 1966 by an association of public and private benefactors and today houses an **Arts Centre** (Collège d'Échanges Contemporains) which stages a number of cultural events, especially in the summer.

★★**Basilica** – 45min. The basilica's construction, on the foundations of a 6C Merovingian church, was begun in 1295 by Charles II, prince of Salerno, future king of Sicily and count of Provence. Work continued until 1316 (chancel followed by five bays of the nave); halted for more than a century, work began again in 1404 when the crypt of the old church was reduced to ground level to allow for the construction of the new basilica floor. From 1508 to 1532 work proceeded and the building took on its present appearance.

Exterior – Devoid of transepts and ambulatory, the basilica has a squat appearance reinforced by the absence of a belfry, its incomplete west front, and the massive buttresses reaching the nave walls high up. It is nonetheless the most important example of the Gothic style in Provence, combining the influences of the north, especially of Bourges, with local architectural traditions.

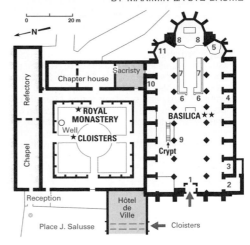

Interior – The building comprises a nave, chancel and two aisles of remarkable height. The two-storey, 29m/95ft high nave has pointed vaulting; its keystones bear the arms of the counts of Provence and kings of France; the very large chancel is closed off by a pentagonal apse. The aisles, which were only 18m/59ft high to allow for a clerestory, end with quadrangular apsidal chapels. The side chapels were raised less than the aisles so as to allow the light to filter through.

1) The organ, which has a double case and still has the pipes saved by Lucien Bonaparte, was made by the lay Dominican, Isnard of Tarascon and ranks with the one in Poitiers' cathedral, as one of the finest 18C instruments in France.

2) Fine gilded wood statue of John the Baptist.

3) 15C altarpiece of the Four Saints: Lawrence, Anthony, Sebastian and Thomas Aquinas.

4) Reliquary containing the sumptuous cope of St Louis of Anjou, bishop of Toulouse (1274-97); 30 silk embroidered medallions of different colours illustrating the lives of Christ and the Virgin encircled by four winged cherubim *(electric switch on the pillar)*.

5) Rosary altar adorned with 18C gilded wood statue of the Virgin; 16C altar front carved with four low reliefs recounting the life of Mary Magdalene.

6) 17C choir screen carved in wood with wrought iron inlets emblazoned with the arms of France.

7) Choir stall panelling enclosing 94 stalls, decorated with 22 medallions of saints of the Dominican Order, carved in the 17C by the lay brother, Vincent Funel.

8) 17C stucco decoration by J. Lombard before which stand, to the right, a terracotta of Mary Magdalene's communion, to the left, a marble of the saint's ecstasy and, at the centre, the altar surmounted by a glory.

9) Pulpit carved in 1756 by the Dominican, Louis Gaudet, with representations on the sounding board, of immense size, of the ecstasy of Mary Magdalene, and on the staircase, panels of her life. The rail is cut from a single piece of wood and is a masterpiece in itself.

10) 15C Provençal School predella (lower part of the altarpiece) illustrating the beheading of John the Baptist, St Martha taming the Tarasque on Tarascon Bridge and Christ appearing to Mary Magdalene.

11) 16C painted wood **retable★** by Ronzen of the Crucifixion, surrounded by 18 medallions.

Crypt – The crypt was the funeral vault of a late 4C-early 5C Roman villa. It contains 4 sarcophagi of the 4C: Saint Mary Magdalene, Saints Marcella and Susan, Saints Maximinus and Cedonius.

Sarcophagus of St Cedonius (detail) in the Basilica of St-Maximin

G. Gaud/PIX

At the back there is a 19C reliquary containing a cranium long venerated as that of Mary Magdalene. Four marble and stone tablets depict carved figures of the Virgin, Abraham and Daniel (c 500).

★Royal Monastery ⊘ – Started in the 13C at the same time as the basilica against which it has been built to the north, the former royal monastery was completed in the 15C. The elegant **cloisters★** include 32 bays. At their entrance note the 1C milestone. Its garden contains an abundance of foliage: boxwood, yew, lime and cedars. It serves as the stage set for the St-Maximinus Musical Evenings (Soirées Musicales de St-Maximin – *see Calendar of events at the end of the guide*) in the summer. The conventual buildings include a chapel with fine vaulting in the form of a depressed arch, the refectory of five bays (on the north wall note the lectern) and the **chapterhouse**, with its lovely pointed vault above slender columns ending in foliated capitals and held by very low corbels; it is entered through a door flanked by two windows. The large 17C guest-house now houses the town hall.

Old Quarter – South of the church opens a covered passageway which joins Rue Colbert; lined with 14C arcades, it indicates the location of the old Jewish ghetto. On the street's other side is the house lived in by Lucien Bonaparte from 1793 to 1794, and the old hospital. Retrace your steps to reach a small square dominated by the clock tower and its bell cage. On the right on the way to Rue de Gaulle, there is a fine 16C house with a corbelled turret.

Abbaye de ST-MICHEL-DE-FRIGOLET

Michelin map 81 fold 11 or 245 fold 29 or 246 fold 25
18km/11mi south of Avignon

The abbey nestles in a hollow, fragrant with rosemary, lavender and thyme, sheltered by cypresses, pines and olives.

Ten centuries of pilgrimages – The abbey was founded in the 10C by monks from Montmajour, who came to this idyllic spot to recover from the fevers they contracted while draining the marshes around their mother house. They dedicated the chapel to Our Lady of Goodly Remedy (Notre-Dame-du-Bon-Remède), which became the object of a pilgrimage which continues even to this day.

Monks from different orders inhabited the conventual buildings before everything was confiscated and sold during the Revolution. The abbey was converted into a boarding school which **Frédéric Mistral** attended from 1839 to 1841. The school shut down in 1841 and the abbey was abandoned. In 1858 the abbey was bought and the Premonstratensians took up residence. The owner, a certain R.P. Edmond, had the idea in the mid 19C of surrounding the abbey with a neo-medieval curtain wall complete with towers, crenellations and machicolations. Vast pilgrim guest-houses as well as a farm, workshops and a lavishly ornate church were added.

Expulsions – In 1880 religious persecution drove the monks out and the abbey underwent a real siege at that time. The religious community was once again dispersed in 1903, as a result of the Law of Congregations: the Premonstratensians fled to Belgium. During the First World War the abbey was converted into a military round-up camp; later the Premonstratensians returned to their abbey.

ABBEY *45min*

Simple, beautiful religious ceremonies are among the abbey's charms.

Église Abbatiale and Notre-Dame-du-Bon-Remède ⊘ – Built in the 19C by R.P. Edmond, the abbey church possesses lavish decoration.

The 11C **Chapelle de Notre-Dame-du-Bon-Remède** *(see illustration of retable on p 41)*, which was the abbey's precursor, serves as the apse of the church's north aisle; it contains lovely gilt **panelling★**, a gift from Anne of Austria, on pilgrimage to ask for a son after many years of childless marriage; her son, Louis XIV, was born in 1638. The panelling includes 14 framed canvases attributed to the School of Nicolas Mignard. In the hall, added in the 19C, onto which opens the refectory, note the handsome modern *santon* figures in olive-wood.

Cloisters (Cloître) ⊘ – Early 12C. In the north gallery a number of Roman ruins have been collected: friezes, capitals, masks.

Chapterhouse (Salle Capitulaire) – 17C. The monks who resisted expulsion were arrested in this chapterhouse in 1880.

Museum (Musée) – The museum contains Provençal furniture, a fine collection of 18C-19C pharmacy jars and the chapel's Renaissance doorway.

Église St-Michel – This very plain 12C church was once the monastery's church. It has a fine stone roof topped by an openwork crest. The façade was redone in the 19C. The interior was heightened by 1.5m/4ft, thus modifying the building's equilibrium.

ST-RÉMY-DE-PROVENCE★

Population 9 340
Michelin map 84 fold 1 or 245 fold 29 or 246 fold 26
Local map see Les ALPILLES – Facilities

Gateway to the Alpilles, St-Rémy symbolises beautifully the essence of Provence, whether it be through its decor of boulevards shaded by plane trees, fountains splashing in the squares, charming old town alleyways or the atmosphere which reigns especially on market day and during traditional fairs.

The village, founded after the destruction of Glanum *(see below)*, developed under the protection of the Abbaye de St-Rémi of Reims, from whence it got its name.

It is a town of gardeners, in keeping with the region which is a great fruit and market gardening centre, and has long specialised in the production and trade of flower and vegetable seeds. However, its main source of income is tourism, encouraged by its thyme and rosemary-scented streets and by the presence of moving Roman ruins.

Birthplace of the famous astrologist **Michel Nostradamus**, St-Rémy has been dazzled by the genius of Van Gogh and by the inspiration of the Provençal poets from Roumanille to Marie Mauron.

★★PLATEAU DES ANTIQUES *1hr 30min*

Leave St-Rémy by ③ on the town plan.

The Roman monuments lie on a plateau below the Alpilles' last foothills, 1km/0.5mi south of St-Rémy. In this pleasant spot, from where the view extends over the Comtat plain, Durance valley and Mont Ventoux, stood the prosperous city of Glanum. It was abandoned after Barbarian invasions at the end of the 3C; two magnificent monuments – the mausoleum and commemorative arch – remain.

★★Roman Monuments

★★ **Mausoleum** – This monument is 18m/60ft high and is one of the most outstanding in the Roman world and the best preserved; it lacks but the pinecone finial crowning its dome. For a long time it was believed to have been built as a sepulchre for a noble from Glanum and his spouse. However, the excavations conducted by Henri Rolland have established that it was not a tomb but a cenotaph; that is to say, a monument built in memory of the deceased.

Low reliefs representing battle and hunting scenes adorn the four walls of the square podium. The first storey, pierced by four arches, bears on the frieze (depicting naval scenes) of the northern architrave an inscription which says "Sextius, Lucius, Marcus, sons of Caius of the Julii family, to their parents". This suggests a posthumous dedication in honour of Emperor Augustus' grandsons, Caius and Lucius, known to have been nicknamed the Princes of Youth. The second storey is made up of a rotunda with a Corinthian colonnade which encloses the statues of the two figures.

D. Faure/DIAF

Mausoleum – The Dome

The archeologists date the mausoleum to c 30 BC and attribute it to a Rhône valley workshop under the direction of Italian master craftsmen.

★ **Arc Municipal** – Perhaps contemporary with the mausoleum, that is to say the first years of Augustus' reign; this arch is the oldest Roman arch of the Narbonensis region. It indicated, on the great way of the Alps, the entrance to Glanum. Its perfect proportions (12.50m/40ft long, 5.50m/17ft wide and 8.60m/27ft high) and the exceptional quality of its carved decoration show Greek influence, quite evident at Glanum.

The sole arcade is carved with a lovely festoon of fruit and leaves; inside, it is adorned with a finely-carved hexagonal coffered ceiling. On either side of the opening are allegorical symbols of victory and on the sides groups of two prisoners, men and women, down by the victors' booty. The despondency of these figures is well rendered.

Art historians feel that the unique form of this arch, mutilated very soon after construction, has inspired some of the 12C Romanesque doorways such as St-Trophime at Arles. The tiled roof was added in the 18C.

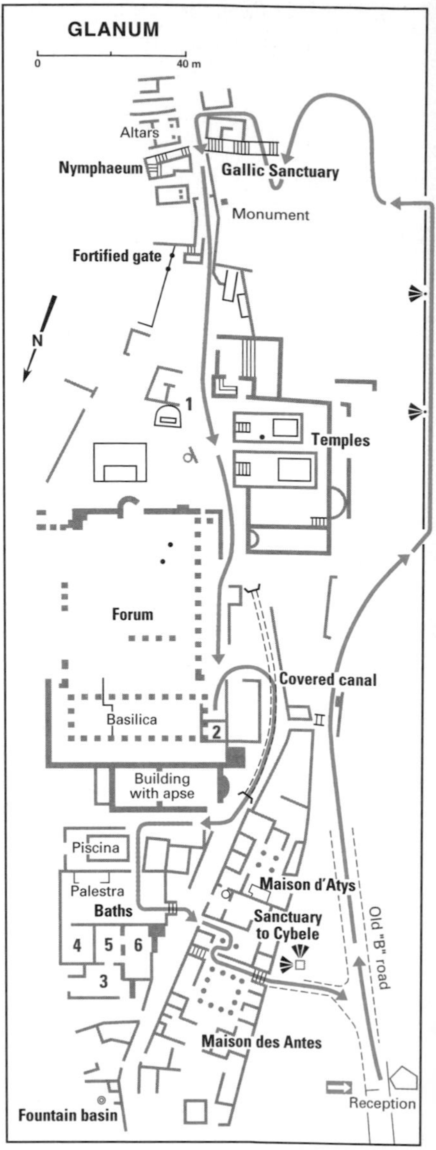

★ **Glanum** ⊘

History of the site – The excavations, unearthed since 1921, are located at the main gap of the Alpilles, which dominate them. The site consists of a group of complex structures reflecting several different periods of occupation, grouped by archeologists into three phases. The origin of the site is a sanctuary venerated by Celtic-Ligurian people known as the Glanics. This native settlement rapidly came into contact with the merchants of Massalia owing to its location close to two important roads.

Glanon (or Glanum I) developed under Hellenistic influence as can be seen in the construction, particularly in the technique of bonding (large carved blocks of stone perfectly set without mortar) in the 3C and 2C BC. This Hellenistic community included public buildings (temple, agora, assembly hall, a rampart, which was probably ceremonial and controlled the procession to the sanctuary), houses with peristyles, and a fortified district to the south (sanctuary).

GLANUM

The second phase (Glanum II) began with the Roman conquest during the late 2C and with the occupation of the country by Marius' army which stopped the Teutonic army. The town most probably suffered when the Teutons passed through; the new buildings were then made by the bonding of irregular stones and the majority of the public buildings disappeared.

The last phase (Glanum III) follows the conquest of Marseille by Caesar in 49 BC. Romanisation intensified, and under Augustus the town was rebuilt.

In the centre, the old buildings were razed, their debris levelled and filled to make room for a vast horizontal esplanade on which were erected the great public buildings: forum, basilica, temples, baths etc. The private dwellings, which had not disappeared, were adapted and transformed; others were built. The walls were in regular ashlar work bonded with mortar.

In c 270, Glanum fell prey to the Germanic tribes and it was abandoned. The canals, no longer maintained, clogged up, and the alluvium descending from the Alpilles slowly covered the site. The excavations unearthed with caution an enormous quantity of ruins, the interpretation of which still today is based on a number of theories: the vestiges discovered are exhibited at the Hôtel de Sade *(see below)*. In the Visitors' Centre *(ticket office)*, two models of the site, reconstructed frescoes and various fragments of architecture and domestic objects all help to shed further light on the different phases of the site's history.

Viewpoints (Belvédères) – These offer a good overall view of the site.

Gallic Sanctuary – Set up in terraces, orientated towards the rising sun, this sanctuary dates from the 6C BC. In this area were uncovered kneeling warriors and stelae with carved skulls identical to those found in the great Salian towns.

Nymphaeum – The source round which Glanum possibly developed is marked by a pool with masonry walls of large, Greek-style stones. In 20 BC Agrippa built right next to it a temple dedicated to Valetudo, goddess of health (ruins of three fluted columns). A staircase leads to the bottom still fed with water from the spring. On the south side, a sanctuary to Hercules was established; a statue of the demi-god and several votive altars have been discovered (casts).

Fortified Gate – This remarkable Hellenistic vestige used, like at St-Blaise, the Massaliote technique of large well-matched rectangular blocks of stone with merlons and gargoyles. The ramparts, which succeeded at least two protohistoric ramparts, defended the sanctuary and included a postern with a zigzag passageway and a carriage gate.

Temples – Southwest of the forum (on the left as you go north) stood twin temples surrounded by a *peribolus*, the southern section of which partially covered an assembly hall (the Greek bouleuterion) with its tiered seats. These Roman public buildings, the oldest of their kind in Gaul, date back to 30 BC. Important vestiges of their lavish decoration (blocks of cornice, roof decorations etc) as well as exquisite sculpture (particularly the portraits of Octavian and Julia which will be found in the Hôtel de Sade) have been excavated. These vestiges have made it possible, partially, to reconstruct the smaller of the two temples. A monumental fountain (**1**) stood opposite the temples in front of the forum and here a trapezoidal square belonging to a hellenistic building was laid out, surrounded by magnificent head capital colonnades (exhibited at the Hôtel de Sade).
Facing the temples, in front of the forum, was a triangular square with a paved platform and a monumental fountain. Further east was the theatre district.

Forum – The forum was built on the ruins of pre-Roman buildings which the archeologists are seeking to identify. It was closed to the north by the basilica (a multi-purpose building mostly for commercial and administrative activities) of which 24 foundation pillars remain and under which Sulla's House was discovered. In the house were uncovered mosaics (**2**), most likely the oldest ones found in Gaul. South of the basilica lay the forum square lined on each side by a covered gallery and closed to the south by a great decorated apsidal-ended wall. Discovered underneath the square were a house and a large hellenistic building *(see above)*. A spring identical to that next to the Gallic sanctuary has recently been discovered under the forum (not on view at present).

Covered Canal – This remarkable work, probably a channel which drained the water from the valley and the town, was so constructed that the stone covering also served as Glanum's main street pavement. It skirts an apsed building near which a great number of altars dedicated for the most part to Silvanus, the god with the mallet, were found.

Baths – These baths date back to the time of Julius Caesar. Their clear plan followed the classical route: a *gymnasium* (**3**), *frigidarium* (**4**), *tepidarium* (**5**), *caldarium* (**6**), *palestra*, set up for physical exercise and athletic games, once lined with porticoes, cold swimming pool perhaps, finally, with running water.

Maison d'Atys – This house was divided, in its primitive period, into two parts (peristyled court to the north and pool to the south) joined by a large door. Consequently, a sanctuary to Cybele was set up in the area where the peristyle stood; note the votive altar dedicated to the goddess' ears.

Maison des Antes – Beside Maison d'Atys, this lovely house of the Greek type, built according to the 2C BC taste, was laid out around a peristyled central courtyard and cistern. The entrance bay of one of the rooms has preserved its two pilasters *(antes)*. The ruins of a staircase and the low columns suggest that the house had one storey. It was modified during the Gallo-Roman period.

Fountain Basin – Elegant 2C BC fountain.

Additional Sights on the Plateau des Antiques

Ancien Monastère de St-Paul-de-Mausole ⊙ – *Access via ③ on the map.* Located near the Roman monuments, to which its name is linked, this monastery of Augustinian and later Franciscan canons was transformed into a convalescent home in the mid 18C. It preserves the memory of **Vincent Van Gogh** who demanded to be interned here from 3 May 1889 to 16 May 1890. He had a workroom on the ground floor and a bedroom on the first floor. While here he painted: his life at the hospital, nature *(Cypress Trees, The Sower)*, self-portraits; and copied great masters such as Rembrandt, Millet, Delacroix, Gustave Doré *(The Prisoners' Watch)* and the extraordinary work *Starry Night*.

ST-RÉMY-DE-PROVENCE

Lafayette (R.) .... **Z** 6

Carnot (R.).................. **Y**
Combette (Ch. de la). **Z**
Commune (R.) .... **Z** 2
Durant-Maillane (Av.). **Z**
Fauconnet (Av.)......... **Z**
Favier (Pl.) .... **Y**
Gambetta (Bd) .... **Y**
Gras (Av. F.)............... **Y**
Hoche (R.)................. **Z** 4
Jaurès (Pl. J.)............. **Z**
Libération (Av. de la) . **Y** 7
Marceau (Bd)............ **Y**
Mirabeau (Bd)........... **YZ** 8
Mistral (Av. F.) .... **Y**
Mistral (Av. L.) .... **Y**
Nostradamus (R.)....... **Y** 10
Parage (R.) .... **Y** 12
Pasteur (Av.)............. **Z**
Pelissier (Pl. J.) .... **Z**
République (Pl. de la) **Z**
Résistance (Av.)........ **Z** 13
Roux (R.) .... **Z** 14
Salengro (R. R.) .... **Y** 15
Schweitzer (Av. A.) .... **Y**
Taillandier
  (Av. G. St-René) ..... **Y**
Victor-Hugo (Bd) .... **Z**
8-Mai-1945 (R. du) ..... **Z** 16

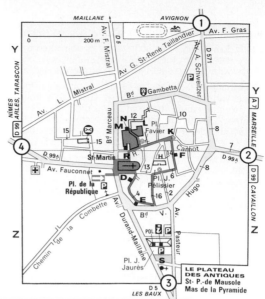

D	Maison natale de Nostradamus
E	Ancien hôpital St-Jacques
F	Hôtel Estrine
	(Centre d'Art-Présence Van Gogh)
K	Fontaine Nostradamus
L	Hôtel de Sade
M	Musée des Alpilles Pierre-de-Brun
N	Hôtel de Lagoy
R	Hôtel d'Almeran-Maillane
S	Chapelle Notre-Dame-de-Pitié

The small church dates from the end of the 12C (18C façade) and has a fine square bell tower with Lombard arcades. Beside it the **cloisters★** present a fine Romanesque decor: the capitals of the small columns are carved with varied motifs (foliage, animals, masks etc) in a style similar to that of Montmajour and St-Trophime in Arles.

Mas de la Pyramide ⊙ – *Via ③ on the map, 200m/219yd from the Monastery of St-Paul-de-Mausole.* This troglodytic *mas* with its unusual interior layout was built for the most part in the old Roman quarries from materials which were also used for the neighbouring town of Glanum. The rooms house a museum of rural life which includes displays of the tools and agricultural equipment once used by local peasants.

At the centre of the estate, the vertical, 20m/66ft tall "pyramid" rock is a lone reminder of the old ground level of the site before mining work in the quarries was begun.

THE CITY OF ST-RÉMY-DE-PROVENCE *1hr*

Place de la République (Z) – Beside the ring road, this square is on the site of the medieval ramparts and is the heart of the town, animated by its café terraces and the bustle on its market days.

Collégiale St-Martin (Z) – This collegiate church with its striking façade was rebuilt around 1820 after it had partially caved in. The only remaining 14C feature is the bell tower crowned with a crocketed spire. The lovely organ case in the gallery inside was reconstructed in 1983. The organ is used every year during the festival of organ music *(see Calendar of events at the end of the guide)*.

The vestiges of the old fortifications line Rue Hoche; these include, in poor condition, the **Maison Natale de Nostradamus** (Nostradamus' Birthplace) **(D)** and the 17C **Ancien Hôpital St-Jacques (E)**.

On Place Jules-Pélissier stands the town hall, which was formerly a 17C monastery.

Hôtel Estrine ⊙ **(Z F)** – This handsome private mansion was built in the 18C for Marquis Joseph de Pistoye and was subsequently purchased by Louis Estrine, a master rope-maker from Marseille, from whom the house gets its name. Recent renovation work has restored the residence to its former glory, and it now houses the **Centre d'Art–Présence Van Gogh** ⊙.

The mansion, built on three storeys from ashlar masonry, features a central concave section on its façade into which opens the doorway, surmounted by an elegant wrought iron balcony. Inside, the grand stone staircase leads up to the rooms on the first floor, which are paved with floor tiles and decorated with plasterwork. The ground floor is devoted to Vincent Van Gogh: an audiovisual display and thematic exhibitions illustrate his work and the time he spent at St-Rémy. The upper floors are given over to interesting temporary exhibitions of contemporary art.

On the corner of Rue Carnot and Rue Nostradamus is the 19C **Fontaine Nostradamus** (**K**), decorated with a portrait of the famous medic and astrologer.

A couple of yards further on, Place Favier (Le Planet or the former herbal market place) is lined with fine 15C and 16C hôtels, converted into museums.

Hôtel de Sade ⊘ (**Y L**) – This 15C-16C townhouse boasts a rich and extensive **archeological stone collection★** (part of which is open to the public) where remarkable finds from the Glanum excavations can be seen. Ground floor: Gallic funerary stelae in the form of obelisks, votive altars, sarcophagi, columns, acroterions and cornice fragments from the temples of Caius and Lucius. In the back of the courtyard are remains of 4C baths and a 5C baptistery, evidence of the origins of St-Rémy. On the first floor are: capitals, a very fine acroterion from the temple dedicated to the goddess Valetudo (represented with a torque or necklace), miscellaneous votive offerings, votive altars, a statue of a captured Gaul, a statue of Hercules from Hercules' sanctuary, a lovely low relief with the effigy of Hermes and Fortuna. The second floor displays objects evoking daily life at Glanum from the Greeks to the Gallo-Roman occupation: tools, bronze and wood objects, funerary urns, pottery, oil lamps (among them note the rare candelabrum with two rows of lamps, one above the other), jewellery (note the magnificent ring made of rock crystal adorned with the finely carved head of a woman); as well as a prehistoric collection (flints, bones).

Musée des Alpilles Pierre-de-Brun ⊘ (**Y M**) – This museum is located in the vast 16C Mistral de Mondragon mansion built round a fine courtyard with a round turreted staircase and overlooked by loggias, next to the 17C **Hôtel de Lagoy** (**N**). The exhibits relate to popular arts and traditions. Documents concerning Nostradamus as well as minerals from the Alpilles are also displayed.

Hôtel d'Almeran-Maillane (**YZ R**) – Charles Gounod gave his first hearing of "Mireille" here in 1863, an event which is commemorated in a stone high relief work.

Chapelle Notre-Dame-de-Pitié ⊘ (**Z S**) – Beneath the pointed vaulting of this small country chapel (nave dating originally from the 12C to 13C, side aisles added in the 17C and porch in the 18C) are the tapestry of the "Shroud" as well as 11 *Paintings of the Agony*, a bleak work of branches and trunks of trees juxtaposed in black and white, evoking the Crucifixion of Christ. An alternating display of copper engravings, prints, Indian ink drawings on paper on the subject of the Alpilles etc completes this bequest made to the French state by **Mario Prassinos** (1916-1985), a Greek artist who settled at Eygalières.

Massif de la STE-BAUME★★

Michelin map 84 fold 14 or 114 folds 30 and 31 or 245 folds 45 and 46

Ste-Baume is the name of a forest and of a cave – *baoumo* is Provençal for cave. The cave, where Mary Magdalene retired, and which subsequently gave its name to this massif, is now a well-known place of pilgrimage. The forest is magnificent and unique for several reasons. The massif forms at its summit a long crest, one of the peaks of which, St-Pilon (alt 994m/3 261ft), offers a splendid panorama.

The massif – The most extensive and the highest of the Provençal mountain ranges, Massif de la Ste-Baume reaches an altitude of 1 147m/3 763ft at the Signal de la Ste-Baume beacon. It is an example of the general east-west orientation of the mountain system of Pyrenean origin which predominates in Provence *(see details on land formation in the Introduction)*. The asymmetrical relief, common in this region, is very accentuated, as around the Montagne Ste-Victoire, but in the opposite sense.

The arid and barren southern face climbs in a gentle slope from the Bassin de Cuges up to the 12km/7.5mi long crest; the northern face, a steep vertical slope approximately 300m/984ft high shelters the famous cave; below lies the state forest beside the permeable plateau of the Plan d'Aups similar to the Causses.

This massif, typically Provençal with its poor soil and brilliantly white rocky ridge, is surprisingly northern in aspect because of its forest cover.

Mountaineers can climb from the Pic de Bertagneto the eastern extremity of the chain; peaks of more than 100m/328ft (some rise 250m/820ft).

The forest – Sprawled over 100ha/247 acres and varying in altitude from 680 to 1 000m/2 231 to 3 281ft, this forest holds an exceptional position among French forests. Of glaciary origin, the forest was most probably a sacred wood at the time of the Gauls and this tradition has come down over the centuries. From time immemorial Ste-Baume has been protected from being cut down, a protection which is still enforced. The continuation of each species is carefully monitored.

Its other unique aspect is its forest cover: giant beech, enormous lime trees intermingled with maples. Their light foliage forms a canopy over the thick, dark undergrowth of yew, spindle, ivy and holly. It is astonishing to see a forest cover typical of the forests of Île-de-France deep in the heart of Provence. This can be explained by the fact that the shade cast by the steep cliff, which on the southern side overlooks the wooded area, creates a cold and humid, typically northern climate. As soon as this ridge ends Mediterranean foliage reappears.

Mary Magdalene – Mary Magdalene led a dissolute life until the day she heard Christ preaching. The repentant sinner became a follower of Christ; she stood by His Cross at Calvary and was the first to see the risen Christ on Easter morning. She has been identified by some as Lazarus and Martha's sister and according to local oral tradition she was driven from Palestine with the two of them, St Maximinus and other saints at the time of the early Christian persecutions by the Jews. They were set adrift in a boat without sails and came ashore at Stes-Maries-de-la-Mer. Mary Magdalene preached all over Provence and finally came to Ste-Baume, a popular place of pilgrimage to fertility goddesses. She retired to a cave for 33 years to a life of prayer and contemplation and as her death drew near she went down into the plain to receive the final communion from Maximinus, who later buried her. On the right of the road coming down from Ste-Beaume, a short distance before the Abbaye de St-Maximin, a monument, the Petit Pilon, stands on the spot where, according to tradition, her last communion took place.

The pilgrimage – The cave has been venerated from the earliest centuries, and in the 5C the monks of St Cassien settled here and in Abbaye de St-Maximin. Its fame attracted a number of pilgrims, some of them illustrious.

Then in the 11C, it was said that the relics of Mary Magdalene were stolen and taken to Vézelay which became one of the main pilgrim centres of Christianity *(see Michelin Green Guide Burgundy-Jura)*. But in 1279 Charles of Anjou discovered the saint's remains at St-Maximin abbey and the Provençal pilgrimage replaced the one at Vézelay. A number of French kings (including St Louis), several popes (especially those from Avignon), thousands of lords and millions of the faithful flocked to Ste-Baume. One of Good King René's first public appearances was to go to the cave, accompanied by his nephew Louis XI. Tradition has it that each engaged couple built, on the path up to the cave, a pile of rocks; the number of rocks in the pile meant the number of children desired in the future household. Beside the proud rock piles stood unassuming menhirs.

As of 1295 the Dominicans were the guardians of the cave. Their guest-house situated right next to the cave was burned down during the Revolution. Traces of its site are still visible on the rock side.

In 1859 Père Lacordaire brought the Dominicans back to the cave and to St-Maximin abbey. The guest-house was rebuilt according to his directions below the plateau. It functions under the spiritual direction of the Dominicans except for a lay director, who is there to supervise all the technical services.

On Whit Monday a pilgrimage from all over Provence takes place. In honour of the feast of Mary Magdalene there is an evening entertainment on 21 July and a Mass on 22 July. At Christmas, Midnight Mass is celebrated in the cave.

ROUND TOUR FROM GÉMENOS

69km/43mi – about 3hr (not including ascent of St-Pilon)

Gémenos – Facilities. The small town, where the 17C château now serves as the town hall, stands where the small green St-Pons valley opens into the larger Huveaune.

Drive 3km/2mi up D 2 along St-Pons valley.

★**Parc de St-Pons** – *Park the car before the bridge and walk along the path beside the stream.*

An old watermill fed by St-Pons stream, a Vauclusian spring, and the extensive ruins of a 13C Cistercian abbey, abandoned in the 15C, are set in a wooded park of beech, hornbeam, ash and maple, uncommon trees for so southerly a latitude. In the spring there are Judas trees in flower.

The road climbs the steep and bare southern slope cut into a deep circus.

★**Col de l'Espigoulier** – *Alt 728m/2 390ft.* The views from this pass extend over the Ste-Baume massif itself, Aubagne plain, Chaîne St-Cyr, Marseille and the Chaîne de l'Étoile.

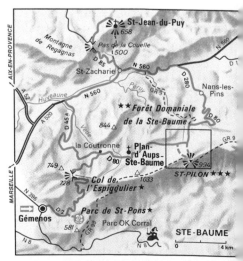

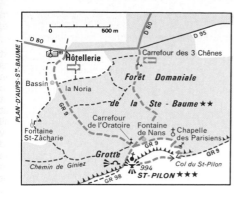

The descent down the north face offers further views of the Étoile and of Montagne Ste-Victoire beyond Fuveau basin. *At La Coutronne turn right onto D 80.*

Plan-d'Aups-Ste-Baume – The small health resort has a Romanesque church.

Hôtellerie – The guest-house, 675m/2 215ft up on the plateau in the lee of the forest, was rebuilt in 1863, and continues to house pilgrims. It became a cultural and spiritual centre in 1968; in 1972 a chapel was created in the elegant vaulted hall, the original pilgrim shelter. To the left of the guest-house is the austere cemetery.

Access to the Grotte – *1hr 30min return on foot. There are two alternative starts to the route: the first is along a path left of the guest-house and through the Canapé, a group of moss-covered rocks; the second, which is easier, is from D 80-D 95 or the three Oak Trees crossroads (Carrefour des Trois-Chênes), along the "Kings' Way" (Chemin des Rois).*

After a pleasant walk through the lovely Ste-Baume forest cover, the two paths meet at the Oratory crossroads (Carrefour de l'Oratoire), where a wide path on the right leads to a flight of steps cut into the rock face; halfway up there is a door decorated with a pretty shield with fleur-de-lis and a bronze Calvary nestling in a niche to the left.

Terrace – The stairway *(150 steps)* ends at a terrace on which a stone Cross and bronze *Pietá* (it has been set up as the 13th Station of the Cross) stand. The terrace itself commands a **view**★ of Montagne Ste-Victoire, Mont Aurélien, which extends it to the right, and in the foreground Plan d'Aups, the Hôtellerie and dense woodland.

Grotte – The semicircular cave lies north of the terrace at an altitude of 946m/3 105ft. Inside, to the right of the high altar, is a shrine with relics of Mary Magdalene brought from the Abbaye de St-Maximin-la-Ste-Baume; behind the altar, 3m/10ft up the wall, is an irregular cavity, the only dry place in the cave, known as the Place of Penance, which contains a recumbent statue of the saint.

★★**St-Pilon** – *2hr return on foot. Start at the Oratory crossroads (Carrefour de l'Oratoire). Pass in front of the oratory and follow the right-hand path (red and white GR 9 signs) which climbs to the abandoned Chapelle des Parisiens and continues by a zigzag route and a turn to the right to the Col du St-Pilon (pass).*

A column, since replaced by the small chapel, formerly marked the summit – hence the name. According to legend, angels bore Mary Magdalene to this spot seven times a day so that she might listen to the music of paradise.

From St-Pilon (alt 994m/3 261ft) a magnificent **panorama**★★★ *(viewing table)* can be enjoyed: to the north the Hôtellerie in the foreground, Mont Ventoux in the distance, the Luberon, Montagne de Lure, the Briançonnais region, Mont Olympe and nearer Mont Aurélien; to the southeast the Massif des Maures; southwest onto Massif de la Ste-Baume and La Ciotat bay; northwest on to the Alpilles and Montagne Ste-Victoire.

Return to the car and make for Nans-les-Pins along D 80.

The road as it descends through the woods affords views of Mont Regagnas.

In Nans-les-Pins turn left onto D 280 which crosses a pinewood before meeting N 560; turn left to travel the upper Huveaune valley to St-Zacharie.

Oratoire de St-Jean-du-Puy – *9km/6mi from St-Zacharie, plus 15min return on foot.* Turn right onto D 85 from which, as it climbs by means of hairpin bends, there are views of St-Zacharie basin and, in the distance, the Ste-Baume massif. Shortly after the Pas de la Couelle, a narrow track on the right leads up a short slope to a military radar post. Park the car and continue on foot to the oratory. From the site there is a good **view**★ of Montagne Ste-Victoire and the St-Maximin plain to the north, the Maures and Ste-Baume massifs to the southeast, Mont Regagnas in the foreground and the Chaîne de l'Étoile and Aix countryside to the west.

Continue along N 560 to Le Pujol; turn left onto D 45ᴬ.

The road first ascends the valley of the Vede, a stream at the foot of terraced hillsides, before turning aside to overlook the bare, rock-walled gorges.

At La Coutronne turn right for Gémenos along the road taken in the opposite direction at the outset.

Montagne STE-VICTOIRE★★

Michelin map 84 folds 3 and 4 or 114 folds 16 and 17 or 245 fold 32

East of Aix-en-Provence lies Montagne Ste-Victoire, a limestone range which reaches an altitude of 1011m/3297ft at its peak, the Pic des Mouches. Orientated west to east, this range forms on its south side a sheer drop down to the Arc basin, whereas on its north side it slopes gently in a series of limestone plateaux towards the Durance plain. A striking contrast exists between the bright red clay of the foot of the mountains and the white limestone of the high mountain ridges, especially between Le Tholonet and Puyloubier.

The mountain, immortalised by **Paul Cézanne** *(see p 63)* in his paintings, was the site of the battle in which Marius' legions overcame the Teutons as they were about to start an advance on Rome *(see p 61)*.

ROUND TOUR STARTING FROM AIX-EN-PROVENCE

74km/46mi – allow 1 day (not including tour of Aix) – local map see below

★★ **Aix-en-Provence** – *4hr. See AIX-EN-PROVENCE.*

Leave Aix-en-Provence on D 10 going east; turn right towards the Barrage de Bimont.

Barrage de Bimont – This vaulted dam across the River Infernet is the principal undertaking on the Canal de Verdon extension. It stands in a beautiful, wooded site at the foot of Montagne Ste-Victoire.

Downstream, superb gorges descend *(1hr return on foot)* to the Barrage Zola (a dam built by engineer François Zola, father of the famous author, Émile Zola), the second undertaking in the scheme which supplies water to local towns and villages and irrigation to some 60 local communes.

Return to D 10 and turn right.

The road offers fine views of the dam.

★★★ **Croix de Provence** – *3hr 30min return on foot. Park the car to the right of the road at Les Cabassols farm and walk along the Venturiers path, a mule track which rises rapidly through a pinewood before easing off into a winding path (easier walking).*

The road offers fine views of the reservoir up the hillside. The first staging post is at 900m/2950ft, the Notre-Dame de Ste-Victoire priory, built in 1656 and occupied until 1879. It comprises a chapel, a conventual building and parts of cloisters; a terrace laid in a breach in the wall gives a **view** of the Arc basin and Étoile chain. Bear left of the cloisters to make the short climb to the 945m/3100ft high summit marked by a 17m/56ft Cross (croix) upon an 11m/36ft base.

The **panorama★★★** of Provençal mountains includes: Massif de la Ste-Baume and Chaîne de l'Étoile to the south, then towards the right the Vitrolles, Crau plain, Durance valley, Luberon, Provençal Alps and more to the east the Pic des Mouches.

To the east on the crest is **Gouffre du Garagaï**, a chasm 150m/492ft deep, a source of legends and superstitions *(see Introduction: Legends and tales)*.

Château de Vauvenargues – *(Not open to the public).* The 17C château stands on a rock spur overlooking the Infernet valley. **Pablo Picasso**, who lived here at the end of his life (1881-1973), is buried in the park in front of the château.

Beyond Vauvenargues turn left onto D 11 towards Jouques continuing for about 1km/0.5mi.

The road follows lovely steep **gorges★**.

Return to D 10.

The road goes up the wooded Infernet gorges, overlooked on the left by the 723m/2370ft high Citadelle, and reaches Col des Portes pass. During the descent, the Alpine foothills can be distinguished on the horizon.

Southern slope of the Montagne Ste-Victoire

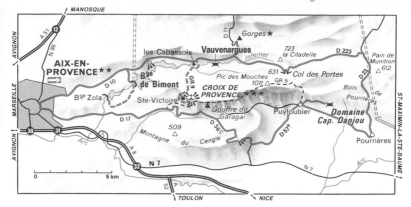

Take D 23 to the right which skirts Montagne Ste-Victoire on its eastern side and crosses the Bois de Pourrières (woods), to your left is the Pain de Munition (alt 612m/2 005ft).

In Pourrières turn right to Puyloubier.

The region is a grape-growing area.

Domaine Capitaine Danjou ⊘ – In Puyloubier, a path to the right leads to Château le Général, now the Foreign Legion's Pensioners' Hospital *(see AUBAGNE)*. The tour includes the workshops (pottery, book-binding, ironworks) and a small museum.

Return to Puyloubier and take D 57B; then turn right onto D 56.

More good views of Montagne Ste-Victoire, also of Trets basin and Massif de la Ste-Baume can be enjoyed before the road climbs the slopes of Montagne du Cengle. The D 17, on the left, winds between the imposing mass of Montagne Ste-Victoire and the Cengle plateau to reach Aix.

Les STES-MARIES-DE-LA-MER ★

Population 2 232
Michelin map 83 fold 19 or 245 fold 41 or 246 fold 27
Local map see La CAMARGUE – Facilities

Between the Mediterranean and the Launes and Impérial lagoons, at the heart of the Camargue, Les Stes-Maries-de-la-Mer can be distinguished by its fortified church. A new marina extends to the west.

The "Saintly Ship" – According to Provençal legend, the boat abandoned to the waves in c 40 by the Jews of Jerusalem, which, without the aid of sail or oar, landed safely on the shore where Les Saintes-Maries is now situated, carried Mary, the mother of James, Mary Magdalene, Martha and her brother Lazarus, St Maximinus, Mary Salome, the mother of James Major and John, and Cedonius, the man born blind. Sarah, the two Marys' black servant left behind on the shore, wept aloud until Mary Salome threw her mantle on the water so that Sarah could walk over it to join the others. The legend continues that after erecting a simple oratory to the Virgin on the shore, the disciples separated; Martha went to Tarascon, Mary Magdalene to Ste-Baume. The two Marys and Sarah remained in Camargue and were buried in the oratory.

Nineteen centuries of pilgrimage – The saints' tomb rapidly became the object of a cult attracting pilgrims from afar, whereas gypsies and other nomads developed a particular veneration for Sarah.

By the mid 9C the oratory (believed to date from the 6C) had been replaced by a fortified church which, in 869, was being incorporated into the town ramparts under the personal supervision of the archbishop of Arles, when suddenly the Saracens made a lightning raid and carried off the archbishop.

In the short time it took to collect the ransom of 150 *livres* of silver, 150 mantles, 150 swords and 150 slaves, the prelate died; unperturbed, the Saracens returned with the corpse, set it apart on a throne with a great show of respect as if nothing were wrong, and departed with the ransom before the Arlesians discovered their loss.

In the 11C the monks of Montmajour established a priory and in the 12C rebuilt the church which was at the same time incorporated into the fortifications. At the end of the 14C the church's fortress-like appearance was reinforced by the addition of machicolations.

During the Barbarian invasions the saints' remains were buried under the chancel. In 1448, King René ordered the exhumation of the saints, whose relics were then enshrined with great ceremony and have remained the object of a deep and widespread veneration ever since.

Les Saintes-Maries-de-la-Mer's feast days – Two vast celebratory pilgrimages are still held here each year for the Virgin Mary's two half-sisters: on 24 and 25 May, the **Gypsy Celebration ★★**, for Mary, the mother of James, and the Sunday in October closest to 22 October for Mary Salome *(see the Calendar of events at the end of the guide)*. On the afternoon of the first day, the shrines are brought down from the upper chapel to the chancel. The next day the saints' statues, preceded by the women of Arles in costume, surrounded by Camargue *gardians* on horseback, are marched in procession through the streets, to the beach and into the sea. Finally, after vespers, the shrines are returned to their chapel on high.

Les Stes-Maries-de-la-Mer – Gypsy Celebration

Aubanel (R. Théodore) .... **A** 2
Baroncelli
(Pl. Marquis de) .... **A** 4
Bizet (R. Georges) .... **A** 6
Châteaubriand (R.) .... **A** 10
Château d'eau (R. du) .... **A** 12
Église (Pl. de l') .... **A** 17
Espelly (R.) .... **A** 18
Étang (R. de l') .... **A** 20
Ferrade (R. de la) .... **B** 22
Fouque (R. du Capitaine) .... **A** 23
Gambetta (Av. Léon) .... **AB** 25
Lamartine (Pl.) .... **A** 27
Pénitents-Blanc
(R. des) .... **A** 30
Portalet (Pl.) .... **A** 32
Razeteurs (R. des) .... **A** 34

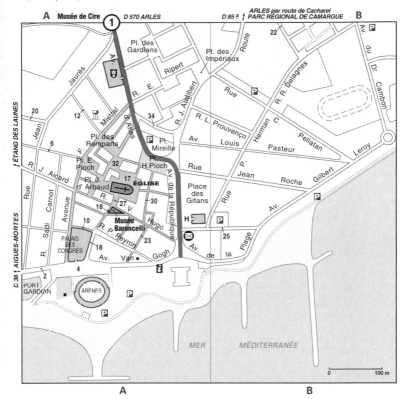

The arrival of gypsies who come here from all over the world adds to the picturesque charm of these festivities. They take over the church's crypt where their patron saint, Sarah, lies. They, too, on the first day march the richly dressed statue of Sarah through the streets to the sea. They elect their queen here every three or four years.

The 26 May is Baroncelli-Javon Memorial Day *(see Musée Baroncelli below)*: It is one of much celebration and local colour. Camargue *gardians* with the women of Arles in traditional costume take part in such events as the local dance, the *farandole*, the round-up *(ferrade)*, horse racing and bull running.

SIGHTS

★ Église – From the exterior, the massive crenellated walls of this fortified church are decorated with Lombard arcades at the east end. The keep-like structure of the upper chapel, surrounded at the base by a watchpath and crowned by a crenellated terrace, is dominated by a bell gable (restored in the early 20C).
On the south side note the two fine lions devouring their prey which are believed to have supported a porch.

Interior – *Enter through the small door on Place de l'Église.* The Romanesque nave (extended by two bays in the 15C) is very dark. The chancel raised when the crypt was constructed has blind arcading held up by eight marble columns with splendid carved capitals, two of which are historiated – one illustrating the Incarnation, the other Abraham's Sacrifice of Isaac – and the other six decorated with leaf-work, masks and busts of men.
South of the nave, protected by a wrought iron railing, is a well of fresh water for use in time of siege. In the third bay on the north side, above the altar is the Saints Marys' boat which is carried in procession by the gypsies in May and the parishioners in October. South of this altar note the Saints' Pillow, a worn block of marble incorporated in a column and discovered during the excavations of 1448 when the saints' relics were discovered. In the fourth north bay is a pagan altar.

Crypt – Built under the sanctuary. The altar has been built with part of a sarcophagus; it holds the reliquary containing the presumed relics of St Sarah. Right of the altar stands the statue of Sarah and ex-votos offered by the gypsies.

Upper Chapel – The chapel is richly panelled in bright green and gold in the Louis XV style. It houses the reliquary shrine of the two Marys, which is exposed on the nave's clerestory sill, except during pilgrimages. Frédéric Mistral set the final scene of his romance *Mirèio* in the chapel where his heroine, Mireille, came to pray for help. There is a statue of *Mireille* by A. Mercié standing in the main square.

Watchpath (Chemin de Ronde) ⊘ – *53 steps.* Climb to the paved watchpath which encircles the church roof, commanding an unforgettable **view** of the sea, the town, and the vast Camargue plain.

Musée Baroncelli ⊘ – This is located in the 19C town hall, the side façades of which feature two marble medallions (remnants of the original 17C building) depicting on one side the coats of arms of France and Navarre, and on the other side those of the Saint Marys. The literature collected by **Marquis Folco de Baroncelli-Javon** (1869-1943), a genuine Camargue *manadier* who revived Camargue traditions, is on the subject of the agro-pastoral way of life in the Camargue and on the history of the town of Les Saintes-Maries. The exhibition comprises also: dioramas illustrating Camargue fauna, including a herons' nesting site; 18C Provençal furniture; display cases devoted to Van Gogh and the marquis de Baroncelli.

SALON-DE-PROVENCE★

Population 34 054
Michelin map 84 fold 2 or 245 fold 30 or 246 fold 12 – Facilities

The town lies at the heart of France's olive growing country. The olive oil industry was established here in the 15C and developed by Colbert. Today mineral oils hold an important position in the town's commerce.

A large agricultural market centre, Salon is also the seat of the officers' training school for the French Air Force, which was established in 1936. The French Air Patrol, which is based at Salon, usually has training sessions on Tuesdays between noon and 2pm. The town is in two parts: the old city climbing up the hill to the castle *(see below)*, and the new district which lies at its feet, divided by a broad belt of tree-shaded avenues. On 11 June 1909 the area from Salon to Aix was badly shaken by a severe earth tremor destroying the villages of Vernègues and Rognes and damaging parts in Salon, Lambesc and St-Cannat; some 60 people died.

The French Air Patrol, which is based at Salon, usually has training sessions on Tuesdays between noon and 2pm.

The Salon **Festival de Jazz** has gained a solid reputation and is the basis for much of the town's events in the summer *(see the Calendar of events at the end of the guide).*

Adam de Craponne – A native son of Salon, the civil engineer Adam de Craponne, (1527-76) made the region fertile through the construction of the irrigation canal bearing his name which carries water from the Durance along the original river course through the Lamanon gap to the Étang de Berre and the sea – *see Basse Vallée de la DURANCE.*

SALON-DE-PROVENCE

Carnot (Cours)	AY 4
Crousillat (Pl.)	BY 12
Frères-Kennedy (R. des)	AY
Gimon (Cours)	BZ
Victor-Hugo (Cours)	BY 38

Ancienne Halle (Pl.)	BY 2
Capucins (Bd des)	BZ 3
Centuries (Pl. des)	BY 6
Clemenceau (Bd Georges)	AY 7
Coren (Bd Léopold)	AY 8
Craponne (Allées de)	BZ 10
Farreyroux (Pl.)	BZ 13
Ferrage (Pl.)	BZ 14
Fileuses-de-Soie (R. des)	AY 15
Gambetta (Pl.)	BZ 18
Horloge (R. de l')	BY 20
Ledru-Rollin (Bd)	AY 22
Massenet (R.)	AY 23
Médicis (Pl. C. de)	BZ 24
Mistral (Bd Frédéric)	BY 26
Moulin d'Isnard (R.)	BY 27
Nostradamus (Bd)	AY 28
Pasquet (Bd)	BZ 30
Pelletan (Cours Camille)	AY 32
République (Bd de la)	AY 33
Raynaud-d'Ursule (R.)	BZ 34
St-Laurent (Square)	BY 35

F	Porte Bourg-Neuf
H	Hôtel de ville
K	Porte de l'Horloge
M¹	Musée Grévin de Provence
M²	Maison de Nostradamus

Michel Nostradamus – Nostradamus chose Salon as his home. Born in St-Rémy-de-Provence in 1503, he studied medicine in Montpellier and travelled for twelve years in Europe and the Far East to try to improve the remedies which he kept secret; he also studied esoterism.

The success he achieved with his remedy for the plague epidemics of Aix and Lyon aroused the jealousy of his colleagues. When the epidemics ceased, he retired to Salon (1547) and took up astrology. His book of predictions entitled *Centuries*, written in the form of verse quatrains, was fantastically successful and attracted the attention of Catherine de' Medici. She came to him and had him read Charles IX's horoscope, showering him profusely with gifts. Nostradamus then attempted meteorology and his *Almanach* was also successful. He died in Salon in 1566. His son César wrote a remarkable work entitled *Stories and Chronicles of Provence*.

TOWN CENTRE *2hr*

Follow on foot the itinerary indicated on the town plan

Château de l'Empéri ⊘ **(BYZ)** – Built on top of Puech rock, this massive castle dominates the old town. Once the residence of the archbishops of Arles, lords of Salon, the castle was begun in the 10C, rebuilt in the 12C and 13C and remodelled in the 16C; it was transformed into barracks in the 19C but damaged during the 1909 earthquake. A vaulted passage leads to the courtyard decorated with a Renaissance gallery.

The 12C Chapelle Ste-Catherine, the main reception room with its finely carved chimney and some 20 rooms house the Empéri Museum.

★★Musée de l'Empéri ⊘ **(BYZ)** – This museum presents the collections of Raoul and Jean Brunon acquired in 1967 by the Musée de l'Armée in Paris *(see Michelin Green Guide Paris)*. It covers the history of the French army from the time of Louis XIV to 1918. The fine rooms enhance the pleasant display of 10 000 items (uniforms, flags, decorations, cutting and thrusting weapons and firearms, cannons, paintings, drawings, engravings, figures on foot or on horseback) which illustrate the military past with special reference to the Napoleonic years.

Musée de l'Empéri, Salon-de-Provence

Musée de l'Empéri

Musée Grévin de Provence ⊘ **(BY M¹)** – Some 2 600 years of the history of Provence are retraced here, in the form of 15 paintings, from the legendary marriage of Gyptis and Protis which, with the foundation of Marseille, sealed the union between the Celtic-Ligurians and the Phocaeans, until the 20C and the literary creation reinterpreted for the cinema in the character of Manon des Sources.

Hôtel de Ville (BY H) – This elegant 17C mansion with two corner turrets and a carved balcony nowadays houses the town hall.

On Place de l'Hôtel-de-Ville stands the statue of Adam de Craponne (fountain).

Porte Bourg-Neuf (BY F) – This gate is all that is left of the old 13C ramparts.

Église St-Michel (BY) – This 13C church possesses two bell towers: a fine five-bay arcaded tower and another tower added in the 15C. Note the portal's (12C) carved tympanum where, in the centre, St Michael surrounded by two snakes stands above the Paschal lamb in a stylised floral decoration.

In the chancel there is an imposing gilded wooden altar (17C); and in the third south chapel the statue of the Virgin (17C).

Maison de Nostradamus ⊘ **(BY M²)** – This is the house in which Nostradamus spent the last 19 years of his life. Ten animated tableaux with audiovisual back-up illustrate his life and work. Themes treated include historical context, where he grew up, a reconstruction of his study and old editions of *Centuries* and his other works.

Porte de l'Horloge (BY K) – 17C ruins of the old ramparts.

Fontaine moussue (BY) – On Place Crousillat stands this charming 18C fountain.

Collégiale St-Laurent (BY) – Of the 14C and 15C, this church is a good example of southern French Gothic.

Inside, the first chapel north of the chancel contains a monolithic 15C polychrome *Descent from the Cross*; the third north chapel has a 16C alabaster Virgin and Nostradamus' tomb; in the fifth chapel is a 15C low relief in marble.

Leave the centre of town on D 17 towards the east, then turn left onto the Val de Cuech road, and immediately left again into Rue du Pavillon (route is signposted).

Musée de Salon et de la Crau ⊘ – This museum is in a huge 19C mansion, known as the "Pavillon", and is concerned with local history and the popular arts and traditions of Salon and the surrounding area at the end of the 19C. A model illustrates the natural environment and its evolution over the years. Traditional activities and everyday customs are evoked thematically: sheep-raising, the manufacture of local household soap known as *savon de Marseille*, popular worship etc. The natural history section has diorama displays of a variety of naturalised birds.

NORTHEAST OF SALON *Round tour of 51km/31.5mi – allow 3hr*

Leave Salon-de-Provence on D 17 heading east.

Musée de Salon et de la Crau – *See above.*

Continue along D 17; in Pélissanne turn left onto D 22ᴬ.

★**Château de La Barben** – *See Château de La BARBEN.*

Continue along D 22ᴬ and turn left onto D 572.

The road follows the fertile Touloubre valley and passes beneath the Canal de Marseille *(see Basse Vallée de la DURANCE)* before offering a lovely view of the Trévaresse range before you.

St-Cannat – The town was the birthplace of **Admiral Suffren** (1729-88), who was engaged in constant and usually successful action against the Royal Navy throughout a career which spanned the Seven Years War and the American War of Independence. The house in which Suffren was born is now the town hall (small **museum** ⊘). In the church a fine ancient reliquary chest, decorated with small figures carved in high relief, now serves as the stoup.

Lambesc – The small town, now by-passed by N 7, has a large 18C church which incorporates a 14C bell tower of an earlier sanctuary. The spire collapsed in the 1909 earthquake. On a 16C gate is a belfry with a clock and Jack.

Continue along N 7, in Cazan turn left onto D 22.

Château-Bas – *See CHÂTEAU-BAS.*

Continue along D 22 and turn right onto D 22ᶜ.

As the road rises a very fine view extends to include, besides the Luberon and Durance valley, the Chaîne des Côtes and Aix countryside.

Vernègues – The post-1909 village was built on the plateau after the earthquake had destroyed the original hill-top settlement.

Vieux-Vernègues – The uphill road circles the village *(the ruins are not open to the public)* and goes on to the small tower from where there is a vast **panorama**★ *(viewing-table)* of a large area of Provence; the Alpilles stand out in the west.

Return to Vernègues, bear right on D 22ᴮ and left on D 68.

The road leads into the small Cuech valley with its lovely gorges.

At the entrance to Pélisanne turn right onto D 17.

SAULT

Population 1 206
Michelin map 81 fold 14 or 245 fold 18 – Local map see Mont VENTOUX

The town is built in a semicircle, 765m/2 510ft up on a rock promontory at the west end of the Vaucluse plateau above the Gorges de la Nesque. Its position makes it an ideal centre for excursions to Mont Ventoux and the Baronnies and Lure mountains. It is at the centre of an important lavender-growing region and is known for its nougat and honey.

SIGHTS

Church (Église) – The 12C-14C building has a fine elevation and a gabled transept; the nave is remarkable for the arches of its broken barrel vaulting which descend on to tall engaged columns. The Gothic chancel is lined with 17C panelling.

Terrace – *At the north end of the town.* From here there is a lovely **view** of the Vaucluse plateau, the entrance to the Nesque gorges and Mont Ventoux.

Museum ⊙ – Located on the first floor of the library, the museum contains prehistoric and Gallo-Roman remains, coins, arms, geological finds and a collection of old documents, as well as a mummy and other Egyptian artefacts.

★★★MONT VENTOUX

Ascent via the eastern face – 30km/19mi – allow 2hr. Leave Sault on D 164. Description and local map see Mont VENTOUX.

PLATEAU D'ALBION

Round tour of 30km/19mi – 1hr 30min. Leave Sault on D 30 towards St-Christol.

The Albion plateau, with its fissured calcareous landscape, has all the physical characteristics of a limestone *causse*. Over 200 underground caves or *avens* have been discovered here, many with narrow openings which are difficult to spot. The most beautiful viewed from above is the "Crirvi" cave near St-Christol; the deepest in the region include the Aven Jean-Nouveau with its 168m/550ft vertical shaft at its entrance, and the 600m/1970ft deep Aven Autran, also near St-Christol, with abundant flowing water at its base. The distinctive feature of these caves is their ability to absorb rainwater down into the branches of an underground system buried deep in the calcareous rock: the main branch of this vast system emerges in the famous "Fontaine de Vaucluse".

An underground missile base has also been built on the plateau where several vertical shafts have been converted into nuclear rocket silos.

The road passes the entrance to the Plateau d'Albion military base.

St-Christol – This small town on the edge of the Plateau d'Albion (also known as the Plateau de St-Christol) has a **church** built in the 12C by Benedictines from the Abbaye St-André in Villeneuve-lès-Avignon. It was enlarged by the addition of an aisle in the 17C. The most interesting feature is the carving in the oven vaulted apse: the blind arcading is supported on six fluted columns, chiselled with reliefs of leaves, fruits and birds; above are foliated capitals; below are bases decorated with masks and fantastic animals. The Carolingian altar is carved on three sides.

Turn back on D 30 towards Sault, then turn right onto D 95.

St-Trinit – A 12C **church** is all that remains of an old medieval priory which was accountable to the Abbaye St-André at Villeneuve-lès-Avignon. The chevet with its cut-off corners punctuated by bare pilasters is adorned with a window framed by two cabled columns with Corinthian capitals.

In the interior, both the oven vaulted pentagonal apse and the bay of the chancel are supported by discharging arches dating from the church's initial construction.

Continue to Aurel on D 950 towards Sault, then take D 1 which branches off to the right, and finally D 95.

Aurel – From D 95 the village, overlooking the Sault plain and its fields of lavender, appears suddenly below, along with its old fortifications and robust church with its light-coloured stone. A hospice was built here by the Knights of St John of Jerusalem.

Abbaye de SÉNANQUE★★

Michelin map 81 fold 13 or 245 fold 17 or 246 fold 11

Nestling in the hollow of a small canyon of the Senancole, which opens onto the Vaucluse plateau, the harmonious ensemble of buildings of the Abbaye de Sénanque (lovely view coming from Gordes on D 177) stands in a desolate **site★**. On arrival, as one takes in the abbey church's east end, set, in the summer, in a sea of lavender and bathed in sunlight, one feels perfectly in tune with the tranquil atmosphere which this seat of Cistercian monasticism exudes.

Foundation and development – The foundation, in 1148, of Sénanque by a group of monks who had come from Abbaye de Mazan (Haut-Vivarais) fits into the great Cistercian expansion of the 12C. This monastic movement, directed and inspired by St Bernard of Clairvaux, preached an ascetic ideal and prescribed the strict application of the early Benedictine rule in its monasteries: isolation, poverty and simplicity must lead the monk to purity and beatitude.

The way of life of the Cistercians was thus very demanding, very difficult even: divine service, prayer and pious reading alternated with manual labour to fill very long days where time of rest did not exceed seven hours; meals taken in silence were frugal and the monks slept in a common dormitory without any comfort. Cistercian austerity influenced the architectural and artistic conceptions of the Order. St Bernard decreed that buildings be exceedingly plain and stripped of all ornamentation that could divert the attention of those who prayed: no coloured stained glass windows, statues, paintings, or carved tympana and proud bell towers. This sparse ornamentation is echoed in the other two Provençal abbeys, daughter-houses of Sénanque: Abbaye du Thoronet *(see Michelin Green Guide French Riviera)* and Abbaye de Silvacane. They have come down to us almost as they were at the height of the Cistercian movement.

Sénanque prospered very rapidly to the point that, as early as 1152, the community had enough members to found another abbey in Vivarais. It profited from numerous gifts starting with the land of the Simiane family and later the land of the lords of Venasque. The monastery rapidly set up, sometimes quite far away, outlying farms *(granges)* worked by lay brothers recruited from the peasant population, who performed the duties essential to the running of a farm.

Sénanque's golden age occurred in the early 13C, but as elsewhere, success and prosperity caused corruption. As with the Cluny Order in the past, the Cistercian Order accumulated wealth incompatible with its vow of poverty: disorder ensued.

Decadence and renaissance – In the 14C Sénanque entered a decadent period. Recruitment and fervour diminished while lack of discipline increased. And yet, thanks to the energetic rule of an abbot during the end of the 15C, the situation improved and until the mid 16C the monastery once more strove to respect the ideals of its founders.

Unfortunately, in 1544, Sénanque fell victim to the Vaudois revolt: monks were hanged by the heretics and several buildings were razed. This was the final blow; the abbey was never able to recover.

At the end of the 17C, in spite of the deserving efforts of the abbots, the community numbered only two monks. Nevertheless the south wing of the monastery was rebuilt at the beginning of the 18C.

Abbaye de Sénanque

Sold as state property in 1791, Sénanque miraculously fell into the hands of an intelligent owner who not only preserved it from destruction but also consolidated it. Bought by an ecclesiastic in 1854, it was returned, soon after, to its monastic vocation; new buildings were added flanking the older ones and 72 monks were installed. The anticlerical beliefs of the Third Republic brought about their eviction twice. In 1927 a dozen monks returned and remained for some 40-odd years, then moved for a period to the Lérins Islands (St-Honorat) and finally returned to resume monastic life in the abbey in October 1989.

TOUR ⏱ allow 1hr

This is a fine example of Cistercian architecture. The early monastery is almost complete with the exception of the lay-brothers' range, which was rebuilt in the 18C. The medieval parts are built in local ashlar stone. The abbey church has kept its original roof of limestone slabs *(lauzes)* surmounted by a small square bell tower; contrary to custom it was built orientated not to the east but to the north, as the builders had to compensate for the rigours of the local terrain.

The tour starts on the first floor of the dormitory, northwest of the cloisters.

Dormitory (Dortoir) – This vast pointed barrel vaulted room with transverse arches, lit by a 12-lobed oculus and narrow windows, is paved in brick. This is where the monks slept fully dressed on a simple straw pallet. They were roused in the middle of the night for the first service (nocturns) which took place at 2am, soon followed by matins at dawn. The dormitory now houses an exhibition on the abbey's construction.

★**Abbey Church (Église)** – Begun in 1160 with the sanctuary and transept, the church was completed in the early 13C with the nave. The purity of line and great and austere beauty, emphasised by the absence of all decoration, create a place of worship and meditation.

Stand at the back of the nave to admire the harmony of the proportions and masses. The façade did not have the customary central door, as one entered through two small doors opening onto the aisles; this indicated that the church was not made to receive flocks of worshippers in this secluded spot. The five-bayed nave is roofed with pointed barrel vaulting without transverse arches, the aisles are in rampant pointed barrel vaulting, and are joined to the nave's arches by great arcades with double recessed orders. The transept crossing is crowned by a large dome on elaborate squinches (small arches, curved stone slab, fluted pilasters which recall the style of churches from Velay and Vivarais). The sanctuary ends with a semicircular apse pierced by three windows, symbolising the Trinity, and flanked by four apsidal chapels, which on the outside have been incorporated into a great rectangular structure. The four side altars and high altar are the original ones. In the east arm of the transept, the wall of which is opened by a window with 10 rays, is the tomb of a Venasque lord, one of the abbey's benefactors in the early 13C. Nave, transept and aisles are covered with flat stones resting on the vault itself. Note the lack of all ornamentation which left the monk undistracted as he worshipped God.

Off the north façade is the sacristy.

★**Cloisters (Cloître)** – Late 12C. The cloisters' galleries are covered with rounded bar-

rel vaulting with transverse arches held up by carved brackets. Under great relieving arches are two groups of small twinned columns alternating with square pillars. Decoration appears on the capitals (leaf-work, flowers, rope and palm-leaf moulding and interlacing) and yet it remains discreet.

The cloisters open onto the different rooms of the conventual buildings, each of which has its specific function.

★**Conventual buildings (Bâtiments conventuels)** – An extension of the abbey church's west transept arm including: chapterhouse, warming house, dormitory *(see above)* upstairs; to the west and south are the refectory and lay-brothers' range.

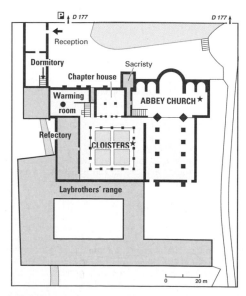

249

Chapterhouse (Salle capitulaire) – The room is roofed with six-pointed vaults held up at the centre on two pillars flanked by four small engaged columns. Under the abbot's leadership the monastic community met here to read and comment on the Scriptures, receive the novices' vows, to keep vigil over the dead and to make important decisions. The monks sat on the tiers.

Warming Room (Chauffoir) – Access via a narrow passage (parlour or day room), the warming house (calefactory) is roofed with groined vaulting which is held up by a massive central pillar perched on a plinth. One of the two original chimneys remains in a corner. The heat was essential to the transcribers who were bent over their manuscripts all day.

Refectory (Réfectoire) – Parallel to the west gallery of the cloisters. It was extensively damaged in the 16C and has recently been restored to its original appearance.

Lay-brothers' Range (Bâtiment des Convers) – South of the cloisters, this building which was remodelled in the 18C housed the lay-brothers, who lived separately from the monks, meeting them only during certain services or when working in the fields.

Abbaye de SILVACANE ★★

Michelin map 84 folds 2 and 3 or 114 folds 1 and 2 or 245 fold 31 or 246 fold 12
Local map see Basse Vallée de la DURANCE

Set in a pastoral landscape on the Durance's south bank, the Abbaye de Silvacane, with its pink-tiled roofs and small mutilated square bell tower, offers a beautiful example of plain Cistercian beauty.

From its founding to the present – In the 11C the monks from St-Victor of Marseille established themselves on this insalubrious land surrounded by "a forest of reeds" *(Sylva cana)*, from which the monastery derives its name.

The monastery became affiliated with Cîteaux and in 1144 received a donation from two benefactors: Guillaume de la Roque and Raymond de Baux, while a group of Cistercians from the Abbaye de Morimond (an abbey which has since disappeared, located on the boundary of Champagne and Lorraine) settled here.

Protected by Provence's great lords, the abbey prospered; it accomplished large land improvement projects in the region and in turn founded Abbaye de Valsainte near Apt. In 1289 a violent confrontation occurred between it and the powerful Abbaye de Montmajour of the Benedictine Order; monks pursued each other and some were even taken as hostages. The affair ended in a trial and Silvacane was returned to its rightful owners, the Cistercians.

But even more serious were the pillaging of the abbey in 1358 by the lord of Aubignan and the severe frosts of 1364 which destroyed the olive and wine crops. This set of a period of decline which ended in 1443 with the annexation of the abbey to the chapter of Cathédrale St-Sauveur in Aix.

It became the village of Roque-d'Anthéron's parish church in the early 16C, and suffered during the Wars of Religion. When the Revolution broke out the buildings were already abandoned; the abbey was sold as state property and converted into a farm. In 1949 the buildings were bought by the state and are gradually being restored: on the foundations discovered in 1989, to the west, the monastic buildings, the fortified wall in coated quarry-stone, and the monks' guest-house have all now been restored.

TOUR *about 1hr*

Access through ticket office built on the site of the old inn

Church (Église) – The church, which was built on a slope between 1175 and 1230, features different levels which are noticeable when one is viewing the west façade. This façade is pierced by openings: a central door (on the tympanum the canons of St-Sauveur placed their coat of arms), two side doors topped with small off-centred windows, three windows and an oculus adorned with mouldings on the upper floor. The three-bayed nave ends in a flat east end. Each arm of the transept has two orientated chapels.

The vaulting is surprisingly varied: pointed barrel with transverse arches in the nave, rampant barrel in the aisles except the third north bay which is half-barrel, transverse barrel vaulting for the arms of the transept, pointed vaulting for the transept crossing and apsidal chapels.

The chancel is illuminated by three round-arched windows surmounted by an oculus; the south aisle is also lit by an opening in each bay. Note how the architect had to take into account the very steep slope of the land by placing at different levels the south aisle, nave, north aisle and cloisters. As at Sénanque all decoration was forbidden; the simplicity of the building is in keeping with the rigid Cistercian rule. In the north chapel of the north arm of the transept (**1**) are the fragments of the tomb of Bertrand de Baux, grandson of the founder, who began the church's construction.

Cloisters – Located at a lower level (1.6m/4.5ft) than the church, the cloisters date from the second half of the 13C. Nevertheless, the gallery vaulting is still Romanesque with rounded barrel vaulting on transverse arches, except for three corners which have pointed vaulting. Powerful rounded arches open on to the yard; they were originally adorned with paired bays.

Conventual buildings – Except for the refectory these were all built from 1210 to 1230.

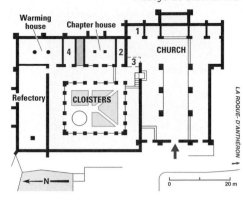

The **sacristy** (**2**) is a long narrow room next to the **library** (**3**) located under the north arm of the transept. The **chapterhouse** *(see plan on p 39 under Art: Architectural Terms)* recalls the one at Sénanque: six-pointed vaults falling on two different central pillars: one flanked by four small columns, the other with fluted rope moulding. After the **parlour** (**4**), which was used as a passage to the exterior, comes the **warming house** (calefactory); also with pointed vaulting, it has kept its chimney. Above is the **dormitory**.

The large and magnificent **refectory** was rebuilt from 1420 to 1425. The capitals are more decorated than in the other rooms; the room is well lit by high windows and a large rose window; the pulpit remains.

The lay-brothers' range has completely disappeared. Excavations have uncovered, outside, the ruins of the gatehouse and the abbey's precinct wall.

SUZE-LA-ROUSSE

Population 1 422

Michelin map 81 fold 2 or 245 fold 16 or 246 fold 23 – Facilities

Suze-la-Rousse, picturesquely terraced on the south bank of the Lez, was, during the Middle Ages, the most important town of Tricastin.

The hill is dominated by its imposing feudal castle. One of its lords, wounded during the siege of Montélimar in 1587, was hoisted on to his mare, also wounded, and before returning home, kindly said to her, "Come on, my grey, let us go and die at Suze." The former town hall displays a lovely 15C and 16C façade.

Castle (Château) ⊙ – Crossing a plantation of truffle oaks (some 30ha/74 acres) an alley leads to the castle's only entrance.

It dates for the most part from the 14C, and its towers are a good example of military architecture of this period. It was remodelled inside during the Renaissance. The main courtyard features fine Renaissance façades.

The ground floor houses the staff and service quarters, the stables and 12C kitchen. The apartments are reached by a monumental grand staircase. Note the Four Seasons Room, and the armoury with its painted ceiling and great chimney flanked by two frescoes (restored) representing the siege of Montélimar.

In one of the corner towers there is an octagonal room. A fine view of Mont Ventoux, Lance mountain and the Dauphiné pre-Alps can be had.

The castle houses the "**University of Wine**" ⊙, founded by professionals, which is equipped with a laboratory and a tasting room and which offers courses in oenology.

TARASCON★

Population 10 826

Michelin map 83 fold 10 or 245 fold 28 or 246 fold 26

A tradition dating back some 2 000 years has created Tarascon, the city of the Tarasque. Last century the French writer **Alphonse Daudet** brought fame to the town through his character **Tartarin** (a fat, bearded figure invented in 1872). And yet the city has its own claim to fame in the shape of its magnificent castle, with walls which drop straight down to the swift-flowing River Rhône.

The city is on the boundary of a rich market gardening region and has thus become an important fruit and vegetable dispatching centre.

The Tarasque monster – Massalia's trading post, Tarascon was established on an island in the Rhône. The Romans took it over after the defeat of the Massaliotes. The present castle stands on the site of the Roman camp built by the legionaries.

According to a Provençal legend, an amphibious creature periodically climbed out of the Rhône into the town, where it devoured children and cattle and killed anyone attempting to cross the river. To save the town, St Martha came from Les Stes-Maries-de-la-Mer and subdued the beast with the sign of the Cross; the now docile beast was thereupon captured by the townspeople.

In celebration of the miracle, Good King René, who often resided in the castle, organised stupendous festivities in 1474. The legend is recalled in an annual fête and procession. A huge model of the Tarasque with champing jaws and swinging tail is paraded through the streets; with a snap of its tail, the monster knocks down those it can reach.

Tarasque

Tartarin – The city of Tarascon inevitably brings to mind the legendary figure of Tartarin whom Alphonse Daudet invented in 1872. This stout, bearded character, often seen as a symbol for naïvety and pompousness, was invariably portrayed setting off for some fashionable location, sporting either his colonial hunter's gear for an African safari, or else the outfit of the perfect climber – complete with goggles, cap, ice pick and crampons – staunchly determined to tackle the vertiginous heights of the French Alpilles.

★★CASTLE (Y) *1hr*

Its location on the banks of the Rhône, its massive appearance which contrasts with its inside architecture, and its exceptional state of preservation, make this building one of the finest medieval castles in France. In the 13C, the castle, opposite the royal city of Beaucaire, defended Provence's western boundary. Captured by Raymond de Turenne in 1399, it was restored soon after to its owners, the Anjou family; Louis II, father of René, decided to have it entirely rebuilt.

Construction began with the fortified walls and towers built from 1400 to 1406 and continued under Louis III from 1430 to 1435 with the inner courtyard and the east and southeast wings; the master craftsman was the Provençal architect Jean Robert. From 1447 to 1449, **King René** completed the building, which was his favourite residence, contributing all his taste and refinement to the interior decoration.

Here he organised splendid festivities (notably the famous tournament, Pas de la Bergère, which went on for three days in June 1449), wrote the *Tournaments Treatise*, composed music and received prominent guests, such as the future Louis XI and Charles of Orléans, the famous troubadour.

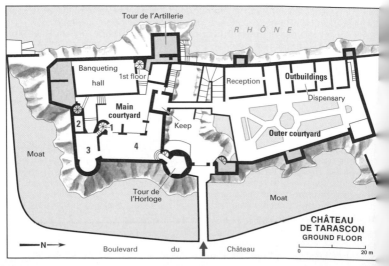

TARASCON

Halles (R. des) .... **YZ**
Mairie (Pl. de la) .... **Y** 15
Monge (R.) .... **Y**
Pelletan (R.E.) .... **Z** 19
Proudhon (R.) .... **Z** 20
Victor-Hugo (Bd) .... **Z**

Aqueduc (R. de l') .... **Y** 2
Berrurier (Pl. Colonel) .... **Z** 3
Blanqui (R.) .... **Z** 4
Briand (Crs Aristide) .... **Z** 5
Château (Bd du) .... **Y** 6
Château (R. du) .... **Y** 7
Hôpital (R. de l') .... **Z** 9
Jaurès (R. Jean) .... **Y** 12
Jeu de Paume (R. du) .... **YZ** 14
Millaud (R. Ed.) .... **YZ** 16
Mistral (R. Frédéric) .... **Z** 18
Raffin (R.) .... **Z** 23
République (Av. de la) .... **Z** 24
Salengro (Av. R.) .... **Y** 25

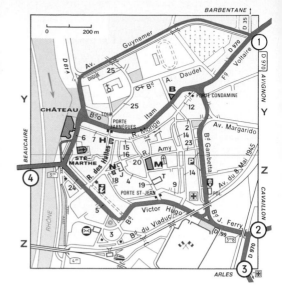

B Maison de Tartarin
H Hôtel de ville
M Musée Charles-Deméry
N Cloître des Cordeliers

More or less abandoned, Tarascon castle became a famous prison in the 17C. It exercised this rather sinister function until 1926. Since restored, it has rid itself of its numerous accretions and its moats have been cleared, giving the castle the appearance it had 500 years ago. It is made up of two independent buildings: the seigneurial living quarters on the south side flanked by round towers on the town's side and square towers on the Rhône side, offering a compact mass of walls rising up 48m/157ft (towers and curtain wall were of the same height, which facilitated artillery movement on the terraces built for that purpose); and the inner courtyard on the north side, defended by shorter rectangular towers (see illustration on p 42 under Art: Architectural Terms).

Outer Courtyard – A wide moat crossed by a bridge (once a drawbridge) isolates the two groups of buildings from the rest of the city. An annexe of the castle which it joins, but independent of, this section includes the service buildings. Recently remodelled, these buildings house the Hospital of St-Nicolas' **dispensary**: in a finely-panelled 18C room there are 200 apothecary jars (ceramics from St-Jean-du-Désert and Montpellier).

Seigneurial Living Quarters – Enter the seigneurial living quarters through the keep's zigzag passageway to the main courtyard, around which are the apartments with their lovely, finely-carved façades adorned with mullioned windows. A graceful polygonal staircase turret (**1**) serves the different floors; near it a niche shelters the busts of King René and Jeanne of Laval, his second wife. Still on the south side of the main courtyard, climb up some steps to the Flamboyant screen of the chantry (**2**); opening onto the corner tower is the lower chapel (**3**), and above it the upper chapel.

To the east and north lie the L-shaped main living quarters which partly overlook the town and include the private apartments, which rise above a lovely gallery (**4**) with pointed barrel vaulting, and communicate with the clock tower (which had a military function). To the west stands the Tour de l'Artillerie which juts out over the bank of the Rhône.

The tour of the west wing, which rises above the river, is a visit through the state rooms: the ground floor – banqueting hall (two chimneys); first floor – reception hall (two vast rooms with painted wood ceilings). Then continue to the King's Bedroom (in the southwest tower) with a chimney and heating platter; on the second floor are the Audience Chamber and Council Room, which were vaulted to support the terraces. In these rooms there are several fine 17C Flemish tapestries, the subject of which is: *"Scipio Africanus'Gesture"*.

Return to the south wing to see the Chaplain's Room (sacristy, host oven, corner for the treasury) and the royal chapel, which has kept the king's and queen's oratories and from where they could hear the chantry voices.

Terrace – The terrace offers a wide **panorama**★★ of Beaucaire, Tarascon, the Rhône, Vallabrègues undertaking, the Montagnette hills, the Alpilles, Fontvieille, the Abbaye de Montmajour, Arles and St-Gilles plain. It was through the crenellations of this platform that Robespierre's local partisans were thrown into the river in 1794. These terraces were dominated by a fort, crowning the keep; its base remains.

Go back down by the clock tower; the ground floor houses the Galley Room, named to commemorate the graffiti and boat drawings made by past prisoners.

ADDITIONAL SIGHTS

★Église Ste-Marthe ⊘ **(Y)** – Founded in c 10C, this church was rebuilt in the 12C when the saint's body was found, then largely rebuilt once more in the 14C and modified over the following centuries. The church was restored having been partly destroyed in 1944. The south door is a fine example of the Romanesque style; unfortunately, its lovely carved decoration has partially disappeared.

Inside among the numerous paintings hanging in the side chapels note: *St Thomas Aquinas and St Catherine of Siena* by Pierre Parrocel *(third south chapel)* and the works of Vien and Nicolas Mignard retracing the life of St Martha. Found in the north aisle are a fine 15C triptych (last bay's chapel); *St Francis of Assisi* by Carle Van Loo, a reliquary bust and a marble recumbent figure from a 17C mausoleum *(Ste-Marthe's Chapel, second bay)*.

In the staircase to the crypt is the Renaissance-style tomb of Jean de Cossa (former Seneschal of Provence), attributed to the school of Francesco Laurana.

The crypt itself contains the sarcophagus (3C-4C) of St Martha, ornamented with carvings.

Musée Charles-Déméry (Souleiado) ⊘ **(Z M)** – This interesting museum, established on the same site as the family business, contains several rare pieces of printed cloth, popular 18C-19C Provençal costumes and a large collection of earthenware, pottery and paintings.

Hôtel de Ville (Y H) – This 17C building features an elegantly carved façade enhanced by a stone balcony.

In the nearby **Rue des Halles** are picturesque arcaded houses (15C).

Maison de Tartarin ⊘ **(Y B)** – Arranged in homage to the most famous of Tarascon citizens, the fictitious Tartarin, this house consists of three rooms decorated in the 1870s style. On the ground floor are the office and living room, above is the bedroom. Costumed models, furniture and documents help relive the atmosphere of Daudet's novel: *The New Don Quixote or the Wonderful Adventures of Tarascon.* Behind the house is a tropical garden. A conservatory here contains an effigy of the Tarasque with a "tarascaire" (knight of the Tarasque).

Cloître des Cordeliers (Z N) – The 17C galleries of this old cloister have alternating ribbed and hemispheric vaulting on a square plan. An access corridor leads to the gallery, with its gothic arched bays decorated with garlands of flowers sculptured in stone. The charming, flower-decked inner courtyard, bordered by arcades surmounted by balustrades, is often the setting for cultural events.

Le THOR

Population 5941

Michelin map 81 fold 12 or 245 fold 17 or 246 fold 11

Once the capital of the white dessert grape, Chasselas, Le Thor has diversified its agricultural activities to include market gardening and tree and shrub growing. The bridge over the Sorgue, the church and its precinct create a picturesque scene. Remaining from the Middle Ages are the ruins of the ramparts and the belfry.

★Church (Église) ⊘ – *15min.* Completed in the early 13C, the church as a whole is Romanesque in style, yet its single nave is covered with Gothic vaulting which counts among the most ancient in Provence. The exterior is imposing with its massive buttresses supporting the tall nave, its apse adorned with Lombard arcades and its heavy unfinished central bell tower. The doors were directly inspired by Antique art, particularly the south door.

The austere interior consists of a single nave and a fine dome on squinches. Note the keystone at the entrance to the four-sided apse: the Lamb of God encircled by five eagles.

Grotte de Thouzon ⊘ – *3 km/2mi to the north; the trail to the cave branches off D 16.* The cave opens at the foot of the hill crowned by the ruins of Thouzon castle and a monastery (small Romanesque chapel quite close by). It was discovered in 1902 by chance after a blast on the site of a former quarry. The visitor walks 230m/755ft along the bed of the old underground river, which carved this gallery, to a not very deep chasm.

On the cave roof, which rises to 22m/72ft, are delicate stalactites of rare quality. In addition the cave presents oddly-shaped, beautifully-coloured concretions.

Michelin Maps, Red Guides and Green Guides
are complementary publications
to be used together.

La TOUR-D'AIGUES

Population 3 328
Michelin map 84 fold 3 or 245 fold 32 – 6km/3.5mi northeast of Pertuis

Nestling at the foot of the Luberon, Aigues country, open onto Aix-en-Provence, appears to be a favoured region: its delightful countryside made up of fertile and well exposed land where vineyards, orchards (cherries) and market produce grow, contrasts with the wild barrenness of the neighbouring mountains.

Founded in the 10C or 11C, the town owes its name to a tower (*tour* in French) which was a precursor of the keep of the present castle. In high season the Festival du Sud Luberon is held here.

Château ⊘ – The château was rebuilt from 1555 to 1575 in the Renaissance style by an Italian architect (Ercole Nigra) on the foundations of a medieval castle. It occupies 1 400m²/15 070sq ft on a vast terrace overlooking the Lèze. Burned in 1782 and again in 1792 when it was ruined, it is now being progressively restored by the Vaucluse *département*.

The monumental **Entrance Gate** takes the form of a richly-decorated triumphal arch: Corinthian columns and pilasters, a frieze of the attributes of war and an entablature surmounted by a triangular pediment. On either side rises an imposing square pavilion with three storeys of windows (the pavilion on the left has preserved its tall chimney). In the centre of the bailey is the keep restored to its 16C Italian plan; in a corner the chapel.

Inside, the network of underground cellars now house exhibition, projection and conference rooms as well as collections from the two museums below.

Musée des Faïences ⊘ – During the course of the restoration work carried out on the château's cellars a large quantity of glazed earthenware was discovered. The finest pieces from these finds have been brought together in this museum which offers the visitor a comprehensive illustration of the work produced in Jérôme Bruny's Tour-d'Aigues factory between 1750 and 1785. The collection contains some fine examples of faience ware, white stanniferous-enamelled faience, tableware emblazoned with the coat of arms of the Bruny family, and polychrome and *en camaïeu faïence*, including an oval dish representing a fox-hunting scene in orange-tinted monochrome from an engraving by Jean Bernard Oudry. Examples of 18C European (Delft, Moustiers, Marseille) and Asian (China, Japan) porcelain are also displayed, as well as 16C marble medallions of laurel-crowned heads, and 17C-18C enamalled terracotta ornamental tiles.

Musée de l'Histoire du Pays d'Aigues ⊘ – This museum contains a modern display drawing heavily on audiovisual methods: a history of Provençal man's evolution from his origins to the present. Slides, illuminated maps, miscellaneous objects (early casts, tools, reconstruction of a silkworm farm) and models depict the development of local rural life.

Church (Église) – This unusual building possesses a Romanesque nave with an apse which served as the main entrance until 1961. It has been restored and is now used as originally intended. The transept and the chancel are 17C additions.

Château de la Tour-d'Aigues – Entrance Gate

UZÈS★★

Population 7 649
Michelin map 80 fold 19 or 245 fold 14 or 246 fold 25 – Facilities

Set in the severe yet charming *garrigues* countryside, Uzès established itself at the tip of a limestone plateau, overlooking the Alzon valley.

A ducal seat, bishopric and consular seat, Uzès has preserved its lay-out as a medieval stronghold, which in the 17C and 18C embellished itself as a result of economic prosperity (acquired through the manufacture of linen, serge and silk). The town has overflowed its former fortifications, now replaced by boulevards, and has developed on the plateau. It has been restored to its earlier appearance as a result of the renovation work undertaken in the protected district.

The duchy of Uzès – The old House of Uzès goes back to Charlemagne through its women. In 1486 the last heir of the lords of Uzès married the count de Crussol, governor of Dauphiné; one of their descendants, Antoine de Crussol, received from Charles IX in 1565 the title of Duke of Uzès. After the execution, in 1632, of the Duke of Montmorency in Toulouse, the Duke of Uzès became the first duke and peer of the kingdom.

As long ago as 1547 a powerful Protestant church was established in Uzès. From then on there began a long period of religious wars which resulted in the submission and exile of Huguenots under Louis XIII and Louis XIV. Since then a sullen rivalry has divided the Uzès religious population of Catholics and Protestants until quite recently.

Poet in exile – Uzès has its place in the history of French literature, because it was here that **Jean Racine** (1639-99) stayed in 1661 when he was 22 years old.

Having been educated under the severe discipline of Port-Royal and the Jansenist College of Harcourt in Paris, Racine sought a change. His family, who watched with horror as their son considered a career in the theatre, sent him to his uncle, vicar general of Uzès. To entice him away from his worldly associations, his uncle promised him an allowance once he had taken holy orders. Racine spent rather more than a year at his uncle's. In his letters, full of humour, he spoke little of theology but much of the countryside, the food, the local dialect (which he could not understand) and his first poems.

A trial was brought concerning his proposed allowance; Racine did not understand a thing and lost. This pettifoggery is said to have been the origin of his only comedy *Les Plaideurs* (*The Litigants*, a three-act play written in 1668).

The young poet did not pursue the religious vocation so desired by his family, but returned to Paris to become France's greatest classical dramatist.

The Gide family – Uzès is also the birthplace of the Gides. **Paul Gide** (1832-80), an eminent lawyer, and **Charles Gide** (1847-1932), the famous economist, were both born in Uzès and were respectively the father and uncle of the author **André Gide** (1869-1951) who was awarded the Nobel Prize for Literature in 1947. Gide spent his holidays with his grandmother in Uzès and recounts his sojourns in *If It Die... (Si le Grain ne Meurt)*.

★★OLD TOWN *2hr 30min*

Start at Avenue de la Libération and turn right onto Boulevard des Alliés.

Église St-Étienne ⊘ (**A**) – This church was built in the 18C in the Jesuit style, based on the design of the architect Pierre Bondon. It occupies the site of an earlier church which was destroyed during the Wars of Religion. It features a curvilinear façade decorated with pilasters with Ionic capitals and with flame ornamentation. The rectangular bell tower is the only remnant of the 13C building.

On Place de l'Église stands the house (**A D**) where Charles Gide *(see above)* was born.

Rue St-Étienne (**A 25**) – No 1. An imposing Louis XIII-style faceted door. Further on to the left in a blind alley is a fine Renaissance façade.

★**Place aux Herbes** (**A**) – This picturesque, asymmetrical square is surrounded by covered walkways and has plane trees growing in it. Among the medieval houses, which were converted in the 17C and 18C, notice set back on the west side of the square the **Hôtel d'Aigaliers** (**A E**), dating from the 17C, and to the north a corner house (**A F**) decorated on the side with a turret on squinches.

At the end of the square turn right into an alleyway.

It leads to the unusual and narrow **Rue Pélisserie** (**A 18**).

Go forward into Rue Entre-les-Tours.

Tour de l'Horloge (**A**) – This clock tower dates from the 12C and is crowned with a wrought-iron bell cage. It was the bishop's tower; it confronted the duke's tower and king's tower at a time when these three powers shared Uzès.

Hôtel Dampmartin (**A K**) – *On the corner of Rue Jacques-d'Uzès and Place Dampmartin.* This mansion displays a Renaissance façade flanked by a round tower; a carved frieze surrounds the first-floor window. Enter into the Renaissance courtyard (staircase).

Cross Place Dampmartin.

UZÈS

Alliés (Bd des)	**A** 2	Boucairie (R.)	**B** 4	Marronniers (Prom.)	**B** 16		
Gambetta (Bd)	**A**	Collège (R. du)	**B** 6	Pascal (Av. M.)	**B** 17		
Gide (Bd Ch.)	**AB**	Dampmartin (Pl.)	**A** 7	Pélisserie (R.)	**A** 18		
République (R.)	**A** 23	Dr-Blanchard (R.)	**B** 8	Plan-de-l'Oume (R.)	**B** 19		
Uzès (R. J.-d')	**A** 29	Duché (Pl. du)	**A** 9	Port-Royal (R.)	**B** 20		
Vincent (Av. Gén.)	**A**	Entre-les-Tours (R.)	**A** 10	Rafin (R.)	**B** 21		
		Évêché (R. de l')	**B** 12	St-Étienne (R.)	**A** 25		
		Foch (Av. Mar.)	**A** 13	St-Théodorit (R.)	**B** 27		
		Foussat (R. Paul)	**A** 14	Victor-Hugo (Bd)	**A** 32		
				4-Septembre (R.)	**A** 35		

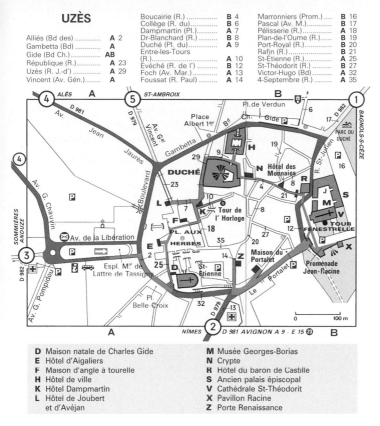

D	Maison natale de Charles Gide	**M**	Musée Georges-Borias
E	Hôtel d'Aigaliers	**N**	Crypte
F	Maison d'angle à tourelle	**R**	Hôtel du baron de Castille
H	Hôtel de ville	**S**	Ancien palais épiscopal
K	Hôtel Dampmartin	**V**	Cathédrale St-Théodorit
L	Hôtel de Joubert	**X**	Pavillon Racine
	et d'Avéjan	**Z**	Porte Renaissance

Hôtel de Joubert et d'Avéjan (**A L**) – *No 12 Rue de la République.* Fine Henri II-style façade (restored).
Return to Rue Jacques-d'Uzès and turn left.

★**Duché** ⊙ (**A**) – From the outside, the ducal palace appears as a feudal mass with buildings of various periods exemplifying the rise of the Uzès family.

Courtyard – From left to right are: Tour de la Vicomté (14C tower) with its octagonal turret, commemorating the lords of Uzès' elevation to a viscounty in 1328; Tour Dermonde, a square 11C keep, the top of it, damaged during the Revolution, was rebuilt in the 19C. To the right, at a right angle, lies the Renaissance **façade**★ erected by the first duke in c 1550 based on plans by Philibert Delorme (c 1510-c 1570). It is one of the first examples of the superimposition of the classical orders – Doric, Ionic and Corinthian. At the façade's far end stands a Gothic chapel (restored in the 19C).

Tour Bermonde – This tower is entered up a spiral staircase *(135 steps)*.
From the terrace the **panorama**★★ which unfolds over the old roofs of Uzès, burnt by the sun, and the *garrigues* landscape is really beautiful; the bell cage of the clock tower can be seen nearby.

Cellars (Caves) – The enormous 11C vaulted cellars house a waxwork reconstruction of the marriage of Jacques de Crussol and Simone d'Uzès in 1486.

Apartments – To get into these, go through the doorway in the façade, which is surmounted by the coats of arms and the motto of the Uzès family: *"ferro non auro"* (by iron and not by gold). The doorway opens onto the beautiful Renaissance main staircase, which has coffered, diamond-pointed vaulting.
Particularly worth including in the visit are: the Louis XV great hall, decorated with plasterwork and a Trianon console (gilded with gold-leaf and carrying a beautiful Delft vase); the library containing memoirs of the Duchess of Mortemart de Rochechouart; the dining room decorated with Renaissance and Louis XIII furniture; and the 15C chapel, which was renovated in 19C (15C *Virgin and Child*).
On the left as you leave notice the 12C **Tour de la Vigie**.

Hôtel de Ville (**AB H**) – This dates from the 18C and has a finely laid-out courtyard. From the façade on the side of the château there is a view of the enormous outline of the Ducal Palace and the chapel roof of varnished tiles.

Crypte ⊙ (**AB N**) – Note the baptistery and the two low reliefs: one of the low relief's figures has been given glass eyes; in the 4C early-Christian sanctuary the niches were intended to hold cult objects.
Continue along Rue Boucairie.

At the corner of Rue Rafin stands the **Hôtel des Monnaies** (Old Mint) (**B**); a sign reminds us that the bishops of Uzès were permitted to strike their own coins during the Middle Ages.

Hôtel du Baron de Castille (**B R**) – The late-18C front of this mansion is preceded by a colonnade – a particular predilection of the baron's, it would seem, since his other residence, Château de Castille, is similarly adorned.

Ancien Palais épiscopal (**B S**) – This sumptuous episcopal palace was built at the end of the 17C; its right wing houses the public library and museum.

Musée Municipal Georges-Borias ⊘ (**M**) – The museum's collections include archeological finds, popular arts and traditions, old documents; pottery from St-Quentin-la-Poterie; paintings by Sigalon, Chabaud and Borias; engravings by Subleyas; and souvenirs of André Gide (manuscripts, rare editions).

Cathédrale St-Théodorit (**B V**) – The 17C cathedral behind a 19C remodelled west front contains a fine Louis XIV-style **organ★** *(see illustration on p 41 under Art: Architectural Terms)*. It has preserved many of its 18C pipes; in the past, during Lent, painted shutters were closed over the instrument (they can still be seen). Note also the triforium gallery with wrought iron rails above the tall arcades, and in the chancel, on the left, the handsome 17C lectern.

★★Tour Fenestrelle (**B**) – This tower which abuts the cathedral's south wall is 12C and is the only relic of the former Romanesque cathedral destroyed during the Wars of Religion.

This kind of round bell tower is unique in France: it rises 42m/138ft above a square base with six storeys which recede one above the other. The variety of the openings adds elegance and avoids monotony.

Promenade Jean-Racine (**B**) – This avenue, which runs into Promenade des Marronniers, overlooks the ducal park, the *garrigues*, and the Alzon valley where the River Eure was tapped at its source by the Romans and diverted along the Pont du Gard aqueduct to provide water for Nîmes.

To the left stands the **Pavillon Racine** (**B X**), an old tower, once part of the fortifications, restored in the late 18C.

Maison du Portalet (**B**) – *No 9 Le Portalet.* This is a pretty Renaissance house.

Turn right into Rue Paul-Foussat.

At no 3 there is the lovely Renaissance door of the mansion (**A Z**) where Grimoard du Roure lived before becoming Pope Urban V.

EXCURSIONS

Uzès National Stud (Haras National d'Uzès) ⊘ – *3.5km/2.2mi west. Leave Uzès on ④ on the map, the Alès road. After 2km/1mi turn left onto the Chemin du Mas-des-Tailles (signposted).*

This stud was established in 1974 on a property which included, among other things, a large house dating from the end of the 19C, outbuildings and stables. Modern installations were added to enhance the premises, namely a riding school, race courses and an obstacle course for the dressage and training of their 64 stallions. The circumscription of the Uzès stud includes the regions of Corsica, Languedoc-Roussillon and Provence-Alps-French Riviera.

Uzès – Tour Fenestrelle

Moulin de Chalier ⊘ – *4km/2.5mi. Leave Uzès on D 982, the Anduze road. Turn right just before Arpaillargues onto a road running downhill.*

This 18C stone mill houses the **Musée 1900** with its collection of vehicles, posters and other objects evoking daily life during the Belle Époque. Exhibits include a wide range of vehicles dating from 1870 onwards: a 1907 Renault, luxury limousines from the 1930s, 1950s motorbikes; fire-fighting equipment (including an 1850 Parisian fire engine). The early days of cinema, photography and radio are also represented by magic lanterns (1870), a photo enlarger (1880) and crystal receivers, as well as an entire section devoted to traditional agricultural activities in the region (18C oil mill).

The nearby **Musée du Train et du Jouet** (Toy and Train Museum), entertainingly-set out in the decor of a recreated railway station, houses a 400m/1 300ft long miniature railway as well as models of the region's most impressive sites: the amphitheatre at Nîmes, the Pont du Gard aqueduct and the fortifications at Aigues-Mortes.

St-Quentin-la-Poterie – *5km/3mi. Leave Uzès by ① on the map, the Bagnols-sur-Cèze road. After 2km/1mi turn left onto D 5 and then left again onto D 23.*

The excellent quality of its clay sub-soil gave rise to the rapid development of the pottery industry in the village, particularly during the 14C when over 110 000 glazed earthenware tiles were made for the decoration of the Palais des Papes at Avignon. Large-scale production continued up to the beginning of this century; the last brick factory closed its doors in 1954 and the last pipe factory stopped operating in 1974. Since 1983, ceramists, along with glass artists, have been attracted to the village to continue the tradition.

An old oil mill in the centre of the village houses the Maison de la Terre (Clay Centre) where, adjoining a workshop housing a rotating group of potters of all nationalities, stands the **Galerie Terra Viva** ⊘ with its displays of contemporary ceramic art. The small **Musée des Terrailles**, on the first floor, provides an overview of the history of St-Quentin pottery, the growth of which was undoubtedly aided by the proximity of Beaucaire Fair. A display case, facing the reconstruction of a typical farm kitchen in which a number of ceramic items have been arranged, exhibits fragments of jars and pieces of broken glass and bottles from the Neolithic period, as well as some 1C Gallo-Roman remains.

Every year, the gallery organizes temporary exhibitions of pieces crafted by some of the greatest names in contemporary ceramics. The large **Terralha** pottery fair, which is held annually around 14 July (*see p 295*), brings together around 100 exhibitors attracting thousands of visitors.

VAISON-LA-ROMAINE★★

Population 5 663
Michelin map 81 fold 2 or 245 fold 17 or 246 fold 9
Local maps see DENTELLES DE MONTMIRAIL and Mont VENTOUX – Facilities

Built along the banks of the River Ouvèze, in the middle of a corrie of wooded hills, Vaison-la-Romaine, a small Provençal town full of charm, will enchant those who love old historical places. Rarely does a town offer such a complete and picturesque ensemble: vast fields of ancient ruins, Romanesque cathedral and cloisters, old district dominated by its castle etc.

As well as becoming a busy tourist centre during the music festivals *(see the Calendar of events at the end of the guide)*, Vaison thrives as an agricultural centre where wine, fruit and mountain produce (honey, lavender, truffles) are the source of prosperous trading.

At 11 o'clock on the morning of 22 September 1992, huge gushes of water swept through the town, transforming the River Ouvèze into a destructive torrent. The consequences were devastating; 37 people lost their lives, 150 houses were destroyed and the town's industrial estate was completely washed away. With the exception of its parapet which has since been rebuilt, the Roman bridge alone was able to withstand the river's onslaught. The town has bravely risen out of its ruins and has now recaptured its pleasing air.

HISTORICAL NOTES

The city of the Vocontii – Southern capital of the Vocontii, a Celtic tribe, Vaison (Vasio Vocontiorum) became part of Roman Provence which was conquered at the end of the 2C BC and covered all southeastern Gaul. Very early on it received the status of federated city (and not colony) which allowed it a great deal of autonomy. Allied with Caesar during the Gallic Wars (58-1 BC), the Vocontii lived side by side with the Romans; and among them illustrious men appeared: the historian Trogus-Pompeius and Nero's tutor Burrhus.

Cited as one of the Narbonensis' most prosperous cities under Roman rule, Vaison covered some 70ha/173 acres and had a population of approximately 10000. Unlike the colonial examples of Arles, Nîmes, Orange etc the city did not expand with a Romanised urban plan, as was customary, because a pre-existing rural plan prevented the surveyors from tracing a regular grid plan and placing living quarters and public buildings in their rightful place. The result was a very loose urban lay-out.

Immense dwellings were built right in the centre of the city, replacing the earlier buildings.

It was not until the last third of 1C AD, under the Flavians, that it was decided to create straight streets: properties had to be remodelled accordingly, the façades of houses were realigned and their axes modified, while porticoes and colonnades were erected. The large public buildings, except for the theatre and baths, have not been traced.

The archeologists have established that the luxurious *domi* were much larger than those in Pompeii. They were built over a period of 250 years, and yet Vaison was not restricted to just this kind of dwelling; excavations have unearthed small palaces, modest dwellings, huts and tiny shops.

Over the centuries – Partially destroyed in the late 3C, Vaison rose again during the 4C with a reduced urban plan. The seat of a bishopric, it ranked highly in the 5C and 6C in spite of Barbarian occupation, and two synods took place here in 442 and 529. The following centuries were marked by a sharp decline and by the desertion of the lower town, to the profit of the old town on the river's south bank where the count of Toulouse built a castle. The medieval upper town was protected; it was abandoned in the 18C and 19C and the modern town fortified the Gallo-Roman city. Excavations began in the 1840s, and Mérimée (the Minister of Culture at that time) came to the site. And yet the major part of the work was accomplished from 1907 to 1955 by Canon Sautel, to whom we owe the discovery and uncovering of two districts and the theatre. His work is still being pursued by a highly qualified team of archeologists. At the same time, the upper town is under restoration, thanks to private donations, and is taking on a new appearance with an atmosphere of days past.

★★ROMAN RUINS ⊘ (Y) *about 2hr*

The ancient ruins are spread over 15ha/37 acres. The centre of the Gallo-Roman city (forum and precincts) is covered by the modern town, and therefore only the peripheral quarters, rich with information on life at Vaison in the 1C AD, especially its private life, have been uncovered.

The excavations progress on the one hand towards the cathedral in the La Villasse quarter and on the other hand around Puymin hill, where a shopping district and a sumptuous *domus*, the Peacock villa *(see below)* with its mosaics, were recently unearthed. On the northern boundary of the ancient town, the excavated baths (some 20 rooms) have revealed that they were used until the late 3C and then destroyed.

Quartier de Puymin

Maison des Messii ⊘ – This *domus*, a large urban dwelling belonging to a wealthy Vaison family (partly buried under the modern road network), features a very elaborate interior which favoured a sumptuous and comfortable lifestyle. As one enters, via the Roman street, a vestibule then a corridor lead to the *atrium* (**1**) around

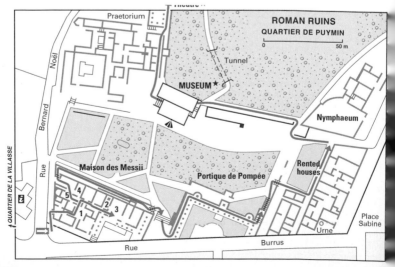

which the various rooms have been laid out, including the *tablinum* (study and library reserved for the head of the family). The atrium had in its centre, under the open section, a square basin *(impluvium)* which caught the rainwater.

Note the room (**2**) where Apollo's head (in the museum; *photograph p 22*) was found, the main reception hall or oecus (**3**), the peristyle and its basin. The annexes include the kitchen (**4**) with its twin hearths, and the private bath (**5**) with its three rooms: *caldarium, tepidarium, frigidarium.*

Portique de Pompée – This elegant public promenade, a sort of public garden, 64m by 52m/210ft by 171ft, consisted of four galleries with niches *(exedra)*, covered originally with a lean-to-roof, surrounding a garden and pool, in the centre of which stood a square aedicule. *For the definition of terms used in this guide see Introduction: Art and Architectural terms.*

The well-excavated north gallery presents three exedra into which were placed the casts of the statues of Sabina, Diadumenos (Roman copy of the statue by Polyclitus which is exhibited at the British Museum) and Hadrian.

The west gallery is also almost entirely excavated, while the other two galleries are buried under the modern buildings.

Rented Houses – This residential complex consists of a block of dwellings (to rent) several storeys high, for citizens of modest means. Note the large urn *(dolium)* for provisions.

Empress Sabina

Nymphaeum – This features various buildings of a cistern set around a spring, which was collected into an elongated basin, called a *nymphaeum.*

Further on to the east the shopping district and Peacock villa were excavated *(not open to the public).*

★**Musée Archéologique Théo-Desplans** ⊘ (**M**) – This fascinating and pleasant archeological museum displays the finds excavated at Vaison. Different aspects of Gallo-Roman civilization are presented thematically: religion (altars, funerary inscriptions, dedications), living quarters, pottery glassware, arms, tools, ornaments, toiletries and Imperial coins. The statues are remarkable. They are all in white marble; in chronological order: Claudius (dating from 43) wearing a heavy oak crown, Domitian in armour, naked Hadrian (dating from 121) in a majestic pose in the Hellenistic manner, Sabina, his wife, represented more conventionally as a great lady in state dress. The headless statues are those of municipal figures whose heads were interchangeable. Two other pieces are worthy of interest: the 2C marble head of Apollo crowned with laurel leaves, a 3C silver bust of a patrician and mosaics from the Peacock Villa.

Go to the theatre by following the west slope of the Puymin.

★**Théâtre Romain** – The theatre was built in the 1C, repaired in the 3C and dismantled in the 5C. Its dimensions (95m/312ft diameter, 29m/95ft high) reveal that it was slightly smaller than the one in Orange (103m/338ft, 36m/118ft); it had a seating capacity of 6 000 people (Orange held 9-10 000 spectators). Also like the theatre in Orange, it was built against the hillside, but its tiers were rebuilt by Jules Formigé (1879-1960; Inspector-General of Historical Monuments). The entire stage was hewn out of the rock and the pits containing the machinery and curtain have been well preserved. Discovered amid the ruins were the fine statues exhibited in the museum. Another feature, unique among the Roman theatres in Provence, is the existence of part of a top gallery portico.

Quartier de La Villasse

Main street and baths – On entering the site of the excavations, walk on the paved main street, under which runs a drain going down towards the Ouvèze and the modern buildings. On the west side of the street is a parallel passageway lined with colonnades reserved for pedestrians only; shops, located in the main houses' outbuildings, lined it. On the east side of the street lie the baths – for a long time thought to be a basilica – which are surrounded by deep drains. The great room 12.5m/40ft wide has a pilastered arcade.

Maison au Buste d'Argent (House of the Patrician of the Silver Bust) – Across from the baths in the shop street is the entrance (**1**) to the vast *domus*, in which was discovered the silver bust *(see museum above)* of its opulent owner.

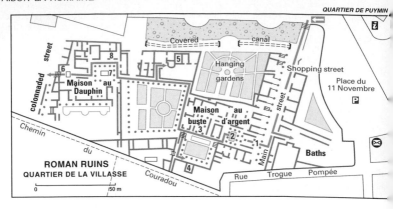

Sprawled over about 5000m²/53820sq ft, the *domus* is complete: paved vestibule, *atrium* (**2**), *tablinum* (**3**), a first peristyle with garden and pool and then a second, larger peristyle also enhanced with garden and pool.

On the south side of the house stands another where mosaics (**4**) were found as well as frescoes around an *atrium*. North of the second (larger) peristyle is the private bath (**5**) which is preceded by a courtyard. Nearby, to the east, lies a large hanging garden which enhanced the wealthy property. *For the definition of the above terms and more, see p 38. An explanation of the Roman house with a drawing appears on p 48.*

Maison au Dauphin (Dolphin House) – In its early stages c 40 BC, this house occupied the north-eastern section of a large enclosure in a non-urban setting. The main residence was enclosed by a peristyle, whereas an outbuilding housed the first private baths known of in Gaul.

The central part of this vast house, which covers 2700m²/29060sq ft, is laid out around a peristyle (**7**) decorated by a pool in dressed stone. To the north, covering 50m²/538sq ft, there are the private baths (**8**) with the *triclinium*, a large dining room used for banquets, along the west edge. The *atrium* (**6**) led into the colonnaded street; this was one of the entrances to the house.

To the south stands another peristyle, a pleasant garden complemented by a large pool, with three exedra and faced with white marble, as well as fountains and formal gardens.

Colonnaded street – Not completely excavated, this street borders the Maison au Dauphin along 43m/141ft. It was not a paved street; its surface, like many other street surfaces, was made of gravel.

ADDITIONAL SIGHTS

Ancienne Cathédrale Notre-Dame-de-Nazareth (**Y**) – *See plan on p 39 under Art Architectural Terms.* This beautiful Provençal Romanesque style building still has its 11C chevet, made from a solid rectangular block of masonry, its apsidal chapels and its walls, reinforced in the 12C at the same time that the nave was covered in by a barrel-vault. The discovery of Gallo-Roman architectural fragments leads experts to believe that the cathedral was built on the ruins of a civic building with a basilical ground plan.

In the foundations of the chevet capitals, column drums and reused blocks of carved stone have been found; below the level of the chevet there are the remains of a low semicircular wall with small stone courses (end of 1C-beginning of 2C); finally, in the north side aisle a fluted column has been uncovered resting on a stylobate (base).

Outside, the chevet is decorated with cornices and foliated friezes imitating Antique decoration. The apsidal chapels are of unequal size and the square bell tower is off-centre.

Inside, the nave includes two bays with pointed barrel vaulting and one bay topped by an octagonal dome on squinches decorated with the symbols of the Evangelists. It is lit through windows cut at the base of the vaulting. The central apse (11C), covered by half-domed vaulting, is decorated with arcading supported on Antique columns. The 11C capitals are similar to those at Venasque and St-Victor in Marseille. The apse still retains its original layout, with the episcopal cathedra surrounded by the three stone steps of the presbyterial bench. On the ground, the sarcophagus discovered in 1950 is thought to be that of St Quenin, bishop of his birthplace Vaison. The white marble **high altar★**, supported by four small columns, probably dates from the 11C. Notice in the north side aisle another tabular marble altar.

★**Cloître** ⊘ (**Y B**) – The cloisters are adjacent with the north side of the cathedral and were built in the 12C and 13C. The galleries (one of which, the southeast one, is a 19C reconstruction) follow the same pattern: they run beneath vast semicircular arcades from which windows open off in threes, resting on the capitals of twinned colonnettes. Those in the east arcade are the most elaborately decorated: acanthus leaves, interlaced designs or figures.

From the courtyard of the cloisters there is a view of the bell tower and the north gutter-bearing wall of the cathedral, on which there is a decorative inscription in Latin. This has provoked lively discussion among scholars, who cannot agree on a translation.

Various archeological finds are on display here: tabular altars; a marble Christian sarcophagus; tomb stones; Merovingian or Carolingian decorative plaques; and medieval sculptures, including a beautiful 15C double-sided cross.

★**Chapelle de St-Quenin** ⊘ (**Y**) – The unusual triangular chevet and its remarkable decoration have given rise to a number of theories from the archeologists. Some see it as a temple of Diana, others as a Merovingian chapel. It is now believed to be a Romanesque building constructed in the 12C with older elements. The nave was rebuilt in the 17C. Paleochristian and Merovingian decoration has been reused above and to the left of the door.

Pont Romain (**Z**) – The Roman bridge has but one arch, 17.20m/56.5ft wide. Apart from the parapet, reworked after the dramatic flood on 22 September 1992, the bridge is as it was 2000 years ago.

★**Haute Ville** (**Upper Town**) (**Z**) – Start from Place du Poids and walk through the maze of alleyways and small squares of the upper town, which dates from the 13C and 14C.

The 14C fortifications which surround the city's steeply sloping streets, once used as calades for exercising horses, were built in part using stones from the ruins of the Roman town. The successful restoration of the warm-coloured stone houses roofed with old Roman tiles, evokes a typical Provençal village of yesteryear.

Go through the 14C fortified gateway, dominated by the belfry tower and its 18C wrought iron bell cage. Take the time to amble through the charmingly picturesque streets (Rue de l'Église, Rue de l'Évêché, Rue des Fours) and squares (Place du Vieux-Marché) decorated with lovely fountains.

The **church**, which was the cathedral until the Revolution, dates from the 15C and was remodelled in the 17C and 18C (façade). Mont Ventoux can be seen from the parvis.

A steep path leads to the castle.

The **castle**, built by the counts of Toulouse at the end of the 12C and converted in the 15C to keep pace with developments in military architecture, overlooks the upper town. There is a fine **view** of Mont Ventoux from the foot of the building.

VAISON-LA-ROMAINE

Fabre (Cours H.) .... Y 13
Grande-Rue .... Y 18
Montfort (Pl. de) .... Y 25
République (R.) .... Y 32

Aubanel (Pl.) .... Z 3
Burrus (R.) .... Y 4
Cathédrale (Pl. de la) .... Y 5
Chanoine-Sautel (Pl.) .... Y 6
Coudray (Av.) .... Y 9
Église (R. de l') .... Z 10
Évêché (R. de l') .... Z 12
Foch (Quai Maréchal) .... Z 14
Gontard (Quai P.) .... Z 17
Horloge (R. de l') .... Z 21
Jaurès (R. Jean) .... Y 22
Mazen (Av. J.) .... Y 23
Mistral (R. Frédéric) .... Y 24
Noël (R. B.) .... Y 27
Poids (Pl. du) .... Z 29
St-Quenin (Av.) .... Y 34
Taulignan (Crs.) .... Y 35
Victor-Hugo (Av.) .... Y 36
Vieux-Marché (Pl. du) .... Z 38
Ville Haute (chemin de la) ... Y 39
11-Novembre (Pl. du) .... Y 40

B Cloître
M Musée archéologique
      Théo-Desplans

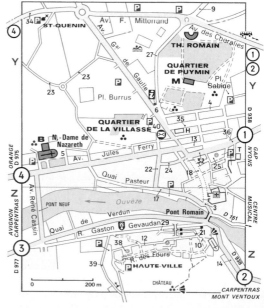

EXCURSIONS

★**Dentelles de Montmirail** – *Round tour of 60km/37mi – allow half a day. Leave Vaison-la-Romaine on ③ on the town plan and after 5.5km/3.4mi take D 88 to the left. See DENTELLES DE MONTMIRAIL for description of sight.*

Rasteau – *17km/11mi west – allow 1hr. Leave Vaison-la-Romaine on ④ on the town plan, D 975.*
The vineyards of Rasteau produce wines under the two official *appellations* of Côtes-du-Rhône and Rasteau (dessert wines known as *vins doux naturels*). The **Musée du Vigneron** ⊘ with a display of winegrowing equipment used long ago and a large collection of vintage Châteauneuf-du-Pape will certainly be of interest to amateur oenologists.

Chartreuse de VALBONNE

Michelin map 80 fold 9 or 245 fold 15 or 246 fold 23

The Valbonne charterhouse with its glazed-tile roofs lies deep in a thick forest Founded in 1203, rebuilt in the 17C and 18C, the charterhouse is now a hospital. In the middle of a long building, flanked by two Provençal-style turrets, is the main gate A 17C door leads to the central courtyard, in the corner of which (on the right) is a door with rustication dating from the reign of Henri II, which leads to small cloisters Facing the entrance door stands the Baroque church.

TOUR *30min*

The **interior decoration**★ is sumptuous: in the middle of the stucco-decorated chancel is the Baroque high altar surmounted by a small baldachin with small wreathed columns. The white stone rose-patterned vaulting is of rare workmanship.
A passage opening onto the church's south side leads into the immense glassed in cloisters, offering a perspective more than 100m/328ft long, which were once lined with monk's cells. A **monk's cell** ⊘ has been recreated and contains furnishings and items evoking the life of the Carthusian monks.

VALLON-PONT-D'ARC

Population 1 914
Michelin map 80 fold 9 or 245 fold 1 or 246 fold 23
Local map see Gorges de l'ARDÈCHE – Facilities

An outdoor pursuits resort, Vallon is the recommended starting point for travelling down the Gorges de l'Ardèche by boat. Southeast, on the hillside, stand the ruins of old Vallon, a feudal village.

Town Hall Tapestries ⊘ – The town hall *(mairie)* is located in an old Louis XIII style mansion. In a ground floor gallery hang seven Aubusson tapestries remarkable for their bright colours. Six of them depict episodes from the deliverance of Jerusalem; the seventh tapestry, the ancient art of grafting a tree.

"Grotte Chauvet" Exhibition ⊘ – *No 1, Rue de Mariou.* With a view to preserving the invaluable heritage discovered in the Grotte Chauvet in 1994, a huge exhibition has been organised to enlighten visitors on this major breakthrough dating back to the Upper Paleolithic Era. A display of photographs, explanatory documents and films explore the various representations of art in the decorated caves of the Ardèche, as well as the daily life of nomadic hunters back in those Prehistoric days (reconstituted scenes).

Silkworm Farm (Magnanerie) ⊘ – *3km/2mi towards Ruoms on D 579. Access along a road branching off to the left coming from Vallon.*
In the village of **Les Mazes** one of the last Vivarois silkworm farms still in operation can be seen.
From the covered terrace *(couradou)* visit the cocoonery, a vast room containing silkworms on trays made of reeds. The tour shows the development of the silkworm from a tiny larva, the size of a pinhead, to a cocoon enveloped in silken threads. These cocoons are then sent to the Alès Institute of Silkworm Breeding

Many camp sites have shops, bars, restaurants and laundries; they may also have games rooms, tennis courts, miniature golf courses, playgrounds, swimming pools. Consult the current edition of the Michelin Camping Caravaning Guide.

VALRÉAS

Population 9069

Michelin map 81 fold 2 or 245 folds 3 and 4 or 246 fold 9 – Facilities

Lying in the fertile Coronne valley, Valréas is an important centre for agriculture and light industry (printers, factories making metal furniture, cardboard or plastic articles etc).

The papal enclave – The papacy located in Avignon wanted to possess Valréas, a neighbour to the Comtat Venaissin.

In 1317, John XXII bought Valréas from the Dauphin Jean II, Visan in 1318, Richerenches in 1320 and Grillon in 1451; and yet a strip of land still separated the two pontifical states.

Worried about the expansion of the papal lands in this region, King Charles VII forbade further sales of land to the popes, thus creating this papal enclave. In 1791, after a referendum, France annexed the territory.

Valréas, once an enclave, is a now a *canton* of Vaucluse *département* entirely surrounded by the Drôme *département*.

Le Petit St-Jean (Little St John) – This is a charming tradition which has survived 500 years. Every year, on the night of 23 June, a small boy (3-5 years old) is crowned Le Petit St-Jean. Symbolising the relics of St Martin, the city's patron saint, Le Petit St-Jean parades through torch-lit streets on a litter, blessing people along the way. A procession of 300 costumed figures follows him in a colourful and animated atmosphere. For one year Valréas is placed under his protection.

SIGHTS

The town lies within plane tree-shaded boulevards planted on the site of former ramparts of which only the Tour du Tivoli (**B**) remains.

Hôtel de Ville ⊘ (**H**) – This former 18C mansion belonged to the Marquis de Simiane, who married Pauline de Grignan, granddaughter of Mme de Sévigné. The oldest part of the mansion dates back to the 15C; a majestic façade overlooks Place Aristide-Briand.

The first floor contains the **Salle du Conseil** (Council Room) which has a painted ceiling and friezes. The library with its 17C wood panelling from the former hospital contains papal bulls and manuscripts.

The second floor room with its fine timber ceiling contains works by the Austrian painter Scharf (1876-1943) who retired to Valréas.

Église Notre-Dame-de-Nazareth – This 11C and 12C Provençal Romanesque church was remodelled in the 14C and 15C (transept crossing and side chapels). It is most interesting for its south door of four recessed orders resting on small columns. The interior features a 16C organ.

Chapelle des Pénitents Blancs ⊘ (**E**) – On Place Pie a lovely wrought-iron gate announces the way to the 17C chapel. Enter the section reserved for the faithful. The chancel is adorned with carved stalls and a lovely flowered coffered ceiling. The garden is overlooked by Château Ripert or clock tower (**F**); from the terrace there is a lovely view of old Valréas and the hills of the Tricastin.

VALRÉAS

Ancien-Collège (R. de l')........... 2
Borello (R. Charles)................... 3
Château-Robert (R.).................. 5
Daurand (R. J.-F.) 6
Échelle (R. de l')....................... 7
Fabre (Pl. Henri)....................... 9
Faye (R. Jules)......................... 10
Ferry (Pl. Jules)........................ 12
Foch (Av. Maréchal)................. 13
Grande-Rue.............................. 14
Gutenberg (Pl.) 15
Maury (Pl. Cardinal)................. 16
Meynard (Av.)........................... 17
Niel (R. Jules) 18
Pasteur (R. Louis)..................... 19
Recluse (Pl. de la) 21
Recluse (R. de la) 22
République (Pl. de la).............. 23
St-Antoine (R.) 24
St-Jean (R.).............................. 25

B Tour du Tivoli
E Chapelle des Pénitents Blancs
F Tour de l'Horloge
H Hôtel de ville
K Hôtel d'Aultane
M Musée du Cartonnage et de l'Imprimerie
N Hôtel d'Inguimbert
R Château Delphinal

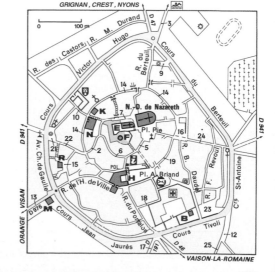

Prov. ang. 10

265

Old houses – At No 36 Grande-Rue is the Hôtel d'Aultane (**K**) – its door is topped by a coat of arms; on the corner of Rue de l'Échelle is Hôtel d'Inguimbert (**N**) adorned with modillions and mullioned windows; on Place Gutenberg stands Château Delphinal (**R**) with machicolations.

Musée du Cartonnage et de l'Imprimerie ⊙ (**M**) – Valréas, an important centre of cardboard production, offers tourists interested in the manufacturing industries a chance to follow the different processes involved in the manufacture of cardboard since the 19C in this instructive museum. There are reconstructed workshops, tools and iconographic documents all illustrating the history of the "cardboard box", that familiar object found daily in contexts such as pharmacy, jewellery, perfumery and confectionery.

EXCURSIONS

Round tour of 40km/25mi – allow 2hr

Leave Valréas west on D 941.

★**Grignan** – *See GRIGNAN.*

Take D 541 and turn left onto D 71.

Chamaret – A clock tower, converted from a fine belfry, relic of the massive castle perched high on a rock, dominates the landscape with an all-encompassing view of Tricastin.

Continue along D 71.

The road is bordered by fields of lavender separated by truffle oaks and cypresses.

Montségur-sur-Lauzon – The modern village stands at a crossroads.

In front of the town hall, take the street on the left, turn right and then take the uphill path to the hillock on which lies the old village.

A network of streets through the old town leads to the old troglodyte-Romanesque church (restored).

From the watchpath, a fine **panoramic view** of the Tricastin countryside, Baronnies and Mont Ventoux unfolds.

Take D 71⁸ going east.

There are good views of Montagne de la Lance and the Nyons countryside.

Richerenches – This former commandery was founded in the 12C by the Knights Templars. It was a place of work and worship; they raised horses and sheep and subsisted on the sale of wool and wheat. The town is now an important truffle market. Built on a rectangular plan, it still retains its fortified wall flanked by four round corner towers; go through the belfry, a rectangular machicolated tower with a heavy nailed door.

Left of the church lie important temple ruins.

D 20, southeast, crosses Visan and continues on to Notre-Dame-des-Vignes.

Chapelle Notre-Dame-des-Vignes – The nave of this 13C chapel is decorated with 15C panelling; in the chancel is a 13C polychrome wood statue of the Virgin, the object of a popular pilgrimage on 8 September.

Go past Visan and take D 976 to return to Valréas.

VENASQUE

Population 785

Michelin map 81 fold 13 or 245 fold 17 or 246 fold 11

Venasque, built on a foothill of the Vaucluse plateau, dominates the Carpentras plain. The village was, before Carpentras, the Comtat's bishopric and gave its name to the Comtat Venaissin.

★**Baptistery** ⊙ – *Entrance right of the presbytery.* The baptistery, most likely from the 6C or the Merovingian period and remodelled in the 11C, is one of France's oldest religious buildings. The Greek cross plan, with groined vaulting over the centre square, has unequal arms ending in apsidal chapels, each oven-vaulted with blind arcading on slender marble columns with Antique or, in the case of the east apsidal chapel, Merovingian capitals. The hollow in the floor was for the font.

Église Notre-Dame – The church, which is 12C and 13C with considerable 15C-18C alterations, contains, in the chancel, a 17C carved altarpiece and a tabernacle door of the Resurrected Christ appearing to the disciples of Emmaus. In the second north chapel is a 15C Avignon School Crucifixion.

ROUTE DES GORGES

10km/6mi east on D 4 towards Apt.

This winding yet picturesque road through the **Forêt de Venasque** goes up the **gorges**★ which are often dry but quite pleasant. After climbing some 400m/1 312ft the road reaches **Col de Murs** pass (alt 627m/2 057ft). Beyond the pass the first bends on the way down to Murs reveal extended views of Apt basin and Roussillon.

Mont VENTOUX★★★

Michelin map 81 folds 3, 4, 13 and 14 or 245 folds 17 and 18 or 246 fold 10

Mont Ventoux is the most dominant feature of Provence's Rhône valley. It proudly commands the Rhône valley to the west, Vaucluse plateau to the south and the small Baronnies range to the north.

The climb to Mont Ventoux is one of the loveliest excursions of Provence; the panorama from the peak is immense. With a height of only 1909m/6263ft, Mont Ventoux cannot rival the Alps or Pyrenees for altitude; yet its location in front of the Alps, far from any rival peak, its bold outline above Carpentras plain and the Vaucluse plateau, all combine to give it an astonishing majesty.

Weather – There is nearly always a wind on Mont Ventoux, as its name suggests (*vent* means wind), particularly when the *mistral* is blowing. The temperature at the top is on average 11°C/20°F lower than at the foot; rainfall is twice as heavy and filters through the fissured limestone of Vaucluse Plateau. In winter the temperature may drop at the observatory to – 27°C (-17°F), the mountain is usually snow-capped above 1300m/4265ft to 1400m/4593ft from December to April, and the slopes at Mont Serein on the north side and Chalet-Reynard on the south provide good skiing.

Mont Ventoux

Vegetation – The lower slopes are covered with the trees and plants typical of Provence, while at the summit polar species such as Spitzbergen saxifrage and Icelandic poppy flourish. The flowers are at their best the first fortnight in July. The forests which once covered the mountainside were felled from the 16C on, to supply the naval shipyards in Toulon; replanting has been going on since 1860. Aleppo pine, holm and downy oaks, cedar, beech, pitch pine, fir and larch from a forest cover which at about 1600m/5249ft is replaced by a vast field of white shingle.

During the autumn a climb to the top through the multicoloured landscape is enchanting.

The conquest of the summit – From 1902 to 1973 the road between Bédoin and the summit was used for motorcar hill trials; the pre 1914-18 record established by Boillot in a Peugeot was 17' 38" (73kph/45mph); in 1952 Manzon in a Simca-Gordini was 13' 17" 7/10 (averaging 97.480kph/60mph); in 1973 Mieusset in a March was 9' 03'' 6/10 (averaging 142.278kph/90mph). The summit is sometimes included in the Tour de France cycle race.

In 1994, Mont Ventoux, with its abundant flora and fauna, was classified a Biosphere reserve by UNESCO.

★★ASCENT OF THE NORTH FACE ⊘

① Round Tour Starting from Vaison-la-Romaine

63 km/39mi – allow 1 day – local map below

The itinerary ⊘ uses D 974, a road made in 1933 for tourists ascending **Mont Ventoux**. Although the incline is similar to the one on the south side, it is less trying during the hot summer months because of the breeze. During a storm, the road can be obstructed by fallen earth for the last 3km/2mi but does not stop traffic. These conditions simply require more attention on the part of the driver.

So as not to strain the engine it is advisable to go up this way, and take the Bédoin road down.

★★**Vaison-la-Romaine** – *See VAISON-LA-ROMAINE.*

Leave Vaison-la-Romaine on ② on the town plan, D 938.

The road goes up the charming Groseau valley overlooked on the west by the Dentelles de Montmirail.

Entrechaux – *3km/2mi on D 54.* The village, overlooked by the ruins of a castle with its 220m/700ft defensive keep, was formerly a possession of the bishops of Vaison.

Return to the Malaucène road via D 13.

Malaucène – *See DENTELLES-DE-MONTMIRAIL.*

Leave Malaucène east on D 974.

Chapelle Notre-Dame-du-Groseau – (*not open to the public*). This chapel is all that is left of a Benedictine abbey, a dependant of St-Victor's of Marseille. The square building is the 12C abbey church's former chancel; the nave has been destroyed. In the early 14C, Clement V, first of the dynasty of French popes at Avignon, liked to stay in this charming spot.

Source vauclusienne du Groseau – This spring forms a pool of clear water as it emerges from several fissures at the foot of a steep slope (over 100m/328ft), beneath trees to the left of the road. The Romans built an aqueduct to carry the water to Vaison-la-Romaine.

The road continues up the northern slope revealing a good view of the Vaucluse plateau, climbing up the steepest and most ravined face of the mountain; it crosses pastures and pinewoods near the Mont Serein refuge.

The viewpoint beyond the Ramayettes hut offers a fine **view★** of the Ouvèze and Groseau valleys, the Massif des Baronnies and Plate summit.

Mont Serein – Winter sports resort: chalets are charmingly set in the snow fields; and it is well equipped with ski-lifts.

The panorama becomes wider and includes the Dentelles de Montmirail and the heights along the Rhône's west bank. Two more long hairpin bends lead to the top.

★★★**Mont Ventoux Summit** – The summit, which rises to an altitude of 1 909m/6 263ft, is spiked with scientific equipment: an air force radar station and a television mast. In summer the summit may be shrouded in cloud or midday mist; it is advisable to set out early or remain at the top until sunset. In winter the atmosphere tends to be clearer but the last stage of the ascent should be made on skis. The view from the car park extends over the Alps and particularly the Vercors range *(viewing table)*. The platform on the south side offers an almost circular **panorama★★★** *(viewing table)*: it swings from the Pelvoux massif to the Cévennes by way of the Luberon, Ste-Victoire, Estaque hills, Marseille, the Étang de Berre, the Alpilles and the Rhône valley.

On very clear days the Canigou is visible way over to the southwest in the Pyrenees. At night the Provençal plain is a wonderful sight as it is transformed into a dark carpet studded with clusters of glittering lights. The sight extends to the Étang de Berre and coast where the lighthouses regularly probe the darkness.

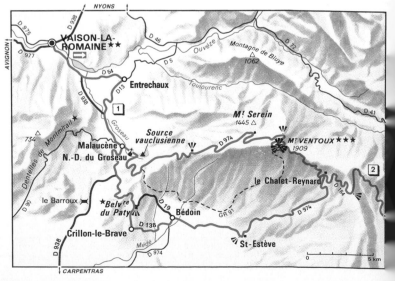

The *corniche* road, which winds down the south face through a vast tract of shining white shingle to woods, is the oldest road built (c 1885) to serve the observatory. In 22km/13.5mi of hairpin bends to Bédoin (alt 310m/1017ft), it descends 1600m/5249ft.

Le Chalet-Reynard – Excellent local slopes have made Le Chalet-Reynard a popular resort for skiers from Avignon, Carpentras and other nearby towns.
The road goes through the forest; pine trees, beeches, oaks and cedars give way to vines, peach and cherry orchards and a few small olive groves. The view extends across the Comtadin plain; beyond Vaucluse plateau appears the Luberon.

St-Estève – From the famous sharp bend, now straightened, which featured in the Ventoux car racing competition to the summit, there is a good **view**★ on the right of the Dentelles de Montmirail, the Comtat plain, and left onto Vaucluse plateau.

Bédoin – This village, which is perched on a hill, has picturesque small streets, leading to the classical Jesuit-style church, which contains several elegant altars.
Take D 138.

Crillon-le-Brave – Nestling on a overhang facing the Mont Ventoux, Crillon-le-Brave is a quaint perched village with vestiges of its former fortifications. Beside the Town Hall stands the fascinating **Maison de la Musique Mécanique** ⊘, where you can see and hear a bird flageolet (1740), a 1900 orchestrion featuring nine instruments, several barrel organs, an organ used for merry-go-rounds at funfairs...
North of the village, take the untarred road leading up to the Belvédère du Paty, running perpendicular to D 138.

★**Belvédère du Paty** – From this viewpoint, there is a panoramic **view**★ down onto the picturesque terraced village of Crillon-le-Brave and the ochre clay quarries; to the right emerge the Alpilles, and opposite them the Comtat Venaissin, bounded by the Vaucluse plateau, and to the left is Mont Ventoux.
Take D 19, which crosses a wooded area, and D 938 to return to Vaison-la-Romaine.

★★ASCENT BY THE EAST FACE

② Round Tour Starting from Sault *28km/17mi – about 2hr*

Sault – *See SAULT.*
Leave Sault on D 164.

The road travels through the upper, cultivated valley of the Nesque before ascending the pine-covered east face of Mont Ventoux. From the belvedere on the lefthand side of the road there is an extensive **view** across the Sault countryside and the Vaucluse plateau.

Le Chalet-Reynard – *See above.*

★★★**Mont Ventoux Summit** – *See above.*

The descent can be made either by D 974 towards Malaucène and Vaison-la-Romaine (description of the journey in the opposite direction p 150) or via D 974 towards Bédoin (description above).

VILLENEUVE-LÈS-AVIGNON★

Population 10730
Michelin map 81 folds 11 and 12 or 245 fold 16 or 246 fold 25 – Facilities
Plan of the conurbation of Avignon in the current Michelin Red Guide France

A tour of Villeneuve-lès-Avignon is the natural complement to a visit to Avignon. This town, the "City of the Cardinals", offers a view over the "City of the Popes" which is one of the most famous in the Rhône valley. It is at the end of the afternoon, beneath a setting sun, that Avignon appears in all its splendour.

Historical notes – In 1271 after the Albigensian Crusade, the King of France, Philip III the Bold, acquired the county of Toulouse which extended to the banks of the Rhône. On the opposite shore was Provence and the Holy Roman Empire.
The river belonged to the crown, which raised the thorny question of rights: whenever the river flooded parts of Avignon, the French king claimed them as his territory and demanded taxes from the unfortunate citizens.
At the end of the 13C, Philip the Fair founded a new town (in French: *ville neuve*) on the plain, and its population grew rapidly. Grasping the great military importance of the spot, he built a powerful fortification at the entrance to Pont St-Bénézet.
The cardinals, arriving at the papal court in the 14C and finding no suitable accommodation in Avignon, began to build magnificent residences *(livrées)* across the river in Villeneuve, until eventually there were fifteen of these.

The prosperity, which the cardinals' patronage of churches and monastic houses brought to the town, remained long after the papal court had returned to Rome. The kings John the Good and Charles V had built Fort St-André in order to watch over the neighbouring papal kingdom. In the 17C and 18C fine *hôtels* lined the Grande-Rue. In the monasteries, which developed into real museums, an active and brilliant life style flourished until the Revolution swept away the aristocratic and ecclesiastic regimes.

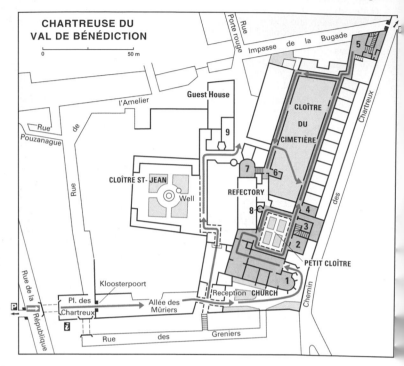

★CHARTREUSE DU VAL DE BÉNÉDICTION *1hr*

In 1352 the papal conclave met in Avignon and elected the General of the Carthusian Order as Pope, but he refused the throne out of humility. To commemorate this gesture Innocent VI, who became Pope instead, founded a charterhouse on his *livrée* in Val de Bénédiction. The house, enlarged by the Pope's nephews after his death, became the most important one in France.

The Carthusian Order was founded in 1084 by St Bruno. It consisted of Fathers, who used the title Dom, and Brothers, who lived a communal life like monks in other orders. The Fathers, however, lived singly in cells spending their time in prayer, study and manual work. Three times a day the monks met in chapel to sing the offices; they took their meals alone except on Sundays when brief periods of conversation were allowed.

The charterhouse now houses colloquia and seminars and also the **Centre National des Écritures du Spectacle** (CNES), established to promote the act of writing for public performance (plays, opera, songs etc).

Enter at n° 60 Rue de la République through the monumental door.

A plaque on the right of the door marks the highest flood level reached by the Rhône on 1 May 1856.

Porte du cloître – The cloister door separates Place des Chartreux from Allée des Mûriers. The proportions and ornamentation of the 17C door can be admired from inside: fluted consoles supporting balconies, lions' heads, fir cones decorating the pediment, etc.

Pass through the reception area and skirt the church's south side.

Church – Go through the nave; the apse opens out with a view on to Fort St-André. On the north side, the apse of the other nave and a bay contain the tomb of Innocent VI (**1**): the white marble recumbent figure lies on a high plinth of Pernes stone decorated with arcading; the Flamboyant Gothic canopy has been restored. The next two chapels, dedicated to St Michael and St Bruno, are open only during exhibitions.

Petit Cloître – The east gallery opens into the chapterhouse (**2**) and the Sacristans' yard (**3**) with its well and picturesque staircase.

Cloître du Cimetière – The great cloisters, 80m/262ft x 20m/66ft, with their warm Provençal colouring, are lined with cells for the Fathers, each cell consisting of a small open court and two rooms, one of which communicates with the cloisters by a hatch. The first cell (**4**) can be visited. At the northeast end of the cloisters a passage leads to the *bugade* (**5**), the depressed groin-vaulted wash-room, which has preserved its well and chimney for drying clothes. Opening off the west gallery is a small chapel of the dead (**6**) off which is another chapel (**7**) which was part of Innocent VI's *livrée*; it is decorated with lovely frescoes attributed to Matteo Giovanetti (14C), one of the decorators of the Palais des Papes *(see AVIGNON)*. They illustrate scenes from the life of John the Baptist and the life of Christ. Particularly fine are the Presentation in the Temple and the Entombment.

Cross the Graveyard Cloisters and go along the north side of the Petit Cloître.

The **lavabo** (**8**) is a small circular building with a beautiful 18C dome.

Refectory – *(Not open to the public)*. The Tinel (18C) is used for concerts.

Pass by the church and reception office to reach Cloître St-Jean.

Cloître St-Jean – The cloisters' galleries have disappeared; however, several of the Fathers' cells remain. In the centre stands the monumental Fontaine St-Jean (18C) which has kept its well and lovely old basin. On leaving the cloisters, skirt the crenellated east end of the Tinel; note the bakery (**9**) with its hexagonal tower. On the northeast side, the **guest house**, remodelled in the 18C, features a lovely façade on its north side.

ADDITIONAL SIGHTS

★**Fort St-André** ⊙ – In the Middle Ages, St-André hill, called Mount Andaon, was still an island with a hermitage and later a monastery on it.

The tributary of the Rhône which circled it on the landward side dried up and was taken by the local people.

The fort, built in the second half of the 14C by John the Good and Charles V, includes: a magnificent **Porte Fortifiée** (Fortified Gate)★, flanked by twin towers (**B**) – this is one of the finest examples of medieval fortifications to be seen – and a fortified wall which included a Benedictine abbey, the 12C Romanesque Chapelle **Notre-Dame-de-Belvézet** (**D**) *(not open to the public)* and the village of St-André, of which there remain but a few walls.

Access to the west tower of the fortified gate allows the visitor to discover the chamber from which the portcullises were controlled, and a 18C bakery.

The terrace *(85 steps)* commands a very beautiful **view**★★ of Mont Ventoux, the Rhône, Avignon and the Palais des Papes, the Comtadin plain, the Luberon, the Alpilles and Tour Philippe-le-Bel.

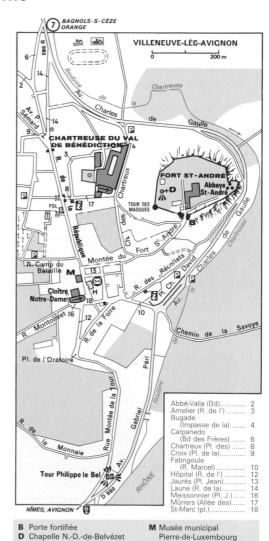

Abbé-Valla (Bd)	2
Amelier (R. de l')	3
Bugade (Impasse de la)	4
Carpanedo (Bd des Frères)	6
Chartreux (Pl. des)	8
Croix (Pl. de la)	9
Fabrigoule (R. Marcel)	10
Hôpital (R. de l')	12
Jaurès (Pl. Jean)	13
Laune (R. de la)	14
Meissonnier (Pl. J.)	16
Mûriers (Allée des)	17
St-Marc (pl.)	18

B Porte fortifiée
D Chapelle N.-D.-de-Belvézet

M Musée municipal
Pierre-de-Luxembourg

Abbaye St-André ⊘ – Of the Benedictine abbey founded in the 10C on the old pilgrims' way to St Casarie (6C – patron saint of Villeneuve) then partly destroyed during the Revolution, there remain the entrance gate, left wing and terraces, held up by massive vaulting. Walk through the pleasant Italian-style gardens; the upper terrace gives a lovely **view**★ of Avignon, the Rhône valley and Mont Ventoux.

Église Notre-Dame ⊘ – This collegiate church dedicated to Our Lady was founded in 1333. The tower which ends the building on the east side was built as a separate belfry, the ground floor of which straddled the public footpath. The monks obtained permission to redirect the path. They blocked off the belfry arcade, converted it into a chancel and linked it to the existing church by adding an extra bay to the nave. Inside, a number of works of art can be found: starting from the back of the church note the tomb of Cardinal Arnaud de Via, rebuilt with its original 14C recumbent figure (second north chapel), a copy of the famous *Pietà* kept in the Louvre since 1904 (third south chapel), *St Bruno* by Nicolas Mignard and a *Calvary* by Reynaud Levieux (above the chancel's entrance).

The 18C high altar is adorned with a low relief of *Christ Laid in the Tomb* from the charterhouse; to the right of the high altar is an old abbot's chair (18C) from St-André monastery. Note also the nave's finely carved corbels (partly destroyed).

14C polychrome ivory
Virgin with Child,
Villeneuve-lès-Avignon Museum

Cloître ⊘ – These cloisters date from the late 14C.

Rue de la République – The street is lined with a number of *livrées* (nos 1, 3, 45 and 53). One of these palaces (recently restored), which belonged to Cardinal Pierre de Luxembourg, a cardinal who died having already won saintly repute at the early age of 19 (in 1387), houses the local museum.

Musée Municipal Pierre-de-Luxembourg ⊘ **(M)** – This museum displays magnificent works of art on four floors. On the ground floor is the 14C polychrome ivory **Virgin**★★, carved from an elephant's tusk; it is one of the finest works of its kind. Also worth admiring are: the marble Virgin with two faces from the School of Nuremberg (14C); the death mask of Jeanne de Laval, second wife of King René, by Laurana; the chasuble said to have belonged to Innocent VI; and the 17C veil of the Holy Sacrament, adorned with small pearls. The first floor houses the museum's most beautiful work of art: **Coronation of the Virgin**★★, painted in 1453 by Enguerrand Quarton, from Laon; this artist painted in Aix, then Avignon (from 1447). Fascinated by landscapes and Provençal light, he used bright colours which emphasised the scene's majesty. The Virgin with her large cloak dominates this composition which encompasses heaven and earth in the subjects painted; the Holy Spirit is symbolised by a dove, whose open wings unite God the Father and His Son. Interesting paintings by Nicolas Mignard (*Jesus in the Temple*, 1649) and Philippe de Champaigne (*Visitation* c 1644).

The second and third floors exhibit works by Nicolas Mignard, Reynaud Levieux (*Crucifixion*), Simon de Châlons, Parrocel (*St Anthony and the Infant Jesus*) and Reynaud Levieux, miscellaneous items (17C door, 17C cupboard) from the charterhouse and pewter from the guest house.

Tour Philippe-le-Bel ⊘ – Built on a rock, near the Rhône, this tower was the key structure in the defence work at the west end of Pont St-Bénézet, on royal land. When it was first built (1293-1307) it was the present one storey-high building. The second floor and watch turret were added in the 14C. The upper terrace *(176 steps)* gives a lovely **view**★★ of Villeneuve and Avignon, Mont Ventoux, the Montagnette hills and the Alpilles.

VITROLLES

Population 35 397

Michelin map 84 fold 2 or or 114 fold 14 or 245 folds 31, 44 or 246 fold P

Local map see Étang de BERRE

Located east of the Étang de Berre and overlooking motorway A 7, which links Lyon to Marseille, Vitrolles lies in a zone (240ha/593 acres) of light industry: metal construction, chemical products and foodstuffs. Near the industrial zone is a large long- and short-haul lorry depot. These activities have created, around the old town, a vast residential zone of warm ochre-coloured houses.

The town is also known for the unusual ruiniform rock that dominates it.

WALK TO THE ROCK

1/4 hour on foot Rtn. Take the path around the rock, leave the car in front of the cemetery's main gate and climb 75 steps.

At the top of the rock, on the southernmost tip, there is a Saracen tower (11C), and on the opposite side a chapel dedicated to Notre-Dame-de-Vie, the aviators' guardian.

★**Panorama** – This immense panorama embraces to the southwest the lagoons of Berre and Bolmon, the Chaîne de l'Estaque separated from St-Mitre heights by the Caronte depression, and the port and oil installations of Lavéra. On the banks of the lagoons can be seen the mouth of the Arles canal, Fos-sur-Mer, La Mède and its refinery, Marignane and the airport, Berre and its factories. To the southeast lie the Chaîne de l'Étoile and Pilon du Roi; further to the east looms the impressive bulk of Montagne Ste-Victoire.

Practical
information

Planning your trip

Passport – Visitors entering France must be in possession of a valid national passport. Citizens of one of the European Union countries need only a national identity card. In the event of loss or theft, report to your embassy or consulate and the local police.

Visa – No **entry visa** is required for US and Canadian citizens as long as their stay in France does not exceed three months. Australians and New Zealanders must apply for one at the nearest French consulate. For other countries, check with a French consulate or travel agent. US citizens should obtain the booklet **Your Trip Abroad**, which provides useful information on visa requirements, customs regulations, medical care etc for international travellers. Contact the Superintendent of Documents, PO Box 371954, Pittsburgh, PA 15250-7954 ☎ (202) 512-1800.

Customs – Apply to the Customs Office (UK) for a leaflet entitled **A Guide for Travellers** on customs regulations and the full range of duty-free allowances. The US Customs Service, PO Box 7407, Washington, DC 20044 ☎ (202) 927-5580, offers a free publication **Know Before You Go** for US residents. There are no customs formalities for holiday-makers bringing caravans into France for a stay of less than six months. No customs document is necessary for pleasure boats and outboard motors for a stay of less than six months, but the registration certificate should be kept on board.

French Tourist Offices – For information, brochures, maps and assistance in planning a trip to France, travellers should contact the official tourist office in their own country:

Australia-New Zealand
Sydney – BNP Building, 12 Castlereagh Street
Sydney, New South Wales 2000
☎ (61) 2 231 52 44 – Fax (61) 2 221 86 82.

Canada
Montreal – College Suite 490
Montreal PQ H3A 2W9
☎ (514) 288-4264 – Fax (514) 845 48 68.

Eire
Dublin – 38 Lower Abbey St, Dublin 1
☎ (1) 703 40 46 – Fax (1) 874 73 24.

United Kingdom
London – 179 Piccadilly, London WI
☎ (0891) 244 123 – Fax (0171) 493 6594.

United States
East Coast: New York – 444 Madison Avenue, NY 10022
☎ 212-838-7800 – Fax (212) 838 7855.
Mid-West: Chicago – 676 North Michigan Avenue, Suite 3360, Chicago, IL 60611
☎ (312) 751 7800 – Fax (312) 337 6339.
West Coast: Los Angeles – 9454 Wilshire Boulevard, Suite 715, Beverly Hills, CA 90212
☎ (310) 271 2693 – Fax (310) 276 2835.

When to go – The region of Provence is blessed with mild weather throughout the year, especially along the coast. However, in winter it can be very cold when the *mistral* is blowing. Obviously the summer months attract permanent crowds to this attractive and

Mean Temperatures

			January		February		March		April		May		June	
min	max	°F	33°	50°	35°	52°	38°	59°	44°	62°	52°	62°	57°	79°
min	max	°C	1°	10°	2°	11°	5°	15°	7°	17°	11°	21°	14°	26°

			July		August		September		October		November		December	
min	max	°F	62°	82°	62°	82°	57°	77°	50°	66°	42°	57°	37°	50°
min	max	°C	17°	28°	17°	28°	14°	25°	10°	19°	6°	14°	3°	10°

Precipitation

	January	February	March	April	May	June
Average monthly fall	43mm	32mm	43mm	42mm	46mm	24mm

	July	August	September	October	November	December
Average monthly fall	11mm	34mm	60mm	76mm	69mm	66mm

increasingly popular region, which is most charming at this time. Spring or autumn are less fiercely hot and can be rainy and the *mistral* may suddenly influence temperatures.

For further information on the region (hotel reservation, transport, etc) American tourists can use the Provence Hotline (☎ 800-292-0219) open from 8am to 6pm Monday to Friday. They can also write to Provence Travel Reservation, 275 Madison Avenue, NY, NY 10016.

Time – France is one hour ahead of Greenwich Mean Time (GMT), except between the end of September and the end of October, when there is no difference.

When it is **noon in France**, it is 11am in London

      11am in Dublin
      6am in New York
      3am in Los Angeles
      7pm in Perth
      9pm in Sydney
      11pm in Auckland

In France "am" and "pm" are not used but the 24-hour clock is widely applied.

Getting there

By air – The various national and other independent airlines operate services to **Paris** (**Roissy-Charles-de-Gaulle** and **Orly** airports). North Americans can fly to **Nice** on a direct flight from New York (operated by Delta Airlines). Daily connecting flights are available from **Orly** to **Marseille** (operated by Air Inter, TAT European Airlines, AOM and Air Liberté), **Nîmes** (Air Inter) and **Avignon** (Air Inter).

There are daily direct flights from **London** to **Marseille** (operated by British Airways and Air France).

There are also package tour flights with a rail or coach link-up as well as Fly-Drive schemes. Information, brochures and timetables are available from the airlines or travel agents.

By rail – **British Rail** and **French Railways** (SNCF) operate a 3hr daily service via the Channel Tunnel on Eurostar in 3 hours between **London** (Waterloo International Station) and **Paris** (Gare du Nord). There are trains from **Paris** (Gare de Lyon) to **Marseille** (4hr), **Avignon** (3hr 20min), and **Nîmes** (3hr 45min). There are also direct services from **Lille** to **Marseille** (5hr 30min), **Avignon** (4hr 30min) and **Nîmes** (5hr).

There are rail passes offering unlimited travel and group travel tickets offering services for parties. **Eurailpass, Flexipass** and **Saver Pass** are options available in the US for travel in Europe and must be purchased in the US – ☎ 212 308 3103 (information) and 800 223 636 (reservations). In the UK information and booking from French Railways, 179 Piccadilly, London, W1V 0BA ☎ 0891 515 477 and from main British Rail Travel Centres and Travel agencies.

Tickets bought in France must be validated *(composter)* by using the orange automatic date-stamping machines at the platform entrance.

You can always buy the **Thomas Cook European Rail Timetable**, which gives all the train schedules throughout France and useful information on train travel (US ☎ 1 800 367 7984).

By coach – The Provence region can be reached by coach via Paris. **Eurolines** has daily services to the towns of Marseille, Avignon and Nîmes. For further information, contact:

London: 52 Grosvenor Gardens, Victoria, London SW1 0AU ☎ 0171 730 8235.

Paris: 28 Avenue du Général-de-Gaulle, 93541 Bagnolet ☎ 01 49 72 51 51.

By car – Drivers from the British Isles can easily travel to France and Provence by car. Numerous cross-Channel services (passenger and car-ferries, hovercraft, SeaCat and via the Channel Tunnel) operate across the English Channel and St George's Channel. For details contact travel agencies or:

Stena Line, Charter House, Park Street, Ashford, Kent TN24 8EX, ☎ 0990 707070.

P&O Stena Line (Ferries), Channel House, Channel View Road, Dover CT17 9TJ, ☎ 0990 980 980 or 01304 863 000 (Switchboard).

Hoverspeed, International Hoverport, Marine Parade, Dover, Kent CT17 9TG;, ☎ 0990 240 241.

Brittany Ferries, The Brittany Centre Wharf Road Portsmouth, Hampshire PO2 8RU, ☎ 0990 360 360.

Portsmouth Commercial Port, George Byng Way, Portsmouth, Hampshire PO2 8SP, ☎ 01705 297391.

Le Shuttle-Eurotunnel ☎ 0990 353535.

To choose the most suitable route between one of the ports along the north coast of France and Provence, use the Michelin Motoring Atlas France, Michelin map 911 (which gives travel times and mileage) or Michelin maps from the 1:200 000 series (yellow cover).

Getting around

Motoring in France

Documents – Nationals of European Union countries require a valid national driving licence. Nationals of non EU countries should obtain an international driving licence (obtainable in the US from the American Automobile Association, cost for members: US$10, for non-members US$22). For the vehicle, it is necessary to have the registration papers (log-book) and a nationality plate of the approved size.

Insurance – Certain UK motoring organisations (AA, RAC) offer accident insurance and breakdown service schemes for members. Europ-Assistance (252 High St, Croyden CRO 1NF ☎ 0181 680 1234) has special policies for motorists. Members of the American Automobile Association should obtain the free brochure *Offices To Serve You Abroad*.

Highway code – The minimum driving age is 18 years old. Traffic drives on the right. It is compulsory for front-seat passengers to wear **seat belts** and it is also compulsory for back-seat passengers to do so when the car is fitted with them. Full or dipped headlights must be switched on in poor visibility and at night; use side lights only when the vehicle is stationary.
In the case of a **breakdown**, a red warning triangle or hazard warning lights are obligatory. Drivers should watch out for unfamiliar road signs and take great care on the road. In built-up areas priority must be ceded to vehicles coming from the right. However, traffic on main roads outside built-up areas (indicated by a yellow diamond sign) and on roundabouts has priority. Vehicles must stop when the lights turn red at road junctions and may filter to the right only where indicated by a flashing amber arrow.
The regulations on **drinking and driving** (limited to 0.50 g/l) and **speeding** are strictly enforced – usually by an on-the-spot fine and/or confiscation of the vehicle.

Speed limits – Although liable to modification, these are as follows:
– toll motorways *(autoroute à péage)* 130kph/80mph (110kph/68mph in rainy weather);
– dual carriage roads and motorways without tolls 110kph/68mph (100kph/62mph in rainy weather);
– other roads 90kph/56mph (80kph/50mph in rainy weather) and in towns 50kph/31mph;
– outside lane on motorways during daylight, on level ground and with good visibility, minimum speed limit of 80kph/50mph.

Parking regulations – In town there are zones where **parking** is either restricted or subject to a fee; tickets should be obtained from the ticket machines (*horodateurs* – small change necessary) and displayed inside the windscreen on the driver's side; failure to display may result in a heavy fine or even the offending vehicle being towed away. In some towns you can find blue parking zones *(zone bleue)* marked by a blue line on the pavement or a blue signpost with a P and a small square underneath. In this particular case you have to display a "time disc", which will allow you to stay for 1hr 30min (2hr 30min hours over lunchtime) for free. You can buy these "time discs" in supermarkets or petrol stations (ask for a *disque de stationnement*).

Route planning – For round-the-clock road traffic information dial 01 56 96 33 33 or consult Minitel **3615 CODE ROUTE** (1.29F/min).
www.michelin-travel.com. is the Michelin Web page, with a service for plotting an itinerary and finding a hotel or restaurant on the route.
The road network is excellent and includes many motorways. The roads are very busy during the holiday period (particularly weekends in July and August) and to avoid traffic congestion it is advisable to follow the recommended secondary routes *(Bison Futé-itinéraires bis)*.

Tolls – In France, most motorway stretches are subject to a toll *(péage)*. This can be expensive, especially if you drive all the way south (Calais to Marseille around 400F for a car). You can pay in cash or with a credit card (Visa, Mastercard).

Car rental – There are car rental agencies at airports, railway stations and in all large cities throughout France. European cars usually have manual transmission, but automatic cars are available on demand (advance reservation recommended). It is relatively expensive to hire a car in France; Americans in particular will notice the difference and should consider either booking a car from home before leaving or else taking advantage of Fly-Drive schemes.
Central Reservation in France: **Avis** 01 46 10 60 60.; **Hertz** 01 47 88 51 51; **Europcar** 01 30 43 82 82; **Budget** 01 46 86 65 65; **Baron's Limousine and Driver** 01 45 30 21 21.

Petrol – In France you will find three different types of petrol *(US:gas)*:
super unleaded 98 *(sans plomb 98)*
super unleaded 95 *(sans plomb 95)*
diesel *(diesel/gazole)*
Petrol in France is more expensive than in the United States or even the United Kingdom.

Tourist Information

Local tourist offices – To find the addresses of local Tourist Information Centres throughout France, contact the **Fédération Nationale des Comités Départementaux de Tourisme**, 280 Boulevard St-Germain, 75007 Paris ☎ 01 44 11 10 20.
Useful brochures and information are available at the regional tourist offices:
Comité Départemental du Tourisme de l'Ardèche, 4 Cours du Palais, B.P. 221, 07002 Privas ☎ 04 75 64 42 55.
Comité Départemental du Tourisme des Bouches-du-Rhône, "Le Montesquieu", 13 Rue Roux-de-Brignoles, 13006 Marseille ☎ 04 91 13 84 13.
Comité Départemental du Tourisme de la Drôme, 31 Avenue du Président-Herriot, 26000 Valence ☎ 04 75 82 19 26.
Comité Départemental du Tourisme du Gard, 3 Place des Arènes, B.P. 122, 30010 Nîmes Cedex ☎ 04 66 36 96 30.
Comité Départemental du Tourisme du Var, 1 Boulevard Maréchal-Foch, B.P. 99, 83003 Draguignan Cedex ☎ 04 94 50 55 50.
Chambre Départementale du Tourisme du Vaucluse, B.P. 147, 84008 Avignon Cedex 1, ☎ 04 90 80 47 00.

Travellers with special needs – Useful information on transportation, holidaymaking and sports associations for the disabled is available from the *Comité National Français de Liaison pour la Réadaptation des Handicapés* (CNRH), 236 bis rue de Tolbiac, 75013 Paris. Call their international information number ☎ 01 53 80 66 44, or write to request a catalogue of publications. Web-surfers can find information for slow walkers, mature travellers and others with special needs at www.access-able.com and www.handitel.org. For information on museum access for the disabled contact La Direction, *Les Musées de France, Service Accueil des Publics Spécifiques*, 6, rue des Pyramides, 75041 Paris Cedex 1, ☎ 01 40 15 35 88.
The **Michelin Red Guide France** and the **Michelin Camping Caravaning France** indicate hotels and camp sites with facilities suitable for physically-handicapped people.

Cyberspace

www.info.france-usa.org
The French Embassy's Web site provides basic information (geography, demographics, history), a news digest and business-related information. It offers special pages for children, and pages devoted to culture, language study and travel, and you can reach other selected French sites (regions, cities, ministries) with a hypertext link.

www.ottowa.ambafrance.org
The Cultural Service of the French Embassy in Ottawa has a bright and varied site with many links to other sites for French literature, news updates, E-texts in both French and English.

www.fr.holidaystore.co.uk
The new Travel Centre in London has gone on-line with this service, providing information on all of the regions of France, including updated special travel offers and details on available accomodation.

www.visiteurope.com
The European Travel Commission provides useful information on travelling to and around 27 European countries, and includes links to some commercial booking services (le vehicle hire), rail schedules, weather reports and more.

Accommodation

Places to stay – The **Places to Stay** map at the front of this book indicates recommended places for overnight stops and may be used in conjunction with the **Michelin Red Guide France**, which lists a selection of hotels and restaurants. Loisirs Accueil is a booking service that has offices in most French *départements*. For information, contact **Réservation Loisirs Accueil**, 280 Boulevard St-Germain 75007 Paris ☎ 01 44 11 10 44. The brochure **Logis et Auberges de France** is available from the different French Tourist Information Centres *(see list p 276)*.

Rural accommodation – The **Maison des Gîtes de France** has a list of self-catering accommodation where you can stay in Provence (and the rest of France). This usually takes the form of a cottage or apartment decorated in the local style where you will be able to make yourself at home. Gîtes de France have offices in:
London: 178 Piccadilly, London W1 ☎ (0891) 244 123.
Paris: 59 Rue St-Lazare, 75009 Paris ☎ 01 49 70 75 75.

Bed and breakfast – Gîtes de France *(see above)* publish a booklet on bed and breakfast accommodation *(chambres d'hôtes)* which includes a room and breakfast at a reasonable price. You can also contact two associations that provide addresses of such accommodation throughout Provence:
Bed & Breakfast (France), International Reservations Centre, PO Box 66, Henley-on-Thames, Oxon, RG9 1XS ☎ (01491) 578 803, fax (01491) 410 806.

Eating out – The **Guide Rouge Michelin France** provides a broad selection of restaurants, for all tastes and pocketbooks, serving the finest specialities in Provence as well as the rest of France. When the word *repas* (meal) is printed in red, it refers to a high-quality but reasonably-priced meal. Pictograms indicate places with a charming decor, a beautiful view, or a quiet setting.

Youth Hostels – There are two main youth hostel *(auberge de jeunesse)* associations in France.
– **Ligue Française pour les Auberges de Jeunesse**, 38, boulevard Raspail, 75007 Paris, ☎ 01 45 48 69 84, Fax 01 45 44 57 47.
– **Fédération Unie des Auberges de Jeunesse**, 27, rue Pajol, 75012 Paris, ☎ 01 44 89 87 27, Fax 07 44 89 10, Internet: www.Fuaj.org.

Holders of an International Youth Federation card should contact the IYHF in their own country for information and membership applications (US ☎ 0202 783 6161; UK ☎ 1727 855215; Canada ☎ 613-273 7884; Australia ☎ 61-2-9565-1669; Internet www.iyhf.org).

Camping – There are numerous officially-graded sites with varying standards of facilities throughout Provence. The **Michelin Guide Camping Caravaning France** lists a selection of camp sites. An international Camping Carnet for caravans is useful but not compulsory; it may be obtained from motoring organisations or the Camping and Caravanning Club (Greenfield House, Westwood Way, Coventry CV4 8JH ☎ 01203 694 995).
The **Fédération Française des Stations Vertes de Vacances** publishes an annual list of rural localities selected for their tranquillity and the outdoor activities available. Information from the Federation, 16 Rue Nodot, 21000 Dijon ☎ 03 80 43 49 47.

Thalassotherapy – *The health spas in the region covered by this guide are indicated on the Places to Stay map, see pp 8-9.*
Thalassotherapy uses the virtues of seawater to prevent or cure certain disorders and conditions. The healing properties of the marine climate (iodine, radiant light, etc), seawater, sea mud, algae and sand have given rise to a variety of therapeutic cures: fitness programmes, beauty treatments, cures for pregnant women and young mothers, as well as for those suffering from backache, stress and addiction to smoking. The mild Mediterranean climate is particularly suitable for people who are prone to fatigue.

Thalacap Camargue, Avenue du Docteur-Cambon, 13460 Les Stes-Maries-de-la-Mer ☎ 04 90 99 22 22 or by Minitel **3615 THALACAP**.

Les Bains de Mer Chauds, 96 Corniche du Président Kennedy, 13007 Marseille ☎ 04 91 52 01 03.

Bains de Mer de l'Estaque, 149 Plage de l'Estaque, 13016 Marseille ☎ 04 91 04 06 69.

Le Grand Large, 42 Avenue du Grand-Large, 13008 Marseille ☎ 04 91 73 25 88.

Thalassa Port Camargue, Route des Marines, Plage Sud, Port-Camargue, 30240 Le Grau-du-Roi.

Fédération Mer et Santé, 8 Rue de l'Isly, 75008 Paris ☎ 01 44 70 07 57 or by Minitel **3615 THALASSO**.

Maison de la Thalassothérapie, 230 Rue du Faubourg-St-Honoré, 75008 Paris ☎ 01 45 63 16 15.

Basic information

Electricity – The electric current is 220 volts. Circular two-pin plugs are the rule. You should buy adaptors before leaving home. They are on sale at most airports.

Medical treatment – First aid, medical advice and chemist's night service rota are available from chemists/drugstores (*pharmacie* identified by a green cross sign).
It is advisable to take out comprehensive insurance cover as tourists undergoing medical treatment in French hospitals or clinics have to pay for it themselves. Nationals of non-EU countries should check with their insurance companies about policy limitations. Reimbursement can then be negotiated with the insurance company according to the policy held. All prescription drugs should be clearly labelled; it is recommended to carry a copy of prescriptions. American Express offers a service only to its cardholders, "Global Assist", for any medical, legal or personal emergency ☎ 01 47 16 25 29.
British and Irish citizens should apply to the Department of Health and Social Security for **Form E111**, which entitles the holder to urgent treatment for accident and unexpected illness in EU countries. A refund of part of the costs of treatment can be obtained on application in person or by post to the local Social Security offices (*Caisse Primaire d'Assurance Maladie*).

Tipping – Since a service charge is automatically included in the price of meals and accommodation in France, it is not necessary to tip in restaurants and hotels. However taxi drivers, bellboys, doormen, filling station attendants or anyone who has been of assistance are usually tipped at the customer's discretion. Most French people give an extra tip in restaurants and cafés (about 2 francs for a drink and around 10 francs for a meal). There is no tipping in theatres.

Currency – There are no restrictions on the amount of currency visitors can take into France. Visitors wishing to export currency in foreign banknotes in excess of the given allocation from France should complete a currency declaration form on arrival.

French francs *(see illustration following)* are subdivided into 100 centimes. European currency units known as **euros** are being printed, and as of January 1999 the banking and finance industries began making the changeover. Banknotes are scheduled to go into circulation in January 2002, with national instruments phased out by July of that year. In the meantime, both euro and franc values (1 euro is about 6 francs 50 centimes) are given in more and more instances (store and restaurant receipts, bank documents, etc)

Banks – Banks are generally open from 9am to noon and from 2pm to 4pm and are closed on Mondays or Saturdays (except on market days). Banks close early on the day before a bank holiday. A passport is necessary for identification when cashing cheques (travellers' or ordinary) in banks. Commission charges vary and hotels usually charge more than banks when cashing cheques for non-residents.

Most banks have **cash dispensers** (ATM) that accept international credit cards. These are easily recognizable by the CB logo. American Express cards can only be used in dispensers at no 11 Rue Scribe (Amex office) and inside the Gare de Lyon and the Gare Montparnasse train stations.

Credit cards – American Express, Visa, Mastercard-Eurocard and Diners Club are widely accepted in shops, hotels, restaurants and petrol stations. If your card is lost or stolen, call the following 24-hour hotlines: **American Express** ☎ 01 47 77 72 00, **Visa** ☎ 08 36 69 08 80, **Mastercard/Eurocard** ☎ 01 45 67 84 84, **Diners Club** ☎ 01 49 06 17 50.

You must also report any loss or theft to the local police who will issue you with a certificate (useful proof to show the credit card company).

Post – Main Post Offices are open Mondays to Fridays from 8am to 7pm, Saturdays from 8am to noon. Smaller branch post offices generally close at lunchtime between noon and 2pm and at 4pm.

Postage via airmail for letters (20g): UK 3F, North America 4.40F, Australia and NZ 5.20F.

Stamps are also available from newsagents and *bureaux de tabac*. Stamp collectors should ask for *timbres de collection* at any post office.

Public Holidays – The following are days when museums and other monuments may be closed or may vary their hours of admission:

1 January	New Year's Day *(Jour de l'An)*
	Easter Day and Easter Monday *(Pâques)*
1 May	May Day
8 May	V E Day
40 days after Easter	Ascension Day *(Ascension)*
7th Sun after Easter	Whitsun *(Pentecôte)*
14 July	France's National Day (Bastille Day)
15 August	Assumption *(Assomption)*
1 November	All Saints' Day *(Toussaint)*
11 November	Armistice Day
25 December	Christmas Day *(Noël)*

Local radios – These usually give frequent updates on traffic, local demonstrations etc as well as information on regional cultural events.

Radio France can be picked up on the FM frequency band (90.2 at Nîmes and 98.8 at Avignon).

Embassies and consulates

Australia: Embassy – 4 Rue Jean-Rey, 75015 Paris ☎ 01 40 59 33 00, fax 01 40 59 33 10.

Canada: Embassy – 35 Avenue Montaigne, 75008 Paris ☎ 01 44 43 29 00, fax 01 44 43 29 99.

Eire: Embassy – 4 Rue Rude, 75016 Paris ☎ 01 44 17 67 00. fax 01 45 00 84 17.

New Zealand: Embassy – 7 ter Rue Léonard-de-Vinci, 75016 Paris ☎ 01 45 00 24 11, fax 01 45 01 26 39.

UK: Embassy – 35 Rue du Faubourg-St-Honoré, 75008 Paris ☎ 01 42 66 91 42, fax 01 42 66 95 90.
Consulate – 16 Rue d'Anjou, 75008 Paris ☎ 01 42 66 06 68 (visas).
Consulate – 24 Avenue Prado, 13006 Marseille ☎ 04 91 15 72 10, fax 04 91 37 47 06.

USA: Embassy – 2 Avenue Gabriel, 75008 Paris ☎ 01 43 12 22 22, fax 01 42 66 97 83.
Consulate – 2 Rue St-Florentin, 75008 Paris ☎ 01 42 96 14 88.
Consulate – 12 Boulevard Paul-Peytral, 13006 Marseille ☎ 04 91 54 92 00.

Conversion tables

Weights and measures

1 kilogram (kg)	2.2 pounds (lb)	2.2 pounds
1 metric ton (tn)	1.1 tons	1.1 tons

to convert kilograms to pounds, multiply by 2.2

1 litre (l)	2.1 pints (pt)	1.8 pints
1 litre	0.3 gallon (gal)	0.2 gallon

to convert litres to gallons, multiply by 0.26 (US) or 0.22 (UK)

1 hectare (ha)	2.5 acres	2.5 acres
1 square kilometre (km²)	0.4 square miles (sq mi)	0.4 square miles

to convert hectares to acres, multiply by 2.4

1 centimetre (cm)	0.4 inches (in)	0.4 inches
1 metre (m)	3.3 feet (ft) - 39.4 inches - 1.1 yards (yd)	
1 kilometre (km)	0.6 miles (mi)	0.6 miles

to convert metres to feet, multiply by 3.28. kilometres to miles, multiply by 0.6

Clothing

Women							Men
	35	4	2½	40	7½	7	
	36	5	3½	41	8½	8	
	37	6	4½	42	9½	9	
Shoes	38	7	5½	43	10½	10	Shoes
	39	8	6½	44	11½	11	
	40	9	7½	45	12½	12	
	41	10	8½	46	13½	13	
	36	4	8	46	36	36	
	38	6	10	48	38	38	
Dresses &	40	8	12	50	40	40	Suits
Suits	42	12	14	52	42	42	
	44	14	16	54	44	44	
	46	16	18	56	46	48	
	36	08	30	37	14½	14,5	
	38	10	32	38	15	15	
Blouses &	40	12	14	39	15½	15½	Shirts
sweaters	42	14	36	40	15¾	15¾	
	44	16	38	41	16	16	
	46	18	40	42	16½	16½	

Sizes often vary depending on the designer. These equivalents are given for guidance only.

Speed

kph	10	30	50	70	80	90	100	110	120	130
mph	6	19	31	43	50	56	62	68	75	81

Temperature

Celsius (°C)	0°	5°	10°	15°	20°	25°	30°	40°	60°	80°	100°
Fahrenheit (°F)	32°	41°	50°	59°	68°	77°	86°	104°	140°	176°	212°

To convert Celsius into Fahrenheit, multiply °C by 9, divide by 5, and add 32.
To convert Fahrenheit into Celsius, subtract 32 from °F, multiply by 5, and divide by 9.

Notes and coins

500 Francs featuring
scientists
Pierre and Marie Curie
(1858-1906), (1867-1934)

200 Francs featuring
engineer Gustave Eiffel
(1832-1923)

100 Francs featuring
Post-Impressionist painter
Paul Cézanne
(1839-1906)

50 Francs featuring
pilot and writer
Antoine de Saint-Exupéry
(1900-1944)

20 Francs

10 Francs

5 Francs

2 Francs

1 Franc

50 Centimes

20 Centimes

10 Centimes

5 Centimes

Telephoning

Public Telephones – Most public phones in France use pre-paid phone cards *(télé-cartes)*. Some telephone booths accept credit cards (Visa, Mastercard/Eurocard; minimum monthly charge 20F). *Télécartes* (50 or 120 units) can be bought in post offices, branches of France Télécom, *bureaux de tabac* (authorised cigarette sales points) and newsagents, and can be used to make calls in France and abroad. Calls can be received at phone boxes where the blue bell sign is shown; the phone will not ring, so keep your eye on the little display screen.

National calls – When calling within France dial the 10-digit correspondent's number. The French ringing tone is a series of long tones and the engaged (busy) tone is a series of short beeps. All French telephone numbers have 10 digits. The five different area codes are as follows: Paris region – 01; northwest France – 02; northeast France – 03; southeast France and Corsica – 04; southwest France – 05.

Toll-free numbers – In France numbers beginning with 0800 are toll-free.

Emergency numbers – Police 17; Fire Brigade (Pompiers) 18; Ambulance (SAMU) 15.

International calls – To call France from abroad, dial the country code (33) + the correspondent's 9-digit number (omit the initial 0). When calling abroad from France dial 00, then dial the country code, followed by the area code and number of your correspondent. For international inquiries dial 00 33 12 + country code (be prepared to wait for up to an hour). For local directory assistance, dial 12.
To use your personal calling card dial: **AT&T** 0800 99 00 11; **Sprint** 0800 99 00 87; **MCI** 0800 99 00 19; **Canada Direct** 0800 99 00 16.

International dialling codes – Australia 61; Canada 1; Eire 353; New Zealand 64; United Kingdom 44; United States 1.

Minitel – France Télécom operates a system offering directory enquiries (free of charge up to 3min), travel and entertainment reservations, and other services (cost varies between 0.37F - 5.57F/min). These small computer-like terminals can be found in some post offices, hotels and **France Télécom** agencies and in many French homes. **3614 PAGES E** is the code for Directory assistance in English (turn on the unit, dial 3614, hit the "connexion" button when you get the tone, type in "PAGES E", and follow the instructions on the screen). For route planning, use Michelin services **3615 MICHELIN** (tourist and route information) and **3617 MICHELIN** (information sent by fax). **3615 HORAV** provides general airline information and flight schedules from and to Paris, **3615 TCAMP** will give you camping information, and weather reports are available on **3615 METEO**. As for those British tourists who are feeling homesick, **3614 BBC** will supply them with the latest BBC news.

Cellular phones – In France mobile phones have numbers beginning with 06. Two watt (lighter, shorter reach) and eight-watt models are on the market, using the Itinéris (France Télécom) or SFR network. **Mobicartes** are pre-paid phone cards that fit into mobile units. Cell phone rentals (delivery or airport pickup provided):

Ellinas Phone Rental ☏ 01 47 20 70 00
Rent a Cell Express ☏ 01 53 93 78 00.

Shopping in Provence

General Information

Opening hours – Department stores and chain stores are open Mondays to Saturdays 9am to 6.30pm-7.30pm. Smaller, more specialised shops may close during the lunch hour. Food stores (grocers, wine merchants and bakeries) are open from 7am to 6.30pm-7.30pm. Some open on Sunday mornings. Many food stores close between noon and 2pm and on Mondays. Supermarkets are usually open until 9pm-10pm.

What to bring back – There are so many things to bring back that to list them all would be too long. However tourists should bring back among other things the famous *santons* from Aubagne, Arles or Marseille. Tarascon is famous for its Provençal cloth, although this can be bought throughout the entire region. As far as food is concerned, Provence is famous for its candied fruit (Apt) or its olive oil (Alpilles region).

Travellers to America cannot bring back food and plant products, especially cheese and fruit. Americans are allowed to return with up to US$400 worth of tax-free goods, Canadians up to CND$300, British up to £136, Australians up to AUS$400 and New Zealanders up to NZ$700.

Provençal markets

The picturesque markets of Provence, which liven up both city streets and village squares, are much appreciated by foreign visitors, who are impressed by the variety and quality of the local produce and crafts (fruit and vegetables, flowers, spices, Provençal herbs, olives, honey, cheese, Provençal fabric etc) as well as by the loquacious stallholders and their broad southern accent.

Carcanague/IMAGES TOULOUSE

Provençal market stall selling aromatic herbs

Aigues-Mortes – Traditional market Wednesdays and Sundays.

Aix-en-Provence – Traditional market on Place Richelme every day.
Flower market on Place des Prêcheurs Mondays, Wednesdays, Fridays and Sundays.
Flea market on Place Verdun Tuesdays, Thursdays and Saturdays.
Market offering biological produce on Place de la Croix-Verte at Jas-de-Bouffan on Thursdays.

Apt – Traditional market Saturdays.
Farmers' market Tuesdays May to November.

Arles – Traditional market Wednesdays (Boulevard Émile-Combes) and Saturdays (Boulevard des Lices and Boulevard Clémenceau).
Flea market on Boulevard des Lices the first Wednesday of each month.

Aubagne – Traditional market on Cours Voltaire Tuesdays, Thursdays, Saturdays and Sundays.
Flea market at La Tourtelle the last Sunday of each month.

Avignon – Traditional market daily except Mondays at les Halles.
Flower market on Place des Carmes Saturdays.
Flea market on Place Crillon Saturdays.

Beaucaire – Traditional market Thursdays and Sundays.

Bédoin – Provençal market Mondays.

Cadenet – Farmers' market Mondays and Saturdays.

Carpentras – Traditional market around the station every day.
Truffes market Fridays, November to March.

Cavaillon – Traditional market Mondays.

La Ciotat – Handicraft market every evening 8pm to midnight at the Vieux Port in July and August.

Fontvieille – Handicraft market once a week 4pm to 9pm in June, July and August.

Gardanne – Traditional market in the town centre Wednesdays, Fridays and Sundays.

Graveson – Farmers' market on Place du Marché 4pm to 8pm Fridays from 21 May to 31 October.

L'Isle-sur-la-Sorgue – Traditional market Thursdays and Sundays.
Flea market Sundays.

Marseille – *See p 176.*

Ménerbes – *Truffes* market on the last Sunday in December.
Honey market on the third Sunday in July.
Artists and artisans market on the second Sunday in August.

Nîmes – Traditional market Mondays.

Nyons – Traditional market Thursdays.

Orange – Traditional market Thursdays.

Pertuis – Traditional market Fridays.
Farmers' market Wednesdays and Saturdays.

Ruoms – Traditional market Fridays and Saturdays.

St-Rémy-de-Provence – Traditional market Wednesdays on Place de la République and Place Pélissier.

Les Stes-Maries-de-la-Mer – Traditional market on Place des Gitans, Mondays and Fridays.

Salon-de-Provence – Traditional market on Place Morgan and along the Cours, Wednesdays.
Flea market on Place Morgan the first Sunday of each month.

Tarascon – Traditional market in the town centre Tuesdays.

Uzès – Traditional market Saturdays.

Vaison-la-Romaine – Traditional market Tuesdays.
Provençal market in the upper town Sundays, June to September.

Vallon-Pont-d'Arc – Traditional market Thursdays.

Valréas – Traditional market Wednesdays and Saturdays.
Truffes market Wednesdays, November to March.

Sport and recreation

ALONG THE COAST

Marinas

Most of the seaside resorts lying between Le Grau-du-Roi and La Ciotat *(see Places to Stay at the beginning of the guide)* have well-equipped marinas. The main ones, running from west to east, are: Aigues-Mortes, Le Grau-du-Roi, Port-Camargue, Les Stes-Maries/Port Gardian, Port-St-Gervais to Fos-sur-Mer, Martigues, Les Heures Claires at Istres, Carro, Sausset-les-Pins, Carry-le-Rouet, L'Estaque, Le Frioul, Marseille Pointe Rouge and Le Vieux Port, Cassis and La Ciotat.

Les Stes-Maries/Port Gardian and Port-Camargue have been awarded the label **Pavillon Bleu d'Europe**, granted on the basis of the following criteria: clean site and surroundings, special equipment and amenities, reception and information services, educational facilities.

Sailing

Most seaside resorts have sailing schools where courses are organised. It is possible to hire, in season, boats with or without a crew. For further information, contact the local harbour-master's office or the **Fédération Française de Voile**, 55 Avenue Kléber, 75784 Paris Cedex 16 ☎ 01 44 05 81 00. Between Le Grau-du-Roi and La Ciotat, most resorts *(see the Places to Stay map at the beginning of the guide)* have well-equipped marinas. The largest are, from west to east, Aigues-Mortes, le Grau-du-Roi, Port-Camargues, Stes-Maries/Port Gardian, Port St-Gervais to Fos-sur-Mer, Martigues, Les Heures Claires, Istres, Carro, Sausset-les-Pins, Carry-le-Rouet, l'Estaque, Le Frioul, Marseille, Pointe Rouge, Cassis and La Ciotat.

Sea canoeing

This new sport uses the same equipment as traditional canoeing, except that the boats are longer and narrower. It enables tourists to visit small coves that cannot be reached by land. It is forbidden to stray from the beach for more than one nautical mile. During your first trip you will be accompanied by experienced sailors. Apply to the **Fédération Loisirs-Accueil des Bouches-du-Rhône**, which offers 3-day excursions including a tour of the Marseille calanques and a special "marine itinerary".

The Quality of Seawater in Provence

Tests are carried out on the waters fit for swimming every year from the month of June. They classify the water in four categories:
A: good quality
B: fair quality
C: risk of occasional pollution
D: poor quality
The results of these tests are available on Minitel 3615 INFOPLAGE.

Scuba diving

Marseille and its surroundings have always been a privileged setting for diving activities. It was here that Jacques-Yves Cousteau and Émile Gagnan achieved their record-breaking performances that paved the way for modern diving with the invention of the Aqualung.

The most popular spot for deep-sea diving are the calanques around Marseille, where the seabed is truly a feast for the eyes. Six exceptional sites can be explored: *Le Chauoen*, a Moroccan cargo ship which ran aground on the Île du Planier (off Marseille); *La Drôme*, a shipwreck lying at a depth of 51m/168ft; *Le Liban*, a liner that

---

Safety Measures for Deep-Sea Divers

The growing popularity of scuba-diving along the Mediterranean coast, where one can admire superb underwater landscapes, must not detract from the potential hazards of this sport. To protect yourself against the risk of an accident, the consequences of which may be serious, you should bear in mind the following instructions. It is highly inadvisable to dive on your own, after a heavy meal, after an alcoholic meal, after consuming fizzy drinks, or when you are tired. Also, make sure to avoid the fairways used by boats and the areas frequented by windsurfers. When diving, it is essential that you respect the decompression stops. In the event of an accident, give precise details of what happened to the emergency team on land so that they can provide appropriate care in a hyperbaric chamber (the only solution to decompression problems, however slight).

---

sunk in front of the Île Maïre in 1903; *Les Impériaux*, a site renowned for its huge gorgonian fish; La Cassidaigne, a seaway teeming with fish at the foot of the light-house (4 nautical miles from Cassis); Île Verte, an islet with luxuriant vegetation peopled with myriads of fish.

This sport requires a lengthy and challenging training which can only be provided by fully-trained instructors holding nationally-recognised diplomas. For a list of clubs offering scuba-diving courses, contact the local branch of the **Fédération Française d'Études et de Sports Sous-Marins**, 24 Quai de Rive-Neuve, 13007 Marseille ☎ 04 91 33 99 31, or consult the Minitel on **3615 FFESSM**. This federation publishes *Subaqua*, a bimestrial journal on diving in France. The **Centre UCPA** in Niolon is Europe's biggest training centre for deep-sea diving: Centre UCPA, Niolon, 13740 Le Rove ☎ 04 91 46 90 16.

Books about diving can be found at the Librairie Maritime bookshop, 26 Quai de Rive-Neuve, 13007 Marseille ☎ 04 91 54 79 26.

Cassis – View of the harbour

Sea fishing

There are fewer fish in the Mediterranean than in the other seas bordering the French coast, but shoals of rock fish nonetheless abound: scorpion fish (an essential ingre-dient in a *bouillabaisse*), red mullet, conger and moray eels as well as numerous octopuses, spider crabs, various squid and even the odd crayfish. In the shallower, sandy waters there are skate, sole and dab. Offshore, shoals of sardines, anchovies and tuna fish intermingle with sea bream, bass and grey mullet. No permit is neces-sary for sea angling, provided that the day's catch is for personal consumption only.

Boat trips

By sea – Leaving from Marseille, you can visit the Château d'If, the Îles du Frioul and the Calanques; leaving from Cassis, you can visit the calanques at Port-Miou, Port-Pin and En-Vau. *See the section on Admission times and charges under the heading Les CALANQUES.*

Leaving from La Ciotat, you can visit the Île Verte (*see the section on Admission times and charges under the heading La CIOTAT*). The excursions leaving from La Ciotat are on board a catamaran-type boat with views of the sea depths cruising among the calanques of La Ciotat, between Cassis and Marseille. For details apply to **Les Amis des Calanques**, 6 Place de la Liberté, 13600 La Ciotat ☎ 04 42 83 54 50.

Leaving from the Tour de Constance in Aigues-Mortes, *Le Pescalune* will take you on a trip along the canals and the Vidourle, a coastal river. For details, apply to M. Griller, B.P. 76, 30220 Aigues-Mortes ☎ 04 66 53 79 47.

Along the River Rhône – *See the section on Admission times and charges under the headings AVIGNON and La CAMARGUE.*

Rambling

Exploring Provence on foot is an enchanting way of discovering the all-encompassing brightness of Provençal light as it sets off the beauty of the landscape to perfection, both in its natural, unspoiled state, and featuring the evidence of man's passage through village and countryside. Leave the car behind and experience a different, more relaxed pace of life in a landscape which rings with the echoes of days gone by.

Many long-distance footpaths *(sentiers de Grande Randonnée – GR)* cover the area described in this guide. The GR 4 crosses the lower Vivarais country as far as Mont Ventoux; GR 42 leads along the valley of the Rhône; GR 6 follows the River Gard as far as Beaucaire and then plunges into the Alpilles and Luberon ranges; GR 9 takes the line of the north face of Mont Ventoux, then crosses the Vaucluse plateau, the Luberon range, Montagne Ste-Victoire and the massif of Ste-Baume. Further variations on the above are offered by the GRs 63, 92, 97 and 98. Besides the long-distance footpaths, there are short to medium-distance paths ranging from walks of a few hours to a couple of days. Topo-guides to footpaths in France are published by the **Fédération Française de la Randonnée Pédestre** and are on sale from the Information Centre at 64 Rue de Gergovie, 75014 Paris ☎ 01 45 45 31 02, or by mail order from McCarta, 15 Highbury Place, London N 5 1QP ☎ (0171) 354 1616. They give detailed maps of the paths and offer valuable information to ramblers.

The **Comité Départemental du Tourisme des Bouches-du-Rhône** publishes a map called *Ballades et Randonnées dans les Bouches-du-Rhône*: it gives addresses of rambling clubs and provides details concerning accommodation as well as other miscellaneous subjects. Details of short walks are provided by local Tourist Information Centres. Ramblers can consult the guide entitled *Gîtes et Refuges France et Frontières* by A. and S. Mouraret (Éditions La Cadole, 74 Rue Albert-Perdreaux, 78140 Vélizy ☎ 01 34 65 10 40). The guide has been written mainly for those who enjoy rambling, riding and cycling holidays. The national guide *Bienvenue à la Ferme* (Editions Solar) includes the addresses of farmers who have signed a charter drawn up by the Chambers of Agriculture. *Bienvenue à la Ferme* farms, vetted for quality and meeting official standards, can be identified by the yellow flower which serves as their logo.

A French bylaw rules that access to forests and other wooded massifs is strictly forbidden between 1 July and the second weekend in September, and when winds blow at over 40kph/25mph.

Stepping smart

Choosing the right equipment for a rambling expedition is essential: flexible hiking shoes with non-slip soles, a rain jacket or poncho, an extra sweater, sun protection (hat, glasses, lotion), drinking water (1-2l per person), high energy snacks (chocolate, cereal bars, banana ...), and a first aid kit. Of course, you'll need a good map (and a compass if you plan to leave the main trails). Plan your itinerary well, keeping in mind that while the average walking speed for an adult is 4kph/2.5mph, you will need time to eat and rest, and children will not keep up the same pace. Leave your itinerary with someone before setting out (innkeeper or fellow camper).

Respect for nature is a cardinal rule and includes the following precautions: don't smoke or light fires in the forest, which are particularly susceptible in the dry summer months; always carry your rubbish out; leave wild flowers as they are; walk around, not through, farmers' fields; close gates behind you.

If you are caught in an electrical storm, avoid high ground, and do not move along a ridge top; do not seek shelter under overhanging rocks, isolated trees in otherwise open areas, at the entrance to caves or other openings in the rocks, or in the proximity of metal fences or gates. Do not use a metallic survival blanket. If possible, position yourself at least 15m/15yd from the highest point around you (rock or tree); crouch with your knees up and without touching the rock face with your hands or any exposed part of your body. An automobile is a good refuge as its rubber tires ground it and provide protection for those inside.

Riding

The **Délégation Nationale au Tourisme Équestre** (30 Avenue d'Iéna, 75116 Paris ☎ 01 53 67 44 44) publishes an annual handbook called *Tourisme et Loisirs Équestres en France* covering the whole of France, divided into regions and *départements*. You may also consult the Minitel on **3615 FFE** or apply to the **Association Régionale de Tourisme Équestre de Provence**, 28 Place Roger-Salengro, 84300 Cavaillon ☎ 04 90 78 04 49. In the Camargue, the land of the horse, there are various opportunities to visit the lagoons on horseback. *For details see p 132.*

Cycling

The **Fédération Française de Tourisme** (5 Rue de Rome, 93561 Rosny-sous-Bois Cedex ☎ 01 49 35 69 45 or by Minitel on **3615 CENTRES VTT** or **3615 CENTRES FFC**) publishes a handbook that lists 17 000km/10 600mi of signposted trails for those who enjoy mountain bike riding.

The **Fédération Française de Cyclotourisme** (8 Rue Jean-Marie-Jégo, 75013 Paris ☎ 01 44 16 88 88) provides detailed information on specific cycling routes: mileage, degree of difficulty, touristic sights. Tourist Information Centres should be able to provide lists of local firms which hire bicycles.

The firm **Europbike** offers bike rental facilities seven days a week to discover the Provençal countryside leaving from the city of Avignon: Europbike, Station Shell, Les Remparts, 16 Boulevard St-Michel, 84000 Avignon ☎ 04 90 86 54 47.

Skiing

You can practice both downhill and cross-country skiing at the Mont-Serein resort (the secondary peak of Mont Ventoux, 1 445m/4 741ft high). For details apply to the town hall (Mairie) in Beaumont-du-Ventoux (84340), Tuesdays, Thursdays and Fridays ☎ 04 90 65 21 13 or the Reception Chalet (Chalet d'Accueil) ☎ 04 90 63 42 02.

Rock-climbing

This can be done all year up the Dentelles de Montmirail or the cliffs in the calanques near Marseille (bear in mind that access to the calanques is forbidden from 1 July to the second Saturday in September). The local branch of the **Club Alpin Français de Provence** (12 Rue Fort-Notre-Dame, 13007 Marseille ☎ 04 91 54 36 94) organises accompanied climbing trips.
General information can be obtained from the **Fédération Française de la Montagne et de l'Escalade**, 10 Quai de la Marne, 75019 Paris ☎ 01 40 18 75 50.

Caving and pot-holing

The region is rich in caves and pot-holes. Serious speleologists as well as informed amateurs will be enchanted by the diversity of the local underground network. Apply to the "Section Spéléologie" of the **Club Alpin Français de Provence** *(see address above)*. General information can be obtained from the **Fédération Française de Spéléologie**, 130 Rue St-Maur, 75011 Paris ☎ 01 43 57 56 54.

Bird's eye views

One way of discovering the beautiful landscapes of Provence from above is gliding. There are several associations throughout the region that organise air trips:
Association Vélivole de Carpentras, BP 129, 84204 Carpentras Cedex ☎ 04 90 60 08 17.
Association Vélivole du Luberon, 26 Avenue de la Fontaine, 13370 Mallemort ☎ 04 90 57 43 86. Aerodrome.
Aéro-Club St-Rémy-les-Alpilles, Aérodrome du Romarin, 13210 St-Rémy-de-Provence ☎ 04 90 92 08 43. Gliding school, courses and flights for beginners.
Centre de Vol à Voile de la Crau, Aérodrome Salon-Eyguières, BP 81, 13651 Salon Cedex ☎ 04 90 42 00 91.
General information can be obtained from the **Fédération Française de Planeur Ultra-Léger Motorisé**, 96 bis Rue Marc-Sangnier, B.P. 341, 94709 Maisons-Alfort Cedex ☎ 01 49 81 74 43.

Freshwater fishing

Those interested in freshwater fishing should bear in mind that the inland water supply in Provence is both relatively sparse and subject to variation in water levels. Many small rivers dry up without rainfall. However, rivers such as the Ardèche, the Gard or the Durance (not to mention the Rhône) and canals or reservoirs (Cadarache, Brinon) are home to trout, chub, carp, tench and pike. In general, the upper reaches of a river are classed as first category and the middle and lower reaches as second category. For full details of regulations and fishing permits, contact Tourist Information Centres or the Water and Forest Authority (Eaux et Forêts). A brochure and folding map *Pêche en France* (Fishing in France) is published and distributed by the **Conseil Supérieur de la Pêche** (134 Avenue de Malakoff, 75116 Paris ☎ 01 45 02 20 20). In each *département*, the Fishing Federations and Associations for the Preservation of Aquatic Sites also provide maps and general information to the public.

Canoeing

This is a good way of exploring the less accessible stretches of the Ardèche, Cèze, Gardon, Durance and Sorgue rivers.
As far as the **Gorges de l'Ardèche** are concerned, conditions for hiring boats are mentioned in the section on Admission times and charges under the heading Gorges de l'Ardèche; bear in mind that the stretch between Charmes and Sauze has been designated a natural reserve and special rules are enforced: no windsurfing; no boats with more than three people allowed, compulsory life jackets. Camping is possible only in Gaud and Gournier, for no longer than two nights. For further practical information, contact the **Maison de la Réserve** at Gournier ☎ 04 75 38 63 00.
The Association de Protection des Gorges de l'Ardèche publishes a plasticated map showing difficult stretches of river and possible "refuelling" stops along the river. (It can be found at local Tourist Information Centres).
The association **CAPCANOE** organises four trips along the River Cèze (4, 8, 15 and 30km/2.5, 5, 9 and 19mi). 30500 St-Ambroix ☎ 04 66 24 25 16.
Upstream from the Pont du Gard, you can safely practise canoeing on the Gardon (4 trips of 6, 11, 22 and 29km/3.5, 7, 14 and 19mi). **KAYAK VERT**, 30210 Collias ☎ 04 66 22 84 83.
Between Fontaine-de-Vaucluse and Isle-sur-la-Sorgue, a 8km/5mi trip on the Sorgue will enable you to discover the beauty of the local landscape. **KAYAK VERT**, 84800 Fontaine-de-Vaucluse ☎ 04 90 20 35 44.

Vallon Pont d'Arc

In conjunction with the **Fédération Française de Canoë-Kayak** (87 Quai de la Marne, 94344 Joinville-le-Pont ☎ 01 45 11 08 50), IGN publishes a map called *France, Canoë-Kayak et Sports d'Eau Vive* which lists all the different excursions, classifying them in terms of difficulty. Further information can be obtained from the Minitel on **3615 CANOË PLUS**.

Bullfighting events

The Camargue area, and especially the famous Camargue bull, have always been at the heart of French bullfighting tradition. *Cocarde* races (also called *courses camarguaises* or *courses libres*) involve going down into the arena in a bid to remove the trappings that are fixed to and between the horns of the animal. These events take place in Arles (April to early October - *Cocarde d'Or* on the first Monday in July), Beaucaire (late July), Les Stes-Maries-de-la-Mer (April to August), St-Martin-de-Crau (May and October) and Châteaurenard (May to October). Newspapers give the dates for these events, which are widely reported in the local press.

Originally, bullfighting was a Spanish tradition but it gradually spread to Provence. *Corridas* and *novilladas* are usually held during *ferias*, large celebrations that bring huge crowds to the arenas and create a lively atmosphere in the town centre: *abrivados* (bulls are let loose on the streets), *peñas* (brass bands) playing along pavements and in the *bodegas* (bars), dances, etc. The city of Nîmes hosts three *ferias* every year and Arles stages the famous Feria de Pentecôte at Easter. In Les Stes-Maries-de-la-Mer, the *corridas* are performed on horseback (Feria du Cheval). To attend a *corrida* or a *novillada*, it is best to book in advance by calling one of the following offices – Nîmes: Bureau de Location des Arènes, Rue Alexandre Ducros, 30000 Nîmes ☎ 04 66 67 28 02; Arles: Location Arènes d'Arles, B.P. 216, 13635 Arles Cedex ☎ 04 90 96 03 70; Les Stes-Maries-de-la-Mer: Arènes des Stes-Maries-de-la-Mer ☎ 04 90 97 85 86; Camargue: Arènes de Méjanes ☎ 04 90 97 10 60. The best seats are in the front row, on the side of the arena.

Small Bullfighting Lexicon

Aficionado: enthusiastic spectator; expert in tauromachy

Bravo: said of an aggressive bull

Chaquetilla: short embroidered jacket; an essential part of the matador's outfit

Coleta: small plait worn by the torero during bullfights

Faena: series of passes that the bullfighter performs with the muleta

Matador de toros: Master of Bulls who confronts the bull during a corrida

Montera: bullfighter's hat

Muleta: square of red material affixed to a wooden mast that the matador brandishes during the faena

Novillada: fight with a young bull under four years of age; the first stage in a bullfighter's career

Rejoneador: bullfighter who performs on horseback

Zapatilla: shoes traditionally worn by the matador

Thematic trips

DISCOVERING NATURE

Nature parks

Parc Naturel Régional de Camargue – Centre d'Information de Ginès, Pont de Gau, 13460 Les Stes-Maries-de-la-Mer ☎ 04 90 97 86 32; Musée Camarguais, Mas du Pont de Rousty, 13200 Arles ☎ 04 90 97 10 82. Information can also be obtained from Tourist Information Centres in Arles, Salin-de-Giraud and Les Stes-Maries-de-la-Mer and on the Minitel **3615 CAMARGUE** *(see p 132 for details on the park's activities)*.

Parc Naturel Régional du Luberon – Maison du Parc, 60 Place Jean-Jaurès, B.P. 122, 84404 Apt ☎ 04 90 04 42 00 and by Minitel on **3615 LUBERON**. You can also apply to local Tourist Information Centres *(see p 168 for details on the park's activities)*.

Marine parks

Marine parks feature preserved areas where fishing and diving activities, as well as boat anchoring, are strictly regulated and where experiments with artificial reefs are being carried out. The aim of these parks is to fulfil a number of well-defined objectives: protecting the natural environment (controlling all activities concerned with the development and survival of vegetal and animal species); exploiting the available resources (immersion of artificial reefs to encourage the growth of fauna and flora); installing blocks to hinder illicit trawling and providing information (increasing public awareness of ecological issues).

Parc Régional Marin de la Côte Bleue – Lying west of Marseille harbour, it laps the Massif de la Nerthe, a rocky mountain range separating the Étang de Berre from the sea. Information can be obtained from the Parc Régional Marin de la Côte Bleue, Club de la Mer, B.P. 37, 13960 Sausset-les-Pins ☎ 04 42 45 45 07 or from local Tourist Information Centres in Carry-le-Rouet, Ensuès-la-Redonne, Martigues, Le Rove and Sausset-les-Pins.

Parc Régional Marin de la Baie de La Ciotat – The park is defined by La Ciotat bay. The underwater topography is remarkably varied: rocks, sand, sloping ledges, underwater slabs and mossy beds of posidonia, home to a great many small molluscs. Information available from the Parc Régional Marin de la Baie de La Ciotat, Hôtel de Ville, 13712 La Ciotat ☎ 04 42 83 90 09 or apply to the Tourist Information Centre in La Ciotat.

Remember to Protect the Sea!
Never forget that the marine environment is extremely fragile and needs to be respected by all those who venture near it. Make a point of observing the following rules:
Do not throw away plastic bags;
Throw the fish you have caught back into the sea;
Do not damage or remove the long, green posidonia leaves which cleanse seawater by renewing its oxygen (avoid pulling them out with your hands or dragging an anchor through them).

Olives and the oil industry

There exist several types of olive in Provence: the *tanche* or *olive de Nyons*, the only one to enjoy the AOC label, is delicious when served pickled in brine; the *angladau* is pressed for its oil; the *grossane* is a big, black, fleshy olive; the *salonenque* or *olive des Baux* is a green variety served crushed; the *picholine*, a long, narrow green olive, is crushed and then pickled.
Provence offers two thematic circuits that focus on the olive, the **Route de l'Olivier en Baronnies**, covering the area around Nyons and Buis-les-Baronnies *(see Michelin Green Guide Alpes du Sud in French)* and the **Route de l'Olivier des Alpilles et de la Vallée des Baux**. These tours include visits to olive groves, mills, presses and museums.
Information can be obtained from the **Comité Économique Agricole de l'Olivier**, Maison des Agriculteurs, 22 Avenue Henri-Pontier, 13626 Aix-en-Provence Cedex 1 ☎ 04 42 23 01 92. The Éditions La Manufacture publishes a guidebook in which these two routes are described at great length - *Guide des Routes de l'Olivier*.

Lavender fields

Created by the Regional Tourist Committee of the Provence-Alpes-Côte d'Azur area, the **Route de la Lavande** enables you to visit a great many places associated with the growing and processing of lavender around the Mont Ventoux, the Luberon and the

Provençal Drôme. This circuit is complemented by various festivities: Fête de la Lavande in Sault on 14 and 15 August, the **Corso Nocturne de la Lavande** in Valréas on the first Saturday and the first Monday in August. The association Routes de la Lavande (2 Avenue de Venterol, 26111 Nyons Cedex ☎ 04 75 26 65 91) publishes a handbook with general information as well as cards with practical data about each site which can be picked up from local Tourist Information Centres.

Pays de Sault et du Ventoux – Ferme St-Agricol in Savoillans: tour of the farmhouse and botanical gardens, practical demonstration of distillation techniques ☎ 04 75 28 86 57.
Lavender garden in Sault: collection of lavender plants. Hameau de Verdolier ☎ 04 90 64 14 97.
You can also visit a cooperative at the Maison des Producteurs de Sault ☎ 04 90 64 08 98.
Pays d'Apt and Luberon – There is a lavender distillery at Lagarde d'Apt. Guided tours available on request ☎ 04 90 75 01 42.
Lavender farm at Lagarde d'Apt: tour by foot of a lavender field and visit of the distillery. Château du Bois ☎ 04 90 76 91 23.
Lavender Museum in Coustellet (see the section on Admission times and charges under the heading Montagne du LUBERON).
Provençal Drôme – Bleu Provence Distillery in Nyons ☎ 04 75 26 10 42.
Jardin des Arômes in Nyons: collection of aromatic plants, promenade along the pier ☎ 04 75 26 04 30.

Tours of wine cooperatives

Tours of cooperative wine cellars (caves) are offered all over the wine-producing regions: the east and west banks of the Rhône, areas surrounding Aigues-Mortes (caves de Listel, see the section on Admission times and charges under the heading AIGUES MORTES and Le GRAU DU ROI), Aix, Les Baux de Provence, Cassis, etc.
The addresses of wine cellars and domains can be obtained from wine merchants and associations. Details about events linked to vineyards are available from Tourist Information Centres.

Aix-en-Provence wines – Fête des Vins in Rognes around mid-July; Fête des Coteaux d'Aix at Aix-en-Provence in late July; Fête des Côtes de Provence Ste-Victoire in Trets in late June; numerous other festivities linked to wine in the Bouches-du-Rhône département. Syndicat des Coteaux d'Aix-en-Provence, Maison des Agriculteurs, Avenue Henri-Pontier, 13100 Aix-en-Provence ☎ 04 42 23 57 14; Syndicat des Vins de Palette, Château Simone, 13590 Meyreuil ☎ 04 42 66 92 58.

Baux-de-Provence wines – Procession des Bouteilles in Boulbon in early June. Fête du Vin et de l'Artisanat in St-Rémy-de-Provence in late July. Syndicat des Vignerons des Baux, Château d'Estoublon, 13990 Fontvieille ☎ 04 90 54 64 00.

Cassis wines – A wine feast with a procession and tasting sessions takes place in September. Apply to the Syndicat des Vignerons de Cassis, Château de Fontcreuse, 13 Route de La Ciotat 13260 Cassis ☎ 04 42 01 71 09.

Southern Côtes du Rhône wines – Fête de la Véraison in Châteauneuf-du-Pape on the first Sunday in August; Fête des Côtes du Rhône primeurs in Avignon around mid-November. Syndicat des Côtes du Rhône, Maison des Vins, 6 Rue des Trois Faucons, 84000 Avignon ☎ 04 90 27 24 24.

Luberon wines – Syndicat Général des Vins du Luberon, Le Château, 84240 La Tour-d'Aigues ☎ 04 90 07 34 40.

THEMATIC ITINERARIES

Historical itineraries

The historical itineraries, known as Routes Historiques, are intended to present France's architectural heritage in its historical context.
Five important historical itineraries cover the region: the **Route Historique Via Domitia** (M. Delran ☎ 04 67 69 75 02), the **Route Historique des Comtes de Provence** (Tourist Information Centre in Salon-de-Provence ☎ 04 90 56 27 60), the **Route Historique des Hauts Lieux de Provence** (Tourist Information Centre at Arcs-sur-Argens ☎ 04 94 73 37 30), the **Route Historique du Patrimoine Juif du Midi de la France** (Direction de la Chambre Départementale du Tourisme du Vaucluse in Avignon ☎ 04 91 54 92 66), the **Route Historique des Vaudois en Luberon** (M. Sarre, Hôtel de Ville at Mérindol ☎ 04 90 72 81 07). You may also be interested in the **Route Historique Musicale** (M. Goven, CRMH de Provence-Alpes-Côte d'Azur in Aix-en-Provence ☎ 04 42 27 98 40) and part of the **Route Historique du Gévaudan au Golfe du Lion** (Château de Flaugergues ☎ 04 67 65 51 72).
These itineraries are clearly indicated along country roads by means of signposts. All of them are detailed in handbooks available from Tourist Information Centres or from the associations concerned with the Routes Historiques (see above).

Other itineraries

Painters' itineraries – The **Route des Peintres de la Lumière en Provence** offers an introduction to the region through the various sites painted by artists who from 1875 to 1920, became renowned for their radiant works suffused with light *(see the chapter on 19C and 20C art in the Introduction)*. For details apply to the Comité Régional de Tourisme Provence-Alpes-Côte d'Azur.
The Tourist Information Centres in Aix-en-Provence and St-Rémy de Provence organise two circuits – "**Cézanne**" and "**Visiting the Sites Painted by Van Gogh**".

Writers' itineraries – The Tourist Information Centre in Aubagne stages a **Circuit Marcel Pagnol** which shows you the places where this author/director spent his childhood and the landscapes which served as backdrops to some of his films *(see the section on Admission times and charges under the heading AUBAGNE)*.
The Tourist Information Centre in Fontvieille organises a **Circuit Alphonse Daudet** that revisits the places where the writer lived and which he used as a setting for his famous work *Lettres de mon Moulin*.

Archeological excavations

Provence is packed with archeological sites which welcome voluntary diggers during the summer. Every spring the journals *Archeologia*, *L'Archéologue* and *Archéologie* list sites which are looking for new recruits. Contact regional archeology departments (Services Régionaux de l'Archéologie) for details.
Ardèche and Drôme: **DRAC Rhône-Alpes**, 6 Quai St-Vincent, 69283 Lyon Cedex 01 ☎ 04 72 00 44 50. Bouches-du-Rhône, Var and Vaucluse: **DRAC Provence-Alpes-Côte d'Azur**, 21-23 Boulevard du Roy-René, 13167 Aix-en-Provence ☎ 04 42 16 19 40. Gard: 5 Rue de la Salle-l'Évêque, BP 2051, 34026 Montpellier Cedex ☎ 04 67 02 32 71.

SPECIALITIES FROM PROVENCE

Crafts and specialised workshops

Numerous craft workshops can be found along the coast and inland, offering a wide variety of cottage industries. Most of them welcome visitors during the summer but it is always advisable to book in advance.

Provençal cloth – Annie Sotinel, Les Pourquiers, Route de Goult, 84220 Gordes ☎ 04 90 72 05 71 (weaving by hand).
Shops: Souleiado, 39 Rue Proudhon, 13150 Tarascon ☎ 04 90 91 08 80. Les Olivades, Avenue Barberin, 13103 St-Étienne-du-Grès ☎ 04 90 49 19 19.

Soaps – Savonnerie Rampal-Patou, 71 Rue Félix-Pyat, 13300 Salon-de-Provence ☎ 04 90 56 07 28. Savonnerie Marius Fabre, 148 Avenue Paul-Bourret, 13300 Salon-de-Provence ☎ 04 90 53 24 77.

Santons and faience pottery – Ateliers Marcel Carbonel *(santons)*, 47 Rue Neuve-Sainte-Catherine, 13007 Marseille ☎ 04 91 54 26 58.
Maison Chave *(santons)*, 37 Rue Frédéric-Mistral, 13400 Aubagne ☎ 04 42 70 12 86 or 14 Rond-Point des Arènes, 13200 Arles ☎ 04 90 96 15 22.

Hand-painting *santons*

Santons Fouque, 65 Cours Gambetta, 13100 Aix-en-Provence ☎ 04 42 26 33 38. Atelier d'Art-Maison Sicard (*santons* and faience), 2 Boulevard Émile-Combes, 13400 Aubagne ☎ 04 42 70 12 92.
Poterie Ravel (faience), Avenue des Goums, 13400 Aubagne ☎ 04 42 03 05 59.
Établissement Vernin Carreaux d'Apt (tiles in baked clay), Quartier du Pont St-Julien RN 100, 84480 Bonnieux ☎ 04 90 04 63 04.

Provençal furniture – Meubles Provençaux Mélani et Fils, Route d'Eyguières, Pont de Crau, 13200 Arles ☎ 04 90 93 61 09 (tour of workshops for small groups by appointment).
Meubles Bonjean, Route de l'Isle-sur-la-Sorgue, 84250 Le Thor ☎ 04 90 33 82 94 (tour of workshops during the week).

Antiques – Those with a passion for antique furniture will enjoy browsing at l'Isle-sur-la-Sorgue, where no less than 160 dealers have set up shops in five separate "villages". The largest one is the Village des Antiquaires de la Gare, 2 bis Avenue de l'Égalité, 84800 L'Isle-sur-la-Sorgue ☎ 04 90 38 04 57.
Village des Antiquaires du Quartier de Lignane, RN 7, Lignane, 13540 Puyricard ☎ 04 42 92 50 03.

Sweetmeats – Calissons du Roy-René, La Pioline, 13545 Aix-en-Provence ☎ 04 42 39 29 89.
Ciprial-Aptunion (candied fruit): *see the section on Admission times and charges under the heading APT.*
Miellerie des Butineuses (honey, nougat, gingerbread), 189 Rue de la Source, 84450 St-Saturnin-les-Avignon ☎ 04 90 22 47 52.
Production centre for *berlingot* sweets: apply to the Tourist Information Centre in Carpentras.

Liquor – Distillerie Liqueur Frigolet *(Élixir du Révérend Père Gaucher)*, 26 Rue Voltaire, 13160 Châteaurenard ☎ 04 90 94 11 08.

Fairs and exhibitions

Arles – Santonmakers' Fair *(Salon International des Santonniers)* late November to mid-January ☎ 04 90 18 41 22.

Aubagne – Santon and Ceramics Fair *(Foire aux Santons et à la Céramique)* July and August and early December to early January ☎ 04 42 03 49 98.
Ceramics Fair *(Argilla)* the third weekend in August every two years (next edition in 1999) ☎ 04 42 03 49 98.

Barjac *(Michelin map no 81 fold 12)* – Antique Fair *(Foire aux Antiquités)* on Easter weekend and on 15 August ☎ 04 66 24 50 09.

L'Isle-sur-la-Sorgue – Antiques Fair *(Foire aux Antiquités)* Easter Sunday and the Sunday around 15 August ☎ 04 90 38 04 78.

Marseille – International Fair early September.
Santon Fair *(Foire aux Santons)* at La Canebière from the last Sunday in November to 31 December ☎ 04 91 13 89.

St-Quentin-la-Poterie – Biennial Pottery Fair *(Terralha)* around 14 July (next editions in 1998, 2000 etc).

MICHELIN GUIDES

The Red Guides (hotels and restaurants)
Benelux - Deutschland - España Portugal - Main Cities Europe - France -
Great Britain and Ireland - Italia - Suisse

The Green Guides (fine art, historical monuments, scenic routes)
Austria - Belgium and Luxembourg - California - Canada - England : the West Country - France - Germany - Great Britain - Greece - Ireland - Italy - London - Mexico - Netherlands - New England - New York - Paris - Portugal - Quebec - Rome - Scotland - Spain - Switzerland - Tuscany - Washington
..and the collection of regional guides for France.

Books and films about Provence

Books

A Guide to Provence *by M. Jacobs (Viking Penguin)*
A Little Tour in France *by H. James (Sidgwick & Jackson)*
Aspects of Provence *by J. Pope-Hennessy (Penguin)*
A Spell in Wild France *by B. and L. Cooper (Methuen)*
A Year in Provence *and* Toujours Provence *by P. Mayle (Hamish Hamilton)*
Caesar's Vast Ghost (Aspects of Provence) *by L. Durrell (Faber & Faber)*
Food Lover's Guide to France *by P. Wells (Eyre and Spottiswoode)*
French Dirt *by R. Goodman (Pavilion)*
Gardens in Provence *by L. Jones (Flammarion)*
My Father's Glory *and* My Mother's Castle *by M. Pagnol (English-language edition from Picador)*
Next Time Round in Provence: The Vaucluse and the Bouches-du-Rhône *by I. Norrie (Aurum Press)*
Provence *by F.M. Ford (Ecco)*
Provence and the Côte-d'Azur *by J. Bentley (Aurum Press)*
When the Riviera was Ours *by P. Howarth (Century)*
South of France *by A. Lyall (Collins)*
The Camargue *by C. Dix (Victor Gollancz)*
The Roman Remains of Southern France *by J. Bromwich (Routledge)*
The Time of Secrets *and* The Time of Love *by M. Pagnol (English-language edition from Deutsch)*
The Water of the Hills *by M. Pagnol (English-language edition from Picador)*
Two Towns in Provence *by M.F.K. Fisher (Chatto and Windus)*
Van Gogh: Letters from Provence *ed M. Bailey (Clarkson N. Potter)*
Wild France: A Traveller's Guide *ed D. Botting (Aurum Press)*

Literature in French

Jean de Florette, Manon des Sources, Marius, Fanny, César, Topaze, La Gloire de mon Père, Le Château de ma Mère, Le Temps des Secrets, Le Temps de l'Amour *by M. Pagnol (Éditions de Fallois, collection Fortunio)*
Lettres de mon Moulin, Tartarin de Tarascon *by A. Daudet (Paris, Presses Pocket)*
Regain, Le Grand Troupeau, Le Chant du Monde *by J. Giono (Paris, Gallimard "Folio" or "Pléiade")*

Films

Manon des Sources *(1952) by Marcel Pagnol*
Borsalino *(1970) by Jacques Deray*
Jean de Florette *(1985) by Claude Berri*
Manon des Sources *(1986) by Claude Berri*
La Gloire de mon Père *(1990) by Yves Robert*
Le Château de ma Mère *(1990) by Yves Robert*
Marius et Jeannette *(1996) by Robert Guédiguian*

Raimu and Fernandel in *La Fille du Puisatier*

Calendar of events

The number and fold of the relevant Michelin map are given for places not described in the guide

Traditional celebrations

First Sunday in February

Nyons .... Festival of New Oil.

2 February

Marseille .... Candlemas Procession *(Fête de la Chandeleur)* in the Basilique St-Victor.

Sunday before Lent

Graveson .... Carnival Procession of Floats *(Corso carnavalesque)*.

Last weekend in February

Nîmes .... Spring Festival *(Feria de Primavera)*. ☎ 04 66 67 28 02.

Feria in Nîmes

Easter to early October

Arles .... Easter Festival *(Feria Pascale)*. Spanish style bullfights.

Easter Monday

Le Beaucet 81 fold 13 . Pilgrimage to the sanctuary of St Gentius.

Early May

Villeneuve-lès-Avignon . Feast of St Mark (patron saint of winegrowers). A beribboned stump of vine is paraded through town.

May

Arles .... Gardians' Festival. ☎ 04 90 18 41 20.

Sunday after 16 May

Monteux .... Feast of St Gentius. Costumes, celebrations punctuated by shots, sermon in Provençal.

Le Beaucet 81 fold 13 . Pilgrimage to the sanctuary of St Gentius.

24 and 25 May

**Les Stes-Maries-
e-la-Mer** .... Gypsy Pilgrimage *(see p 242)* on 24 May, procession down to the beach and blessing of the sea on 25 May. ☎ 04 90 97 82 55.

Whitsun

Apt .... *Cavalcade* (horses). Music Festival.

Nîmes .... Whitsun Festival. ☎ 04 66 67 28 02.

Whit Monday

St-Rémy-de-Provence ... Transhumance Festival.

1 June

Boulbon .... Bottle Procession; canticles in honour of St Marcellinus an blessing of wine. ☎ 04 90 91 03 52.

23 June

Valréas .... Feast of Little St John. ☎ 04 90 35 04 71.

Around 24 June

Allauch .... Provençal Festival of St John. Blessing of the animals an decorated carts. ☎ 04 91 05 31 21.

Late June

Courthézon 81 fold 12 Vine Stock Festival *(Fête de la Souche)*. Children's Parade Dancing and singing of 1493 Hymn to the Graces.

Last weekend in June

Tarascon .... Tarasque Festival. Folklore procession with Daudet's characte Tartarin. Bullfights *(see p 251)*. ☎ 04 90 91 03 52.

Late June

Martigues .... Fishermen's Festival on St Peter's Day. ☎ 04 42 42 31 10

First Monday in July

Arles .... *Course de la Cocarde d'Or* (Provençal-style bullfights ☎ 04 90 96 03 70.

First Friday in July

Arles .... *Pegoulado*. Night-time procession in traditional costume ☎ 04 90 96 47 00.

First Saturday in July

Martigues .... Venitian Festival. Fireworks display and nocturnal flotilla o decorated boats. ☎ 04 42 42 31 10.

Around first Sunday in July

Châteaurenard .... St Eligius' cart, decorated and drawn by 40 horses i Saracen harness. Bullfights. ☎ 04 90 94 23 27.

First week in July

Salon-de-Provence .... Historical re-enactment surrounding the character Mich Nostradamus.

Second week in July

Les Stes-Maries-de-la-Mer .... *Feria du Cheval*. Competitive events for thoroughbreds, games in the arena. ☎ 04 90 97 82 55.

Saturday before 14 July

Nyons .... International Olive Festival.

14 July

Châteaurenard .... Celebration of Old Trades *(Journée des Vieux Métiers* Blacksmith, sheep shearer, washerwoman.

Mid-July

Carpentras .... Nocturnal procession of floats *(Corso de Nuit)*.

21 and 22 July

Ste-Baume .... Festivities in honour of Mary Magdalene in the cave. ☎ 04 42 04 54 84.

Last weekend in July

Graveson .... Feast of St Eligius. ☎ 04 90 95 71 05.

First Saturday and Monday in August

Valréas .... Lavender Festival. Nocturnal procession of floats.

One week in early August

Châteaurenard .... Feast of Mary Magdalene. Ploughs decked with flower ☎ 04 90 94 23 27.

15 August

St-Rémy-de-Provence ... *Feria*. Provençal-style bull runs and bullfights.

Third weekend in August

Séguret .... Provençal Festival and Winegrowers' Fair.

Tuesday after fourth Sunday in August
Monteux........................ St John's Fireworks Display. Monteux is renowned for its fireworks.

Weekend around 25 August
Aigues-Mortes.............. Feast of St Louis. ☎ 04 66 53 73 00.

Every Sunday in September
Le Beaucet 81 fold 13. Pilgrimage to the sanctuary of St Gentius.

First fortnight in September
Arles............................ Rice Festival. Procession of floats. ☎ 04 90 96 03 70.

Last but one weekend in September
Nîmes.......................... Grape Harvest Festival. ☎ 04 66 67 28 02.

Weekend around 22 October
Les Stes-Maries-de-la-Mer .... October Pilgrimage. Procession to the beach and blessing of the sea. ☎ 04 90 97 82 55.

Early December
Istres............................ Shepherds' Festival. Migrant shepherds march through the streets with their herds.

24 December
Allauch .... Provençal Midnight Mass; shepherds come down from the hill of Notre-Dame du Château.

Les Baux de Provence . Shepherds' Festival. Midnight Mass in Provençal.

Arles............................ Christmas Eve watch and Midnight Mass in Provençal. ☎ 04 90 18 41 20.

St-Michel-de-Frigolet ... Midnight Mass in Provençal. ☎ 04. 90.95 70 07.

St-Rémy-de-Provence .. Midnight Mass in Provençal with pastorale.

Ste-Baume .... Midnight Mass in Provençal in the cave. ☎ 04 42 04 54 84.

Les Stes-Maries-de-la-Mer .... Midnight Mass with offerings from shepherds, *gardians*, fishermen and rice growers. ☎ 04 90 97 82 55.

Séguret .... Enactment of the "*Li Bergié de Séguret*" Mystery. ☎ 04 90 46 91 08.

Tarascon .... Midnight Mass in Provençal.

Festivals

June to September
Nîmes........................... *L'Été de Nîmes*. Summer festival of music, theatre, dance, art exhibitions. ☎ 04 66 67 28 02.

Early July
Îles du Frioul .... *Atout Frioul*. Jazz, variety entertainment, folklore. ☎ 04 91 54 91 11.

Festival d'Avignon – Scene from *Andromaque*

July

Fontaine-de-Vaucluse,
L'Isle-sur-la-Sorgue,
Lagnes, Le Thor .... *Festival de la Sorgue.* Music, theatre, dance.

Aix-en-Provence .... Dance Festival. ☎ 04 42 96 05 01.

Villeneuve-lès-Avignon . International Summer Events at the Charterhouse. Theatre.
☎ 04 90 15 24 24.

July-August

Valréas .... Evenings of the Papal Enclave *(Nuits de l'Enclave des Papes).* Theatre.

Early July to early August

Avignon .... Festival of Theatre, Dance and Music. ☎ 04 90 27 66 50
(see p 96 and p 100).

Early July to late August

La Tour-d'Aigues .... Festival of South Luberon.

July to September

Cabrières d'Avignon,
Fontaine-de-Vaucluse
Goult, Roussillon,
Abbaye de Silvacane .... International String Quartet Festival in the Luberon.
☎ 04 90 75 89 60.

St-Rémy-de-Provence .. Organa Festival. Organ concerts. ☎ 04 90 92 49 67.

First fortnight in July

Arles .... International Photography Show.

Marseille .... International Folklore Festival at Château-Gombert.
☎ 04 91 05 15 65.

Mid-July to early August

Orange .... *Chorégies.* Opera, symphonic concerts. ☎ 04 90 51 83 83.

Second fortnight in July

Aix-en-Provence .... International Festival of Opera and Music *(see p 63).*

Carpentras .... *Les Estivales.* International Festival of Theatre, Opera and Dance. ☎ 04 90 60 46 00.

Marseille .... *Boules* competition held in the Parc Borély.

Salon-de-Provence .... Jazz Festival. ☎ 04 90 56 00 07.

Uzès .... *Nuits Musicales d'Uzès.* Evening music concerts.
☎ 04 66 22 68 88.

Mid-July to mid-August

Vaison-la-Romaine .... *L'Été de Vaison.* Theatre, dance, music concerts.
☎ 04 90 28 84 49.

Mid-July to late August

Bollène .... *Polymusicales de Bollène.* Music Festival.
☎ 04 90 40 51 17.

Martigues .... International Folk Festival. ☎ 04 42 42 12 01.

First three weeks in August

La Roque-d'Anthéron
Abbaye de Silvacane .... International Piano Festival. ☎ 04 42 50 51 15.

First fortnight in August

Vaison-la-Romaine .... *Choralies.* International Music Festival staged every 3 years
(next edition in 2001). ☎ 04 72 19 83 40.

Orange .... *Nuits d'Été au Théâtre Antique.* Opera, dance, variety entertainment.

Second fortnight in August

Pont-St-Esprit .... *Rencontres Musicales.* Classical concerts.
☎ 04 66 39 44 45.

Third week in September

St-Maximin-
la-Ste-Baume .... Autumn Festival. Organ concerts. ☎ 04 94 78 00 09.

Early November

Vaison-la-Romaine .... Gastronomic Festival. ☎ 04 90 36 02 11.

Useful French words and phrases

ARCHITECTURAL TERMS

See the ABC of Architecture in the Introduction

SIGHTS

abbaye	abbey	marché	market
beffroi	belfry	monastère	monastery
chapelle	chapel	moulin	windmill
château	castle	musée	museum
cimetière	cemetery	parc	park
cloître	cloisters	place	square
cour	courtyard	pont	bridge
couvent	convent	port	port/harbour
écluse	lock (canal)	porte	gateway
église	church	quai	quay
fontaine	fountain	remparts	ramparts
halle	covered market	rue	street
jardin	garden	statue	statue
mairie	town hall	tour	tower
maison	house		

NATURAL SITES

abîme	chasm	grotte	cave
aven	swallow-hole	lac	lake
barrage	dam	plage	beach
belvédère	viewpoint	rivière	river
cascade	waterfall	ruisseau	stream
col	pass	signal	beacon
corniche	ledge	source	spring
côte	coast, hillside	vallée	valley
forêt	forest		

ON THE ROAD

car park	parking	petrol/gas station	station essence
driving licence	permis de conduire	right	droite
east	Est	south	Sud
garage (for repairs)	garage	toll	péage
left	gauche	traffic lights	feu tricolore
motorway/highway	autoroute	tyre	pneu
north	Nord	west	Ouest
parking meter	horodateur	wheel clamp	sabot
petrol/gas	essence	zebra crossing	passage clouté

TIME

today	aujourd'hui	week	semaine
tomorrow	demain	Monday	lundi
yesterday	hier	Tuesday	mardi
		Wednesday	mercredi
winter	hiver	Thursday	jeudi
spring	printemps	Friday	vendredi
summer	été	Saturday	samedi
autunm/fall	automne	Sunday	dimanche

NUMBERS

0	zéro	10	dix	20	vingt
1	un	11	onze	30	trente
2	deux	12	douze	40	quarante
3	trois	13	treize	50	cinquante
4	quatre	14	quatorze	60	soixante
5	cinq	15	quinze	70	soixante-dix
6	six	16	seize	80	quatre-vingt
7	sept	17	dix-sept	90	quatre-vingt-dix
8	huit	18	dix-huit	100	cent
9	neuf	19	dix-neuf	1000	mille

SHOPPING

bank	banque	fishmonger's	poissonnerie
baker's	boulangerie	grocer's	épicerie
big	grand	newsagent, bookshop	librairie
butcher's	boucherie	open	ouvert
chemist's	pharmacie	post office	poste
closed	fermé	push	pousser
cough mixture	sirop pour la toux	pull	tirer
cough sweets	cachets pour la gorge	shop	magasin
entrance	entrée	small	petit
exit	sortie	stamps	timbres

FOOD AND DRINK

beef	bœuf	lamb	agneau
beer	bière	lunch	déjeuner
butter	beurre	lettuce salad	salade
bread	pain	meat	viande
breakfast	petit-déjeuner	mineral water	eau minérale
cheese	fromage	mixed salad	salade composée
chicken	poulet	orange juice	jus d'orange
dessert	dessert	plate	assiette
dinner	dîner	pork	porc
fish	poisson	restaurant	restaurant
fork	fourchette	red wine	vin rouge
fruit	fruits	salt	sel
sugar	sucre	spoon	cuillère
glass	verre	vegetables	légumes
ice cream	glace	water	de l'eau
ice cubes	glaçons	white wine	vin blanc
ham	jambon	yoghurt	yaourt
knife	couteau		

PERSONAL DOCUMENTS AND TRAVEL

airport	aéroport	railway station	gare
credit card	carte de crédit	shuttle	navette
customs	douane	suitcase	valise
passport	passeport	train/plane ticket	billet de train/d'avion
platform	voie	wallet	portefeuille

CLOTHING

coat	manteau	socks	chaussettes
jumper	pull	stockings	bas
raincoat	imperméable	suit	costume
shirt	chemise	tights	collants
shoes	chaussures	trousers	pantalons

USEFUL PHRASES

goodbye	au revoir	yes/no	oui/non
hello/good morning	bonjour	I am sorry	pardon
how	comment	why	pourquoi
excuse me	excusez-moi	when	quand
thank you	merci	please	s'il vous plaît

Do you speak English?	Parlez-vous anglais?
I don't understand	Je ne comprends pas
Talk slowly	Parlez lentement
Where's...?	Où est...?
When does the ... leave?	À quelle heure part...?
When does the ... arrive?	À quelle heure arrive...?
When does the museum open?	À quelle heure ouvre le musée ?
When is the show?	À quelle heure est la représentation ?
When is breakfast served?	À quelle heure sert-on le petit-déjeuner ?
What does it cost?	Combien cela coûte?
Where can I buy a newspaper in English?	Où puis-je acheter un journal en anglais ?
Where is the nearest petrol/gas station?	Où se trouve la station essence la plus proche?
Where can I change traveller's cheques?	Où puis-je échanger des traveller's cheques ?
Where are the toilets?	Où sont les toilettes ?
Do you accept credit cards?	Acceptez-vous les cartes de crédit ?

Admission times and charges

Every sight for which times and charges are listed is indicated by the symbol ⊙ in the text in the main part of the guide.

Admission times and charges are liable to alteration without prior notice. Due to fluctuations in the cost of living and the constant change in opening times, the information below is given only as a general indication. The information was correct when this guide went to press; however, for some sights, the updated details were not available, in which case the text appears in italics. Dates given are inclusive.

The information applies to individual adults and, whenever possible, children. For parties, however, special conditions regarding times and charges are common, and arrangements should be made in advance. In some cases admission is free on certain days, e.g. Wednesdays, Sundays or public holidays. Ticket offices often close 30 to 45 minutes before the actual closing time.

Churches and chapels are usually closed from noon to 2pm and do not admit visitors during services; tourists should therefore refrain from visits while services are being held. Times are indicated if the interior is of special interest or if the church or chapel has unusual opening times. Visitors to chapels are often accompanied by the person who keeps the key. Donations are welcome.

Where there are regular, organised lecture tours of towns or their historic districts – usually during the tourist season – such details are indicated below.

When guided tours are indicated, the departure time of the last tour of the morning or afternoon will be up to an hour before the actual closing time. Most tours are conducted by French-speaking guides, but in some cases the term "guided tours" may cover group-visits with recorded commentaries. Some of the larger and more frequented sights may offer guided tours in other languages. The symbol ▲ indicates that a tour is given by a lecturer from the Historic Monuments Association. Enquire at the ticket office or book stall. Other aids for the foreign tourist are notes, pamphlets and audio-guides.

Sights which have comprehensive facilities for disabled tourists are indicated by the symbol &.

Ensure that no valuables are left in unattended vehicles.

Enquire at the Tourist Information Centre (Syndicat d'Initiative) – the address follows the symbol ☐ – for local religious holidays, market days etc.

A

AIGUES-MORTES   ☐ Porte de la Gardette 30220 ☎ 04 66 53 73 00

Tour de Constance and Remparts – Open May-Sept 9.30am-7pm (June-Aug 9.30am-8pm); Oct-Apr 10am-5pm (Feb-Apr and in Oct 10am-6pm). Closed 1 Jan, 1 May, 1 and 11 Nov, 25 Dec. 32F. ☎ 04 66 53 61 55.

Chapelle des Pénitents Blancs – Guided tours Mon, Wed and Fri 10-11.30am. Apply to the Tourist Information Centre.

Chapelle des Pénitents Gris – Guided tours Mon, Wed and Fri 10-11.30am. Apply to the Tourist Information Centre.

Excursions

Salins du Midi – Guided tours (4hr) by bus July and Aug, Wed and Fri 1.30pm; early Apr to end of Aug guided tours (45min) in small tourist train, departures every hour. Closed public holidays. 50F (bus), 35F (tourist train), 28F (child). Apply to the Aigues-Mortes Tourist Information Centre one day before.

Caves de Listel - & Guided tours (30min) and wine tasting sesssions Apr-Sept 10am-6.30pm; Oct-Mar daily (except Sat-Sun and public holidays) 10-11.30am and 2-5pm. Last departure 45 min before actual closing time. No charge. ☎ 04 66 51 17 00.

Château de Teillan – Park and grounds open to the public and guided tours of the interior (1hr 30min) daily(except Mon) mid-June to mid-Sept 2-6pm. 30F. ☎ 04 66 88 02 38.

AIX-EN-PROVENCE   ☐ 2, Place du Général-de-Gaulle 13100 ☎ 04 42 16 11 61

Guided tours of the town ▲ – Apply to the Tourist Information Centre.

"Cézanne Tour" (Circuit Cézanne) – Guided tours of the town and its outskirts, centering on a chosen theme, are available to visitors: apply to the Tourist Information Centre. It is possible to complete the tour on your own with the aid of a brochure *(Sur les Pas de Cézanne)* available from the Tourist Information Centre.

Muséum d'Histoire Naturelle – Open year round 10am-noon and 1-5pm, 10am-6pm during temporary exhibitions. Closed 1 Jan, 1 May and 25 Dec. 10F. ☎ 04 42 26 23 67.

Musée du Vieil Aix – Open Apr-Sept daily (except Mon) 10am-noon and 2.30-6pm; Nov-Mar daily (except Mon) 10am-noon and 2-5pm. Closed public holidays and in Oct. 15F. ☎ 04 42 21 43 55.

Hôtel de Châteaurenard – Open Mon-Fri 9am-noon and 2-5pm. No charge.

Musée des Tapisseries – Open year round daily (except Tues) 10am-noon and 2-5pm; Apr-Oct 10am-noon and 2-6pm. Closed 1 Jan, 1 May and 25 Dec. 10F. ☎ 04 42 21 05 78.

Cloître St-Sauveur – Open year round 9.30-11.30am and 2-4.30pm. Closed Sun (during services) and public holidays. Contact the cathedral attendant. ☎ 04 42 21 10 51.

Cathédrale St-Sauveur – Open year round Mon-Fri.

Aix-en-Provence – Tour de l'Horloge

Musée Bibliographique et Archéologique Paul Arbaud – Open year round Tues and Thur 2-5pm. Closed public holidays. Call for information regarding the other days of the week. 15F. ☎ 04 42 38 38 95.

Musée Granet – Open year round daily (except Tues) 10am-noon and 2-6pm. Closed public holidays. 10F. ☎ 04 42 38 14 70.

Pavillon de Vendôme – Open Apr-Oct daily (except Tues) 10am-noon and 2-6pm; Feb-Mar daily (except Tues) 10am-noon and 1.30-5.30pm; Nov-Jan 10am-noon and 1-5pm. Closed 1 Jan, 1 May and 25 Dec. 10F. ☎ 04 42 21 05 78.

Cité du Livre: Fondation St-John-Perse – ♿ Open year round Tues-Fri 2-6pm. Closed public holidays. No charge. ☎ 04 42 25 98 85.

Vidéothèque Internationale d'Art Lyrique et de Musique – Open Tues-Sat 1-6pm, Sat 10am-noon and 1-6pm. Closed public holidays. ☎ 04 42 37 70 89.

Fondation Vasarely – Open mid-Mar to end of Oct 10am-1pm and 2-7pm, Sat-Sun 10am-7pm; Nov to mid-Mar 9.30am-1pm and 2-6pm, Sat-Sun 9.30am-6pm. Closed 1 Jan, 1 Mayand 25 Dec. 35F. ☎ 04 42 20 01 09.

Atelier Paul-Cézanne – Open year round daily 10am-noon and 2-5pm ; Apr-Sept 10am-noon and 2-6pm. Closed 1 Jan, 1 Mayand 25 Dec. 25F. ☎ 04 42 21 06 53.

Oppidum d'Entremont: Excavations – Open daily (except Tues) 9am-noon and 2-6pm. Closed 1 Jan, 1 May, 1 and 11 Nov, 25 Dec. No charge. ☎ 04 42 21 97 33.

Excursions

Jardins d'Albertas – ♿ Open June-Aug 3-7pm; May, Sept and Oct Sat-Sun and public holidays 2-6pm. Closed the rest of the year. 20F. ☎ 04 42 22 29 77.

Château de la Pioline – Open year round 3-6pm. No charge. ☎ 04 42 20 07 81.

ALLAUCH

Musée du Vieil Allauch – *Closed for restoration work.*

Les ALPILLES

Chapelle St Gabriel – Contact the Tourist Information Centre in Tarascon (400F deposit and identification papers required). ☎ 04 90 91 03 52.

Panorama de la Caume - Guided tours on "nature themes" on request. Apply to the Tourist Information Centre in St-Rémy-de-Provence. ☎ 04 90 92 05 22.

ANSOUIS

Château – Guided tours (45min) Feb to 1 Novat 2.30pm; mid-July to end of Aug at 11am and 2.30pm; 1 Novto Easter daily (except Tues) at 2.30pm. Closed in Jan. 30F (adult), 15F (child). ☎ 04 90 09 82 70.

Musée Extraordinaire – Guided tours (30min) Apr-Sept daily (except Tues) 2-7pm; the rest of the year 2-6pm. Closed Jan-Feb. 22F. ☎ 04 90 09 82 64.

APT
🇧 Avenue Philippe-de-Girard 84400 ☎ 04 90 74 03 18

Centre d'Art Contemporain – Temporary exhibitions. Apply to the Tourist Information Centre.

Crystallised Fruit Factory – Open Mon-Sat 9-11am and 2-6pm, Fri 9-11am on request. Closed public holidays and three weeks over July and Aug. It is necessary to reserve at least one week in advance. No charge. ☎ 04 90 76 31 43.

Ancienne Cathédrale Sainte-Anne – Open year round daily 10am-noon and 3-5pm (4pm in winter).
Treasury – ♿ Guided tours (15min) July to mid-Sept 11am-noon and 5-6pm; mid-Sept to end of June on request. No charge. ☎ 04 90 04 61 71.

Musée Archéologique – Open June-Sept daily (except Tues) 10am-noon and 2-5pm, Sun 2-6pm; Oct-May daily (except Sun and Tues) 2-5pm, Sat 10am-noon and 2.30-5.30pm. Closed public holidays. 12F. ☎ 04 90 74 00 34.

Maison du Parc Naturel Régional du Luberon – Open mid-Apr to mid-Sept daily (except Sun) 8.30am-noon and 1.30-6pm, Sat 8.30am-noon. ☎ 04 90 04 42 00.

Gorges de l'ARDÈCHE

Grotte des Huguenots – Open mid-June to end of Aug 10am-7pm. Closed the rest of the year. 20F (adult), 12F (child). ☎ 04 74 96 11 63.

Aven de la Forestière – Guided tours (1hr 15min) Apr-Sept 10am-6pm (July-Aug 10am-7pm); Oct-Mar Sat-Sun and public holidays only 10am-noon and 2-6pm. Closed 1 Janand 25 Dec. 33F (adult), 16F (child). ☎ 04 75 38 63 08.

Labastide-de-Virac: Castle – Open Easter to end of Sept daily (except Wed) 2-6pm; July-Aug daily 10am-7pm. 29F. ☎ 04 75 38 61 13.

Descent of the Gorges by boat or canoe – Depending on the season and the water level, allow 6 to 9 hours for the descent (no departures after 6pm). Some difficult passages (rapids) require certified experience of handling canoes or boats. Being able to swim is essential. Navigation regulations can be consulted at rental firms, town halls, Tourist Information Centres and *gendarmeries*.
It might also be useful-obtain the map-guide of the Gorges, *Plan-Guide des Gorges de l'Ardèche*, published by Association Tourena.
It is possible to stop for a picnic anywhere along the river, but camping is only allowed on the official sites at Gaud and Gournier (25F to 35F per person per night) as the river flows through a nature reserve. Longer stays are possible at the Templiers campsite (naturist) and the Grottes St-Marcel. About 50 rental firms located at Vallon-Pont-d'Arc, Salavas, Ruoms, St-Martin and St-Remèze have offers for the descent of the gorges, either for independent hire or for guided trips lasting 1 to 2 days and costing 120F to 150F.
Request the list of rental firms from the Tourist Information Centre in Ruoms (Rue Alphonse-Daudet, 07120 Ruoms ☎ 04 75 93 91 90), Vallon-Pont-d'Arc (Cité Administrative, 07150 Vallon-Pont-d'Arc ☎ 04 75 88 04 01) or St-Martin-d'Ardèche (Rue de la Mairie, 07700 St-Martin-d'Ardèche ☎ 04 75 98 70 91).

Descent on foot – The map-guide of the Gorges published by Association Tourena *(see above)* gives valuable information about footpaths through the gorges. If taking the footpath along the north bank of the river, it is advisable to get the latest report on the water level from the local *gendarmeries* or the Service Départemental d'Alerte des Crues *(département flood warning service)* ☎ 04 75 64 54 55 before setting out.

ARLES
🇧 Esplanade Charles-de-Gaulle 13200 ☎ 04 90 18 41 20

Marais du Viguelret – Allow 6hr and remember to take a picnic with you. Apply to the Tourist Information Centre.

Guided tours of the town 🄰 – Apply to the Tourist Information Centre.

ARLES

Roman Sights in Arles – Open Apr-Sept 9am-0.30pm and 2-7pm, mid-June to mid-Sept 9am-7pm; Mar and Oct 10am-0.30pm and 2-5.30pm; Nov 10am-0.30pm and 2-5pm; Feb10am-noon and 2-5pm; Dec-Jan 10am-noon and 2-4.30pm. Closed 1 Jan, 1 Nov and 25 Dec. 55F (combined ticket including access to all Roman sites, available from any of the sites). ☎ 04 90 18 41 22.

Amphitheatre – ♿ See "Roman Sights in Arles" above. Closed during bullfights. 15F. ☎ 04 90 49 36 74.

Roman Theatre – See "Roman Sights in Arles" above. 15F. ☎ 04 90 49 38 34.

Cloître St-Trophime – See "Roman Sights in Arles" above. 15F. ☎ 04 90 49 36 74.

Cryptoporticus – See "Roman Sights in Arles" above. 15F. ☎ 04 90 49 36 74.

Museon Arlaten – Open June-Aug 9.30am-1pm and 2-6.30pm (last admission 1hr before actual closing time); Jun closed Mon; Sept-May daily (except Mon) 9.30am-0.30pm and 2-5pm; Apr-May and Sept closed at 6pm. Closed 1 Jan, 1 May, 1 Nov and 25 Dec. 20F. ☎ 04 90 96 08 23.

Musée Réattu – ♿ Open Apr-Sept 9am-0.30pm and 2-7pm; Mar and Oct 10am-0.30pm and 2-5.30pm; Nov 10am-0.30pm and 2-5pm; Feb 10am-noon and 2-5pm; Dec-Jan 10am-noon and 2-4.30pm. Closed 1 Jan, 1 Nov and 25 Dec. 15F. ☎ 04 90 49 36 74.

Palais Constantin – ♿ See "Roman Sights in Arles" above. 15F. ☎ 04 90 49 36 74.

Musée de l'Arles Antique – ♿ Open Apr to mid-Sept 9am-7pm; the rest of the year 9.30am-noon and 1.30-6pm. Closed 1 Jan, 1 May, 1 Nov and 25 Dec. 35F (adult), 25F (child). ☎ 04 90 18 88 88.

Les Alyscamps – ♿ See "Roman Sights in Arles" above. 15F. ☎ 04 90 49 36 74 .

Fondation Vincent Van Gogh-Arles – Open Easter-Oct 10am-7pm; Nov-Easter 9.30-noon and 2-5.30pm. Closed 1 Jan and 25 Dec. 30F. ☎ 04 90 49 94 04.

Espace Van-Gogh – Garden and galleries open all year 7.30am-7.30pm. No charge.

AUBAGNE   🄱 Avenue Antide-Boyer 13400 ☎ 04 42 03 49 98

Guided tours of the historical town centre – Apply to the Tourist Information Centre.

Santon and Ceramics Workshops – Some twenty independent workshops can be visited during the day. Contact the Tourist Information Centre for the list of addresses and visiting times.

Ateliers Thérèse-Neveu – ♿ Open year round daily (except Mon) 9am-noon and 2-6pm. No charge. ☎ 04 42 03 43 10.

Le Petit Monde de Marcel Pagnol – Exhibition open mid-Feb to mid-Nov and Dec to early Feb 9am-0.30pm and 2.30-6pm. No charge. ☎ 04 42 84 10 22.

Marcel Pagnol Walks – The Aubagne Tourist Information Centre offers guided tours for groups which take in the main areas of Marcel Pagnol's childhood and the location sites of films based on his works. Short tour with little walking, including lunch and a visit of the Ateliers Thérèse-Neveu as well as a santon workshop (140F). 9km/5.5mi-walk, allow one day and bring a picnic. 20km/12.5mi-hike, allow one day and bring a picnic. In July and Aug on Wed, and Sat-Sun at 4pm there is a coach tour (2hr 30min) with commentary for tourists who do not belong to a group (40F).

Musée de la Légion Étrangère – Open May-Sept daily (except Mon) 10am-noon and 3-7pm, Fri 10am-noon; Oct-Apr Wed and Sat-Sun 10am-noon and 2-6pm. No charge. ☎ 04 42 18 82 41.

Excursion

Parc d'attractions OK Corral – Open mid-June to early Sept daily; Apr to mid-June open Wed, Sat-Sun, public holidays and school holidays; Sept open Wed and Sat-Sun; Mar and Oct open Sun; Nov open the first two Sun and public holidays. Closed mid-Nov to mid-Mar. Call to enquire about times of admission. 83F (adult), 65F (child measuring under 1.40m/4ft 5in). ☎ 04 42 73 80 05.

AURIOLLES

Mas de la Vignasse – Guided tours (1hr) Apr to 1 Nov. 30F. For details call ☎ 04 75 39 65 07.

AVIGNON   🄱 41, Cours Jean-Jaurès 84000 ☎ 04 90 82 65 11

Guided tours of the town 🄰 – Apply to the Tourist Information Centre.

Boat trips on the Rhône –-Cruise down the Rhône as far as the Camargue, apply to "Grands Bateaux de Provence", Allée de l'Oulle ☎ 04 90 85 62 25.

Palais des Papes – Open Apr-Oct 9am-7pm; the rest of the year 9.30am-6.30pm. 45F (55F during exhibitions). ☎ 04 90 27 50 74.

Petit Palais – Open July-Aug daily (except Tues) 10.30am-6pm; the rest of the year daily (except Tues) 9.30am-noon and 2-6pm. Closed 1 Jan, 1 May, 14 July, 1 Nov and 25 Dec. 30F (no charge Sun Oct to end of Feb). ☎ 04 90 86 44 58.

Pont St-Bénézet – Open Apr-Oct 9am-7pm; Nov-Mar 9.30am-5.45pm. 17F. ☎ 04 90 27 50 73.

Église St-Agricol – Open Sat 3-5pm, Sun 8-10.30am.

Palais du Roure – Guided tours of the apartments (1hr 15min) Tues at 3pm or by appointment. It is advisable to book one week in advance. Closed public holidays and in Aug. 20F. ☎ 04 90 80 80 88.

Musée Calvet – Open year round daily (except Tues) 10am-1pm and 2-6pm. Closed 1 Jan, 1 May and 25 Dec. ☎ 04 90 86 33 84.

The Pink Blouse by Modigliani

Fondation Angladon-Dubrujeaud

Muséum Requien – Open Tues-Sat 9am-noon. The library is open Mon-Fri 9am-noon and 2-6pm. Closed public holidays. No charge. ☎ 04 90 82 43 51.

Musée Lapidaire – Open year round daily (except Tues) 10am-1pm and 2-6pm. Closed 1 Jan, 1 May and 25 Dec. 10F. ☎ 04 90 86 33 84.

Chapelle des Pénitents Gris – Open year round daily 8am-noon and 2.30-6.30pm, Sun 8am-noon.

Fondation Angladon-Dubrujeaud – Open July-Aug daily (except Mon and Tues) 1-7pm; the rest of the year 1-6pm, 3-6pm on public holidays. 30F. ☎ 04 90 82 29 03.

Musée Théodore-Aubanel – ♿ Guided tours (1hr) Mon-Fri by appointment. Closed public holidays and in Aug. 20F. Apply to Mme Aubanel. ☎ 04 90 86 35.02

Chapelle des Pénitents Noirs – Open by appointment only. Apply to the Tourist Information Centre.

Musée Louis-Vouland – Open June-Sept Tues-Sat 10am-noon and 2-6pm; Oct-May Tues-Sat 2-6pm. Closed public holidays. 20F. ☎ 04 90 86 03 79.

Excursion

Parc du Soleil et du Cosmos – ♿ Guided tours (1hr 15min) year round daily (except Mon and Tues) 2.30-4pm. Closed 24 Dec to 2 Jan. 40F (adult), 25F (child). ☎ 04 90 25 66 82.

B

BAGNOLS-SUR-CÈZE

🅱 Esplanade du Mont-Cotton 30200 ☎ 04 66 89 54 61

Musée d'Art Moderne Albert-André – Open mid-June to mid-Sept daily (except Mon) 10am-0.30pm and 2-6.30pm; the rest of the year daily (except Mon) 10am-noon and 2-6pm. Closed public holidays and in Feb. 20F. ☎ 04 66 50 50 56.

Musée d'Archéologie Léon-Alègre – ♿ Open mid-June to mid-Sept Thur-Sat 10am-0.30pm and 2-6.30pm; the rest of the year Thur-Sat 10am-noon and 2-6pm. Closed public holidays and in Feb. 20F. ☎ 04 66 50 50 56.

La BARBEN

Château – Guided tours (45min) Apr-Sept 10am-noon and 2-6pm; Feb-Mar daily (except Tues) 10am-noon and 2-5.30pm, Mon 10am-noon; Oct-Dec daily (except Tues) 10am-noon and 2-5pm, Mon 10am-noon, Sat-Sun and public holidays 10am-noon and 2-5.30pm. Closed 25 Dec and in Jan. 40F. ☎ 04 90 55 25 41.

Vivarium and Parc Zoologique – ♿ Open 10am-6pm. 55F (adult), 25F (child). ☎ 04 90 55 19 12.

BARBENTANE

Château – Guided tours (45min) Easter-Oct daily (except Wed) 10am-noon and 2-6pm; July-Sept daily 10am-noon and 2-6pm; Nov-Easter Sun and public holidays 10am-noon and 2-6pm. Closed 1 Jan and 25 Dec. 35F. ☎ 04 90 95 51 07.

Les BAUX-DE-PROVENCE
🛈 Îlot Post Tenebras Lux 13520 ☎ 04 90 54 34 39

Les Baux Vineyards – To visit the various vineyards apply for details to the Syndicat des Vignerons des Baux-de-Provence, Château Romanin, 13210 St-Rémy-de-Provence ☎ 04 90 92 45 87 or the Tourist Information Centre of Les Baux-de-Provence or St-Rémy.

Car park – 20F for any length of stay, 15F for card mentioning parking times *(horodateur)*.

Musée Yves-Brayer – Open Apr-Sept 10am-0.30pm and 2-5.30pm; Oct-Mar daily (except Tues) 10am-0.30pm and 2-6pm (Mar closed at 5pm). Closed Jan-Feb. 25F. ☎ 04 90 54 36 99.

Fondation Louis-Jou – Guided tours (45min) on request 8am-10pm. 20F. Apply to Mr Corbillon. ☎ 04 90 54 34 17.

Château and Musée d'Histoire des Baux – Open Mar-Oct 9am-7.30pm (July-Aug 9am-8.30pm); Nov-Feb 9am-6pm (5pm in winter). 36F (adult), 20F (child). ☎ 04 90 54 55 56.

Cathédrale d'Images – ♿ Audio-visual shows mid-Feb to mid-Jan 10am-6pm (Mar-Sept 10am-7pm). 43F (adult), 27F (child). ☎ 04 90 54 38 65.

BEAUCAIRE
🛈 24, Cours Gambetta 30300 ☎ 04 66 59 26 57

Guided tours of the town – Apply to the Tourist Information Centre.

Musée du Cheval de Trait – Open year round daily 10am-noon and 2-7pm. Closed Tues (except during school holidays). 42F (adult), 20F (child). ☎ 04 66 59 30 06.

Beaucaire Power Station – *Open to visitors for guided tours on weekdays only. Closed public holidays. Written applications should be sent at least a fortnight in advance to La Société Patchwork* ☎ 04 78 24 16 16. Specify the number and type of participants (minimum age limit 9/10 years), minimum number of 10 participants.

Château – Only the grounds and the two curtain walls can be visited (same times of admission as for the Musée Auguste-Jacquet below). During the shows of birds of prey, closing time is after the end of the last show. ☎ 04 66 59 47 61.

Shows of birds of prey in flight – These medieval shows of birds of prey take place at the château in July and Aug at 3pm, 4pm, 5pm and 6pm; Mar-June daily at 2pm, 3pm, 4pm and 5pm; Sept-Oct daily at 2.30pm, 3.30pm and 4.30pm. No shows on Wed (except during school holidays). Closed Nov-Mar. 45F (adult), 25F (child). ☎ 04 66 59 26 72.

Musée Auguste-Jacquet – Open Apr-Oct daily (except Tues) 10am-noon and 2.15-6.45pm; Nov-Mar daily (except Tues) 10.15am-noon and 2-5.15pm. Closed public holidays. 13F. ☎ 04 66 59 47 61.

Excursions

Abbaye de St-Roman – Open Apr-Sept 10am-6pm (July-Aug 10am-6.30pm); Oct-Mar Sat-Sun, public holidays and school holidays 2-5pm. 20F. ☎ 04 66 59 52 26.

Mas des Tourelles – ♿ Open July-Aug 10am-noon and 2-7pm, Sun 2-7pm; Apr-June and Sept-Oct 2-6pm; Nov-Mar Sat only 2-6pm. 27F. ☎ 04 66 59 19 72.

Étang de BERRE

Musée Archéologique d'Istres – Open year round daily 2-6pm. Closed 1 Jan, 1 May, 24, 25, 26, 30 and 31 Dec. 10F (15F during exhibitions). ☎ 04 42 55 50 08.

Château des Covet – Guided tours (1hr) on request Mon-Fri 10am-noon and 2.30-4.30pm. It is advisable to book two weeks in advance. Closed public holidays. ☎ 04 42 09 78 83.

Musée d'Arts et Traditions Populaires - Open Tues and Sat 9am-noon, Wed 2-5pm, Thur and Fri on request only. Closed public holidays . 10F. ☎ 04 42 09 78 83.

BOLLÈNE

🛈 Place Reynaud-de-la-Gardette 84500 ☎ 04 90 40 51 45

Collégiale St-Martin – Guided tours for groups. Apply to the Tourist Information Centre.

Excursion

Mornas: Fortress – Guided tours with historical reconstitution (1hr) July-Aug daily (except Sat) 10am-0.30pm and 1.30-7pm; Mar-June Mon-Fri on request, Sun and public holidays 10am-0.30pm and 1.30-6pm. 30F. Guided tours of the premises July-Aug Sat 10am-6pm ; Mar-June Wed and Sat 10am-5pm; Sept-Oct daily 10am-5pm; Feb and Nov Sun and public holidays 1.30-5pm. 17F. Closed Dec-Jan. ☎ 04 90 37 01 26.

BONNIEUX

🛈 Place Carnot 84480 ☎ 04 90 75 91 90

Musée de la Boulangerie – Open Apr-Sept daily (except Tues) 10am-noon and 3-6.30pm; Oct Sat-Sun only.10am-noon and 3-6.30pm. Closed the rest of the year. 20F. ☎ 04 90 75 88 34.

C

CADENET

🛈 Place du Tambour-d'Arcole 84160 ☎ 04 90 68 38 21

Church – Open July to end of Aug Mon, Tues, Wed and Sat 10.30am-noon and 5.30-7pm; the rest of the year enquire at the presbytery next to the church.

Musée de la Vannerie – ♿ Open Apr to end of Oct daily (except Tues) 10am-noon and 2.30-6.30pm, Sun 2.30-6.30pm. Closed 1 May. 20F. ☎ 04 90 68 24 44.

Les CALANQUES

Boat trips from Marseille – The boat leaves at 2pm (4hr trip with commentary) from 1 Quai des Belges, Le Vieux Port. 120F. ☎ 04 91 55 50 09.

Boat trips from Cassis 45min round trip from Cassis Port to Port-Miou, Port-Pin and En-Vau *calanques*. 50F. ☎ 04 42 01 71 17.

La CAMARGUE

Seawall – 20km/12mi of footpaths and cycle paths can be accessed from the Comtesse car park, near the Phare de Gacholle (lighthouse). Motor traffic is forbidden along the seawall.

Musée Camarguais – ♿ Open Apr-Sept daily; Oct-Mar daily (except Tues). Closed 1 Jan, 1 May and 25 Dec. 25F. Enquire for admission times. ☎ 04 90 97 10 82.

Château d'Avignon – Guided tours (45min) Apr-Oct daily (except Tues) 10am-5.30pm. Closed 1 May. 20F. ☎ 04 90 97 58 60 or 04 90 97 58 58.

Centre d'Information Ginès/François Hüe – No charge for the permanent exhibition, the room with the view and the information resources Apr-Sept daily (except Fri) 9am-6pm, Oct-Mar daily (except Fri) 9.30am-5pm. Closed 1 Jan, 1 May and 25 Dec. For films upstairs a contribution of 5F is requested. Literature is available in the centre. ☎ 04 90 97 86 32.

Massif des Calanques

E. Baret

Parc Ornithologique du Pont de Gau – ♿ Open Apr-Sept 9am to sunset; Oct-Mar 10am to sunset. Closed 25 Dec. 35F (adult), 18F (child). ☎ 04 90 97 82 62.

Boat trip on the Petit Rhône – Service operates between mid-Mar and mid-Nov (1 to 5 departures a day depending on the season). 60F (adult), 30F (child). Information and reservations from Tiki III, 13460 Les Saintes-Maries-de-la-Mer ☎ 04 90 97 81 68.

Méjanes – Riding organised by the mas at 70F/hour. Trips in the little train 20F (adult), 15F (child). Eating facilities available.

La Capelière: Réserve Nationale de Camargue – Open Apr-Sept 9am-1pm and 2-6pm; Oct-Mar daily (except Tues) 9am-1pm and 2-5pm. Closed 1 Jan and 25 Dec. 20F. ☎ 04 90 97 00 97.

Salin-de-Badon: Réserve Nationale de Camargue – Camargue national reserve observatories are available to visitors with a permit from La Capelière *(see above)*. Open Mar-Oct daily (except Wed) from sunrise to 10am and from 4pm to sunset; Nov-Feb from sunrise to 11am and from 3pm to sunset. 20F (adult), 10F (child). ☎ 04 90 97 20 74 or 04 90 97 00 97.

Domaine de la Palissade – Open year round 9am-5pm. Closed public holidays. Anti-mosquito spray or cream recommended. No drinking water available on the estate. 15F. ☎ 04 42 86 81 28.

Musée du Riz – Open year round 9am-noon and 1.30-5.30pm. 15F. ☎ 04 90 97 20 29.

CARPENTRAS
₹ 170, Allée Jean-Jaurès 84200 ☎ 04 90 63 00 78

Guided tour of the town 🅰 – Apply to the Tourist Information Centre.

Ancienne Cathédrale St-Siffrein – Guided tours year round Mon-Fri 10am-noon and 2-4pm (6pm in summer) by appointment. Apply to Mme Battel. ☎ 04 90 63 04 92. **Treasury** – Open Apr-Sept daily (except Tues) 10am-noon and 2-6pm; the rest of the year 10am-noon and 2-4pm. Closed public holidays. 2F. ☎ 04 90 63 04 92.

Palais de Justice – Guided tours (1hr) in summer, spring and during school holidays. No guided tours during assizes. Contact the Tourist Information Centre for details.

Museums – Open Apr-Sept daily (except Tues) 10am-noon and 2-6pm; the rest of the year 10am-noon and 2-4pm. Closed public holidays. ☎ 04 90 63 04 92.

Hôtel-Dieu – Open Mon, Wed and Thur 9-11.30am on request. Closed public holidays. 8F. ☎ 04 90 63 80 00.

Synagogue – Open Mon-Fri 10am-noon and 3-5pm, Fri 10am-noon and 3-6pm. Closed during Jewish religious festivals.

Excursion

Mazan: Local Museum – Guided tours (1hr) mid-June to end of Sept daily (except Tues) 3.30-6.30pm. No charge. ☎ 04 90 69 84 74.

CASSIS
₹ Place Baragnon 13260 ☎ 04 42 01 71 17

Musée d'Arts et Traditions Populaires – Open Wed, Thur and Sat 2-5.30pm; Apr-Sept Wed, Thur and Sat 3.30-6.30pm. Closed 1 Jan, 1 Mayand 25 Dec. No charge. ☎ 04 42 01 88 66.

CAVAILLON
₹ Place François-Tourel 84300 ☎ 04 90 71 32 01

Synagogue – Synagogue and Jewish Comtat Venaissin Museum open daily (except Tues) Apr-Oct 9.30am-0.30pm and 2.30-6.30pm; Nov-Mar Mon, Wed, Thur and Fri 9am-noon and 2-5pm. Closed 1 Jan, 1 May, 25 Dec. 20F. ☎ 04 90 76 00 34.

MusZée de l'Hôtel-Dieu – Open Apr-Oct daily (except Tues) 9.30am-0.30pm and 2.30-6.30pm; Nov-Mar by appointment only. Closed 1 Jan, 1 Mayand 25 Dec. ☎ 04 90 76 00 34.

CHÂTEAU-BAS

Temple Romain – Open year round 9.30am-0.30pm and 1.30-6.30pm, Sun and public holidays 10am-0.30pm and 2.30-6.30pm. Closed 1 Jan and 25 Dec. Access is through the vault. No charge. ☎ 04 90 59 13 16.

CHÂTEAUNEUF-DU-PAPE
₹ Place du Portail 84230 ☎ 04 90 83 71 08

Musée des Outils de Vignerons – ♿ Open July and Aug daily 9am-7pm; the rest of the year 9am-noon and 2-6.30pm. Closed 1 Jan, 1 Nov and 25 Dec. No charge. ☎ 04 90 83 70 07.

CHÂTEAURENARD

🛈 1, Rue Roger-Salengro 13160 ☎ 04 90 94 23 27

Château Féodal: Tour du Griffon – Guided tours (30min) May-Sept daily (except Fri) 10am-noon and 3-6.30pm, Sat 3-7pm, Sun and public holidays 10am-noon and 3-7pm; Oct-Apr daily (except Fri) 10am-noon and 3-5pm, Sat 3-5pm. Closed 1 Jan, 1 May, 1 Novand 25 Dec. 20F. ☎ 04 90 94 23 27.

La CIOTAT

🛈 Boulevard Anatole-France 13600 ☎ 04 42 08 61 32

Musée Ciotaden – Open mid-June to mid-Sept daily (except Tues) 4-7pm; the rest of the year 3-6pm. Closed Easter and 25 Dec. 15F. ☎ 04 42 71 40 99.

Parc du Mugel – Open 9am-8pm in summer, 9am-6pm in winter. There is an information centre on marine environment (Atelier Bleu). It is necessary to book 3 days in advance. ☎ 04 42 08 07 67.

Île Verte – Ferry crossings start during the Easter weekend. There are crossings Sat and Sun in Apr (weather permitting) and daily May-Sept. Contact the boat owners at the landing stage. Price of return ticket: 30F (adult), 15F (child).

Grotte de la COCALIÈRE

&. Guided tours (1hr) Apr-Sept 10am-5pm. 44F (adult), 22F (child). ☎ 04 66 24 01 57.

Plaine de la CRAU

Écomusée de la Crau – &. Open year round daily 9am-noon and 2-6pm. Closed 1 Jan and 25 Dec. No charge. ☎ 04 90 47 02 01.

D – E

DENTELLES DE MONTMIRAIL

Le Barroux: Castle – Open July-Sept 10am-8pm; June and Oct 2.30-7pm; Apr-May Sat-Sun and public holidays only 10am-7pm. Closed Nov-Mar. 20F. ☎ 04 90 62 35 21.

Basse Vallée de la DURANCE

Rognes: Church – Guided tours Wed 9.30-10.30am by appointment only. Apply to the Tourist Information Centre. ☎ 04 42 50 13 36.

La Roque-d'Anthéron: Musée de Géologie Provençale – Open July to mid-Sept Mon-Fri 10am-noon and 3-7pm; mid-Sept to end of June Tues, Thur and Sun (except the first Sunday of each month) 10am-noon and 2-6pm. 10F. ☎ 04 42 50 47 87.

Chartreuse de Bonpas – Grounds are open in summer daily (except Sun) 9am-noon and 3-6.30pm, public holidays 3-6.30pm; open in winter daily (except Sun) 9am-noon and 2-5pm, public holidays 2-5pm. Closed 1 Jan and 25 Dec. 15F. ☎ 04 90 23 09 59.

Chaîne de l'ESTAQUE

Port-de-Bouc: Musée Morales – &. Open year round daily (except Tues) 9am-noon and 2.30-6pm. Closed 1 Jan and 25 Dec. 25F. ☎ 04 42 06 49 01.

F

FONTAINE-DE-VAUCLUSE

🛈 Chemin de la Fontaine 84800 ☎ 04 90 20 32 22

Musée d'Histoire (1939-1945) – &. Open July and Aug daily (except Tues) 10am-7pm; Sept to mid-Oct daily (except Tues) 10am-0.30pm and 2-6pm; mid-Oct to end of Dec Sat-Sun only 10am-0.30pm and 2-6pm; Mar-June daily (except Tues) Sat-Sun only 10am-noon and 2-6pm. Closed Jan and Feb, 1 May and 25 Dec. 20F. ☎ 04 90 20 24 00.

Le Monde Souterrain de Norbert Casteret – &. Guided tours (45min) May-Aug 10am-noon and 2-6pm; the rest of the year 10am-noon and 2-5pm. 30F (adult), 20F (child). ☎ 04 90 20 34 13.

Santon Museum – &. Open July and Aug 10am-7pm; the rest of the year 10am-0.30pm and 2-6pm. 20F (adult), 10F (child). ☎ 04 90 20 20 83.

Musée-Bibliothèque Pétrarque – Open June to Sept daily (except Tues) 10am-0.30pm and 1.30pm to 6pm; Apr-May daily (except Tues) 10am-noon and 2-6pm; Oct Sat-Sun 10am-noon and 2-5pm or 2-6pm. Closed Nov to Mar and 1 May. 20F. ☎ 04 90 20 37 20.

Bassins de FOS

Centre d'Information du Port Autonome de Marseille (CIPAM) – Exhibition and video films shown weekdays 9am-noon and 1-5pm by appointment. Closed public holidays. To reserve call ☎ 04 91 39 47 24.

Tour of the Port – For guided bus tours of the port (2hr 30min) Mon-Fri contact the Service Communication et Relations Publiques, Section Visites, Port Autonome de Marseille, 23 Place de la Joliette, BP 1965 13226 Marseille Cedex 02 ☎ 04 91 39 47 24 at least a fortnight in advance.

G – I

GORDES
🖪 Place du Château 84220 ☎ 04 90 72 02 75

Château: Musée Pol Mara – Open July and Aug daily 10am-noon and 2-6pm; the rest of the year open daily (except Tues) at the same times. Closed 1 Jan and 25 Dec. 25F. ☎ 04 90 72 02 75.

Excursions

Village des Bories – ♿ Open from 9am to sunset. 30F. ☎ 04 90 72 03 48.

Le GRAU-DU-ROI
🖪 30, Rue Michel-Rédarès 30240 ☎ 04 66 51 67 70

Guided tours of the town – Apply to the Tourist Information Centre.

Excursion

Salins du Midi and Caves de Listel – Coach tours (2hr 30min) July and Aug, Tues-Thur at 2pm. No coach tours on public holidays. 50F. Apply to the Information Tourist Centre in Le Grau-du-Roi three days in advance. ☎ 04 66 51 67 70.

GRIGNAN
🖪 Grande Rue 26230 ☎ 04 75 46 56 75

Château – Guided tours (1hr) July and Aug 9.30-11.30am and 2-6pm; Apr-Oct 9.30-11.30am and 2-5.30pm; Nov-Mar daily (except Tues) 9.30-11.30am and 2-5.30pm. Closed 1 Jan and 25 Dec. 30F. ☎ 04 75 46 51 56.

Église St-Sauveur – Organ concerts are given here on 1 Jan, Easter Monday and during summer. Pretty, animated Christmas crib in Dec. Apply to the Tourist Information Centre for details.

L'ISLE-SUR-LA-SORGUE
🖪 Place de l'Église 84800 ☎ 04 90 38 04 78

Église Notre-Dame-des-Anges – Open June-Aug 9am-7.30pm; Sept-May daily (except Mon) 10am-noon and 3-6pm by appointment. Apply to Père Marin at the presbytery.

Hôtel Donadeï de Campredon – Open July-Sept daily (except Mon) 10am-1pm and 3-6.30pm; Oct-June 9.30am-noon and 2-6pm. Closed between exhibitions and 1 Jan, 1 May, 14 July, 25 Dec. 35F (no charge for children). ☎ 04 90 38 17 41.

Hôpital – Closed for restoration work.

L

LOURMARIN
🖪 17, Avenue Philippe-de-Girard 84160 ☎ 04 90 68 10 77

Château – Guided tours July to mid-Sept every 30min 10-11.30am and 3-6pm; Apr-June and mid-Sept to end of Sept at 10am, 11am, 2.30pm, 3.30pm, 4.30pm and 5.30pm; Oct-Mar at 11am, 2.30pm, 3.30pm and 4.30pm. Closed 1 Jan and 25 Dec. 30F. ☎ 04 90 68 15 23.

Montagne du LUBERON

Prieuré de Carluc – Guided tours year round on request (July 3.30-7pm). 10F. ☎ 04 42 54 22 70.

Cucuron: Museum – Open June-Sept 9am-noon and 3-6pm; the rest of the year 9am-noon and 3-5pm. Closed Thur, Tues morning and Sun afternoon. No charge. ☎ 04 90 77 25 02.

Fort de Buoux – Open from sunrise to sunset. 10F. For further details call ☎ 04 90 74 25 75.

Abbaye de St-Hilaire – Open year round 10am-6pm, 10am 5pm in winter. No charge.

Coustellet: Musée de la Lavande – ♿ Open June-Sept 10am-noon and 2-7pm; the rest of the year 10am-noon and 2-6pm. Closed Jan and Feb. 15F. ☎ 04 90 76 91 23.

M

Grotte de la MADELEINE

Guided tours (1hr) Apr to end of Oct 10am-6pm; July-Aug 9am-7pm. Closed the rest of the year. 40F (adult). 24F (child). ☎ 04 75 04 09 52.

MAILLANE

Museon Mistral – Guided tours (30min) Apr-Sept daily (except Mon) 9.30-11.30am and 2.30-6.30pm; Oct-Mar daily (except Mon) 10-11.30am and 2-4.30pm. Closed public holidays. 20F. ☎ 04 90 95 75 06.

MARCOULE

Nuclear Power Centre: Exhibition – ♿ The halls are open July-Aug 10am-noon and 3.30-7.30pm; Apr-June and in Sept Wed and Sat-Sun 2.30-6pm; Jan-Mar Wed and Sat-Sun 2.30-5pm; Oct-Dec Sun 2.30-5pm. Closed 1 Jan and 25 Dec. No charge. ☎ 04 66 79 51 55.

MARSEILLE   🅱 4, La Canebière 13001 ☎ 04 91 13 89 00

Guided tours of the town 🅰 – Apply to the Tourist Information Centre.

Tourist train rides – There are two tours: one runs between the Vieux Port and Notre-Dame-de-la-Garde via the Basilique St-Victor; the other one follows a route through old Marseille (Le Panier and Vieille Charité districts). Departure from Quai des Belges.

Ferry-boat – This operates daily from Place des Huiles to the Hôtel de Ville 8am-6.30pm (8.30pm Sat-Sun in summer). Single ticket 3F, return ticket 5F.

Musée d'Histoire de Marseille – ♿ Open Mar-Oct daily (except Sun) noon-7pm; Nov-Feb daily (except Sun) 10am-5pm. Closed and public holidays. 12F. ☎ 04 91 90 42 22.

Musée du Vieux Marseille – Closed for restoration work.

Musée des Docks Romains – Open June-Sept daily (except Mon) 11am-6pm; Oct-May daily (except Mon) 10am-5pm. Closed public holidays. 12F. ☎ 04 91 91 24 62.

Cathédrale de la Major – Open mid-June to mid-Aug 9am-6.30pm; mid-Aug to mid-June daily (except Mon) 9am-noon and 2-5.30pm. ☎ 04 91 90 53 57.

Ancienne Cathédrale de la Major – Temporarily closed to the public.

Centre de la Vieille Charité – Open June-Sept daily (except Mon) 11am-6pm; Oct-May daily (except Mon) 10am-5pm. Musée d'Archéologie Méditerranéenne 12F; Musée des Arts Africains, Océaniens et Amérindiens 12F; temporary exhibitions 18F. ☎ 04 91 56 28 38.

Basilique de Notre-Dame-de-la-Garde – Guided tours on request. For details contact ☎ 04 91 13 40 80.

Musée de la Marine et de l'Économie de Marseille – Open year round 10am-6pm. 12F. ☎ 04 91 39 33 33.

Musée de la Mode – ♿ Open year round daily (except Mon) noon-7pm. Closed public holidays. 18F. ☎ 04 91 56 59 57.

Ville ce Marseille – DR

Marseille faience Veuve Perrin

MARSEILLE

Musée Cantini – Open June-Sept daily (except Mon) 11am-6pm; Oct-May daily (except Mon) 10am-5pm. Closed public holidays. 12F. ☎ 04 91 54 77 75.

Musée Grobet-Labadié – Open June-Sept daily (except Mon) 11am-6pm; Oct-May daily (except Mon) 10am-5pm. Closed public holidays. 12F. ☎ 04 91 62 21 82.

Musée des Beaux-Arts – Open June-Sept daily (except Mon) 11am-6pm; Oct-May daily (except Mon) 10am-5pm. Closed public holidays. 12F. ☎ 04 91 14 59 30.

Muséum d'Histoire Naturelle – Open year round daily (except Mon) 10am-5pm. Closed public holidays. 12F. ☎ 04 91 14 59 50.

Parc Borély: Botanical Gardens – ♿ Open May-Sept 9.30am-noon and 1-5.30pm, Sat-Sun and public holidays 11.30am-7pm; Oct-Apr 9am-noon and 1-5.30pm, Sat-Sun and public holidays 9.30am-noon and 1-5.30pm. Closed 1 May and 24 Dec to 2 Jan. 10F. ☎ 04 91 55 24 96.

Musée d'Art Contemporain – ♿ Open June-Sept daily (except Mon) 11am-6pm; Oct-May daily (except Mon) 10am-5pm. Closed public holidays. 18F. ☎ 04 91 25 01 07.

Musée de la Faïence – ♿ Open June-Sept daily (except Mon) 11am-6pm; Oct-May daily (except Mon) 10am-5pm. Closed public holidays. 12F. ☎ 04 91 62 21 82.

Train rides – A little train will take you to the museum June-Sept daily (except Mon) 11am-5.30pm; Oct-May 10am-4.30pm. Departures every 30min. Return ticket 8F.

Port: The Docks – Guided tours (2hr) Mon-Fri 9am-5pm. It is necessary to book at least two weeks in advance. Apply to the Port Autonome de Marseille, Service Communication et Relations Publiques, Section Visites, 23 Place de la Joliette, BP 1965, 13002 Marseille Cedex 2 ☎ 04 91 39 47 24.

Excursions

Château d'If – Boat trips (1hr 30min, including tour of the château). Embark at Quai des Belges, in the Vieux Port. Departures every 60min in summer, every 90min in winter. 50F. Admission times for the château are dependent on the timetables for boat trips: Apr-Sept 9am-5.40pm; Oct-Mar 9.15am-6.45pm. 25F. Apply to the Groupement des Armateurs Côtiers Marseillais, 1 Quai des Belges, 13001 Marseille ☎ 04 91 55 50 09.
This company also organises trips to the Îles du Frioul. 80F (combined ticket for Château d'If and Îles du Frioul).

Musée des Arts et Traditions Populaires du Terroir Marseillais – Open year round daily (except Tues) 2.30-6.30pm. Closed public holidays, 1 Jan and 25 Dec. 20F. ☎ 04 91 68 14 38.

MARTIGUES

🛈 2, Quai Paul-Doumer 13500 ☎ 04 42 80 30 72

Guided tours of the town – Guided tours (1hr) by appointment. Apply to the Musée Ziem *(see below)*.

Aven de Marzal

Musée Ziem – Open July-Aug daily (except Tues) 10am-noon and 2.30-6.30pm; Sept-June daily (except Mon and Tues) 2.30-6.30pm. Closed 1 Jan, Easter Sunday and Monday, 14 July, 1 and 11 Nov, 25 Dec. No charge. ☎ 04 42 80 66 06.

Chapelle de l'Annonciade – Guided tours (1hr) Wed mornings at 10.30am by appointment. Meeting-point in front of the chapel. No charge. ☎ 04 42 80 66 06.

Aven de MARZAL

Musée du Monde Souterrain – ♿ Open Apr-Oct 10am-6pm; Mar and Nov Sun and public holidays 11am-5pm. No charge. ☎ 04 75 04 12 45 or 04 75 55 14 82.

Chasm and Cave – Guided tours (1hr) Apr-Oct 10am-6pm; Mar and Nov Sun and public holidays 11am-5pm. 42F (adult), 27F (child). ☎ 04 75 04 12 45 or 04 75 55 14 82.

Delon/PIX

Prehistoric Zoo – ♿ Open Apr-Oct 10am-6pm; Mar and Nov Sun and public holidays 11am-5pm. 42F (adult). 27F (child). ☎ 04 75 04 12 45 or 04 75 55 14 82.

MÉNERBES

Musée du Tire-Bouchon – ♿ Open Apr-Sept Mon-Fri 9am-noon and 2-7pm. Sat-Sun and public holidays 10am-noon and 3-7pm; Oct-Mar daily (except Sun) Mon-Fri 9am-noon and 2-6pm. Sat 9am-noon. 24F. ☎ 04 90 72 41 58.

La MONTAGNETTE

Musée des Arômes et des Parfums – Open year round daily 10am-noon and 2-6pm. Closed 1 Jan and 25 Dec. 10F. ☎ 04 90 95 81 55.

Graveson: Musée Auge-Chabaud – Open June-Sept 10am-noon and 1.30-6.30pm; Oct-May 1.30-6.30pm. Closed 1 Jan and 25 Dec. 20F. ☎ 04 90 90 53 02.

Abbaye de MONTMAJOUR

Open Apr-Sept daily 9am-7pm; Oct-Mar daily (except Tues) 10am-1pm and 2-5pm. Closed 1 Jan, 1 May, 1 and 11 Nov, 25 Dec. 35F.

Chapelle Ste-Croix – Guided tours by appointment only. Apply to the reception area of the abbey. ☎ 04 90 54 64 17.

MOULIN DE DAUDET

Open Apr-Sept 9am-7pm; Oct-Mar 10am-noon and 2-5pm. Closed Jan. 10F. ☎ 04 90 54 60 78.

N

Oppidum de NAGES

Musée Archéologique – For visiting details contact Nages-et-Solorgues town hall (*Secrétariat de la Mairie*) on weekdays. ☎ 04 66 35 05 26.

NÎMES
🖪 6, Rue Auge 30000 ☎ 04 66 67 29 11

Guided tours of the town 🄰 – Apply to the Tourist Information Centre.
A three-day pass is available for the main sites in Nîmes. 60F (adult). 30F (child). Contact the Tourist Information Centre for details.

Amphitheatre – Open June-Sept 9am-6.30pm; Oct-May guided tours (30min) 9am-noon and 2-5.30pm. Closed 1 Jan, 1 May, at Pentecost, 25 Dec, during shows and bullfights and during the Feria. 28F. ☎ 04 66 76 72 77.

Maison Carrée – Open June-Sept 9am-noon and 2.30-7pm; Oct-May 9am-0.30pm and 2-6pm. Closed 1 Jan, 1 May, 25 Dec. No charge. ☎ 04 66 36 26 76.

Carré d'Art – ♿ Open year round daily (except Mon) 10am-6pm. Closed 1 Jan, 1 May, 25 Dec. 28F. ☎ 04 66 76 35 70.

Tour Magne – Open June-Sept 9am-7pm; Oct-May 9am-5pm. Closed 1 Jan, 1 May, 25 Dec. 15F. ☎ 04 66 67 65 56.

Musée du Vieux Nîmes – Open year round daily (except Mon) 11am-6pm. Closed 1 Jan, 1 May, 1 and 11 Nov, 28 Dec. 26F. ☎ 04 66 36 00 64.

Muséum d'Histoire Naturelle – Open year round daily (except Mon) 11am-6pm. Closed 1 Jan, 1 May, 1 and 11 Nov, 25 Dec. 28F. ☎ 04 66 67 39 14.

Musée Archéologique. – Open year round daily (except Mon) 11am-6pm. Closed 1 Jan, 1 May, 1 and 11 Nov, 25 Dec. 28F. ☎ 04 66 67 25 57.

Hôtel Fontfroide – Guided tours only. Apply to the Tourist Information Centre.

Musée des Beaux-Arts – ♿ Open year round daily (except Mon) 11am-6pm. Closed 1 Jan, 1 May, 1, 25 Dec. 28F. ☎ 04 66 67 38 21.

Excursion

Source Perrier – Guided tours (30min) July and Aug Mon-Fri 9.30-10.30am and 1-6pm. Sat-Sun 10-10.30am and 1-4.30pm; Sept-June 9.30-10.30am and 1-4pm, Sat-Sun 1.30-5pm. Closed 1 May and mid-Dec to end of Jan. 20F. It is advisable to book in advance. ☎ 04 66 87 61 01.

NYONS
🖪 Place de la Libération 26110 ☎ 04 75 26 10 35

Moulin Ramade – ♿ Open daily (except Sun) 9am-noon and 2-7pm. Closed public holidays. No charge. ☎ 04 75 26 08 18.

NYONS

Vieux Moulins – Guided tours (30min) Tues-Sat 10am-noon and 2.30-6pm, daily in July and Aug. Closed Jan and 25 Dec. 23F. ☎ 04 75 26 11 00.

Coopérative Oléicole et Viticole – Guided tours (1hr) July and Aug 8.30am-1pm and 2-7.30pm, Sun 9.30am-0.30pm and 3-7pm; Sept-June 8.30am-0.30pm and 2-7pm, Sun 9.30am-0.30pm and 2.30-6.30pm. Closed 1 Jan, 1 May, 25 Dec. No charge. It is advisable to book two weeks in advance. ☎ 04 75 26 03 44.

Musée de l'Olivier – ♿ Open June-Oct daily (except Sun) 10-11.30am and 2.45-6pm; Mar-June daily (except Sun) 2.45-6pm; Nov-Dec daily (except Sun and Mon) 2.45-6pm. 12F. ☎ 04 75 26 12 12.

ORANGE
🚩 Cours Aristide-Briand 84104 ☎ 04 90 34 70 88

Guided tours of the town 🅰 – Apply to the Tourist Information Centre.

Roman Theatre – ♿ Open Apr-Sept 9am-6.30pm; Oct-Mar 9am-noon and 1.30-5pm. Closed 1 Jan and 25 Dec. 30F. ☎ 04 90 34 70 88.

Musée Municipal – Open Apr-Sept 9.30am-7pm; Oct-Mar 9.30am-noon and 1.30-5.30pm. Closed 1 Jan and 25 Dec. 30F (combined ticket including access to the Roman Theatre). ☎ 04 90 51 18 24.

Excursion

Harmas J.-H. Fabre – Guided tours (1hr) daily (except Tues and Sun) 9-11.30am and 2-6pm. Closed Oct and public holidays. 15F. ☎ 04 90 70 00 44.

Aven d'ORGNAC

Guided tours (1hr) Mar to mid-Nov 9.30am-noon and 2-5pm; Apr-Sept closed at 6pm; July-Aug 9.30am-6pm. 45F (adult), 29F (child). ☎ 04 75 38 62 51.

Musée de Préhistoire – ♿ Open July and Aug 10am-7pm; Apr-Sept 10am-0.30pm and 2-6.30pm; Mar and Oct to mid-Nov 10am-noon and 2-5pm. 30F. ☎ 04 75 38 65 10.

P

PERNES-LES-FONTAINES
🚩 Place du Comtat Venaissin 84210 ☎ 04 90 61 31 04

Tour Ferrande – Guided tours (15min) by appointment only. Apply to the Tourist Information Centre. 15F. ☎ 04 90 61 31 04.

Tour de l'Horloge – Open year round daily 9am-5pm.

PEYROLLES-EN-PROVENCE

Église St-Pierre – Guided tours by appointment 8am-noon and 2-5pm. Apply to Mme Vidal at the Mairie. ☎ 04 42 57 89 82.

PONT DU GARD

Access to the bridge – Call for programme and admission charges of cultural activities (guided tours, exhibitions, films etc). Charge for car park. ☎ 04 66 76 34 42.

PONT-ST-ESPRIT
🚩 Rue Vauban 30130 ☎ 04 66 39 44 45

Musée d'Art Sacré du Gard – ♿ Open July-Sept daily (except Mon) 10am-noon and 2-7pm; the rest of the year 10am-noon and 2-6pm. Closed public holidays and in Feb. 20F. ☎ 04 66 90 75 80.

Musée Paul-Raymond – Open July-Sept daily (except Mon) 10am-noon and 3-7pm; Oct-June Wed, Thur and Sun 10am-noon and 2-6pm. Closed public holidays and in Feb. 20F. ☎ 04 66 90 75 80.

R

ROCHEFORT-DU-GARD

Excursion

Sanctuaire Notre-Dame-de-Grâce: Chapel and outbuildings – Guided tours Sun 3-4.30pm (except during services). Apply to the south porch. ☎ 04 90 31 72 01.

S

Site Archéologique de ST-BLAISE

Excavations – *Open in summer 9am-noon and 2-7pm, in winter daily (except Tues) 2-5pm.*

ST-GILLES

🚹 Place Frédéric-Mistral 30800 ☎ 04 66 87 33 75

Guided tours of the town – Apply to the Tourist Information Centre on Place de l'Église. ☎ 04 66 87 41 31.

St-Gilles Abbey: Ancien Chœur, Crypte and Vis de St-Gilles – Open Apr-Sept daily (except Sun) 9am-noon and 2-7pm; the rest of the year daily (except Sun) 9am-noon and 2-5pm. Closed public holidays. 20F. ☎ 04 66 87 41 31.

Cellier des Moines – Closed to the public.

Maison Romane – Open July and Aug daily (except Sun) 9am-noon and 3-7pm; the rest of the year 9am-noon and 2-5pm. Closed public holidays and in Jan. ☎ 04 66 87 40 42.

Grotte de ST-MARCEL

Guided tours (45min) mid-Mar to end of Sept 10am-6pm (July and Aug 10am-7pm); Oct to mid-Nov 10am-5pm. 37F (adult), 22F (child). ☎ 04 75 04 38 07.

ST-MAXIMIN-LA-STE-BAUME

🚹 Hôtel de Ville 83470 ☎ 04 94 54 89 59

Royal Monastery – Open 9am-6pm. No charge. ☎ 04 94 86 55 66.

Abbaye de ST-MICHEL-DE-FRIGOLET

Église Abbatiale and Notre-Dame-du-Bon-Remède – Open Apr-Oct 8-11am and 1.30-7pm; the rest of the year 8-11am and 1.30-6pm. ☎ 04 90 95 70 07.

Cloisters – Guided tours (1hr) Mon-Fri at 2.30pm, Sun at 4pm. No guided tours Sat and public holidays. No charge. ☎ 04 90 95 70 07.

ST-RÉMY-DE-PROVENCE

🚹 Place Jean-Jaurès 13210 ☎ 04 90 92 05 22

Guided tours of the town – Apply to the Tourist Information Centre.

Glanum – Open Apr-Sept 9am-7pm; Oct-Mar 9am-noon and 2-5pm. Closed 1 Jan, 1 May, 1 and 11 Nov, 25 Dec. 32F. ☎ 04 90 92 23 79.

Ancien Monastère de St-Paul-de-Mausole – ♿ Open May-Oct daily (except Sun and Mon) 9am-7pm, public holidays 10am-6pm; Nov-Apr 9am-5.30pm, Sat 9.30am-5.30pm, public holidays 10am-6pm. 15F. ☎ 04 90 92 77 00.

Mas de la Pyramide – ♿ Open in summer 9am-noon and 2-7pm; in winter 9am-noon and 2-5pm. 20F. ☎ 04 90 92 00 81.

Hôtel Estrine: Centre d'Art-Présence Van Gogh – Open mid-Mar to end of Oct and in Dec daily (except Mon) 10.30am-0.30pm and 2.30-6.30pm. 20F. ☎ 04 90 92 34 72.

Hôtel de Sade – Open Apr-Sept 10am-noon and 2-6pm (July and Aug closed at 7pm); Oct-Mar 10am-noon and 2-5pm. Closed 1 Jan, 1 May, 1 and 11 Nov, 25 Dec. 15F. ☎ 04 90 92 64 04.

Musée des Alpilles Pierre-de-Brun – Open July and Aug 10am-noon and 2-7pm; Mar-Oct 10am-noon and 2-6pm; Nov-Dec 10am-noon and 2-5pm. Closed Jan and Feb, 1 May and 25 Dec. 18F. ☎ 04 90 92 68 24.

Chapelle Notre-Dame-de-Pitié – Open July and Aug 10am-noon and 3-7pm; Sept-June 2-6pm. Closed Jan and Feb, 1 May, 1 and 11 Nov and 25 Dec. No charge. ☎ 04 90 92 35 13.

Montagne STE-VICTOIRE

Domaine Capitaine Danjou – ♿ *Tours of the workshops Mon-Fri 9am-noon and 2-5pm. Shop open daily (except Mon) 10am-noon and 2-5pm. Closed in Aug. No charge.* ☎ 04 42 66 31 41.

STES-MARIES-DE-LA-MER

Watchpath – Open Apr to mid-Nov 10am-noon and 2-6pm; mid-Nov to end of Mar Wed and Sat-Sun 10am-noon and 2-5pm. 10F. ☎ 04 90 97 82 55.

Musée Baroncelli – Open Apr to mid-Nov 10am-noon and 2-6pm. 10F. ☎ 04 90 97 82 55.

SALON-DE-PROVENCE

🚹 56, Cours Gimon 13300 ☎ 04 90 56 27 60

Guided tours of the town – Apply to the Tourist Information Centre.

The "Saintly Ship"

Château de l'Empéri – Open Apr-Sept daily (except Tues) 10am-noon and 2.30-6.30pm; Oct-Mar daily (except Tues) 10am-noon and 2-6pm. Closed 1 Jan, 1 May and 25 Dec. 25F. ☎ 04 90 56 22 36.

Musée Grévin de Provence – Open year round Mon-Fri 9am-noon and 2-6pm, Sat-Sun 2-6pm. Last admission 30min before actual closing time. Closed public holidays. 20F ☎ 04 90 56 36 30.

Maison de Nostradamus – Open 9am-noon and 2-6pm, Sat-Sun 2-6pm. Closed Easter, 1 and 8 May, Ascension Day and 14 July. 20F. ☎ 04 90 56 64 31.

Musée de Salon et de la Crau – Open July and Aug daily (except Tues, Saturday mornings and Sunday mornings) 10am-noon and 2-6.30pm; the rest of the year 10am-noon and 2-6pm, Sat-Sun 2-6pm. Closed public holidays. 15F. ☎ 04 90 56 28 37.

Excursion

St-Cannat: Museum – Open May-Sept Tues-Fri 2-5pm, the first Sunday of each month 10.30am-noon and 2.30-4pm; Oct-Apr the first Sunday of each month 10.30am-noon and 2.30-4pm. Closed public holidays. 15F. ☎ 04 42 50 82 00.

SAULT

Museum – Open July-Aug daily (except Sun) 3-6pm. No charge. ☎ 04 90 64 02 30.

Abbaye de SÉNANQUE

Open Mar to Oct 10am-noon and 2-6pm (last admission 30min before actual closing time), Sun and public holidays 2-6pm; Nov-Feb 2-5pm, Sat-Sun and public holidays 2-6pm. Closed Good Friday, the Thursday morning nearest Ascension Day, other religious holidays (mornings) and 25 Dec. 30F. ☎ 04 90 72 05 72.

Abbaye de SILVACANE

Church, cloisters and conventual buildings – Open Apr-Sept 9am-7pm; Oct-Mar daily (except Tues) 10am-1pm and 2-5pm. Closed 1 Jan, 1 May and 25 Dec. 32F (no charge for children). ☎ 04 42 50 41 69.

SUZE-LA-ROUSSE

Castle – Guided tours (45min) Apr-Oct 9.30-11.30am and 2-5.30pm (6pm July and Aug); Nov-Mar daily (except Tues) 9.30-11.30am and 2-5.30pm. Closed 1 Jan and 25 Dec. 17F. ☎ 04 75 04 81 44.

University of Wine – Guided tours (45min) daily (except Tues) 9.30-11am and 2-5.30pm (daily Apr-Oct); July and Aug 9.30-11am and 2-6pm. Closed 1 Janand 25 Dec. 17F. ☎ 04 90 91 03 93.

T

TARASCON   🖪 59, Rue des Halles BP 9 13150 ☎ 04 90 91 03 52

Guided tours of the town – Apply to the Tourist Information Centre.

Castle – Open Apr-Sept 9am-7pm; Oct-Mar daily (except Tues) 9am-noon and 2-5pm. Closed 1 Jan, 1 May, 1 and 11 Nov, 25 Dec. 32F. ☎ 04 90 91 01 93.

Église Ste-Marthe – Guided tours available on request. Apply to the Tourist Information Centre. ☎ 04 90 91 09 50.

Musée Charles-Deméry (Souleiado) – Open May-Sept 10am 6pm (last admission 1hr before actual closing time); Oct-Apr daily (except Sat-Sun and public holidays) 10am-5pm. Closed 1 Mayand during Christmas and New Year celebrations. 40F. It is advisable to book at least one week in advance. ☎ 04 90 91 50 16.

R. Mazin/TOP

Maison de Tartarin – Open mid-Apr to mid-Sept daily (except Sun) 10am-noon and 2-7pm; mid-Mar to mid-Dec daily (except Sun) 10am-noon and 1.30-5pm. Closed 1 May. 10F. ☎ 04 90 91 05 08.

Le THOR

Church – *Open daily (except Mon) 8.30am-noon and 2-6pm, Sun 8.30am-noon.*

Grotte de Thouzon – Guided tours (45min) July and Aug 10am-6.30pm; Apr-Oct 10am-noon and 2-6pm; Mar and Nov Sun and public holidays only 2-6pm. 38F (adult), 26F (child). ☎ 04 90 33 93 65.

La TOUR-D'AIGUES

Château: Musée des Faïences and Musée de l'Histoire du Pays d'Aigues – Open July-Aug daily 10am-1pm and 3.30-6.30pm; Apr to June and in Sept 9.30-11.30am and 3-6pm, Sat-Sun and public holidays 3-6pm; Oct-Mar 9.30-11.30am and 2-5pm, Sat-Sun and public holidays 2-5pm. Closed 1 Jan and 25 Dec. 25F. ☎ 04 90 07 50 33.

U – V

UZÈS
🏛 Avenue de la Libération 30700 ☎ 04 66 22 68 88

Guided tours of the town 🄰 – Apply to the Tourist Information Centre.

Église St-Étienne – Guided tours organised by the Tourist Information Centre.

Duché – Guided tours (45min) of palace July-Aug 10am-6.30pm; the rest of the year guided tours 10am-noon and 2-6pm. During the same period visitors have free access-the keep. 55F (palace and keep), 20F (keep) ☎ 04 66 22 18 96.

Crypte – Tour included in the guided tour of the town organised by the Tourist Information Centre. See the chapter on Practical Information.

Musée Municipal Georges-Borias – Open Feb-Oct daily (except Mon) 3-6pm; Nov-Dec daily (except Mon) 2-5pm. Closed Jan, 1 Nov and 25 Dec. 10F. ☎ 04 66 22 40 23.

Excursions

Uzès National Stud – Guided tours (1hr) July-Feb 2-5pm; Mar-June daily (except Sun and public holidays) 2-5pm. 15F. ☎ 04 66 22 33 11.

Moulin de Chalier: Musée 1900 and Musée du Train et du Jouet – ♿ Open July-Aug 9-7pm; the rest of the year 9am-noon and 2-7pm. 30F (adult), 20F (child). Combined ticket providing access to both museums: 55F (adult), 36F (child). ☎ 04 66 22 58 64.

St-Quentin-la-Poterie: Galerie Terra Viva – ♿ Open July-Aug daily 10am-1pm and 2.30-7pm; the rest of the year 10am-1pm and 2.30-6pm. Closed Jan-Mar and 25 Dec. No charge. ☎ 04 66 22 48 78.

VAISON-LA-ROMAINE
🏛 Place du Chanoine-Sautel 84110 ☎ 04 90 36 02 11

Guided tours of the town – Apply to the Tourist Information Centre.

Roman Ruins: Maison des Messii – Open July-Aug: Puymin 9.30am-7pm, Villasse 9.30am-noon and 2.30-7pm; June-Sept: Puymin 9.30am-6pm, Villasse 9.30am-noon and 2.30-6pm; Mar-May and Oct: 10am-0.30pm and 2-6pm; Nov-Feb: daily (except Tues) 10am-noon and 2-4.30pm. Closed 1 Jan and 25 Dec. Combined ticket including access to all monuments: 40F (adult), 14F (child). ☎ 04 90 36 02 11.

Musée Archéologique Théo-Desplans – ♿ Open Mar-Oct 10am-0.30pm and 2.30-6pm; July-Aug 9.30am-7pm; June and Sept 9.30am-6pm; Nov-Feb daily (except Tues) 10-11.30am and 2-4pm. Closed 1 Jan and 25 Dec. Combined ticket including access-all monuments: 40F (adult), 14F (child). ☎ 04 90 36 51 31.

Cloisters – Open July-Aug 9.30am-noon and 2-6.30pm; June and Sept 9.30am-noon and 2-5.30pm; Mar-May and Oct 10am-noon and 2-5.30pm; Nov-Feb 10am-noon and 2-4pm. Closed 1 Jan and 25 Dec. 8F. ☎ 04 90 36 51 30 or 04 90 36 51 31.

Chapelle de St-Quenin – Apply to the Tourist Information Centre.

Excursion

Rasteau: Musée du Vigneron – ♿ Open July-Aug daily (except Tues) 10am-6pm; Easter to June and Sept-Oct daily (except Tues) 2-6pm. Closed Nov to Easter. 10F. ☎ 04 90 46 11 75.

Chartreuse de VALBONNE

Open June-Sept 10am-1pm and 2-7pm; mid-Mar to end of May 9am-noon and 2-6pm; Oct to mid-Nov 10am-noon and 1.30-5pm; mid-Nov to mid-Mar 9am-noon and 1.30-5.30pm, Sat 1.30-5.30pm. Closed 1 Jan and 25 Dec. 18F. ☎ 04 66 90 41 24.

Monk's Cell – This can only be seen as part of a guided tour (1hr). 23F.

VALLON-PONT-D'ARC   🄱 Cité Administrative 07150 ☎ 04 75 88 04 01

Town Hall Tapestries – & Open Mon-Fri 10-11am and 3.30-4.30pm Closed public holidays. 15F. ☎ 04 75 88 02 06.

"Grotte Chauvet" Exhibition – & Open July and Aug daily (except Mon) 10am-1pm and 3-8pm; mid-Mar to mid-Nov daily (except Mon) 10am-noon and 2-5.30pm. 25F (adult), 15F (child). ☎ 04 75 37 17 68.

Silkworm Farm – & Guided tours (1hr) mid-Apr to end of Sept 9am-noon and 2-6pm. Closed the rest of the year. 25F (adult), 15F (child). ☎ 04 75 88 01 27.

VALRÉAS   🄱 Château de Simiane 84600 ☎ 04 90 35 04 71

Guided tours of the town – Apply to the Tourist Information Centre.

Hôtel de Ville – Open July-Aug during the Salon des Arts Plastiques daily (except Tues) 10.30am-0.30pm and 4-8pm; Sept-June guided tours (30min) daily (except Sun) 3-5pm. Closed public holidays. No charge. ☎ 04 90 35 00 45.

Chapelle des Pénitents Blancs – Guided tours July-Aug Wed and Fri 4-6pm. ☎ 04 90 35 04 71.

Musée du Cartonnage et de l'Imprimerie – Open Apr to end of Oct daily (except Tues) 10am-noon and 3-6pm, Sun 3-6pm. Closed public holidays (except 14 July and 15 Aug). 20F. ☎ 04 90 35 58 75.

VENASQUE   🄱 Grand'Rue 84210 ☎ 04 90 66 11 66

Baptistery – Open mid-Mar to mid-Nov daily (except Wed) 10am-noon and 2-6pm, Sun 2-6pm (June-Sept closed at 7pm); mid-Nov to mid-Feb daily (except Wed) 10am-noon and 2-5pm, Sun 2-5pm. Closed mid-Feb to mid-Mar. 10F. ☎ 04 90 66 62 01.

Mont VENTOUX

Ascent of the North Face – For information on snowfall on the roads of the Ventoux Massif (snow may block roads between Nov and May) contact ☎ 08 36 68 02 84 (French Meteorological Services - commentary in French).

Crillon-le-Brave: Maison de la Musique Mécanique – & Guided tours (1hr) Easter-Sept 3-7pm; Oct-Easter Sun only 3-7pm. Last admission 1hr before actual closing time. 28F. ☎ 04 90 65 93 53.

VILLENEUVE-LÈS-AVIGNON   🄱 1, Place Charles-David 30400 ☎ 04 90 25 61 33

Guided tours of the town – Apply to the Tourist Information Centre.

A combined ticket (45F) called "Passeport pour l'Art" is available from the entrances to the following sights: Chartreuse du Val de Bénédiction, Fort St-André, the Cloisters in the Église Notre-Dame, Tour Philippe-le-Bel and the Musée Pierre-de-Luxembourg. It can also be bought from the Tourist Information Centre.

Chartreuse du Val de Bénédiction – Open Apr-Sept 9am-6.30pm; the rest of the year 9.30am-5.30pm. Closed 1 Jan, 1 May, 1 and 11 Nov, 25 Dec. 25F. ☎ 04 90 15 24 24.

Fort St-André – Open Apr-Sept 10am-0.30pm and 2-6pm; Oct-Mar 10am-noon and 2-5pm. Closed 1 Jan, 1 May, 1 and 11 Nov, 25 Dec. 25F. ☎ 04 90 25 45 35.

Abbaye St-André – *Open Apr-Sept daily (except Mon) 10am-0.30pm and 2-6pm; Oct-Mar daily (except Mon) 10am-noon and 2-5pm; July to end of Sept guided tours (1hr 30min) of the abbey buildings Wed and Sat at 4pm. 20F or 35F (guided tours).* ☎ 04 90 25 55 95.

Église Notre-Dame – *Open Apr-Sept daily (except Mon) 10am-0.30pm and 3-7pm (open daily mid-June to mid-Sept); Oct-Mar daily (except Mon) 10am-noon and 2-5.30pm. Closed 1 and 2 Jan, 1 May, 1 and 11 Nov, 25, 26 Dec and in Feb.* ☎ 04 90 27 49 66.

Cloisters – Open Apr-Sept daily (except Mon) 10am-0.30pm and 3-7.30pm (open daily mid-June to mid-Sept); Oct-Mar daily (except Mon) 10am-noon and 2.30-5pm. Closed 1 Jan, 1 May, 1 and 11 Nov, 25 Decand in Feb. 7F. ☎ 04 90 27 49 85.

Musée Municipal Pierre de Luxembourg – & Open Apr-Sept daily (except Mon) 10am-0.30pm and 3-7pm (open daily mid-June to mid-Sept); Oct-Mar daily (except Mon) 10am-noon and 2-5pm. Closed 1 Jan, 14 July, 1 and 11 Nov, 25 Dec and in Feb. 20F. ☎ 04 90 27 49 66.

Tour Philippe le Bel – Same times and charges as for as the Église Notre-Dame *(see above)*. 10F.

Index

Cadenet *Vaucluse* ....

Puget, Pierre ....

Towns, sights and tourist regions followed by the name of the *département*.

People, historical events and subjects.
Isolated sights (caves, castles, châteaux, abbeys, dams,....) are listed under their proper name.

A

ABC of Architecture 38
Accommodation 6, 279
Adrets, Baron des 125
Agriculture 12
Aigues-Mortes *Gard* 58
Aigues-Mortes (Plain) *Gard* 163
Aiguèze *Ardèche* 81
Aïoli 32
Aires (Col) *Vaucluse* 126
Aix-en-Provence *Bouches-du-Rhône* 61
  Ancienne Chapelle des Jésuites 70
  Ancienne Halle aux Grains 67
  Atelier Paul-Cézanne 71
  Cathédrale St-Sauveur 67
  Cité du Livre 70
  Cloître St-Sauveur 67
  Cours Mirabeau 65
  Église Ste-Marie-Madeleine 70
  Église St-Jean-de-Malte 69
  Fondation Vasarely 70
  Fontaine d'eau thermale 65
  Fontaine des Neuf Canons 65
  Fontaine des Prêcheurs 70
  Fontaine des Quatre Dauphins 69
  Fontaine du Roi René 66
  Hôtel Boyer de Fonscolombe 67
  Hôtel Boyer d'Éguilles 66
  Hôtel d'Agut 70
  Hôtel d'Albertas 66
  Hôtel d'Arbaud 66
  Hôtel d'Arbaud-Jouques 68
  Hôtel de Boisgelin 69
  Hôtel de Caumont 69
  Hôtel de Châteaurenard 67
  Hôtel de Forbin 65
  Hôtel de Marignane 69
  Hôtel de Maynier d'Oppède 67
  Hôtel de Panisse-Passis 70
  Hôtel de Roquesante 70
  Hôtel de Ville 66
  Hôtel de Villeneuve d'Ansouis 69
  Hôtel d'Isoard de Vauvenargues 65
  Hôtel du Poët 66
  Hôtel Maurel de Pontevès 65
  Hôtel Peyronetti 66
  Musée Bibliographique et Archéologique Paul-Arbaud 69
  Musée des Tapisseries 67
  Musée du Vieil Aix 67
  Musée Granet 69
  Muséum d'Histoire Naturelle 66
  Old Aix 64
  Oppidum d'Entremont 71
  Pavillon de Vendôme 70
  Place d'Albertas 66
  Place de l'Hôtel de Ville 66
  Place Richelme 66
  Quartier Mazarin 68
  Rue de l'Opéra 69
  Thermes Sextius 70
Albaron *Bouches-du-Rhône* 135
Albertas (Jardins) *Bouches-du-Rhône* 72
Albion (Plateau) *Vaucluse* 247
Allauch *Bouches-du-Rhône* 73
Almonds 13
Les Alpilles *Bouches-du-Rhône* 73
Amphitheatres 46
Ancient architecture 38
Ancient art 45
André, Albert 111
Anglais et de Vaulx (Promenade) *Drôme* 212
Anjou, Charles of 23, 51
Anne of Austria 77
Ansouis *Vaucluse* 76
Apt *Vaucluse* 76
Aqueducts 48
Arc (Vallée) *Bouches-du-Rhône* 72
Architectural terms 44
Ardèche (Gorges) *Bouches-du-Rhône and Gard* 79
Aristide-Dumont (Station de Pompage) *Gard* 229
Arles *Bouches-du-Rhône* 84
  Allée des Sarcophages 93
  Amphitheatre 86
  Boulevard des Lices 93
  Clock Tower 89
  Cloître St-Trophime 88
  Collégiale Notre-Dame-la-Major 93
  Commanderie Ste-Luce 91
  Cryptoporticus 89
  Église St-Honorat 93
  Église St-Trophime 87
  Espace Van-Gogh 94
  Fondation Vincent Van Gogh-Arles 93
  Fouilles de l'Esplanade 93
  Hôtel de Ville 89
  Les Alyscamps 92
  Musée de l'Arles Antique 91
  Musée Réattu 91
  Museon Arlaten 89
  Palais Constantin 91
  Place du Forum 91
  Ramparts 93
  Théâtre Antique 86
Arômes et du Parfum (Musée) *Bouches-du-Rhône* 197
Art terms 44
Aubagne *Bouches-du-Rhône* 94
Aubanel, Théodore 110
Aurel *Vaucluse* 247
Auriolles *Ardèche* 95
Autridge (Belvédères) *Ardèche* 79
Avignon *Vaucluse* 96
  Cathédrale Notre-Dame-des-Doms 103
  Chapelle des Pénitents Gris 109
  Chapelle des Pénitents Noirs 110
  Chapelle St-Nicolas 106
  Clocher des Augustins 111
  Clock Tower 107
  Couvent des Célestins 110
  Église de la Visitation 110
  Église St-Agricol 107
  Église St-Didier 110
  Église St-Pierre 110
  Église St-Symphorien 111
  Fondation Angladon-Dubrujeaud 109
  Hospice St-Louis 110
  Hôtel de Rascas 110
  Hôtel de Sade 108
  Hôtel des Monnaies 103
  Hôtel de Ville 107
  Livrée Ceccano 110
  Musée Calvet 108
  Musée Lapidaire 108
  Musée Louis-Vouland 110
  Musée Théodore-Aubanel 110
  Muséum Requien 108
  Old Avignon 107
  Palais des Papes 98
  Palais du Roure 108
  Petit Palais 103
  Place de l'Horloge 107
  Place des Carmes 111
  Place du Palais 105
  Place St-Jean-le-Vieux 110
  Pont St-Bénézet 106
  Promenade des Papes 101
  Quartier de la Balance 106
  Remparts 107
  Rocher des Doms 103
  Rue Banasterie 110
  Rue de la Balance 106
  Rue de la Masse 109
  Rue de la République 108
  Rue des Lices 109
  Rue des Teinturiers 109
  Rue des Trois Pilats 111
  Rue du Roi-René 109
  Rue Joseph-Vernet 108
  Rue Ste-Catherine 111
  Rue Viala 107
Avignon (Château) *Bouches-du-Rhône* 135

B

Bagnols-sur-Cèze *Gard* 111

Banne *Ardèche* 219

Barbegal (Aqueducs) *Bouches-du-Rhône* 74

La Barben (Château) *Bouches-du-Rhône* 113

Barbentane *Bouches-du-Rhône* 111,114

Barigoule 33

Baroncelli-Javon, Folco de 26,135,136, 244

Le Barroux *Vaucluse* 150

Bastides 55

Le Bas-Vivarais 112

Les Baux-de-Provence *Bouches-du-Rhône* 115

Bauxite 115

Beaucaire Gard 119

Beaucaire Fair 119

Beaume (Gorges) *Ardèche* 166

Beaumes-de-Venise *Vaucluse* 150

Beaumes-de-Venise wine 34, 150

Bédoin *Vaucluse* 269

Bellaud de la Bellaudière 25

Benedict XIII 97

Bénézet 28

Bernus, Jacques 52, 141

Berre (Étang) *Bouches-du-Rhône* 121

Berre-l'Étang *Bouches-du-Rhône* 124

Bimont (Barrage) *Bouches-du-Rhône* 240

Birdwatching 132

Blanqui, Auguste 135

Bollène *Vaucluse* 125

Bonaparte, Lucien 230

Bonaparte, Napoléon 218

Bonnefoy, Antoine 37

Bonnieux *Vaucluse* 126

Bonpas (Chartreuse) *Vaucluse* 154

Bories 168

Bories (Village) *Vaucluse* 161

Bosco, Henri 137

Boterie, Raymond 222

Bouillabaisse 32

Boulbon *Bouches-du-Rhône* 198

Brandade de morue 202

Brantes *Vaucluse* 126

Braque, Georges 53

Brayer, Yves 53,116

Bretoul (Moulin) *Bouches-du-Rhône* 114, 198

Bullfighting 84, 202, 205

Buoux (Fort) *Vaucluse* 170

C

Cabestaing, Guillem de 27

Cadarache (Barrage) *Bouches-du-Rhône* 152

Cadarache (Research Centre) *Bouches-du-Rhône* 152

Cadenet *Vaucluse* 127

Caderousse *Vaucluse* 216

Caesarius, Saint 27

Caesar, Julius 20

Calanques 12

Calanques (Massif) *Bouches-du-Rhône* 127

Calès (Site) *Bouches-du-Rhône* 131

Calissons 12, 33, 61

Callelongue *Bouches-du-Rhône* 130

Calvisson *Gard* 210

Camargue *Bouches-du-Rhône and Gard* 84, 132

Camargue (Museum) *Bouches-du-Rhône* 135

Camargue (Parc Naturel Régional) *Bouches-du-Rhône* 132

Camargue (Réserve Nationale) *Bouches-du-Rhône* 136

Camaron 94

Camoin, Charles 53

Camoins-les-Bains *Bouches-du-Rhône* 157

Camus, Albert 167

Canaille (Cap) *Bouches-du-Rhône* 148

La Capelière *Bouches-du-Rhône* 136

Capitaine Danjou (Domaine) *Bouches-du-Rhône* 242

Carbonnière (Tour) *Gard* 58,138

Cardinal (Tour) *Bouches-du-Rhône* 74

Carluc (Prieuré) *Alpes-de-Haute-Provence* 170

Carpentras *Vaucluse* 139

Carro *Bouches-du-Rhône* 155

Carry-le-Rouet *Bouches-du-Rhône* 155

Cassis *Bouches-du-Rhône* 141

Castellet *Vaucluse* 169

Casteret, Norbert 196

Castille (Château) *Gard* 161

Cathédrale (Belvédère) *Ardèche* 80

Caume (Panorama) *Bouches-du-Rhône* 75

Cavaillon *Vaucluse* 142

Cave formation 19

Caveirac *Gard* 210

Caves 18

Caves de Listel *Gard* 60

Cayron (Col) *Vaucluse* 150

Céreste *Alpes-de-Haute-Provence* 170

Cézanne, Paul 53, 61, 63, 240

Chabaud, Auguste 53, 198

Le Chalet-Reynard *Vaucluse* 269

Chamaret *Drôme* 266

Chansons de geste 27

Chapels 49

Char, René 165

Chasms 18

Chassezac (Corniche) *Ardèche* 218

Château-Bas *Bouches-du-Rhône* 143

Châteauneuf-du-Pape *Vaucluse* 144

Châteauneuf-du-Pape wine 34

Châteaurenard *Bouches-du-Rhône* 145

Chauvet (Grotte) *Ardèche* 83,264

Christmas Cribs 28

Churches 49

La Ciotat *Bouches-du-Rhône* 145

CIPAM 160

Cire (Rocher) *Vaucluse* 201

Cistercian Order 247,250

Civil architecture 43

Clay pottery 94

Clay quarries 94

Clement IV 229

Clement V 97, 139, 144, 268

Clement VI 97

Clement VII 97

Clérissy, Joseph 37

Climate 6

Coast 12

La Cocalière (Grotte) *Gard* 146

Cocardes 135

Cœur, Jacques 58

Colombier (Belvédère) *Ardèche* 80

Comtat Venaissien *Vaucluse* 141

Comtat Venaissin *Vaucluse* 147

Concluses (Gorges) *Gard* 147

Corniche des Crêtes *Bouches-du-Rhône* 148

Cornillon Gard

Cornillon-Confoux *Bouches-du-Rhône* 123

Costumes 30

Côtes de Provence wine 34

Côtes du Rhône vineyards 34, 112

Couronne (Cap) *Bouches-du-Rhône* 155
Courts of Love 115
Coustellet *Vaucluse* 172
Coutelle (Belvédère) *Ardèche* 80
Craponne (Canal) *Bouches-du-Rhône* 151
Craponne, Adam de 244
Crau (Plaine) *Bouches-du-Rhône* 148
Crestet *Vaucluse* 151
Cribs 28
Crillon-le-Brave *Vaucluse* 269
Les Crottes *Ardèche* 81
Crusades 58
Cubism 53
Cucuron *Vaucluse* 170

D

Daube 33
Daudet, Alphonse 95,199
David, Félicien 127
Dentelles de Montmirail *Vaucluse* 149
Domitian Way 202
Dumas, Alexandre 193
Durance (Basse Vallée) *Alpes-de-Haute-Provence, Bouches-du-Rhône and Vaucluse* 151
Durance River 151
Durand, Marie 59

E

Eccentrics 19
Éguilles *Bouches-du-Rhône* 71
Embarbe (Tour) *Vaucluse* 169
Ensuès-la-Redonne *Bouches-du-Rhône* 155
Entrechaux *Vaucluse* 268
Entreconque (Rochers) *Bouches-du-Rhône* 75
En-Vau (Calanque) *Bouches-du-Rhône* 131
Ernst, Max 53
Espigoulier (Col) *Bouches-du-Rhône* 238
Espiguette (Phare) *Gard* 163
Estaque (Chaîne) *Bouches-du-Rhône* 155
L'Estaque *Bouches-du-Rhône* 194
Estienne, André 127
Étoile (Chaîne) *Bouches-du-Rhône* 157

Extraordinaire (Musée) *Vaucluse* 76
Eygalières *Bouches-du-Rhône* 76
Eyguières *Bouches-du-Rhône* 76

F

Fabre, Jean-Henri 216
Faience 94
Falcons 122
Fangassier (Étang) *Bouches-du-Rhône* 137
Faraman (Phare) *Bouches-du-Rhône* 133
Farandoles 30
Fauchier 37
Félibrige 26
Festivals 30
Figuerolles (Calanque) *Bouches-du-Rhône* 146
Fishing 14
Flassan *Vaucluse* 201
Flavien (Pont) *Bouches-du-Rhône* 124
Fléchier 219
Fontaine-de-Vaucluse *Vaucluse* 157
Fontvieille *Bouches-du-Rhône* 74
Forest fires 18
Forestière (Aven) *Ardèche* 81
Forests 16
Fos (Bassins) *Bouches-du-Rhône* 159
Fos-sur-Mer *Bouches-du-Rhône* 160
Foulque, Guy 229
Franque, Jean-Baptiste 120
French Air Force 244
French Foreign Legion 94
Froment, Nicolas 52

G

Gacholle (Phare) *Bouches-du-Rhône* 137
Galabert (Étang) *Bouches-du-Rhône* 137
Galoubet 30
Garagaï (Gouffre) *Bouches-du-Rhône* 240
Gardanne *Bouches-du-Rhône* 157
Gardians 55,135
Gardon (Gorges) *Gard* 161
Garrigue 18,168
Les Garrigues *Gard* 160

Gaud (Belvédères) *Ardèche* 79
Gauguin, Paul 53
Géants (Chaussée) *Vaucluse* 225
Gémenos *Bouches-du-Rhône* 238
Gide, André 256
Gide, Charles 256
Gide, Paul 256
Gigondas *Vaucluse* 150
Gigondas wine 34, 150
Giles, Saint 227
Ginès-François-Hüe (Centre d'Information) *Bouches-du-Rhône* 135
Gordes *Vaucluse* 161
Gothic art 51
Goudargues *Gard* 112
Les Goudes *Bouches-du-Rhône* 130
Gournier (Belvédères) *Ardèche* 80
Grand Belvédère *Ardèche* 80
Granet, François-Marius 53, 69
Le Grau-du-Roi *Gard* 162
Graveson *Bouches-du-Rhône* 197
Great Plague 177
Gregory XI 97
Grignan *Drôme* 163
Groseau (Source Vauclusienne) *Vaucluse* 268
Guidon du Bouquet *Gard* 112
Guigou, Paul 53
Guihen l'Orphelin 28
Gyptis 27, 174

H – I

Harmas Jean-Henri Fabre *Vaucluse* 216
Haute Corniche *Ardèche* 80
Heracles 27
Herbs of Provence 33
Hills 10
Histoire du Verre et du Vitrail (Musée) *Vaucluse* 162
Var 239
House of Anjou 23
Huguenots 24,227
Huguenots (Grotte) *Ardèche* 79
Impressionism 53
Industrialisation 14
L'Isle-sur-la-Sorgue *Vaucluse* 165
Istres *Bouches-du-Rhône* 123

J

Jalès *Ardèche* 218
Jean de l'Ours 28
Jeanne, Queen 62
Joly, Robert de 18, 196, 216
Jouques (Power Station) *Bouches-du-Rhône* 152
Julien (Pont) *Vaucluse* 78

L

Labastide-de-Virac *Ardèche* 82
Labeaume *Ardèche* 166
Lacoste *Vaucluse* 171
Lagnel, Jean-Louis 28
Lambesc *Bouches-du-Rhône* 246
Lançon (Viewing Table) *Bouches-du-Rhône* 124
Language 25
Lauris *Vaucluse* 127
Lauzes 168
Lavender 13
Lavendin 13
Legends and tales 27
Leroy 37
Listel wine 34
Literature 25
Lombard, Alfred 53
Loubon, Émile 53
Louis IX or Saint Louis 58
Lourmarin *Vaucluse* 167
Luberon (Montagne) *Alpes-de-Haute-Provence and Vaucluse* 167
Luberon (Parc Naturel Régional) *Alpes-de-Haute-Provence and Vaucluse* 77, 167
Lussan *Gard* 112

M

Madeleine (Grotte) *Ardèche* 172
La Madrague-de-Gignac *Bouches-du-Rhône* 155
Maillane *Bouches-du-Rhône* 173
Maladrerie (Belvédère) *Ardèche* 80
Malaucène *Vaucluse* 150
Mallemort (Power Station) *Bouches-du-Rhône* 154
Manades 134
Marcoule *Gard* 173
Marignane *Bouches-du-Rhône* 122, 124
Marius 61, 84, 212, 240

Marseille *Bouches-du-Rhône* 174
Alcazar 187
Ancienne Cathédrale de la Major 184
Basilique Notre-Dame-de-la-Garde 187
Basilique St-Victor 186
Belvédère St-Laurent 184
Botanical Gardens 190
La Canebière 187
Cathédrale de la Major 183
Centre de la Vieille Charité 184
Château Borély 190
Château d'If 193
Cité Radieuse 178
Clocher des Accoules 183
Corniche J.-F.-Kennedy 190
Cours Honoré-d'Estienne-d'Orves 186
Cours Julien 188
Dôme-Nouvel Alcazar 193
Église St-Vincent-de-Paul 188
Église St-Ferréol 179
Ferry boat 178
Fort St-Jean 184
Fort St-Nicolas 184
Four des Navettes 187
Hôtel de Cabre 180
Hôtel du Département 193
Hôtel-Dieu 180
Hôtel de Ville 179
Jardin des Vestiges 178
La Joliette Docks 193
Longchamp District 189
Montée des Accoules 181
Monument aux Morts de l'Armée d'Orient 190
Musée d'Art Contemporain 191
Musée des Arts Africains, Océaniens, Amérindiens 185
Musée des Arts et Traditions Populaires du Terroir Marseillais 193
Musée des Beaux-Arts 189
Musée Cantini 188
Musée des Docks Romains 179
Musée de la Faïence 191
Musée Grobet-Labadié 189
Musée d'Histoire de Marseille 179
Musée de la Marine et de l'Économie de Marseille 187
Musée de la Mode 187
Musée du Vieux Marseille 179
Palais Longchamp 189
Parc Borély 190
Parc du Pharo 190
Pavillon Daviel 180
Place de Lenche 184
Place Thiars 186
The Port 191
Promenade de la Plage 190
Quai des Belges 178
Quai de Rive-Neuve 186
Quartier de l'Arsenal 186
Quartier du Panier 181
Rue du Panier 181
Rue Longue-des-Capucins 188
Rue St-Ferréol 188
Southern Districts 190
Théâtre National de Marseille - La Criée 186
Vallon des Auffes 190
Vieux Port 178

Marseille (Canal) *Bouches-du-Rhône* 151
Marseille-Provence (Airport) *Bouches-du-Rhône* 122, 124
Martel, Charles 23, 96
Martel, Édouard-Alfred 18, 196
Martigues *Bouches-du-Rhône* 194
Martini, Simone 102
Mary Magdalene 238, 242
Marzal (Aven) *Ardèche* 196
Mas 54, 134
Massalia 22, 174
Massifs 10
Masson, André 53
Mauron, Marie 233
Mayle, Peter 197
Mazan *Vaucluse* 141
Mazan (Massif) *Vaucluse* 79
Mazel, Abraham 59
Les Mazes *Ardèche* 264
Mazet-Plage *Ardèche* 219
Méandre de Gaud (Belvédère) *Ardèche* 82
La Mède *Bouches-du-Rhône* 124
Méjanes *Bouches-du-Rhône* 136
Ménerbes *Vaucluse* 197
Meyrargues *Bouches-du-Rhône* 153
Military architecture 42
Mimet *Bouches-du-Rhône* 157
Mirabeau 62, 177
Mirabeau (Défilé) *Bouches-du-Rhône and Vaucluse* 152
Mirabeau (Pont) *Bouches-du-Rhône and Vaucluse* 152
Miramas-le-Vieux *Bouches-du-Rhône* 123
Mistral, Frédéric 26, 89, 141, 145, 173, 232
Mistral wind 7, 138
Monde Souterrain (Musée) *Ardèche* 196
Monieux *Vaucluse* 201
Monségur-sur-Lauzon *Drôme* 266
La Montagnette *Bouches-du-Rhône* 197
Montclus *Gard* 112
Monteux *Vaucluse* 141
Montfavet *Vaucluse* 111
Montfort, Simon de 202, 227
Montmajour (Abbaye) *Bouches-du-Rhône* 198
Morgiou *Bouches-du-Rhône* 130
Mornas *Vaucluse* 125
Moulin de Chalier *Gard* 259

Moulin de Daudet
  Bouches-du-Rhône 199
Moulins des Bouillons
  (Musée) *Vaucluse* 162
Mourre Nègre *Vaucluse*
  169
Mugel (Calanque)
  Bouches-du-Rhône 146
Murs (Col) *Vaucluse* 267

N

Nages (Oppidum) *Gard*
  200
Narbonensis 22,205
Nesque (Gorges) *Vaucluse*
  201
Nîmes *Gard* 202
  Amphithéatre 204
  Carré d'Art 206
  Castellum 207
  Cathédrale Notre-Dame et
    St-Castor 208
  Chapelle des Jésuites 209
  Fontaine Pradier 209
  Galerie Taurine 209
  Hôtel Fontfroide 209
  Jardin de la Fontaine 206
  Maison Carrée 205
  Maison Natale d'Alphonse
    Daudet 209
  Musée Archéologique 209
  Musée des Beaux-Arts 209
  Musée du Vieux Nîmes 208
  Muséum d'Histoire Naturelle
    209
  Old Nîmes 208
  Porte d'Auguste 208
  Rue de l'Aspic 209
  Rue de Bernis 209
  Rue du Chapitre 208
  Rue de la Madeleine 209
  Temple de Diane 207
  Tour Magne 207
Niolon *Bouches-du-Rhône*
  155
Norbert Casteret (Monde
  Souterrain) *Vaucluse*
  158
Nostradamus, Michel 21,
  233, 237, 245, 246
Notre-Dame-d'Aubune
  (Chapelle) *Vaucluse* 150
Notre-Dame-de-
  Beauregard (Chapelle)
  Bouches-du-Rhône 218
Notre-Dame-de-Grâce
  (Sanctuaire) *Gard* 224
Notre-Dame-de-la-Garde
  (Chapelle) *Bouches-du-
  Rhône*
Notre-Dame-de-Lumières
  Vaucluse 172
Notre-Dame-de-Pitié
  (Chapelle) *Bouches-du-
  Rhône* 237
Notre-Dame-des-Marins
  (Chapelle) *Bouches-du-
  Rhône* 196
Notre-Dame-des-Vignes
  (Chapelle) *Vaucluse* 266

Notre-Dame-du-Groseau
  (Chapelle) *Vaucluse* 268
Noves *Bouches-du-Rhône*
  154
Novilladas 203
Nyons *Drôme* 210

O

Occitan 25
Occitanian Provence 23
Ochre 15, 225
Ochre Tour *Vaucluse* 78
Oc language 25
Oïl language 25
Oil mills 210
OK Corral (Parc
  d'Attractions) *Bouches-
  du-Rhône* 95
Olive oil 15, 210
Olives 13, 33, 210
Oppède-le-Vieux *Vaucluse*
  172
Orange *Vaucluse* 212
Orgnac (Aven) *Ardèche*
  216
Orgon *Bouches-du-Rhône*
  218

P

Pagnol, Marcel 26, 94,
  157
Painting 51
Païolive (Bois) *Ardèche*
  218
Palissade (Domaine)
  Bouches-du-Rhône 137
Pas du Mousse (Rock)
  Ardèche 79
Pasteur, Louis 125
Paty (Belvédère) *Vaucluse*
  269
Pax Romana 22
Pernes-les-Fontaines
  Vaucluse 219
Perrier (Source) *Gard*
  210
Pertuis *Vaucluse* 153
Petrarch 25, 97, 157
Petroleum port 121
Peyrolles-en-Provence
  Bouches-du-Rhône 220
Picasso, Pablo 53, 241
Piémanson (Plage)
  Bouches-du-Rhône 138
Pierre of Provence 27
Pine trees 16
Piolenc, Guillaume de 222
Pioline (Château)
  Bouches-du-Rhône 72
Plains 10
Plan-d'Aups-Ste-Baume
  Var 239

Plateaux 10
Pollution 18
Pont-d'Arc *Ardèche* 79
Pont de Gau (Parc
  Ornithologique)
  Bouches-du-Rhône 136
Pont du Gard *Gard* 221
Pontifical Court 97
Pont-St-Esprit *Gard* 222
Port-Camargue *Gard* 163
Port-de-Bouc *Bouches-
  du-Rhône* 155
Port-Miou *Bouches-du-
  Rhône* 131
Port-Pin *Bouches-du-
  Rhône* 131
Port-St-Louis-du-Rhône
  Bouches-du-Rhône 160
Poulx *Gard* 161
Pradier, Jacques 209
Prassinos, Mario 237
Préhistoire (Musée)
  Ardèche 217
Prehistoric art 264
Protis 27,174
Provençal fabric 31
Provençal food 32
Provençal furniture 36
Provençal wines 34, 144,
  264
Provence (Canal)
  Bouches-du-Rhône 152
Provence (Croix)
  Bouches-du-Rhône 240
Puget, Pierre 52, 179,
  189, 189
Pyramide (Mas) *Bouches-
  du-Rhône* 236
Pytheas 27

R

Racine, Jean 256
Ramade (Moulin) *Drôme*
  210
Rambot, Jean-Claude 52
Ranc-Pointu (Belvédère)
  Ardèche 80
Rasteau *Vaucluse* 264
Raymond IV of Toulouse
  227
Raymond VI of Toulouse
  119, 227
Réaltor (Réservoir)
  Bouches-du-Rhône 72
Réattu, Jacques 91
Régalon (Gorges)
  Vaucluse 154
Religious architecture 39
Remoulins *Gard* 161
Renaissance art 52
René, King 24, 34, 51,
  61, 115, 176, 220,
  242, 252
Rhône (Delta) *Bouches-
  du-Rhône* 132

Rhône River 135
Rice 84
Richerenches *Vaucluse* 266
Rièges (Îlots) *Bouches-du-Rhône* 134
Rieu, Charloun 118
Riz (Musée) *Bouches-du-Rhône* 138
Robert, Gaspard 37
Rochecourbière (Grotte) *Drôme* 164
Rochefort-du-Gard *Gard* 224
Rognes *Bouches-du-Rhône* 153
Roman aqueducts 222
Roman baths 47
Roman circuses 47
Romanesque art 49
Roman houses 48
Roman orders 46
Roman public buildings 46
Roman roads 48
Roman temples 47
Roman theatres 46, 213
Roman towns 45
La Roque-d'Anthéron *Bouches-du-Rhône* 153
Roquefavour (Aqueduc) *Bouches-du-Rhône* 72
Roquemartine (Castelas) *Bouches-du-Rhône* 75
Roquemaure *Gard* 144
La Roque-sur-Cèze *Gard* 224
Le Rouet-Plage *Bouches-du-Rhône* 155
Roumanille, Joseph 26
Roussillon *Vaucluse* 225
Rouvière (Belvédère) *Ardèche* 80
Rove (Canal Souterrain) *Bouches-du-Rhône* 156
Ruoms *Ardèche* 166
Ruoms (Défilé) *Ardèche* 166
Rural architecture 54
Rustrel (Colorado) *Vaucluse* 78

S

Saboly, Nicolas 25
Sabran *Gard* 112
Sabran, Saint Eleazarius de 27, 76
Sade, Marquis de 141, 159, 171
Saignon *Vaucluse* 169
Saillans, Comte de 218
Saints 27
St-Blaise (Site Archéologique) *Bouches-du-Rhône* 225
St-Cannat *Bouches-du-Rhône* 246
St-Chamas *Bouches-du-Rhône* 124
St-Chamas (Power Station) *Bouches-du-Rhône* 124
St-Christol *Vaucluse* 247
St-Christophe (Bassin) *Bouches-du-Rhône* 153
Ste-Baume (Grotte) *Var* 239
St-Estève *Vaucluse* 269
St-Estève-Janson (Power Station) *Bouches-du-Rhône* 153
St-Eutrope (Colline) *Vaucluse* 215
Ste-Victoire (Montagne) *Bouches-du-Rhône* 63
St-Gabriel (Chapelle) *Bouches-du-Rhône* 74
St-Gilles *Gard* 226
St-Gilles (Écluse) *Gard* 138
St-Hilaire (Abbaye) *Vaucluse* 172
St-Jean-de-Garguier (Chapelle) *Bouches-du-Rhône* 95
St-Jean-du-Puy (Oratoire) *Var* 239
St-Julien *Bouches-du-Rhône* 155
St-Julien-le-Montagnier *Var* 229
St-Laurent-des-Arbres *Gard* 113
St-Marcel (Grotte) *Ardèche* 230
St-Martin-d'Ardèche *Ardèche* 81
St-Maximin-la-Ste-Baume *Var* 230
St-Michel (Église) *Vaucluse* 216
St-Michel-de-Frigolet (Abbaye) *Vaucluse* 232
St-Mitre-les-Remparts *Bouches-du-Rhône* 122
St-Nicolas (Église) *Bouches-du-Rhône* 124
St-Nicolas (Pont) *Gard* 161
St-Pantaléon *Vaucluse* 162
St-Paul-de-Mausole (Ancien Monastère) *Bouches-du-Rhône* 235
St-Pilon *Var* 239
St-Pons (Parc) *Bouches-du-Rhône* 238
St-Quentin-la-Poterie *Gard* 259
St-Rémy-de-Provence *Bouches-du-Rhône* 233
St-Roman (Abbaye) *Gard* 121
St-Saturnin-lès-Apt *Vaucluse* 78
St-Sixte (Chapelle) *Bouches-du-Rhône* 76
St-Sulpice (Chapelle) *Ardèche* 81
St-Trinit *Vaucluse* 247
St-Véran (Église) *Vaucluse* 159
St-Victor-la-Coste *Gard* 113
St-Vincent-de-Gaujac (Oppidum) *Gard* 112
Ste-Baume (Massif) *Var* 237
Ste-Croix (Chapelle) *Bouches-du-Rhône* 199
Ste-Victoire (Montagne) *Bouches-du-Rhône* 240
Les Stes-Maries-de-la-Mer *Bouches-du-Rhône* 242
Salin-de-Badon *Bouches-du-Rhône* 137
Salin-de-Giraud *Bouches-du-Rhône* 137
Salins du Midi *Gard* 60
Salon-de-Provence *Bouches-du-Rhône* 244
Salt marshes 15, 59, 133
Sampzon (Rocher) *Ardèche* 166
Santons 28, 94
Saoupe (Mont) *Bouches-du-Rhône* 148
Sarrians *Vaucluse* 141
Sault *Vaucluse* 246
Saumane-de-Vaucluse *Vaucluse* 159
Sausset-les-Pins *Bouches-du-Rhône* 155
Sautadet (Cascade) *Gard* 224
Séguret *Vaucluse* 149
Sénanque (Abbaye) *Vaucluse* 247
Serein (Mont) *Vaucluse* 268
Serre de Tourre (Belvédère) *Ardèche* 79
Sévigné, Mme de 163
Sextius 61
Signac, Paul 53
Silvacane (Abbaye) *Bouches-du-Rhône* 250
Soleil et Cosmos (Parc) *Gard* 111
Sorcery 27
Sormiou *Bouches-du-Rhône* 130
Speleology (Museum) *Ardèche* 196
Speleology 216
Staël, Nicolas de 53
Stalactites 19
Stalagmites 19
Suffren, Admiral 246
Sugiton *Bouches-du-Rhône* 131
Suze-la-Rousse *Drôme* 251

T

Tambourin 30
Tapenade 33
Tarascon *Bouches-du-Rhône* 251
Tarasque 251
Tartarin 252
Tartarin (Maison) *Bouches-du-Rhône* 254
Taulignan *Drôme* 165
Tavel wine 34
Teillan (Château de) *Gard* 61
Templiers (Balcon) *Ardèche* 80
Teutons 61
Le Thor *Vaucluse* 254
Thouzon (Grotte) *Vaucluse* 254
La Tour d'Aigues *Vaucluse* 255
Tourelles (Mas Gallo-Romain) *Gard* 121
Transalpine 22
Trees 13, 15, 16
La Treille *Bouches-du-Rhône* 127
Triumphal arches 47
Troglodyte dwellings 131
Troubadours 25,27
Truffles 13
Tunnels (Grotte) *Ardèche* 79
Turenne, Raymond de 24, 115

U – V

Underground rivers 18
Urban V 97
Uzès *Gard* 256
Uzès, Duchy of 256
Uzès (National Stud) *Gard* 258

V

Vaccarès (Étang) *Bouches-du-Rhône* 136
Vaison-la-Romaine *Vaucluse* 259
Valbonne (Chartreuse) *Gard* 112,264
Val d'Enfer *Bouches-du-Rhône* 119
Valdès 24
Val des Fées (Aiguilles) *Vaucluse* 225
Vallon-Pont-d'Arc *Ardèche* 264
Valréas *Vaucluse* 265
Van Gogh, Vincent 53, 85, 94, 235
Van Loo, Carle 52
Van Loo, Jean-Baptiste 61
Vasarely, Victor 70
Vaudois 24,167,248
Vauvenargues (Château) *Bouches-du-Rhône* 240
Vegetation 15
Venasque *Vaucluse* 266
Venasque (Forêt) *Vaucluse* 266
Ventabren *Bouches-du-Rhône* 72
Ventoux (Mont) *Vaucluse* 268
Verdon (Canal) *Bouches-du-Rhône* 151
Vernègues *Bouches-du-Rhône* 246
Vernet, Joseph 52
Verte (Île) *Bouches-du-Rhône* 146
La Veuve Perrin 37
Vieux-Vernègues *Bouches-du-Rhône* 246
Vilar, Jean 96
Villeneuve-lès-Avignon *Gard* 111, 269
Villes-sur-Auzon *Vaucluse* 201
Vitrolles *Bouches-du-Rhône* 273
Vocontii 259

W – Z

Water infiltration 18
Waterways 12
Winds 7
World War II 21
Ziem, Félix 53,194

Notes